Treatment Issues and Innovations in Mental Retardation

APPLIED CLINICAL PSYCHOLOGY

Series Editors: Alan S. Bellack, *Medical College of Pennsylvania at EPPI, Philadelphia, Pennsylvania,* and Michel Hersen, *University of Pittsburgh, Pittsburgh, Pennsylvania*

HANDBOOK OF BEHAVIOR MODIFICATION WITH THE MENTALLY RETARDED
Edited by Johnny L. Matson and John R. McCartney

THE UTILIZATION OF CLASSROOM PEERS AS BEHAVIOR CHANGE AGENTS
Edited by Phillip S. Strain

FUTURE PERSPECTIVES IN BEHAVIOR THERAPY
Edited by Larry Michelson, Michel Hersen, and Samuel M. Turner

CLINICAL BEHAVIOR THERAPY WITH CHILDREN
Thomas Ollendick and Jerome A. Cerny

OVERCOMING DEFICITS OF AGING: A Behavioral Approach
Roger L. Patterson

TREATMENT ISSUES AND INNOVATIONS IN MENTAL RETARDATION
Edited by Johnny L. Matson and Frank Andrasik

In preparation

SOCIAL SKILLS ASSESSMENT AND TRAINING WITH CHILDREN
An Empirically Based Handbook
Larry Michelson, Don P. Sugai, Randy P. Wood, and Alan E. Kazdin

BEHAVIORAL ASSESSMENT AND REHABILITATION OF THE TRAUMATICALLY BRAIN DAMAGED
Edited by Barry A. Edelstein and Eugene T. Couture

COGNITIVE BEHAVIOR THERAPY WITH CHILDREN
Edited by Andrew W. Meyers and W. Edward Craighead

A Continuation Order Plan is available for this series. A continuation order will bring delivery of each new volume immediately upon publication. Volumes are billed only upon actual shipment. For further information please contact the publisher.

Treatment Issues and Innovations in Mental Retardation

Edited by

Johnny L. Mutson
Northern Illinois University
DeKalb, Illinois

and

Frank Andrasik
State University of New York
Albany, New York

Plenum Press • New York and London

Library of Congress Cataloging in Publication Data

Main entry under title:

Treatment issues and innovations in mental retardation.

(Applied clinical psychology)
Includes bibliographical references and index.
1. Mentally handicapped—Rehabilitation—Addresses, essays, lectures. 2. Behavior therapy—Addresses, essays, lectures. I. Matson, Johnny L. II. Andrasik, Frank, 1949– . III. Series. [DNLM: 1. Mental retardation—Therapy. WM 300 Y7846]
RC570.T7 1982   362.3'8   82-22275
ISBN 0-306-40935-6

© 1983 Plenum Press, New York
A Division of Plenum Publishing Corporation
233 Spring Street, New York, N.Y. 10013

All rights reserved

No part of this book may be reproduced, stored in a retrieval system, or transmitted in any form or by any means, electronic, mechanical, photocopying, microfilming, recording, or otherwise, without written permission from the Publisher

Printed in the United States of America

This book is dedicated with love to our wives and families
for their continued patience and support

Deann and Meggan Matson
Sarah and Meghan Andrasik

Contributors

GENE G. ABEL, Department of Psychiatry, Columbia University, New York, New York.

KARL ALTMAN, Children's Rehabilitation Unit, University of Kansas Medical Center, Kansas City, Kansas

MICHAEL G. AMAN, Department of Psychiatry, School of Medicine, University of Auckland, P.B., Auckland, New Zealand

FRANK ANDRASIK, Department of Psychology, State University of New York at Albany, Albany, New York

ROWLAND P. BARRETT, Western Psychiatric Institute and Clinic, University of Pittsburgh School of Medicine, Pittsburgh, Pennsylvania

D. KIRBY BROWN, Department of Educational Psychology, University of Arizona, Tucson, Arizona

JAN BRUNO, Center for Developmental and Learning Disorders, University of Alabama, Birmingham, Alabama

BRIAN M. CAMPBELL, Department of Psychology, Nova University, Fort Lauderdale, Florida

ALBERT R. CAVALIER, Partlow State School and Hospital, Tuscaloosa, Alabama and National Research and Demonstration Institute, Association for Retarded Citizens, Avenue J, Arlington, Texas.

EMILY M. COLEMAN, Department of Psychiatry, University of Tennessee, Center for the Health Sciences, Memphis, Tennessee

THOMAS M. DILORENZO, Department of Psychology, West Virginia University, Morgantown, West Virginia

DANIEL M. DOLEYS, Behavioral Medicine Services, 2018 Brookwood Medical Center Drive, Suite 109, Birmingham, Alabama

James E. Favell, Western Carolina Center, Morganton, North Carolina

Ralph, Feretti, Cognitive Studies, 406 Hall Health, GS-27, University of Washington, Seattle, Washington

Ronald F. Gaines, Palo Alto Veterans Administration Hospital, Palo Alto, California

Raymond P. Garris, University of Pittsburgh, Division of Specialized Professional Development, Pittsburgh, Pennsylvania

Michael L. Jones, Western Carolina Center, Morganton, North Carolina

Linda Katz-Garris, Western Psychiatric Institute and Clinic, Psychiatric Rehabilitation Services, University of Pittsburgh School of Medicine, Pittsburgh, Pennsylvania

Johnny L. Matson, Department of Learning and Development, Northern Illinois University, DeKalb, Illinois

Ronald B. McCarver, Partlow State School and Hospital, Tuscaloosa, Alabama

Christopher R. Milar, University of North Carolina Medical Center, Chapel Hill, North Carolina

Mary Mira, Children's Rehabilitation Unit, University of Kansas Medical Center, Kansas City, Kansas

Richard J. Morris, Department of Special Education, University of Arizona, Tucson, Arizona

James A. Mulick, Child Development Center, Rhode Island Hospital, Brown University, Providence, Rhode Island

William D. Murphy, Department of Psychiatry, University of Tennessee, Center for the Health Sciences, Memphis, Tennessee

Dennis H. Reid, Western Carolina Center, Morganton, North Carolina

Todd R. Risley, Western Carolina Center, Morganton, North Carolina

STEPHEN SCHRODER, *Director of Research, Division for Disorders of Development and Learning, University of North Carolina Medical Center 220H, Chapel Hill, North Carolina*

FRANK D. SCOTT, *School Psychology Program, University of Rhode Island, Kingston, Rhode Island*

EDWARD S. SHAPIRO, *Department of Educational Psychology, University of Arizona, Tucson, Arizona*

DONALD STACY, *University of Alabama, Birmingham, Alabama*

Foreword

The field of mental retardation represents an area of tremendous diversity. Multiple disciplines, areas of research, and specialities which might otherwise operate independently are united toward a central theme. Within the areas of treatment and habilitation, several disciplines have converged to improve the impact of what currently can be done for persons in need of assistance and special programming for their daily functioning. The impetus for innovation has stemmed from several sources. Innovations have been required to meet the changing philosophies toward institutionalization and education of mentally retarded persons. Legal and legislative influences have set new challenges that require restructuring several facets of treatment, education, and care. At the same time, saltatory breakthroughs in treatment have expanded the limits of what can be accomplished in training persons for normalized, institutional, and intermediate living conditions.

It would be misleading to imply that several influences have melliflously coalesced into a single theme from which a set of innovative treatments have emerged. The field is replete with debate, controversy, and significant issues, many of which evolve with rapid developments in the area of social policy. Perhaps the innovations that have emerged can be traced in part to the intellectual clashes the field has generated and the practical and social demands the subject matter dictates.

The present book is unique in bringing together an impressive list of contributors whose collective expertise spans many areas central to habilitation of the mentally retarded. The breadth of coverage is reflected in detailed elaboration of multiple conceptual positions, interventions, populations, and settings. Broad coverage is essential to encompass the issues relevant to different subpopulations referred under the rubric of mentally retarded persons. For example, for some persons, issues and potential benefits raised by de-institutionalization and normalization may be quite relevant. On the other hand, for other persons, these notions are less germane than is the progress on institutional design and development of prosthetic devices. The present book conveys innovative treatments to meet the demands of many different subgroups within the general area of research.

The treatment approaches include behavioral techniques, environmental design, pharmacotherapy, and others. These interventions are applied to self-care, social interaction, community living, deviance, and psychopathology. Ethical and legal issues and the philosophical and social positions they reflect elaborate the current contexts of treatment development.

Although several specific areas are covered, there is an overriding theme the separate contributions reflect, namely, that substantive advances have been made in the approaches and procedures available to help mentally retarded persons. Also, the thrust is on empirical evidence and the combined benefits of science and technology. Scientific research, of course, provides improved understanding of the development of physical and psychological handicaps and the conditions that can promote adaptive functioning; technology translates basic advances as soon as possible to have impact on the urgent problems of living.

Matson and Andrasik have made a distinct contribution in bringing this text to fruition. The topics they have presented are of extremely high interest not only because of the urgent problems current treatments address, but also because the topics convey progress in mental retardation as a basic and applied discipline. The book consolidates existing advances into a central source to bring the information to the widest professional audience. The direct and marked contribution of this text is to describe the current status of treatment and habilitation. Its indirect contribution will be to point to the limits of what is currently known and hence what needs to be pursued more vigorously.

ALAN E. KAZDIN

University of Pittsburgh, School of Medicine

Preface

Methods for treating problems of the mentally retarded have greatly expanded in the past few years. This change has been stimulated, in large part, by the realization that many heretofore untreated problems could benefit from behavioral programming. Equally instrumental in this accelerated growth, however, have been the recent ethical-legal developments and philosophical shifts in treatment concepts, such as normalization.

Given this unprecedented expansion and the possibility of continued marked development in research with mentally retarded persons, the present authors set out to prepare a volume that would reflect some of the recent developments in humane care that are on the forefront of the treatment of the mentally retarded. We do not presume that the topics selected for coverage here constitute the only important new advances and changes in philosophy stimulating change that are in the country at present. However, the diversity of topics described in this volume does give an idea of the expanded scope of treatment which until only a few years ago focused almost solely on educational and self-help skills, with the latter being confined almost exclusively to institutional populations.

The authors for each chapter are persons noted for their research in these developing areas. Therefore, the reader is being presented with an up-to-date evaluation prepared as only a person intimately familiar with a specific research area can do.

It is particularly hard to systemize chapters in a book of this type where a diversity of topics is presented. The only attempt at systemization was to present the McCarver and Cavalier chapter first, since we feel it gives a useful introduction as to how we arrived at our current thinking in at least some areas of treatment with the mentally retarded. This presentation is followed by chapters on a variety of topics concerning the application of particular treatment technologies. The chapters subsequent to the first are not ordered in any systematic basis, and so the reader should not equate order with perceived importance or significance.

This book is primarily for the reader with some level of expertise in the field of mental retardation. Thus, graduate students, researchers, college professors, and practitioners in the field are the primary audience. We hope this book will prove of value to these persons as a means of "keeping up" with new developments in the field and as a means of stimulating future research.

JOHNNY L. MATSON
FRANK ANDRASIK

Contents

1
*Philosophical Concepts and Attitudes Underlying Programming
for the Mentally Retarded* 1
RONALD B. MCCARVER AND ALBERT R. CAVALIER

2
Implementing Behavioral Programs in the Community 37
DONALD STACY, DANIEL M. DOLEYS, AND JAN BRUNO

3
*Legal and Ethical Issues in Behavior Modification with
Mentally Retarded Persons* 61
RICHARD J. MORRIS AND D. KIRBY BROWN

4
*Litigation and Legislative Regulations Impacting on the
Treatment of the Developmentally Disabled* 97
LYNDA KATZ-GARRIS AND RAYMOND P. GARRIS

5
*The Effects of Lead on Retardation of Cognitive and
Adaptive Behavior* 129
CHRISTOPHER R. MILAR AND STEPHEN R. SCHROEDER

6
Behavioral Assessment of the Mentally Retarded 159
EDWARD S. SHAPIRO AND ROWLAND P. BARRETT

7
*Trends and Issues in Behavioral Research on Training Feeding
      and Dressing Skills* 213
DENNIS H. REID

8
*A Critical Assessment of Overcorrection Procedures with
      Mentally Retarded Persons* 241
RALPH P. FERRETTI AND ALBERT R. CAVALIER

9
Training Parents of Developmentally Disabled Children 303
KARL ALTMAN AND MARY MIRA

10
Socioecological Programming of the Mentally Retarded 373
MICHAEL L. JONES, JAMES E. FAVELL, AND TODD R. RISLEY

11
*A Review of Behavior Modification Procedures for Treating Social
      Skill Deficits and Psychiatric Disorders of the Mentally Retarded* .. 415
JOHNNY L. MATSON, THOMAS M. DILORENZO, AND FRANK ANDRASIK

12
Psychoactive Drugs in Mental Retardation 455
MICHAEL G. AMAN

13
*Devices and Instrumentation for Skill Development and Behavior
      Change* 515
JAMES A. MULICK, FRANK D. SCOTT, RONALD F. GAINES,
AND BRIAN M. CAMPBELL

14
Human Sexuality in the Mentally Retarded 581
WILLIAM D. MURPHY, EMILY M. COLEMAN, AND GENE G. ABEL

Index 645

1 Philosophical Concepts and Attitudes Underlying Programming for the Mentally Retarded

Ronald B. McCarver and Albert R. Cavalier

Philosophy in Action: Historical Programming Efforts

Workers in the field of mental retardation are intimately aware of the effects of prevailing public opinion on treatment provided the mentally retarded. Public laws often dictate the professional behavior of those responsible for their care and incorporate philosophical positions representing the will of those speaking for the people. Standards and guidelines related to research and treatment proliferate in the field, and concepts such as normalization and de-institutionalization have found their way into the language of court orders. At no other time in history have the fields of mental health and mental retardation occupied so large a share of the public limelight.

The care of deviant individuals has always had its underpinnings in philosophical beliefs, but the zeitgeist is often hard to determine other than in retrospect. We shall have to wait for someone with the advantage of hindsight to elucidate completely the spirit of our time. However, certain guiding lights can now be identified. In this chapter, we shall attempt to take an objective look at these and describe their effects on programming. The services provided to a fictitious mentally retarded individual who reappears at several different points in recent history will be used as a vehicle throughout the chapter to highlight the interplay between philosophy and action. For expository purposes,

---

Ronald B. McCarver and Albert R. Cavalier • Partlow State School and Hospital, Tuscaloosa, Alabama 35401. The authors also hold adjunct appointments in the Department of Psychology at the University of Alabama.

the characteristics of this individual will remain constant—only the times will change.

Alicia is a 21-year-old female with Down's syndrome. If given the Stanford-Binet (she was around before it was), she would obtain a score of 40, placing her in the moderate range of mental retardation according to current terminology of the American Association on Mental Deficiency (AAMD), (Grossman, 1977). Alicia is more socially adept than would be predicted on the basis of her IQ score. She can take care of her personal needs, count to 20, read and write her name, carry on a simple conversation, find her way to and from familiar places, and perform a variety of tasks with minimal supervision. She has no striking maladaptive behaviors and generally gets along well with other people. When she does not get her way, however, she has occasional temper tantrums, some rather severe.

On June 6, 1876, the Association of Medical Officers of American Institutions of Idiotic and Feebleminded Persons was established. Included in its constitution was a statement indicating that the association would lend its influence to the establishment of institutions for the management and training of idiots and feebleminded individuals and research related thereto (Sloan & Stevens, 1976). Initially, most of these schools followed the lead of Samuel Howe, a Boston neuropsychiatrist who introduced Seguin's "physiological method" to the United States when he became director of the first facility for the mentally retarded in this country. Sequin, a Saint-Simonist interested in social reform, espoused an optimistic treatment package for the mentally retarded. In brief, he proposed development of the senses and training of certain motor movements that would permit undamaged areas of the brain to take over the function of damaged areas. This method was enthusiastically embraced by many of the early leaders in the field. Thus, early institutions were founded on the belief that the mentally retarded could be trained to function at a higher level, that is, could be "cured" (Kanner, 1964). Many states established age limits for admission and accepted only those individuals who were likely to profit from training (Sloan & Stevens, 1976).

If Alicia had happened to be in the right place at the right time, she might have been admitted to one of the new training schools for the feebleminded. She would have met the admission criteria for most, but practitioners and facilities were few in number, and both were soon overburdened with intractable caseloads. There were 15 American institutions serving slightly over 4,000 people in 1868 (Baumeister, 1970). The government and most citizens were more concerned with reconstruction than mental retardation. Most mentally retarded people, including Alicia, received no special services. She lived at home with her parents on a small farm just outside a medium-sized city in the Midwest. Several siblings, ranging in age from 4 to 25 years, also lived at home. Alicia caused no particular problems. She helped care for her younger brothers and sisters, and, although she was given simple chores and had to be reminded of them often, she did them well. She had never attended school, but few girls her age did at the time. Alicia was considered "slow" by the community, and some of her peers played simple-minded and sometimes cruel jokes on her. She had never shown any interest in boys, though most girls her age were married. Alicia's mother had once taken her to a doctor in town. He said that Alicia might be a "mongol"; he read that a Dr. Down had identified such a condition. "It might be a throwback," were the physician's words that stuck with Alicia's mother. She never told anyone else of the visit. Alicia's father had long since given up punishing his daughter for her occasional tantrums. After these incidents she was either cajoled or ignored, depending on who was present at the time. In sum, Alicia received the special services that society at large deemed necessary for her at the time—none whatsoever.

In 1912, the superintendent of Midwest State School heard a paper by Walter E. Fernald at the annual meeting of the American Association for the Study of the Feebleminded (AASF), and, immediately on returning home, began a campaign for the enlargement of his entire institution and the establishment of a completely new annex for females of childbearing age. The fact sheet circulated in the state legislature was taken almost entirely from Fernald's paper. It stated, among other things, that at least 80% of mental defects were inherited, and described the mentally retarded as "a parasitic and predatory class never capable of supporting themselves or managing their own affairs . . . a menace and danger to the community . . . a potential criminal." High-grade female imbeciles were seen as especially dangerous being "twice as prolific as the normal woman," and "certain to become sexual offenders and to spread venereal disease or to give birth to degenerate children" (Sloan & Stevens, 1976, p. 76). Work was started within the year, and the new wing for "feebleminded" females was ready for occupancy late in 1914.

We now turn to Alicia in 1915. Her mother took her to a local doctor, who made an initial diagnosis of Down's syndrome and strongly recommended that Alicia be taken to Midwest State School for further evaluation. The director of the institution, who was also the chief physician, confirmed the diagnosis, and a newly employed psychologist pronounced that her IQ was 40 as determined by the Binet-Simon test. The prognosis was bleak, and immediate institutionalization was recommended for both Alicia's benefit and the welfare of the community. After much family debate and the encouragement of the local doctor,

Alicia was admitted to the new female dormitory several months later. The institution was about 60 miles from her home, an ideal distance according to institutional planners of the time. They wanted some involvement with the family, but did not want frequent visits (Sloan & Stevens, 1976).

The year of Alicia's admission, 1915, marked the beginning of a period of the most rapid rise in rate of institutionalization in history (Baumeister, 1970). Barr's plea to the mothers of America was being heeded at an ever-increasing rate:

> For the idiot, unimprovable, nothing is needed beyond the asylum, giving that care and attention found in every well-regulated nursery of delicate children, the *sine qua non* being regular hours, simple nourishing foods, frequent baths and tender mothering. As numbers can be cared for here with more efficiency and greater ease than one in the ordinary family, and as the child very often does not recognize the hand that administers to its physical want, the mother herself is forced to admit that the asylum is best, not only for the good of the child but also for the welfare of the home. (Barr, 1913)

However, Alicia was not admitted to provide her with better care nor to remediate her condition. The "feebleminded" were now generally regarded as a menace to society, a menace that should be segregated for their own protection and for the well-being of society. The prevalent notion that moral and mental "defectiveness" were closely related had recently been reinforced by the findings of Goddard (1912) and Estabrook (1916). This belief, along with the absence of any real cures in the early experimental schools, dovetailed nicely with the eugenics movement. The control of the spread of mental retardation by segregation was the preferred alternative to sterilization, according to the Research Committee of the Eugenics Section of the American Breeder's Association (Baumeister, 1970), and leaders in the field did their best to follow this guideline.

Alicia's new home housed 400 other mentally retarded individuals, and plans were underway for new dormitories. She was delivered by her mother and an older brother, who talked briefly with the director, toured her dormitory and the training area, and then left. The curriculum at Midwest State School was similar to that of other institutions of the time. Cognitive development was not expected, and academic instruction was a minimal part of the program. Residents were expected to work within the institution in order to decrease the burden on society for their upkeep. Consequently, females were trained in such things as knitting, basket weaving, sewing, darning, lace making, ironing, domestic work, and gardening. Graduates were expected to work as domestics, or in the mending room, kitchen, dining room, laundry, etc.,

(Thompson & Grabowski, 1972). Some received minimal pay for their services. For example, at the 15th annual meeting of the AASF, one member reported payments of 25 cents per week to a resident worker who was a driver, and another reported that residents working as aides were paid 1 cent per day (Sloan & Stevens, 1976).

Initially, Alicia's mother visited her fairly often, but her visits became less frequent. She gradually accepted the psychologist's statement that her visits were disruptive (Alicia would become homesick for a few days afterward), and the superintendent's pronouncement that her condition could not be improved and would necessitate lifelong care. Alicia adjusted fairly well to institutional life except for periodic bouts of depression and an occasional temper tantrum.

It was almost immediately apparent that the "menace of the feebleminded" was not to be erased by placing them in institutions. As early as 1913, Goddard indicated that control was not to be accomplished by dealing only with those in institutions. He strongly advocated studying families of the "feebleminded," presumably similar to his own treatise on the Kallikaks (Sloan & Stevens, 1976). A social worker visited Alicia's home a few years after admission. She interviewed Alicia's parents and younger brother, who was the only child remaining at home, the others having moved to the city. Her brother was identified as a "moron" by the social worker using Goddard's classification system. A special file was established for possible action, but it was soon lost among hundreds of others.

By 1920, leaders in the field were aware that it would be economically impossible and perhaps socially undesirable to completely segregate the "feebleminded." Fernald had already begun to change his position and by 1923 had completely recanted (Sloan & Stevens, 1976). The successful community adjustment of some previous clients of Waverly State School (mainly escapees) surprised him (Fernald, 1919). He later admitted that there were both good and bad "defectives" and that, contrary to his own predictions, the good ones were in the majority. Shortly before he died, Fernald stated that newer knowledge based on unselected cases indicated the existence of many more "feebleminded" people than previously estimated, that many of their parents were well-to-do and industrious, and that there were causes other than heredity (Sloan & Stevens, 1976).

The general hue and cry in the professional community over eugenics and the relationship between mental retardation, poverty, and antisocial behavior faded during the 1920s. A state plan for the care of the mentally defective submitted by Fernald to the AAMD in 1920 was very similar to many now in existence and included recommendations for a broad-based service delivery system of which institutional care was only one component. However, the public, having so readily accepted the seemingly easy solution of permanent institutionalization, was not as pliable as Fernald. At the beginning of the Great Depression, there were no other services available on a large scale. Special programs in the schools had been started in the 1890s and grew slowly until 1930, when they served almost as many people as institutions did (i.e., 34,000). However, the lack of any spectacular successes, the John Dewey-inspired belief that the regular classroom teacher could handle all types of students, and shrinking school budgets stopped this growth. The result was a diminution of special education programs in many areas of the country (Baumeister, 1970). However, the rate of institutionalization continued to grow and has only recently begun to level off (Baumeister, 1970; Scheerenberger, 1976, 1979). The public demand for institutional care actually increased during the depression, perhaps because of the inability of families to care for their own (Sloan & Stevens, 1976).

Alicia's situation did not change much during the Depression and the ensuing war years. It became more likely that her condition would be recognized at birth. This diagnosis was almost invariably accomplished by a gloomy prognosis and a recommendation of early institutionalization before the family could become attached to the child. However, waiting lists were long, and by the time she was offered admission, her mother was against commitment. But the family members were concerned about what would happen when they were unable to take care of her, and so they accepted the opening when it was available.

Alicia's life in the institution changed gradually over the years. Institutions were somewhat insulated from the economic realities of the day by virtue of their large farms, cheap labor pool (the residents), indestructible buildings (some built in the early 1900s have only recently begun to deteriorate), and at least some public subsidy. Eventually, years of neglect took their toll. More residents were admitted but few buildings added. The dorm in which Alicia lived was originally designed for 40 females; in 1950 it housed 80. Fewer professionals were hired, and these were frequently underpaid and undertrained. Alicia still worked in the institution, but she usually received no specific training for the job. The trend to admit only lower-level or problematic defectives (noted by Fernald in 1922) continued, and, as a consequence, her job often consisted of taking care of her less fortunate peers. Crowded conditions, unmanageable residents, and inadequate supervision eventually led to harsher discipline, locked doors, and an increase in incidents of abuse. At the close of World War II, virtually every state could boast of a "snakepit" and had little else in terms of care and habilitation to offer its mentally retarded citizens.

Largely because of this abysmal state of affairs, three distinct but intertwined movements emerged: the development of behavior modification, the formation of consumer groups, and the start of what might be called "humanistic legalism." Behavior modifiers systematized available knowledge about the acquisition of behavior and made the first large-scale optimistic claims for the trainability of the mentally retarded in almost a century. Consumer groups, most notably the National Association for Retarded Citizens (NARC), which held its first meeting in 1950 with six parents in attendance, rapidly attracted a following and spoke loudly and clearly about the needs of the retarded. The first major influence of such groups was to spur development of new services and facilities, primarily in the community. More recently, their primary area of concern has been the quality of services, best represented by the adoption of the philosophy of normalization. Humanistic legalism has always been around, but in the last 25 years it has become an extremely potent influence on the field. It includes judicial (*Brown* v. *Board of Education*; *Wyatt* v. *Stickney*), political (President's Committee on Mental Retardation), and legislative (Developmental Disabilities Assistance and Bill of Rights Act; Education for All Handicapped Children Act) aspects.

The philosophy underlying these influences is by no means new. The spirit of social reform and the treatment advocated by Sequin and others of like mind in the mid-1800s is not qualitatively different from the underlying motives of behavior modifiers, normalizers, and legal activists. "Liberté, egalité, fraternité" is a time honored slogan. The difference now is financial. The United States in particular has enjoyed a general level of prosperity in recent times that has never before been equaled on such a large scale. The philosophy is not new, but the wherewithal to do much more than talk about it is.

At this point, we are going to leave Alicia for a while. She is still a working resident in an overcrowded and understaffed institution, receives little by way of treatment, and has little chance of discharge. For all intents and purposes she is disenfranchised and has not enjoyed the concern of society for decades. The picture will soon be quite different. We revisit Alicia after describing what we see as the three major contemporary influences on programming for the mentally retarded: behavior modification, normalization, and humanistic legalism.

Behavior Modification

The term *behavior modification* refers to a collection of techniques derived from the models of classical conditioning, social learning, and operant conditioning, with heavy emphasis on the last. The philosophical underpinnings of the behavior modification model are many and diverse. Before the sixteenth century, the movements of human beings, infrahumans, and even inanimate objects were held to be primarily determined by intentions and desires. Largely because of the influence of Galileo, the movement of physical bodies came to be viewed as machine-like and predictable, based on the effects of external forces. Descartes applied this view to the behavior of living organisms. Involuntary behavior was mechanical, the basis for which was association by nervous connections of a stimulus and a response. Voluntary behavior was rational and not governed by physical laws.

Associationism/empiricism as espoused by Locke (1690) and Hobbes (1650) maintained that one set of laws accounted for both the actions of the mind and the behavior of the body. Their focus was mental activity. The basic doctrine held that (1) all knowledge is derived from sensory experience, (2) all complex ideas are constructed from and reducible to simple ideas, (3) the mind is machine-like with no mysterious components, and most importantly, (4) ideas are acquired or connected solely through association by contiguity in experience.

In the realm of biology, Darwin (1859) put forth a theory of evolution with two central components: random variation among members of a species and natural selection of the most adaptive characteristics. Spencer (1880) suggested "that organisms engaged in essentially random activity. Some of that activity resulted in pleasurable consequences. These pleasurable consequences worked to select the activities which preceded them" (Schwartz, 1978, p. 21). With these influences from biology, the pragmatic William James and John Dewey shifted the approach from the association of antecedent and consequent ideas of Locke and Hobbes to the association of ideas and practical action. This functionalist view reflected and fostered great optimism that changes in human nature could be accomplished, with consequences for changes in educational and social practices, and, in so doing, became the direct forerunner of contemporary behavioristic views.

From the real-world relevance of the functionalists, John B. Watson (1924) began to focus on observable stimuli and responses, thereby lifting American psychology out of the realm of mentalism. Much of the impetus for this move was innovative work conducted in Russia. While Pavlov (1927) and Bechterev

(1913) pioneered investigations into classical conditioning from which some current programmatic interventions are derived (e.g., Rachman & Teasdale, 1969; Wolpe & Lazarus, 1966), Russians also studied the influence of consequences on behavior (Ivanov-Smolensky, 1927; Pavlov, 1932). At about the same time, Thorndike (1911) was involved in a program of research on the effect of consequences on behavior, which culminated in his formulation of the law of effect; that is, responses followed by satisfying consequences are more likely to be repeated. The experimentation of Pavlov, his colleagues, and Thorndike is the foundation of modern behaviorism. These researchers were not the first to discover the influence of reinforcing and punishing consequences on behavior, but they were the first to conduct systematic investigations.

The early Romans put eels in wine cups as an aversive therapy for alcoholism (Zilboorg & Henry, 1941). In the twelfth century, students received figs and honey for reciting religious lessons (Birnbaum, 1962). In the sixteenth century, Erasmus suggested fruit and cake to facilitate teaching Greek and Latin (Skinner, 1966). Itard trained the wild boy of Aveyron to recognize words using his "physiological" method in which correct responses were rewarded with milk. Sequin gave his students apples to cool their bruised hands and to reward them after a difficult perceptual-motor ladder-climbing task. Following Watson's lead in utilizing the classical conditioning model, Jones (1924), English (1929), and Jersild and Holmes (1935) treated young children's fears and Mowrer and Mowrer (1938), enuresis.

In 1938, B. F. Skinner published data from an extensive number of investigations of operant conditioning using laboratory animals as subjects. Conceptually, the operant conditioning approach was extended to human behavior and social institutions in Skinner's subsequent writings (Skinner, 1948, 1953). Empirical demonstrations of some of these contentions soon followed. If the work of Pavlov and Thorndike is the foundation of behavior modification, the work of Skinner is its cornerstone.

Fuller (1949) trained a simple arm-raising response in an 18-year-old "vegetative idiot" using sugar milk as a reward. In 1953, important applications were made by Skinner and Lindsley with psychotic patients at the Metropolitan State Hospital in Waltham, Massachusetts (Lindsley, 1956, 1960; Lindsley & Skinner, 1954; Skinner, 1954). In general, they demonstrated that the behavior of the patients was orderly and followed normal psychological laws. Ferster and DeMyer (1961, 1962) reported similar results with autistic children. The primary focus of these studies was the testing of laboratory principles with nonlaboratory humans. At this point, the transition from experimental investigation to clinical research and applied intervention began.

Behavioral programs for maladaptive and adaptive behaviors were first used by Ayllon and his colleagues with psychotic and neurotic adults at Saskatchewan Hospital in Canada (Ayllon, 1963; Ayllon & Azrin, 1964; Ayllon & Haughton, 1962, 1964; Ayllon & Michael, 1959). The procedures were applied on a broader scale to the behaviors of a ward of chronic psychotic residents at Anna State Hospital in Illinois (Ayllon & Azrin, 1965). During this same period of time, pioneering articles on the application of operant conditioning principles to the training of the mentally retarded began to appear (Barrett & Lindsley, 1962; Bijou, 1963; Bijou & Orlando, 1961; Ellis & Pryer, 1958; Ellis, 1962, 1963; Ellis, Barnett, & Pryer, 1960; Girardeau, 1962; Headrick, 1963a,b; Lindsley, 1964; Orlando, 1961a, b; Orlando & Bijou, 1960; Zeaman, House, & Orlando, 1958). A token economy program focusing on a wide variety of behaviors was established for mentally retarded females at Parsons State Hospital and Training Center (Girardeau & Spradlin, 1964). A token economy system was applied to a classroom of mentally retarded children at the Rainier School in Washington by Birnbrauer and Lawler (1964) and Birnbrauer, Wolf, Kidder, and Tague (1965). These initial reports indicated that it was possible to manage longstanding maladaptive behaviors and to train new behavior patterns in some mentally retarded individuals. In 1966, Bijou wrote the "biblical" account of the behavior modification approach to the mentally retarded, and now, 15 years later, the number of published interventions is immense, including single case and group designs utilized in homes, schools, institutions, and community settings (see Birnbrauer, 1976, and Whitman & Scibak, 1979).

Contemporary behavior modification embodies many explicitly defined concepts and implicitly held assumptions. The central tenets are that (1) the appropriate focus of study and intervention is behavior, (2) complex behaviors are usually reducible to more elementary behaviors, (3) behavior is lawful, (4) behavior is a function of its consequences, and (5) the primary area of concern is the conditions maintaining the presence or absence of the target behavior.

The behavior modification model holds that, with rare exception, behavior is learned via certain principles, and, therefore, maladaptive behavior is acquired and maintained in the same way as adaptive behavior. Consequently, the sole target of intervention efforts is adaptive behavior or maladaptive behavior. The concern is not with presumed underlying internal causes such as repressed desires, minimal brain dysfunction, low ego strength, etc. Instead behavior modifiers are concerned with antecedent and consequent stimuli, systematic task analysis, and precise specification of target behaviors

Philosophical Concepts

and goals. In general, the approach is imbued with profound optimism.

> The focus is always upon improvement. No limit is set on what an individual can learn, other than the limits of his own rate of progress. Some individuals may progress quickly, others more slowly, but all are capable of learning. (Thompson & Grabowski, 1972, p. 18)

The rise of behavior modification was largely a result of the interplay of various philosophical influences and a reaction to various aspects of the medical model. The behavior modification model and the medical model differ primarily in their conception of the causes of retarded behavior and their implications for remediation. The medical model holds that structural damage or difference is the cause of the behavior, which in turn is only a symptom of the underlying problem. Information collected by investigators operating within the medical model may be valid, but it typically provides little direction to those involved in programmatic efforts (MacMillan, 1973). In contrast, the behavior modification model provided a dynamic, learning-based conception of retarded behavior. Workers in the field were quick to recognize that an abundant amount of information on learning derived from years of laboratory research was available to guide the development of programs for behavioral change (MacMillan, 1973). This action-oriented approach, bolstered by its explicit optimism, led to quick acceptance of the model.

It should be noted that, contrary to popular opinion, the medical model is not dead (see Clarke & Clarke, 1977). It is true that physicians are seldom in charge of institutions or community-based programs. However, the traditional medical approach to intervention, which can be described as grouping people on the basis of common diagnosis, assigning a label, providing a prognosis, prescribing a treatment (if any is available), and searching for the cause, has been more productive in recent years than ever before. A few dramatically effective treatments are now available, such as those for phenylketonuria and hydrocephaly, and medical researchers have been especially productive in the area of prevention. Congenital syphillis and kernicterus are two examples of syndromes that have been relegated to the past. Advances in prenatal care and genetics have also been rapid in recent years. Some physicians certainly impeded progress with gloomy predictions and recommendations for lifelong custodial care, but others were in the laboratory and substantive results have begun to emerge.

Currently, the behavior modification model dominates programming efforts for the mentally retarded. It has not been without its critics, however. Baumeister (1969), perhaps, best expresses the views of those opposed to the wholesale acceptance of this approach:

> Perhaps it would be fair to say operant conditioning has become something of a fad, particularly among those who are involved in institutional programming. ...Whether this popularity is warranted is quite another matter (p. 49)....Frequently, operant conditioners, in the interests of rigorously defining their response units, have taken a particularly restrictive view of what constitutes an adaptive response....The operant conditioner's definition of toilet training — and many other things, for that matter — probably would not be very comforting to most mothers. ...It is one thing to show that certain well defined response sequences can be shaped in a highly structured, controlled, and atypical environment and quite another matter to demonstrate that operant conditioning can produce permanent adaptive changes in complex areas of adjustment over a wide variety of environmental circumstances. (p. 50)

Other writers (MacMillan, 1973; MacMillan & Forness, 1970; Maehr, 1968) have commented on the limitations of the subject matter and the explanatory power of the approach. It is not uncommon to read a behavior modification report which targets very limited behaviors in selected mentally retarded persons over very short periods of time, and a blanket conclusion such as 'This was shown to be a highly effective procedure for use with the mentally retarded.

> Enthusiasm over reported successes of behavior modification. . . .coupled with the desperation of those working with the retarded has led to a somewhat uncritical acceptance of this technique as a panacea. Some have been blinded to what behavior modification does not, or cannot do. (MacMillan & Forness, 1973, p. 198)

In addition, journals which publish information-processing articles are replete with investigations of complex cognitive variables which have increasingly strong educational implications out of the realm of behavior modification (see reviews by Mercer & Snell, 1977, and Rohwer & Dempster, 1977).

Deitz (1978) leveled a strong caution about the widespread use of behavior modification procedures before they have been adequately researched. He claims that there has not been enough applied science for there to be a sound and finalized technology, and further states that applied behavior analysis differs from basic operant research only in the type of behavior studied: both seek to determine what controls the target behavior. According to Deitz, some recently expressed views run counter to the theoretical basis of applied behavioral analysis and have caused confusion about its purpose. Those by Azrin (1977) were cited as an example:

> Our guiding principle outcome, or in more familiar language, "cure" (p. 141). ...This outcome oriented research strategy places the emphasis on the benefit resulting from treatment rather than on the conceptual variables. (p. 145)

The net effect of this change in philosophy is to restrict advances. "If the goal is to cure rather than investigate, it will become more difficult to discover new cures" (Deitz, 1978, p. 807). Many of the severely and profoundly mentally retarded of yesterday can be found among the severely and profoundly retarded of today despite repeated attempts at behavioral "cures."

The philosophical shift to an outcome orientation also entails a potential conflict of interests. Traditionally, operant conditioners have avoided firm hypotheses about human behavior (Sidman, 1960). However,

> When the purpose of behavioral efforts is to promote a cure, once one makes the assumption that one *can* promote a cure, quite firm hypotheses are stated. Holding firm hypotheses then leads to the problem of completing research in order to confirm these hypotheses. (Deitz, 1978, p. 808)

These problems are magnified when behavior modifiers have products to sell in the form of behavior management and training packages which are founded on their research (e.g., Gold, 1980, Foxx & Azrin, 1973; Watson, 1972, 1978).

Pierce and Epling (1980) essentially agree with the arguments presented above and suggest that the contingencies on investigators' behavior set by institutions and service agencies and the editorial policies of leading applied journals may, in large part, be responsible for the shift in orientation. Other behavior modifiers have noted the increasing trend from more conceptual to purely technical aspects of behavior modification and have reiterated the caution that, as a result, the actual applied impact of the field may be severely limited (Birnbrauer, 1979; Hayes, 1978; Hayes, Rincover, & Solnick, 1980).

From a different perspective, Holland (1978) is strongly critical of the assumptions and methods of some of his fellow behavior modifiers. The problem is often considered to be the client who exhibits the behavior rather than the stimuli maintaining the behavior. Also, the methods used to effect cure often involve artificial contingencies operating in isolation, rather than a restructuring of the prevailing conditions. In Holland's words, "lasting behavior change requires the modification of the contingencies that produce and maintain the original behavior" (1978, p. 164).

The behavior modification model has also been criticized for its neutral stance on the specification of habilitative goals (e.g., Hewett, Taylor, & Artuso, 1969; MacNamara, 1977; MacMillan & Forness, 1973; Winett & Winkler, 1972; Wood, 1968).

> Like many "tools," behavior modification techniques are themselves morally blind. Like a stout sword, they work equally well in the hands of hero or tyrant. Any person of moderate intelligence can, with assistance if not independently, apply them with great effectiveness for good or ill. (Wood, 1968, p. 14)

Only after someone has decided on the target behavior, independent of the model, can the techniques be implemented. Other models (e.g., Montessori, Piaget, Kohlberg, Wolfensberger) are needed to assist in determining goals and in outlining a program of tasks and skills. Without such guidance, there is a real danger that behaviors which facilitate the smooth operation of the educational/institutional system will be increased, and that behaviors which annoy the trainers will be decreased, whether or not they enhance or interfere with a person's progress. Winett and Winkler (1972) label this the "be still, be quiet, be docile" approach to programming.

Behavior modifiers have also been strongly criticized for frequently choosing reinforcers for their own convenience rather than for the client's best interests (Ferster, 1967; MacMillan, 1969; MacMillan & Forness, 1970). MacMillan (1969) proposed a continuum of consequences, ranging from the most primitive and artificial to the most mature and natural, along which clients should be advanced.

The above-mentioned shortcomings have drawn the attention of many coworkers. Our belief is that the majority of problems discussed here are not due to any limitations in behavior modification principles, but to the ineptitude or misdirection of many of those who use the principles in programmatic efforts.

The previous discussion is a prelude to a critical issue in the use of behavior modification techniques in habilitative programs, that is, legal and ethical responsibilities concerning control. Recent landmark court decisions have argued that mentally retarded citizens possess rights previously accorded only to nonretarded citizens (Martin, 1975). Violations of those rights have sometimes involved the use of behavior modification techniques, particularly punishment. This has resulted in legal strictures and occasional social and professional mandates against the use of punishment in programmatic interventions (e.g., Hewett, 1968; *Wyatt* v. *Stickney*).

Rejection of the use of punishment would not be lamentable if more benign and effective techniques for dealing with severe problems were available. However, such is not always the case. Repp and Deitz (1978), who have contributed much to the study of positive reinforcement reductive procedures, stated:

> A journal reader might presume the technology of applied behavior analysis has advanced to a level commensurate with the severity of behavioral problems presented by retarded persons. However, those working directly with retarded clients in institutions...consistently discuss problems not solved by these newer methodologies. In these cases, there appears to be a clear need for seeking a judicious use of punishment techniques when circumstances suggest the client will benefit more from such treatment than from absence of such treatment. (p. 250)

And Baer (1970) pointedly commented, "Not to rescue a person from an unhappy organization of his behavior is to punish him, in that it leaves him in a state of recurrent punishment" (p. 246). Although withholding aversive treatment can be considered unethical for these reasons, it may also be illegal when it precludes movement to a less restrictive environment. As Martin (1975) explains, "When a person is confined, the quid pro quo for allowing confinement, according to *Donaldson* v. *O'Connor,* is treatment sufficient to qualify for release" (p. 71). Interestingly, whereas advocates of the normalization principles are often the most outspoken against the use of punishment, normalization could dictate the use of some punitive procedures with mentally retarded persons comparable to those operative in the normal society, for example, reprimands, frowns, fines, suspensions, loss of privileges, spankings (Tennant, Huttersley, & Cullen, 1978).

In summary, the behavior modification approach is the result of a confluence of numerous philosophical and scientific orientations extending far back into history. The central tenets are that overt behavior is the appropriate subject matter and that behavior is a function of its consequences. Intervention techniques derived from the model focus on the antecedent and consequent stimuli. Critics of the approach have claimed that (1) typical target behaviors have been rather restricted in scope, (2) efficacy has been prematurely overstated, (3) habilitative goals are not specified, permitting programmatic misdirection, and (4) the philosophical shift from analysis and cure solely to cure will severely curtail future technological advances. We believe that the validity of any of these claims can be attributed in large part to a lack of understanding, poor training, or misdirection of many of those who apply the behavior modification principles, rather than to limitations in the principles themselves.

Critics notwithstanding, behavior modification techniques are the most widely adopted in programming efforts. We now turn to the most popular contemporary positions which dictate the objectives to which these techniques have been applied, that is, normalization and related concepts.

Normalization

In 1961, representatives of the recently formed President's Panel on Mental Retardation (PPMR) traveled to several European countries. Their purpose was to gather information about services for the mentally retarded so that the panel could better plan the needs of mentally retarded citizens in the United States. Enthusiastic reports were received from the delegation to the Scandinavian countries and the Netherlands (PPMR, 1962). The attitudes and services they described (now embodied in the principle of normalization) were quickly embraced by many leaders in the field and have become an almost universal standard for service providers and consumers.

Normalization as a concept was first promulgated by Bank-Mikkelson, who was instrumental in having the principle included in the 1959 Danish legislation governing services for the mentally retarded. To Bank-Mikkelson, normalization meant "letting the mentally retarded obtain an existence as close to normal as possible" (Wolfensberger, 1972, p. 27). The first systematic presentation of the principle was a monograph by Bengt Nirje sponsored by the President's Committee on Mental Retardation. This paper was translated into Swedish and was the first significant treatment of the topic in the Scandinavian literature (Wolfensberger, 1972). Nirje's conception of normalization, slightly different from Bank-Mikkelson's original idea, was "making available to the mentally retarded, patterns and conditions of everyday life which are as close as possible to the norms and patterns of the mainstream of society" (Nirje, 1969, p. 181). A more significant change in the concept was made by Wolfensberger (1972), whose definition is probably the most widely accepted today. To allow for the "broadest adaptability to human management in general," he proposed the following definition of the normalization principle: "Utilization of means which are as culturally normative as possible, in order to establish and/or maintain personal behaviors and characteristics which are as culturally normative as possible" (Wolfensberger, 1972, p. 28; see Wolfensberger, 1980, for a more recent definition with only superficial changes). Thus, Wolfensberger's principle included both a means and an end in contrast to Nirje's, which emphasized only the means.

The provision of services which are as culturally normative as possible is a philosophical commitment. Whether or not "normal" services will lead to more normal behavior is an empirical question. The necessity for making a distinction between the means (normal services) and the end (normal behavior) has been discussed by Roos (1972), Miller (1974), and Throne (1975). Their main concern is that culturally normative services might not always be the best way to achieve the goals of the developmental model.[1]

[1]The developmental model has different meanings for different people. The term *developmentally retarded* was, to our knowledge, first used by Cameron and Margaret (1951). It was adopted by Bijou and his colleagues in their functional analysis of behavior (Bijou, 1963, 1966; Orlando, 1961a; Orlando & Bijou, 1960; Orlando, Bijou, Tyler, & Marshall, 1961). A "developmental theory" of mental retardation was most forcefully stated by Zigler and holds that mentally retarded persons progress through the developmental sequence more slowly than normal persons and often reach a lower asymptote of development (Zigler, 1966, 1967, 1969). In the late 1960s, Roos, Menalascino, and others were discussing the "developmental model," which, in essence, simply holds that mentally retarded people develop. By 1972, NARC had adopted this model.

The developmental model is "based on the assumption that all retardates have potential for growth, learning, and development" (Roos, 1971, p. 23). Further premises are that the mentally retarded, like all human beings, develop in a sequential and predictable way throughout their life span, and that a teacher's task is to determine the developmental level of each individual client and to provide experiences appropriate for that level. The model is not logically associated with the concept of normalization. However, even a cursory perusal of the literature indicates that the two are typically associated. According to Roos (1979), there is a consensus that mental retardation should be approached from a developmental perspective and that for most mentally retarded people this means adherence to the principle of normalization. However, it does not necessarily follow that all mentally retarded people will develop maximally by the "utilization of means that are as culturally normative as possible."

Roos (1972) was forced to take issue with the inclusion of means in the definition of normalization in order to reconcile the techniques of behavior modification with the principle. He felt that nonnormal experiences were certainly appropriate if designed to foster normal behavior. Miller (1974) reiterated Roos's objection and pointed out other inconsistencies in Wolfensberger's treatment of the concept of normalization, for example, how to determine what is normal? By professional fiat? According to central tendency? Although there have been many critics of normalization, the most comprehensive indictment of the principle belongs to Throne (1975):

> To speak of normalizing the retarded by treating them normally is a contradiction in terms; treating them normally will leave them functioning as retarded. Retarded by definition means retarded under ordinary conditions. Only extraordinary conditions — nonnormal can result in diminishing retarded states, i.e., making the retarded more normal. (p. 23)

NARC had already accepted the fact that nonnormal procedures could be used if they had been demonstrated to be more effective (NARC, 1972). Throne maintains that this position is in error and concludes that "specialized procedures must logically have priority, if we really believe in their right to develop normally to the fullest extent possible" (1975, p. 25).

Throne's argument was substantially reiterated by Aanes and Haagenson (1978), who stated that normalization as a means becomes relevant only if normal means are the best path to a desirable outcome. Rhoades and Browning (1977) argued that Wolfensberger advocates the elimination of deviancy by simply removing it from public awareness and that the ultimate goal of normalization is socially isolated independent living. Mesibov (1976) indicated that the application of normalization has been directed more toward service agencies than the clients of those agencies. Isaacson (1977) presented a convincing argument that recognition of a mentally retarded person's deficiency is a prerequisite for humanely meeting his or her needs.

Wolfensberger (1980) has recently responded to all the above criticicisms and others not mentioned here. He claims that most critics are unaware of the basic literature (i.e., his own writings) and either fail to relate to any of the specific definitions (i.e., Bank-Mikkelson's, Nirje's, or his own) or fail to recognize the differences between them. His attempt to clarify the issues includes the following elaborations of his conception of normalization (1) the goal of normalization is culturally valued treatment as opposed to statistically normative treatment, (2) social integration necessarily involves "intimate, positive one-to-one relationships with ordinary (un-paid) citizens," and (3) nonnormative techniques can be used if the outcome justifies the "damage inflicted by nonnormative means." He further contends that Throne and others are clinically wrong in their contention that normal treatment will perpetuate a client's retarded behavior, because "often, the impairment itself is only the result of denormalized treatment in the first place" (Wolfensberger, 1980, p. 87). Wolfensberger concludes his rebuttal by admonishing critics to distinguish between process and outcome, allow for different degrees of normalization, distinguish between physical and social integration, and recognize that normalization corollaries may clash with one another (sic).

Criticism of the principle notwithstanding, the programmatic recommendations which Wolfensberger made in 1972 now serve as a standard (albeit a very incomplete one) for many service providers. Most of the recommendations that supposedly are derived from the principle of normalization have to do with residential services. This is no surprise, considering Wolfensberger's writing (e.g., 1969, 1971a, b) previous to his formulation of the normalization principle. In fact, most of his 1972 pronouncement was a restatement of his already established position that large residential institutions should be replaced by small community facilities. The only substantive difference was a philosophical position upon which to hang his hat. He posited five major implications of normalization for group residential services; (1) they should be integrated in the community with easy access to generic services; (2) they should be small; (3) they should be specialized so that all residents requiring the same degree of supervision and/or care live together; (4) residents should not live and work at the same place; and (5) there should be a continuum of services with individual placement representing the ideal. Several other programmatic implications, often related to these, can be found scattered throughout his treatise. He stated that the nonnormal should be surrounded by the normal, that mentally retarded children should not associate with mentally retarded adults, that the name of a facility should be chosen to foster a perception of nondeviancy, that males and females should mingle, that useful work should be performed by the mentally retarded to the extent of their capabilty, that the daily routine of the mentally retarded should be comparable to that of the nonretarded, and finally, that the mentally retarded should be educated with the nonretarded (Wolfensberger, 1972). In 1980, more advice has been added. For example, he now also proposes that community living arrangements should not be in close proximity to "devalued" neighborhoods, that the mentally retarded should not work in cemeteries or funeral parlors, and that the handicapped should not work on things for other handicapped people or do classical institutional work (e.g., upholstery or shoe repair). Wolfensberger's programmatic guidelines designed to implement the normalization principle stand almost alone. Other writers have tended either to restate or criticize rather than extend them.

Most of the advice presented above could be subsumed under two related positions, *de-institutionalization* and *mainstreaming*. Both of these positions are closely allied to the current conception of normalization. It is hard to find a proponent of normalization who is not also an advocate of small, community-based residential facilities and of integration in education. However, de-institutionalization and mainstreaming both have their own roots and would likely be potent in the field today if we had never heard of normalization.

The de-institutionalization movement began when the deplorable conditions existing in many public facilities for the mentally retarded were exposed and publicized in the 1950s and 1960s (e.g., Blatt & Kaplan, 1966). In 1969, Wolfensberger clearly tied this movement to the emerging principle of normalization. In 1971, he proposed that institutions, as he defined them, should fade away, and went so far as to say that the goal of superintendents should be to phase out their institutions and to replace them with small group homes, utilizing existing housing where possible (Wolfensberger, 1971a, b). The position Wolfensberger espoused was fairly pervasive by 1971 when President Nixon issued what has been called his "de institutionalization statment." Nixon called for all Americans to help achieve two goals: to reduce by half the occurence of mental retardation and to reduce by one-third the population in institutions. The movement steamrolled with little opposition and has been incorporated into standards, laws, proclamations, etc., as documented in the next section. The major target has been large institutions, even though Wolfensberger himself did not use size *per se* as one of the criteria for defining those facilities that should fade away.

We were reminded by Throne (1979) that small or medium-sized community-based residential facilities, group homes, foster homes, and nuclear families are also institutions. Evidence is equivocal concerning the relationship of size of a residential facility and the quality of life of those who live there. Balla (1976) reviewed the available literature, found only a handful of citable studies, and concluded that there was not enough information to decide one way or another. Landesman-Dwyer, Sackett, and Kleinman (1980) agreed with Balla and reported that the only difference among group homes ranging in size from 6 to 20 residents was in favor of the larger ones. Baroff (1980) reviewed essentially the same studies and concluded that small facilities are associated with more individualized resident-care practices. The controversy is not over. Nevertheless, the move against large institutions and toward community-based facilities continues, not because they have been demonstrated to lead to more normal behavior, but because they look more normal.

Mainstreaming is the counterpart to de-institutionalization within the field of education. The term has different meanings for different people. Mercer (1974) places the concept on a continuum of special education services ranging from totally segregated special classes to no special assistance whatsoever. Others (e.g., MacMillan, Jones, & Meyers, 1976) are much more specific and suggest several criteria, including attendance in a regular class at least half the day and the absence of any label or classification. Most recommend it only for "borderline" and mildly retarded children in line with Dunn's (1968) far-reaching criticism of special education. Jones and Moe (1980) advocate mainstreaming at the college level for even the severely and profoundly retarded. The only thing approaching consensus about mainstreaming is that it refers to the idea that at least some of the mentally retarded should attend regular classes some of the time.

Mainstreaming, which is hardly a new idea, was espoused by a few professionals in the early 1900s (Sloan & Stevens, 1976). Until the last decade or so, only a very small percentage of the mentally retarded have received any special services in the school system. The vast majority were excluded from public school, and those who were admitted either succeeded on their own or were socially promoted until they dropped out (Dunn, 1973; Gearhart & Weishahn, 1976). However, this state of affairs existed more by default than by intent. Most teachers and other professionals perceived a need for separate classes for mentally retarded and normal students for their mutual benefit. Consequently, special-education classes developed rapidly when money and political support became available after World War II.

In 1948, 86,980 mentally retarded individuals were enrolled in special-education classes provided by public school systems. By 1971, this figure had multiplied more than tenfold (Dunn, 1973). About this time, the movement *against* self-contained special classes began in earnest. The attack occurred on several fronts (see Corman & Gottlieb, 1978, for a review of the area). One argument was their failure to demonstrate better academic achievement for students placed in special classes (e.g., Blatt, 1960; Dunn, 1968; Goldstein, Moss, & Jordan, 1965; Hammons, 1972); another, the concern for possible detrimental social effects of being labeled mentally retarded and being isolated from one's peers (e.g., MacMillan, Jones, & Aloia, 1974; Mercer, 1973). Another argument was seen in the overrepresentation of minority groups in special-education classes (e.g., Blanton, 1975; Franks, 1971; Mercer, 1973). This attack is viewed by many as the most critical. In the words of Blatt, "It is my impression that the mainstreaming movement grew out of the civil rights movement, out of concern for the right of all people to enjoy educational opportunities and in as normal a societal structure as possible" (1979, p. 304). The concept of mainstreaming has been adopted by most advocates of the normalization model, despite Wolfensberger's (1980) disclaimer. We believe that this allegiance is one of the most significant factors contributing to the current popularity of mainstreaming.

Support for the mainstreaming movement is broad-based but is not beyond criticism. One major objection is a corollary to the one Throne (1975) made against the overall principle of normalization and has been presented in various forms (e.g., MacMillan *et al.*, 1976). The gist of the argument is that the typical mentally retarded person placed in a special-education class was, after all, failing in the regular class (MacMillan, 1971). School systems do not begin a testing process until an individual is identified as failing in a regular class (Meyers, Sundstrom, & Yoshida, 1974). Why, then, do we now expect the regular class to accommodate them? According to MacMillan and Borthwick (1980), "mainstreaming is feasible only for a very small percentage of the mentally retarded population when a restrictive definition is employed" (p. 158). This argument has been countered in two ways. Some critics (e.g., Dunn, 1968; Mercer, 1973) maintain that the regular class has changed and that new resources are now available whereas others (e.g., Blatt, 1979; Wolfensberger, 1972) simply place the burden of proof on those who would provide special, that is, nonnormal services.

Childs (1979) presented a different sort of argument against mainstreaming. He maintains that the mentally retarded require a different curriculum than that offered in a regular class. The emphasis in special classes immediately before the mainstreaming movement was on practical skills needed for independent living. According to Childs, the curriculum for a mainstreamed mentally retarded child has now become the same as the one for a regular class student, that is, reading, writing, and arithmetic. He further argues that most of the data indicating success in a regular class are from borderline or slow-learning individuals who probably should never have been placed in a special class in the first place. He also pleads for research on the proper curriculum for the mildly retarded. Childs was countered by Warren (1979), who believes that decisions must be made on "legal, philosophical, and ethical bases" in the absence of research, and by Blatt (1979), who maintains that research has nothing to do with the issue and that we need merely to pledge ourselves to the idea.

The philosophical positions described above are certainly not the only ones affecting current efforts in programming for the mentally retarded. However, they are the most influential and pervasive. It also seems likely that, if a national survey of professionals and consumers were conducted, the majority would agree with them in one form or another. There are also many who would disagree in one form or another. This is as it should be. No positions to date have provided a complete solution to the problem of habilitating the mentally retarded; if one is to emerge, it will have to go beyond established modes of thought. Consequently, we, as service providers, are gravely concerned about the growing tendency to "dogmatize" opinions of the majority, before efficacy is adequately demonstrated on scientific grounds. There is a serious danger that this will impede programmatic progress. To this and related issues we now turn.

Humanistic Legalism

A third movement with increasingly profound impact on programming for mentally retarded persons is what we term *humanistic legalism*. This is defined as the reification, via advocacy position statements, proclamations, court orders, and legislation, of philosophical positions and programmatic orientations. The guiding and noble spirit is equality in justice: that regardless of the limitations of mentally retarded persons, as human beings they are entitled to dignity, respect, and the rights of other citizens, unless these are suspended for good reason and through due process of law (Allen, 1969). The concept is not new. More than 250 years ago an English law book read:

> It is not certain that our Law hath a very great and tender consideration for Persons naturally Disabled. ...The Law protects their Persons, preserves their rights and Estates, Excuseth their Laches, and assists them in the Pleadings. (The Infant's Lawyer, 1712, as cited in Allen, 1969)

Today this movement can be seen as part of a larger concern with constitutional rights of minorities, beginning formally with *Brown* v. *Board of Educa-*

tion (1954). It gained impetus from the rise of consumer advocacy groups, most notably NARC, and the increased sensitivity to the problem of the mentally retarded by President Kennedy, resulting in the formation of the President's Committee on Mental Retardation. In the beginning, the primary concern was improvement of services for the mentally retarded, untainted by any particular programmatic orientations. More recently, the emphasis has shifted.

In October of 1970, a class action suit (*Wyatt* v. *Stickney*) was filed in a district court in Alabama on behalf of the 5,000 mental patients at Bryce Hospital. In August of 1971, nearby Partlow State School and Hospital for the mentally retarded was added to the case at the request of the plaintiffs. After hearing evidence of the abhorrent conditions there, Judge Johnson issued a landmark decision which focused on three main areas of deficiency (1) a humane physical and psychological environment, (2) qualified staff in numbers sufficient to provide adequate treatment, and (3) an individual habilitation plan (IHP) for each resident. Johnson was the first to enunciate a "right to treatment" and to prescribe a set of standards for minimally acceptable care and medical and treatment conditions in public facilities for the mentally retarded. These 49 standards were formulated by attorneys representing both the plaintiffs and defendants, in conjunction with representatives of a number of national professional organizations, including the American Psychological Association, the American Orthopsychiatric Association, and the American Association on Mental Deficiency. Many of these standards delineate requirements for adequate physical facilities and habilitative services. Others, however, are statements of philosophy which include the principle of normalization, de-institutionalization, and the developmental model.

Wyatt marks the beginning of the intertwining of legal rights and programmatic philosophies. The flurry of litigation and legislation following *Wyatt* is an unprecedented and "extraordinary reliance on the courts as agencies of reform" (Cohen, 1976). The Mental Health Law project has played a central role. This group was formed in 1972 by the attorneys who represented the *amicus curiae* organizations in the *Wyatt* case and some of the experts who worked on the standards. A few examples will elucidate the main thrust of most of this action.

The consent decree accepted in *The New York State Association for Retarded Children* v. *Carey* (1975) specified the primary goals of the Willowbrook Developmental Center as the development of each resident, preparation for their living in the community, and the establishment of less restrictive community facilities for more than half of the residents. This case also established a second constitutional principle for mentally retarded persons: the right to protection from harm. *The Developmental Disabilities Act* (P.L. 94-103) signed by President Ford in 1973 states that "the treatment, services and habilitation for a person with developmental disabilities . . . should be provided in the setting that is least restrictive of the person's personal liberty." *The Education for All Handicapped Children Act* of 1975 (P.L. 94-142) stresses a similar point with respect to education. In *Halderman v. Pennhurst State School and Hospital* (1977), the district court ruled that the very existence of the institution violated the law and that it must be closed and replaced by a network of community facilities.

Actions like these have accomplished an extraordinary amount and have become the major force in combating numerous tragic examples of inhuman treatment. In many cases, the final efforts have yet to be realized and the work must continue. However, we contend that many recent decisions have potentially tragic consequences for advances in programmatic services. Judges have, at the persistent urging of public-interest lawyers and certain experts, extended their decisions (and consequently their domain) from the concerns of human rights, to particular programmatic beliefs and orientations.

Ordering an increase in the programmatic services provided a person to ensure his rights is quite different from ordering that a particular programmatic orientation be adopted. The latter is inappropriate, particularly when that programmatic orientation is under debate by professionals with expertise in the area. This removes the critical decisions from those most capable of making them, allows for the official sanction of fads, and potentially limits investigation of other, possibly more beneficial, positions. The foremost example of this is the principle of normalization as a process to accomplish habilitation (Wolfensberger, 1972). We maintain that, even though the goal of normalization is noble, it is inappropriate for a judge to order normalization as the process to achieve that goal.

Statements such as the following obscure individual differences among mentally retarded people, ignore differences of opinion among professionals, and add little to enlightened discovery:

> Understanding and applying the principle of normalization at an operational level is *essential* in the establishment of new service models, especially community residential facilites. . . . The principle of normalization is deceptively simple, *requiring* that service delivery practices enable a person considered different by society to function within the acceptable norms of his community. Thus, the means employed for training should be as culturally normative as possible . . . the program processes and content that are used should be as close as possible to those typically utilized in the normal culture. *Only* in this way will retarded citizens develop more normal adult behavior and improve their relations with others. (Glenn, 1976, pp. 500–501, emphasis added)

A majority of the residents currently found in institutions are profoundly retarded, some of whom have resisted the best habilitative attempts yet devised. No matter what a principle claims, it cannot simply require that residents function normally and expect it to materialize. There is no compelling evidence that application of the principle of normalization is "essential, that program processes must be as normal as possible, that "only in this way" will optimal habilitation be realized. And yet, court testimony such as this has emerged in the proclamation of judges. A few decades ago, progressive professionals in the field of mental retardation were zealously encouraging institutionalization. Should the courts join sides in this pendulumlike process of discovery which often characterizes science?

In the *Pennhurst* case, Judge Broderick, who was obvioulsy caught up in this spirit, observed that

> Since the early 1960s there has been a distinct humanistic renaissance, replete with the acceptance of the theory of normalization for the habilitation of the retarded. . . . As the Court has heretofore found, Pennhurst does not provide an atmosphere conducive to normalization which is so vital to the retarded if they are to be given the opportunity to acquire, maintain, and improve thier life skills.

We contend that programmatic services for the mentally retarded will be advanced only if the courts act to steadfastly preserve constitutional rights, and if social scientists act to discover and refine particular methods for their actualization. In the continuing *Wyatt* litigation, Judge Johnson succinctly stated a similar position, concerning de-institutionalization:

> From the evidence it is clear that there is debate within the profession concerning the beneficial effects of community placement for the severely and profoundly retarded. The Court will not choose sides in this debate, nor should it. In 1972, the Court ordered defendants to implement certain standards only after there had been a finding of widespread constitutional violations. . . . Determining the ideal mode of treatment, or ordering state institutions to implement the best system, is beyond the province of the Court. (*Wyatt* v. *Ireland*, 1979)

In this important ruling, the court modified some of the standards and acknowledged that an institution may be the least restrictive environment for some residents. Also, the U.S. Court of Appeals, Third Circuit, recently stayed the ruling of the district court in *Pennhurst* to close the institution. Judge Gibbons stated that the trial court should have considered whether or not the needs of individual residents would be better served in the community and allowed for the possibility that some might be better served in the institution. The issue will eventually be heard by the U.S. Supreme Court. Ultimately, the question to be answered is: Who makes the programmatic decisions concerning habilitation?

> Unlike voter registration or school desegregation or equal access to public facilities, no court order can permanently accomplish the ultimate and only real purpose of litigation over the provision of social services: fair, adequate, and humanitarian treatment. That goal is and will remain the primary responsibility of those professionals who have been trained and have chosen to serve those in need of their particular knowledge and skills. (Johnson, 1975, p. 347)

In conclusion, humanistic legalism has had a profound influence on the programmatic services provided mentally retarded persons. Whereas it may spring from good faith and intention, there are drawbacks to the reification of philosophical and programmatic orientations which in the long run could have negative consequences for the very people on whose behalf the action is taken. Clearly, we are advocating that specific programmatic doctrines be excluded from court and legislative proclamations unless they are concerned with specific infringements of a mentally retarded person's constitutional rights.

Philosophy in Action: Current Programming Efforts

We now return to Alicia, the fictional character introduced at the start of this chapter, to depict some of the effects of the previously discussed movements on services for the mentally retarded.

At the time we left her, Alicia was a resident at Midwest State School. The institution was overcrowded and understaffed and had a long waiting list. New admissions were exceptional and typically granted more for political purposes than treatment concerns. A newly formed chapter of NARC from a nearby city toured the facility in 1956, and individual members selected specific cases for review. Alicia's was one of those selected.

Several things were determined from Alicia's record and conversations with staff who knew her. Included in periodic psychological evaluations were recommendations for training in a vocationally oriented skill. When questioned about the lack of follow-up on these, the facility's psychologist said that he and his two staff members barely had time to test the 1,400 residents. He assumed that ward staff, if anyone, would implement their recommendations and further indicated that his department had little to offer from a programmatic standpoint. An aide assigned to Alicia's living unit said that Alicia's daily routine consisted mainly of helping ward personnel perform their duties, which she occasionally refused to do. The principal of the school program on campus said that Alicia had attended for several months, but was dropped in favor of a higher-level resident.

Medical records indicated that Alicia had been taking a daily dose of chlorpromazine for several years in an attempt to control her tantrums and to alleviate her stubbornness. No mention was made of the success of this regimen. This was not an unusual situation. As recently as 1969, more than half of the population residing in institutions for the mentally retarded were receiving psychotropic medication (Lipman, 1970). The NARC member also visited briefly with Alicia and found her to be pleasant but relatively uncommunicative. When asked if she wanted anything, Alicia said, "When my momma coming?" According to Alicia's social worker, the family did not visit often because of transportation problems. Permanent home placement was not considered feasible, because both of her parents worked, and there were no services for the mentally retarded in her home community.

The NARC discussed conditions at the institution at great length during their next meeting. The group as a whole was not shocked; conditions of Midwest State School were in no way comparable to the horror stories about other institutions that some members had heard at the last annual meeting of NARC. However, they were very concerned about their firsthand evidence of public indifference and legislative neglect. They pledged themselves to support upgrading of the institution, development of community programs, and research regarding treatment and prevention. The subsequent efforts of many groups like this one led, in large part, to the first significant improvements in services for mentally retarded citizens in decades. They accomplished this by acting as a lobbying group at the state and national level and by providing direct services in the community. They also played a significant part in creating an optimistic attitude about the trainability and potential productivity of all mentally retarded citizens.

Alicia's lot gradually changed for the better. A new institution was built in another part of the state, and 200 residents were transferred there from Midwest State School. More community programs and special education classes became available. As a result, the crowded conditions and the pressure for admissions were eased somewhat. A few of the oldest dormitories at Midwest State School, including Alicia's, were renovated to meet the standards required for participation in the Title XIX of The Social Security Act (1974).

The adoption of these standards led to several significant changes. These included (1) the provision of an individual plan of active treatment designed to foster the skills necessary for community living for every resident, (2) the cessation of Alicia's housekeeping duties, (3) the development of a daily schedule of activities which approximated a "normal" routine, and (4) the procurement of enough qualified staff to accomplish the above. One of the new staff members was a psychologist from the University of Washington, who introduced behavior modification to the facility.

The first application of behavior modification techniques was a token system in Alicia's living unit similar to the ones described in Birnbrauer and Lawler (1964) and Ayllon and Azrin (1968). Alicia earned points for her participation in ward maintenance tasks, for punctuality at the dining room, for maintaining her grooming skills, and for a multitude of other behaviors. She could redeem the points for snacks, radios, dolls, TV time, visits to the campus hairdresser, passes to the weekly dance, and a host of other commodities and activities. She was fined points whenever she had a tantrum. Some of the aides on Alicia's ward wanted to use electric shock to control these: they had heard that "shock therapy" was working well on the behavior control unit. The psychologist, however, did not think Alicia's behavior was serious enough to warrant the use of shock. Alicia's response to the program was generally good, except that she occasionally tore up her point card and refused to participate.

A great change was brewing for Alicia in the late 1960s and early 1970s. In response to local pressure, federal guidelines, and the national clamor generated by the recently concluded *Wyatt* v. *Stickney* case, her state joined the de-institutionalization and normalization movements at their height. The development of a full range of community services was encouraged at the state level and largely funded by federal dollars. An adult activity center and two group homes were built in Alicia's home community. Today, many states have a broad array of community services; others do not (Bruinicks, Hauber, & Kudla, 1980).

At Midwest State School the programmatic efforts for Alicia shifted to emphasize the skills necessary for her eventual participation in a work activity center and placement in a community group home. Professionals were uncertain, however, about which skills were necessary for successful community placement (e.g., McCarver & Craig, 1974; Heal, Sigleman, & Switsky, 1978), so they followed the recommendations of several directors of community programs.

Alicia still had her tantrums and periods of noncompliance, for which she was now "timed-out" in addition to being fined. Time-out rooms had to be modified to ensure adequate lighting, temperature, and supervision. Staff members were becoming increasingly disinclined to use the procedure now that they had to personally hold the time-out door shut when she was inside. Professional staff attended an increasing number of workshops and, after one of them, returned very enthusiastic about a new technique which was said to reduce maladaptive behaviors, instill responsibility for one's actions, and teach adaptive behaviors. Although her stubbornness remained unchanged, this overcorrection procedure reduced the frequency of her tantrums somewhat;

however, staff were observed sometimes to "look the other way" during these episodes, apparently to avoid applying the techniques.

In her annual interdisciplinary team meeting, it was recommended that Alicia be referred for placement in the community. Subsequently, a social worker arranged a meeting with Alicia's mother to elicit her support for Alicia's potential outplacement. At the beginning of the meeting, Alicia's mother did not favor community placement. She supported community programs in general, but felt that her daughter might not receive the close supervision she required if she lived in a group home. This is not an atypical parental attitude (e.g., Ferrara, 1970; Meyer, 1980). She was also concerned about what would happen to Alicia if the group home closed. The social worker, a staunch advocate of normalization, countered by saying that Alicia could never realize her true potential from a developmental perspective while she lived in an institution and gave her a copy of Perske's article on the dignity of risk (1972). She also emphasized that Alicia would be much closer to her parents in the group home. In the end, Alicia's mother agreed to support the transfer, at least on a trial basis. A case summary was then prepared and sent to the local agency for review. The first paragraph read as follows:

> Alicia is a 21-year-old female with Down's syndrome. On the Stanford-Binet, she obtained a score of 40, placing her in the moderate range of mental retardation according to current terminology of the American Association on Mental Deficiency (Grossman, 1977). Alicia is more socially adept than would be predicted on the basis of her IQ score. She can take care of her personal needs, count to 20, read and write her name, carry on a simple conversation, find her way to and from familiar places, and perform a variety of tasks with minimal supervision. She has no striking maladaptive behaviors and generally gets along well with other people. When she doesn't get her way, however, she has occasional temper tantrums, some rather severe.

References

Aanes, D., & Haagenson, L. Normalization: Attention to a conceptual disaster. *Mental Retardation*, 1978, *16*, 55–56.

Allen, R. C. Legal rights of the institutionalized retardate: Equal justice for the unequal. *Mental Retardation*, 1969, *7*, 2–5.

Ayllon, T. Intensive treatment of psychotic behavior by stimulus satiation and food reinforcement. *Behavior Research and Therapy*, 1963, *1*, 53–61.

Ayllon, T. Some behavioral problems associated with eating in chronic schizophrenic patients. In L. P. Ullman & L. Krasner (Eds.), *Case studies in behavior modification*. New York: Holt, Rinehart & Winston, 1965.

Ayllon, T., & Azrin, N. H. Reinforcement and instructions with mental patients. *Journal of the Experimental Analysis of Behavior*, 1964, *7*, 327–331.

AYLLON, T., & AZRIN, N. H. The measurement and reinforcement of behavior of psychotics. *Journal of the Experimental Analysis of Behavior*, 1965, *8*, 357-380.

AYLLON, T., & AZRIN, N. H. *The token economy: A motivational system for therapy and rehabilitation.* New York: Appleton-Century-Crofts, 1968.

AYLLON, T., & HAUGHTON, E. Control of the behavior of schizophrenics by food. *Journal of the Experimental Analysis of Behavior*, 1962, *5*, 343-352.

AYLLON, T., & HAUGHTON, E. Modification of symptomatic verbal behavior of mental patients. *Behaviour Research and Therapy*, 1964, *2*, 87-97.

AYLLON, T., & MICHAEL, J. The psychiatric nurse as a behavioral engineer. *Journal of the Experimental Analysis of Behavior*, 1959, *2*, 323-334.

AZRIN, N. H. A strategy for applied research: Learning based but outcome oriented. *American Psychologist*, 1977, *32*, 140-149.

BAER, D. M. A case for the selective reinforcement of punishment. In C. Neuringer & J. Michael (Eds.), *Behavior modification in clinical psychology.* New York: Appleton-Century-Crofts, 1970.

BALLA, D. Relationship of institution size to quality of care: A review of the literature. *American Journal of Mental Deficiency*, 1976, *81*, 117-124.

BARR, M. W. *Mental defectives: Their history, treatment, and training.* Philadelphia, Pa.: P. Blakiston, 1913.

BAROFF, G. On size and quality of residential care: A second look. *Mental Retardation*, 1980, *18*, 113-118.

BARRETT, B., & LINDSLEY, O. R. Deficits in acquisition of operant discrimination and differentiation shown by institutionalized retarded children. *American Journal of Mental Deficiency*, 1962, *67*, 424-426.

BAUMEISTER, A. A. More ado about operant conditioning—or nothing? *Mental Retardation*, 1969, *7*, 49-51.

BAUMEISTER, A. A. The American residential institution: Its history and character. In A. A. Baumeister & E. C. Butterfield (Eds.), *Residential facilities for the mentally retarded.* Chicago: Aldine, 1970.

BECHTEREV, V. M. *La psychologie objective.* Paris: Alcan, 1913.

BIJOU, S. W. Theory and research in mental (developmental) retardation. *The Psychological Record*, 1963, *13*, 95-110.

BIJOU, S. W. A functional analysis of retarded development. In N. R. Ellis (Ed.), *International review of research in mental retardation* (Vol. 1). New York: Academic Press, 1966.

BIJOU, S. W. & ORLANDO, R. Rapid development of multiple schedule performances with retarded children. *Journal of the Experimental Analysis of Behavior*, 1961, *4*, 7-16.

BIRNBAUM, P. (Ed.). *A treasury of Judaism.* New York: Hebrew Publishing, 1962.

BIRNBRAUER, J. S. In H. Leitenberg (Ed.), *Handbook of behavior modification and behavior therapy.* Englewood Cliffs, N.J.: Prentice-Hall, 1976.

BIRNBRAUER, J. S. Applied behavior analysis, service, and the acquisition of knowledge. *The Behavior Analysit*, 1979, *2*, 15-21.

BIRNBRAUER, J. S., & LAWLER, J. Token reinforcement for learning. *Mental Retardation*, 1964, *2*, 275-279.

BIRNBRAUER, J. S., WOLF, M. M., KIDDER, J. D., & TAGUE, C. Classroom behavior of retarded pupils with token reinforcement. *Journal of Experimental Child Psychology*, 1965, *2*, 219-235.

BLANTON, R. L. Historical perspectives on classification of mental retardation. In N. Hobbs (Ed.), *Issues in the classification of children*, (Vol. 1). San Francisco: Jossey-Brass, 1975.

BLATT, B. Some persistently recurring assumptions concerning the mentally subnormal. *Training School Bulletin*, 1960, *57*, 48-59.

BLATT, B. A drastically different analysis. *Mental Retardation,* 1979, *17,* 303-306.
BLATT, B., & KAPLAN, F. *Christmas in purgatory.* Boston: Allyn & Bacon, 1966.
Brown v. Board of Education, 347, U.S., *483,* 19-54.
BRUINICKS, R. H., HAUBER, F. A., & KLUDA, M. J. National survey of community residential facilities: A profile of facilities and residents in 1977. *American Journal of Mental Deficiency,* 1980, *84,* 470-478.
CAMERON, N., & MARGARET, A. *Behavior pathology.* New York: Houghton Mifflin, 1951.
CHILDS, R. E. A drastic change in curriculum for the educable mentally retarded child. *Mental Retardation,* 1979, *17,* 299-301.
CLARKE, A. D. & CLARKE, A. M. Prospects for prevention and amelioration of mental retardation. *American Journal of Mental Deficiency,* 1977, *81,* 423-533.
COHEN, F. Advocacy. In M. Kindred, J. Cohen, D. Penrod, & T. Shaffer (Eds.), *The mentally retarded citizen and the law.* New York: Free Press, 1976.
CORMAN, L., & GOTTLIEB, J. Mainstreaming mentally retarded children: A review of research. In N. R. Ellis (Ed.), *International review of research in mental retardation* (Vol. 9). New York: Academic Press. 1978.
DARWIN, C. *The origin of species,* 1859.
DEITZ, S. M. Current status of applied behavior analysis. *American Psychologist,* 1978, *33,* 805-814.
Donaldson v. O'Connor, 493 F. 2d. 507 (5th Cir. 1974), vacated and remanded on the issue of immunity, 95 S. Ct. 2486 (1975).
DUNN, L. M. Special education for the mildly retarded: Is much of it justifiable? *Exceptional Children,* 1968, *35,* 5-22.
DUNN, L. M. An overview. In L.M. Dunn, (Ed.), *Exceptional children in the schools* (Vol. 2). New York: Holt, Rinehart, & Winston, 1973.
ELLIS, N. R. Amount of reward and operant behavior in mental defectives. *Journal of Comparative and Physiological Psychology,* 1962, *6,* 595-599.
ELLIS, N. R. Toilet training the severely defective patient: An S-R reinforcement analysis. *American Journal of Mental Deficiency,* 1963, *68,* 98-103.
ELLIS, N. R. & PRYER, M. Primary versus secondary reinforcement in simple discrimination learning of mental defectives. *Psychological Reports,* 1958, *4,* 67-70.
ELLIS, N. R., BARNETT, C. S., & PRYER, M. W. Operant behavior in mental defectives: Exploratory studies. *Journal of the Experimental Analysis of Behavior,* 1960, *3,* 63-69.
ENGLISH, W. Three cases of contitioned fear response. *Journal of Abnormal Psychology,* 1929, *24,* 221-225.
ESTABROOK, A. H. *The Jukes in 1915.* Washington, D.C.: Carnegie Institution, 1916.
FERNALD, W. E. After-care study of the patients discharged from Waverly for a period of twenty-five years. *Ungraded,* 1919, *5,* 25-31.
FERNALD, W. E. Discussion. *Journal of Psycho-Asthenics,* 1922, *27,* 74.
FERRARA, D. M. Attitudes of parents of mentally retarded children toward normalization activities. *American Journal of Mental Deficiency,* 1979, *84,* 145-151.
FERSTER, C. B. Arbitrary and natural reinforcement. *Psychological Record,* 1967, *17,* 341-347.
FERSTER, C. B., & DEMEYER, M. K. The development of performances in autistic children in an automatically controlled environment. *Journal of Chronic Diseases,* 1961, *13,* 312-345.
FERSTER, C. B., & DEMEYER, M. K. A method of the experimental analysis of the behavior of autistic children. *American Journal of Orthopsychiatry,* 1962, *32,* 89-98.
FOXX, R. M., & AZRIN, N. H. *Toilet training the retarded.* Champaign, Ill.: Research Press, 1973.
FRANKS, D. J. Ethnic and social class characteristics of children in EMR and LD classes. *Exceptional Children,* 1971, *37,* 537-538.

FULLER, P. R. Operant conditioning of a vegetative human organism. *American Journal of Psychology*, 1949, *62*, 587–590.
GEARHART, B. R., & WEISHAHN, M. W. *The handicapped child in the regular classroom*. St. Louis: Mosby, 1976.
GIRARDEAU, F. L. The effect of secondary reinforcement on the operant behavior of mental defectives. *American Journal of Mental Deficiency*, 1962, *67*, 441-449.
GIRARDEAU, F. L. & SPRADLIN, J. E. Token rewards in a cottage program. *Mental Retardation*, 1964, *2*, 345–351.
GLENN, L. The least restrictive alternative in residential care and the principle of normalization. In M. Kindred, J. Cohen, D. Penrod, & T. Shaffer (Eds.), *The mentally retarded citizen and the law*. New York: Free Press, 1976.
GODDARD, H. H. *The Kallikak family*. New York: MacMillan, 1912.
GOLD, M. C. *Marc Gold: "Did I say that?"* Champaign, Ill.: Research Press, 1980.
GOLDSTEIN, H., MOSS, J. W. & JORDAN, L. J. *The efficacy of special class training on the development of mentally retarded children*. Urbana: University of Illinois, Institute for Research on Exceptional Children, 1965.
GROSSMAN, H. (Ed.). *Manual on terminology and classification in mental retardation*. Washington, D.C.: American Association on Mental Deficiency, 1977.
Halderman v. Pennhurst State School and Hospital, F. Supp. (E.D. Pa. 1977).
HAMMONS, G. W. Educating the mildly retarded: A review. *Exceptional Children*, 1972, *38*, 565–570.
HAYES, S. C. Theory and technology in behavior analysis. *The Behavior Analyst*, 1978, *1*, 35–41.
HAYES, S. C., RINCOVER, A., & SOLNICK, J. V. The technical drift of applied behavior analysis. *Journal of Applied Behavior Analysis*, 1980, *13*, 275–285.
HEADRICK, M. W. Effects of instructions and initial reinforcement on fixed-interval behavior in retardates. *American Journal of Mental Deficiency*, 1963, *68*, 425–432. (a)
HEADRICK, M. W. Operant conditioning in mental deficiency. *American Journal of Mental Deficiency*, 1963, *67*, 924–929. (b)
HEAL, L. W., SIGELMAN, C. K., & SWITSKY, H. N. Research on community residential alternatives for the mentally retarded. In N. R. Ellis (Ed.), *International review of research in mental retardation* (Vol. 9). New York: Academic Press, 1978.
HEWETT, F. M. *The emotionally disturbed child in the classroom*. Boston: Allyn & Bacon, 1968.
HEWETT, F. M., TAYLOR, F. D., & ARTUSO, A. A. The Santa Monica project: Evaluation of an engineered classroom design with emotionally disturbed children. *Exceptional Children*, 1969, *35*, 523–529.
HOBBES, T. Human nature. In W. Molesworth (Ed.), *The English works of Thomas Hobbes* Vol. 4. London: Bohn, 1840. (Originally published, 1650.)
HOLLAND, J. G. Behaviorism: Part of the problem or part of the solution. *Journal of Applied Behavior Analysis*, 1978, *11*, 163–174.
ISAACSON, R. *Meeting the needs of the retarded*. Niles, Ill.: Argus Communications, 1977.
IVANOV-SMOLENSKY, A. G. Neurotic behavior and the teaching of conditioned reflexes. *American Journal of Psychiatry*, 1927, *84*, 483–488.
JERSILD, A., & HOLMES, F. Methods in overcoming children's fears. *Journal of Psychology*, 1935, *1*, 75–104.
JOHNSON, F. M., JR. Court decisions and the social services. *Social Work*, 1975, *20*, 343–347.
JONES, L. A., & MOE, R. College education for mentally retarded adults. *Mental Retardation*, 1980, *18*, 59–60.
JONES, M. C. The elimination of children's fears. *Journal of Experimental Psychology*, 1924, *7*, 382–390.
KANNER, L. *A history of the care and study of the mentally retarded*. Springfield, Ill.: Charles C Thomas, 1964.

Landesman-Dwyer, S., Sackett, G., & Kleinman, J. Relationship of size to resident and staff behavior in small community residences. *American Journal of Mental Deficiency*, 1980, 85, 6–17.

Lindsley, O. R. Operant conditioning methods applied to research in chronic schizophrenia. *Psychiatric Research Reports*, 1956, 5, 118–139.

Lindsley, O. R. Characteristics of the behavior of chronic psychotics as revealed by free-operant conditioning methods. *Diseases of the Nervous System* (Monograph Supplement), 1960, 21, 66–78.

Lindsley, O. R. Direct measurement and prosthesis of retarded behavior. *Journal of Education*, 1964, 147, 62–81.

Lindsley, O. R., & Skinner, B. F. A method for the experimental analysis of behavior of psychotic patients. *American Psychologist*, 1954, 9, 419–420.

Lipman, R. S. The use of psychopharmacological agents in residential facilities for the retarded. In F. J. Menolascino (Ed.), *Psychiatric approaches to mental retardation*. New York: Basic Books, 1970.

Locke, J. *An essay concerning human understanding* A. S. Pringle-Pattison, (Editor). Oxford: Clarendon Press, 1924. Originally published, 1690.

MacMillan, D. L. Behavior modification: A teacher strategy to control behavior. *Report of the Proceedings of the Forty-fourth Meeting of the Convention of American Instructors of the Deaf*, 1969, 68–76.

MacMillan, D. L. Special education for the mildly retarded: Servant or savant? *Focus on Exceptional Children*, 1971, 2, 1–11.

MacMillan, D. L. *Behavior modification in education*. New York: MacMillan, 1973.

MacMillan, D. L., & Forness, S. R. Behavior modification: Limitations and liabilities. *Exceptional Children*, 1970, 37, 291–297.

MacMillan, D. L., & Forness, S. R. Behavior modification: Savior or savant? In G. Tarjan, R. K. Eyman, & C. E. Meyers (Eds.), *Sociobehavioral studies in mental retardation*. Washington, D.C.: American Association on Mental Deficiency, 1973.

MacMillan, D. L., & Borthwick, M. The new educable mentally retarded population: Can they be mainstreamed? *Mental Retardation*, 1980, 18, 155–158.

MacMillan, D. L., Jones, R. L., & Aloia, G. F. The mentally retarded label: A review of research and theoretical analysis. *American Journal of Mental Deficiency*, 1975, 79, 241–261.

MacMillan, D. L., Jones, R. L., & Meyers, C. E. Mainstreaming the mildly retarded. *Mental Retardation*, 1976, 2, 3–10.

MacNamara, R. The compleat behavior modifier: Confessions of an overzealous operant conditioner. *Mental Retardation*, 1977, 15, 34–37.

Maehr, M. L. Some limitations of the application of reinforcement theory to education. *School and Society*, 1968, 96, 108–110.

Martin, R. *Legal challenges to behavior modification: Trends in schools, corrections, and mental health*. Champaign, Ill.: Research Press, 1975.

McCarver, R. B., & Craig, E. M. Placement of the retarded in the community: Prognosis and outcome. In N. R. Ellis (Ed.), *International review of research in mental retardation* (Vol. 7). New York: Academic Press, 1974.

Mercer, C. D., & Snell, M. E. *Learning theory research in mental retardation. Implications of teaching*. Columbus, Ohio: Charles E. Merrill, 1977.

Mercer, J. R. *Labelling the mentally retarded*. Berkeley: University of California Press, 1973.

Mercer, J. R. The who, why, and how of mainstreaming. Paper presented at the Joint Education–Psychology Division Luncheon, American Association on Mental Deficiency, Toronto, June 1974.

Mesibov, G. B. Alternatives to the principle of normalization. *Mental Retardation*, 1976, 14, 30–32.

Meyer, R. J. Attitudes of parents of institutionalized mentally retarded individuals to de-institutionalization. *American Journal of Mental Deficiency*, 1980, *85*, 184–187.

Meyers, D. E., Sundstrom, P. E., & Yoshida, R. K. The school psychologist and assessment in special education. *School Psychology Monograph*, 1974, *6*, 377–381.

Miller, M. A review of *The principle of normalization in human services* by Wolf Wolfensberger. *American Journal of Mental Deficiency*, 1974, *78*, 505–506.

Mowrer, O. H., & Mowrer, W. M. Enuresis—a method for its study and treatment. *American Journal of Orthopsychiatry*, 1938, *8*, 436–459.

National Association for Retarded Citizens. *1972 Annual Report*. Arlington, Tex. 1973.

New York State Association for Retarded Children v. Carey, 393 F. Supp. 715 (E.D.N.Y. 1975), 357 F. Supp. 752 (E.D.N.Y. 1973).

Nirje, B. The normalization principle and its human management implications. In R. B. Kugel & W. Wolfensberger (Eds.), *Changing patterns in residential services for the mentally retarded*. Washington, D.C.: President's Committee on Mental Retardation, 1969.

Orlando, R. Component behaviors in free operant temporal discrimination. *American Journal of Mental Deficiency*, 1961, *65*, 615–619. (a)

Orlando, R. The functional role of discriminative stimuli in free operant performance of developmentally retarded children. *Psychological Record*, 1961, *11*, 153–162.(b)

Orlando, R., & Bijou, S. W. Single and multiple schedules of reinforcement in developmentally retarded children. *Journal of the Experimental Analysis of Behavior*, 1960, *3*, 339–348.

Orlando, R., Bijou, S. W., Tyler, R. M., & Marshall, D. A. A laboratory for the experimental analysis of developmentally retarded children. *Psychological Reports*, 1961, *7*, 261–267.

Pavlov, I. P. *Conditioned reflexes*. (G. V. Anrep, Editor and Translator). London: Oxford University Press, 1927.

Pavlov, I. P. The reply of a physiologist to psychologists. *Psychological Review*, 1932, *39*, 91–127.

Perske, R. The dignity of risk and the mentally retarded. *Mental Retardation*. 1927, *10*, 24–27.

Pierce, W. D., & Epling, W. F. What happened to analysis in applied behavior analysis. *The Behavior Analyst*, 1980, *3*, 1–9.

President's Panel on Mental Retardation. *Report of the Mission to the Netherlands*. Washington, D.C.: U.S. Government Printing Office, 1962.

Rachman, S., & Teasdale, J. *Aversion therapy and behaviour disorders*. Coral Gables, Fla.: University of Miami Press, 1969.

Repp, A. C., & Deitz, D. E. Ethical issues in reducing responding of institutionalized mentally retarded persons. *Mental Retardation*, 1978, *16*, 45–46.

Rhoades, C., & Browning, P. Normalization at what price? *Mental Retardation*, 1977, *15*, 24.

Rohwer, W. D., Jr., & Dempster, F. N. In R. V. Kail, Jr. & W. W. Hagen (Eds.), *Perspectives on the development of memory and cognition*. Hillsdale, N.J.: Lawrence Erlbaum, 1977.

Roos, P. Misinterpreting criticisms of the medical model. *Mental Retardation*, 1971, *2*, 22–24.

Roos, P. Reconciling behavior modification procedures with the normalization principle. In W. Wolfensberger (Ed.), *The principle of normalization in human services*. Toronto: National Institute on Mental Retardation, 1972.

Roos, P. Custodial care for the "subtrainable" — revisiting an old myth. *Law and Psychology Review*, 1979, *5*, 1–4.

Scheerenberger, R. C. A study of public residential facilities. *Mental Retardation*, 1976, *14*, 32–35.

Scheerenberger, R. C. *Public residential facilities for the mentally retarded*. National Association of Superintendents of Public Residential Facilities for the Mentally Retarded, 1979.

Schwartz, B. *Psychology of learning and behavior*. New York: Norton, 1978.

SIDMAN, M. *Tactics of scientific research.* New York: Basic Books, 1960.
Skinner, B. F. *The behavior of organisms: An experimental analysis.* New York: Appleton Century, 1938.
SKINNER, B. F. *Walden two.* New York: MacMillan, 1948.
SKINNER, B. F. *Science and human behavior.* New York: Free Press, 1953.
SKINNER, B. F. A new method for the experimental analysis of the behavior of psychotic patients. *Journal of Nervous and Mental Disease,* 1954, *120,* 403-406.
SKINNER, B.F. The phylogeny and ontogeny of behavior. *Science,* 1966, *153,* 1205-1213.
SLOAN, W., & STEVENS, H.A. *A history of the American association on mental deficiency, 1875-1976.* Washington, D.C.: American Association on Mental Deficiency, 1976.
SPENCER, H. *Principles of psychology* (3rd ed.), 1880.
TENNANT, L., HUTTERSLEY, J., & CULLEN, C. Some comments on the punishment relationship and is relevance to normalization for developmentally retarded people. *Mental Retardation,* 1978, *16,* 42-44.
THOMPSON, T., & GRABOWSKI, J. (Eds.) *Behavior modification of the mentally retarded.* New York: Oxford University Press, 1972.
THORNDIKE, E.L. *Animal intelligence: Experimental studies.* New York: MacMillan, 1911.
THRONE, J.M. The normalization principle: Right ends, wrong means. *Mental Retardation,* 1975, *13,* 23-25.
THRONE, J.M. Deinstitutionalization: Too wide a swath. *Mental Retardation,* 1979, *17,* 171-175.
WARREN, S.A. What is wrong with mainstreaming? A comment on drastic change. *Mental Retardation,* 1979, *17,* 301-303.
WATSON, J.B. *Behaviorism.* New York: Norton, 1924
WATSON, L.S. *Teaching self-help skills to children with behavioral disorders* (videotape or 16-mm film). Columbus, Ohio: Behavior Modification Technology, 1972.
WATSON, L.S. JR. *How to teach independent living skills and manage disruptive behaviors.* Tuscaloosa, Ala.: Behavior Modification Technology, 1978.
WHITMAN, T.L., & SCIBAK, J.W. Behavior modification research with the severely and profoundly retarded. In N.R. Ellis (Ed.), *Handbook of mental deficiency, psychological theory and research.* Hillsdale, N.J.: Lawrence Erlbaum, 1979.
WINETT, R.A., & WINKLER, R.C. Current behavior modifictation in the classroom: Be still, be quiet, be docile. *Journal of Applied Behavior Analysis,* 1972, *5,* 499-504.
WOLPE, J., & LAZARUS, A. A. *Behavior therapy techniques.* Oxford: Pergamon Press, 1966.
WOOD, F.H. Behavior modification techniques in context. *Newsletter of the Council for Children with Behavioral Disorders,* 1968, *5,* 12-15.
WOLFENSBERGER, W. Twenty predictions about the future of residential services in mental retardation. *Mental Retardation,* 1969, *7,* 51-54.
WOLFENSBERGER, W. Will there always be an institution I: The impact of epidemological trends. *Mental Retardation,* 1971, *9,* 14-20. (a)
WOLFENSBERGER, W. Will there always be an institution II: The impact of new service models. Mental Retardation, 1971, *9,* 31-38. (b)
WOLFENSBERGER, W. *The principle of normalization in human services.* Ontario: National Institute on Mental Retardation, 1972.
WOLFENSBERGER, W. The definition of normalization: Update, problems, disagreements, and misunderstandings. In R. J. Flynn & K.E. Nitsch (Eds.), *Normalization, social integration, and community services.* Baltimore: University Park Press, 1980.
Wyatt v. Ireland, Civil action #3195-N, unreported, (M.D. Ala. October 25, 1979).
Wyatt v. Stickney, 325 F. Supp. 781 (M.D. Ala. 1971), 334 F. Supp. 1341 (M.D. Ala. 1971), 344 F. Supp. 373, 387 (M.D. Ala. 1972), aff'd in part, modified in part sub nom., Wyatt v. Anderholt, 503 F. 2d. 1305 (5th Cir. 1974).

Zeaman, D., House, B.J., & Orlando, R. Use of special training conditions in the visual discrimination learning with imbeciles. *American Journal of Mental Deficiency*, 1958, *63*, 453–459.

Zigler, E. Mental retardation: Current issues and approaches. In L.W. Hoffman & M.L. Hoffman (Eds.), *Review of child development research*. (Vol. 2). New York: Russel Sage, 1966.

Zigler, E. Familial mental retardation: A continuing dilemma. *Science*, 1967, *155*, 292–298.

Zigler, E. Developmental versus difference theories of mental retardation and the problem of motivation. *American Journal of Mental Deficiency*, 1969, *73*, 536–556.

Zilboorg, G., & Henry, G. W. *A history of medical psychology*. New York: Norton, 1941.

2 Implementing Behavioral Programs in the Community

DONALD STACY, DANIEL M. DOLEYS, AND JAN BRUNO

INTRODUCTION

The problems encountered in attempting to establish and maintain behaviorally oriented programs are challenging. Along with the general issue of how to ensure effective programming (Kazdin, 1977), special problems unrelated to the nuances of proper application of behavioral principles are encountered in psychiatric (Hersen & Bellack, 1978) and institutional (Grabowski & Thompson, 1972) settings. Formal and informal channels of communication, training of staff, politics, funding, and existing treatment philosophies must be appreciated and reckoned with. Nowhere, however, are all these, plus other obstacles, more prevalent than in the development of programs in community group homes (Berdiansky & Parker, 1977; Gardner, 1977).

De-institutionalization is not a new concept. Follow-up studies on mentally retarded individuals released from the institution to community settings date back to the 1920s (Fernald, 1919). The concept of de-institutionalization, however, appears to have been revitalized and given more emphasis in recent times (Bassuk & Gerson, 1978). Clearly, there is a trend toward community placement of the developmentally disabled individual (Balla, 1976; Brown, Windle, & Stewart, 1959; Gardner, 1977; Menolascino & Eaton, 1980; President's Committee on Mental Retardation, 1976; Rosen & Clark, 1977). It seems

---

DONALD STACY • University of Alabama, Birmingham, Alabama 35291. DANIEL M. DOLEYS • Behavioral Medicine Sciences, Brookwood Medical Center, Birmingham, Alabama 35209. JAN BRUNO • Center for Developmental and Learning Disorders, University of Alabama, Birmingham, Alabama 35209. Preparation of this manuscript was supported in part by Project 910, U.S. Maternal and Child Health, H.S.M.S.A., Department of Health, Education and Welfare, as awarded to the Center for Developmental and Learning Disorders, University of Alabama in Birmingham School of Medicine, Birmingham, Alabama.

to have been propelled into prominence for the mentally retarded by Judge Johnson's decision in the *Wyatt* v. *Stickney* case. The decision in this case mandated a reduction in the number of institutionalized mentally retarded persons. Unfortunately, no financial mechanism was established to carry this out. This resulted in communities competing for already scarce funds (Dorman, 1977).

The advantages of community placement are generally accepted and include (1) increased opportunity for normal social development through daily interaction with the community (Sarason, Zitnay, & Grossman, 1971); (2) more individual attention due to the small size of community (i.e., 8–12 clients); and (3) an opportunity for the community to relate more familiarly to the mentally retarded (Mamula, 1973). "Normalization" is the current philosophy which underlies the community placement movement. Generally, this refers to developing and designing programs for the mentally retarded which treat them as close to normal as possible (Wolfensberger, 1972; Nirje, 1965). However, this philosophy has resulted in a paucity of relevant research which has left many programs wanting for direction. Community placements often took on the character of "boarding homes." As Bassuk and Gerson (1978) noted "the development of community services was not based on data collected by systematic research; rather it was assumed that each center would be shaped by the particular needs of its area as they were perceived by the community itself" (p. 49). Although the federal mandate of de-institutionalization has spurred every state to move in the direction of community-based programs, a few comprehensive systems have been developed which can truly be said to be effective alternatives to institutionalization (Menolascino & Eaton, 1980). More research needs to be conducted in noninstitutionalized settings (Haywood, 1976) to develop effective programs. There is significant variation in the extent to which communities are providing coordinating services to meet the needs of the developmentally disabled individual. However, there are examples of well-coordinated government–consumer coalitions of community-based service systems which provide quality care (ENCOR, 1979). This, then, is the setting into which the behavioral psychologist ventures.

In this chapter we will attempt to enumerate the problems of implementing behavioral community programs in group homes for previously institutionalized mentally retarded adolescents and adults. Some of the clients have been institutionalized for almost 50 years. We will try to discuss the problems encountered from an administrator's and behavioral consultant's point of view.

The Community

Existing Programs

When programs shift from large institutions to small training units in the community, a program administrator oftentimes will not have access to a team of professionals who work under the supervision of one director as in the institution. The various treatment functions, such as psychology, special education, and vocational training, are often based in separate agencies. This fragmentation of services makes it highly important to examine the organizations with whom client training will be shared to determine if training philosophies and approaches are complementary. If the training facilities apply behavioral approaches in client training, then it will be much easier to develop programs that will be compatible and to generalize across settings.

Although the relative superiority of operant techniques for establishing adaptive behaviors in mentally retarded population has been demonstrated (Baker & Ward, 1971; Roos & Oliver, 1969), if the training facilities or agencies are not accepting of behavior modification approaches, and many are not, the program may not be able to deal with certain classes of behavior that must be mastered for community living. Arguments against the use of behavioral techniques include the fear that behavior control will be used to manipulate individuals for self-fulfilling ends (London, 1969) and the thwarting of personal freedom (Wheeler, 1973). The teaching of socially appropriate behavior and the elimination of disruptive behavior in clients become extremely difficult when training centers do not employ procedures designed to maintain new skills from one setting to the next. When contingencies are applied in one setting but not in a second, it is unlikely that the training goals will be achieved even with success in the first setting. In fact, increases in disruptive behavior can occur in the second setting (Doleys & Wells, 1978). This "contrast effect" has been observed in classrooms and other settings (Blanchard & Johnson, 1973; Merbaum, 1973; Risley, 1968). We have observed this informally between group homes, especially when response-reduction procedures were used.

The nongeneralization of skills from one setting to another is not an uncommon phenomenon with the mentally retarded. It is a difficulty that needs interagency discussion and resolution to guarantee that training programs are something more than "expensive babysitting." If interagency cooperation cannot be secured in providing program consistency, development of the training components by the group home staff may be necessary or a more restrictive living setting may be needed for the client. Above all, attempts must be made to ensure that systematic, organized "training" does take place, rather than merely exposing the client to a job or placement setting in the hopes that training will occur (Gold, 1973).

Community Attitudes and Awareness

In their discussion of problems encountered in implementing behavioral programs in the institutional setting, Reppucci and Saunders (1975) cited external pressure as heavily influencing their ability to implement what they considered to be the appropriate training programs. Social, state, and federal governing bodies have become very active in recent years as evidenced by the number of mental health-related court decisions issued during the decade of the seventies (Huey, 1978; *Wyatt* v. *Stickney Court Case*, 1974).

External pressure of a different sort can and often is applied by advocate groups from the community at large, such as the Association for Retarded Citizens. The interest of advocate groups is genuine, but many times in their zeal to ensure the protection of the client's rights, they make decisions that, in fact, impair the ability of service providers to offer reasonable service to clients.

For example, an advocacy group we dealt with took great pride in the fact that they led the fight in the elimination of the use of "behavior modification" techniques at a local school. On close examination of this school, it was found that a child had been secluded in a closet for an afternoon session and was not released until the family arrived to pick him up. Clearly this abuse was in no way related to effective use of behavior modification principles, but rather was indicative of extremely poor judgment and a training gap in the teacher's professional development. This abuse was highlighted by the advocacy group as being commonplace when "behavior modification" was used, and they were successful in eliminating legitimate procedures from being applied. Occurrences of this sort can, and do, damage the relationship between the advocacy group and the school and also instigate the development of an unnecessary adversary relationship between the de-institutionalization project and lay advocacy groups.

To avert negative confrontation and influence concerning program implementation, educating and enlisting the support of the community is vital (Mamula & Newman, 1973). To be successful, positive community relationships must be developed so that the community will accept the mentally retarded resident. Generally, it is the attitude of the community which makes adjustment for the mentally retarded individual difficult. Many have erroneous beliefs about the retarded, for example, that all criminals and epileptics are mentally retarded, that they come from poor home environments, and/or that they are sexually promiscuous (Fanning, 1975). Public relationship (i.e., becoming visible to the community in a positive way through news articles, letters, use of volunteers, and direct discussions with members of the community where the program is located) can be very beneficial in gaining support. This support will be needed when the agency undergoes periods of "bad press." Misinformation concerning behavioral programs has had a detrimental effect on progress in the past. Educating the public concerning program purposes and practices is good "preventive medicine."

Some of the views held by community members regarding the mentally retarded can be abated through education. Concerns over the threat of sexually-acting out are common (Berdiansky & Parker, 1977). Although education may help to clear misconceptions, other fears are more realistic. One of these fears is the possibility of decreasing property value in the neighborhood where a group home is located. Not only might such concerns make admission to a "good" neighborhood difficult, but the persistence of these fears and prejudices places the client in jeopardy of being abused. A second concern is that the clients will display disruptive acting-out behavior. Nihira and Nihira (1975) found that unacceptable behavior is a major problem in caring for discharged mentally retarded residents. This variable has been demonstrated to be a decisive factor in determining successful foster care placement. Although physical violence, property damage, and self-violence seem more prevalent in institutional than in community settings (Eyman & Call, 1977), they do occur in the community. The natural consequences for such behavior may be very severe in the community, especially if performed outside the confines of the group home. The behavioral psychologist must take this charge for educating the public seriously, and must become an active participant in it.

Funding

Community placement is frequently found to be less expensive than institutionalization (Gardner, 1977). For example, Gardner (1977) estimated that in 1975–1976 Ohio spent nearly $40 per diem for residential care in state institutions for the mentally retarded. The cost for group homes in their project averaged $17.54 per diem, which is less than half of what the state institutions cost. The majority of community programs today are publicly funded. These funds can be local, state, federal, or any combination of the three. It is extremely difficult to secure and retain dollars from any of these sources. Even though a major goal for the federal and state government has been de-institutionalization, the dollars have not been supplied in sufficient sums to reasonably implement community programs geared toward reaching these goals (Dorman, 1977). Currently a large number of developmentally disabled individuals are being returned to the community. Considerable evidence indicates that many of these persons are being exploited or neglected because of inadequate community resources. The entire de-institutionalization movement may be in serious jeopardy unless there is mutual community integration of quality services developed simultaneously (Menolascino & Eaton, 1980). Despite the trend for more and more clients to be treated in the community, dollars are still flowing into institutions in increasing rates while the treatment populations are being drastically reduced. In the community, many programs have been doing well to keep the dollars they have, even though the treatment population has been expanded.

Funding has impact on a community program in many ways. First, low salaries do not attract the more competent and well-trained staff. Second, there is a high turnover in staff because of low salaries which has obvious negative effects on program maintenance. Third, low-level funding often means that group homes which are bought or rented will be inadequate and old. Aiello and DeRisi (1978) provided convincing arguments regarding the role of environmental settings in the development of adaptive behaviors. And finally, low-level funding almost ensures that client housing will be located in low-income and often high-crime areas.

Federal Moneys

A substantial amount of federal funds that are available for treatment programs for the mentally retarded come from Title XX of the Social Security Act. In many states the Department of Pensions and Securities (DPS) is the agency responsible for seeing that these funds impact on the target groups as specified in the guidelines for funding beneficial projects. For the provisions of mental illness and mental-retardation programs, DPS (in Alabama) has opted to contract with the State Department of Mental Health (DMH). DMH then contracts with local governing boards to provide services. In some cases there is even a third contract between a local governing board, which handles mental health moneys, and a private community agency. All this can create an administrative nightmare long before service delivery even comes into the picture. And, as expected, an enormous amount of time is spent filling out forms.

Then there are the Title XX regulations to contend with. The point is that these federal dollars demand exorbitant amounts of time to deal with paperwork largely unrelated to the project, and these should be considered in developing the project.

The impact of all these procedures on the behavioral consultant should be an awareness that no matter how well conceived his or her program may be, without money it will not be implemented. Additionally, maintenance of funding is a priority. Program development, expansion, and modification may have to wait its turn. The situation often presents an interesting challenge: how to make the best of what you have got. Usually, there is a great discrepancy between what the behavioral psychologist thinks should be done, what administrators would like to have done, and what there is money to do.

State Funding

Institutional budgets often garnish the majority of the state's dollars that are allocated for mental-retardation programs for adult clients. Securing state dollars to serve clients reentering communities from the institutions has not been an easy accomplishment even when new dollars going into institutional budgets purchase fewer and fewer services. However, state institutions have been required by federal court order to move clients to less restrictive environments, and some money has been made available for this purpose. Using state dollars has been less a problem than utilizing federal dollars.

The community has been guilty for years of "dumping" clients on the institutions, and many still consider total responsibility for mental-health programs to belong to the state. With such misconceptions about the responsibilities of the state government and the local government, lines of responsibility have been prematurely drawn, resulting in tremendous service gaps for institutional clients moving into the community, with neither part accepting adequate responsibility for these individuals. In general, large amounts of time are involved in dealing with funding sources in areas that do not appear to be germane to the operation of the project.

Personnel

Recruitment, Funding, and the "Generalist"

Recruitment of personnel who are knowledgeable and competent in the area of program implementation with the mentally retarded is essential to the development of a sound community-based program. Ongoing in-service programs for staff are needed to ensure that staff members maintain skills, learn new approaches, and keep abreast of research in their field.

These goals do not represent anything new that most administrators would not want for their program. In reality, however, these minimal requirements for staff can be difficult to attain. In some instances, the development of a community program is "sold" to legislators and professionals as a less expensive and more humane way to treat not only the mentally retarded but all those served by the mental-health system. The state institutions nationwide have taken to this idea either on their own or through federal court mandate and have been releasing clients to communities at a very high rate. In Alabama, for example, the population of the state's largest institution for the mentally retarded was reduced from approximately 2,300 clients to about 1,100 clients from 1972 to 1979. This trend has also been reflected in Alabama's major hospitals for the mentally ill. Along with the reduction in number served, however, has come escalating budgets for institutional programs. The moneys to serve these clients, one would logically assume, would follow the treatment setting, that is, into community-based programs. The institutional system has, however, jealously guarded its money and has received increases while serving fewer and fewer clients. The effect of this competition for dollars has put many community programs in the position of having increasing client responsibilities with constant or decreasing dollars on a year-to-year basis for staff and consultants.

Professionals in the community have been caught in their own trap by promising to offer better, and less expensive, care to clients in the community. Given the rapid de-institutionalization rate, it has not been unusual for program directors to be headlong into programming before realizing that they have neither properly trained nor sufficient numbers of staff to provide services above those of a custodial nature.

Inadequate funding for the recruitment of those educated to provide training services to the mentally retarded has forced directors to rely on the use of "generalists" in direct service–delivery positions. Use of a generalist presents the director with another set of problems superimposed on the clinical charge of providing direct service to the mentally retarded. How can personnel be taught to teach the clients and how quickly can this be done? As is well known, inconsistent implementation of programming can sabotage accrued training benefits very quickly. As an example, the program which we eventually became involved with has two major goals in its early stages: (1) employment of clients and (2) movement of clients into independent living. The staff overseeing "progress" to these goals was a melting-pot assortment of well-intentioned individuals with little or no training in even basic behavioral procedures. Each staff person had his or her own idea of what was to be accomplished, with the result that no two staff members implemented even a simple program in a consistent manner. After 1.5 years of operating in this fashion, the program has 0% clients in independent living, 0% clients competitively employed (receiving minimum wage), a 70% job and vocational placement loss rate, and 20% recidivism rate to the state institutions.

The initial use of the generalist in-service delivery positions was not a major success. Use of paraprofessionals has been necessary, but with appropriate in-service and "on-the-job" training, such staff members can, and have become, exceptional employees.

Staff Training

Staff training is a much overlooked and important aspect of effective program development. Although validated training procedures for attendance of mentally retarded individuals in large institutions have been reported (Gardner, 1972; Montegar, Reed, Madsen, & Ewell, 1977; Panyan & Patterson, 1974), there remains a need for validated staff training procedures in the smaller residential facilities in group homes (O'Connor, 1976). In our project, a major effort was undertaken by the administration to educate the staff in behavior-modification principles, direct their work behaviors toward specific goals, and give them feedback on their performance. The training had a classroom component and a "hands-on" component to ensure that academic training was carried over into the actual work setting.

Using outside consultants to aid in providing in-service training can be of benefit. However, caution should be used not to utilize outside consultants to provide a total treatment package for the following reasons. First, the training of staff members in residential programs is a constantly occurring need because turnover in most of these programs is high. If in-service training is contracted for on a one-shot delivery, in six months' time many employee slots could and typically do turnover, requiring the training of new staff. Second, relying totally on outside consultants can lead to the exclusion of administrative personnel from the training setting and can be and often is seen by on-line personnel as a sign of an administrative lack of knowledge in the program area. When the administrator is perceived as not being capable, it is difficult to get staff to implement difficult programs. In fact, in institutions and community programs, it is not at all uncommon for animosity to develop between administrators and direct-care personnel, with the latter accusing the former of being out of touch and unrealistic (Grabowski & Thompson, 1972). This is often a fair judgment when program administrators are totally isolated from the day-to-day grind of program implementation with the mentally retarded.

An approach that we and others have found beneficial is to build an in-service training and monitoring component into the administrative structure of the project. The responsibility of training staff remains in the project, but the staff trainer has access to consultants for a wide variety of problems and issues. Additionally, behavior modification consultants take part in in-service training and are able to provide an independent assessment of performance. These consultants can also enlist the aid of staff and administrative personnel in the process. The effectiveness of behavior modification training to group-home staff of the mentally retarded has been demonstrated by Schinke and Wong (1977). Six group homes where the staff received 8 weeks of on-site training in concepts and applications of social learning theory with the mentally retarded were compared with control group homes. The treatment group had a significant increase in knowledge of behavioral techniques, made better evaluations of the residents, and had less declining job satisfaction.

A major problem in staff training is not only how to teach the necessary skills, but how to motivate staff performance of these skills at a high rate, on a consistent day-to-day basis. Several investigators have noted that merely training staff in the principles of behavior change does not prove effective in changing staff performance. (Kazdin, 1975). As a result, strategies are needed to increase and maintain staff performance. Behavior modification programs can be used with staff as well in meeting programmatic goals. An excellent example of this approach is the Madison County Mental Health Center in Huntsville, Alabama (Turner, Goodson, & Rinn, 1979). At this center, each employee, from maintenance workers to the center director, contracts on a yearly basis for the completion of various job assignments. These contracts are negotiated with each individual supervisor and are ultimately approved by the center director for implementation. Each job assignment is stated in precise fashion in each contract to allow for quantification. Raises and promotions are based on the employees' ability to perform various duties specified in the contract. According to administrative personnel, this has enabled the center to maintain a high level of employment productivity. Other strategies have been utilized to increase staff performance, but the major point to be made is that some system must be devised to motivate staff performance, or else in-service does no good in the long run.

In government-operated programs, it is difficult to get governing boards to accept the use of incentive plans with employees. Bureaucracies tend to be highly resistant to change, and even application of a simple employee–incentive system will be fought. After implementation of the program in the Huntsville system, staff turnover increased to about 50% in the following year. This rate then decreased to around 15% in 3 years, which is a good rate for public programs. It is oftentimes impossible to get employee–incentive programs built into existing personnel policies and public programs. This should not stop administrators from developing specific goals and a sufficient monitoring system to see that these goals are implemented. This type of system probably will not lead to staff performances as high as do incentive systems, but it is a needed step along the way and allows for feedback to on-line staff concerning performance when needed.

Compliance and Supervision

Motivation of staff to carry out programs in the absence of close supervision can be a major stumbling block. Low pay, lack of commitment to the job, inadequate experience, and modest academic or on-the-job training can be contributing factors. Where, because of the particular staffing and living arrangements, "live-in" staff are required or shifts are extended to 12 hours or more, inconveniences and diminished social outlets may reduce morale and yield resentment. Changes in client behavior may be slow and marked by frequent relapses, suggesting to the staff the futility of their attempts, no matter how honorable their intentions. Researchers (Gardner, 1972; Paul & McInnis, 1974; Paul, McInnis, & Mariotto, 1973) have investigated on-the-job performance (following instructions in behavior modification) for mental-health technicians when they received on-the-job supervision with a trained technician as opposed to a professional staff member. On-the-job performance by technicians was found to be superior when they were supervised by a trained technician.

In the face of all this, there are several things which can be done in an attempt to maintain staff performance. Some of these have already been discussed by Grabowski and Thompson (1972).

1. Incorporate staff into treatment plans (Miller, 1978). Individuals are much more likely to carry out a project if they have been involved in the developmental and planning stages of the project. This gives them some sense of "ownership." According to Stevens (1977), face-to-face interaction with consultants leads to increased adoption of evaluation methods advocated.

2. Be sure that plans are fully understood. Projects and treatments should be as basic as possible. Stages of programming should be clearly delineated so that the staff members know exactly what is expected of them. Numerous behavior–modification training programs for workers are currently on the market (Andrasik, Klare, & Murphy, 1976; Andrasik, Edlund, Butz, & Klare, 1980; Andrasik & Murphy, 1977).

3. Appreciate staff experience. In many cases staff members are not trained well enough to describe their experiences, hypotheses, or thoughts in behavioral terms. Nonetheless, if they have been working with retarded clients, they may have valuable suggestions.

4. Minimize paperwork. Many programs involve detailed paperwork for administrators and supervisors. This can detract from the program itself and leave the staff member feeling that he or she is working for some large bureaucracy.

5. Make data collection relevant. There is a tendency on the part of some behaviorally oriented therapists to collect all data possible on a project so as to be sure not to miss any treatment effects. Although in a research setting, with sufficient number of staff members or technicians, this may be a reasonable approach, in a communtiy setting, the more data that are collected, the greater the chance for "burnout" on the part of staff. Data collected should be specifically relevant to the project and not made more complicated than necessary.

6. Reinforce staff behavior even if the client's behavior does not change. Oftentimes, unfortunately, staff members evaluate their own performance on the basis of whether or not they were able to change a client's behavior. Patient improvement does not always provide sufficient reinforcement to motivate continued staff adherence to behavior treatment programs (Loeber, 1971; Panyan, Boozer, & Morris, 1970). Administrators should be very careful about reinforcing staff for compliance to the program and not making reinforcement contingent on the client's behavior change.

7. Do not "kick a dead horse." If the behavior is recalcitrant, change the strategy or target a new behavior. Sometimes in an attempt to change one behavior, we persist at the expense of ignoring other more immediate concerns and more modifiable behaviors.

8. Be reasonable. Requests of staff members and behaviors that you are attempting to change should be very reasonable. Changes are likely to be slow, generalization may be minimal, and competing contingencies are likely to be enormous.

9. Review all data collected. When several programs are ongoing simultaneously, the program coordinators or consultants may forget about or only in-

termittently review the data collected by the staff. Even though it may not be necessary for program changes, sitting down with the staff member on a regular basis and reviewing the data that are collected may be helpful to the staff member, assuring him that such data are important and, therefore, his time in collecting the data is valuable and important.

10. Maintain regular in-service training. Staff should have the benefit of regular in-service training programs designed to enhance and facilitate their skills. Individuals who have participated in specific projects may be utilized to train other staff. In our own program, for example, one staff member develops a package for training clients in shopping skills. Attempts were made to formalize this package and to have that staff member participate in the training of other staff.

11. Recognize staff effort (Mamula, 1973). Either letters or certificates of commendation from administrators can be used. A simple letter from the administrator, of whom staff are aware, but do not often see, may be very reinforcing. The letter need only state the administrator's awareness of a staff member's diligence in carrying out a difficult job. Greene, Willis, Levy, and Bailey (1978) reported that praise and feedback from the program director to direct-care staff for engaging and training interactions with the mentally retarded resident resulted in a moderate, albeit unstable, increase in training interactions. Montegar, Reed, Madsen, and Ewell (1977) provide strong support for the use of praise. Public posting of individual performance has generally resulted in the desired staff behavior (Quilitch, 1978; Shook, Johnson, & Uhlman, 1978).

12. In regard to the above, attach staff names to papers. Convention papers, published papers, etc., that come from a project should include as coauthor the names of those staff members who participated in the project.

THE OPEN ENVIRONMENT

In the past, the training and education of the mentally retarded, as with other groups of individuals, has been done in such artificial settings as institutions or schools where the learning environment differs very drastically from the environment in which the mentally retarded client is expected to exhibit learning skills. An example is the teaching of work skills. These skills, it is hoped, are taught to all individuals in an institution before their placement in a competitive-work environment. Many times the skills learned in the training center do not apply in the natural-work environment, resulting in subsequent termination from work.

This last step, placement of the mentally retarded out of training and into a natural setting, has not been given the attention needed by investigators, but this transition is critical to the mentally retarded client who is expected to adjust to a new work and living setting that he or she has not been exposed to previously.

Community-based group homes are generally minimally restricted environments. The client's basic daily needs, access to community activities, and social interactions are provided. Therefore, the degree of environmental control often exercised in more restricted settings (such as in institutions) is lessened. The term "open token economy" has been used to describe a token-economy system implemented in such a setting (Welch & Gist, 1974). The word "open" signifies that a program is community-based and the training effects result from limited contact with the client in a moderately restrictive environment.

The effects of token-reinforcement programs have been demonstrated repeatedly with a variety of populations (Kazdin, 1975, 1977). Token systems and behavioral strategies have been effective with mentally retarded in a number of academic, social, and vocational-training settings. Most of these programs, however, have been applied in institutional or highly restrictive environments such as classrooms and workshops. Implementing such behavioral programs in a less restrictive community or "open" setting poses many problems. The first of these is that program contingencies must compete with natural contingencies that exist in the community. Since clients in such a setting have open access to the community, they may find it more reinforcing than having to respond to the demands of a training program. Second, contingencies cannot always be applied immediately in a less restrictive environment. Although this is certainly a problem in almost any setting, community programs tend to experience it to a much larger degree. Third, the contingencies which are applied may not always be those which are planned. Because group homes tend to be scattered around the community, supervision of program implementation oftentimes is less regular than in a more confined treatment setting. This is complicated by the fact that the staff often must implement and monitor multiple programs for a relatively large number of clients. The staff is also responsible not only for training of the clients, but for the clients' general welfare, which includes knowledge of each client's whereabouts throughout the day. This multiplicity of responsibilities and duties creates a heavy burden, particularly for inexperienced and minimally trained staff.

Programs

A multitude of target behaviors must be considered when dealing with individuals in community facilities (Gardner, 1977). Selection of initial behaviors to be modified is often guided by practical considerations. For example, the development of basic pedestrian skills (Matson, 1980) and instruction in the use of transportation and communications systems (Leff, 1975) are required early as "survival" skills. In contrast to the institutional setting, development of these behaviors is necessary for survival of the client in the community.

Many community facilities are located in the more rundown sections of the community. The development of social and assertive skills (Meredith, Saxon, Doleys, & Kyzer, 1980; Stacy, Doleys, & Malcolm, 1979) is also required. Clients who are able to move about the community freely are often taken advantage of. This presents major problems in the establishment of reinforcement systems, as the contingencies which can be arranged within the community group home may not be powerful enough to deter the client from interacting in maladaptive ways with individuals in a community. It is not unusual, for example, to find that they have freely given their money in exchange for some social reinforcement or have been cajoled into engaging in petty thievery or other unlawful acts.

Although many times it is assumed that mentally retarded individuals placed in community facilities are functioning at a higher level than they would be in an institution, the absence of such basic skills as grooming behavior has often been noted (Doleys, Stacy, & Knowles, in press). This situation is found in spite of the fact that personal appearance and hygiene has been demonstrated to be highly coorelated with successful adjustment to the community and employment (Badham, 1955; Goldstein, 1964). Boyan (1978) emphasized that the rehabilitative efforts for the mentally retarded have stressed vocational training at the expense of independent living skills. He argues that independent living skills should be of major concern, beginning early in training and then later balanced with vocational skills. A survey by Nihira and Nihira (1975) suggests that caretakers are primarily concerned with their residents being able to care for themselves. It might be helpful if "exit wards" (Hunt, Fitzhugh, & Fitzhugh, 1968) were established to train "basic personal readiness skills." This would free the community staff to focus more on community and independent living skills.

Training Difficulties

It is difficult to execute behavioral programs in a more natural setting where reinforcement contingencies operating outside the immediate programming may be more powerful than those within the program. Unlike the institutional setting, it is very difficult if not impossible to restrict a client to the community facility. Clients are often exposed to inappropriate yet potentially reinforcing models. A client may respond to attempts to implement restrictive programs, particularly those which may involve an aversive aspect such as response cost, "fleeing" to the community.

Individuals in the immediate community may object to programs of which they have little understanding. We experienced one situation which revolved around a money-management program. The client was expected to turn his daily or weekly earnings over to the staff. Money was allotted to him in certain amounts. At the end of the day he was expected to account for all expenditures. The amount of money given was increased as he demonstrated control over spending and the ability to account for his spending. In the midst of the program, the staff was notified that an adult living next door became aware of some aspects of the money-management program and felt that the client was being "robbed." The community member was under the impression that the staff was taking the money from the client and informed the client that he should not allow this to happen, that he was old enough to keep whatever money he earned, and that he should seek legal action against the staff and administrators of the project.

The consequences for inappropriate social behavior can be much more severe in the community than in the institution. One client was known to approach people inappropriately as they walked by the group home, introducing himself, and wanting to shake their hands. Once, when a car pulled up to the corner, the client walked to the open window of the car and introduced himself to the two female passengers who, frightened by his sudden appearance, filed a report with the local police. Such episodes are difficult to control, and more often than not the client may be encouraged by others in the environment to engage in such behavior and reinforced for doing so. Numerous studies (Doleys, Meredith, Poire, Campbell, & Cook, 1977; Gibson, Lawrence, & Nelson, 1976; Meredith, Saxon, Doleys, & Kyzer, 1980; Nelson, Gibson, & Cutting, 1973; Stacy, Doleys, & Malcolm, 1979) have reported positive effects from social-skills training for the mentally retarded individual. Stacy, Doleys, and Malcolm (1979) specifically examine social-skills training of previously institutionalized mentally retarded subjects residing in community group homes. When compared with a control group, the treatment group showed significant improvement in the observed behaviors. These and other authors (Rinn & Wise, 1975) caution that the acquisition of assertive behaviors may be overgeneralized and misapplied to the disadvantage of the individual.

Maintenance and Generality of Training

Maintenance and generality of behavior change has been a critical problem in controlled environment (Doleys, Stacy, & Knowles, in press; Stacy, Doleys, & Malcolm, 1979). It becomes more of an issue in community settings, where clients are much freer to move about and where training is often interrupted by any one of a number of problems. One study (Doleys, Stacy, & Knowles, in press) demonstrated the effectiveness of token reinforcement in two community group homes in the modification of a variety of behaviors. Token reinforcement was removed for one behavior while two other classes of behaviors continued to be reinforced during the 16-week follow-up. At the end of the follow-up, the behavior class no longer under reinforcement conditions dropped to below baseline levels, while those being maintained on tokens continued at their posttreatment level. Perhaps in no other setting is the philosophy of programming generalization more true than in the community setting.

INDEPENDENT LIVING

One of the major goals of any community program, whether behaviorally oriented or not, is to have as many clients as possible live independently or in the least restrictive environment possible (Menolascino & Eaton, 1980). "Independent living" is not defined just by reduced supervision. It should be the terminal link in a long chain of events marked by successful demonstration of prerequisite behaviors. These behaviors include self-maintenance and the full array of self-care behavior and appropriate social skills. But more than this, the client must be able to demonstrate abilities to (1) grocery shop, (2) cook, (3) clean, (4) manage money, and (5) maintain a job.

There are at least two ways of approaching this goal of independent living. One is to place the client in an independent living situation to determine whether or not he or she is able to survive. The other is to perform a functional analysis of the behaviors required in independent living, arrange these in a hierarchy, and then develop a sequence of behavioral programs to be built in each of these desired behaviors. Because of all the factors identified above, including inadequate personnel, funding, poor housing, etc., the latter is often a very difficult thing to accomplish. One common problem is the mixture of skill levels found in any given group home. For example, a group home which maintains eight or nine mentally retarded clients might have some who are much more adaptive than others. There are likely to be some programs such as grooming which are too rudimentary and unnecessary for some of the clients but are needed for others. This can create a good deal of difficulty for the program developer as well as for the staff.

We attempted one possible solution by arranging three adult group homes according to skill level. All new clients entering the community from the institution were placed in Group Home A. At this initial group home, the clients' skills were assessed. Those who were able to demonstrate proper grooming and self-care with some minimal level of social skills were then moved to Group Home B. Individuals who did not have skills remained in Group Home A and were given extensive training. If they were not able to acquire these skills or became unmanageable, attempts were made to return them to the institutions, indicating that they were not appropriate candidates for placement in the community. This is an important option for programs to have. There should be an entry-level home or an exit ward where clients can be evaluated. If considered unsuitable or not having enough necessary skills, they should not be forced to be maintained in a community, since their presence can create great difficulties in management and delay the acquisition of necessary skills by other clients because of the strong demands placed on staff to attend to the maladaptive behavior of clients not ready for community placement.

Group Home B in our sequence was established as a place to develop social skills more firmly and explore vocational training or workshop opportunities. Clients also shared cooking and cleaning chores, and were totally responsible for the maintenance of their living quarters and for their laundry. Individuals who achieved criterion performance on all the above tasks were then advanced to Group Home C.

Group Home C was somewhat unique in that it had an apartment suitable for two adults located below the house itself. Clients in Group Home C who were able to attain some type of regular employment and who were able to show all the skills necessary for entrance into Group Home C were then allowed a trial period in the apartment. In this apartment, supervision was minimal, but regular. The clients were watched closely for their ability to manage money, develop menus, carry out the necessary grocery shopping, and maintain the apartment. When criterion performance was accomplished on all these tasks, a search was initiated to try to find a dwelling in the community.

Although movement of the clients through these various group homes and then into the community was somewhat time-consuming, and although it ultimately resulted in a relatively small proportion of individuals entering the community, this plan seems to be very effective. Those individuals who did acquire independent living accommodations adapted successfully to the community with only periodic (once every 2 to 4 weeks) visits from staff.

Another similar program reported by Gardner (1977) consisted of four levels of training. These levels are hierarchical, with advancement to one level dependent on performance in the previous level. Goals of Level 1 include self-help, social, prevocational, and rudimentary academic skills. Also included were adaptations to a home living environment and knowledge of the neighborhood and local transportation. Goals of Level 2 were adequate academic, social, and elementary vocational skills. Level 3 goals consisted of semi-independent living with complete academic and social skills. This level required self-management with some supervision. The final level was independent living with minimal supervision. This 1977 revision included a fifth level, independent living. Results indicate greater client progress when compared with institutionalized clients. In 1975–1976, of the 116 clients handled, 53 made progress by moving to a higher level, 34 moved to independent living, 12 moved to family or friends, and 17 lost ground.

As shown, all clients will not achieve the goal of independent living. Some of these in our program have been institutionalized for such long periods of time (up to 40 years) that modification of their "institutional personality" (Rosen, Floor, & Baxter, 1971) would take more time, staff, and money than available to most community programs. This highlights the need for more creative and systematic assessment regarding the selection of candidates for community placement. Although the follow-up studies of mentally retarded individuals placed in the community after periods of institutionalization date as far back as 1919 (Fernald, 1919), there still appear to be major gaps in our knowledge and ability to predict successful outcome (cf. McCarver & Craig, 1974).

It would seem as though there is a deep abiding need for research money to be applied in this area. If we are to examine and gain knowledge of how to effectively apply behavioral technology toward successful community placement, then it would seem to make the most sense to examine the probem *in vivo*. Answers are not going to be found very effectively if we try to examine the problem through the establishment of research programs in institutional or academic settings.

Summary

In recent years, applied behavior programs for the mentally retarded and mentally ill have been extended into more naturalistic settings in communities, such as group homes or halfway houses designed specifically for the de-institutionalization of these populations. Many clients, however, have not succeeded in this setting (cf. McCarver & Craig, 1974). There are also many clients who have moved from the backwards of institutions to the urban poverty-stricken disaster areas of inner cities where the aftercare, if any, is suspect.

Although the shift in emphasis from closed ward and isolated institutional settings to community settings can produce serious problems, many of these problems can be anticipated and adequately planned for before the implementation of a program. It is highly recommended that the service delivery methodology be examined closely in the early stages of developing the program. Many times it is assumed that the service delivery system will immediately fall into place after the administration of requirements, such as appropriate room, board, transportation, and hiring of staff, has been handled. This is seldom the case.

Community placement may offer advantages and opportunities over the maintenance of many mentally retarded individuals in institutional settings. Community, state, and federal support is required to make sure that we are not moving individuals from the back wards of institutions to the back streets of cities. Unless the proper financial resources are provided so as to ensure quality living conditions and staff, the potential effectiveness of community programs can be reduced so greatly that we will, in effect, have merely modified institutional settings such that highways separate the wards rather than hallways. There can be no substitute for paving the way for the implementation of behavioral programs through the education of administrators, staff, and community.

Acknowledgments

We would like to express our appreciation to Peggy Holly and Sandra Castner for their secretarial and editorial assistance.

References

Aiello, J. R. & DeRisi, D. T. *Toward successful community placement: environmental assessment or residential settings for the mentally retarded.* Paper presented at the Gatlinburg Conference on Research in Mental Retardation, Gatlinburg, Tenn. November 1978.

ANDRASIK, F., & MURPHY, W. D. Assessing the readability of thirty-one behavior modification test books and primers. *Journal of Applied Behavior Analysis*, 1977, *10*, 341–344.

ANDRASIK, F., KLARE, G. R., & MURPHY, W. D. Readability and behavior modification tests: Cross-comparisons and comments. *Behavior Therapy*, 1976, *7*, 539–543.

ANDRASIK, F., EDLUND, S. R., BUTZ, R. A., & KLARE, G. R. *Readability of behavior modification training test*. Manuscript submitted for publication, 1980.

BADHAM, J. N. The outside employment of hospitalized mentally defective patients as a step towards resocialization. *American Journal of Mental Deficiency*, 1955, *59*, 666–680.

BAKER, B. L., & WARD, M. H. Reinforcement therapy for behavior problems in severely retarded children. *American Journal of Orthopsychiatry*, 1971, *41*, 124–135.

BALLA, D. A. Relationship between institution size to quality of care: A review of the literature. *American Journal of Mental Deficiency*, 1976, *81*(2), 117–124.

BASSUK, E. L., & GERSON, S. Deinstitutionalization and mental health services. *Scientific American*, 1978, *238*, 46–54.

BERDIANSKY, H. A., & PARKER, R. Establishing a group home for the adult mentally retarded in North Carolina. *Mental Retardation*, 1977, *15*, 8–11.

BLANCHARD, E. B., & JOHNSON, R. A. Generalization of operant classroom control procedures. *Behavior Therapy*, 1973, *4*, 219–229.

BOYAN, C. A flexible approach to career development: Balancing vocational training and training for independent living. *Education and Training of the Mentally Retarded*, 1978, *13*(2), 209–213.

BROWN, S. J., WINDLE, C., & STEWART, E. Statistics on a family care program. *American Journal of Mental Deficiency*, 1959, *64*(5), 535–542.

DOLEYS, D. M., & WELLS, K. C. Situation generality of overcorrective functional movement training. *Psychological Reports*, 1978, *43*, 759–762.

DOLEYS, D. M., MEREDITH, R. L., POIRE, R., CAMPBELL, L. M., & COOK, M. Preliminary examination of assessment of assertive behavior in retarded persons. *Psychological Reports*, 1977, *41*, 855–859.

DOLEYS, D. M., STACY, D., & KNOWLES, S. Modification of grooming behavior in adult retarded: Token reinforcement in a community based program. *Behavior Modification*, 1981, *5*, 119–128.

DOLEYS, D. M., STACY, D., & KNOWLES, S. Effects of token reinforcement in community group homes. *American Journal of Mental Deficiency*, in press.

DORMAN, L. B. Community mental health services in Alabama after Wyatt. *Hospital and Community Psychiatry*, 1977, *28*, 364–366.

EASTERN NEBRASKA COMMUNITY OFFICE OF RETARDATION ACTION PLAN: *For we have promises to keep . . . and miles to go before we sleep*. Omaha, Neb: Eastern Nebraska Community Office of Retardation, January 1979.

EYMAN, R. K., & CALL, T. Maladaptive behavior and community placement of mentally retarded persons. *American Journal of Mental Deficiency*, 1977, *81*, 137–144.

FANNING, J. W. *A Common Sense Approach to Communty Living Arrangements for the Mentally Retarded*. Springfield, Ill.: Charles C Thomas, 1975.

FERNALD, W. E. After-care study of the patients discharged from Waverly for a period of 25 years. *Ungraded*. 1919, *5*, 25–31.

GARDNER, J. M. Teaching behavior modification to nonprofessionals. *Journal of Applied Behavior Analysis*, 1972, *5*, 517–521.

GARDNER, J. M. Community residential alternatives for the developmentally disabled. *Mental Retardation*, 1977, *15*, 3–8.

GIBSON, R. W., LAWRENCE, P. S., & NELSON, R. O. Comparison of three training procedures for teaching sound responses to developmentally disabled adults. *American Journal of Mental Deficiency*, 1976, *81*, 379–387.

GOLD, M. W. Research on the vocational habilitation of the retarded: The present, the future. In N. R. Ellis (Ed.), *International review of research in mental retardation*. (Vol. 6). New York: McGraw-Hill, 1973.

GOLDSTEIN, H. Social and occupational adjustment. In H. A. Stevens & R. Huber (Eds.), *Mental Retardation*. Chicago: University of Chicago Press, 1964.

GRABOWSKI, J., & THOMPSON, T. Implementing behavior modification programs. In T. Thompson & J. Grabowski (Eds.), *Behavior modification of the mentally retarded*. New York: Oxford University Press, 1972.

GREENE, G. F., WILLIS, B. S., LEVY, R., & BAILEY, J. S. Measuring client gains from staff implemented programs. *Journal of Applied Behavior Analysis*, 1978, *11*, 395-412.

HAYWOOD, H. C. The ethics of doing research and of not doing it. *American Journal of Mental Deficiency*, 1976, *81*, 311-317.

HERSEN, M., & BELLACK, A. S. Staff training and consultation. In M. Hensen & A. S. Bellack (Eds.), *Behavior therapy in the psychiatric setting*. Baltimore: Williams & Wilkins, 1978.

HUEY, K. Placing the mentally retarded: Where shall they live? *Hospital and Community psychiatry*, 1978, (9), 596-602.

HUNT, J. G., FITZHUGH, L. C., & FITZHUGH, K. B. Teaching "exit-ward" patients appropriate personal appearance behaviors by using reinforcement techniques. *American Journal of Mental Deficiency*, 1968, *73*, 41-45.

KAZDIN, A. E. Recent advances in token economy research. In M. Hersen, R. M. Eisler, & P. M. Miller (Eds.), *Progress in behavior modification*, (Vol. 1). New York: Academic Press, 1975.

KAZDIN, A. E. *The token economy*, New York: Plenum Press, 1977.

LEFF. R. B. Teaching TMR children and adults to dial the telephone. *Mental Retardation*, 1975, *13*, 9-12.

LOEBER, R. Engineering the behavioral engineer. *Journal of Applied Behavior Analysis*, 1971, *4*, 321-362.

LONDON, P. *Behavior control*. New York: Harper & Row, 1969.

MAMULA, R. A., & NEWMAN, N. *Community placement of the mentally retarded*. Springfield, Ill.: Charles C Thomas, 1973.

MATSON, J. L. A controlled study of pedestrian-skill training for the mentally retarded. *Behavior Research and Therapy*, 1980, *18*, 99-106.

MCCARVER, R. B., & CRAIG, E. M. Placement of the retarded in the community: Prognosis and outcome. In N. R. Ellis (Eds.), *International Review of Research in Mental Retardation*. (Vol. 7). New York: Academic Press, 1974.

MENOLASCINO, F. J., & EATON, L. F. Future trends in mental retardation. *Child Psychiatry & Human Development*, 1980, 10, *3*, 156-168.

MERBAUM, M. The modification of self-destructive behavior by a mother-therapist using aversive stimulation. *Behavior Therapy*, 1973, *4*, 442-447.

MEREDITH, R. L., SAXON, S., DOLEYS, D. M., & KYZER, B. Social skills training with mildly retarded young adults. *Journal of Clinical Psychology*, 1980, *36*, 1000-1009.

MILLER, L. M. *Behavior management: The new science of managing people to work*. New York: Wiley, 1978.

MONTEGAR, C. A., REED, D. H., MADSEN, C. H., Jr., & EWELL, M. D. Increasing institutional staff to resident interactions through in-service training and supervisor approval. *Behavior Therapy*, 1977, *8*, 533-540.

NELSON, R., GIBSON, F., Jr., & CUTTING, D. S. Video taped modeling: The development of three appropriate social responses in a mildly retarded child. *Mental Retardation*, December 1973, 24-28.

NIHIRA, L., & NIHIRA, K. Normalized behavior in community placement. *Mental Retardation*, 1975, *12*, 9-13.

NIRJE, B. The normalization principle and its human management implications. In R. B. Kugel & W. Wolfensberger (Eds.), *Changing patterns in residential services for the mentally retarded*, President's Committee on Mental Retardation, Washington, D.C., 1965.

O'CONNOR, G. Home is a good place: A national perspective of community residential facilities for developmentally disabled persons. *Monograph of the American Association on Mental Deficiency*, 1976 (No. 2).

PANYAN, M. C., & PATTERSON, E. T. Teaching attendants the applied aspects of behavior modification. *Mental Retardation*, 1974, *12*, 30-32.

PANYAN, M., BOOZER, H., & MORRIS, N. Feedback to attendants as a reinforcer for applying operant techniques. *Journal of Applied Behavior Analysis*, 1970, *3*, 1-4.

PAUL, G. L., & MCINNIS, T. L. Attitudinal changes associated with two approaches to training mental health technicians in milieu and social-learning programs. *Journal of Consulting and Clinical Psychology*, 1974, *42*, 21-33.

PAUL, G. L., MCINNIS, T. L., & MARIOTTO, M. J. Objective performance outcomes associated with two approaches to training mental health technicians in milieu and social-learning programs. *Journal of Abnormal Psychology*, 1973, *82*, 523-532.

PRESIDENT'S COMMITTEE ON MENTAL RETARDATION. Report to the President. *Mental Retardation: Century decision*. Washington, D.C.: Government Printing Office, 1976.

QUILITCH, H. R. Using a simple feedback procedure to reinforce the submission of written suggestions by mental health employees. *Journal of Organizational Behavior Management*, 1978, *1*, 155-163.

REPPUCCI, N. D., & SAUNDERS, J. T. Social psychology of behavior modification: Problem of implementation in natural settings. In A. L. Graziano (Ed), *Behavior therapy with children* (Vol. II). Chicago: Aldine, 1975.

RINN, R.C., & WISE, M. J. *Developing assertive responses in retarded adults. An analog study*. Unpublished manuscript, Huntsville-Madison County Community Health Center, 1975.

RISLEY, T. R. The effects and side effects of punishing the autistic behaviors of a deviant child. *Journal of Applied Mental Deficiency*, 1968, *1*, 21-34.

Roos, R., & OLIVER, M. Evaluation of operant conditioning with institutionalized retarded children. *American Journal of Mental Deficiency*, 1969, *74*, 325-330.

ROSEN, M., & CLARK, G. R., *Habilitation of the handicapped*. London. University Park Press, 1977.

ROSEN, M., FLOOR, L., & BAXTER, D. The institutional personality. *British Journal of Mental Subnormality*, 1971, *17*, 125-131.

SARASON, S., ZITNAY, G., & GROSSMAN, F. *The creation of a community setting*. Syracuse: Syracuse University Division of Special Education and Rehabilitation and the Center on Human Policy, 1971.

SCHINKE, S. F., & WONG, S. E. Evaluation of staff training in group homes for retarded persons. *American Journal of Mental Deficiency*, 1977, *82*(2), 130-136.

SHOOK, G.L., JOHNSON, M., & UHLMAN, W. F. The effect of response effort reduction, instructions, group and individual feedback and reinforcement on staff performance. *Journal of Organizational Behavior Management*, 1978, *1*, 206-215.

STACY, D., DOLEYS, D. M., & MALCOLM, R. Effects of social skills training in a community based program for adult retarded. *American Journal of Mental Deficiency*, 1979, *84*, 152-158.

STERNLICHT, M. Variables affecting foster care placement of institutionalized retarded residents. *Mental Retardation*, 1978, *2*, 25-28.

STEVENS, W. F. *An assessment of the impact of staff involvement and face-to-face consultation on adoption of innovative program evaluation methods*. Unpublished doctoral dissertation, Michigan State University, 1977.

TURNER, A. J., GOODSON, W. H.,& RINN, R.C. (Eds.).*The Huntsville Experience: Accountability and community mental health*, Cambridge, Mass.: Research Media, 1979.

WELCH, M. W., & GIST, J. W. *The open token economy system.* Springfield, Ill.: Charles C Thomas, 1974.
WHEELER, H. (Ed.). *Beyond the punitive society,* San Francisco: Freeman, 1973.
WOLFENSBERGER, W. *The principle of normalization in human services.* University of York, Toronto: National Insititute on Mental Retardation, 1972.
Wyatt, v. *Strickney Court Case.* In B. J. Ennis & P. P. Friedman (Eds.), *Legal rights of the mentally retarded.* (Vol. 1). New York: Practicing Law Institute, 1974.

3 Legal and Ethical Issues in Behavior Modification with Mentally Retarded Persons

RICHARD J. MORRIS AND D. KIRBY BROWN

Introduction and Overview

There have been many changes in recent years in the field of mental retardation. Great strides can be found in the educational, vocational, and community services provided retarded persons, as well as in state and federal laws guaranteeing quality education for all handicapped children. Changes can also be found in state residential service programs, where the emphasis is now away from the overpopulated, barren, and dehumanizing institution which typified residential programs in the United States from the early 1900s to the middle 1970s (e.g., Baumeister, 1970; Blatt, 1968, 1970; Blatt & Kaplan, 1966; Wolfensberger, 1969), and toward the alternative of de-institutionalization and the establishment of group homes, developmental homes, and independent living apartments in the community (e.g., Birenbaum & Re, 1979; Birenbaum & Seiffer, 1976; de Silvia & Faflak, 1976).

We are also finding a major redirection in our society's attitude toward and concern for persons who are mentally retarded. Following the articulate (and sometimes pictorial) descriptions of the inhumane and degrading conditions in many institutions for the mentally retarded (e.g., Blatt, 1968; Blatt & Kaplan, 1966; *New York Association for Retarded Children* v. *Rockefeller*, 1973; *Wyatt* v. *Stickney*, 1971), our society began to demand closer scrutiny of the therapeutic, educational, and vocational services provided retarded per-

---

RICHARD J. MORRIS • Department of Special Education, University of Arizona, Tucson, Arizona 85721.   D. KIRBY BROWN • Department of Educational Psychology, University of Arizona, Tucson, Arizona 85721. Portions of this chapter are based on material presented as part of a symposium entitled "Behavior Modification in an Institution for Mentally Handicapped Persons: Issues and Problems," at the 87th Annual Meeting of the American Psychological Association, New York, September 1979.

sons. Specifically, accountability on the part of professionals providing these services, a normal living and work environment for people receiving these services, and, generally, the return of these people's dignity and self-respect were demanded.[1]

Consistent with this societal trend, and following the earlier controversies regarding the general use of behavior modification with people in institutional settings (e.g., Ball, 1968; Bragg & Wagner, 1968; Cahoon, 1968; Lucero, Vail, & Scherber, 1968; Miron, 1968; Schaefer, 1969; Vogler & Martin, 1969), professionals and laypersons began in the early 1970s to critically discuss and scrutinize behavior modification programming (e.g., Krapfl & Vargas, 1977; Martin, 1975; National Association for Retarded Citizens, 1975; Repp & Deitz, 1978; Roos, 1974). In fact, by the mid-1970s, a number of national professional associations, state residential institutions, city school districts, and states began writing guidelines and/or position statements regarding the use of behavior modification procedures—written either specifically for mentally retarded and other developmentally disabled persons or as general guidelines regarding professional conduct in the use of these procedures with any person (e.g., Association for Advancement of Behavior Thearapy, 1977; National Association for Retarded Citizens, 1975; National Society for Autistic Children, 1975; State of Minnesota, 1978; State of Wisconsin, 1977). Numerous legal decisions were also written during the 1970s regarding the treatment and educational services provided mentally retarded persons which had direct impact on behavior modification programming (e.g., Martin, 1975, 1979; Stolz, Wienckowski, & Brown, 1975).

The present chapter will summarize some of the recent legal decisions and ethical issues regarding the educational and treatment services provided mentally retarded persons, and discuss the implications of these decisions and issues on the use of behavior-modification procedures with people who are mentally retarded.

Ethical and Human Rights Issues in Behavior Modification

The focus of many discussions regarding ethics and the use of behavior modification with mentally retarded persons has often centered on (1) the issue of controlling people who have difficulty gaining countercontrol over their environment; and (2) the value or belief that these procedures are being used in

[1] Interestingly, these societal demands (circa 1970) are not appreciably different from the views of Edward Sequin, Samuel G. Howe, and others during the 1840s (see, for example, Baumeister, 1970; Kraft, 1961; Wolfensberger, 1969).

the "best interests" of a client to assist him or her in progressing developmentally. Ethics, therefore, in behavior modification and mental retardation involve the control of mentally retarded persons' behaviors by other persons, using treatment strategies which emphasize control and prediction of behavior. For example, Braun (1975) raised the following questions regarding behavior modification: "Who shall have the power to control behavior? Towards what end shall the controlling power be used? How shall the power to control behavior be regulated (p. 51)?" And to this one might add: Should the power of control be regulated? If so, under what conditions? Do aversive conditioning techniques constitute dehumanizing and abusive practices? Do the ends warrant the means? (See Roos, 1974, pp. 3-4).

Rights, on the other hand, refer to "the use of oneself, others, or things to obtain various reinforcers or to avoid particular punishing situations" (Vargas, 1975, p. 179). Implied here is that a rights question arises when an individual obtains reinforcement (or avoids punishment), or effects a change in the behavior of another person, by manipulating someone without that person having control over his or her involvement in that manipulation. Here the person is being treated as an object and not as someone who has a choice in initiating a countercontrolling operation. For example, if the means used to control a behavior was intolerable to a mentally retarded person and the person did not indicate that he or she elected to be involved in this process, then a rights question would result. In contrast, a question which would not result in either an ethics or rights issue would be: Is this procedure significantly more effective than other available treatment procedures. Here the answer is based primarily on statistical findings rather than issues involving who controls whom or one's beliefs and values.

Ethics and rights begin to interact when a group of people sharing the same ethics, called the "ethical community," intervene in behalf of a retarded person (Farkas, 1980; Vargas, 1975). If, for example, the ethical community decided that a client should not be required to wash dishes each night before she can watch television, the community would be exercising its rights in behalf of the client. The problem here is that the client is still being denied her rights, because she has not been asked to give her consent regarding the washing dishes–television contingency. Similarly, the ethical community may make the statement: All programs involving aversive conditioning must be reviewed by an independent review committee, and client consent must be obtained—again imposing their rights position into the treatment realm. This statement conveys their view or value that positive programs (e.g., programs involving only reinforcement procedures) do not have to be reviewed independently and client consent is not necessary. Again, however, the client is being denied his rights since he has not been asked to give his consent. In both examples, the ethical community is treating the person as an object by not providing him or her with the opportunity the community members decided to give themselves, namely, the initiation of a countercontrolling operation.

Legal Issues and Behavior Modification

Various legal decisions and issues over the past 10 years have had direct impact on the use of behavior modification procedures. For example, legal decisions have determined particular fundamental rights of persons who are mentally retarded—the right to balanced meals each day, shelter, privacy, and access to such common activities as watching television. The legal issues which have arisen over the past several years include the notion of informed consent; due process; and the right to "appropriate" evaluations, outside consultation, placement in the least restrictive setting, and treatment and/or educational placement.

With respect to mentally retarded persons residing in institutional settings, the major legal issue has centered on the assurance that mentally retarded people receive due process. This procedure attempts to balance institutional costs and benefits with guaranteed client rights. Behavior modification comes under legal scrutiny when client-guaranteed rights and liberties are used as reinforcers by service providers, where the obtainment of these reinforcers by clients is made contingent on the performance of specific target behaviors (Wexler, 1973). To avoid such legal scrutiny (and possible legal sanctions), Goldiamond (1974) has suggested that service providers who use behavior modification procedures should obtain a client's informed consent before initiating treatment.

In Table I, we have summarized some of the major legal decisions which relate to the general area of legal issues and behavior modification with mentally retarded and other handicapped persons. We have also selected a few cases for extended discussion. These latter cases are particularly salient in that they have formed the basis of a legal precedent regarding the provision of therapeutic and educational services to mentally retarded and other handicapped persons, and have implications for the use of behavior modification.[2]

---

[2]The reader should note that different states and local school districts have interpreted these judicial decisions differently; therefore, uniformity across states, etc., with respect to conformity to these legal decisions cannot be assured.

Wyatt v. Stickney 1971

This seminal case has defined the majority of rights for mentally retarded persons living in institutional settings. The complaint alleged that because of staff reductions (staff being fired), adequate care of clients was impossible. The original decision specified a humane physical and psychological environment, appropriate numbers of qualified staff to provide adequate treatment, and individualized treatment plans. The court enumerated many client rights, among which were the following: (1) the right to the least restrictive treatment conditions; (2) the right to be free from isolation (of longer than 1-hour duration); (3) the right to require informed consent for research; (4) the right not to be subjected to treatments such as lobotomies, electroconvulsive shock, aversive conditioning, or other unusual or hazardous treatment without express and informed consent following consultation with counsel; (5) the right to be paid the minimum wage for institutional maintenance work; (6) the right to a comfortable bed, locker or closet, changes of linen, and to privacy; (7) the right to have access to a day room with television and other recreational facilities; (8) the right to a nutritionally adequate diet; (9) the right to use one's own clothes and to keep one's own personal possessions (except in those cases where a qualified mental health professional who is responsible for the client's program has determined that such items are dangerous or otherwise inappropriate to the treatment program); (10) the right to interact with the opposite sex and to be outdoors at regular and frequent intervals; (11) the right to adequate heating, air conditioning, ventilation, and thermostatically controlled hot water.

The court in reference to behavior modification specified that no behavior could be eliminated before certification by a physician that the behavior was not organic in origin and, therefore, not medically treatable. In addition, no behavior may be extinguished or developed solely for the benefit of the institution. In a related case involving juvenile delinquents (*Morales v. Turman*, 1973), the court reaffirmed a time limitation on time-out procedures—that time-out not exceed more than 50 minutes.

In a review of the *Wyatt* case seven years later (*Wyatt v. Ireland*, 1979), the U.S. District Court ordered Partlow State School to be placed into receivership. The court cited "substantial and serious noncompliance with minimum constitutional rights" regarding client treatment services and habilitation. For example, the court noted that (1) staff were insufficiently trained; (2) there was inadequate programming for clients; (3) there were "serious differences" in the programming for severly and profoundly retarded persons; and (4) there was a failure to protect clients from staff abuse. With regard to programming for

TABLE I
Summary of Selected Legal Decisions Regarding Mentally Retarded and Other Handicapped Persons

Case	Client characteristics				Allegations	Decision
	Diagnosis	Number	Age	Sex		
Dixon v. Attorney General (1970–1971)	—	7	—	1 M 6 F	Procedural safeguards denied when clients involuntarily committed to institutions	Mentally retarded persons subject to commitment entitled to notice and a hearing, assistance of counsel, mental exam by expert (court appt.)
Wyatt v. Stickney (1971); Wyatt v. Aderholt (1973, 1974); Wyatt v. Hardin (1979); Wyatt v. Ireland (1979)	—	—	—	—	Right to habilitation of involuntarily committed. Limits on unusual or hazardous procedures and experiments	Involuntarily committed clients have constitutional right to treatment that will give a realistic opportunity to lead "useful and meaningful life and to return to society." *Established*: (1) provision against institutional peonage, (2) the right to a humane psychological environment, (3) minimum staff, (4) detailed physical care standards, (5) minimum nutrition standards, (6) individual evaluations, (7) habilitational care, (8) least restrictive alternative setting, (9) formation of human rights committee to review intervention procedures

Case	Condition	N	Age	Sex	Issue	Ruling
Pennsylvania Association for Retarded Children v. Commonwealth of Pennsylvania (1971)	Mentally retarded	—	8–17	—	Clients excluded from public education on grounds that they were unable to benefit from education	All children, no matter how retarded, can benefit from education. State agreed to least restrictive alternative plan. Clients given due process and reevaluated every 2 years with notice and hearing
Mills v. Board of Education of District of Columbia (1972)	Behavior problems Mentally retarded MBD Hemiplegia	2 3 1 1	12–13 8–12 8 13	M M M F	Clients excluded from public education solely on grounds that they were behavior problems, mentally retarded, emotionally disturbed or hyperactive	All school-age children are entitled to public education, and they should be assigned to regular public classrooms. Reassignment only if alternative is more suited to educational needs and only after notice and a hearing
New York State Association for Retarded Children v. Carey (1973, 1975)	—	—	—	(Class action suit)	Bruised and beaten, infected wounds, inadequate medical care, cruel restraints, inappropriate clothing. Conditions of clients had worsened after institutionalization	Clients have right to protection from harm. Consent decrees forbids seclusion, corporal punishment, degradation, medical experiments, and routine use of restraints. Individual plans for education, therapy, care, and development by a 7-member consumer advisory board
Souder v. Brennan (1973)	Mentally retarded/Mentally ill	3	20	—	Retarded clients not paid for work in accord with Fair Labor Standards Act	Where work assignment is for institutional maintenance without therapeutic value and where institution receives economic benefit, minimum wage must be paid. Decision directs Secretary of Labor to apply federal minimum wage guidelines to nonfederal hospitals, homes, and institutions for mentally ill

TABLE I (continued)

Case	Client characteristics				Allegations	Decision
	Diagnosis	Number	Age	Sex		
In Re Downey (1973)	—	1	—	M	Client denied equal protection of law when state did not provide for an appropriate education	Parents granted tuition refund for money advanced for their son to attend a private school when no public facility was appropriate
In Re K (1973)	—	1	—	M	Client's right to free public education includes reimbursement for tuition to a private school when public facility is not available	It would be a denial of right of equal protection not to reimburse parents of a handicapped child for money advanced to a private school when public facilities were not available
Larry P. v. Riles (1974)	EMR	—	—	—	Clients claim that they are being deprived of 14th Amendment rights by IQ tests which are culturally biased	Students who are wrongfully placed in EMR class as a result of a culturally biased test suffer irreparable harm. School district could not show that IQ tests were validly related to segregating students according to their ability to learn in regular classroom
Bartley v. Kremens (1975)	—	—	19	—	Clients rights violated by mandatory commitment	In absence of evidence that clients' interests have been fully considered, parents may not waive child's constitutional rights. Established 7 minimal constitutional (procedural) safeguards

Case	Disability				Allegation	Holding
Fialkowski v. Shapp (1975)	Multihandicapped	2	5	M	Clients allege that they are denied equal protection because nature of educational programs offered to them is such that no chance exists for them to benefit	Clients entitled, constitutionally, to a certain minimal level of education to acquire basic skills. Sets out standards and procedures for appropriate education
J. L. v. Parham (1976)[a]	MBD Mentally retarded (borderline)	1 1	12 13	M M	Clients allege that they and other class members had been deprived of liberty without procedural due process	Voluntary commitment by parents of minor children unconstitutional under 14th Amendment. Children must be cared for in less drastic, nonhospital environment if available
Hairston v. Drosick (1976)	Spina bifida	1	—	—	Child excluded from regular classroom without bona fide educational reason	School system in violation of Title V P. L. 93-112 Rehabilitation Act of 1973, 29 USC 794. Exclusion from regular classroom a last resort. Cannot be for administrative convenience. Child has right to attend hearing
Davis v. Wynne (1977)	EMR	1	17	M	Illegal exclusion under guise of expulsion for disruptive behavior. Client argues he was left in regular class when he qualified for special education	Expulsion was barred, and client must be returned to proper placement
Donnie R. v. Wood (1977)	—	1	13	M	Client argues that suspension was discriminatory because it was based on his handicapped condition	Consent decree required school to evaluate and place client in appropriate program

TABLE I (continued)

Case	Client characteristics			Allegations	Decision
	Diagnosis	Number	Age	Sex		
Halderman v. Pennhurst (1977) Halderman v. Pennhurst (1979)	Mentally retarded	— (Class action suit)	—	—	State institution violates state and federal statutes as well as 1st, 8th, 9th, and 14th Amendments by not providing education, training, and care required by retarded to reach maximum development	Institutions for retarded inherently unconstitutional because they are too restrictive. They isolate clients from normal population and subject them to regimens that are counterrehabilitative. Also hold that (1) retarded residents had constitutional right to minimally adequate habilitation, to be free from harm, and to nondiscriminatory habilitation
Mattie T. v. Holladay (1979)	Mentally retarded	—	—	F	School system in violation of P.L. 94-142	Consent decree specified (1) movement of children out of institutions into less restrictive environments, (2) the use of surrogate parents to protect children's rights, (3) the conditions under which a child may be removed from a special education program, (4) how the state education agency must investigate complaints of local district noncompliance with federal law, (5) the use of compensatory education to help certain children who have been victims of discrimination

severely handicapped persons, the court stated that the state should provide programming to these people "to maximize the [plaintiff's] human abilities and to enhance his ability to cope with his environment." These latter points not withstanding, the court also listened to suggestions that "in a very limited number of circumstances" those persons who are diagnosed as borderline or mildly mentally retarded cannot always be satisfactorily placed in the community. The court, however, chose not to comment directly on this point.

Dixon v. Attorney General (1971)

This case detailed the rights of mentally retarded persons regarding such areas as involuntary commitment, availability of legal counsel, hearing notice, and independent evaluation.

Pennsylvania Association for Retarded Children (PARC) v. Commonwealth of Pennsylvania (1971)

This decision struck down a state statute which said that children who were determined to be unable to benefit from education could be refused schooling. The ruling determined that all children, no matter how retarded, could benefit from education and training. Retarded children could not be denied a free public education. The children, it was agreed, were to be placed in the least restrictive alternative, with the regular classroom being the least restrictive option. Due-process procedures were to be followed for all placements. Due process included notification of parents, the right to a hearing, the right to legal counsel, the right to examine records, the right to present evidence and to cross-examine, and the right to independent evaluation. In a related decision (*Mills* v. *Board of Education of the District of Columbia*, 1972), the court reaffirmed the *PARC* decision—stating that all school-age children are entitled to public education in regular classrooms. Students could be reassigned only if the alternative educational placement was more suitable and only with appropriate due process.

New York State Association for Retarded Children v. Rockefeller (1973)

The plaintiffs were residents of Willowbrook State School, who alleged that since confinement, their physical, mental, and emotional condition had deteriorated. The consent decree signed by both parties in 1975 prohibited seclusion, corporal punishment, degradation, medical experimentation, and routine use of restraints. Furthermore, residents were to be prepared for return to the community. To attain normalization, both litigants consented to the formation of individual plans for the education, therapy, care, and development of each resident. The decree also created a seven-member consumer advisory board to hear complaints of illegal practices. The Willowbrook case marks the first occasion that the "right to protection from harm" (based on the Eighth Amendment of the U.S. Constitution) was applied to the mentally retarded. This right goes beyond the Fourteenth Amendment right to habilitation, which applied only to individuals who had been involuntarily institutionalized.

Souder v. Brennan (1973)

The plaintiff in this case had been institutionalized for 30 years. He worked a total of 64½ hours per week, was paid $2 per month, and received 2 days off per month. The court decision mandated that the plaintiff receive a minimum wage, extending the payment of minimum wages to all nontherapeutic work of economic benefit to the institution.

Halderman v. Pennhurst (1977)

The court ruled that institutions for mentally retarded persons are too restrictive. It was further stated that mentally retarded persons have a federal statutory right to individualized programming and habilitation, and that such services be provided preferably outside of an institutional setting. In a review of this decision in 1979, the court sustained its earlier ruling and reiterated its stand that institutions are too restrictive, but acknowledged that some programming for some clients may have to take place within an institutional setting.

In conclusion, most of the court cases which have been reviewed are concerned with mentally retarded persons residing in residential settings. The decisions, however, have implications for the treatment and educational services provided all mentally retarded persons. For example, the updated review of the *Wyatt* v. *Stickney* case (*Wyatt* v. *Ireland*, 1979) suggests that severely and profoundly retarded persons should receive as intensive programming as any other mentally retarded person, and the *Halderman* v. *Pennhurst* decision suggests that such programming be provided, if at all possible, outside of the residential setting. At the same time, in establishing programs for these clients, the *Wyatt* case clearly states that service providers cannot restrict those reinforcers which the courts have ruled as rights. As such, for example, clients cannot earn tokens to watch television, cannot lose their meals contingent on disruptive or aggressive behavior, cannot earn tokens to purchase meals, and cannot have the use of perfumes, colognes, etc., restricted. Furthermore, the *Morales* decision stipulated an upper time limit for the use of time-out (no longer than 50 minutes), and the *New York State ARC* case stated that clients shall not be secluded or be exposed to corporal punishment. What also emerged from these decisions was that clients should receive the least restrictive treatment possible within the least restrictive environment. Martin (1975) has stated that these decisions also have direct implications for those treatment procedures which are not clearly defined, namely, they may not meet the standards developed for providing "adequate treatment" to clients.

Guidelines for the Conduct of Behavior Modification

Because behavior modification emphasizes the control of environmental variables, and because of its reported effectiveness in controlling a diversity of behaviors (see, for example, Gardner, 1971, 1977; Kazdin, 1980; Morris, 1976), it has become highly visible within the past 10 years. Furthermore, as a result of increased public and professional awareness of the general areas of ethics, human rights, and the law and the handicapped, reported abuses of behavior modification practices have been noted (e.g., Stolz & Associates, 1978). As a result of these developments, as well as the *Wyatt* case and the Willowbrook consent decree, various national associations, institutions, and states began writing guidelines and position statements regarding the use of behavior modification with mentally retarded and other developmentally disabled persons (e.g., National Society for Autistic Children, 1975; State of California, 1977; State of Wisconsin, 1977).

In 1975, May, Risley, Twardosz, Bijou, and Wexler, under the sponsorship of the Florida State Division of Retardation and Florida State University, wrote a set of guidelines regarding the use of behavior modification procedures in residential settings for mentally retarded persons (National Association for Retarded Persons, 1975). After a short discussion of the historical antecedents of behavioral approaches, institutions and programs for the retarded, and legal safeguards, the authors began a review of behavioral procedures with documented effectiveness for use with the retarded.

The discussion includes qualifications of personnel, procedures for strengthening behavior, procedures for weakening inappropriate behavior,

TABLE II
Summarization of Behavior Modification Guidelines[a]

Goal of procedure	Descriptive name of procedure	Essential characteristics of procedure	Disadvantage of procedure
Strengthening behavior(s)	1. Intrinsic or natural reinforcement a. Refers to acts which produce their own rewards	Consistent with normalization process; natural and frequent consequence to many social behaviors	Cannot be used as initial consequence for shaping many behaviors, e.g., riding bike, reading book, self-help skills, etc.
	2. Social reinforcement a. Social response of another person to client (e.g., smiling, verbal praise, touch, etc.)	Can be used in many contexts to shape and strengthen a variety of behaviors. Critical to the generalization of the behaviors	May not function as reinforcer for some clients. May have to be paired with more tangible or appetitive reinforcers

	3. Artificial reinforcement
	   a. Tokens
	   b. Points
		Used as a means to a defined behavioral objective for clients not responsive to social reinforcement. Should be paired with social or intrinsic reinforcers.	May not be effective for clients who only respond to appetitive reinforcements. May be misconstrued as the objective rather than a means to a behavioral objective

	4. Appetitive reinforcement
	   a. Foods
	   b. Liquids
		Used when client is not amenable to intrinsic or social reinforcers. Meals may be broken down into minimeals	Use of appetitive reinforcers may necessitate deprivation. Staff must guarantee normal intake of nutritional food. Cannot be used to decrease a behavior.

Weakening behavior(s)

1. Avoidance of inappropriate behavior (environmental engineering)

   Examine client's environment in which problem occurs. Provide materials, activities, and social interaction appropriate to each client's interest levels and skills. Modify environment to decrease probability of inappropriate behavior.

   A lengthy and thorough analysis of client's environment must be conducted.

2. Extinction of inappropriate behavior while concurrently reinforcing appropriate behavior

   Staff observe systematically to determine attentional/nonattentional behaviors which contribute to appropriate/inappropriate behavior. Staff must learn to be precise and skillful in consequating behavior. Considered to be essential ingredient in daily staff-client interactions.

   Difficult to use after a client has developed a high rate of maladaptive behavior. Inappropriate behavior may increase during initial phase of extinction. Care must be taken that peer group does not continue to reinforce inappropriate behavior. Even though a technique is effective, it may not be used if it is not publicly acceptable. These procedures are susceptible to social abuse and should only be used by trained staff under controlled conditions.

3. Specific prescriptive procedures
   a. Time-out
   b. Response cost
   c. Application of pain-producing stimuli

   Remedial, as opposed to preventive, procedures for client behaviors which cause harm to self or others or greatly disrupt the environment.

   Susceptible to social abuse and can be used inappropriately.

TABLE II (*continued*)

Goal of procedure	Descriptive name of procedure	Essential characteristics of procedure	Disadvantage of procedure
Weakening behaviors(s) (continued)	4. Contingent education procedures 　a. Contingent observation 　b. Educational fines 　c. Overcorrection	Developed to weaken inappropriate behavior by teaching alternative forms of acceptable behavior.	Potential for mild to substantial abuse. Explicit monitoring is necessary.

[a]Developed by May *et al.*, and adopted by the National Association for Retarded Citizens.

TABLE III
Guidelines for the Qualifications of Personnel Who Administer or Supervise Behavior Modification Programs[a]

Job title	Job qualifications	Training/skill requirements
Resident Life Assistant (RLA)	High school graduate or equivalent	Must demonstrate basic skills of differential reinforcement and extinction in the context of maintaining a minimum level of interaction of one contact per minute with clients.
Resident trainer	High school graduate or equivalent	Successful completion of requirements for RLA and demonstrated skill in all of the training procedures appropriate to that population and in keeping records on client progress.
Unit manager or director	2 years of college or equivalent	Demonstrated competence in duties of RLA and resident trainer. Successful supervision of RLAs in implementing training procedures.
Supervisor	4 years of college and experience	Experience in successfully supervising others in implementing all of the training procedures and health care routines relevant to the population. Supervisor should be able to give feedback on staff performance, particularly inadequate performance, and be able to write reports on client progress.
Director of residential training progress	Master's degree	Formal training including practicum experience in all behavioral procedures relevant to the population, ability to locate information and training packages, and supervisory skills. No additional administrative responsibilities.
Director of programs and services or outside consultant	Ph.D.	All the skills of the director of residential training programs as well as knowledge of all other institutonal programs and the skill to integrate them into a coordinated, full-day program.

[a] See National Association for Retarded Citizens (1975). A summarization of May et al.

and contingent-education procedures. A summary of this discussion is presented in Tables II and III. The review also contains guidelines for the use of more severe treatment procedures such as seclusion time-out and contingent electric shock. A final section provides specific recommendations for devloping procedures for obtaining informed consent and for reviewing treatment programs—such as the Peer Review Committee and the Committee on Legal and Ethical Protection. These guidelines were published in 1976 by the National Association for Retarded Citizens and adopted as their recommended guidelines for the use of behavior modification procedures.

In a 1975 policy statement, the American Association on Mental Deficiency (AAMD, 1975) discussed the increased effectiveness of psychological principles when applied in a systematic manner to affect the behavior of mentally retarded persons. Although noting that no mentally retarded person should be denied effective treatment, the association recognized a potential for abuse in these principles. To assure that the adequacy and efficacy of any treatment would be evaluated for each individual, the AAMD suggested several recommended procedures. First, a client should participate in selecting his or her program goals and procedures—with reasonable indications that informed consent has been obtained. Second, program goals and techniques should be periodically reviewed to determine the program's overall purpose and level of restrictiveness. Third, each client's habilitation program should be continually documented to assess priorities among goals, explanations of intervention strategies and client progress.

The AAMD statement also established a program review procedure consisting of two parts. First, a review body composed of professionals should determine the technical appropriateness and validity of goals and techniques. Second, a human rights review and protection board should assess ethical and legal implications of proposed behavioral goals. Goals and techniques were classified by their degree of acceptability as opposed to their degree of risk.

Following these and other guidelines, the Association for Advancement of Behavior Therapy (AABT) published their *Ethical Issues for Human Services* (1977). Although not a set of guidelines, (that is, it does not prescribe or proscribe what service providers should do), the list is of ethical importance to service providers using behavior modification or behavior therapy procedures. Some of the questions raised in the AABT guidelines are: "Have the goals of treatment been adequately considered?" "Is confidentiality protected?" "Has the choice of treatment methods been adequately considered?" "Is client participation voluntary?" "Is the therapist qualified to provide treatment?" The AABT maintains that service providers can give ethical services if they follow the recommendations inherent in these questions.

Another set of guidelines was published one year later by the Accreditation Council for Services for Mentally Retarded and Other Developmentally Disabled Persons, titled *Standards for Services for Developmentally Disabled Individuals* (1978). The *Standards* are regulations covering extensive areas such as individual program planning and implementation, alternative living arrangements, achieving and protecting rights, individual program support, safety and sanitation, and research. Regulations pertaining to behavior management and behavior modification are found under the section "Individual Program Planning and Implementation." Here the *Standards* list 63 specific prescriptions and/or proscriptions to be met when modifying the behavior of developmentally disabled persons. Some of the standards which relate specifically to behavior modification are listed in Table IV. This rather extensive list suggests that there is a well established movement by the ethical community toward regulating the use of behavior modification and behavior-management procedures with mentally retarded persons.

Factors to Consider in Providing Behavior Modification Services

It is our belief that before any behavior modification procedure is initiated, the service provider must first conduct an extensive behavioral analysis to (1) identify those antecedents, consequences, setting characteristics, and related client and interactional factors which are contributing to the client's target behavior(s); (2) determine which factors, if any, can be manipulated; and (3) collect data reflecting frequency, intensity, and duration of the target behavior(s). Once this is accomplished, the service provider should develop a treatment program.

Before initiating any program, however, the service provider should make sure of the following (1) the program is consistent with the available treatment literature and does not represent any novel intervention approaches (if a new treatment method is being proposed where there are no data to support its relative effectiveness, the person may want to propose the treatment program as an experimental procedure); (2) the program is consistent with the overall treatment objectives for the client and is in the client's best interests; (3) the program involves the least restrictive alternative program for the client; (4) the program can be carried out easily, given the number of staff available and the level of staff training and competence; (5) the client's progress will be monitored using a specific procedure, and the client will be observed closely for possible adverse side effects of the program; (6) the staff have been trained to a criterion level to ensure the provision of quality treatment; and (7) informed consent has been obtained from the client or, in the case of incompetent clients, from the client's advocate(s) and guardian. Of these factors, three which appear to pose some difficulty for service providers are adequacy of staff training,

TABLE IV
Examples of Items Included in the Behavior Management Section of the Standards for Services for Developmentally Disabled Individuals[a]

Corporal punishment and verbal abuse (shouting, screaming, swearing, name calling, or any other activity that would be damaging to an individual's self-respect) are prohibited by written policy and are not employed.

Seclusion (defined as the placement of an individual alone, in a room or other area from which egress is prevented, not under observation as part of a systematic time-out program that meets all applicable standards) is not employed.

When food is provided or withheld as part of a behavior management program, its effect on nutrition and dental status is considered.
1. Foods that may be deleterious to health are not used as rewards unless it is documented that alternative rewards have been tried without success.
2. Behavior management programs do not employ, or result in, denial of a nutritionally adequate diet.

The agency has a written policy that defines the use of behavior modification programs, the staff members who may authorize their use, and a mechanism for monitoring and controlling their use.

When maladaptive or problem behaviors are to be modified, the individual's program plan includes provisions to teach the individual the circumstances under which the behaviors can be exhibited appropriately, to channel the behaviors into similar but appropriate expressions, or to replace the behaviors with behaviors that are adaptive and appropriate.
1. Each plan to modify maladaptive behaviors specifies...the behavioral objectives of the program...the method to be used...the schedule for use of the method...the person responsible for the program, and...the data to be collected to assess progress toward the objectives.
2. Whenever restraint, behavior-modifying drugs, or behavior modification techniques involving the use of time-out devices or aversive stimuli are employed to eliminate maladaptive or problem behaviors, the individual's record documents the fact that less restrictive methods of modifying or replacing the behavior have been systematically tried and have been demonstrated to be ineffective.

Except when used as a time-out device, in accordance with applicable standards, physical restraint is employed only when absolutely necessary to protect the individual from injury to him or herself or to others, and restraint is not employed as punishment, for the convenience of staff, or as a substitute for program.

TABLE IV *(continued)*

Each behavior modification program that involves the use of aversive conditioning or time-out devices is:
1. Reviewed and approved prior to implementation
2. Conducted only with the written consent of the affected individual and/or the individual's family, as appropriate
3. Described in the individual's program plan
4. When a time-out device is employed, the individual's record documents the fact that the situation from which the individual is removed for time-out provides consistent and positive reinforcement of desired, adaptive behaviors.
5. Removal from a situation for time-out purposes occurs only during the conditioning program and only under the direct observation of the persons conducting the program...Removal from a situation for time-out purposes is for not more than one hour, except in extraordinary instances (ordinarily occurring only in the beginning of a time-out program) that are personally approved at the time of occurrence by a member of the individual's interdisciplinary team.
6. Restraints employed as time-out devices are applied only during conditioning sessions and only in the presence of the persons conducting the program...Restraints employed as time-out devices are applied for not more than fifteen minutes, except in extraordinary instances (ordinarily occurring only in the beginning of a time-out program) that are personally approved at the time of occurrence by a member of the individual's interdisciplinary team...Key locks are not employed on rooms in which individuals are confined for time-out...Aversive conditioning is used only in those extreme, last-resort situations in which withholding it would be contrary to the best interests of the individual because his or her behavior is dangerous to him or herself or to other persons and is extremely detrimental to his or her development, and because the individual's failure to respond to positive reinforcement procedures has been documented in his or her record.

[a]From *Standards for Services for Developmentally Disabled Individuals* (1978), pp. 31–35.

service provider is giving the client the opportunity to change under minimally intrusive and restrictive conditions. Since there have been few comparative providing the least restrictive treatment, and obtaining informed consent.

With regard to staff training, a service provider should first ensure that all participating staff are sufficiently trained to a specific program implementation competency level to provide the best available services to the client. One method for training all participating staff is to make use of role-playing situations involving feedback to the participants. The staff could also observe the trainer in real life or on videotape and be encouraged to model the trainer under supervision. Also, daily charts should be kept and notes taken so that the supervisor or trainer can assess progress, identifying potential treatment problems, and evaluate staff consistency.

By providing the client with the least restrictive alternative program, the

TABLE V

Examples of Guidelines (or Proposed Guidelines) for Use of Behavior Modification Procedures with Developmentally Disabled Persons

Region	Number of levels of behavioral procedures	Descriptive name of levels	Criteria for use of particular procedure
State of Arizona (1979)	2	Positive procedures requiring no special review Aversive procedures requiring special review	Least restrictive/intrusive procedures should be used first. Effectiveness of a procedure is not an absolute argument for its use
State of California (draft version, January 1977)	3	Alternatives to restrictive or aversive therapy Mildly restrictive procedures Moderately restrictive or aversive procedures Highly restrictive or aversive procedures	Clinical, ethical, legal, administrative considerations. Least restrictive procedures first. Interdisciplinary team decision. Effectiveness of procedures is not absolute argument for its use
Province of Manitoba, Canada (1978)	1	Time-out	Applies only to behaviors that fall under the category of physically aggressive behavior, destruction of property, and/or temper tantrums
State of Massachusetts (1978)	4	Phase I—aversive or deprivation procedure not required for review by local review committee Phase II—involve greater intrusion into actions or freedom of movement of client but have low potential for abuse Phase III—significantly more intrusive with higher potential for abuse Certain procedures not to be approved	Less restrictive procedures must be demonstrated to be ineffective. Procedures cannot be used which are regarded as dehumanizing or socially unacceptable, or having high potential for permanent physical or psychological harm

State of Michigan (1978)	2	Minor levels of aversive and deprivation procedures Major levels of aversive and deprivation procedures	Compelling need to clearly benefit recipients, after positive reinforcement procedures have been systematically used and documented as ineffective. Level of intensity of procedure shall correspond to intensity of behavior to be modified
State of Minnesota (1978)	3	Mild aversion and deprivation Moderate aversion and deprivation Intense aversion and deprivation	Mild—little or brief manual guidance; Moderate—more than 15 minutes/day or manual guidance, physical restraint; Intense—activities which require special training, equipment, procedures, or interdisciplinary monitoring to ensure client protection
State of Ohio (1978)	3	Minor aversive interventions Major aversive interventions Other behavioral interventions	Minor—positive reinforcers utilized and proved ineffective or not feasible for use; Major—documentation that positive reinforcers and minor aversive stimuli were utilized and proved ineffective; Other—includes use of positive reinforcers and other nonaversive behavioral interventions
State of Wisconsin (1977)	0	None	Behavioral management programs shall make documented attempt to use behavioral procedures designed to strengthen appropriate behavior via use of positive reinforcement and other behavior-strengthening techniques, in combination with, and where feasible, before trying procedures which involve the use of aversive stimuli

TABLE VI
Proposed Levels of Restrictiveness/Intrusiveness and Aversiveness of Behavior Modification Procedures with Mentally Retarded Persons[a]

Level I Procedures

Reinforcement
Shaping
Modeling
Token economy system
Ecological behavioral engineering
Self-control
Reinforcement of incompatible behaviors
Extinction

Level II Procedures

Contingent observation
Exclusion time-out
Response cost
Contact desensitization

Level III Procedures

Overcorrection
Seclusion time-out
Negative practice
Satiation
Physical punishment

[a] This level system is based on a system developed at the Arizona Division of Developmental Disabilities—District II, Tucson, Arizona.

treatment studies published in behavior modification with mentally retarded persons (e.g., Morris, 1978), service providers are not in a strong position to advocate the use of more restrictive/intrusive or aversive procedures before less restrictive/intrusive or reinforcement methods have been unsuccessfully tried. We recognize that the constructs "restrictiveness" and "intrusiveness" are somewhat ambiguous. Several authors have attempted to clarify this ambiguity. "Restrictiveness" has been defined by Friedman (1975) in terms of "a loss of liberty." Similarly, Friedman (1975) has defined "intrusiveness" in terms of placing a person at risk, using force to modify the behavior of a person, invading someone's body, or the loss of personal autonomy.

Two sets of criteria have been proposed regarding the concept of intrusiveness or restrictive therapeutic methods. For example, Shapiro (1974) has listed six criteria for evaluating the intrusive nature of a particular therapy in the field of mental health. With slight modification, these criteria can be adapted for the use of behavior modification in the field of mental retardation. The following criteria then emerge: (1) whether the effect of the therapy procedure is reversible; (2) whether the effect of the therapy results in behavior(s) which would be judged to be maladaptive and/or inconsistent with "normal" functioning; (3) how quickly the behavioral change occurs following the initiation of the therapetuic procedure; (4) the extent to which a person can avoid behaving in the planned manner; and (5) the duration of the resulting behavior change. A second set of criteria has been developed by Speece (1972) to evaluate the intrusiveness of behavioral and other therapeutic procedures with prisoners and psychiatric patients. Again, with slight modifications, these criteria can be applied to the field of mental retardation to provide the reader with a perspective on the constructs of "intrusiveness" and "restrictiveness" as they relate to behavioral procedures: (1) the nature and intensity of the collateral behaviors and other side effects which develop as a result of the procedure, as well as the duration of the effect on the targeted behavior, (2) the extent to which an uncooperative client can avoid the procedure, that is, exert countercontrol vis-à-vis the therapeutic procedure; and (3) the extent to which the procedure involves the introduction of physical contact with the body of the client.

Given these criteria for intrusiveness and restrictiveness, no behavioral procedure—whether it is planned for use to increase or decrease behavior—can escape being defined as intrusive or restrictive. For instance, touching another's body whether to "pat" or to "slap" is intrusive. Unfortunately, neither writers of guidelines nor the courts have specifically defined levels of intrusiveness or restrictiveness. Table V summarizes some of the different level systems which have been developed by various states. Table VI represents a system which we are proposing, based on a series of discussions with administrators, service providers, and consultants who are associated with providing residential treatment services, vocational services, and community resource services to mentally retarded people. This system varies along both the dimensions of restrictiveness/intrusiveness and aversiveness (defined in terms of the frequency, intensity, duration, and topography of the aversive stimulus which is introduced to decrease the client's target behavior).

In general, service providers should demonstrate that the Level I procedures have been ineffective in controlling a behavior before proceeding to the use of Level II procedures. Similarly, before Level III procedures are used, the service provider must show that Level II procedures have been ineffective. Whichever procedure is used, however, it is our belief that the service provider should obtain client (or advocate or guardian) informed consent, and that the procedure should be independently reviewed by the institution's, school's, or clinic's review board and by an external human rights and ethics board. The purpose of the program review board is to ensure the appropriateness and technical feasibility of the intervention procedure. The purpose of the human rights and ethics review committee is to ensure that the rights of clients (both from the ethical community view and from the viewpoint of the client through informed consent) are maintained in the treatment program.

A potential problem, however, with these review committees is that they may not be used to protect the client. One critic (Blatt, 1980), who was instrumental in the human rights movement regarding mentally retarded persons, questions whether the work of these committees is not more devoted to protecting the maintenance of institutional systems than to protecting the rights of individual clients. It would seem that this is a question needing further study. For example, one might examine how members of program review boards construe their respective roles, and how their respective constructions compare with what they actually do—both individually and as a group—during their meetings. Also, one might investigate how therapy staff, administrators, and parents or guardians construe the purpose, activities, etc., of these review boards, and whether there are differences between these groups in their respective views.

With respect to obtaining informed consent, the question which arises is, Can one ever obtain "truly" informed consent from people who are mentally retarded? That is, is a mentally retarded person "informed" after she or he has been provided with information about the treatment program to which she or he will be exposed? Is it possible for a person who lives in a residential setting for mentally retarded persons to be in a position to ever give his or her consent without coercion and under no duress or deceit? Related to these questions is, how do we obtain informed consent from a retarded person who is judged incompetent to give such consent? In many cases, as is discussed in the consent manual of the AAMD, substitute consent can be obtained from a person's parent or legal guardian. In other cases, especially where guardianship has not been established, Roos (1980) suggests that a group or committee external to the agency should assign an advocate to the client to assist him or her in determining whether he or she will accept the treatment program. This alternative, as well as those involving a client's parents' or guardians' signing of a consent form for treatment, still removes the client from the option of refusing treatment.

Even in those situations involving competent clients, can one assume that by informing a client about his or her treatment that he or she is, in fact, "informed"? Stuart (1978) and Gray (1975) have suggested, regarding people of normal intelligence, that just because participants are told about the various aspects of an experiment and sign a consent form with regard to their participation, this does not necessarily mean that they *know* what will be happening to them in the experiment. If people of normal intelligence have difficulty understanding the nature and objectives of the research project for which they have given their "informed" consent, then we might hypothesize that persons who are mentally retarded would have similar difficulties with regard to their agreement to receive treatment.

Finally, a factor which has not yet been discussed, and one which is not often discussed in the literature, is a client's refusal of treatment. Specifically, does a client have the right to refuse *all* treatment, and, if so, what are the conditions under which clients can elect not to participate in behavior modification treatment? Our position is that clients do have the right to refuse treatment, as they have the right to refuse participation in research, but that the right to provide treatment to a client also exists. Therefore, if a client (or guardian, etc.) and the service provider(s) are in disagreement regarding the receipt or provision of treatment, then it would seem that the final decision should be made in a court of law.

A Model for Monitoring Behavior Modification Programming in Applied Settings[3]

It would seem that behavior modification programs could be monitored appropriately in applied settings within a committee system like that proposed by AAMD (1975) and discussed by NARC (1976). Similarly, behavior modification and other therapy research could be reviewed in the same fashion. In essence, each agency or school would have to develop an *internal review board* (e.g., the program review committee, or for research, the research review committee) and an *external review board* (e.g., the human rights and ethics committee).

---

[3]This section is based on a program review and human rights committee system established at the Arizona Division of Developmental Disabilities—District II, Tucson, Arizona.

Program Review (PR) Committee

The PR committee would review all behavioral programs planned for a particular client or student, whether these programs involved Level I, II, or III intervention strategies (see Table VI This committee would *not* function as an adversary group to agency staff or classroom teachers but, rather, as a "helping" or advocacy committee in which the goal was to provide staff or teachers with the best available advice regarding the adequacy and appropriateness of the proposed program plan. As such, the committee would base its approval or disapproval of a program plan on (1) the available literature supporting the treatment procedure; (2) the clarity with which the procedure is described and whether the program is consistent with the overall treatment or educational objectives for the client or student; (3) whether the procedure involves the least restrictive/intrusive and least aversive level of programming possible; (4) whether, in those cases where more restrictive and/or aversive procedures are being proposed, data are available to show that less restrictive and aversive procedures were not effective; (5) whether the staff is sufficiently trained to implement the program and if there are sufficient staff to maintain program consistency; (6) what data will be collected and how often the client will be monitored for possible side effects of the program; and, (7) the committee's best judgment of whether the program is in the best interests of the client and will, in fact, change his or her behavior. These criteria are consistent with the Willowbrook consent decree, the *Wyatt* decision, and interpretations of various legal decisions (e.g., Martin, 1975, 1979).

If the PR committee did not approve a particular procedure, its next function would be to offer suggestions or advice on how the procedure could be improved, and ask the staff to resubmit the program plan at a later date. The program suggestions could come from the committee or from a *technical assistance team*. This team would function as a direct services/consultation arm of the PR committee, and would be available for programming assistance whenever necessary. This team would have to be staffed by people who were thoroughly trained in the area of behavior modification—with an extensive background in special education, psychology, medicine, and/or rehabilitation.

The PR committee's membership would be very important. In addition to the directors of client services (in residential or clinic settings) or area principals (in special education schools), the committee should consist of a parent(s) of a retarded person and recognized experts from psychology, special education, and medicine, each of whom is also knowledgeable in behavior modification procedures. If such people are not available locally, then the search for these people should be expanded to the regional and state level. The outside experts would provide the committee with the necessary technical and theoretical knowledge as well as the particular setting's sociopolitical perspective. The parent(s) provides an obviously important perspective and one which no other committee member could necessarily provide.

Human Rights and Ethics (HRE) Committee

The HRE committee would provide independent, external monitoring of the maintenance of the rights of all clients receiving therapeutic and educational services. The committee would also review allegations by any client, staff member, parent or guardian, or community agency of violation of the rights of a client receiving these services. Whereas the PR committee's major purpose would be the review of client program plans regarding their technical feasibility and appropriateness, the HRE committee's primary function would be to serve as an external and independent group to assure that the rights of clients were protected.

Since members of the HRE committe would be essentially external to the agency or school and would not have had responsibility for approving or disapproving a particular program, they would be less likely to support it if a rights or ethics question was raised. The membership of the HRE committee would be quite diverse, consisting of lawyers knowledgeable in the area of law and the handicapped, the parent(s) of a mentally retarded person, people from the local or state client protection and advocacy agency, and psychologists, special educators, physicians, or social workers. Thus, by being concerned with issues which are separate from the PR committee, the HRE committee could more objectively determine which human rights issues, if any, would be raised by a particular treatment plan and whether any action would seem indicated. Some of the questions and issues which the HRE committee could address would be the following:

1. Are clients and/or their advocates, parents, or guardians encouraged to participate fully in any decision making regarding the client's educational and therapeutic programming?
2. Is the current educational and therapeutic programming prescribed for the client consistent with the immediate and long-term goals which have been established for that person?
3. Do clients have the right to refuse treatment, and, if so, what are the conditions under which clients have this right?

4. If a client is judged to be incompetent, and a parent or guardian cannot be located to sign a consent form (or chooses not to be involved in any decision making regarding the person), what steps should the institution or school follow to ensure that the client's rights are protected in all current and future educational and therapeutic programming?
5. How often and under what conditions and for what purposes should members of the HRE committee perform on-site visits to residential living units or school classrooms?
6. Are there specific educational or therapeutic procedures, independent of the circumstances and conditions under which they are used, which should not be practiced in the institution or school?
7. Under what circumstances should psychotherapeutic drugs be used with a client in conjunction with behavior programming?
8. What procedure should be followed in the review of allegations of abuse or neglect of clients by staff or teachers?
9. (For residential settings.) Is the institution committed to returning clients to the community—for example, through the establishment of group homes and other types of independent living centers; by advocating the provision of quality educational services in the public school to all school-age clients; by providing parent training and home consultation services to parents (or foster parents) who want their son or daughter to live at home; and/or by providing vocational consultation services to industry for those businesses which want to employ retarded persons?

It would seem that the major factor which might influence the relative effectiveness of the PR and HRE committees would be the extent to which each was independent of the other, and how independent the HRE members were from the particular applied setting.

Research Review (RR) Committee

An integral function of most agencies or schools which provide services to mentally retarded persons is also to stimulate, encourage, and facilitate research. Related to this emphasis on research should be the encouragement by administrators for their staff to explore the use of behavioral and other therapeutic or educational procedures which have little or no empirical support in the research literature. Certainly, such research would need to be monitored, and it would seem that these efforts could be reviewed within a committee structure similar to the program review and the human rights and ethics committees (AAMD, 1975; Morris & Hoschouer, 1980).

The research review committee would review all research proposals before they were initiated—including those projects involving the use of experimental therapeutic or experimental educational procedures. The proposals would be reviewed with regard to their purpose and rationale, methodology, and potential contribution to the agency and field of mental retardation. The human rights and ethics committee, on the other hand, would review each proposal on the basis of (1) whether the research project has made sufficient provision for obtaining client/subject or guardian informed consent, for providing clients/subjects and guardians with a debriefing period, and for assuring clients/subjects that they may withdraw from the research project at anytime; and (2) whether the experiment raises any ethical issues independent of clients/subjects' rights. The membership of the RR committee would be composed of agency or school personnel and professionals from the community who were knowledgeable in experimental design, intervention strategies, and the field of mental retardation. In instances where members of the agency's or school's PR committee were also knowledgeable in research methodology, it is conceivable that the program and research committees could be combined under one committee, the program and research review committee.

As in the case of the program review committee, the RR committee should function as an advocacy rather than an adversary group. Its purpose should be not only to review research proposals, but also to encourage and assist staff in the formulation of a scientifically sound research project.

Although one cannot deny that these research review procedures, as well as the obtaining of informed consent from each client/subject, add to the length of a research project, take time on the part of the facility's or school's staff and consultants, and are costly, they nevertheless ensure that ethical practices will be followed in the conduct of behavior modification and other therapeutic or educational research with mentally retarded persons. These review procedures also assure the ethical community that clients will only receive treatment which is based on, or an integral part of, an empirical investigation(s). The potential benefits of these review procedures to the research clients/subjects and to the field of mental retardation would seem to outweigh any potential "discomforts" to a particular agency or researcher.

Conclusion and Future Directions

As we mentioned earlier, it was because of the effectiveness of behavior modification procedures, its emphasis on controlling behavior, its specific objective, and the fact that it was used initially with severely handicapped children that ethical and legal questions arose concerning its use with persons who are mentally retarded. It seems clear that the various guidelines written were also in reaction to the ethical questions and criticisms raised concerning these procedures. What has also become clear is that those treatment procedures which de-emphasize control, the specificity of their treatment methods, and the relative effect of their treatment variables on the outcome of treatment have not been as subject to ethical questions by the professional community.

It appears that the field of mental retardation has stigmatized behavior modification because it emphasizes specificity—of behavior, objectives, treatment, and outcome measures—and gives tacit support, in many cases, to those methods involving rather ambigious procedures (often phrased in humanistic, relationship, or psychodynamic terms). This seems discriminatory. Any intervention program, whether it involves behavior modification, psychotherapeutic drugs, Adlerian therapy, hyperventilation therapy, or Rogerian play therapy, should be subject to the same rights and ethics issues and scrutiny by professional and layperson review boards. If our ultimate goal is the protection of our clients from unsafe, ineffective, and potentially dangerous therapy practices, then we should make sure that all treatment methods receive the same detailed review to ensure that we as service providers are offering the best possible services to clients/students while, at the same time, documenting the agency's or school's compliance with court-mandated review procedures and federal and state guidelines regarding the provision of educational and treatment services to mentally retarded persons.

Acknowledgments

The authors wish to express their gratitude to Burton Blatt, Thomas R. Kratochwill, Vinnie P. Morris, and Steven J. Obringer for critically reading various preliminary drafts of this chapter. Appreciation is also due Ronald S. Barber, Program Manager, Arizona Division of Developmental Disabilities—District II, and his staff for their input at various stages in the preparation of this chapter.

References

Accreditation Council for Services for Mentally Retarded and Other Developmentally Disabled Persons. *Standards for services for developmentally disabled individuals.* Chicago: Joint Commission on Accreditation of Hospitals, 1978.

American Association on Mental Deficiency. Human rights review and protection boards. *Mental Retardation,* 1975, *13,* C-3-C-8.

Association for Advancement of Behavior Therapy. Ethical issues for human services. *Behavior Therapy,* 1977, *8,* v-vi.

Ball, T. S. Issues and implications of operant conditioning: The reestablishment of social behavior. Hospital and Community Psychiatry, 1968, *19,* 229-230.

Bartley v. Kremens. 402 F. Supp. 1039 (1975)

Baumeister, A. A. The American residential institution: Its history and character. In A. A. Baumeister & E. Butterfield (Eds.), *Residential facilities for the mentally retarded.* Chicago, Aldine, 1970.

Birenbaum, A., & Re, M. A. Resettling mentally retarded adults in the community almost four years later. *American Journal of Mental Deficiency,* 1979, *83,* 323-329.

Birenbaum, A., & Seiffer, S. *Resettling retarded adults in a managed community.* New York: Praeger, 1976.

Blatt, B. The dark side of the mirror. *Mental Retardation,* 1968, *6,* 42-44.

Blatt, B. *Exodus from pandemonium.* Boston: Allyn & Bacon, 1970.

Blatt B. *Personal communication,* March 1980.

Blatt, B., & Kaplan, F. *Christmas in purgatory: A photographic essay on mental retardation.* Boston: Allyn & Bacon, 1966.

Bragg, R. A., & Wagner, M. K. Issues and implications of operant conditioning: Can deprivation be justified? *Hospital and Community Psychiatry,* 1968, *19,* 229-230.

Braun, S. H. Ethical issues in behavior modification. *Behavior Therapy,* 1975, *6,* 51-62.

Cahoon, D. D. Issues and implications of operant conditioning: Balancing procedures against outcomes. *Hospital and Community Psychiatry,* 1968, *19,* 228-229.

Davis v. Wynne S. D. Ga. (1977).

De Silvia, R. M., & Faflak, P. From institutions to community. *Mental Retardation,* 1976, *14,* 25-28.

Dixon v. Attorney General. 313 F. Supp. 653 (1970); 325 F. Supp. 966 (1971).

Donnie R. v. Wood. DSC (1977)

Farkas, G. M. An ontological analysis of behavior therapy. *American Psychologist,* 1980, *35,* 364-374.

Fialkowski v. Shapp. 405 F. Supp. 946 (1975)

Friedman, P. *The rights of the mentally retarded.* New York: Avon, 1975.

Gardner, W. I. *Behavior modification in mental retardation.* Chicago: Aldine, 1971.

Gardner, W. I. *Learning and behavior characteristics of exceptional children and youth: A humanistic behavioral approach.* Boston: Allyn & Bacon, 1977.

Goldiamond, I. Toward a constructional approach to social problems. *Behaviorism,* 1974, *2,* 1-84.

Gray, B. H. An assessment of institutional review committees in human experimentation. *Medical Care,* 1975, *13,* 318-328.

Hairston v. Drosick. 423 F. Supp. 180 (1976).

Halderman v. Pennhurst. 446 F. Supp. 1295 (1977).

Halderman v. Pennhurst. 612 F. 2d84 (1979).
In Re Downey. 340 NYS 2d 271 (1973).
In Re K. 347 NYS 2d 271 (1973).
Larry P. v. Riles. 323 F. Supp. 1306 (1972); aff'd 502 F. 2d 963 (1974)
J. L. v. Parham. 412 F. Supp. 112 (1976).
KAZDIN, A. E. *Behavior modification in applied settings* (2nd ed.). Homewood, Ill.: Dorsey Press, 1980.
KRAPFL, J. E., & VARGAS, E. A. *Behaviorism and ethics.* Kalamazoo, Mich.: Behaviordelia, 1977.
Larry P. v. Riles. 343 F. Supp. 1306 (1972; aff'd 502 F. 2d 963 (1974).
LUCERO, R. J., VAIL, D. J., & SCHERBER, J. Regulating operant-conditioning programs. *Hospital and Community Psychiatry,* 1968, *19,* 53-54.
MARTIN, R. *Legal challenges to behavior modifications: Trends in schools, corrections, and mental health.* Champaign, Ill.: Research Press, 1975.
MARTIN, R. Comments on the "Wisconsin experience." *The Behavior Therapist,* 1979, *2,* 7.
Mattie T. v. Holladay. N.D. Miss (1979).
Mills v. Board of Education of District of Columbia. 348 F. Supp. 866 (1972).
MIRON, N. B. Issues and implications of operant conditioning: The primary ethical consideration. *Hospital and Community Psychiatry,* 1968, *19,* 226-228.
Morales v. Turman. 383 F. Supp. 53 (1973).
MORRIS, R. J. *Behavior modification with children: A systematic guide.* Cambridge, Mass.: Winthrop Publishers, 1976.
MORRIS, R. J. Treating mentally retarded children: A prescriptive approach. In A. P. Goldstein (Ed.), *Prescriptions for child mental health and education.* New York: Pergamon, 1978.
MORRIS, R. J., & HOSCHOUER, R. L. Current issues in applied research with mentally retarded persons. *Applied Research in Mental Retardation,* 1980, *1,* 85-93.
NATIONAL ASSOCIATION FOR RETARDED CITIZENS. Guidelines for the use of behavioral procedures in state programs for retarded persons. *M. R. Research,* 1975, *1,* 1-71.
NATIONAL SOCIETY FOR AUTISTIC CHILDREN. *White paper on behavior modification with autistic children.* Mimeo., June 1975.
New York State Association for Retarded Children v. Rockefeller. 357 F. Supp. 752 (1973).
Pennsylvania Association for Retarded Children v. Commonwealth of Pennsylvania. 334 F. Supp. 1257 (1971).
PROVINCE OF MANITOBA, DEPARTMENT OF HEALTH AND SOCIAL DEVELOPMENT. The Manitoba School. *Time-out guidelines.* Mimeo., 1978.
REPP. A. C., & DEITZ, D. E. D. On the selective use of punishment—suggested guidelines for administrators. *Mental Retardation,* 1978, *16,* 250-254.
Roos, P. Human rights and behavior modification. *Mental Retardation,* 1974, *12,* 3-6.
Roos, P. Personal communication April 1980.
SCHAEFER, H. H. The ethics of deprivation. In D. R. Rubin & C. M. Franks (Eds.), *Advances in behavior therapy 1968.* New York: Academic Press, 1969.
SHAPIRO, M. H. Legislating the control of behavior control: Autonomy and the coercive use of organic therapies. *Southern California Law Review,* 1974, *47,* 237-356.
Souder v. Brennan. 367 F. Supp. 808 (1973).
SPEECE, R. G. Conditioning and other technologies used to "treat?" "rehabilitate?" "demolish?" prisoners and mental patients. *Southern California Law Review,* 1972, *45,* 616-681.
SHAPIRO, M. H. Legislating the control of behavior control: Autonomy and the coercive use of organic therapies. *Southern California Law Review,* 1974, *47,* 237-356.
Souder v. Brennan. 367 F. Supp. 808 (1973).
SPEECE, R. G. Conditioning and other technologies used to "treat?" "rehabilitate?" "demolish?" prisoners and mental patients. *Southern California Law Review,* 1972, *45,* 616-681.

STATE OF ARIZONA. Division of Developmental Disabilities and Mental Retardation Services. District II. *Behavior modification methodology.* Mimeo., February 1979.

STATE OF CALIFORNIA. *Draft of guidelines for the use of behavioral procedures in community care and health facilities for developmentally and mentally disabled children.* Mimeo., 1977.

STATE OF MICHIGAN. *Aversive and deprivation procedures.* Mimeo., 1978.

STATE OF MINNESOTA. DPW Rule 39—Draft. *Conditions for the use of aversive and deprivation procedures.* Mimeo., 1978.

STATE OF MASSACHUSETTS. *Use of aversive and deprivation procedures,* Mimeo., 1978.

STATE OF OHIO. *Regulation of behavior modification programs in state institutions.* Mimeo., 1978.

STATE OF WISCONSIN, Division of Community Services. *Behavior management guidelines.* Mimeo., July 1977.

STOLZ, S. B., & ASSOCIATES. *Ethical issues in behavior modification.* San Francisco; Jossey-Bass, 1978.

STUART, R. B. Protection of the right of informed consent to participate in research. *Behavior Therapy,* 1978, 9, 73–82.

VARGAS, E. A. Rights: A behavioristic analysis. *Behaviorism,* 1975, 3, 178–190.

VOGLER, R. E., & MARTIN, P. L. In defense of operant conditioning programs in mental institutions. *Psychological Record,* 1969, 19, 59–64.

WEXLER, D. Token and taboo: Behavior modification, token economies, and the law. *California Law Review,* 1973, 61, 81–109.

WOLFENSBERGER, W. The origin and nature of our institutional models. In R. B. Kugel & W. Wolfensberger (Eds.). *Changing patterns in residential services for the mentally retarded.* Washington, D.C.: U.S. Government Printing Office, 1969.

Wyatt v. *Stickney* 325 F. Supp. 781, 334 F. Supp. 1341 (1971); 344 F. Supp. 373, 387 (1971) affirmed in part, remanded in part sub nom *Wyatt* v. *Aderhold* 503 F. 2d 1305, (1978, 1974) *Wyatt* v. *Hardin,* M.D. Ala. (1979), *Wyatt* v. *Ireland,* M.D. Ala. (1979).

4 Litigation and Legislative Regulations Impacting on the Treatment of the Developmentally Disabled

LYNDA KATZ-GARRIS AND RAYMOND P. GARRIS

INTRODUCTION

The task of writing a chapter on a subject which has within the last 10 years produced literally thousands of legal briefs, scholarly treatises, government regulations, judicial decisions, major state-of-the-art reports, and training conferences could easily be viewed as naive, obviously superficial, and probably redundant. Such was not the case, however, less than a decade ago. The world of the developmentally disabled emerged dramatically in the law, following the footsteps of one of the major pieces of mental health legislation passed by the U.S. Congress. While the concept of developmentally disabled was still in an embryonic stage, the evolutionary process continued to evolve and spew forth a Partlow, a Willowbrook, more pieces of federal legislation, and, as of this writing, a Supreme Court ruling, involving a Pennsylvania institution (Pennhurst).

The seeds for this revolutionary spirit with regard to rights of the disabled emerged from the civil rights movement of the 1960s, the War on Poverty, the social activism of student groups, and the Vietnam war era. In the name of civil liberties and individual rights we entered the age of the minority. Among the multitude of minorities which coexist in a pluralistic society, the minority of the disabled and of the mentally, physically, and emotionally impaired has come come center stage in the last two decades. As citizens, these persons have needs

---

LYNDA KATZ-GARRIS • Western Psychiatric Institute and Clinic, Psychiatric Rehabilitation Services, University of Pittsburgh, Pittsburgh, Pennsylvania 15261.   RAYMOND P. GARRIS • University of Pittsburgh, Division of Specialized Professional Development, Pittsburgh, Pennsylvania 15260.

for the basic human services provided to all in a democratic humanistic society. Of particular importance is the fact that developmentally disabled have special needs. Whether called treatment, education, habilitation, or rehabilitation, to provide them with a standard of excellence, professionals must understand the legal constraints and mandates within which they must function.

With the realization that this chapter may be outdated before it can be published, we shall attempt to highlight major judicial decisions and legislative mandates which have influenced treatment of the developmentally disabled. Further, it is our intention that, in reviewing these materials, the treatment implications will elucidate understanding, cognition, and voluntariness in the providers of treatment who can then be said to have given "informed consent," respective to their role in treatment of the developmentally disabled.

A Definition and Its Historical Evolution in the Courts

> Treatment: 1. The act or manner of treating something, such as a person or subject. 2. The application of remedies with the object of effecting a cure; therapy. (American Heritage, 1969, p. 1367)

The concept of treatment entered the courts in 1966 with the case of *Rouse v. Cameron* [373 F. 2d 451 (D.C. Cir. 1966)], but its definition therein derived from its absence.

> The purpose of involuntary hospitalization is treatment not punishment.... absent treatment, the hospital is "transform[ed]...into a penitentiary where one could be held indefinitely for no convicted offense, and this even though the offense of which he was previously acquitted because of doubt as to his sanity might not have been one of the more serious felonies" or might have been, as it was were, a misdemeanor. (p. 452)

Because providing treatment was the rationale for confinement in a hospital, failure in this area raised the constitutional issues of due process, equal protection, and cruel and unusual punishment. However, the court in *Rouse* did not deal with these issues but instead based its decision on existing statutory law (Stick, 1976).

The District of Columbia's statute regarding treatment read: "A person hospitalized in a public hospital for mental illness shall, during his hospitalization, be entitled to medical and psychiatric care and treatment" [D.C. Code Ann. 21-562 (1967)]. The statute provided that treatment need not cure or improve the condition of the patient, but rather there should be a bona fide effort to do so; that the treatment provided was adequate in light of existing knowledge; and that initial and periodic reviews be made concerning the patient's condition in order that treatment suitable to the patient's needs be provided.

It was left to other courts to deal with constitutional violations inherent in the process of institutionalization or confinement for treatment purposes. Since the individual has a right not to be institutionalized under the Fifth and Fourteenth Amendments, when a state exercises its *parens patria* power "effective treatment must be *quid pro quo*" [*Martarella* v. *Kelly,* 349 F. Supp. 575, 600 (S.D. N.Y. 1972)].

Although the "right to treatment" began to emerge in the field of mental health law, this right was extended to the mentally retarded in the courtroom of Judge Johnson in the landmark *Wyatt* v. *Stickney* [344 F. Supp. 387, 396 (M.D. Ala. 1972)] case. The Court concluded on December 10, 1971, that the defendant's (State of Alabama) treatment program was deficient in three fundamental areas: (1) a humane psychological and physical environment; (2) qualified staff in numbers sufficient to administer adequate treatment; and (3) individualized treatment plans. More specifically, the Court found that many conditions, such as nontherapeutic, uncompensated work assignments and the absence of privacy, constituted dehumanizing factors contributing to the degeneration of the patient's self-esteem (Brooks, 1974). A humane psychological and physical environment under the Court order was further specified by delineating a series of "rights" for the patients which included rights (1) to enjoy privacy and dignity; (2) to live under the least restrictive conditions necessary to achieve the purposes of commitment; (3) to seek legal proceedings to establish incompetency; (4) to have visitation, use the telephone, and send sealed mail; (5) not to have unnecessary or excessive medication; (6) to be free from physical restraint and isolation except for emergency situations; (7) not to be subject to experimental research without the express and informed consent of the patient or his guardian; (8) to receive prompt and adequate medical treatment for physical ailments; (9) to freely choose and wear their own clothing and have access to personal belongings; (10) to enjoy religious worship; and (11) to have suitable opportunities, with adequate supervision, to interact with members of the opposite sex.

In addition, qualified and sufficient staffing was specified as well as standards for labor considered therapeutic. The individualized treatment plan was outlined and included among other standards that such a plan contain (1) a statement of the nature of the specific needs and problems of the patient; (2) a statement of the least restrictive treatment condition necessary to achieve the purposes of commitment; (3) a description of intermediate and long-range treatment goals with a projected timetable for their attainment; (4) a statement and rationale for the plan of treatment to achieve these goals; (5) specification of staff responsibility and involvement in attaining these goals; and (6) criteria for release to less restrictive treatment conditions, criteria for discharge, and an individualized posthospitalization plan.

In the order relating to Bryce Hospital for mentally ill patients, education suited to the needs of children and young adults was specifically included as one of "the minimum constitutional standards for adequate treatment of the mentally ill." In addition, Judge Johnson found that "[in] the context of the right to appropriate care for people civilly confined to public mental institutions, no viable distinction could be made between the mentally ill and mentally retarded" [344 F. Supp. (1982) at 390]. In a separate order directed at Partlow State School and Hospital for the mentally retarded, the court issued a similar order regarding "the minimum constitutional standards for adequate habilitation" (McClung, 1974, p. 163). In the words of the court habilitation was defined as

> The process by which the staff of the institution assists the resident to acquire and maintain those life skills which enable him to cope more effectively with the demands of his own person and of his environment and to raise the level of his physical, mental, and social efficiency. Habilitation includes but is not limited to programs of formal, structured education and treatment. [344 F. Supp. (1972) at 395]

By defining *habilitation* in this manner, the court facilitated the argument that the state must afford to handicapped children opportunities for cognitive as well as social growth because it offers these opportunities (called *education*) to other children (Burt, 1975). By conceiving of habilitation as training to enable the individual to cope with his environment, the court closely approximated the definition of *education* adapted in *Brown* v. *The Board of Education* and *Pennsylvania Association for Retarded Children* v. *Pennsylvania (P.A.R.C.)*. The Supreme Court in *Brown* stated:

> Today, education is perhaps the most important function of state and local governments.... It is the very foundation of good citizenship. Today it is a principal instrument in awakening the child to cultural values, in preparing him for later professional training, and in helping him to adjust normally to his environment. [347 U.S. 483 (1954) at 493]

The *P.A.R.C.* consent decree declared:

> all mentally retarded persons are capable of benefiting from a program of education and training; that the greatest number of retarded persons, given such education and training, are capable of achieving self-sufficiency, and the remaining few, with such education and training, are capable of achieving some degree of self-care [334 F. Supp. 1257 (1971) at 1259].

Before the consent decree had been formulated, expert witnesses in *P.A.R.C.* had provided the Court with the definition of education:

> [E]ducation cannot be defined solely as the provision of academic experiences to children. Rather, education must be seen as a continuous process by which individuals learn to cope and function within their environment. Thus, for children to learn to clothe and feed themselves is a legitimate outcome achieveable through an educational program. (Weintraub & Abeson, 1972, p. 1046)

While the right to treatment seemed to have a secure constitutional basis, the Supreme Court in *Rodriguez* v. *San Antonio Independent School District* [411 U.S. 1 (1973)] held that the right to an equal education was not a fundamental right. However, they reserved the decision on whether some minimum amount of education was fundamental. In addition, the Court apparently accepted the analogy between exclusion from education and exclusion from such fundamental activities as voting and criminal appeal (Flanagan, 1974). "Proceeding from this analogy, exlcusion from education because a child cannot afford to pay a fee is clearly unconstitutional. So also is a pattern of exclusion in which there is a sufficient correlation between those who are excluded from education and those who are poor" (Flanagan, p. 545).

The issue of treatment, on the other hand, which arose more specifically among those who were civilly committed as discussed by the courts as "massive curtailment of liberty" in such cases as *Humphrey* v. *Cody* [405 U.S. 504 (1972)] and *Jackson* v. *Indiana* (406 U.S. 715 (1972)], received constitutional sanction in the famous Donaldson case [*O'Connor* v. *Donaldson*, 422 U.S. 563 (1975)]. Donaldson, which began as a right-to-treatment case, reached the U.S. Supreme Court as a right-to-liberty case with the court ruling that there was a constitutional right to liberty and that a person who was not dangerous could not be confined in a mental hospital against his will. The Supreme Court emphasized that adequacy of treatment could be investigated by the court.

One of the most recent cases involving the court's defintion of treatment is found in *Vitek* v. *Jones* [100 S.Ct. 1254 (1980)]. This case involved the necessity for procedural due process before the transfer of a prisoner to a psychiatric hospital. In the words of the court:

> The loss of liberty produced by an involuntary commitment is more than a loss of freedom from confinement. It is indisputable that commitment to a mental hospital "can engender adverse social consequences to the individual" and that "[w]hether we label this phenomena 'stigma' or choose to call it something else . . . we recognize that it can occur and that it can have very significant impact on the individual." Also, "among the historic liberties" protected by the Due Process Clause is the "right to be free from, and to obtain judicial relief for, unjustified intrusions on personal security." Compelled treatment in the form of mandatory behavior modification programs, to which the District Courts found Jones was exposed in this case, was a proper factor to be weighed by the District Court. (Perlin & Martin, 1980, p. 26)

Intrinsically intertwined among the various important legal concepts which have been applied in securing treatment (broadly defined by now) for those committed to institutions and those outside of institutions bound by compulsory school attendance statutes including due process, cruel and unusual punishment standards, suspect classification, etc., is the concept of least restrictive alternative (environment). For a thorough discussion of this concept, see Chambers (1972). This concept entered the arena of mental health litigation for the first time in *Lake* v. *Cameron* [364 F. 2d 657 (1966)] by the civil analogue of the "cruel and unusual punishment doctrine" which had been given constitutional dimension in *Shelton* v. *Tucker* [364 U.S. 479 (1960)]: "even though the government's purpose be legitimate and substantial, that purpose cannot be pursued by means that broadly stifle fundamental liberties when the end can be more reasonably achieved" [364 U.S. 479 (1960) at 488]. The U.S. Court of Appeals for the District of Columbia Circuit ordered that alternatives to hospitalization for the mentally ill be explored in all cases and used where appropriate. Actualizing the concept "least restrictive alternative," while surfacing in *Wyatt* and later in *Willowbrook* [*New York Association for Retarded Children, Inc.* v. *Rockefeller*, 357 F. Supp. 756 (E.D.N.Y. 1973)], by and large was confined to inside of the institution's walls. With *Halderman* v. *Pennhurst State School and Hospital* [612 F. 2d 84 (3d Cir. 1979)], the concept has seemingly broken down the institutional confines of treatment and has emerged as de-institutionalization. While currently awaiting a Supreme Court decision on an appeal from the U.S. Court of Appeals for the Third Circuit by the original defendants in the case, the lower court's ruling stands thusly:

> Naturally, nothing we have said here should be understood to disapprove the interim measures ordered by the trial court for the improvement of Pennhurst. Quite the reverse: state and federal laws plainly require that if Pennhurst is to remain open for at least some patients, it must be dramatically improved so as to provide adequate habilitation. Neither should our willingness to permit retention of Pennhurst as an institution available for those who cannot be treated in any less restrictive environment be construed as an invitation to the appellants to desist from opening up alternative community facilities. As we have said, institutionalization is a disfavored approach to habilitation. Only where the court or the Master finds that an improved Pennhurst is the only appropriate place for individual patients should it be used. For all other patients, CLA's (Community Living Arrangements) must be provided. [612 F. 2d 84 (3d Cir. 1979) at 107]

We shall discuss *Pennhurst* in more detail, following the discussion of major federal legislation involving the developmentally disabled, as this case was litigated under the provisions of federal as well as state statutes.

The logical corollary to de-institutionalization as a connotative meaning of "treatment" is the institutionalized person's right to refuse treatment. In the words of Perlin and Martin (1980):

> More controversial than the right to treatment is the right to refuse treatment. This issue—often the focal point of pitched "turf" battles between patients and lawyers on one hand and hospital administrators and mental health professionals on the

other—encompasses virtually every important issue involving the regulation of mental health practice: Issues of freedom of choice, informed consent, privacy, dignity, autonomy, self-sufficiency, and the right to control one's own thought processes are all involved in the explosive area of the right to refuse treatment. (p. 65)

The right was originally litigated in cases which involved the use of experimental drugs as part of aversive training programs [*Mackey v. Procunier*, 477 F. 2d 877 (9th Cir. 19783)] and in a psychosurgery case [*Kaimowitz v. Department of Public Health of Michigan, U.S. Law Week* 2063 (1973)]. Subsequent cases [*Scott v. Plante*, 532 F. 2d 939 (3d Cir. 1976); *Rennie v. Klein*, 462 F. Supp. 1131 (D.N.J. 1978), Modified, 476 F. Supp. 129 (D.N.J. 1979); *Roger v. Okin*, 478 F. Supp. 1342 (D. Mass. 1979)] have involved antipsychotic medications as treatment.

In the words of the court in *Rogers v. Okin* (1979):

> The only purpose, therefore, of forced medication, in a non-emergency, is to help the patient. The desire to help the patient is a laudable if not noble goal. But, a basic premise of the right to privacy is the freedom to decide whether we want to be helped, or whether we want to be left alone. It takes a grave set of circumstances to abrogate that right. That a non-emergency injection in the buttocks may be therapeutic does not constitute such a circumstance.

In an amicus brief, the Massachusetts Psychiatric Society argues:

> If forbidden to use certain standard, effective modalities, they (hospital staffs) will be caught in the situation of having a legal obligation which they cannot carry out.
>
> That argument suffers from a faulty premise. The state has a duty to make treatment available. It has no duty to impose treatment on a competent involuntary patient who prefers to refuse medication, regardless of its potential benefit. (Perlin & Martin, 1980, p. 86)

The definition of treatment, whether in a mental health or educational setting, has largely been a matter of form rather than content. In the legal context, the definition parallels the concept of procedural rather than substantive due process. The courts have set the parameters within which treatment is to occur, that is, least restrictive setting, psychological and humane environment, individualized treatment goals, staffing ratios, and limits within which treatment can be imposed on a nonwilling party. The substantive issue, what is appropriate education or individualized treatment, the courts have left to the professionals involved in the treatment or education process to define. The one area that appears to be the exception is the forced use of medication or, in some instances, intrusive management techniques or methods which involve substantive rather than procedural issues.

Of final significance is the fact that the courts, through the litigation process, have broadened the scope of education to include training in basic life skills and socialization. The definition of treatment, at last removed from the historical vestiges of custodial care, has also been enlarged to include the concept of habilitation which is defined not only as a skills acquisition or maintenance function but also as a remedial process. The general review presented is an effort to give the logical sequence of legal events in a succinct fashion. Court litigation is a long, arduous, and costly process; perhaps for that reason we have, as citizens, another means for accessing rights and reaping benefits from those mandated rights. We shall now turn to a discussion of those major pieces of federal legislation which have influenced the treatment of the developmentally disabled.

Legislative Mandates to Provide Treatment to the Developmentally Disabled

According to Martin (1980), with the successful conclusion of cases such as *P.A.R.C.* and *Mills* v. *The Board of Education of the District of Columbia* [348 F. Supp. 866 (D.D.C. 1972)] and the filing of 36 additional right-to-education cases, the time had come for the federal government to declare well-delineated and systematic standards. The congressional measures took two routes, one involving nondiscrimination applied to all programs and the other an amendment of federal education laws. Whereas the Congress had created the Bureau of Education for the Handicapped in Public Law 91-230, the Education of the Handicapped Act, that act was expanded in the 1974 amendments which laid the basis for comprehensive planning for the states and the protection of handicapped children's rights through due process. Such congressional efforts culminated in the Education for All Handicapped Children Act. P.L. 94-142, (20 U.S.C. 1401 *et seq.*, 89 Stat 773) and the subsequent regulations for the implementation of P.L. 94-142 [45 C.F.R. § 121a *et seq.*, (1979)].

The corollary legislation to secure civil rights for the handicapped, known as the Rehabilitation Act of 1973, P.L. 93-112, contained within it a section which has been interpreted as the counterpart of Title VI of the Civil Rights Act of 1964. That final section of the act, Section 504 (29 U.S.C. 194), stated:

> No otherwise qualified handicapped individual in the United States, as defined in section 7 (6), shall, solely by reason of his handicap, be excluded from the participation in, be denied the benefits of, or be subjected to discrimination under any program or activity receiving Federal financial assistance.

Among the handicapped were persons classified as developmentally disabled. Under P.L. 91-517, the Developmental Disabilities Services and Facilities Construction Act of 1970 (89 Stat. 773), the definition of developmental disabilities was extended to individuals substantially handicapped by disability of neurological origin, beginning in childhood, and expected to continue indefinitely. Mental retardation, epilepsy, and cerebral palsy were specifically named in the act together with "other neurological conditions." Then in 1974 the Senate committee which reviewed the act recommended adding autism and severe specific learning disabilities. The definition was further expanded to include conditions closely related to mental retardation, such as lowered general intellectual functioning, impaired adaptive behavior, or other conditions necessitating treatment similar to that required for mentally retarded individuals.

The ensuing legislation, P.L. 94-103, The Developmentally Disabled Assistance and Bill of Rights Act of 1975, (42 U.S.C. §§ 6000 et seq., 89 Stat. 486) expanded the definition again to the following formulation:

> The term "developmental disability" means a disability of a person which (A) (i) is attributable to mental retardation, cerebral palsy, epilepsy, or autism;
>
> (ii) is attributable to any other condition of a person found to be closely related to mental retardation because such condition results in similar impairment of general intellectual functioning or adaptive behavior to that of mentally retarded persons or requires treatment and services similar to those required for such persons; or
>
> (iii) is attributable to dyslexia resulting from a disability described in clause (i) or (ii) of this subparagraph;
>
> (B) originates before such person attains age 18;
>
> (C) has continued or can be expected to continue indefinitely; and
>
> (D) constitutes a substantial handicap to such person's ability to function normally in society. (89 Stat. 497)

In addition, the act required state plans to contain priorities and goals frequently mandated. Namely, the inappropriate institutional placement of persons with developmental disabilities was to be reduced and eventually eliminated. Additional required goals included the improvement of the quality of care on habilitation and rehabilitation of the developmentally disabled; early diagnosis and screening; counseling and program coordination of follow-along services; protective services and personal advocacy; support of community program establishment; alternatives to institutionalization; promotion of human rights, and the provision of interdisciplinary intervention in training programs for the multiplyhandicapped individual (Vandamn, 1979).

Lastly, under Section III of the Developmentally Disabled Assistance and

Bill of Rights Act (42 U.S.C. § 6010), Congress made the following findings with respect to the rights of persons with developmental disabilities:

1. Persons with developmental disabilities have a right to appropriate treatment, services, and habilitation for such disabilities.
2. The treatment, services, and habilitation for a person with developmental disabilities should be designed to maximize the developmental potential of the person and should be provided in the setting that is least restrictive of the person's personal liberty.
3. The Federal Government and the States both have an obligation to assure that public funds are not provided to any institution or other residential program for persons with developmental disabilities that
   (A) does not provide treatment, services, and habilitation which is appropriate to the needs of such persons; or
   (B) does not meet the following minimum standards;
       (i) Provision of a nourishing, well-balanced daily diet to the persons with developmental disabilities being served by the program.
       (ii) Provision to such persons of appropriate and sufficient medical and dental services.
       (iii) Prohibition of the use of physical restraint on such persons unless absolutely necessary and prohibition of the use of such restraint as a punishment or as a substitute for a habilitation program.
       (iv) Prohibition on the excessive use of chemical restraints on such persons and the use of such restraints as punishment or as a substitute for a habilitation program or in quantities that interfere with services, treatment, or habilitation for such persons.
       (v) Permission for close relatives of such persons to visit them at reasonable hours without prior notice.
       (vi) Compliance with adequate fire and safety standards as may be promulgated by the Secretary.
4. All programs for persons with developmental disabilities should meet standards which are designed to assure the most favorable possible outcome for those served, and
   (A) in the case of residential programs serving persons in need of comprehensive, health-related, habilitative, or rehabilitative services, which are at least equivalent to those standards applicable to intermediate care facilities for the mentally retarded promulgated in regulations of the Secretary on January 17, 1974 (39 Fed. Reg. pt. II), as appropriate when taking into account the size of the institutions and the service delivery arrangements of the facilities of the programs;
   (B) in the case of other residential programs for persons with developmental disabilities, which assure that care is appropriate to the needs of the persons being served by such programs, assure that the persons admitted to facilities of such programs are persons whose needs can be met through services provided by facilities, and assure that the facilities under such programs provide for the humane care of the residents of the facilities, are sanitary, and protect their rights; and
   (C) in the case of nonresidential programs, which assure the care provided by such programs is appropriate to the persons served by the programs.

> The rights of persons with developmental disabilities described in findings made in this section are in addition to any constitutional or other rights otherwise afforded to all persons.

According to Burgdorf (1980) "at least one federal court has held that the requirements of § 6010 may be enforced by a private right of action, *Naughton* v. *Bevilacqua*, 458 F. Supp. 610 (D.R.I. 1978). The impact on this section of the practices of state institutions is as yet largely unmeasured, but it seems to hold significant potential" (p. 701).

With the adoption of P.L. 95-602 in 1978, developmental disabilities joined forces with rehabilitation legislation in the Comprehensive Rehabilitation Services and Developmental Disabilities Amendments of 1978. However, the regulations to implement the developmental disabilities amendments have not been promulgated as of this writing. (This issue will be addressed more fully later.)

The 1978 act again expanded the definition of developmental disabilities but did so this time by not enumerating a list of specific impairments. The Senate version of the bill was adopted ultimately by a joint committee which emphasized that previously enumerated groups were not to be deprived of their eligibility:

> The conferees stress, however, that the definition agreed to is intended to cover everyone currently under the definition and is also intended to add other individuals with similar characteristics. In this definition, individuals with conditions currently listed in the law—autism, cerebral palsy, dyslexia, or mental retardation—would be included if they meet the following criteria: Manifestation prior to age 22, expectation of continuing indefinitely, substantial functional limitation, and need for multiple services for an extended period. It is not the intent to exlcude anyone who legitimately should have been included under the definition in current law. (Burgdorf, 1980, p. 31)

Having now dealt with the handicapping conditions of those individuals who have been defined under the law as developmentally disabled, we shall turn to a discussion of the major components of the Education for all Handicapped Children Act, P.L. 94-142, and the Rehabilitation Act of 1973, and its amendments of 1978, with particular emphasis on Section 504.

Public Law 94-142

The Supreme Court decision in *Brown* v. *The Board of Education* [347 483 (1954)] provided the impetus for significant growth in special education. From that decision, the right to an education for all children emerged.

Educators hailed the decision not only for blacks but for all disadvantaged children (Weintraub & Abeson, 1972). By the late 1960s, the trend requiring school districts to educate handicapped children had been firmly established. In 1971, there were 899 bills promoting the education of handicapped children introduced in state legislatures; 237 of these were enacted into law. By 1973, 40% of the states had enacted laws mandating educational programs to handicapped children (Casey, 1973).

While interest in the handicapped child has been attributed to *Brown* and its progeny of desegragation cases, in addition, professional attitudes toward the handicapped child and an increase in the number of advocates asserting their rights (Gilhoul, 1973) have been contributing factors. The educator's emerging attitude, referred to as the "zero reject" concept, basically states that all handicapped persons can learn, develop, and benefit from appropriate educational programs (Burgdorf, 1972). This meant that programs had to be developed for the estimated 1,750,000 handicapped individuals of school age who as of 1975 were totally excluded from public school education programs. It also came to mean that something had to be done for the 2,200,000 handicapped children attending schools, but not being provided with special programs suited to their needs. This latter category included the learning disabled child and the educationally mentally retarded child. Although some of these children were included in the classroom, without appropriate programming they were in effect constructively excluded from the education process.

Congress passed P.L. 94-142 in response to the need for increased funding brought about by the widespread recognition by courts and state legislatures of the right of the handicapped child to an adequate education. The act itself sets forth the general requirements that states must meet in order to qualify for receipt of federal funds; it does not prescribe the specific educational programs local schools must make available in order to fulfill those requirements. Instead, the heart of the federal control mechanism is a system of procedural safeguards which provide for parental involvement in placement decisions. In effect, the act guarantees procedures whereby parents might challenge the appropriateness of their child's educational program but provides only the most general guidelines for resolving the substantive questions such challenges may present.

In passing the act, Congress codified and expanded the broadest procedural rights accorded handicapped children in earlier litigated cases. In addition, Congress authorized large annual appropriations to aid the states in providing expensive new services for handicapped children. Finally, the act gave courts and administrative hearing officers broad authority to prescribe the details of educational policy in individual cases [20 U.S.C. § 1415 (e) (2) (1976)]; however, the authority of hearing officers is never defined in the act. Presumably, either a judge or hearing officer could order implementation of whatever program was deemed appropriate. Although there are broad substantive guidelines, these guidelines would not entirely overcome the difficulties encountered by courts in constitutional litigation in fashioning remedies for individual children.

The act requires states to provide a "free appropriate public education" to all handicapped children between the ages of 3 and 18 years by September 1, 1978, and between 3 and 21 by September 1, 1980 [(20 U.S.C. § 1412 (2) (B)]. Avoiding any attempt at prescribing specific educational programs, the Act defines appropriate education as "special education and related services which... are in conformity with an IEP" [20 U.S.C. § 1401 (18)]. An IEP, or individualized educational program, is a "written statement for each handicapped child" developed in a meeting with the child's parents, teacher, and qualified school representative [20 U.S.C. § 1401 (19)].

Each IEP must be reviewed and/or revised at least on an annual basis. Section 121a. 346 requires the IEP to include the following elements:

1. A statement of the child's present levels of educational performance;
2. A statement of annual goals, including short-term instructional objectives;
3. A statement of the specific special education and related services to be provided to the child, and the extent to which the child will be able to participate in regular educational programs;
4. The projected dates for initiation of service and the anticipated duration of the services;
5. Appropriate objective criteria and evaluation procedures and schedules for determining, on at least an annual basis, whether the short-term instructional objectives are being achieved.

Although the IEP is not a legally binding contract and no agency, teacher, or other person may be held accountable if the child does not achieve the projected progress based on the annual goals and objectives, this section of the law (§ 121a. 349) does not relieve agencies and teachers from making good-faith efforts to teach the child (Turnbull & Turnbull, 1979).

Exhibiting "good faith" in the IEP conference, the writers of the act set forth no guidelines for determining substantive content of an appropriate program. To direct placement decisions, it includes a statement that handicapped children should be educated together with the nonhandicapped "to the maximum extent appropriate" [§1412 5 (B)]. To reduce misclassification, the act prohibits racially or culturally biased tests and forbids reliance on any single criterion—such as IQ tests—in determining a handicapped child's placement [§ 1412 (5) (C)].

To secure the right of handicapped children, the act established detailed procedural safeguards. It granted parents the right to present a complaint with regard to any matter relating to the identification, evaluation, educational placement, and provision of free appropriate public education to their handicapped children [§ 1915 (b)(I)(E)]. Parents are entitled to an impartial due process hearing before a hearing officer who is not an employee of the agency involved in the education of the child [§ 1915 (b) (2)]. If the hearing initially takes place at a local level, an aggrieved party may appeal to a state agency for review of the local decision [§ 1415 (c)]. The act does not state whether the state appeals officer is to make an entirely independent determination or is to rely on the decision of a local examiner if supported by substantial evidence in the record.

When administrative procedures fail to resolve conflict, the act provides that any party aggrieved by a state determination may bring a civil action in a state or federal court [20 U.S.C. § 1415 (e)]. During the pendancy of the case, the act provides a "stay-put" requirement that allows the child to remain in his or her current placement pending the outcome of administrative or judicial proceedings [§ 1415 (e) (3)]. Finally, any child applying for initial admission to a public school is entitled to be placed in a regular school program unless parents and the school agree to do otherwise [§ 1415 (e) (3)].

Public Law 94-142 contains, then, the major components of previously litigated right to education cases, including the concept of "zero reject," the least restrictive educational setting, provision for a due process hearing and the right to appeal, fair classification and nonculturally biased testing procedures, and parental participation in the placement process. In addition, the act set forth content guidelines for a written individualized educational program plan, a stay-put clause to allow children continued educational programming until the administrative or judicial proceedings conclude, and a definition of special education and/or related services. As the issue of related services directly spans the education-treatment continuum, we shall deal more fully with it in later discussion.

This, in summary form, is a synopsis of the major provisions of P.L. 94-142. For a much more detailed and extensive legal analysis of the act, see Martin (1980). For a comprehensive historical and sociopolitical analysis of educational handicap and public policy in its historical perspective, see Sarason and Doris (1979). We shall now turn to a review of the major provisions of the Rehabilitation Act and its 1978 amendments which have particular impact on the treatment of the developmentally disabled and mentally retarded.

Public Law 93-112, Section 504

Section 504 of the Rehabilitation Act of 1973, as amended by P.L. 93-516, P.L. 94-230, and P.L. 95-602, guarantees specific rights in federally funded programs and activities to persons who qualify as "handicapped." Under the 1978 amendements,

> the term "handicapped individual" means... any person who (i) has a physical or mental impairment which substantially limits one or more of such person's major life activities, (ii) has a record of such an impairment, or (iii) is regarded as having such an impairment. For purposes of Section 503 and 504 as such sections relate to employment, such term does not include any individual who is an alcohol or drug abuser... [Section 7 (6) (B)]

The Office of Standards Policy and Research (OSPR) in a memorandum dated April 20, 1979, Section 84.3, defines "physical or mental impairment" as

> (A) any physiological disorder or condition, cosmetic disfigurement, or anatomical loss affecting one or more of the following body systems: neurological, musculoskeletal, special sense organs: respiratory, including speech organs, cardio-vascular, reproductive, digestive, genito-urinary, hemic and lymphatic, skin, and endocrine, or (B) any mental or psychological disorder, such as mental retardation, organic brain syndrome, emotional or mental illness, and specific learning disabilities. *Handicapped Requirements Handbook*, 1980, App. III: C: 3

and "major life activities" as "caring for one's self, performing manual tasks, walking, seeing, hearing, speaking, breathing, learning, and working" (*Handicapped Requirements Handbook*, 1980, App. III: C:3). This law requires that all recipients of federal funds review and, if necessary, modify their programs and activities so that discrimination based on handicaps is eliminated. Section 504 does not provide for the rehabiliation or personal needs of handicapped persons but, rather, provides for their civil protection against discrimination in areas such as education and employment. The basic concepts which underly Section 504 are those of "otherwise qualified handicapped person," program and architectural accessibility and reasonable accommodation.

In the regulations entitled "Guidelines for Determining Discriminatory Practices" (*Handicapped Requirements Handbook*, 1980) promulgated in order to implement the act, Section 504 has been interpreted as prohibiting not only those practices that are overtly discriminatory but also those that have the effect of discriminating. The issue is one of equal opportunity as opposed to equal treatment. Obviously, the rationale was that in some situations identical treatment of nonhandicapped and handicapped persons could be viewed as discriminatory and that identical treatment might not provide the necessary adjustments or accommodations required to achieve equal opportunity. On the other hand separate or different treatment is permitted only where it can be shown to be necessary to ensure equal opportunity and effective benefits and services. Moreover, equally effective aids, benefits, or services need not produce equal results but rather must provide equal opportunities to achieve equal results. The delivery of these aids, benefits, and services to the handicapped, then, occurs in "the most integrated setting appropriate" [§ 85.51 (b) (2) and § 85.51 (d)]. The regulations stipulate that recipients may not deny a qualified handicapped person the opportunity to participate in programs or activities that are not separate or different despite the existence of permissibly separate or different activities and programs. Therefore, the creation of separate or different programs or activities that were not necessary (based on individually determined needs) for the handicapped persons involved would be a violation of the Section 504 government-wide regulations.

With respect to the concept of reasonable accommodation, it is first necessary to recognize that Section 504 is not an affirmative action statute [*Southeastern Community College* v. *Davis,* 574 F. 2d 1158: 4th Cir. (1978)] as is Section 503 of the act, which specifically mandates affirmative action to employ and continue in employment of qualified handicapped persons of all federal (sub) contractors with (sub) contracts of $2,500 or more. Section 504 mandates equal opportunity and nondiscrimination. In light of this mandate, reasonable accommodations would impose an "undue hardship" on the operation of the program. Factors relating to the determination of such an "undue hardship" include the size of the program, the type of operation, and the nature and cost of accommodations needed. The reasonable accommodation principle also governs accessibility in employment opportunity as the program accessibility standard does not apply to employment functions.

The "program accessibility" concept is perhaps one of the key terms in Section 504, with the above-mentioned exception. The requirement is essentially that programs be accessible; "structural modifications of existing facilities need to be undertaken only when other methods are inadequate to assure that a program is available to handicapped persons (43 *Federal Register* 2138, Jan. 23, 1978, Implementation of Executive order 11914, Nondiscrimination on the Basis of Handicap in Federally Assisted Programs). Moreover, Section 504 does not require recipients to establish a barrier-free environment. Rather, physical barriers may exist in a recipient's facilities as long as these barriers do not hinder the full participation of the handicapped persons in each program and activity when it is viewed in its entirety (43 *Federal Register* 2138, Jan. 13, 1978).

The final concept with which we shall deal in reviewing Section 504 of the act is that of the "qualified handicapped person." The broad criteria for defining a "qualified handicapped person" are essentially threefold: (1) with respect to employment, a handicapped person who, with reasonable accommodation, can perform the essential functions of the job in question; (2) with respect to services, a handicapped person who meets the essential eligibility requirements for the receipt of such services; and (3) with respect to education, a handicapped person who meets the academic and technical standards requisite to admission or participation in the institution's programs and activities. However, the HEW interpretation also emphasizes that factors such as safety may be considered in determining whether a handicapped person is qualified as long as such considerations are based on facts relating to the individual applicant's qualifications rather than assumptions or stereotypes (43 *Federal Register,* 2137, Jan. 12, 1978). An additional criterion is that imposed by the U.S. Supreme Court in the *Davis* case (*Southeastern Community College* v. *Davis,* 1978) when it ruled that a handicapped person may be required to meet the necessary physical qualifications for participation in a program or activity. The Court held that legitimate physical requirements may be taken into account in determining someone's qualifications for program participation, and stated that "[a]n otherwise qualified person is one who is able to meet all of a program's requirements in spite of his handicap" (*Handicapped Requirements Handbook,* 1980).

Subpart D of HEW regulations for the implementation of the 1978 Amendments of the Rehabilitation Act which are codified under Title 45 C.F.R. applies to preschool, elementary, secondary, and adult education programs and activities that receive or benefit from federal financial assistance for the operation of such programs. Regulations for program requirements of educational institutions under the act are covered in Sections 84.32 to 84.39 and include (1) the location and notification of all qualified handicapped persons who may not be receiving a public school education by each recipient school district; (2) the right of all qualified handicapped individuals to receive a free and appropriate public education; (3) the responsibility of the recipient school district for the child's educational program in an appropriate setting even if it lies outside of the recipient's own programs; (4) the development of an individualized educational program as one means of meeting the standards of a free and appropriate education; (5) procedural safeguards;

(6) nonacademic services; (7) preschool and adult education programs; and (8) private education programs.

To summarize our discussions thus far with respect to the particular federal statutes and regulations reviewed, we shall conclude by drawing certain similarities and differences between P.L. 94-142 and Section 504 utilizing the analysis compiled by the Federal Programs Advisory Service (*Handicapped Requirements Handbook*, 1980). Essentially, five basic requirements are common to both P.L. 94-142, and the Section 504 regulations: (1) that handicapped students, regardless of the nature or severity of handicap, be provided a free appropriate education; (2) that handicapped students be educated with nonhandicapped students to the maximum extent appropriate; (3) that educational agencies identify and locate unserved handicapped children; (4) that evaluation procedures be improved to avoid the inappropriate education that results from the misclassification of students; and (5) that procedural safeguards be established to enable parents and guardians to influence decisions regarding the evaluation and placement of their children. On the other hand, as an education statute, enforcement of P.L. 94-142 and subsequent regulations are administered by the Bureau of Education of the Handicapped (BEH). Enforcement of Section 504, because Section 504 is a civil rights statute, is the resonsibility of the Office for Civil Rights (HEW). Also, P.L. 94-142 allows for formula-type grants extending financial aid for programs to educate handicapped children and to monitor such programs. Section 504, as a civil rights law, is concerned with a broader range of issues, including employment discrimination, education at all levels, and the accessibility of federally funded programs and activities. Public Law 94-142 applies to all handicapped children who require special education and related services, between the ages of 3 and 21, inclusive. Section 504 applies to all persons in the United States, regardless of age, and therefore applies to all handicapped children with respect to their public education. Also, Section 504 mandates not only an appropriate education but general program accessibility (access extending to all handicapped children in both regular and special education programs), which may involve the necessity of structural modifications. Public Law 94-142 applies only to states which accept financial assistance under Part B of the Education for All the Handicapped Children Act (P.L. 94-142). If the educational agency receives such funds, it must comply with P.L. 94-142 regulations. This situation is not the case with Section 504 regulations, which contain no authorization of funds, but which apply to all educational agencies receiving federal financial assistance. Also, there is a noteworthy distinction between the definition of "handicapped person" set forth under Section 504 and "handicapped children" as defined under P.L. 94-142. Generally, the term *handicapped person* encompasses more handicapping conditions, including persons with conditions "considered" handicapping. And finally, Section 504 does not by its terms expressly create a private right of action (that is, the right of an individual to sue under the provisions of Section 504); P.L. 94-142 grants such a right, after administrative due process appeals have been exhausted. However, although Section 504 does not explicitly grant the right of private action, it does not prohibit it, and cases brought under Section 504 have successfully challenged discrimination in public education [*Boxall* v. *Sequoia Union High School*, 464 F. Supp. 1104 (N. D. Cal. 1979)] following the precedential case in which a private right of action under Section 504 was established [*Lloyd* v. *Regional Transportation Authority*, 548 F. 2d 1277 (7th Cir. 1977)]. In the *Lloyd* case the court found that the language of Title VI of the Civil Rights Act of 1964 (42 U.S.C. § 2000 d), construed in *Lau* v. *Nichols* [414 U.S. 563 (1974)], created affirmative rights and was particularly similar to the language of Section 504. Further justification for a private remedy was found to be implicit in the statute under the standards established by the Supreme Court in *Cort* v. *Ash* [422 U.S. 66 (1975)]. In *Cort* v. *Ash* four factors were set forth as relevant to determining whether a private remedy was implicit in a statute not expressly providing one. They were:

> First, is the "plaintiff" one of the class for whose *especial* benefit the statute was enacted,"—that is, does the statute create a federal right in favor of the plaintiff? Second, is there any indication of legislative intent, explicit or implicit, either to create such a remedy or to deny one? Third, is it consistent with the underlying purposes of the legislative scheme to imply such a remedy for the plaintiff? And finally, is the cause of action one traditionally relegated to state law, in an area basically the concern of the states, so that it would be inappropriate to infer a cause of action based solely on federal law? (422 U.S. 66 at 78; emphasis supplied)

The court in *Lloyd* found that all four factors established by *Cort* were satisfied and that Section 504, indeed, provided a private right of action. According to Burgdorf (1980) "Judge Cummings's excellent analysis of Section 504 has been accepted by every court to subsequently consider its applicability to transportation systems ... and to other areas touched by Section 504 as well ... [*Southeastern Community College* v. *Davis*, 574 F. 2d 1158 (4th Cir. 1978)(education); *Kampmeier* v. *Nyquist*, 553 F. 2d 296 (2d Cir. 1977) (recreation); *Whitaker* v. *Board of Higher Education of City of New York*, 461 F. Supp. 99 (E.D.N.Y. 1978) (employment)" (p. 490)].

The real difference, then, would appear to be that under Section 504 an aggrieved handicapped person may be entitled to file his or her lawsuit before exhausting any administrative remedies available. Under P.L. 94-142, the plaintiff must first exhaust the administrative remedies available and only then may he or she file the lawsuit. This issue of administrative remedies, however, has not been upheld when the state or local administrative procedures either have not been in place or have not conformed to federal due process guidelines [*Howard S.* v. *Friendswood*, 454 F. Supp. 634 (S.D. Tex. 1978); *Larry P.* v. *Riles*, 343 F. Supp. 1306, No. C-71-2270 RFP (N.D. Col. 1979)], although Section 504 might subsequently become the "preferred route for redress" (Turnbull & Turnbull, 1979, p. 28).

Our final consideration of a federal statute and its implementing regulations which deals with the developmentally disabled involves the Developmental Disabilities Act of 1978 which expires in September 1982. Hearings for reauthorization of the Act still have not been scheduled in either the House or Senate. In one of her final official actions as Health and Human Services Secretary, Patricia Harris signed the developmental disabilities regulations on January 19, 1981. The regulations were to have been previously published one year earlier and set for public hearing along with the Comprehensive Rehabilitation Services and Independent Living Regulations (44 *Federal Register*, Nov. 29, 1979, 68564-68621). They were finally published in May 1980 amid much controversy. However, immediately after assuming his position, Secretary Schweiker withdrew the regulations before they could be published in the *Federal Register*. Because of the possibility of a major reorganization in the Department of Health and Human Services as well as past controversy surrounding the act, there remains a strong probability that the regulations will not be forthcoming. Previously, numerous state and local officials had been critical of the administrative rquirements that states had to satisfy in order to receive funds under the act. When the State of Virginia withdrew from the federal Development Disabilities Program in November 1980, the governor cited requirements in the regulations that states retrain employees of state institutions who lost their jobs when the handicapped moved from institutions to community living arrangements. There was also additional objection to a mandated comprehensive system for evaluating services to the developmentally disabled, which was delineated in the Act as well (Virginia Withdraws, 1980).

As we pointed out at the beginning of this chapter, the life span of federal legislation, particularly in an era that seems to be embarking on a reemphasis or reestablishment of states' rights, may mean that such a review as this will only have historical value at best. This statement is made in recognition of current political-social policy which is promoting the concept of block grants which according to Stockman (1981) "would reduce the multiplicity of rules and regulations (and, thence, Federal direction) that service agencies currently operate under.... The overall result would provide publicly-financed services more effectively at lower costs for those in need" (*Handicapped Americans Report,* 1981, p. 3). According to this same publication, there is also under way a proposal for consolidating special education programs into such a block grant, "virtually eras(ing) the Education for All Handicapped Children Act, P.L. 94-142 and replac(ing) it with string-free... grants that would lump special education programs with other federal... education programs" (p. 3).

Suffice it to say that as we cannot predict the outcome of such governmental policy at this time, we shall return in the final section of this chapter to examine efforts to implement the statutory law of P.L. 94-142 and the Rehabilitation Act as they specifically relate to treatment of the developmentally disabled and mentally retarded. Thus, we again return to the judicial system and litigation efforts to secure and implement statutory rights through the courts.

Litigation Revisited

Following the enactment of the previously discussed federal legislation, the judicial branch of our tripartite system of government had now to exercise its function, that of interpreting the law of the land. Since the court cases number in the hundreds, we will deal only with those that have the most direct bearing on "treatment" (as has been previously broadly defined) issues with respect to the developmentally disabled. Some of the issues are by now familiar to the reader—least restrictive alternative, right to treatment, right to education, labeling, due process, residential placement; others have appeared under new names—change in educational placement, change in treatment setting, affirmative duty, related services. The issues overlap and are interrelated in the case law, so that any classification system would be an arbitrary one. Therefore, we shall highlight cases which raise several issues but which deal specifically with least restrictive alternative in educational and treatment settings and related services as mandated under P.L. 94-142. Our rationale is that the least restrictive alternative concept is so entwined with the right to treatment that it generally presents itself as an issue of law around due process cases, placement decisions, and discriminatory practice litigation. With respect to treatments, "related services" under the educational statute and benefits and services under the Rehabilitation Act are most relevant.

Least Restrictive Alternative

Under the regulations for the implementation of P.L. 94-142 [*Federal Register,* 42473, 42497-42498 (Aug. 23, 1977)], Section 121a.566 states "that to the maximum extent appropriate, handicapped children, including children in public or private institutions or other area facilities, are educated with nonhandicapped children." Until *Mattie T. v. Holloday* [C.A. No. 75-31-S (N.D.) Miss., July 28, 1979] was filed in a U.S. district court, none of the "least restriction" cases relied on federal statutes. *Mattie T.* clearly raised the "least restrictive placement" issue by relying on P.L. 94-142 (20 U.S.C. § 1411), Section 504 (29, (U.S.C. § 794) and T. 1, ESEA of 1965 (20 U.S.C. § 421e)]. The case focused on the provision of inadequate educational services to handicapped children placed in self-contained education classes that isolated them from nonhandicapped children. The case was finally resolved as a consent decree [N. DC-75-31-S (N.D. Miss. Jan. 26, 1979)] which issued strict guidelines for the actualization of "least restrictive environment."

The case of *Stuart v. Nappi* [443 F. Supp. 1235 (1978)] dealt with the issue of least restrictive alternative within the context of a school suspension and proposed expulsion of a high school student with both learning disabilities and emotional difficulties by a local school superintendent and board of education. In its ruling the Court stated that the right to an education in the least restrictive environment could be circumvented if schools were permitted to expel handicapped children and that such expulsions were inconsistent with the procedures established by the Handicapped Act for changing the placement of disruptive children. Burgdorf (1980) commented that the factual situation of *Stuart v. Nappi* epitomized the "child must fit the program" attitude common among old-line educators and that "the concept of least restrictive environment mandated that efforts be made to adapt the program to the special needs of the child" (p. 283).

P-1. v. Shedd [No. 78-58 D. Conn. (Mar. 23, 1979)] culminated in a Consent Decree following an action by six students who claimed violations of procedural safeguards regarding school suspension and expulsion. The Decree specifically outlined a detailed procedure to be followed regarding placement in the least restrictive alternative and discipline. In addition, *P-1. v. Shedd* established that Federal regulations governing methods for changing placements of handicapped students would replace existing state and local policies. Moreover, students not regarded as handicapped but considered for serious disciplinary sanctions had to be referred for evaluation. If these children were found to be handicapped, the special education process had to take place in lieu of disciplinary action.

In *Lora v. Board of Education of City of New York* [456 F. Supp. 1211 (1978)], the court used the educational term "mainstreaming" which is analogous to the legal concept of least restrictive alternative. However, since there is no real consistency with the educational terminology (Burgdorf, 1980), schematic diagrams such as those developed by Reynolds (1962) and Deno (1971) utilizing a "cascade system" to illustrate the range of educational alternatives available to children in order to achieve the goal of education in the least restrictive alternative were employed by the court. The plaintiffs were black and Hispanic students in New York City placed in special schools for aggression. Although the Judge did not order closing the day schools, he did find that evaluation procedures used in placement had violated the constitutional rights of the plaintiffs, relying on Title VI of the Civil Rights Act of 1964, the Education of all Handicapped Children Act and the 1974 Amendments to the Rehabilitation Act of 1973 which extended prohibitions against discrimination to areas such as education.

Hairston v. *Drosick* [423 F. Supp. 180 (S.D. W. Va. 1976)] involved the exclusion of a spina bifida child of normal intelligence from a regular classroom for bowel incontinence. This was the first private right of action case heard under Section 504 against schools. The judge ruled that denying a handicapped child access to a regular public school classroom in receipt of federal financial assistance without compelling educational justification constituted discrimination and a denial of program benefits. The school's desire to place the child in another school to meet her physical needs more easily was not sufficiently "compelling."

The ruling *Hairston* v. *Drosick* was cited in another case involving the least restrictive alternative [*New York State Association for Retarded Children* v. *Carey* [(466 F. Supp. 479 E.D.N.Y. 1978)] which concerned the segregation of residents of Willowbrook who were carriers of hepatitis B and who were being educated in public schools. After the court injunction to stop such exclusionary practice, the School Board formed a Task Force which presented the court a proposal for creating nine special education classes composed solely of mentally retarded hepatitis B carriers. The court found the plan unacceptable since the children would not be placed in the "least restrictive environment" required by Consent Judgment and federal and state law and regulations. The judge then cited *Drosick* which recognized the importance of socialization to the education and development of handicapped persons:

> A child's chance in this society is through the educational process. A major goal of the educational process is the socialization process that takes place in the regular classroom, with the resulting capability to interact in a social way with one's peers. It is therefore imperative that every child receive an education with his or her peers insofar as it is at all possible. (P. 183)

These cases, particularly *Stuart* v. *Nappi, P-1* v. *Shedd, Lora* v. *Board of Education, Hairston* v. *Drosick,* and *New York Association for Retarded Children* v. *Carey* clearly illustrate the court's strict adherence to the concept of least restrictive alternative and should give those involved in the treatment and educational process cause to examine their current practices. Specifically, how often do mental health professionals working with parents of adolescents not previously identified as exceptional students examine a particular school board's decision to suspend or expel a child for disciplinary reasons. Also, how often would a due process hearing for evaluation be the more correct procedure to follow? Moreover, within the institutional setting, do units exclusively designed for hyperaggressive males or sexually promiscuous females parallel efforts to segregate carriers of hepatitis B? Also, are physically handicapped students confined to special schools specifically because they are wheelchair bound or, as in the case of *Hairston,* in need of specialized services involving basic bodily functions? The concept of least restrictive alternatives has far reaching and much more subtle consequences for the provision of treatment than merely a choice between institutional versus noninstitutional setting. As professionals involved in the treatment of the developmentally disabled and mentally retarded, we have an obligation to examine our own segregatory practices. Otherwise, treatment becomes a process reactive to court litigation and legislative mandates rather than an effort directed at meeting the needs of the individuals for whom it is intended.

A fitting conclusion to our discussion under the least restrictive alternative concept is that of *Halderman* v. *Pennhurst State School and Hospital* [612 F. 2d 84 (1979)] currently awaiting a decision on appeal to the U.S. Supreme Court whose ruling is expected by spring of 1981. In the brief for the petitioner, Pennhurst State School and Hospital *et al.,* it is argued in part that the Developmental Disabilities Act imposes no duties on the states to fund "appropriate treatment" or "the least restrictive environment" for developmentally disabled persons and that the Act is a funding statute designed to assist and encourage improved state care for such persons. Whether or not the lower court's ruling is upheld or overrruled, the *Pennhurst* decision in the court of Judge Broderick [446 F. Supp. 1295 (1977)], upheld in large part by the Third Circuit Court of Appeals on December 13, 1979, on statutory grounds (except for the requirement that least restrictive alternative requires the banning of all future admissions and the eventual closing of Pennhurst, regardless of the individual circumstances involved), brings together almost all the legal theories applied to the problem of inhumane residential institutions (Burgdorf, 1980).

According to Burgdorf (1980):

> As the cases cited in Judge Broderick's opinion make clear, Halderman was not the first decision to rely upon the concept of least restrictive alternatives, but it was the first to follow the concept to its logical conclusion—sounding the death knell for large inhumane institutions and forcing state officials to provide services to mentally retarded people in local communities. (p. 687)

Related Services

Under the regulations implementing Section 504 of the Rehabilitation Act [42 *Fed. Reg.* 22682 (May 2, 1977), 45 C.F.R. 84 *et seq.*], related services—"free appropriate public education"—are contained under Section 84.33. The provision of free education "is the provision of educational and related services without cost to the handicapped person or to his or her parents or guardian," either provided directly or through a program not operated by the recipient. As a means of carrying out the "requirements," "the recipient shall ensure that adequate transportaion to and from the program is provided." If placement in a public or private residential program is necessary, "the program, including nonmedical care and room and board, shall be provided at no cost. Disagreements with respect to school and parent or guardian requests for private school placement rather than an available school program are subject to the due process procedures of § 84.36."

Under P.L. 94-142 parents and their handicapped children are entitled to special education and related services at no cost.

> The term "related service" means transportation, and such developmental, corrective, and other supportive services (including speech pathology and audiology, psychological services, physical and occupational therapy, recreation, and medical and counseling services, except that such medical services shall be for diagnostic and evaluation purposes only) as may be required to assist a handicapped child to benefit from special education, and includes the early identification and assessment of handicapping conditions in children. [20 U.S.C. 1401 (17)]

The implementing regulations further define the meaning of transportation to include travel to and from school and between schools, in and around school buildings, and specialized equipment if required to provide special transportation for a handicapped child [45 C.F.R. § 121a 13(b) (13)]. Further subsections [121a 13(b) (2), (4), and (5)] define counseling services, medical services and psychological services. (1) Medical services were defined as those services provided by a licensed physician to determine a child's medically related, handicapping condition; (2) counseling services were those services provided by qualified social workers, psychologists, guidance counselors, or other qualified personnel; and (3) psychological services included test administration and assessment, interpreting assessment results, obtaining, integrating and interpreting information about a child's behavior and those conditions which would relate to learning, consulting with other staff, and planning and managing a program of psychological services, including psychological counseling for children and parents. In addition, the general definition of "related services" contained in Reg. 121a. 13(a) is virtually identical to that found in 20 U.S.C. 1401 (17) except that it omits the word "only" (after the inclusion of medical services). Thus making the definition "open ended." Moreover, the official comment following Section 121a. 13 of the regulations state that the list of related services is not exhaustive and that certain kinds of services might be provided by persons from varying professional backgrounds and with a variety of operational titles, depending upon requirements in individual states.

Possibly the most controversial issue to face the federal special education policy makers was the scope of the definition of related services and specifically whether such related services included the provision of psychotherapy.

> "Psychotherapy" is the term most widely used to refer to a variety of treatment models and therapies used to alleviate severe emotional and/or behavioral disorders. The omission of any reference to psychotherapy in the regulations is the crux of the issue under discussion. If psychotherapy is termed either a "counseling service" or a "psychological service" then no argument ensues as to whether it is a "related service" within the meaning of Part B. If, on the other hand, psychotherapy is related to the status of a medical treatment (whenever it is provided by or under the supervision of a psychiatrist) then it falls outside the range of "related services" and the cost can be charged to parents as a personal (i.e., medical care) expense. (Martin, undated memorandum, p. 10)

The Bureau for the Education of the Handicapped (BEH) still had adopted no formal policy on the distinction between mental health services as ongoing medical treatment as opposed to related services as defined in P.L. 94-142, nor, does one appear forthcoming.

However, cases have been litigated based on the Education of the Handicapped Act Part B requirements [*In re Family A*, 602 P. 2d 157 (Mont. Sup. Ct. 1979; *P-1* v. *Shedd*, C.A. No. H78-58 (D. Conn. 1979) 212178; *North, et al.* v. *District of Columbia Board of Education*, 471 F. Supp. 136 (1979)]. In the Matter of the A Family, the court stated:

> The word "psychotherapy" is not specifically mentioned in the federal statutes or regulations. However, Webster's... Dictionary (1965) defines "psychotherapy" as "treatment of mental or emotional disorder or of related bodily ills by

psychological means." By that definition, psychotherapy comes within the meaning of the term "psychological services." (*Education of the Handicapped Law Review,* 1980, 3, 551: 349)

In general, then, with no official policy as yet established by the Bureau for the Education of the Handicapped, the outcome of case litigation dealing with this particular aspect of related services will vary from state to state.

On the other hand, the office for Civil Rights has interpreted Section 504 of the Rehabilitation Act of 1973 as requiring public educational agencies to provide mental health services to emotionally disturbed children when they are shown to be "necessary to enable a qualified handicapped person to obtain the same result, to gain the same benefit, or to reach the same level of achievement to the maximum extent possible" [Connecticut Department of Education (OCR-10/17/79) 2 EHLR 257:55]. In a second case dealing with complaints alleging that the Berkeley Unified School District (California) failed to provide the related service of psychotheraphy even though it was listed in the child's IEP, the Office of Civil Rights endorsed the office of the General Counsel's legal analysis of the case as consistent with its present policy. That analysis concluded with the following summary statement:

> Psychotherapy is a psychological service which must be provided when it is demonstrated to be necessary to meet the educational needs of handicapped persons as adequately as the needs of nonhandicapped persons. The Berkeley School District, having recognized the educational necessity of psychotherapy in (the complainant's) case, must provide, or reimburse the cost of psychotherapy services, regardless of the status of the service provider. (Martin, undated memorandum, p. 19)

Other state court litigation has dealt with the provision of related services such as music therapy *(Joseph v. Boston Public Schools)*; neurologial examination *(In the Matter of the application of a handicapped child, by his parent, from action of the Board of Education of the Minerva Central School District relating to the provision of special education services,* New York); physical therapy *(Julie C. v. Marshfield Public Schools,* Mass.); catheterization *(Tatro v. Texas),* 481 F. Supp. 1224 (N.D. Tex. 1979) in which catheterization was ruled not to be a "related service", reversed by the Fifth Circuit Court of Appeals (4 MDLR 403); and residential placement [*Rory Capello et al. v. District of Columbia Board of Education et al.; William C. et al. v. The Board of Education of Chicago,* and *North v. District of Columbia Board of Education* 471 F. Supp. 136 (1979)].

North, which will be the final case to be addressed in our discussion, is of particular interest for a number of reasons. The plaintiff was a 16-year-old boy diagnosed as epileptic, emotionally disturbed and learning disabled and whose condition required that he be placed in a residential treatment facility in order to provide appropriate medical supervision, special education and psychological support. The Court ruled that although the child's problems were educational as well as noneducational (emotional and social), the decision as to who would fund his residential placement, a matter of contention between the District of Columbia Board of Education and the Department of Human Resources (whose funding was dependent upon a neglect action), would "not be left to local law" [471 F. Supp. 136 (1979) at 137]. In the words of the Court:

> It may be possible in some situations to ascertain and determine whether the social, emotional, medical, or educational problems are dominant and to assign responsibility for placement and treatment to the agency operating in the area of that problem. In this case, all of these needs are so intimately intertwined that realistically it is not possible for the Court to perform the Solomon-like task of separating them. Since, as noted *supra*, relegation of the plaintiff's to the purely social recourse, i.e., the neglect procedure, is fraught with peril to the child and the family, use of the federal educational laws and placement pursuant to those laws is the only legally available alternative and is clearly required. (471 F. Supp. at 141)

The Court also noted, however, that it would have been preferable to have issues of the type involved in this case attended to by social service agencies rather than by the school authorities thereby reflecting again the unresolved status surrounding psychotherapy as a medical or psychological service.

Conclusion

This chapter had as its purpose an explication of the litigatory process and legislative mandates which have had impact on the treatment of the developmentally disabled and the mentally retarded. As an outgrowth of the civil rights movement, court cases, judicial decisions, and congressional legislation were employed to establish the individual and collective rights of the handicapped population as citizens with equal stature and worth. The actualization of these rights began in the fields of education, mental health, and rehabilitation with the first right to education suit in Pennsylvania, the first right to treatment suit in Alabama, and the Rehabilitation Act of 1973. Although litigation has continued to surround both the P.A.R.C. case and the Partlow decision in *Wyatt* v. *Stickney* since their initial hearing, most of their substantive issues have been given the impact of law with P.L. 94-142, the Developmentally Disabled Assistance and Bill of Rights Act of 1975, the Rehabilitation Amendments of 1978, and subsequent federal court decisions.

Procedural safeguards insuring due process, right to appeal, least restrictive environment, individualized treatment (education) plans, and informed consent are firmly in place. The actualization of rights, however, is only as viable as the knowledge of treatment (education) providers and the individuals whom they serve. The danger facing all implementation efforts lies in the reactive stance of professional service providers who, angered by the court and the legal profession's invasion of their territorial waters, waste needless energy and resources in a defensive posture which implies that their professional integrity is at stake. Such, in actuality is not the case, as the courts have historically left substantive issues to the professionals involved. It is the treatment and education providers who determine the qualities of appropriateness, who have the final say in reasonable accommodation and accessibility and individualization, and who provide the array of services which are deemed least restrictive in nature. The final danger, however, that of fiscal restraint and constraint, may be the most devastating of all. Rights that have taken 15 years to secure can be virtually eliminated overnight if the mechanisms with attached appropriations for funding are without force. And, there can be no doubt that such economic measures in and of themselves will have an impact on the treatment of the developmentally disabled and mentally retarded far less constructive than the most rigorous restraining order from the court or federal regulatory device. We can only hope that an understanding of the law, both judicial and legislative, which we have attempted to provide, will have provoked a more positive view of its beneficence to those who are disabled and/or retarded so that the professionals involved will direct their anger and frustrations collectively on a more appropriate target.

We also hope that this review of the current state of the art, as proscribed and defined within a legal framework, will have relevance to those who propose to be care-givers, advocates, and human service workers in the area of the developmentally disabled. That knowledge translates into meaningful and purposive action we cannot say absolutely, but we know that it is a more worthy goal than well-intentioned but inherently purposeless reaction.

> If you treat an individual as he is, he will stay as he is, but if you treat him as if he were what he ought to be, he will become what he ought to be and could be.
>
> —Goethe

References

THE AMERICAN HERITAGE DICTIONARY OF THE ENGLISH LANGUAGE. W. MORRIS (Ed.), Boston: 1969.
Boxall v. Sequoia Union High School, 464 F. Supp. 1104 (1979).
BROOKS, A. D. The right to treatment. In A. D. Brooks (Ed.), Law, psychiatry and the mental health system. Boston: Little, Brown, 1974.
Brown v. The Board of Education, 347 U.S. 483 (1954).
BURGDORF, R. L. A history of unequal treatment: The qualifications of handicapped persons in a "Suspect Class" under the Equal Protection Clause. Santa Clara Law Review, 1972, 15, 855.
BURGDORF, R. L. The legal rights of handicapped persons. Baltimore: Paul H. Brookes, 1980.
BURT, R. A. Judicial action to aid the retarded. In N. Hobbs (Ed.), Issues in the classification of children (Vol II). San Francisco: Jossey-Bass, 1975.
CASEY, P. J. The Supreme Court and the suspect class. Exceptional Children, 1973, 40(2), 119-125.
CHAMBERS, D. Alternatives to civil commitment of the mentally ill: Practical guides and constitutional imperatives. Michigan Law Review, 1972, 70, 1107.
COMPREHENSIVE REHABILITATION SERVICES AND DEVELOPMENTAL DISABILITIES AMENDMENTS of 1978, P.L. 95-602, 45 U.S.C. §§ 6000-6081 (1979).
COMPREHENSIVE REHABILITATION SERVICES AND INDEPENDENT LIVING REGULATIONS, Federal Register, 1979, 44, 68564-68621.
CONNECTICUT DEPARTMENT OF EDUCATION, OFFICE OF CIVIL RIGHTS (October 17, 1979). Education of the Handicapped Law Review, 1979, 2, 257:55.
Cort v. Ash, 422 U.S. 66 (1975).
DENO, E. Special education as developmental capital. Exceptional Children, 1970, 37(3), 229-237.
DEVELOPMENTALLY DISABLED ASSISTANCE AND BILL OF RIGHTS ACT OF 1975, P. L. 94-103, 42 U.S.C. §§ 6000 et seq., 89 Stat. 486.
THE DEVELOPMENTAL DISABILITIES SERVICES AND FACILITIES CONSTRUCTION ACT OF 1970, P.L. 91-517, 89 Stat. 497.
DISTRICT OF COLUMBIA, CODE ANN. 21-562, 1967.
EDUCATION FOR ALL HANDICAPPED CHILDREN ACT OF 1975, P.L. 94-142, 20 U.S.C. §§1401 et seq., 89 Stat. 773.
FLANAGAN, R. L. The right of handicapped children to an education: The phoenix of Rodriquez. Cornell Law Review, 1974, 59, 519.
GILHOOL, T. K. Education: An inalienable right. Exceptional Children, 1973, 39(8), 597-609.
Hairston v. Drosick, 423 F. Supp. 180, (S.D.W.Va. 1976).
Halderman v. Pennhurst State School and Hospital, 446 F. Supp. 1295 (E.D.Pa. 1977), aff'd. part rev'd. part, 612 F. 2d 84 3d Cir. (1979), cert. granted and argued, 49 U.S.L.W. 3437 (December 16, 1980).
HANDICAPPED AMERICAN'S REPORT. Washington, D.C.: Capitol Publications, 1981.
HANDICAPPED REQUIREMENT'S HANDBOOK. Appendix III: C:3xx, Federal Programs Advisory Service, Washington, D.C., 1980.
HEW REGULATIONS FOR IMPLEMENTATION OF EXECUTIVE ORDER 11914, NONDISCRIMINATION on the basis of Handicap in Federally Assisted Programs, Federal Register, 1978, 43, 2138.
HEW REGULATIONS FOR IMPLEMENTING § 504 OF THE REHABILIATION ACT of 1973, 42 Fed. Reg. 22682 (May 4, 1977), 45 C.R.R. §§ 84 et seq.
Howard S. v. Friendswood, 405 U.S. 504 (1978).
Humphrey v. Cody, 405 U.S. 504 (1972).
In re: Family A, 602 P. 2d 157 (Mont. Sup. Ct. 1979).
In the Matter of the Application of a handicapped child, by his parent from action of the Board of Education of the Minerva Central School District relating to the provision of special educa-

tion services. *Education of the Handicapped Law Review,* 1980, *3,* 501:235.
Jackson v. Indiana, 406 U.S. 715 (1972).
Joseph L. v. Boston Public Schools. *Education of the Handicapped Law Review,* 1980, *3,* 501:133.
Julie C. v. Marshfield Public Schools. *Education of the Handicapped Law Review,* 1980, *3,* 502-170.
Kampmeier v. Nyquist, 553 F 2d 296 (2d Cir. 1977).
Kaimowitz v. Department of Public Health of Michigan. *United States Law Week,* 2063 (1973).
Knecht v. Gilman, 488 F. 2d 1136 (8th Cir., 1973).
Lake v. Cameron, 364 F. 2d 657 (1966).
Larry P. v. Riles, 343 F. Supp. 1306 (N.D.Cal. 1972), preliminary injunction aff'd, 502 F. 2d 963 (9th Cir., 1974), opinion, Larry P. v. Riles, No. C-71-2270 RFP (N.D.Col. October 16, (1974).
Lau v. Nichols, 414 U.S. 563 (1974).
Lloyd v. Regional Transportation Authority, 548 F. 2d 1277 (7th Cir., 1977).
Lora v. Board of Education of City of New York, 456 F. Supp. 1211 (1978)
Mackey v. Procunier, 477 F. 2d 877 (9th Cir., 1973).
Martarella v. Kelly, 349 F. Supp. 575 (S.D.N.Y. 1972).
Martin, E. W. Definition of "Related Services" under 94-142 and the Provision of Mental Health Services to Handicapped Children. Undated Memorandum to Secretary of Education Hufstedter. Department of HEW, Office of Education.
Martin, R. *Educating handicapped children: The legal mandate.* Champaign, Ill.: Research Press, 1980.
Mattie T. v. Holloday, No.D.C. 75-31-S (N.D.Miss. 1979).
McClung, E. Do handicapped children have a right to a minimally adequate education? *Journal of Law and Education,* 1974, *3,* 153-174.
Mills v. The Board of Education of the District of Columbia. 348 F. Supp. 866 (D.D.C. 1972).
New York Association for Retarded Children, Inc. v. Rockefeller, 357 F. Supp. 756 (E.D.N.Y. 1973).
New York State Association for Retarded Children v. Carey, 466 F. Supp. 610 (E.D.N.Y. 1978).
Naughton v. Bevilacqua, 458 F. Supp. 610 (D.R.I. 1978).
North et al. v. District of Columbia Board of Education, 471 F. Supp. 136 (1979).
O'Connor v. Donaldson, 422 U.S. 563 (1975).
P-1 v. Shedd, No H78-58 (D.Conn. 1979).
Pennsylvania Association for Retarded Children v. Pennsylvania, 334 F. Supp. 1257 (1971).
Perlin, M. L., & Martin, R. The impact of recent mental disability litigation: Workshop materials. Champaign, Ill.: Public Law Division, Research Press, 1980.
Regulations for the Implementation of P.L. 94-142, 45 C.F.R. § 121a et seq., 1979.
Rennie v. Klein, 462 F. Supp. 1131 (D.N.J. 1978), Modified, 476 F. Supp. 1294 (D.N.J. 1979).
Reynolds, M. A framework for considering some issues in special education. *Exceptional Children,* 1962, *28*(7), 367-377.
Rodriguez v. San Antonio Independent School District, 411 U.S. 1 (1973).
Rogers v. Okin, 478 F. Supp. 1342 (D.Mass. 1979).
Rory Capello et al. v. District of Columbia Board of Education et al., No. 79-1006 (D.D.C., 1979). *Education of the Handicapped Law Review,* 3, 1980; 551:500.
Rouse v. Cameron, 373 F. 2d 451 (D.C. Cir. 1966).
Sarason, S. & Doris, J. *Educational handicap, public policy, and social history.* New York: Macmillan, 1979.
Scott v. Plante, 532 F. 2d 939 3d Cir. (1976).
Section 504 of the Rehabilitation Act of 1973, P.L. 93-112, 29 U.S.C. 794, 45 C.F.R. §§ 84 et seq.
Shelton v. Tucker, 364 U.S. 479 (1960).

Southeastern Community College v. *Davis,* 574 F. 2d 115(8), (4th Cir. 1978).
STICK, R. S. The handicapped child has a right to an appropriate education, *Nebraska Law Review,* 1976, *55,* 637.
Stuart v. *Nappi,* 443 F. Supp. 1235 (1978).
Tatro v. *Texas,* 481 F. Supp. 1224 (N.D. Tex. 1979) rev'd, 625 F 2d 537 (1980).
TITLE VI OF THE CIVIL RIGHTS ACT of 1964, 42 U.S.C. § 2000d.
TURNBULL, H. R., & TURNBULL, A. P. *Free appropriate public education: Law and implementation.* Denver: Love Publishing, 1979.
VANDAMN, M. D. Developmental disabilities act: An historic perspective, Part 1. *American Journal of Occupational Therapy,* 1979, *33*(6), 355-359.
Virginia Withdraws from Developmental Disabilities Program; New York replaces P & A. Agency. *Mental Disability Law Report,* 1980, *4,* 463.
Witek v. *Jones,* 100 S.Ct. 1254 (1980).
WEINTRAUB, F., & ABESON, A. Appropriate education for all handicapped children: A growing issue. *Syracuse University Law Review,* 1972, *23,* 1037.
Whitaker v. *Board of Higher Education of City of New York,* 461 F. Supp. 99 (E.D.N.Y. 1978).
William C. et al. v. *The Board of Education of Chicago,* 390 N.E. 2d 479 (Ill. App. Ct. 1979). *Education of the Handicapped Law Review,* 1980, *3,* 551:228.
Wyatt v. *Stickney,* 344 F. Supp. 383 M.D. Ala. (1972).

5 The Effects of Lead on Retardation of Cognitive and Adaptive Behavior

Christopher R. Milar and Stephen R. Schroeder

Introduction

Since the advent of the industrial revolution, there has been a steady increase in the use of lead and consequent exposure of human populations to lead. The maximum daily intake of lead for children that does not produce excessive body lead burden is 300 μg (Zarkowsky, 1970). Ingestion of greater amounts of lead causes accumulation in the body tissues and can result in lead poisoning. One of the first noticeable effects of lead is disruption of blood synthesis, resulting in the accumulation of a precursor of hemoglobin—erythrocyte protoporphyrin (EP). The ease of measurement of EP makes it an ideal screening test for children at risk for lead poisoning (Piomelli & Davidow, 1972); unfortunately, EP is also elevated in cases of iron deficiency (Piomelli, Brickman, & Carlos, 1976). For children with an elevated EP, it is necessary to obtain a venous blood sample for determination of blood lead. Both blood lead and EP are measured in micrograms per deciliter of whole blood (μg/dl), and normal values are less than 30 μg/dl for lead and less than 50 μg/dl for EP. On the basis of these two determinations, the Center for Disease Control (1978) has arbitrarily divided children into four categories based on potential risk as shown in Table I. Children falling in Class I are at low risk for lead poisoning, Class II at moderate risk, and Class III at high risk. Children falling into Class IV are at urgent risk

---

Christopher R. Milar • University of North Carolina Medical Center, Chapel Hill, North Carolina 27514.   Stephen Schroeder • Director of Research, Division for Disorders of Development and Learning, University of North Carolina Medical Center 220H, Chapel Hill, North Carolina 27514. We wish to acknowledge NIEHS Grant ES-01104, "Neurobiology on Environmental Pollutants," Martin Krigman, M.D., and Lester D. Grant, Ph. D., principal investigators; USPHS Grant HD-03110 to the Child Development Research Institute; MCH Project 916 to the Division for Disorders of Development and Learning; Wake County Public Health Department, Jane Wooten, M.D., Director.

TABLE I
Risk of Classification for Asymptomatic Children

		Erythrocyte protoporphyrin (μg/dl)			
		59	60–109	110–189	190
Blood	29	I	Ia	Ia	
Lead	30–49	Ib	II	III	III
μg/dl	50–69		III	III	IV
	70			IV	IV

for lead poisoning, and immediate medical evaluation must be provided. Class Ia children are iron-deficient, and Class Ib children appear to have transient, stable, or declining lead levels and are at low risk.

CLINICAL LEAD POISONING

The early symptoms of lead poisoning are fatigue, pallor, anorexia, irritability, abdominal pain, vomiting, and ataxia. Since these early symptoms are similar to other less serious diseases of childhood, incorrect diagnosis and treatment often occur. Symptoms, however, are not always present. Rennert, Weiner, and Madden (1970) found that 90% of the children seen during a 6-month period with lead levels greater than 60μg/dl were asymptomatic. For children falling into Class IV, encephalopathy is always possible, and it may emerge rapidly followed by seizures, coma, cardiorespiratory arrest, and even death. The mortality rates for children with encephalopathy range from 5% (Lewis, Collins, & Wilson, 1955) to 39% (Ennis & Harrison, 1950).

If the child survives, the neurological aftermath of encephalopathy includes cortical atrophy, hydrocephalus, convulsive seizures, mental retardation, and behavior disorders (Smith, 1964; Chisolm & Harrison, 1956). A child who has recovered from encephalopathy and is reexposed to lead almost invariably evidences permanent central nervous system damage (Chisolm & Harrison, 1956).

The consequences of lead poisoning in the absence of encephalopathy were first documented by Byers and Lord (1943). These authors reported on 20 children who had previously evidenced relatively mild lead poisoning. All but one of the children were making unsatisfactory progress in school in spite of a mean IQ of 90 for the group (range 67 to 109). Sensorimotor deficits, short attention span, and behavior difficulties were most frequently reported.

Mellins and Jenkins (1955) followed 15 children who had survived lead poisoning. Unfortunately, the authors fail to indicate the presence or absence of encephalopathy. In all cases, however, symptoms of central nervous system disturbance were evident at the time of hospitalization. The authors obtained pre-illness medical and developmental information from an "intensive interview" with the mother. According to the maternal report, 14 of the children were at or above age level on motor development, there was a question of delayed language development for three, and three children showed partial retardation. The children were then evaluated 6 months subsequent to the illness. The authors state:

> The poisoning episode was associated with a definite setback in mental development. While only 3 seemed in any way below average during early infancy, 14 of the 15 are now seriously below average, as measured by tests of general mental development. (p. 18)

Subsequent gross motor development was reported as normal, but fine motor development and perceptual-motor performance were delayed in 14 of the children. Fourteen of the children also demonstrated short attention span and distractability.

Another follow-up report of lead-poisoned children was by Thurston, Middlekamp, and Mason (1955). Eleven children were followed for 5 to 10 years after hospitalization. Most of the children were symptomatic at the time of hospitalization. Psychological testing was carried out in 1950 and again in 1954. The time interval between the lead-poisoning episode and initial testing ranged from immediately after recovery to 5 years postrecovery. In 1950, the children's average IQ was 94: two of the children below the dull-normal range and two in the bright-average to superior categories on the Stanford Binet. In 1954 the average IQ was 102, and none of the children tested below the dull-normal level of intelligence. At the second testing the children were also administered the Goodenough Draw-A-Man Test in addition to the Stanford Binet. On the Goodenough, the mean IQ for the 11 children was 85. The authors state:

> It would seem that while the overall intelligence of these children remains intact and is developing normally, a definite deficit is seen in their visual-motor functioning. (p. 419)

In 1954, only three of the children were making adequate academic progress in school, and the authors attribute this to deficits in the visual-motor area.

Mellins and Jenkins (1955) found that 13 of the 15 children in their study engaged in pica. Smith, Baehner, Carney, and Majors (1963) attempted to clarify the relationship between lead poisoning and pica. Four groups of 10 subjects each were studied. The encephalopathy group consisted of children who had been diagnosed 5 or more years previously as evidencing encephalopathy. The lead absorption group comprised children who, 5 or more years previously, had shown blood-lead levels greater than 57 μg/dl but were asymptomatic at the time. A third group was composed of children who, based on a history of pica, had been suspected of lead poisoning 5 or more years previously due to a history of pica, but laboratory analysis indicated that these children had lead levels less than 57 μg/dl at the time of the study. A control group was selected from the hospital admissions list and consisted of children hospitalized for acute respiratory infections or elective surgery. Neurological examination demonstrated deficits only in the children who previously had displayed encephalopathy.

A later publication (Smith, 1964) reports that the lead encephalopathy group had an average IQ of 80, compared with an average of 87 for the group of children who had lead poisoning without encephalopathy. Both the control group and the group with a history of pica, but not lead poisoning, had an average IQ of 98. Thus, the lead-exposed children tended to show IQ deficits compared with both the control children and children with a history of pica.

Perlstein and Attala (1966) reported neurological sequelae in 140 of 386 children (37%) following lead poisoning without encephalopathy. The problems reported were mental retardation, seizures, cerebral palsy, and optic atrophy. Visual-perceptual problems were reported in some children with minimal intellectual impairment. It appears that the severity of sequelae is related to the severity of the symptoms. Of these children who were asymptomatic at the time the diagnosis of lead poisoning was made, mental retardation was the only sequela and only 9% of the children were affected.

In summary, the literature is quite definitive that lead poisoning with encephalopathy results in greatly increased incidence of neurologial and cognitive impairments. The study by Perlstein and Attala (1966) strongly supports the viewpoint that children with symptomatic lead poisoning in the absence of encephalopathy also evidence an increased incidence of neurological and behavioral impairments. Unfortunately, the methodological shortcomings of the studies reviewed to this point make it difficult to determine if *asymptomatic* lead poisoning results in neurological, cognitive, or behavioral deficits. The earlier studies (Mellins & Jenkins, 1955; Thurston *et al.*, 1955) failed to distinguish between children with and without encephalopathy. Other studies (Byers & Lord, 1943; Mellins & Jenkins, 1955; Perlstein & Attala, 1966; Thurston *et al.*, 1955) did not include a suitable control group. Lead poisoning typically occurs in children from low socioeconomic status

(SES) families who reside in old, inner-city housing. Robinson and Robinson (1976) point out that "children's IQ's tend to vary with the status of their families" (p. 153). Taking into account the socioeconomic status of the children in the Mellins and Jenkins (1955) study, the distribution of the children's IQ scores may be representative of the population from which these children were drawn. Likewise, the 9% incidence of mental retardation following asymptomatic lead poisoning found by Perlstein and Attala (1966) may be no different than the base rate for a population of that SES. Other shortcomings, such as relying on maternal interview to determine previous development (Mellins & Jenkins, 1955) and failure to take into account base rates of such problems as short attention span, hyperactivity, perceptual-motor deficits, fine-motor deficits, and deficits in test-taking behavior in children of lower SES (Byers & Lord, 1943; Mellins & Jenkins, 1955; Perlstein & Attala, 1966; Thurston et al., 1955), make it difficult to conclude that asymptomatic lead poisoning has a detrimental effect on neurological, behavioral, or cognitive functioning. A review of the literature by Wiener in 1970 came to the same conclusion.

Subclinical Lead Poisoning

In spite of the lack of evidence, authorities have begun to argue that lead exposure at subclinical levels (CDC Classes II and III) has a detrimental effect on children. For example, Needleman (1973) states:

> The number of children known to be lead poisoned who as a result often have profound neurologic and psychologic sequelae, is dwarfed by a much larger group of children with unrecognized body-lead burdens. This paper will argue that this latter group of unidentified asymptomatic children probably has significant neurologic and psychologic impairment. (p. 47)

Waldron (1975) also feels that

> Environmental pollution with lead has reached such a level that body burdens in the general population are not only closer to those which would produce clinical poisoning than any other toxic chemical pollutant, but they are presently producing serious subclinical effects, including abnormalities in behavior. (p. 148)

Two methods of study have typically been used to examine the effects of subclinical lead poisoning: either children previously identified as being atypical in some way (i.e., hyperactive, mentally retarded) have been evaluated to determine the possibility of lead exposure, or children demonstrating elevated lead levels have been studied using various indices of cognitive and neurological functioning.

Lead Levels in Atypical Populations

Since mental retardation is one possible consequence of acute lead intoxication, mentally retarded children have been one group of atypical children investigated. The earliest study of this type is that of Moncrieff, Koamides, Clayton, Patrick, Renwick, and Roberts (1964). Lead levels were determined for a group of children between the ages of 4 months and 14½ years who were not mentally retarded and for a group of children aged 6 months to 14 years who showed evidence of mental retardation or severe behavior disorder. All normal children except two had a lead level below 36 µg/dl, while 45% of the children in the atypical group had levels above 36 µg/dl.

In a more carefully controlled investigation, Gibson, Lam, McCrae, and Goldberg (1967) determined lead levels in three groups of children. There were 20 children aged 3 to 11 years in each group, and they were matched for age. One group comprised normally intelligent children who were being seen at a hospital for orthopedic or cardiac problems. A second group was composed of mentally retarded children with a known etiological cause of retardation. The third group consisted of retarded children with no known etiological cause. There was no difference in average lead level between the group of normal children and the group of mentally retarded children with no known etiology (3 µg/dl vs. 34 µg/dl). Three children in the normal group and six children in the mentally retarded group with no known etiology had lead levels over 40 µg/dl (the upper limit of normal according to the authors). The mentally retarded children with a known etiology had an average lead level of 17 µg/dl, and none of these children had levels over 40 µg/dl. The failure to find a difference between normal children and mentally retarded children with no known etiological causes of mental retardation and the relatively low blood-lead levels of the children in the known etiology group is attributed by the authors to the mobility of the children. Some of the children in the known etiology group had restricted movement owing to the nature of their illness (organic brain damage) and were under closer supervision, while the children in the other two groups were more mobile, thus encountering and ingesting greater quantities of lead.

David, Hoffman, McCann, Sverd, and Clark (1976) reported blood-lead levels of borderline and mildly mentally retarded children seen at a developmental evaluation clinic. The children were divided into two groups based on the presence or absence of a probable etiological factor causing the retardation. The blood-lead concentrations of these children were compared with a control group from a general pediatric outpatient clinic. The children in the three groups ranged in age from 4 to 11 years. The lead levels for the mentally retarded children with no known etiology were significantly higher than for the children in either the control group or the group with a known probable etiology (25.5 µg/dl, 18.8 µg/dl, and 18.7 µg/dl, respectively).

During the prenatal period, human brain growth proceeds at its most rapid pace and the brain is also most vulnerable to insult (Dobbing, 1970). In an effort to implicate low-level lead exposure during this period of development with mental retardation, Beattie, Moore, Goldberg, Finlayson, Mackie Graham, Main, McLaren, Murdoch, and Stewart (1975) compared 77 children with developmental or intellectual quotients below 70 and no known etiology for retardation and 77 matched nonretarded children. The home addresses of the mothers during pregnancy and during the first year of the child's life were obtained and a water sample taken from each address. The authors found that there was a significant increase in the incidence of mental retardation if the lead concentration of the tap water was greater than 800 µg/dl. These authors also obtained blood samples from 37 of the mentally retarded children and compared the lead concentrations with 20 same-aged children hospitalized with diseases not associated with lead. The mean blood-lead level of the mentally retarded children was significantly higher than that of the control children (25.4 µg/dl vs. 17.8 µg/dl). Moore, Meredith, and Goldberg (1977) attempted to determine if the increased availability of lead from the water supply resulted in increased lead levels in the prenatal period for the above children. For most children in the Beattie et al. (1975) study, blood samples on cards used for testing for phenylketonuria during the first 2 weeks of life were available. The samples on these cards were subsequently analyzed for lead concentrations, and the children in the mentally retarded group had significantly higher blood-lead levels than the control children (25.49 µg/dl vs. 20.93 µg/dl). A comparison between the lead concentration in the children's blood and the lead concentration of the water samples also resulted in a significant correlation (r = +0.54). The authors argue that these two studies

> [reinforce] not only the association between water-lead values and blood-lead values, but also the probability that some forms of mental retardation of unknown etiology might be associated with a preventable form of lead exposure—i.e., lead in drinking water. (p. 719)

There are two possible interpretations of the studies on the relationship between lead and mental retardation. One is that mentally retarded children are at a greater risk for increased lead absorption than normal children. Several factors could contribute to this increased risk: possible increased incidence of pica or greater environmental exposure to lead. Both Gibson et al. (1976) and

David, Hoffman, McCann, Sverd, and Clark, (1976) acknowledge this interpretation but stress a second hypothesis, that lead actually contributes to the intellectual deficit of mentally retarded children. As Gibson et al. state:

> it appears possible that the raised blood-lead levels in the present series may have been a factor in the aggravation of mental deficiency though it is considered unlikely that lead poisoning was the primary aetiology in any case. (p. 577)

David, Hoffman, McCann, Sverd, and Clark (1976) also have this to add:

> This report then is not a comment on the relationship between encephalopathic poisoning and mental retardation, but shows that lead at concentrations much lower than those causing the accepted clinical symptoms of lead poisoning may also be causing lead poisoning, albeit a type that is very differently defined. (p. 8)

The problem of increased lead burden has also been studied in autistic children by Cohen, Johnson, and Caparulo (1976). Thirty-four psychotic children were classified as either being autistic ($n = 18$) or exhibiting severe atypical development. The children with atypical development "were less profoundly impaired than the autistic children, were markedly immature, and resembled children often described as 'borderline' psychotic" (p. 47). The age range for both groups of children was 3 to 13 years. The authors used the normal siblings ($n = 10$) of these children as a control group (age range 2 to 13 years). The group of autistic children had significantly higher lead levels than the atypical children and the control siblings, but the atypical group did not differ from the control siblings. The average blood-lead level of the normal children was 15.2 µg/dl compared to 25.4 µg/dl for the autistic and atypical groups of children combined. Unlike Gibson et al. (1967) and David, Hoffman, Sverd, and Clark (1976), Cohen et al. (1976) emphasize the risk to atypical children from lead poisoning rather than possible contributions of lead to the child's deficits.

> There is no indication that increased lead levels are etiologically related to the underlying autistic syndrome, nor that chelation therapy improves the underlying disturbances and... the impulsive autistic child with pica may ingest dangerous amounts of lead, even in environments that are usually considered safe. Thus, all autistic and atypical children should have a blood lead determination as part of their general medical evaluation. (p. 48)

Other authors have attempted to implicate lead in the etiology of hyperactivity. David, Clark, and Voeller (1972) compared blood-lead levels in five groups of children. Children classified as hyperactive on the basis of doctors', teachers', and parents' rating scales were subdivided into three groups on the basis of a possible etiology for hyperactivity. The pure hyperactive group ($n = 54$) comprised those children with no etiological factor to explain the hyperactivity. The remainder of the hyperactive children were subdivided on the basis of a probable cause of hyperactivity ($n = 9$) and a possible cause of hyperactivity ($n = 11$). A fourth group consisted of eight children with a history of lead poisoning. The control group ($n = 37$) was composed of children who were not classified as hyperactive, but no further information is given about the selection of this group. In general, the age ranges for all groups were 3½ to 11 years with a higher population of males. As would be expected, the group with a history of lead poisoning had a significantly higher blood–lead level (41.06 µg/dl) than the other groups. The mean lead levels for the other four groups were 26.23 µg/dl for the pure hyperactive children, 22.89 µg/dl for the probable group. 22.94 µg/dl for the possible cause group, and 22.16 µg/dl for the control group. On a one-tailed t test, the pure hyperactive and possible hyperactive groups showed significantly higher blood–lead levels than the controls. The group with a history of lead poisoning also had significantly higher blood–lead levels than the controls.

Penicillamine is a compound that binds with lead stored in soft body tissues and results in the excretion of lead from the body in urine. David et al. (1972) hypothesized that hyperactive children should excrete more lead following the administration of penicillamine than control children. The results closely parallel the data on blood–lead concentrations in these groups of children. The group with a history of lead poisoning had a mean of 325 µg/dl of lead excreted in the urine; the pure hyperactive group, 146 µg/dl; the probable cause hyperactive children, 46 µg/dl; the possible cause hyperactive children, 189 µg/dl; and the control children, 77 µg/dl. On a one-tailed t test the pure hyperactive and possible cause hyperactive children were significantly higher, respectively, than the control children. Again, the group with a history of lead poisoning was significantly higher than the control children.

Following the above reasoning one step further, David, Hoffman, Sverd, Clark, and Voeller (1976) argued that if lead causes hyperactivity in children, reduction of body lead levels through chelation might result in behavioral improvement. Thirteen hyperactive children were subdivided into two groups on the basis of the presence ($n = 6$) or absence ($n = 7$) of a known probable cause for hyperactivity. The children ranged in age from 6 to 10½ years. Children in both groups were treated with either penicillamine or calcium disodium edetate (CaEDTA) chelating agents. Both groups showed a decrease in blood–lead levels with treatment, and on the basis of teachers' ratings (Conners, 1969), children with no probable cause for hyperactivity showed improvement following treatment, while the known probable cause group of children showed no improvement. There was no differential effect between groups on the parents' ratings (Werry, 1968); both groups showed significant improvement. The authors also used a "Parent Symptom Questionnaire" and state that a description of it could be found in David et al. (1972). There is no description in the earlier publication, and in the absence of such, interpretation of results pertaining to this questionnaire is difficult.

The above studies by David and his associates suffer from many methodological shortcomings; among these are small sample size, concurrent administration of stimulant medication to four of the children (David, Hoffman, Sverd, Clark, & Voeller, 1976), unexplained subject mortality (David, Hoffman, Sverd, Clark, & Voeller, 1976), and possible group differences including degree of hyperactivity, SES, intelligence, and sex. Bullpit (1972) has also criticized the inappropriate use of one-tailed t tests (David et al., 1972) in analyzing the data. The evidence for a relationship between lead and hyperactivity is, at best, only mildly suggestive given the methodological problems of these studies, and replication is needed. David, Hoffman, Sverd, Clark, and Voeller (1976), however, are more definitive in drawing conclusions.

> Our findings indicate that with a child whose hyperactive state is not known to be due to any of the common and/or known etiologies, and who also has a slightly increased body lead burden, treating the condition of the increased lead burden with chelating agents *markedly* ameliorates the hyperactive condition... Approximately 50% of the hyperactive children seen have thereby qualified for treatment, and of these more than half showed a *marked* amelioration in problem behavior over the course of the deleading regimen. (p. 1158; italics added)

A recent study by Milar, Schroeder, Mushak, and Boone (1980) also addressed the issue of the relationship between increased lead level and hyperactivity in preschool children. They compared 40 preschool-aged children evidencing moderately increased lead burden (mean = 42 μg/dl) with 48 preschool-aged children whose blood level was less than 30 μg/dl. Using three of the most widely employed measures of hyperactivity, the Conner's Parent Rating Scale (Conners, 1980), the Werry-Weiss-Peters Activity Scale (WPPAS) (Werry, 1968) and a measure of free-field gross motor activity (Routh, Schroeder, & O'Tuama, 1974), they failed to find any difference between the groups.

In summary, increased blood–lead level is probably not an unusual condition in atypical populations. Two factors could account for this. First, hyperactive children would more frequently encounter sources of lead in the environment than would normally active children in the same environment. This increased contact with lead would result in greater lead burden as in the Gibson et al. (1967) study. Secondly, a difference in the relative incidence of pica in the various groups studied could also account for the results obtained. In order for lead to reach the bloodstream, it is usually necessary that it first be ingested. Children with a higher incidence of pica would show a higher blood–lead level than children who do not engage in pica. For example, in a study by Greenberg, Jacobziner, McLaughlin, Fuerst, and Pellitter (1958), 25% of the children with pica showed evidence of lead poisoning (lead levels 60 μg/dl). Retrospective studies of blood–lead levels in atypical populations have only demonstrated that groups of atypical children tend to have increased lead levels. Such studies have been less than successful in directly implicating lead as a causative or even contributing agent in any of the conditions in spite of oftentimes emotional rather than logical arguments.

Controlled Studies of Children with Elevated Lead Levels

Another method of assessing the effects of lead on children's behavior is to compare children exposed to lead resulting in elevated blood levels with children not exposed to lead using behavioral, psychological, neurological, or medical indices. When a researcher uses this approach, it is essentially to evaluate carefully the possible effects of such variables as sex, age, race, socioeconomic status, and parental intelligence. If a study fails to control for these variables, differences between groups could possibly be attributed to these variables. As the reader will see, this is a problem that plagues many of the studies in this category.

Basically, two approaches have been used. One is to compare children identified as having elevated body burdens of lead with a similar nonexposed group of children, controlling, either through matching or statistics, for possible influence of extraneous variables. These studies will be referred to as cohort studies. The other approach is to use an epidemiological strategy by identifying populations of children and comparing those displaying increased burden with those who do not. Usually the populations identified consist of children living close to a point source of lead such as a smelter.

Cohort Studies

Most of these studies have sought to demonstrate some deficit in intellectual functioning in lead-exposed children through the use of standardized pyschometric evaluations. Two studies by de la Burde and Choate (1972, 1975) are representative of this type of research. In their initial study, they compared 70 4-year-old children who had a blood level of 40 μg/dl or above (mean, 58 μg/dl) or who showed positive radiographic findings consisting of lead lines on the long bones and/or metallic densities in the intestines with 72 4-year-old children with no history of paint or plaster ingestion. Blood–lead levels were not determined for the control children, but the authors state that they came from a home environment which provided little opportunity for ingestion of lead. All children were part of a larger longitudinal project and had been followed since their mother's pregnancy. Children in both groups who showed neurological or developmental problems during the newborn period or at assessments at 4 and 9 months were eliminated from the study, as were children with a history of central nervous system disease or injury. In addition to IQ, assessments were made on fine- and gross-motor functioning, concept formation, and behavior. The results showed that significantly more of the children with lead exposure showed deficits in IQ, fine-motor performance, and behavior. The behavioral characteristics most frequently found were extreme negativism, distractibility, and constant need for attention. The actual difference in IQ between the two groups of children was 5 points (89 for lead-exposed versus 94 for the control children), and the authors do not state if this difference was significant.

In their later study, de la Burde and Choate (1975) reported on the same subjects at 7 years of age. On the Wechsler Intelligence Scale for Children (WISC), significantly more of the lead-exposed children showed deficits in full-scale IQ, but there was no difference in the number of children showing deficits on either the verbal or performance scales of the WISC. The mean IQ for the two groups was 86.6 for the lead-exposed children and 90.1 for the control children. Behavior ratings during the testing situation showed that lead-exposed children were eight times more likely to have their behavior coded as suspect or abnormal. Short attention span and little goal-directed behavior were the most frequent problems cited, but no difference in activity level was noted. A review of the school records also demonstrated academic and behavioral difficulties in school for the lead-exposed children. Of the lead-exposed children, 27.8% were making poor academic progress compared with 4.1% of the controls. Nineteen of the lead-exposed children were described as hyperactive, impulsive, and explosive, and having frequent temper tantrums, while only five of the control children were so described in the school records.

In both studies (de la Burde & Choate, 1972, 1975), the difference in mean IQ between the two groups was approximately 4 to 5 points. T tests based on the data presented by the authors were nonsignificant, but even this small difference in children's IQ could be accounted for by the 4-point difference in IQ of the mothers in the two groups.

The work of Perino and Ernhart (1974) also supports the notion that lead exposure results in intellectual deficits in children. Eighty children between

3 and 5 years of age with blood–lead levels between 10 and 70 μg/dl were divided into two groups. The low-lead group consisted of 50 children with lead levels between 10 and 30 μg/dl. Each child was tested using the McCarthy Scales of Children's Abilities, and the parents were tested with the Quick Test of Gross Intellectual Level (Ammons & Ammons, 1962). The lead-exposed group demonstrated significantly poorer performance in general cognitive ability, on the verbal scale, on the perceptual-performance scale, and on the quantitative scale. Another method of analysis used by the authors was to compare the correlation between child and parental IQ. The authors state that if lead exposure were to result in intellectual deficit, then the usual correlation of 0.50 between child and parental IQ (Burt, 1966) would be affected. For the low-lead group of children, the correlation was 0.52, but for the lead-exposed children the correlation was only 0.10, a statistically significant difference.

Albert, Shore, Sayers, Strehlow, Kreip, Pasternack, Friedhoff, Covan, and Cimino (1974) reported on the psychometric testing of 159 subjects, most of whom were identified from the blood–lead registry of the New York City Health Department. For all children included in the study, deciduous teeth were available, either from extractions at dental clinics or from natural loss. The amount of lead in the teeth is felt to represent cumulative exposure to lead, whereas blood–lead measures reflect more recent exposure. Subjects were divided into five groups: (1) children with a history of lead encephalopathy ($n = 3$); (2) children hospitalized for lead poisoning and treated with chelation therapy but who did not develop encephalopathy ($n = 68$); (3) children who, 3 to 11 years (mean 6.7 years), previously had shown a high blood lead level equal to or above 60 μg/dl ($n = 25$); (4) children with low blood–lead levels who showed high concentrations of lead in their teeth ($n = 24$); and (5) children with low blood–lead levels (less than 50 μg/dl) and also low concentrations of lead in their teeth ($n = 39$). At the time of testing, the children ranged in age from 5 to 15 years. On the standardized psychometric evaluation (WISC), only children with encephalopathy and children wtih high blood–lead levels showed deficits when compared with the children with both low blood and low tooth levels of lead. The authors also checked school records and found that a greater percentage of the children with encephalopathy as well as children with high blood–lead levels were in special classes because of academic or behavior problems, as compared with the children with low blood and low tooth levels of lead. Children with encephalopathy, children hospitalized for treatment without encephalopathy, and children with a history of high blood–lead levels also had higher percentages of psychological referrals and behavior, attention, and concentration problems than children with low blood and low tooth levels of lead. In general, only the children who evidenced encephalopathy and the children who previously had high blood-levels demonstrated consistent deficits. The failure to find deficits in those children who had been hospitalized for lead poisoning in the absence of encephalopathy was unexpected. These hospitalized children had higher lead levels than the group with a previous history of high lead levels, and if lead were responsible for the intellectual and behavioral deficits, there should also have been significant deficits in those children hospitalized for treatment. One possible interpretation is that treatment for lead poisoning prevented the damage incurred by the long-term but lower elevation in lead level of the children with a history of high blood lead.

Other cohort studies have failed to confirm detrimental effects of asymptomatic lead exposure on behavior. Rummo, Routh, Rummo, and Brown (1979) evaluated 90 children with a standard neurological and psychometric battery. The children were divided into four groups: children with a history of lead encephalopathy ($n = 10$); children with long-term lead exposure who had two blood-lead levels greater than $40 \mu g/dl$ on two or more samples 6 months apart or who evidenced lead lines on large bones when X-rayed ($n = 20$); children with short-term lead exposure with only one lead determination greater than $40 \mu g/dl$ ($n = 15$); and children with no known history of lead exposure ($n = 15$). Significant deficits in intellectual performance as measured by the McCarthy Scales, deficits in motor skills, and hyperactivity were evident in the lead encephalopathy group, but there were no significant differences between the long- and short-term exposure groups when compared with the control group. The children in the long-term and short-term lead exposure groups performed at levels intermediate between those of the control group and the encephalopathy group, and the direction of these results (even though nonsignificant) is consistent with the hypothesis that low-level lead exposure causes some impairment.

Two studies by Kotok (Kotok, 1972; Kotok, Kotok, & Heriot, 1977), failed to find significant effects of lead on behavior. In the first study (Kotok, 1972), the lead exposure group consisted of 24 children with a mean blood-lead level of $81 \mu g/dl$ (range of $59-137 \mu g/dl$). None of the children evidenced encephalopathy, but 21 of the 24 children had undergone chelation therapy. The children in the control group ($n = 25$) were from a similar environment visiting a local pediatric clinic and had an average blood level of $38 \mu g/dl$ (range $20-55 \mu g/dl$). On the Denver Developmental Screening Test, the lead exposure group showed no significant deficits when compared with the control group.

In the second Kotok study, Kotok et al. (1977) used a battery of tasks drawn from various standardized psychometric tests to evaluate the development of lead-exposed children. The lead group consisted of 31 children with blood–lead levels between 61 and 200 μg/dl (79.6 mean), and the control group was composed of 36 children with blood–lead levels between 11 and 40 μg/dl (28.3 mean). The age range was from 20 to 67 months (mean 43.4 for the lead group and 42.6 for the control group). There were no significant differences between the groups, but as in the Rummo *et al.* (1979) study, the subjects in the lead group showed consistent deficits in all areas assessed.

Baloh, Sturm, Green, and Gleser (1975), using the WISC and WPPSI, compared children with elevated blood–lead levels ($n = 27$) with a control group selected from the files of an inner-city pediatric clinic ($n = 27$). The elevated lead group was made up of children with two blood–lead levels greater than 50 μg/dl, and the control group children all had blood–lead levels less than 30 μg/dl. The authors found no difference in intelligence quotient (89.2 for the lead group and 89.8 for the control group). They also failed to find any difference on neurological, physical, or behavior evaluations.

Two such studies by Sachs and her associates (Sachs, Krall, McCaughran, Rozenfeld, Youngsmith, Growe, Lazar, Novak, O'Connell, & Payson, 1978; Sachs, McCaughran, Krall, Rozenfeld, & Youngsmith, 1979) followed up children who had been treated for lead poisoning 2 to 8 years previously. The treated children ($n = 47$) were compared with their closest-aged sibling using the Beery-Buktenica Test of Visual Motor Integration, the Ravens Progressive Matrices, figure drawing, and one of three IQ tests: either the WISC, WPPSI, or Stanford Binet. There were no significant differences between the treated children and their siblings on the psychological evaluation. Sachs *et al.* (1979) present basically the same data in their second study, but use a slightly different analysis and reach the same conclusions. Two methodological problems with these studies which make interpretation difficult are (1) the use of three different IQ tests and the combining of these scores for data analysis, and (2) the control siblings were, on the average, 11 months older than the treated children.

The cohort studies reviewed here have all been retrospective in design and present many difficulties in interpretation. Specifically:

1. There was no preexposure measure of intellectual functioning. Without such a measure, it is impossible to determine if lead resulted in a lowered IQ or if children with lower IQ were more likely to ingest significant amounts of lead.
2. In choosing control groups, it is extremely difficult to control for all en-

vironmental variables that could affect intelligence. Low-level lead exposure is most likely to produce a small decrement in intellectual functioning, and the studies reviewed above leave open the interpretation that the decrements found (if found) were due to other, uncontrolled variables.
3. In most of these studies, possible lead exposure of the children in the control group cannot be definitively ruled out. Either no blood lead results were provided for the control children, or in other instances, one or two previous lead determinations were used to assign children to a "nonexposed" control group. It is not unlikely that many of the children in the control groups experienced undetected exposure to lead.

Epidemiological Studies

The controversy surrounding possible effects of low-level lead exposure is well illustrated by two studies conducted in the El Paso, Texas, area in the summer of 1973. The children lived in an area called Smeltertown which was near a large lead-ore smelter. Landrigan, Whitworth, Baloh, Straehling, Barthel, and Rosenblum (1975) studied 124 children aged 3 years 9 months to 15 years 11 months who lived within 6.6. km of the smelter. The children were subdivided into two groups based on blood–lead level: a control group ($n = 46$) and a lead-absorption group ($n = 78$) with 40 µg/dl as the cut point. Children over 5 years of age were evaluated with the WISC (34 in the lead group and 36 in the control group). Children under the age of 5 were evaluated with the Wechsler Preschool and Primary Scale of Intelligence (WPPSI): 12 children in the lead group and 15 in the control group. On the performance portions of both tests, the lead-absorption group showed a significant deficit. In addition, all children were given a battery of neurological tests to evaluate motor functioning. On these tests, only finger-wrist tapping was significantly slower for the lead-absorption group.

A second study by McNeil, Ptasnik, and Croft (1975) included many of the same children used by Landrigan, Whitworth, Baloh, Straehling, Barthel, and Rosenblum (1975) and found quite different results. Their subjects included 138 children ranging in age from 21 months to 18 years (median 9 years) from the Smeltertown group of lead-exposed children and two control groups: one group consisted of children from the city of El Paso, and another group was composed of children from a rural community 20 km from the smelter. The evaluations of the children included a history questionnaire, general physical exam, neurological exam, determination of nerve conduction velocity, teacher evaluation, and psychometric evaluation. The psychometric evaluation consisted of the McCarthy Scales for children under 6 years of age, the WISC for children aged 6 to 15 years, and the Wechsler Adult Intelligence Scale (WAIS) for children 16 to 18 years of age. Other tests included in the evaluation were the Beery Test of Visual Motor Integration, Wide Range Achievement Test, Wepman Test of Auditory Discrimination, Oseretsky Test of Motor Development, Bender, Draw-a-Person, California Test of Personality, and the Frostig Developmental Test of Visual Perception. The authors analyzed their data according to group membership, blood–lead level, and exposure risk factors. No consistent effects of lead were found on any of the dependent variables studied for any of the three methods of data analysis.

In an effort to explain the disparities between these two studies, the Society on Environmental and Occupational Health (1976) commissioned a special committee, which found serious methodological problems with both studies (i.e., nonrandom exclusion of children, questions about selection of control groups), but concluded that there was no detrimental effect of lead on any psychological or neurological variable studied. The committee did caution that "because of inherent problems of study design and the limitations of the tests used, this finding should not lead to a conclusion that low levels of lead have no effects on neuropsychological performance" (p. 41).

The most recent study reporting intellectual and behavioral deficits in children exposed to lead was by Needleman, Gunnoe, Leviton, Reed, Peresie, Maher, and Barrett (1979). Rather than using the traditional measure of blood–lead level, the authors used dentine-lead level as a basis for grouping. Teeth were collected from 3,329 children in the first and second grade. Children whose dentine-lead was either above the 90th percentile or below the 10th percentile were classified as high- or low-lead levels, respectively. Of the children eligible for inclusion, neuropsychologic testing and teachers' behavior ratings were reported on 100 low-lead and 58 high-lead children. The main findings were that the high-lead children's performance on the Wechsler Intelligence Scale for Children—Revised (WISC-R) was significantly lower than the low-lead children. The high-lead children also performed significantly poorer on a reaction-time task than did the low-lead children. Teacher's ratings of the children's classroom behavior also showed an increase in negative ratings with increasing dentine-lead level.

Lansdown, Shepherd, Clayton, Delves, Graham, and Turner (1974) surveyed the entire population of children under the age of 17 who were exposed to excess amounts of lead owing to emissions from a lead smelter in London, England. Children over the age of 6 ($n = 232$) were evaluated using the WISC, the Burt Graded reading test, and a behavior questionnaire. There was a significant positive correlation between the distance of the child's residence from the smelter and the blood–lead level. There was no correlation, however, between blood–lead level and IQ, reading ability, or behavior rating.

There is one study in the literature which reports an association between low-level lead exposure and *increased* intellectual functioning. Hebel, Kinch, and Armstrong (1976) identified from birth records children who had lived from birth in the vicinity of a battery factory. Two comparison groups were children who had lived since birth in an area surrounding a non-lead-related industry and children residing in a residential area. Both comparison areas were of similar social composition. Intellectual ability was assessed using an examination given to all 11-year-old children and consisted of tests of verbal reasoning, English, and mathematics. The subjects were selected from the population of children taking this examination between 1961 and 1964. The authors found no relationship between test results and distance from the battery factory. As a group, however, the children residing in the vicinity of the battery factory performed better on the test than the children in the other two areas, in spite of a lack of difference in social class, birthrank, and maternal age.

In summary, epidemiologial-type studies have also been inconsistent in finding effects of low-level lead exposure. The best controlled study is that of Needleman *et al.* (1979), but like the cohort studies, all the epidemiological-type studies have been retrospective in nature and cannot rule out contributions of other environmental variables to possible deficits attributable to lead. One such unmeasured variable was identified in the study by Hebel *et al.* (1976) The schools in the area close to the battery factory were probably of better quality. It is entirely possible that uncontrolled variables in other studies were also present.

Lead Interactions with Nutritional Factors

Nutritional factors related to lead may play a role in mental retardation in several ways (1) because of persistence of pica and mouthing by mentally retarded people into adulthood (Albin, 1977; Schroeder, Mulick, & Rojahn, 1980); (2) by serving as the nutritional basis for lead pica (Snowdon, 1977); and (3) by altering susceptibility to lead intoxication (Mahaffey & Michaelson, 1980).

Lead and Pica

Epidemiological studies of pica, the ingestion of inedible substances (Barltrop, 1966; Lourie, Layman, & Millican, 1953) suggest that it is quite high (50%) in children at one year of age, but decreases rapidly to less than 10% by age 4. The most frequently ingested items were, in descending order: paper, clothing, dirt, matches, toiletries, plaster, writing materials, tobacco, and other items. The pica was not related to sex, race, family rank, place of birth of the parents, nor to the size or social position of the family, but was related to mouthing, bottle feeding, finger sucking, late weaning, bed-wetting, and siblings who also engaged in pica. These results suggest that home environmental factors affect the prevalence of pica. A similar observation was made by Chisholm and Harrison (1956) that, in many homes, maternal deprivation or disturbed child–parent relationships precipitate the ingestion of nonfood materials including lead (Bicknell, 1967).

Nutrition and Pica

It seems to be fairly well established that there is a higher incidence of pica among inner-city children from low-income families living in substandard housing (Kaliza, Ekvall, & Palmer, 1979). The main sources of lead ingestion by children are canned foods, water from lead-lined tanks or pipes, lead-laden house dust, and fallout from the air. By far the most serious source is from pica of lead-based paint chips, wall dust, and gnawing on objects (Zarkowsky, 1970). The main question is: Does pica cause lead ingestion or vice versa? They are both associated with nutritional deficiencies, especially vitamins C and D, iron, calcium, and phosphorous (Mahaffey, Treloar, Banis, Peacock, & Parekh, 1976; Sorrel, Rosen, & Roginsky, 1977). However, there is not good agreement among studies as to the nature of the relationship between pica and nutritional deficiencies (Gutelius, Millican, Layman, Cohen, & Dublin, 1962; Johnson & Tenuta, 1979; Mooty, Ferr, & Harris, 1975). For instance, Gutelius *et al.* (1962) found that replenishing an iron-deficient diet with intramuscular injections of iron did not reduce children's pica. Obviously, methodological rigor in this area must concede to ethical considerations. Probably case-controlled epidemiological studies in humans will have to be used to address this important question. Animal studies suggest that there could be a nutritional basis for lead pica. Snowdon (1977) showed that rats who had been made deficient in calcium, zinc, and magnesium ingested foods containing more lead, whereas their restoration to a nutritionally adequate diet eliminated lead ingestion. Calcium deficient rats also failed to form a learned aversion to lead acetate, suggesting that mineral deficiency may be a major factor in producing lead pica. How far such animal models can be generalized to children, for whom pica is also related to early feeding practices and home environment, needs to be investigated. It is likely that a complex relationship exists between nutritional and sociocultural factors in placing the child at risk for lead pica and possibly mental retardation.

Lead and Nutrition

There are a few prospective studies of the role of nutrition in predisposing humans to lead poisoning. Kehoe (1961) performed nutritional balance studies in four young adult male volunteers. They ingested low amounts of lead typically found in food so that their normal daily intake was slightly above normal. Absorption rate in the gut of lead from the diet varied between 5% and 10%. Similar studies carried out in children aged 3 weeks to 8 years (Alexander, Delves, & Clayton, 1972) found a 50% net absorption and 18% retention of dietary lead. Ziegler, Edwards, Jensen, Mahaffey, and Fomon (1978) found that retention and absorption were inversely correlated with the calcium content of the diet. Age, environment, and a wide variety of dietary factors may interact to influence absorption, retention, excretion, and distribution of lead in the body. Most of this research has been performed on animals, and we will only summarize it briefly here. Mahaffey and Michaelson (1980) provide an excellent review.

Several dietary factors have been found to have either a protective or a potentiating effect on the body's reaction to lead exposure: (1) quantity and type of dietary fat can result in up to 7- to 14-fold increase in lead content of several tissues; (2) increasing protein in the diet can decrease lead content of liver, kidney, and blood; (3) calcium and phosphorous deficient diets can cause increased gastrointestinal absorption of lead, increased retention of lead, and increased mobilization of lead from bone to soft tissues; (4) increased vitamin D may enhance gastrointestinal absorption of lead and delay the excretion of lead; (5) iron deficiency is related to increased retention in the liver, kidney, and bone; (6) copper seems to interact with the effects of lead, perhaps because lead may induce copper deficiency and thus interfere with iron metabolism; (7) zinc and chromium, on the other hand, have a protective effect against lead, possibly by competing for protein binding sites; and (8) vitamin C and a number of B vitamins, including nicotinic acid, B_{12}, B_6, and folic acid have been found to have a favorable effect on lead poisoning.

Nutrition can affect lead toxicity in a variety of organ systems. The effects of this interaction on development of the CNS and therefore on neurobehavioral consequences like learning and adaptive beahvior is largely uncharted territory in animals, let alone humans. Yet it is known that undernutrition in animals inhibits brain growth, synaptic organization, myelination, and production of biogenic amines (Mahaffey & Michaelson, 1980). Cross-species comparisons, however, must be made with caution. As Weiss (1980) points out, the cluster of complaints associated with low-level lead toxicity in humans features a wide variety of nonspecific symptoms, for example, jitteriness, irritability, paresthesia, hyperactivity, mental retardation, paralysis, peripheral neuropathy, polyneuritis, psychiatric symptoms, somnolence, tremor, disturbed vision, and weakness. Since these symptoms are subjective and ill-defined; they could occur for a variety of reasons. Therefore, generalizations made from laboratory analogues must be made very carefully.

Environmental Factors Contributing to Increased Lead Burden

One predisposing factor resulting in increased lead burden is nutrition. However, there are other factors in the child's environment which could act to place a child at risk for detrimental behavioral effects of increased lead burden. Previous research has hinted that there might be possible deficiencies in the care-giving environment of children who evidence increased lead burden (Chatterjee & Gettman, 1972; Lansdown et al., 1974; Millican, Lourie, & Layman, 1956; Rennert et al., 1970; Rummo et al., 1979). Most studies have attempted to control for possible covariances, for example, social class, age, maternal IQ, pica, etc., but only one study has addressed the question of deficiencies in the care-giving environment and increased lead burden. Milar et al. (1980) compared two groups of children, 12 to 30 months of age and 31 to 78 months of age showing increased lead burden with a sample of children matched for age, sex, and socioeconomic status, but showing no evidence of increased lead burden. The quality of the care giving environment of these children was assessed through the use of the Home Observation for Measurement of the Environment (HOME) Inventory developed by Caldwell, Heider, and Kaplan (1966). A measure of maternal intelligence was also obtained. For the younger children in the sample significant deficits in maternal IQ and quality of the care-giving environment were associated with increased lead burden in the children. The subscales of the HOME Inventory dealing with emotional and verbal responsiveness of the mother and maternal involvement with the child showed significant deficiencies in the care-giving environment of the children with increased lead burden. For the older children, the HOME Inventory also showed deficiencies in the care-giving environment of children with increased lead burden, but the differences were not significant.

As has been pointed out previously, all the research to date on low-level lead effects on behavior has been retrospective in nature. In spite of the seeming equality between lead-exposed children and children in control groups at the time of the study, the early care-giving environment of these children is unknown.

Research in the area of child development has only recently begun to document the powerful influences of the early care-giving environment on subsequent development of the child. Studies by Bradley and Caldwell (1976a,b) have used the HOME Inventory to identify factors in the child's environment during the first two years of life which are related to mental test performance at 36 and 54 months of age. Two of the subscales of the HOME Inventory that were strongly related to later intellectual development were emotional and verbal responsivity of the mother and maternal involvement with the child, These are also the two sub-scales identified by Milar *et al.* (1980) showing significant deficiencies in the environment of children with increased lead burden.

Traditionally the interpretation of the research on lead effects has been that increased lead burden directly results in deficits in cognitive functioning. However, alternative hypotheses are equally plausible. First, given the results of Milar *et al.* (1980), it is possible that the deficits found in children exposed to lead are a direct result of deficiencies in the care-giving environment and are not related to lead at all. The research of Bradley and Caldwell (1976a,b) would tend to support this conclusion.

Second, it is possible that deficiencies in the care-giving environment are responsible for increased lead burden and that the deficiencies are because of lead. A child in an environment where lead is available would be much more likely to ingest significant amounts of lead if left unsupervised by his caregiver. The poor care-giving environment is an antecedent to the lead ingestion, but it is the neurotoxic effects of lead that are responsbile for the deficits in cognitive functioning. Such a situation would be similar to research on malnutrition in children. Severe malnutrition can lead to cognitive deficits (Dobbing, 1970), but it is also known that aspects of the care-giving environment place children at risk for malnutrition (Cravioto & DeLicardie, 1972).

A third hypothesis is that the care-giving environment and lead combine to adversely affect intellectual development. This would be similar to the relationship found by Werner, Honzik, and Smith (1968) between perinatal complications and later psychological development. At 20 months of age the IQ differences between children with and without perinatal complications were only 5–7 points for children from a favorable social background. For infants living in a low socioeconomic environment the IQ differences ranged from 19–37 points. Clearly, perinatal insult and the quality of the child's environment both affected development.

Summary and Conclusions

The Neurobehavioral Toxicology of Lead Exposure

The history of research on lead is instructive. The effects of lead encephalopathy on mental retardation and deficits in motor function have been known for centuries. The amount of ambient lead in the environment increased sharply with the advent of the Industrial Revolution in the nineteenth century, so that now the average blood level considered acceptable in a highly industrialized nation like the United States may be up to 30 µg/dl (Air Quality for Lead, EPA, 1977). This is seven times as high as average blood level in Nepal, an acculturated, but nonindustrialized, society (Piomelli, Corash, Corash, Seaman, Mushak, Glover, & Padgett, 1980). Nevertheless, concern over asymptomatic lead exposure began only about 30 years ago, when the sociopolitical climate set the stage for concern about overpopulation, abuse of natural resources, and environmental pollution. Lead then became the prototype for research on many environmental pollutants. Research emphasis was on adverse health effects, that is, lead toxicity on organ systems of the body. Such research was perforce done primarily on animals. Human research focused on medically oriented epidemiological studies which attempted to locate sources of exposure, the risk populations, and the environmental ecological conditons that could be used to set standards for public policy. The main question addressed by this research was what the threshold level of lead burden in the body is which signals an unacceptable risk for retardation of cognitive and adaptive behavior, primarily minimal brain dysfunction (MBD), as exemplifed by hyperactivity.

Table II examines eleven of the best known studies of neurobehavioral toxic effects of lead exposure where subjects did not show the symptoms of lead encephalopathy. Only two of the studies used standard behavior ratings or neurometric evaluations. The right side of Table II shows whether authors attempted to control for the influences of confounding variables (indicated by a +). Some of the strengths and weaknesses of these studies are (1) while several studies showed statistically significant effects of lead exposure on IQ test performance, the group effects were usually small, that is, less than 6 IQ points, which is near the standard error for these tests. Clinically significant IQ effects would be nearer to 15 IQ points (one standard deviation at least). The IQ test, like other standardized psychometric performance tests (fine motor, reaction time, perceptual-motor tasks) may be too gross a measure to reliably tap sub-

TABLE II
Summary Evaluation of the Eleven Major Studies on Moderate Blood-Lead Levels

	Other measures			Possible confounding variables							
	Standard behavior ratings	In vivo behavior observations	Neurometric evaluations	SES	Age	Pica	Blind evaluations	Home environment	Race	Maternal IQ	Exposure history
de la Burde & Choate (1972)				+	+		+	+	+	+	
de la Burde & Choate (1975)				+	+		+	+	+	+	
Perino & Ernhart (1974)				+	+				+	+	
Pueschel et al. (1972)											
Landrigan et al. (1975)	+			+		+					
Rummo (1979)				+	+		+		+		+
Kotok et al. (1977)				+	+	+		+	+		+
Kotok (1972)					+	+					
Lansdown et al. (1974)						+					+
McNeil et al. (1975)				+	+	+	+		+		+
Needleman et al. (1979)			+							+	+

tle neurobehavioral effects of moderate lead exposure. (2) Only one study used a standardized rating scale for hyperactivity (Rummo et al., 1979). A significant effect of lead encephalopathy, but not asymptomatic lead exposure, was found. More recently, Milar et al. (1981) found no effect on children age 12–72 months. The entire validity of the concept of hyperactivity, as a type of minimal brain dysfunction, has been attacked recently (Rutter, 1980; Schroeder, Milar, Wool, & Routh, 1980). (3) Neurological examinations in these studies were negative for lead exposures below 40 μg/dl. Apparently a more sensitive neurometric measure is needed. Recently, Otto et al. (1980) demonstrated significant amplitude changes in slow-wave potentials of children aged 12–47 months with 30–60 μg/dl, but this effect did not appear in older children (48–75 months). (4) No study evaluated children's intelligent or social behavior with direct observations at home, school, or clinic, although it is recognized that these behaviors are often situation-specific (Routh, 1980). (5) Epidemiological studies have not followed up these children to evaluate the cumulative clinical effects of lead exposure, or reversibility on removal of lead from their home environment. The long-term clinical neurotoxic effects of low and moderate lead exposure on children's development remain largely to be investigated.

The Developmental Perspective

The above epidemiological studies and health effects research on the toxicology of lead have been very valuable for dealing with the active effects of lead exposure, but they have been only modestly helpful in addressing its chronic effects. A developmental perspective, in addition to defining who is an at risk case, what is wrong with the subject, and how the disease can be corrected, also asks what the cumulative risks on functioning at a later age are within one's ecological context and how these adverse effects can be compensated for, reversed, or at least minimized.

Environmental pollution will be a legacy of increasing concern to the development of all children. A research technology needs to be developed that will help policy makers evaluate the trade-offs of short-term benefits to society of utilizing natural resources that produce hazardous wastes against the long-term effects on the development of children and living organisms. The research on the effects of lead on development suggests a glimmer of hope that such a technology is beginning to develop. The assessment of perinatal exposure to environmental pollutants, preventive measures like hazard reduction through occupational and public health policies, and careful monitoring of care-giving practices of families whose children are at risk due to combined sociocultural factors like malnutrition, home environment, and poverty, are likely to be high priorities for research in the future.

ACKNOWLEDGMENTS

Thanks are due to the Department of Pediatrics, North Carolina Memorial Hospital, the Neurotoxicology Lab of the Clinical Studies Branch of the Environmental Protection Agency for their countless examples of support and collaboration in this project, and the Department of Biostatistics for statistical consultation.

REFERENCES

Air quality for lead. Washington, D.C.: U.S. Environmental Protection Agency, EPA-600/77-017, December, 1977.

ALBERT, R. E., SHORE, R. E., SAYERS, A. J., STREHLOW, C., KREIP, T. J., PASTERNACK, B. S., FRIEDHOFF, A. J., COVAN, F., & CIMINO, J. A. Follow-up of children overexposed to lead. *Environmental Health Perspectives*, 1974, 7, 33-40.

ALBIN, J. The treatment of pica (scavenging) behavior in the retarded: A critical analysis and implications for research. *Mental Retardation*, 1977, 15, 14-18.

ALEXANDER, F. W., DELVES, H. T., & CLAYTON, B. E. The uptake and excretion by children of lead and other contaminants. *Proceedings of the International Symposium, Environmental Health Perspectives and Lead*. Amsterdam: Commission of the European Communities, Luxembourg, October 1972.

AMMONS, R. B., & AMMONS, C. H. The Quick Test (QT): Provisional manual. *Psychological Reports*, 1962, 11, 111-161.

ANKU, V. D., & HARRIS, J. W. Peripheral neuropathy and lead poisoning in a child with sickle-cell anemia. *Journal of Pediatrics*, 1974, 85, 337-340.

BALOH, R. R., STURM, B., GREEN, B., & GLESER, G. Neuropsychological effects of chronic asymptomatic increased lead absorption: A controlled study, *Archives of Neurology*, 1975, 32, 326-330.

BARLTROP, D. The prevalence of pica. *American Journal of Diseases of Children*. 1966, 112, 116-123.

BEARD, R. R., & GRANDSTAFF, N. Carbon monoxide and human functions. In B. Weiss & V. Laties (Eds.), *Behavioral toxicology*. New York: Plenum Press, 1975.

BEATTIE, A. D., MOORE, M. R., GOLDBERG, A., FINLAYSON, J. J., MACKIE, T. M., GRAHAM, J. F., MAIN, J. C., McLAREN, P. A., MURDOCH, K. M., & STEWART, F. T. Role of chronic low-level lead exposure in the aetiology of mental retardation. *Lancet*, 1975, 1 (7907), 589-592.

BICKNELL, J. Selective pica and lead poisoning in a severely subnormal child. *Journal of Mental Deficiency Research*, 1967, 11, 278-281.

BRADLEY, R., & CALDWELL, B. Early home environment and changes in mental test performance in children from 6 to 36 months. *Developmental Psychology*, 1976, 12, 93-97. (a)

BRADLEY, R., & CALDWELL, B. The relation of infants' home environments to mental test performance at fifty-four months: A follow-up study. *Child Development*, 1976, 47, 1172-1174. (b).

BROADBENT, D. E. *Decision and stress*. New York: Academic Press, 1971.

Bullpit, C. J. Lead and hyperactivity. *Lancet*, 1972, *1*, 1144.
Burde, de la, B., & Choate, M. S. Does asymptomatic lead exposure in children have latent sequelae? *Journal of Pediatrics*, 1972, *81*, 1088-1091.
Burde, de la, B., & Choate, M. S. Early asymptomatic lead exposure and development at school age. *Journal of Pediatrics*, 1975, *87*, 638-642
Burt, C. The genetic determination of differences in intelligence: A study of monozygotic twins reared together and apart. *British Journal of Psychology*, 1966, *57*, 137-153.
Byers, R. K., & Lord, E. E. Late effects of lead poisoning on mental development. *American Journal of Diseases of Children*, 1943, *66*, 471-490.
Caldwell, B., Heider, J., & Kaplan, B. *The inventory of home stimulation*. Paper presented at the meeting of the American Psychological Association, 1966.
Center for Disease Control. *Preventing lead poisoning in young children*. Atlanta: U.S. Department of Health, Education and Welfare, 1978.
Chatterjee, P., & Gettman, J. H. Lead poisoning: Subculture as a facilitating agent? *American Journal of Clinical Nutrition*, 1972, *25*, 324-330.
Chisolm, J. J., & Harrison, H. E. The exposure of children to lead. *Pediatrics* 1956, *18*, 943-957.
Cohen, D. J., Johnson, W. T., & Caparulo, B. K. Pica and elevated blood lead level in autistic and atypical children. *American Journal of Diseases of Children*, 1976, *130*, 47-48.
Conners, C. K. A teacher rating scale for use in drug studies with children. *American Journal of Psychiatry*, 1969, *126*, 884-888.
Conners, C. K. Symptom patterns in hyperactive, neurotic, and normal children. *Child Development*, 1970, *41*, 667-682.
Cooper, G. P. Electrophysiology. In L. Reiter (Ed.), *The effects of lead exposure on CNS function: A workshop on the animal models*. Hendersonville, N.C.: U.S. Environmental Protection Agency, 1976.
Cravioto, J., & DeLicardie, E. Environmental correlates of severe malnutrition and language development in survivors from Kwashiorkor and marasmus. In *Nutrition: The nervous system and behavior*. Scientific Publication No. 251. Washington, D.C.: Pan American Health Organization, 1972.
David, O., Clark, J., & Voeller, K. Lead and hyperactivity. *Lancet*, 1972, *1*, 900-903.
David, O., Hoffman, S., McCann, B., Sverd, J., & Clark, J. Low lead levels and mental retardation. *Lancet*. 1976, *2*, 1370-1379.
David, O., Hoffman, S. P., Sverd, J., Clark, J., & Voeller, K. Lead and hyperactivity. Behavioral response to chelation: A pilot study. *American Journal of Psychiatry*, 1976, *133*, 1155-1158.
Dobbing, J. Undernutrition and the developing brain. In W. A. Hamwick (Ed.), *Developmental neurology*. Springfield, Ill.: Charles C Thomas, 1970.
Ennis, J. M., & Harrison, H. E. Treatment of lead encephalopathy with BAL (2, 3-dimereaptopropanol). *Pediatrics*, 1950, *5*,, 853.
Gibson, S. L. M., Lam, C. N., McCrae, W. M., & Goldberg, A. Blood lead levels in normal and mentally deficient children. *Archives of Diseases in Childhood*, 1967, *42*, 573-578.
Greenberg, M., Jacobziner, H., McLaughlin, M. C., Fuerst, H. T., & Pellitter, O. A study of pica in relation to lead poisoning. *Pediatrics*. 1958, *22*, 756-760.
Gutelius, M. F., Millican, F. K., Layman, E. M., Cohen, G. J., & Dublin, C. C. Nutritional studies of children with pica. *Pediatrics*, 1962, *29*,1012-1023.
Hebel, J. R., Kinch, D., & Armstrong, E. Mental capability of children exposed to lead pollution. *British Journal of Preventive and Social Medicine*, 1976, *30*, 170-174.
Johnson, N. E., & Tenuta, K. Diets and lead blood levels of children who practice pica. *Environmental Health Research*, 1979, 369-376.
Kalisz, K., Ekvall, S., & Palmer, S. Pica and lead intoxication. In S. Palmer & S. Ekvall

(Eds.), *Pediatric nutrition in developmental disorders.* Springfield, Ill.: Charles C Thomas, 1978.

KEHOE, R. A. The metabolism of lead in health and disease. *Archives of Environmental Health,* 1961, *2,* 418–422.

KOTOK, D. Development of children with elevated blood lead levels: A controlled study. *Journal of Pediatrics,* 1972, *80,* 57–61.

KOTOK, D., KOTOK, D., & HERIOT, J. T. Cognitive evaluation of children with elevated blood lead levels. *American Journal of Diseases of Children,* 1977, *131,* 791–793.

LANDRIGAN, P. J., WHITWORTH, R. H., BALOH, R. W., STAEHLING, N. W., BARTHEL, W. F., & ROSENBLUM, B. F. Neuropsychological dysfunction in children with chronic low-level lead absorption. *Lancet,* 1975, *1,* 708–712.

LANSDOWN, R. G., SHEPHERD, J., CLAYTON, B. E., DELVES, H. T., GRAHAM, P. J., & TURNER, W. C. Blood-lead levels behavior, and intelligence: A population study. *Lancet,* 1974, *1,* 538–541.

LEWIS, B. W., COLLINS, R. J., & WILSON, H. S. Seasonal incidence of lead poisoning in children in St. Louis. *Southern Medical Journal,* 1955, *48,* 298–301.

LOURIE, R. S., LAYMAN, E. M., & MILLICAN, F. K. Why children eat things that are not food. *Children,* 1963, *10,* 143–146.

MCNEIL, J. L., PTASNIK, J. A., & CROFT, D. B. Evaluation of long term effects of elevated blood lead concentrations in asymptomatic children. *Archives of Industrial Hygiene and Toxicology,* 1975, *26,* 1975.

MAHAFFEY, K. R., & MICHAELSON, I. A. The interaction between lead and nutrition. In H. Needleman (Ed.), *Low level lead exposure: The clinical implications of current research.* New York: Raven Press, 1980.

MAHAFFEY, K. R., TRELOAR, S., BANIS, T. A., PEACOCK, B. J., & PAREKH, L. Difference in dietary intake of calcium and phosphorous in children having normal and elevated blood lead concentrations. *Journal of Nutrition,* 1976, *106,* 7.

MELLINS, R. B., & JENKINS, C. D. Epidemiological and psychological study of lead poisoning in children. *Journal of the American Medical Association,* 1955, *158,* 15–20.

MILAR, C., SCHROEDER, S., DOLCOURT, J., MUSHAK, P., & GRANT L. Contributions of the caregiving environment to lead exposure in young children. *American Journal of Mental Deficiency,* 1980, *84,* 339–334.

MILAR, C. R., SCHROEDER, S. R., MUSHAK, P., & BOONE, L. Failure to find hyperactivity in preschool children with moderately elevated lead burden. *Journal of Pediatric Psychology,* 1981, *6,* 85–95.

MILLICAN, F. K., LOURIE, R. S., & LAYMAN, R. M. Emotional factors in the etiology and treatment of lead poisoning. *American Journal of Diseases of Children,* 1956, *91,* 144–149.

MONCRIEFF, A. A., KOAMIDES, O. P., CLAYTON, B. E., PATRICK, A. D., RENWICK, A. G. C., & ROBERTS, G. E. Lead poisoning in children. *Archives of Disease in Childhood,* 1964, *39,* 1–13.

MOORE, M. R., MEREDITH, P. A., & GOLDBERG, A. A retrospective analysis of blood-lead in mentally retarded children. *Lancet,* 1977, *2,* 717–719.

MOOTY, J., FERRAND, C. F., & HARRIS, P. Relationship of diet to lead poisoning in children. *Pediatrics,* 1975, *55,* 636–639.

NEEDLEMAN, H. L. Lead poisoning in children: Neurologic implications of wide-spread subclinical intoxication. *Seminars in Psychiatry,* 1973, *5,* 47–53.

NEEDLEMAN, H. L., GUNNOE, C., LEVITON, A., REED, R., PERESIE, H., MAHER, C., & BARRETT, B. S. Deficits in psychologic and classroom performance of children with elevated dentine lead levels. *New England Journal of Medicine,* 1979, *13,* 680–695.

OTTO, D. A., BENIGNUS, V., MULLER, K., & BARTON, C. Effects of age and body lead burden on CNS function in young children. I. Slow cortical potentials. *Electroencephalography and Clinical Neurophysiology,* 1981, *52,* 229–239.

PERINO, J., & ERNHART, C. B. The relation of subclinical lead level to cognitive and sensorimotor impairment in black preschoolers. *Journal of Learning Disabilities*, 1974, *7*, 26-30.

PERSLSTEIN, M. A., & ATTALA, R. Neurologic sequelae of plumbism in children. *Clinical Pediatrics*, 1966, *5*, 292-298.

PIOMELLI, S., BRICKMAN, A., & CARLOS, E. Rapid diagnosis of iron deficiency by measurement of free erythrocyte prophyrins and hemoglobin: The FEP/hemoglobin ratio. *Pediatrics*, 1976, *57*, 136.

PIOMELLI, S., & DAVIDOW, B. The FEP (free erythroctye protoporphyrin) concentration: A promising screening test for lead poisoning. *Pediatric Research*, 1972, *6*, 366.

PIOMELLI, S., CORASH, L., CORASH, M., SEAMAN, C., MUSHAK, P., GLOVER, B., & PADGETT, R. Blood lead concentrations in a remote Himalayan population. *Science*, 1980, *210*, 1135-1137.

PUESCHEL, S. N., KOPITO, L., & SCHWACHMAN, H. Children with increased lead burden: A screening and follow-up study. *Journal of the American Medical Association*, 1972, *222*,, 462.

RENNERT, O. M., WEINER, P., & MADDEN, J. Asymptomatic lead poisoning in 85 Chicago children. *Clinical Pediatrics*, 1970. *9*, 9-13.

ROBINSON, N. M., & ROBINSON, H. B. *The mentally retarded child*. New York: McGraw-Hill, 1976.

ROUTH, D. K., SCHROEDER, C. S., & O'TUAMA, L. A. Development of activity level in children. *Developmental Psychology*, 1974, *10*, 163-168.

ROUTH, D. K. Developmental and social aspects of hyperactivity. In C. Whalen & B. Henker (Eds.), *Hyperactive children: The social ecology of identification and treatment*. New York: Academic Press, 1980.

RUMMO, J. H., ROUTH, D. K., RUMMO, N. J., & BROWN, J. F. Behavioral and neurological effects of symptomatic and asymptomatic lead exposure in children. *Archives of Environmental Health*, 1979, *34*, 120-124.

RUTTER, M. Raised lead levels and impaired cognitive/behavioral functioning. *Developmental Medicine and Child Neurology Supplement No. 42*, 1980, *22*, 1-26.

SACHS, H. K., KRALL, V., MCCAUGHRAN, D.A., ROZENFELD, I. H., YOUNGSMITH, N., GROWE, G., LAZAR, B., NOVAK, L., O'CONNELL, L., & PAYSON, B. IQ following treatment of lead poisoning: A patient-sibling comparison. *Journal of Pediatrics*, 1978, *93*, 428-431.

SCHROEDER, S. R., MULICK, J. A., & ROJAHN, J. The definition, taxonomy, epidemiology, and ecology of self-injurious behavior. *Journal of Autism and Developmental Disorders*, 1980, *10*, 417-432.

SCHROEDER, S. R., MILLAR, C., WOOL, R., & ROUTH, D. Multiple measurement transituational diagnosis of hyperactivity and the concept of generalized overactivity. *Journal of Pediatric Psychology*, 1980, *5*, 365-375.

SMITH, H. D., BAEHNER, R. L., CARNEY, T., & MAJORS, W. J. The sequelae of pica with and without lead poisoning. *American Journal of Diseases of Children*, 1963, *105*, 609-616.

SNOWDON, C. F. A nutritional basis for lead pica. *Physiology and Behavior*, 1977, *18*, 888-893.

SOCIETY ON ENVIRONMENTAL AND OCCUPATIONAL HEALTH. *An epidemiologic study of a lead contaminated area: SOEH evaluation of the El Paso studies*. Unpublished manuscript, 1976.

SORRELL, M., ROSEN, J. F., & ROGINSKY, M. R. Interactions of lead, calcium, vitamin D and nutrition in lead-burdened children. *Archives of Environmental Health*, 1977, *32*,160-164.

THURSTON, D. L., MIDDLEKAMP, J. N., & MASON E. The late effects of lead poisoning. *Journal of Pediatrics*, 1955, *47*, 413-423.

WALDRON, H. A. Subclinical lead poisoning: A preventable disease. *Preventive Medicine*, 1975, *4*, 135-153.

WEISS, B. Conceptual issues in the assessment of lead toxicity. In H. Needleman (Ed.), *Low level lead exposure: The clinical implications of current research*. New York: Raven Press, 1980.

WERNER, E., HONZIK, M., & SMITH, R. Prediction of intelligence and achievement at ten years from twenty months pediatric and psychological examinations. *Child Development,* 1968, *39,* 1063–1075.

WERRY, J. S. Developmental hyperactivity. *Pediatric Clinics of North America,* 1968, *15,* 581–599.

WIENER, G. Varying psychological sequelae of lead ingestion in children. *Public Health Reports,* 1970, *85,* 19–24.

ZARKOWSKY, H. The lead problem in children: Dictum and polemic. *Current Problems in Pediatrics,* 1970, *6,* 1–47.

ZIEGLER, E. E., EDWARDS, B. B., JENSEN, R. L., MAHAFFEY, K. R., & FOMON, S. J. Absorption and retention of lead by infants. *Pediatric Research,* 1978, *12,* 29–34.

6　Behavioral Assessment of the Mentally Retarded

EDWARD S. SHAPIRO AND ROWLAND P. BARRETT

INTRODUCTION

Behavior therapy has received increasing acceptance as a method of treatment for a variety of pathological conditions in children and adults. Techniques for behavior change have been successfully applied in schools, clinics, laboratories, psychiatric hospitals, correctional settings, and homes. Separating behavior therapy from more traditional means of behavior change is essentially a theoretical approach which diminishes the importance or ignores the use of intrapsychic variables in explaining behavior. This difference in conceptualizing psychopathology and establishing regimes for treating it also requires alterations in the modes of problem behaviors. An outgrowth of behavior therapy has been the development of assessment techniques specific to this theoretical orientation.

Unfortunately, the technological advancements that have been made in behavioral treatment have not been paralleled by similar advances in the requisite assessment techniques (e.g., Ciminero, 1977; Hartmann, Roper, & Bradford, 1979). The methodological rigor established with behavioral treatment approaches has largely been ignored in the assessment of behavior. Most behaviorists while developing their assessment devices have, in the past, ignored such psychometric properties as reliability, validity, and standardization that were necessary in establishing the usefulness of traditional assessment instruments (Goldfried & Linehan, 1977; Hartmann *et al.*, 1979). Although some may argue that it may not be appropriate to apply principles and assumptions established with a divergent, largely intrapsychic theoretical base to behavioral assessment (Nelson & Hayes, 1979), the well-established empirical foundation upon which those principles of test construction were developed is

---

EDWARD S. SHAPIRO • Department of Educational Psychology, University of Arizona, Tucson, Arizona 85721.　ROWLAND P. BARRETT • Western Psychiatric Institute and Clinic, University of Pittsburgh School of Medicine, Pittsburgh, Pennsylvania 15213.

compatible with the empirical tradition of behaviorism (Hartmann *et al.*, 1979). The publishing of recent books (Ciminero, Calhoun, & Adams, 1977; Hersen & Bellack, 1976) and journals (*Behavioral Assessment* and *Journal of Behavioral Assessment*) is indicative of the growing recognition in the field that improving the technology of behavioral assessment is important.

Before discussing the specific mechanics of behavioral assessment, it is necessary to understand how these techniques differ from more traditional assessment strategies. Detailed comparisons between traditional and behavioral assessment are available in the literature, and while a thorough discussion of this topic is beyond the scope of this chapter (Cone & Hawkins, 1977; Goldfried & Kent, 1972; Goldfried & Linehan, 1977; Hartmann *et al.*, 1979; Hersen & Bellack, 1976), a brief overview summarizing the differences between these approaches to assessment will be offered.

The distinction between traditional and behavioral assessment has been consistently noted to be based on the assumptions, methods, and applications of the information obtained. Traditional assessment has generally focused on a search for underlying personality characteristics, the assumption being that observed behavior is important only as it serves to indicate underlying traits which affect behavior across many situations. In addition, the individual's behavior during the assessment is assumed to represent a pattern of global responding which was established at an early age, generally with a heavy genetic disposition toward specific behavior that persists throughout his or her life. Typically, traditional assessment of personality consists of projective (e.g., Rorschach, TAT) or self-report tests (MMPI, CPI) and is used primarily for description, diagnosis, classification, and prediction.

In contrast, behavioral assessment views the individual's behavior as a response to particular stimulus elements that are present at some given point. Inferences from behavior to other traits and settings are avoided and made only to summarize a set of observed behaviors. A history of the individual is unimportant except to provide some information regarding the maintenance or stimulus control of the particular behavior. Unlike traditional assessment which is usually restricted to the administration of standardized tests in a single environment, behavioral assessment will often result in the measurement of the same behavior in a variety of settings (home, school, work), and across different response types (self-report, direct observation, role play).

As previously noted, traditional and behavioral assessments differ most in how information is used. With traditional approaches, assessment is a terminal objective leading to classification and diagnosis. Behavioral assessment, on the other hand, is viewed only as a step toward treatment. The purpose of the assessment is to select specific behavior systematically and to determine the variables that are currently controlling it. Prior to the start of treatment, the naturally occurring rates or frequencies of behavior are determined so that an accurate and unbiased observation of behavior change can be made. This focus on treatment offers an opportunity for on-going assessment and directs the treatment planning of the therapist. Through such data collection methods, accountability and credibility of the prescribed treatment (and the therapist) are made possible.

Most extended discussions of behavioral assessment are oriented around methodologies for the assessment of specific categories of behavioral deficits and excesses, such as social skills, depression, addictive behaviors, sexual dysfunctions, and anxiety based disorders (e.g., Ciminero et al., 1977; Hersen & Bellack, 1976). Even though it is generally assumed that strategies for assessing behavioral pathology will be equally useful among all populations with similar behavioral deficits, mentally retarded persons present difficulties in assessment not typically encountered with nonretarded persons. For example, the use of interviews and self-report measures with mentally retarded populations provide extremely limited information that may also be inaccurate. In many cases, it may not be possible to obtain such data directly from the client. Other behavioral assessment strategies, such as direct observation, checklists, rating scales, and standardized tests, must be adapted to reduce behavioral areas into numerous subcomponents, since many instruments used with nonretarded populations are not designed for the detailed analysis of behavior necessary when assessing the mentally retarded. This is particularly true since mentally retarded populations must be taught in small, discrete steps to enable them to acquire new skills and behavior (Haring & Pious, 1976).

The primary use of assessment measures with the mentally retarded has been for diagnosis. Behaviorists have de-emphasized the use of assessment for diagnosis and classification. Indeed, much of the behavioral movement grew out of dissatisfaction with global observations and subjective impressions often evident in the diagnosis of psychopathology. Those therapists ascribing to a behavioral orientation have largely viewed diagnosis as unnecessary for treatment (Bannister, Salmon, & Lieberman, 1964; Frank, 1975; Hersen, 1976; Kazdin, 1978). Criticisms often levied by behaviorists have been that diagnoses are too global, are unrelated to unknown hypothetical constructs, and most important, cannot be reliably validated. Although dissatisfaction for diagnosis and classification processes have pervaded the field of behavior therapy, some individuals have recognized the usefulness of categorization. In fact, some attempts have been made at developing a behaviorially based classification system. Adams, Doster, and Calhoun (1977) have proposed a scheme, Psychological Response Classification System (PRCS), designed to classify responses according to modalities which have come to be considered distinct from each other in the behavioral literature. Each response modality (motor, perceptual, biological, cognitive, emotional, and social) contains a number of objectively defined response categories which provide a clear taxonomy for describing behaviors targeted for treatment. Adams *et al.* (1977) note the heuristic value of their system as well as the need for future empirical validation.

Cone (1978) has also developed a behavioral classification system, the Behavioral Assessment Grid (BAG), based on the simultaneous assessment of the contents of behavior (motor, cognitive, or physiological), methods that are used to assess the contents (interview, self-report, rating by other, self-observation, analogue: role play, analogue: freely occurring behavior, naturalistic: role play, or naturalistic: freely occurring behavior), and the types of generalizability (across scores, items, time, settings, methods and dimensions) that are established. The three dimensions of assessment are combined into a $3 \times 8 \times 6$ matrix (contents $\times$ methods $\times$ generalization) which provides a means for categorizing the assessment process. Cone (1978) indicates that such a system offers a scheme for organizing as well as contributing to the need for standardization in the entire field of behavioral assessment.

Despite the attempts to establish a behaviorally based classification system, the term *mental retardation* represents a traditional diagnostic category and may seem incompatible with behavioral assessment. However, when one considers the nature of the definition of mental retardation, the term is, to a large degree, a classification of general behavior retardation (Kazdin & Straw, 1976). Mental retardation, as defined by the American Association on Mental Deficiency (Grossman, 1977; Heber, 1961), requires deficits to be noted in both "intelligence" and adaptive behavior. This definition of mental retardation is based on the premise that, when compared to other individuals of similar chronological age on a standardized instrument, the mentally retarded person will perform signficantly below the mean (greater than two standard deviations) on both measures of adaptive behavior and traditional intelligence tests. Unfortunately, many psychologists have ignored the need for the assessment of adaptive behavior and have restricted their definition to deficiencies in "intellectual processes" (Adams, 1973; Baumeister & Muma, 1975; Clausen, 1972). Although the definition of *intelligence* has always been controversial (e.g., Sattler, 1974), individuals offering varying definitions of *adaptive behavior* (e.g., Balthazar, 1973; Heber, 1961; Leland, Nihira, Foster, Shellhaas, & Kagin, 1968; Mercer, 1973; Nihira, 1969a) agree that adaptive behavior is represented by independent functioning in basic needs, maintaining social relationships, and includes deficits in cognitive functioning (i.e., "intelligence"). In the assessment of adaptive behavior, when the degree of the deficit reaches a particular level in comparison to other individuals of the same chronological age, the term mental retardation becomes applicable and thereby is directly related to a behavioral criterion. One cannot avoid the inferential use of the term mental retardation since it indicates that deficiencies in adaptive behavior are not due strictly to deficient learning processes that are based on reinforcement history but rather on an inability to learn at a normal rate, which is unrelated to stimulus control or other environmental variables. However, the translation of the term into specific deficits and the lack of mastery of adaptive behaviors place mental retardation squarely into an empirical, behavioral framework.

A behavioral assessment of mental retardation would primarily emphasize attempts to specify the particular deficits in adaptive behavior which the individual possesses. However, because the proper identification of this population is demanded by law, assessment must include establishing a diagnosis. Coulter and Morrow (1978a) provide a perspective for conceptualizing the psychological assessment of the mentally retarded as involving a two-stage process: assessment for classification/identification and assessment for intervention/programming. Although their conceptualization of the assessment process is not described directly in traditional or behavioral terms, such assessment of the mentally retarded can be perceived as behaviorally oriented.

A behavioral assessment for classification/identification of the population requires the identification of adaptive behavior deficits as compared to norms of chronologically equivalent individuals. As noted previously, because the degree and number of deficits determines whether the individual is categorized as mentally retarded, such classification is based on behavior. In the selection of assessment instruments to make determinations regarding mental retardation, the standardization of the assessment process, the availability of well selected norm-reference groups, and the establishment of other traditional psychometric properties of the instrument become essential in making accurate comparisons. It is interesting to note that the use of norm-referenced instruments is not typically considered in behavioral assessment (Evans & Nelson, 1977).

Once the individual has been identified, behavioral assessment for the purpose of intervention/programming becomes relevant (Coulter & Morrow, 1978a). Assessment of this type is more directly associated with the typical use of behavioral assessment. Individuals are assessed regarding the specific areas in which prescriptive programming to remedy such deficits can be planned. In many ways, assessment of this type is much like criterion-referenced testing (Glaser, 1963) where the determination of deficiencies is not based on comparisons to other same-age individuals but on the basis of meeting some minimal criterion which has been established to determine mastery of that skill or behavior. Instructions and techniques that are used to perform this assessment are different from those needed for classification/identification and will be treated in a later section.

In general, the behavioral assessment of the mentally retarded, while having strong similarities to the behavioral assessment of other populations, has striking differences. The term mental retardation is itself a diagnostic category, something which behaviorists have tended to avoid. However, viewed as a significant deficit in adaptive behavior, mental retardation clearly can be perceived as behavioral retardation. As a result, we take the position that behavioral assessment within this population must include evaluations for both classification/identification and intervention/programming. We would also emphasize that techniques and strategies used to make the assessments will vary based on the assessor's purpose.

The primary objectives of this chapter are to provide a summary of behavioral assessment with mentally retarded persons. After a brief overview of behavioral assessment methodologies, instruments typically used to assess specific skill deficits common to the mentally retarded will be covered in more detail. Implications and needs for future research in the behavioral assessment of the mentally retarded will also be discussed.

Current Strategies for Behavioral Assessment

As mentioned in the previous section, strategies used for behavioral assessment are essentially different from those of traditional assessment. Although the instruments themselves may be the same, it is the manner in which the device is used and the corresponding interpretation of data that defines it as either a behavioral or a traditional assessment technique. The scope of the present section is to review briefly four general strategies of assessment: intelligence and achievement testing, interviewing, checklists and rating scales, and direct observation. Within each strategy area, specific assessment devices commonly used with the mentally retarded will be noted and, where applicable, discussed from both the traditional and the behavioral perspectives. In addition, the use of single-case research designs for evaluating behavior change will be considered.

Intelligence and Achievement Testing

Nowhere is the difference between traditional and behavioral assessment strategies more apparent than in the measurement of general intelligence and school achievement. Both areas provide long-standing examples of the traditional clinical use of standardized psychological testing, particularly with regard to the mentally retarded individual.

Although the traditional use of standardized psychological and psychoeducational tests provides the behaviorally oriented practitioner with little meaningful information and is used chiefly to satisfy state and local laws governing schools and/or institutional placements (Ciminero & Drabman, 1977), the data generated by these instruments are potentially useful if viewed from a behavioral perspective.

Among the most widely used of the psychological assessment devices for measuring intelligence is the Stanford-Binet Intelligence Scale, Form L-M (Terman & Merrill, 1973). Its use with the mentally retarded is particularly frequent because it extends to relatively low levels of ability. The format of the Stanford-Binet is appealing since there are numerous opportunities for successful performance (Robinson & Robinson, 1976). The subtests of the Stanford-Binet include language, memory, conceptual thinking, reasoning, numerical reasoning, visual-motor coordination, and social intelligence (Sattler, 1974). Essentially, individuals are asked to complete tasks purported to sample abilities in each of these areas. Through "the sinking of shafts at (these) critical points" (Terman & Merrill, 1937, p. 4), a global estimate of intellectual ability is obtained. A resultant mental age score is then matched against normative data for chronological age and a corresponding deviation IQ score is obtained.

A second set of instruments for the measurement of intelligence are the Wechsler scales: the Wechsler Preschool and Primary Scale of Intelligence (Wechsler, 1967), the Wechsler Intelligence Scale for Children—Revised (Wechsler, 1974), and the Wechsler Adult Intelligence Scale (Wechsler, 1955). Commonly known as the WPPSI, WISC-R, and WAIS, respectively, these tests are the chief rivals of the Stanford-Binet. They are commonly employed with older children, adolescents, and adults functioning within the moderate and mild ranges of mental retardation but are limited with younger children to those functioning only in the mild range of mental retardation because of the inability of the WISC-R and WPPSI to accurately reflect IQ levels below 60.

Similar to the Stanford-Binet, the Wechsler scales contain subtests corresponding to a number of broadly defined categories which, theoretically, reflect critical areas of intellectual ability (general knowledge, social judgment, numerical reasoning, verbal-conceptual thinking, language, auditory memory, nonverbal reasoning, perceptual organization, visual memory, visual-motor coordination, and motor speed). The subtests of the Wechsler scales are grouped into verbal and performance subscales which yield deviation IQ scores for both in addition to a full scale IQ score that represents collective performance and global intelligence.

With the mentally retarded, the traditional use of such standardized intelligence tests as the Stanford-Binet and the Wechsler scales has involved applying the IQ score for diagnosis and classification of intellectual ability. Derived IQ scores greater than two standard deviations below mean performance for chronological age are indicative of mental retardation. Typically, the diagnosis of mental retardation is further classified according to levels of severity, such as mild, moderate, severe, and profound (see Grossman, 1977), the purpose of which is to standardize the interpretation of test performance vis-à-vis the IQ score. In addition, these tests are commonly employed as devices with which to assess the categorical strengths and weaknesses of the mentally retarded individual and to predict school and vocational performance (Robinson & Robinson, 1976).

It is a well accepted opinion, even in the most conservative of testing circles, that relying solely on the results of intelligence tests (e.g., mental age and IQ) provides insufficient data for the comprehensive assessment of an individual's cognitive abilities. This applies to the intellectually average and gifted as well as to the mentally retarded. As such, additional measures are employed as supplements to intelligence testing.

The achievement test is one such additional measure commonly used with mentally retarded populations as an adjunct to IQ tests. Although achievement tests using a group format are more routinely used with nonretarded school-age children, individually administered achievement tests, such as the Peabody Individual Achievement Test (PIAT) (Dunn & Markwardt, 1970) and the Wide Range Achievement Test (WRAT) (Jastak & Jastak, 1965) are used more extensively with children in the mild range of mental retardation. Achievement tests such as the PIAT and WRAT are comprised of subtests designed to measure abilities in several areas related to educational performance (spelling, reading recognition, reading comprehension, mathematics). Again, as with intelligence tests, the principal intent of the achievement test is diagnostic through the assignment of grade and age equivalents based on normative data. The results of achievement tests are typically used to identify the relative strengths and weaknesses in skill areas that are related to school performance and that underlie the potential of an individual to benefit from academic instruction.

The traditional clinical use of intelligence and achievement test data does little in the way of providing the behaviorally oriented assessor with meaningful information about the individual tested. The diagnosis and classification of an individual on the basis of mental age, IQ, and educational grade equivalents does little more than project a stereotyped image of the tested individual. In no way does it impart the adaptive significance of the individual's intellectual or cognitive skills. Instead, the use of classification schemes implies fixed ability levels which may or may not be a true representation of intellectual or educational potential, and certainly not a valid predictor of educational or vocational competencies that may be gained through intensive habilitation (Kazdin & Straw, 1976).

Nonetheless, the data yielded through standardized intelligence and achievement testing are potentially meaningful if they are assigned a role in a behaviorally oriented assessment "package" that emphasizes treatment in addition to satisfying diagnostic requirements. The data from these tests become useful if performance is viewed as a sample of general behavioral skills that the individual has acquired (or has yet to acquire) through learning and not dependent on the emergence of some underlying hypothetical process or cognitive structure (Ciminero & Drabman, 1977). Standardized tests may be used meaningfully as screening devices preceding the use of additional components of the behavioral assessment package (checklists, rating scales, or direct observation) for the identification of specific areas of concern. Global indications of behavioral assets and deficits, such as those obtained through the "sinking of shafts at critical points," are far too broad to be useful. With the mentally retarded, as with any population, the identification of specific problem behaviors will eventually depend on the direct observation of the response and its antecedent and consequent stimuli. This emphasis on the assessment of discrete behaviors at which intervention is directed is critical to the differentiation between behavioral and traditional (diagnostic) assessment.

Interviews

The clinical interview has long been a principal method of psychological assessment. Typically, it represents the initial contact between therapist and client and sets the stage for ongoing treatment. Interview formats may vary in style from the highly structured to nondirective, free-association methods. Despite major differences in form, the goals of most traditional and behavioral assessment interviews are the same: to investigate and conceptualize the client and his or her presenting problem(s). In this sense, traditional clinical and behavioral interviews differ very little. As with standardized psychological tests, it is not the assessment tool itself that distinguishes the technique, but how the data are interpreted and applied. In this sense, traditional clinical and behavioral approaches to interviewing differ considerably.

As with most psychological assessment devices, the traditional use of the interview is primarily diagnostic. Through a series of interviews, the clinician obtains a thorough developmental history including relevant information about the presenting problem, interprets the symptoms, and makes a suitable diagnosis. A treatment plan is then formulated and directed to resolve the underlying conflict, of which the presenting problem is symptomatic. Quite literally, the traditional therapist may never directly address the behavior that led the client to seek treatment.

The behaviorally oriented practitioner takes quite a different approach to the use of the interview as an assessment device, since he is relatively unconcerned with the understanding, treatment, and resolution of hidden conflict. Rather, the behavior therapist's chief concern rests with a functional analysis of the client's behavior. This procedure requires operationally defining the behavioral excess or deficit that led to referral and obtaining information about the reliable antecedent and consequent events that serve to maintain it. This relatively direct and well-structured approach to information gathering does not imply that the behavioral therapist prefers a lack of understanding of the total individual. On the contrary, extremely rigid, mechanistic, and reductionist formats are strongly discouraged (Meyer, Liddell, & Lyons, 1977). For example, the widely used behavioral interviewing techniques of Kanfer and Saslow (1969), Lazarus (1973, 1976), and Wolpe (1973) place much emphasis on the comprehensive evaluation of the total individual, including historical as well as current life events. Because the penchant for extensive data gathering is great, certain assessors have criticized their complex nature and have called for a more concrete and manageable approach to information gathering (Linehan, 1977; Morganstern, 1976). Unfortunately, comparative research on the various interview formats has yet to be done. Hence, the issue becomes one for future empirical study.

The use of behavioral interviews with the mentally retarded is rather limited. If one were to go by published reports alone, he or she would be forced to conclude that interviews of any type are rarely, if ever, used with this population. The fundamental problem of poor reliability and validity which plague verbal reports in general (Ciminero & Drabman, 1977; Evans & Nelson, 1977; Linehan, 1977; Meyer et al., 1977) is perhaps a principal reason for the current situation. Understandably, if information gathered through interviews with intellectually nonimpaired populations is suspect, then the reliability and validity of verbal self-reports from the mentally retarded are naturally assumed to be even poorer.

Nevertheless, in certain cases mentally retarded individuals are interviewed directly and the process is potentially helpful, if for no other reason than to establish rapport and direct communication between therapist and client. When mentally retarded individuals are interviewed, the format more closely resembles the assessment of child than of adult behavior. As with children, mentally retarded individuals are typically not self-referrals. Instead, they are referred by parents, relatives, or helping professionals (e.g., physicians, social workers, teachers, psychologists) and much the same format for interviewing children is required. It is a common practice that knowledgeable informants be interviewed and asked to provide information pertaining to the client's past and present behavior, in addition to the client's self-report (if applicable). It is important to point out, however, that from the standpoint of reliability and validity, information derived from parents (among others) through interviewing is as suspect as information gathered through the client's self-report (Ciminero & Drabman, 1977). Since parent interviews are understandably subjective and expectedly biased in one way or another, they provide little meaningful information on which to base treatment plans. Although there exists no empirical basis for concluding that reports by parents of mentally retarded individuals are equally unreliable and invalid, there are no data which indicate them to be more objective in evaluating and recounting their children's behavior.

In general, the strategy of interviewing parents and significant others when a mentally retarded client is involved appears more than advisable, given the nature of the referral process. Although useful information in terms of direct treatment planning may not be forthcoming from such a strategy, it is certainly important to establish rapport and direct communication with the person making the referral. In addition, it is widely accepted as an ideal time to reach agreements on the nature and objectives of therapy, defining that individual's role in the therapeutic process, and for obtaining information related to the conceptualization of the client's presenting problem (Meyer et al., 1977).

Checklist and Rating Scales

A frequently used strategy for the assessment of behavior is the problem-oriented checklist and rating scale. It is often used by both traditional and behavior therapists as a standard follow-up device to interviewing. There are several reasons underlying the popular use of checklists and rating scales: they are quick and efficient measures that provide a relatively comprehensive survey of problem areas; they yield easily quantifiable data; and they can be used effectively for a number of clinical purposes including behavioral descriptions, prescriptions, and the evaluation of treatment programs (Ciminero & Drabman, 1977; Walls, Werner, Bacon, & Zane, 1977).

The basic format of the behavior problem checklist and rating scale requires a knowledgeable informant to evaluate, from memory or by direct observation, the various client competencies under sets of given conditions. The user of the checklist and rating scale is instructed to be as objective as possible so that the instrument will yield an accurate description of the client's behavior. As with standardized tests and interviews, the key to the use of the problem-oriented checklist and rating scale as a component of the behavioral assessment package is the requirement that its data be applied for intervention and programming, in addition to the narrowing of problem behaviors in need of treatment.

The use of behavior checklists and rating scales with the mentally retarded is extremely frequent and is often determined by state policies which require descriptive measurements of adaptive behavior beyond standardized intelligence and achievement tests before determining a handicapped condition (Morrow & Coulter, 1978). However, the popularity of such checklists with professionals in the field of mental retardation also stems from the practical advantages of the instruments for prescribing and evaluating treatment, since behavior modification is a primary treatment strategy. Although the number of behavior problem checklists and rating scales used with the mentally retarded is far too great to be reviewed here, there appears to be a select few that are predominantly used with this population (see Walls et al., 1977, for a comprehensive review of checklists and rating scales).

In a study designed to survey state policies regarding the measurement of adaptive behavior, Morrow and Coulter (1978) asked agencies to list specific measures of adaptive behavior of which they were aware. The American Association on Mental Deficiency (AAMD) Adaptive Behavior Scale-Public School Version (Lambert, Windmiller, Cole, & Figueroa, 1974), Vineland Social Maturity Scale (Doll, 1965), the System of Multicultural Pluralistic Assessment-SOMPA (Mercer & Lewis, 1977), and the AAMD Adaptive Behavior Scale—1975 Revision (Nihira, Foster, Shellhaas, & Leland, 1975) proved to be the most frequently mentioned measures.

The oldest, if not the most well-known and widely used of these measures, is the Vineland Social Maturity Scale (Doll, 1965). The Vineland requires a recorder to evaluate client competencies as mastered, emergent, or latent within several classes of behavior (self-help, self-direction, occupation, communication, locomotion, and socialization), based on structured discussion with a knowledgeable informant. The Vineland is organized on the basis of developmental competencies (ages 0–30) and uses a hierarchical format to arrive at a measure of social change. A ratio social quotient can also be calculated, although it is usually ignored.

The newest of the above-mentioned measures is the System of Multicultural Pluralistic Assessment-SOMPA (Mercer & Lewis, 1977). Conceptualized as a total system of assessment, the SOMPA consists of nine sets of measures used within three separate assessment models: medical, social-system, and pluralistic.

Among several measures within the social-system assessment model is the Adaptive Behavior Inventory for Children (ABIC), appropriate for use with children ages 5 through 11 years. Although the ABIC was not designed for use outside of the total SOMPA package (Lewis & Mercer, 1978), it will be briefly discussed without reference to other measures because of its particular relevance to our topic.

The format of the ABIC is similar to that of the Vineland. A recorder categorically rates client competencies (latent, emergent, mastered) in relation to several classes of behavior (family role performance, community role performance, peer group role performance, nonacademic school role performance, earner/consumer role performance, self-maintenance role performance) on the basis of information obtained through a knowledgeable informant (e.g., parent). Like the Vineland, the ABIC uses a developmental-hierarchical format, with items placed in chronological order from the simplest to the most difficult, within each age group. The ABIC also contains a subset of items appropriate for use with clients of all ages. In total, the ABIC consists of 242 items distributed across the 6 role-performance subscales. Raw scores are obtained for each of the subscales and are converted to scaled scores on the basis of normative data. Analysis of the scaled scores indicates the client's level of adaptive ability within each behavior class.

The standard instruments for the assessment of adaptive behavior of the mentally retarded are the AAMD Adaptive Behavior Scales (ABS), the most recent of which is the 1975 revision (Nihira et al., 1975). Originally developed in 1969 to provide operational descriptions and measurements of the adaptive behavior of mentally retarded individuals, the 1975 revised edition of the ABS consists of two parts covering 24 behavioral domains. Part I includes 10 behavioral domains (independent functioning, physical development, economic activity, language development, numbers and time, domestic activity, vocation activity, self-direction, responsibility, and socialization) and 21 subdomains. The behavioral domains are organized within a developmental framework with information gathered in a manner similar to that used by the Vineland and the ABIC (interviewing the most knowledgeable informant). Scoring is accomplished in stepwise fashion with the rater/recorder addressing individual items within each subdomain before computing subdomain totals, and finally, by computing domain totals. The raw domain score for each behavior is then matched against normative data for mentally retarded individuals of similar age (ages 3–69 years) that were obtained in institutions in the United States. The procedure for administering and scoring the 14 additional behavior domains of Part II of the ABS is identical to that used in Part I of the scale. However, since Part II addresses social expectations and the measurement of maladaptive behaviors (violent and destructive behavior, antisocial behavior, rebellious behavior, untrustworthy behavior, withdrawal, stereotyped behavior and odd mannerisms, inappropriate interpersonal manners, unacceptable vocal habits, unacceptable or eccentric habits, self-abusive behavior, hyperactive tendencies, sexually aberrant behavior, psychological disturbances, use of medications), domains are not organized using a developmental format. In sum, the 1975 Revision of the ABS yields a behavioral profile in terms of personal-social responsibility that is intended for use in the formulation of individual treatment plans (Nihira et al., 1975).

Although the Vineland, ABIC, and ABS are among the frequently cited measures of adaptive behavior which were noted in the Morrow and Coulter (1978) survey of state policies, a critical comparison of these instruments is in order. The Vineland is perhaps the most widely used and poorest measure of the three. It has been severely criticized for its lack of usefulness in developing strategies for intervention/programming, lack of comprehensiveness in assessing adaptive behavior, and outdated norms. Despite these criticisms, psychologists will often use the Vineland as a substitute for intelligence tests to assess children found to be "untestable," and then use the overall social age as a measure to establish general cognitive levels. Even when the Vineland is used appropriately in conjunction with a standardized measure of intelligence in assessing the mentally retarded for the purpose of identification/classification, psychologists frequently do not use the Vineland to contribute to the decision-making process of diagnosing mental retardation.

The ABIC is a relatively new instrument and has yet to be critically evaluated. However, because it is not recommended for use apart from the total SOMPA system, the ABIC can only be relevant for those individuals for whom the entire SOMPA can be administered. Decisions based on the results of the SOMPA assessment measures are obtained from the combined information on the parent interview, student evaluation, ABIC, the WISC-R, and the Bender-Gestalt. Since the norm of the entire SOMPA including the ABIC is only nonretarded children between the ages of 5 and 12, and the WISC-R and Bender-Gestalt may not be valid for many mentally retarded children in that age group, the ABIC has very limited usefulness for assessing adaptive behavior of the mentally retarded. Future investigations should be directed toward determining if the ABIC can be used independently of the SOMPA, without diminishing its predictive validity, and also establishing norms for its use with mentally retarded children.

Probably the best instrument of the three for assessing adaptive behavior is the AAMD Adaptive Behavior Scale. Comparisons of profiles can be extremely helpful in assessing areas of strength and weakness necessary for developing strategies targeted for intervention/programming. However, since the ABS does not provide an overall rating of adaptive behavior, the scale is limited in its usefulness in assessments for the identification/classification of mental retardation. In addition to this difficulty, the objectivity of some items on the ABS is questionable.

Certainly, the three instruments briefly reviewed are not representative of the total number of behavior checklists and rating scales commonly used with the mentally retarded; each has its advantages and limitations. However, those instruments that are discussed were chosen because of their frequent use as accepted measures of adaptive behavior (Morrow & Coulter, 1978) and/or their meeting a number of criteria (such as reliability, validity, use of normative data, and opportunities to demonstrate appropriate behaviors) deemed important when selecting a particular device for use in the behavioral assessment package (Ciminero & Drabman, 1977).

In conclusion, it is important to note that, as with the use of interview data and information gathered through standardized psychological tests, checklists and rating scales are not sufficiently precise to be used alone and should be used only as one component of the growing list of strategies in the comprehensive behavioral assessment package.

Direct Observation

The most widely used and well-accepted strategy of behavioral assessment is one that is based on direct observation. Its use as a principal method of psychological assessment is as long-standing as that of the interview. However, the rapid development of empirical data based direct observational procedures during the last 10 to 15 years has distinguished it from its traditional counterpart. Beginning with the *psychiatric* narrative, which resulted in global descriptions of overall behavior within general settings to aid in the formulation of diagnostic clinical impressions, the use of direct observation has evolved to a scientific state of higher-order based on the principles of a behavioral psychology which required observations to be objective, measurable, and treatment-oriented. Indeed, much of the current popularity of direct observational procedures as assessment devices is derived precisely from their ability to yield reliable, valid, and quantifiable data that can be easily applied toward problem description, prescriptive treatment, and the evaluation of ongoing programming.

Although direct observation as an assessment strategy is used frequently with the mentally retarded, it is certainly not applied uniquely to this population. As the cornerstone strategy of the behavioral assessment package, it is nonetheless important to review and summarize certain of the direct observational procedures that are commonly employed with the mentally retarded.

As mentioned previously, to be useful, behavioral assessment must eventually rely on direct observation to be sufficiently precise. This strategy calls for the direct observation of both the behavior selected for modification (response assessment) and the antecedent and consequent conditions that serve to maintain it (stimulus assessment). Careful response assessment is necessary first, to determine objectively the extent to which targeted behaviors occur; second, to control the occurrence of reactive changes in the target behavior attributable to the assessment process; and third, to document changes in the target behavior as a function of treatment (Kazdin & Straw, 1976). Similarly, it is important to accurately assess the stimulus conditions (both antecedent and consequent) reliably associated with the target behavior, to determine objectively the relationship between the target behavior and the stimulus events, and to document the effect of a stimulus manipulation on the behavior targeted for change (Kazdin & Straw, 1976).

Within the direct observation strategy of assessment, there are two well-known methods of measuring and recording behavior: event sampling and time sampling. To be effective as measurement devices, both methods require that the behavior being assessed possess characteristics of objectivity (clearly observable and without reference to inner states), clarity (clearly defined and not subject to observer interpretation), and completeness (well-delineated boundary conditions) (Hawkins & Dobes, 1975; Kazdin & Straw, 1976).

Event sampling is a procedure wherein the frequency or duration of a specific behavior is measured for a given period of time. As a measurement device, event sampling is usually thought of as appropriate only if the behavior in question has a clearly observable beginning and end. To obtain a frequency measure, the observer merely records the number of discrete responses that occur within the given time period. For example, a teacher may want to assess the amount of work each student completes daily. By assigning a specified number of worksheets and counting the number completed per day, the teacher has utilized a form of event sampling.

Some behaviors consume varying amounts of time but still retain a clearly definable beginning and end. Although an event sampling technique employing a frequency count per units of time would be applicable, the behavior would be better suited for duration measurement. For this measure, the observer records the elapsed time that is spent performing the response targeted for treatment, and then calculates a sum total for the given time period. For example, a child's out-of-seat behavior may have different durations. A frequency measure may be misleading if the child is out-of-seat for varying periods of time. By recording a total time out-of-seat per day, a more accurate measure of behavior can be obtained.

In cases where a specific behavior is not discrete, making it difficult to judge when a response ends and another begins, time sampling may provide the assessor with more meaningful data. Time sampling is an assessment method based on units of time rather than events. Among the most common forms of time sampling is interval recording, of which there are two types: *continuous* and *noncontinuous*. In *continuous* interval recording, behavior is sampled for a given block of time (e.g., 20 min) each day with the time block being divided into shorter observation intervals (e.g., 10 sec). The targeted response is then scored as having occurred or not occurred within each separate interval of observation. Target responses are noted as occurring only once per interval and can be readily expressed as a percentage across intervals. For example, if a pupil is out-of-seat at least once during 90 of the 120 10-sec intervals contained in a 20-min observation period, the pupil can be said to be out-of-seat 75 % of the observed intervals. In certain cases where multiple-target behaviors are observed, an observer may find that continuous interval recording does not allow sufficient time for recording data. In this case, noncontinuous interval recording may be used. *Noncontinuous* interval recording is identical to continuous interval recording with the exception of standardized departures from observation to allow the assessor to record data. Using the example above, behaviors would still be sampled for 20 min with 10-sec observation intervals, however, each interval would be followed by a 5-sec pause to record data. Thus, the total number of intervals (120) are reduced by one-third to 80. Given a reasonable degree of response stability, the pupil in our example would be observed out-of-seat during 60 of the 80 10-sec intervals within a 20-min noncontinuous interval sampling period.

As mentioned previously, the strength of direct observation as a strategy for behavioral assessment is derived not only from its good face validity (seeing is believing) and its ability to produce quantifiable data, but also the reliability of the data. As with any assessment method, the role of reliability is extremely important. It is vital to the effective analysis of behavior that everyone is "seeing" and "believing" the same thing. In direct observational procedures, such as those reviewed (frequency and duration measures, interval recording), interobserver agreement is the most commonly applied statistical method for determining reliability estimates. In order to assess the consistency of observations, two raters must simultaneously and independently record behavior. These occasions (known as reliability checks) are important because they contribute to the careful nature of response and stimulus assessments by empirically determining that the behavior under observation is clearly and sufficiently defined, and that it is being rated objectively (Kazdin & Straw, 1976).

In event sampling, interobserver reliability is usually obtained through a comparison of the event totals (frequency or duration) of each observer across a given time period. Reliability is calculated by dividing the smaller total by the larger one and then multiplying the quotient by 100 to form a percentage agreement. Using our example, if one observer recorded a pupil to be out-of-seat 10 times (or for 10 min) across the school day and the second observer rated him as out-of-seat only 9 times (or for only 9 min), the interobserver agreement would equal $9/10 \times 100$ or 90%.

With time sampling, reliability data are typically computed on an interval-by-interval basis of agreement. The number of intervals in which two independent observers agreed that a target response occurred are summed and divided by the number of disagreement plus agreement intervals. This quotient is then multiplied by 100 and expressed as a percentage.

Although this type of calculation of reliability is the one most frequently found in the literature, much effort has been devoted to discussion of the technical problems encountered in both assessment of reliability and biases in data collection obtained through direct observation. Interested readers should consult Hartmann (1977), Kent and Foster (1977), and articles in the Spring 1977 issue of the *Journal of Applied Behavior Analysis*.

In sum, direct observational procedures, such as event sampling and time sampling, have both advantages and disadvantages. Both provide meaningful treatment-related data but involve a commitment on behalf of the clinician to consistent long-term observation which may become inconvenient over time. Frequency and duration recording are direct techniques that are easily learned and require no special equipment beyond a mechanical counter, paper and pencil, and/or a stopwatch. However, as noted previously, these recording techniques are inflexible to changes in the discreteness of response. For example, if the behavior under observation should lose its clearly definable beginning and end, the accuracy of the data is compromised. In this regard, a time-sampling method, such as interval recording, is more flexible to variable response performance. However, interval recording requires such special equipment as coded behavioral sheets and tape recorders to insure the accuracy of observation, which can become cumbersome. In addition, time-sampling methods (including interval observation) have been criticized for not accurately representing the magnitude of the behavior under observation, particularly when the target behavior is subject to high rates of responding or response bursts (Repp, Roberts, Slack, Repp, & Berkler, 1976). The magnitude of a target behavior may be grossly underestimated if it is simply recorded as having occurred or not occurred within each individual interval of observation. For example, a target behavior which occurs more than once within an interval or only once each interval during the baseline observation would be recorded similarly. The number of intervals in which the target behavior occurred would be calculated and expressed as 100% of the observation intervals. By the same token, treatment may be applied and the target behavior "reduced" to a single occurrence within each individual interval, or for only half its duration across the same block of time. The target behavior would continue to be expressed as having occurred during 100% of the observation intervals; since it occurred at least once in each interval, the effect of treatment would not be clearly represented by the data.

Despite these limitations, comprehensive behavioral assessment depends heavily on obtaining the clearest and most descriptive response definition available; one that is meaningful to both treatment prescription and evaluation. To this end, direct observation provides the most effective strategy, particularly if one considers that many of the limitations of data collection methods can either be minimized or eliminated altogether if the clinician takes the time to make a careful, concrete definition of the response targeted for observation and if the clinician is aware of existing alternative methods of direct observational measurement. The particular measure which may reflect a more accurate description of the data cannot be categorically specified. What is more essential, however, is that the clinician be able to match data collection technique to the information to be discussed.

Analysis of Behavior Change

Up to this point, the review of current strategies of behavioral assessment have included the major techniques used to determine the existing levels of behavior prior to the implementation of any programs designed to effect behavior change. As noted previously, one of the critical differences between behavioral and traditional assessment is the focus on treatment rather than on diagnosis. As such, empirical demonstration of the relationship of the intervention strategy to changes in the behavior selected for treatment is one of the most important features of behavioral assessment. In this regard, there exist several single-case

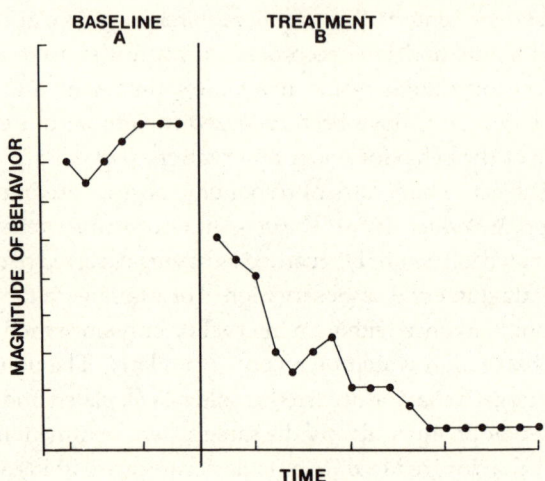

FIGURE 1. An example of the A-B (baseline, treatment) design.

experimental designs that are commonly employed as strategies for studying behavioral change. These include the basic A-B design and A-B-A-B (reversal) design (Baer, Wolf, & Risley, 1968; Hersen & Barlow, 1976), the multiple baseline design (Baer, Wolf, & Risley, 1968; Hersen & Barlow, 1976), and the alternating-treatments design (Barlow & Hayes, 1979), also known as the simultaneous-treatment design (Kazdin & Hartmann, 1978), and the multiple schedule design (Hersen & Barlow, 1976).

The A-B design, an example of which is presented in Figure 1, is the simplest of the single-case strategies. In this design, the magnitude of the behavior targeted for change is measured through repeated observations across two phases of study: baseline (A) and treatment (B). The baseline or A phase represents the natural magnitude of the target behavior under the identified conditions in which treatment will be implemented. The B phase represents the magnitude of the target behavior after the independent variable (treatment) has been introduced or manipulated. Any change in the magnitude of the target behavior during the B phase is attributed to the introduction of treatment and provides a direct ongoing means for assessing the effectiveness of treatment.

An elaboration of the baseline-treatment (A-B) design is the A-B-A-B (reversal) design. Its use is preferable to the simple baseline-treatment approach because it allows for a clear demonstration of experimental control. For the reversal design, the baseline and treatment phases are replicated (A-B-A-B) to assess whether change in the magnitude of the target behavior occurs as a function of the manipulation of the treatment procedure. If, as in Figure 2, the level of the

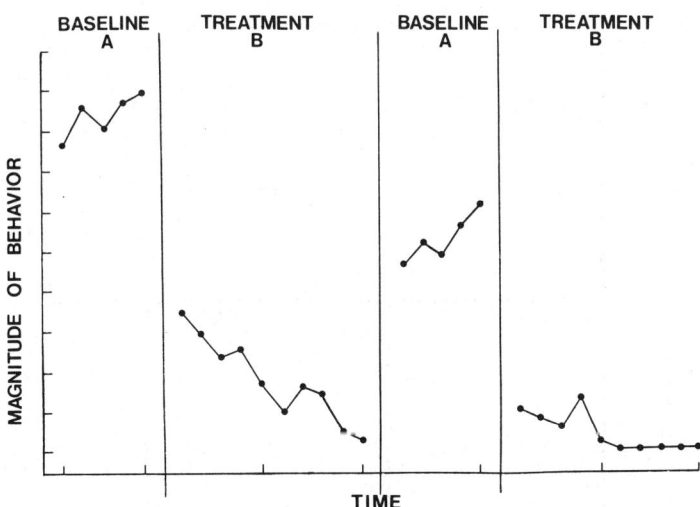

FIGURE 2. An example of the A-B-A-B (baseline, treatment, baseline, treatment) design.

target behavior "reverses" correspondent to first withdrawing and then restoring treatment, a certain degree of experimental control is established, and the conclusion that treatment is the variable affecting the change is strengthened (Hersen & Barlow, 1976). This is important in behavioral assessment since it can provide accountability for both the treatment procedure and the therapist.

The multiple-baseline design is used primarily as an alternative to the A-B-A B design, when for practical or ethical reasons the systematic withdrawal and restoration of treatment is inadvisable. In the multiple-baseline design employing a single subject, separate A-B designs are established for two or more behaviors targeted for change, or for a single target behavior that occurs in two or more settings. A multiple-baseline design across subjects can also be designed by targeting a single behavior presented by two or more subjects in the same setting for change. In Figure 3, the treatment or B phase of the second and succeeding A-B designs is delayed until some effect is evident on the targeted behavior in the first A-B design. Experimental control is established if the magnitude of the behavior(s) targeted for treatment in the second and successive baselines changes only upon the introduction of treatment (B) following the first baseline phase. In turn, each replication of controlled change with the sequential application of treatment enhances experimental control and increases confidence in the effectiveness of the treatment procedure.

Single-case experimental strategies for studying behavior change have been greatly enhanced by the advent of the unique alternating-treatments design which allows for a direct comparison of treatments within the same sub-

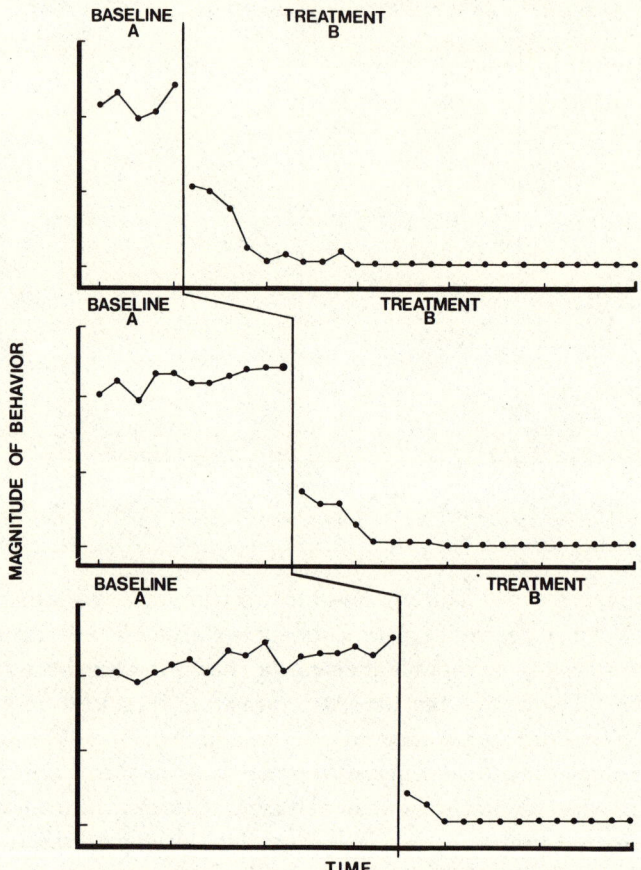

FIGURE 3. An example of the multiple-baseline design.

ject. In this approach, which can be conceptualized as an A-B-B' design, a single target behavior is identified and observed for a baseline phase comprised of alternating stimulus conditions, such as time periods or therapists, which are in accordance with a planned schedule of intervention. After stable response levels across the alternating time periods of baseline (A) are achieved, two or more separate conditions of treatment (B) are implemented. During the B (treatment) phase, each of the separate treatment conditions is presented alternately in counterbalanced fashion across the same stimulus conditions present during baseline. Typically, the design is extended to include a B' phase to allow the more effective treatment to replace the less effective one. Although in its present form this design allows for a direct comparison of treatment effec-

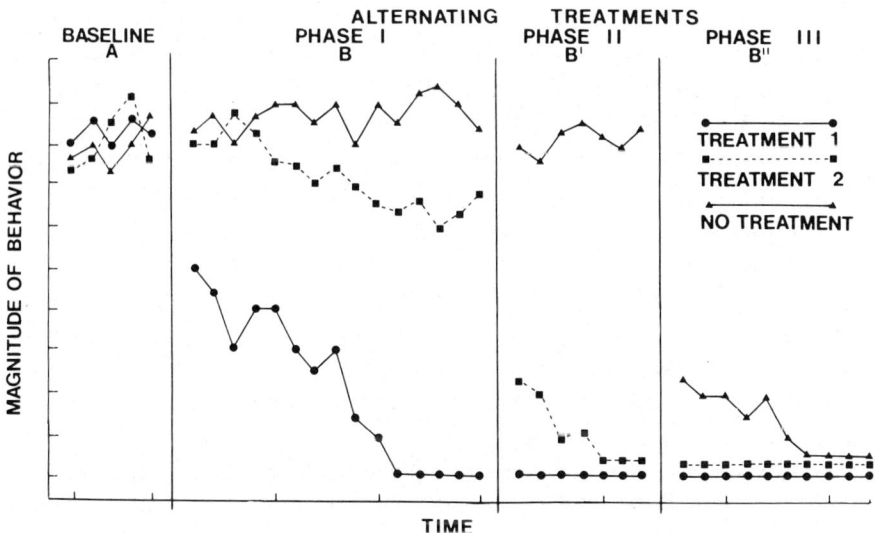

FIGURE 4. An example of the alternating-treatment design.

tiveness, it does not show evidence of experimental control. The simple witnessing of the differential impact of separate treatments does not experimentally rule out the possibility that the target behavior was influenced by extraneous variables during the phases of active intervention (B, B'). Yet, this problem appears to be easily remedied. An ideal example of the alternating-treatments design which will provide a demonstration of functional control is presented in Figure 4. In this example, stable behavior levels across the alternating time periods of baseline (A) have been achieved. During the B (treatment) phase, two separate conditions of treatment and one of no treatment were presented alternately in counterbalanced fashion and in accordance with the observation schedule used during baseline. After it was clear that one of the treatments was more effective, the design was extended to a B' phase and the less effective treatment was replaced by the treatment of choice. The final step of our example extends the design to include a B" phase, wherein the remaining treatment replaces the no-treatment condition. In this respect, the use of a no-treatment condition allows the alternating-treatments design to provide not only valuable information pertaining to the differential impact of separate treatments on a single target behavior, but also a clear demonstration of experimental control as well, if given the relatively stable rates of responding in the no-treatment condition across all phases (A-B-B'-B") of study.

In sum, each of the single-case designs presented here as strategies for assessing behavioral change have both advantages and disadvantages in their use. The A-B design, although simple and straightforward, is actually quasi-experimental (Campbell & Stanley, 1966) in nature and presents no clear evidence of the functional relationship between treatment and behavior change. Thus, changes in behavior which are attributed to treatment are accepted only with "some major reservations." (Hersen & Barlow, 1976, p. 169). The A-B-A-B reversal design, despite its popular use and potential to establish clear experimental control through the systematic withdrawal and restoration of treatment, may be impractical or unethical in some cases, since such a systematic manipulation of treatment procedures may allow behaviors to recover temporarily while treatment is withdrawn, which oftentimes may be undesirable. Conversely, it has been noted that many behaviors which have been therapeutically changed will not reverse upon withdrawal of treatment, perhaps owing to environmental variables which act to maintain the change after some critical level has been achieved (Mann, 1976). Although the multiple-baseline design has a number of advantages, particularly that it demonstrates the functional control of treatment over behavior change without a temporary withdrawal of treatment, it also has disadvantages. In general, two or more baselines of stable response magnitude must be established before treatment can be initiated, and this is time consuming. Even then, because of design characteristics (the same behavior in a different setting, a different behavior in the same setting, or other individuals with the same behavior in the same setting), target behaviors remain unchanged for relative amounts of time throughout the sequential application of treatment. And finally, despite its promise as a most valuable strategy in clinical practice, the alternating-treatments design is subject to threats of internal validity because of multiple-treatment interference (Ullmann & Sulzer-Azaroff, 1975) as well as the difficulties inherent in the feasibility of meeting all the requirements of counterbalancing stimulus conditions.

Nonetheless, each of the designs reviewed provide the clinician with valuable information about the relative effectiveness of treatment. With the exception of the A-B design, each possesses the potential to demonstrate convincingly the functional relationships of treatment procedures to behavior change. Thus, the empirical demonstration of treatment effectiveness is the ultimate goal of behavioral assessment. Moreover, if the clinician is well practiced in the experimental strategies for studying behavioral change, many of the disadvantages can be minimized and in some cases avoided altogether through the knowledge of the most appropriate design.

Behavioral Assessment of Adaptive Behavior: Common Skill Deficits in the Mentally Retarded

As previously noted, a defining characterisitc of mental retardation is deficits in adaptive behavior. In fact, unless deficits in adaptive behavior are present, the diagnostic classification of mental retardation is not appropriate according to the AAMD definition of mental retardation (Grossman, 1977). Some investigators have advocated that children evidencing deficits in intellecutal functioning but not adaptive behavior have been consistently mislabeled as mentally retarded (Mercer, 1973). Because deficits in adaptive behavior are central in identifying this population, the assessment of these deficits takes on an extremely important role.

This section, athough it does not include all behavioral deficits of the mentally retarded, will focus on the specific skill deficits of self-care, classroom behavior, social skills, vocational skills, and language development. A behavioral excess common to many mentally retarded persons, stereotyped behavior, will also be briefly explored. Samples of research related to the strategies of assessing these behaviors will be discussed.

Self-Care Skills

Deficits in self-care skills are particularly prevalent among mentally retarded persons. With younger children and with more severely mentally retarded persons, these deficits are more frequently present in such specific skill areas as eating, dressing, toileting, cleanliness, and other independent living skills. Older children and adolescents often show additional deficits in community-living skills, such as transportation, communication, and economics. Expectations of mastery in each skill area are directly dependent on the level of mental retardation evident, with the persons of higher cognitive ability thereby having more potential to achieve a greater degree of independence. Because deficiencies in self-care are the major characteristic of mentally retarded persons, the assessment of these skills becomes essential.

Numerous instruments have been developed to assess self-care skills in mentally retarded persons but it is beyond the scope of this chapter to cover in detail all these instruments and their related research findings. Interested readers should see Walls et al. (1977). Instead, an attempt will be made to discuss some of the more commonly used assessment instruments, examining the specifics of these scales alone.

Scales which have been developed for the assessment of self-care skills in the mentally retarded have not been developed specifically either for the purpose of identification/classification or intervention/programming. However, professionals using them have found certain scales to be more amenable for identification/classification, whereas others are more pertinent for intervention/programming. As noted earlier, the scale which has probably received the widest notoriety and acceptance, and as a result the assessment tool which is the standard in the field, is the American Association on Mental Deficiency Adaptive Behavior Scale (ABS) (Nihira et al., 1975). The scale (see p. 170) for a description) contains two subscales arranged along developmental lines. One scale provides an assessment of the skills related to personal independence and daily living in 10 domains. The second subscale measures the degree of maladaptive or unacceptable behavior exhibited across 14 domains. Two sets of norms have been developed: one for institutionalized children and adults from ages 3 to 69 functioning in all ranges of retardation, and one for children in public schools between ages 7 and 13 enrolled in classes for educable and trainable mentally retarded, emotionally handicapped, and "normal" children (Lambert et al., 1974). Coulter and Morrow (1978a) note that between the two versions of the ABS, the institutional version is most often used for intervention/programming, whereas the public school version is used for both identification/classification and intervention/programming. However, research examining the predictive validity of the ABS public school version for identification/classification of the mentally retarded is not extensive.

Malone and Christian (1974) examined the utility of the ABS (Part I) as a screening device in the special education placement of 126 institutionalized mentally retarded children and adolescents. Subjects consisted of four educational levels (developmental, primary, intermediate one, intermediate two) as determined to present academic functioning, IQ scores, age, and subjective assessments of behavior by teachers. Correlations of scores on the ABS (Part I), Wide Range Achievement Test (Jastak & Jastak, 1965), and an IQ test (Stanford-Binet, WAIS, or WISC-R) were obtained. Results of this analysis found that the ABS provided differentiation between training levels. The findings suggested that the ABS could be used to discriminate among classifications of mentally retarded persons as well as IQ scores. Unfortunately, Malone and Christian (1974), by summing all subdomain scores on the ABS and subjecting the data to univariate analyses of variance, obscured profile differences of specific combinations of subdomains that discriminate between levels of mentally retarded persons.

Although the efforts of Malone and Christian (1974) were well intentioned, it is important to realize that the ABS was not designed to give one score of overall adaptive behavior (Lambert, 1978). Scores on the ABS are profiled and determinations regarding levels of adaptive behavior could best be established by comparing the individual's scores to those of nonretarded, educably mentally retarded, trainably mentally retarded, or emotionally handicapped children.

Gully and Hosch (1979), in responding to this criticism, used a discriminant analysis technique to analyze the results of the ABS scores of 588 6 to 12-year-old children selected from educably and trainably mentally retarded, and nonretarded classrooms. Their study found the ABS accurately discriminated 91.2% of the nonretarded subjects and 88.2% of the trainable subjects. Educably mentally retarded subjects were most likely to be mislabeled as only 66.1% of these subjects were correctly identified. Overall, their findings tend to support the use of the ABS as a screening instrument in the diagnostic process of identification/classification.

In a further attempt to validate the domain and subdomain components, a number of studies have been performed in which factor analysis of the ABS scales has been the subject of investigation. Nihira (1969a,b), working with institutionalized children, adolescents, and adults, found that the analysis of combined scores on both Parts I and II tend to yield three orthogonal factors in the areas of personal independence, social maladaptation, and personal maladaptation. The presence of these factors made clear the need to include maladaptive behavior as a dimension of adaptive behavior. More recent factor-analytic studies examined adaptive behavior in mentally retarded persons living in the community rather than in institutions. Lambert and Nicoll (1976) used the public school version of the ABS and found two orthogonal factors within Part I of the scale: functional autonomy and social responsibility. In addition, the two factors noted within Part II of the ABS in the Nihira (1969a, b) studies were also evident. Another analysis by Guarnaccia (1976) of mentally retarded adults reported four factors labeled personal independence, personal responsibility, productivity, and social responsibility within Part I of the scale.

Based on the findings of the factor-analytic studies, Nihira (1978) has attempted to develop a new system for classifying Part I of the scale for all mentally retarded persons. As a result, 10 factors were identified and grouped under three general classifications established by previous factor analyses. Table I presents Nihira's reconceptualization of factors in the ABS (Part I). Even though future empirical validation of Nihira's findings is needed, the new classification scheme does provide a straightforward means of interpreting the profiles of the ABS.

Another adaptive behavior scale which has been used as a measure for

TABLE I
Nihira's Factor Analytic Scheme for the ABS (Part I)[a]

Personal self-sufficiency

Factors	Neuromotor (all ages)	Self-help (all ages)	Sensory (child and adolescents)
Items	1. Use of utensils 3. Drinking 24. Body balance 25. Walking and running 26. Control of hands 27. Limb function	5. Toilet trained 6. Self-care, toilet 7. Wash hands and face 8. Bathing 10. Toothbrushing 11. Menstruation 15. Dressing 16. Undressing 17. Shoes	22. Vision 23. Hearing

Community self-sufficiency

Factors	Community-I (all ages)	Community-II (child and adolescents)	Cognitive (child and adolescents)	Communication (child and adolescents)	Speech (adult)
Items	2. Eat in public 18. Sense of direction 21. Miscellaneous independent functioning 30. Errands 31. Purchase 46. Table settings 47. Food preparation 48. Table clearing 49. General domestic	9. Personal hygiene 13. Clothing 14. Care of clothing 19. Public transportation 20. Telephone 45. Laundry	28. Money 29. Budget 32. Write 37. Read 41. Number 42. Time 43. Time concept	33. Preverbal expression 34. Articulation 35. Sentences 36. Word usage 38. Complex instructions 39. Conversations 40. Miscellaneous 41. Numbers	23. Hearing 33. Preverbal expression 34. Articulation 35. Sentences 36. Word usage

Personal social responsibility

Factors	Self-direction (adult)	Socialization (adult)	Personal-Social (child and adult)
Items	51. Self-direction 52. Work habits 53. Initiative 54. Passivity 55. Attention 56. Persistence 57. Leisure time 58. Personal belongings 59. General responsibility	60. Cooperation 61. Consideration 62. Aware of others 63. Interaction 64. Participation in groups	53. Initiative 54. Passivity 55. Attention 57. Leisure time 58. Personal belongings 59. General responsibility 60. Cooperation 61. Consideration 62. Aware of others 63. Interaction 64. Participates in groups

[a] Adapted from K. Nihira, "Factorial Description of the AAMD Adaptive Behavior Scale." In W. A. Coulter & H. W. Morrow (Eds), *Adaptive behavior: Concepts and measurements*, New York: Grune & Stratton, 1978. (Used by permission).

identification/classification is the Adaptive Behavior Inventory for Children (ABIC), which is part of the System of Multipluralistic Asssessment-SOMPA (Mercer & Lewis, 1977). The norm of this scale is a sample of 2,080 children between the ages of 5–11 from three ethnic groups (Anglo, black, Hispanic). Scores on six subtests of the ABIC comprise the adaptive behavior score and norms are available to compare the child directly to a child in the same chronological age group. The scale is not intended to be used as an independent measure but as part of a more elaborate assessment system. At present, no research has been published specifically to examine the scale alone.

Among the other scales commonly used for purposes of identification/classification has been the Vineland Social Maturity Scale (Doll, 1965). The scale provides an overall social quotient based on the total raw score obtained on the instrument. Thus, one is able to establish a social age for the individual and use this score as part of the determination of functioning level. Unfortunately, many investigators have severely criticized the Vineland for conclusions which have often been drawn from correlation studies with IQ scores. Leland, Shellhaas, Nihira, and Foster (1967) note that it is methodologically incorrect to compare scores on the two tests, since the normative distributions from the two tests have different means and standard deviations. In fact, Heber (1962) has stated that the imprecision of the norms of the Vineland forces psychologists to regard the IQ test as a better measure of adaptive behavior. Although Heber's statement is dated and is no longer true because of the proliferation of adaptive behavior scales since that time, many professionals continue to rely on the Vineland Social Maturity Scale as their only measure of adaptive behavior.

Assessment instruments used for the purpose of identification/classification of self-care skills offer the examiner a profile of relative strengths and weaknesses, but provide limited information for designing intervention and remediation strategies. The scales are referenced by norms and give minimal assistance in identifying behavioral objectives for treatment. Instruments which have been used specifically for the purpose of intervention/programming differ in both methodology and number from those designed and used primarily for identification/classification. These instruments are built on the principles of task analysis and are referenced by criteria. Individual subareas of self-care skills are delineated into small, discrete units which lead to the mastery of more complex skills. Assessment is performed primarily through direct observation of the individual under baseline conditions. The person's maximum abilities to perform certain subskills are determined, and programming begins at this point. Most often, assessment instruments of this type are developed by the individual assessor.

However, a variety of published scales do exist. Walls *et al.* (1977) and Coulter and Morrow (1978b) provide detailed lists of some of the available instruments.

The use of these and other individualized assessment scales have been found in the voluminous literature in the self-care area. Programs to teach such skills as toileting (Foxx & Azrin, 1973), buttoning (Adelson-Bernstein & Sandow, 1978), self-feeding (Knapczyk & Livingston, 1977), pedestrian skills (Matson, 1980), telephone use (Leff, 1974, 1975), and comprehensive meal-time behavior (Matson, Ollendick, & Adkins, 1980) have been successfully implemented in all levels and ages of mentally retarded persons. Almost unanimously, these programs have been based on the principles of the operant shaping of behavior.

On the basis of an assessment of skill levels present before beginning treatment, behaviors and skill areas in need of treatment are selected. The specific behaviors are then taught, using the techniques of prompting, shaping, and fading. Essentially, individuals are reinforced for successively better approximation of the targeted behavior until such behavior is demonstrated as consistently present in the person's repertoire. The use of these techniques has consistently been found to be the most effective means for teaching self-care skills to mentally retarded persons of all ages.

Classroom Behavior

Since the passage of laws governing the right-to-education of the handicapped, mentally retarded children at all cognitive levels have been afforded educational experiences. The instructional curriculum is based on the functioning level of the children (educable, trainable, severe/profound) with less emphasis given to academics (reading, writing, and arithmetic) and with more stress on functional daily-living skills and vocational skills as the progression moves from the mild to the profound range of mental retardation. Also, within each level of retardation, increased emphasis is placed on vocational abilities as the child proceeds through adolescence.

Most classroom studies with mentally retarded persons have primarily examined the manipulation of on-task or disruptive behavior. Assessments of these behaviors are obtained within some format of direct behavioral observation. For example, Shapiro and Klein (1980) observed four moderately mentally retarded, severely disturbed children in a classroom setting by observing each child for a 10-sec period in succession and by marking whether they were on-task or not. Attending behavior consisted of sitting in a chair or standing directly in front of the test area, visually attending to the task, and working toward task completion. The child had to be attentive for the entire 10 sec to be scored as on-task. Almost all studies examining this variable have been recorded in a similar manner (Broden, Bruce, Mitchell, Carter, & Hall, 1970; Hill & Strain, 1977; Kazdin, 1977; Kazdin & Geesey, 1977; Strain & Pierce, 1977).

Studies which have focused on the manipulation of disruptive behaviors in the classroom have assessed these behaviors in a manner comparable to the assessment of on-task behavior. For example, O'Leary, Kaufman, Kass, and Drabman (1970) developed a behavioral coding system based on 20-sec observations. The categories of disruptive behavior are: (1) out of chair, (2) modified out of chair, (3) touching other's property, (4) vocalization, (5) playing, (6) orienting, (7) noise, (8) aggression, and (9) time off-task. Their system was designed to be applicable across populations and has been subsequently used in studies of adolescent residents in a psychiatric hospital (Santogrossi, O'Leary, Romancyzk, & Kaufman, 1973; Turkewitz, O'Leary, & Ironsmith, 1975) as well as disruptive moderately to mildly mentally retarded children (Robertson, Simon, Pachman, & Drabman, 1980).

An additional variable which has often been of interest in classroom research with the mentally retarded is the modification of academic performance rates. The assessment of academic behavior is relatively straightforward, using a method of direct observation. Most often, the use of a frequency count of permanent products (e.g., number of math problems solved, number of words identified, number of colors matched) is employed as a dependent measure. An issue which has emerged from this area of research is the relationship between on-task behavior, accuracy, and performance. Klein (1979) provides a comprehensive review of the literature in this area.

Social Skills

One particular area in which mentally retarded persons by definition are deficient is social skills (Grossman, 1977). As conceptualized by behavioral investigators with primarily nonretarded populations, social skills refers to a rather global construct which pertains to a variety of more specific behaviors evident in interpersonal interactions (Curran, 1979; Hersen & Bellack, 1976). Studies examining social skill deficits in nonretarded populations have focused typically on assertiveness (McFall & Lillesand, 1971) or heterosocial behavior (Arkowitz, Lichenstein, McGowen, & Hines, 1975). Within each of these categories of behavior, skills that comprise assertiveness or heterosocial behavior have been varied and dependent on the specific situation in which the skill is studied (Eisler, 1976).

The behavioral assessment of social skills with nonretarded populations has primarily used self-report measures, role-play tests, or direct observation. Self-report measures have consisted primarily of paper-and-pencil inventories. While such methods provide an opportunity to assess social skills through direct client contact, the difficulties inherent in self-report measures are well known. Direct observation, a very common strategy of behavioral assessment, has also been used to examine the relationship between social skills and depression (Lewinsohn, 1975; Lewinsohn & Shaffer, 1971). The advantages of naturalistic and direct observation, however, are contradicted by the economic and practical restrictions imposed by this method. Not only is direct observation costly in terms of time and manpower, but this strategy is obviously not applicable for those individuals treated on an outpatient basis. As a result, behavior therapists have often used role-play tests to assess social skills. Situations analogous to real-life experiences are presented by confederates while trained observers assess the behaviors of the clients. Investigators have used both standardized role-play tests, such as the Behavioral Assertiveness Test (Eisler, Miller, & Hersen, 1973), and role-play tests in which the investigator develops scenes specific to the area under study. Results obtained during the role-played test are assumed to be representative of responses in other similar real-life situations. Recently, however, some evidence casting doubt on this assumption has been found (Bellack, Hersen, & Lamparski, 1979; Bellack, Hersen, & Turner, 1978, 1979).

Social skills, when referring to mentally retarded populations, consist of the same basic skill areas as nonretarded persons but are conceptualized in a more molecular fashion. Such target behaviors as eye contact, making appropriate requests, and voice moderation, which typically are included as subcategories of overall social skills with nonretarded persons, are viewed as entire classes of skill deficits targeted for treatment with the mentally retarded (Marchetti & Matson, 1981).

Strategies which have been used to assess social skills with the nonretarded have typically been used with mentally retarded populations as well, with the exception of most self-report measures. Because of the limitations in demonstrating cognitive functioning, the paper-and-pencil inventories and the interviews are assumed to be of dubious value. Instead, most studies that examine social skills in the mentally retarded have used either direct observation or role-play tests.

In the first study directed at improving social skills in mentally retarded persons, Ross (1969) attempted to increase the recognition of social responses in 32 educably mentally retarded children ranging in ages from 3 to 10 years. The assessment of social skills was performed by presenting 10 social situations to the children. All items were presented in doll-play and live-model formats and consisted of typical child interactions involving play skills. The verbal behaviors of each child were rated based on the completeness of their answers. For example, if the child responded by apologizing, he would receive one point. If he both apologized and made retribution, he received two points. Both attention placebo and nonretarded control groups were included in the study. Treatment consisted of the use of modeling and role playing combined with primary and secondary reinforcement. Results of the study were that the mentally retarded children in the treatment condition made significantly greater improvement in social responsiveness compared to either control group.

Nelson, Gibson, and Cutting (1973) used a role-play test to assess conversation skills in a mildly mentally retarded boy. The child was presented with social situations requiring the use of grammatically correct questions and appropriate conversation. Observers rated the child's behavior on the specific target behaviors. Subsequent training consisted of modeling, instructions, and social reinforcement after the child watched two appropriate peer models on videotape. The training program was found to be highly successful in increasing the target behaviors. These gains were evident at the 3½ month follow-up.

Lee (1977), in a group study, focused on social skills with mentally retarded adults. Social skills were assessed through a combination of standardized rating scales, staff rating, and verbal reports of the subjects. Using institutionalized moderately to mildly retarded persons, training was provided in group counseling sessions dealing with the specific skills of social interaction, personal appearance, physical mannerisms, awareness of feelings, making friends, and social responsibility. In addition to the administration of the AAMD Adaptive Behavior Scale and the Peabody Picture Vocabulary Test, peer nominations of those with whom they would prefer to work and play and the ward staff's rank ordering of the residents according to frequency of socially inappropriate behaviors all served as assessments of social skills. The results of the study found the greatest improvement in pre-postassessment evident for the treatment group on all measurements except staff nominations.

Recently, Matson and his colleagues have developed a complex social skills training package for treating the mentally retarded. The training package and assessment techniques have been successfully implemented in a number of studies with institutionalized mentally retarded adults (Matson & Earnhardt,

1982; Matson & Zeiss, 1978, 1979). The program was first used with four institutionalized, extremely aggressive, mentally retarded adults who were also diagnosed as psychotic (Matson & Stephens, 1978). During the treatment phase, social skills training was provided daily for 10 to 40 minutes. Ten role-played scenes were selected based on the description of events which had been observed to result in fighting in the ward. Six scenes were presented during each training session. Data were also collected by having the ward staff note the number of fights or arguments occurring throughout the day by the target and/or control subjects.

Social skills were assessed by having the therapist present a scene and scoring the response of the subject. Behaviors were recorded as either present or absent during each of the role-played scenes. Target behaviors identified for the subjects consisted of frequency of looking, inappropriate requests, inappropriate laughing, irrelevant comments, and interruptions. In addition, 6 other behaviors were rated by observers on a 1–5 scale (1 = negative or inappropriate, 5 = positive or appropriate). The behaviors rated were: appropriate content, overall assertiveness, physical appearance, facial mannerisms, posture, and appropriate affect.

The results of this extensive effort at training and assessing social skills in institutionalized mentally retarded, psychotic adults show that the treatment package was successful in controlling extremely aggressive behavior. Follow-up data showed that the training effects were maintained at three months post-treatment, although some reduction in the effectiveness of the procedures was evident beyond this time. More importantly, this study provides a strong example of the adaptation of a behavioral assessment technique typically used with nonretarded adults to a mentally retarded population.

Vocational Skills

For mildly retarded adolescents or adults, the appropriate placement into jobs in which they can be successful is a difficult task. Often, the mentally retarded person may possess the ability to perform the required job but may not have attained sufficient social skills to be accepted by fellow workers. In other cases, the mentally retarded person may appear socially appropriate but may not have adequate skills to meet the demands of the job. As a result of this need for proper job placement, the use of vocational evaluation with the mentally retarded has assumed increasing importance.

Within the field of vocational evaluation, contrasting assessment methods have been employed. Historically, one of the most common instruments consists of an endless variety of paper-and-pencil tests which are used to measure hypothesized underlying traits and abilities related to the characteristics of individuals in particular occupations. These types of instruments have obvious limitations when assessing both mentally retarded and nonretarded persons.

Two types of alternative assessment devices to paper–and–pencil tests have been developed. Work-sample assessments consist of a series of tasks assigned to clients. Persons are observed by the evaluator throughout their work and are judged on both performance on the task compared to a normative sample and behavioral characteristics evident during their work. On completion of the entire series of work samples, the evaluator determines the worker's traits, based on the profiles of the individual. By matching those traits with occupations which require such traits, the client is provided with a list of occupations in which they would have a high chance of success. For example, on one such work sample, the Vocational Information and Evaluation Work Sample, if a client shows his best performance on rubber stamping, tile sorting, and nut packing, he would be told that according to the *Dictionary of Occupation Titles* (U.S. Department of Labor, 1965) he would best be suited for jobs as mail-order filler or lining matcher.

A number of standardized work-sample assessment systems have been developed, such as the Comprehensive Occupational Assessment and Training System (Pisauro, 1976), the Hester Evaluation System (Botterbusch, 1975), the Micro-Tower System (Piller, 1976), and the Vocational Information and Evaluation Work Samples (VIEWS) (Rosen, 1977). Among the four mentioned, only the VIEWS has been specifically normed on mentally retarded clients. The VIEWS contains 16 work samples organized around four worker trait groups: elemental areas of work, clerical work, machine work, and crafts work. The entire evaluation process takes 20–35 hours. Clients are also observed regarding such behaviors as punctuality, attendance, responses to instruction, and communication. Norms are available on 104 mentally retarded persons between the ages of 16 and 61 with a median IQ of 50. Recommendations for occupational placement are based on the specific combination of worker traits obtained from the assessment (Botterbusch, 1977).

Although the VIEWS provides a means for evaluating the vocational potential of mentally retarded adults, it is theoretically based clearly on a more traditional approach to assessment. As noted previously regarding traditional assessment, behavior and performance during the evaluation is believed to be representative of a more general response class and not specifically related to the stimuli present when the work sample was collected. The assumption of underlying worker traits is a further indication of the particular traditional viewpoint implicit in work-sample assessment.

Two types of vocational assessment closely analogous to behavioral assessment are on-the-job evaluation and sheltered employment. Evaluations performed on-the-job are conducted by placing the client in one more real work situations with assessments of the client's abilities and behavior provided under actual employment conditions. In sheltered employment, the client is placed in a job situation analogous to conditions evident in competitive employment (Botterbusch, 1977). Unfortunately, no standardized instruments exist for assessing performance in either on-the-job evaluations or sheltered employment assessment. Essentially, evaluators must develop their own instruments and operational definitions of expected behaviors based on general guidelines provided by prospective employers (Botterbusch, 1977). Often, the high cost of this more behaviorally based evaluation system prohibits its use.

Language Development

It is a truism that communication skills are among the behavioral domains considered fundamental to the development of adaptive functioning, particularly regarding social, educational, and vocational skills. As such, a number of speech and language assessment devices have been developed. The majority of these instruments have traditionally focused on the evaluation of receptive (aural input) and expressive (oral output) abilities and the diagnosis of various dysfunctions related to either or both of these skill areas. Since it is beyond the scope of this chapter to review these instruments and their related research findings, an attempt will be made to discuss the topic of language assessment as it relates to the mentally retarded. Interested readers are referred to Darley (1979) for critical reviews of 87 published speech and language tests.

Although tests of speech and language ability have not been developed exclusively for use with the mentally retarded, they are commonly employed with this population because of the prevalence of receptive and/or expressive skill deficits among mentally retarded persons. Spreen (1965) has indicated that language dysfunction occurs in 100% of persons functioning in the profound range of mental retardation, 90% of those within the severe to moderate range, and 45% of the mildly mentally retarded. A survey of 16 separate populations of institutionalized mentally retarded children, as well as those enrolled in special education public school classrooms, found the incidence of speech and language problems to be slightly less prevalent (52%–72% and 8%–26%, respectively), yet still representative of a significant percentage of each population (Keane, 1972).

According to Robinson and Robinson (1976), among the most widely used of the traditional language assessment devices with the mentally retarded is the Illinois Test of Psycholinguistic Abilities (ITPA) (Kirk, McCarthy, & Kirk, 1968; Paraskevopoulous & Kirk, 1969). The instrument is based on Osgood's (1957) model of communication and was designed to assess the speech and language development of children 2½ to 10 years of age along three dimensions of cognitive ability: channels of communication, psycholinguistic processes, and level of organization. The ITPA comprises 12 subtests (auditory reception, visual reception, auditory association, visual association, verbal expression, manual expression, grammatic closure, visual closure, auditory closure, sound blending, auditory-sequential memory, and visual sequential-memory) which attempt to separate and measure various intermodal relationships, receptive and expressive skills, and mediational processes that are related to speech and language development. The ITPA is scored like the traditional intelligence and achievement tests: basal and ceiling levels of performance are established for each of the 12 subtests, which can then be converted to scaled scores or age scores. An overall psycholinguistic age can also be obtained. As with other traditional assessment devices, the ITPA judges the behavior evidenced during the evaluation as related to hypothetical processes and underlying cognitive mechanisms.

A number of criticisms have been made against the ITPA, of which the most notable are: poor standardization technique, low subtest reliability, failure to sample important areas of speech and language development (Robinson & Robinson, 1976), and poor content and construct validity (Brown, 1973; Hulzinga, 1973; Ryckman & Wiergernik, 1969). Despite these weaknesses, many of which pertain directly to the application of the ITPA as a diagnostic tool, there are certain advantages to its use if the data are viewed from a treatment-oriented, behavioral perspective. The ITPA is constructed in a fashion that can be adapted for behavioral interpretation. Its 12 subtests tap content areas which are generally accepted as related to speech and language development in such a way that the data yielded by the ITPA can accrue meaning if they are interpreted as samples of language behavior acquired, or yet to be acquired, through learning. The use of the ITPA may also provide information that is valuable to the clinician in the development of response definitions on which direct observations of overt language behavior are to be based. To this end, it is proposed that the proper (i.e., behavioral) use of the ITPA be such that it focuses on remediation as well as diagnosis and classification. An approach which focuses on the remediation of samples of overt language behavior would allow it to fit better within the behavioral assessment paradigm of response description, treatment prescription, and the ongoing evaluation of intervention and programming. Kirk and Kirk (1971, 1978) provide detailed information pertaining to the remedial and proper uses of the ITPA.

Despite the apparent need for a standardized behavioral system for assessing speech and language development, most programmatic attempts to assess, treat, and evaluate language dysfunction have relied on direct observational procedures. A wide variety of language-related disorders have been assessed and treated by behavioral methods with the mentally retarded. These include receptive skills, such as following instructions (Fjellstedt & Sulzer, 1973; Kazdin & Erickson, 1975; Zimmerman, Zimmerman, & Russell, 1969), understanding adjectives (Baer & Guess, 1971), expressive skills, such as producing plurals (Guess, Sailor, Rutherford, & Baer, 1968), sentence development (Lutzker & Sherman, 1974), question asking (Twardosz & Baer, 1973), and increasing vocabulary and spontaneous use of language (Piene, Gregersen, & Sloane, 1970). Behavioral assessment methods based on direct observational strategies have also been frequently employed to decrease or eliminate inappropriate speech of mentally retarded persons (Barton, 1970; Butz & Hasazi, 1973a; Kazdin, 1971; Schreibman & Carr, 1978) and to develop functional speech where such speech is disordered (Risley & Wolf, 1967) or where there is no speech (Butz & Hasazi, 1973b; Hung, 1976).

Recently, a new aspect of language training has been observed in the teaching of sign language to mentally retarded children who have failed to learn speech. The impetus underlying this approach appears to stem from the successful demonstration that chimpanzees can be taught gestural modes of communication (Linden, 1974) and the positive reports of sign training with "autistic" children (Miller & Miller, 1973). A similar approach, referred to as total communication, which places equal emphasis on the development of gestural, aural receptive, and oral expressive skills, has also been proposed (Smith, 1975). In most cases, the application of behavior analysis to the systematic investigation of the efficacy of total communication in remediating language deficiencies of the mentally retarded has lagged far behind clinical practice.

A refreshing exception is a study by Carr, Binkoff, Kologinsky, and Eddy (1978) in which the authors taught expressive noun labels to four nonverbal autistic boys, ranging in age from 10 to 15 years, who had been institutionalized for periods ranging from 5 to 10 years. These children appeared to meet the behavioral criterion for classification as mentally retarded, but information reported in the study is limited (Vineland mean social age = 2.4 years). Prior to the study, each child had received 1 to 3 years of traditional speech therapy on a twice weekly basis and had failed to develop any effective discriminative vocal imitation. Receptive skills for each child were also judged to be poor. The basic task was to teach each child a specific sign when shown a particular object. The study was designed to evaluate whether prompting and fading techniques that are commonly employed as part of a more complex treatment package in clinical practice (Miller & Miller, 1973) were sufficient in themselves to teach sign language and to determine whether the systematic application of these procedures could result in a child's mastery of several expressive signs.

The results of the study, which utilized the direct observational strategy of a frequency count in a multiple-baseline design across behaviors (signs), demonstrated that a continuous reinforcement schedule using both prompting and fading was sufficient for teaching expressive noun labels for each child studied. In addition, each child was observed to master five expressive noun-sign discriminations based on the systematic application of the treatment package. Carr and his colleagues have continued this line of research with additional success although their results are currently unpublished.

In sum, standardized approaches to the assessment of speech and language development, such as the ITPA, can yield meaningful information if adapted for use as a single component of a comprehensive behavioral assessment package. If used properly as a means of sampling overt speech and language behaviors without inference to underlying language mechanisms, the test data are potentially helpful in the description, prescription, and evaluation of remedial treatment programs. However, as with other standardized approaches to behavioral assessment, its role must be limited to providing supplemental information to that gained through direct observational procedures.

Stereotyped Behavior

Thus far, we have reviewed the behavioral assessment of skill deficits commonly observed in the mentally retarded. However, it is also of value to address the assessment of behavioral excess in the mentally retarded. Such a departure is not only necessary because of the role of behavioral excess in the functional development of learning and social skills deficits (Forehand & Baumeister, 1976; Mann, 1976), but welcomed for providing many excellent examples of behavioral assessment for the mentally retarded.

A common form of behavioral excess, that has been heavily researched and demonstrated to interfere with learning in mentally retarded individuals (Berkson & Mason, 1964; Lovaas, Litrownick, & Mann, 1971), is stereotyped behavior. Such acts, which by definition comprise maladaptive, consistent, and repetitious motor or posturing behaviors, are among the most salient characteristics of the mentally retarded (Baumeister & Forehand, 1973). A number of theories have been espoused to account for the sources of motivation underlying stereotyped responding, which may also include self-injurious behavior (Baumeister & Rollings, 1976). Various reviews of studies examining the mechanisms that are hypothesized in the maintenance of stereotyped behavior are available. Since it is not our aim to review the studies related to the etiology and treatment of behavioral stereotypy in the mentally retarded, it is certainly of interest to note the wide variety of theories and wider range of such behavior that has been treated effectively with behavioral methods. The reader is therefore referred to several excellent reviews on the topic by Baumeister and Forehand (1973), Baumeister and Rollings (1976), Carr (1977), Forehand and Baumeister (1976), and Mann (1976).

From the standpoint of behavioral assessment, the evaluation and treatment of stereotyped behavior with the mentally retarded has relied exclusively on the strategy of direct observation. A number of checklists and rating scales provide for the documentation of stereotyped responding and odd mannerisms (AAMD Adaptive Behavior Scale). These measures are usually far too broad to be used meaningfully in the assessment process of behavioral description, treatment prescription, and the evaluation of ongoing programming. Typically, direct observation procedures utilizing frequency or duration measures and interval recording techniques have been used to accomplish the behavioral assessment, with variables being systematically manipulated according to one of the previously reviewed single-case designs for the purpose of establishing causal relationships between treatment procedures and the target behavior.

Conclusions

In this chapter we have provided a broad examination of the methodology of behavioral assessment and its applicability to the mentally retarded. Even though behavioral assessment is still in its infancy in relation to its predecessor, behavior therapy, a number of specific conclusions can be reached regarding future efforts in the behavioral assessment of the mentally retarded.

The Need for Two Types of Assessment

The mentally retarded will always require assessment for both identification/classification and intervention/programming. The former can be conceptualized from a traditional assessment viewpoint of diagnosis and has often been found to include only an assessment of "intelligence." By definition, this is not enough to determine whether a person is or is not mentally retarded. More specifically, significant deficits must be identified in adaptive behavior as well as "intelligence." Since persons are classed as mentally retarded or nonretarded on the basis of behavioral deficits, the diagnosis of mental retardation is, at least in large part, behavioral retardation. The assessment of adaptive behavior, therefore, must be viewed in terms of behavioral rather than traditional assessment.

To accurately arrive at decisions regarding whether or not they meet the criteria for the category mental retardation, persons must be assessed according to the degree that they possess certain skills in areas of adaptive behavior that are present in nonretarded normative samples of individuals of the same age. The accumulation of behavioral deficits in numerous areas of adaptive behavior which are greater than two standard deviations below the mean identify the population of mentally retarded persons. These comparisons require normative samples of both mentally retarded and nonretarded persons to provide predictive validity in identifying the mentally retarded. Unfortunately, the only scale measuring adaptive behavior that provides norms for both mentally retarded and nonretarded individuals is the American Association on Mental Deficiency Adaptive Behavior Scale. Other norm-referenced instruments which are typically used to assess intellectual functioning with the mentally retarded, as the WISC-R and the Stanford-Binet, were not developed with any intention of measuring adaptive behavior. It is obvious that a strong need exists for the development of additional behaviorally based scales containing normative comparisons to both retarded and nonretarded populations to better assess adaptive behavior in this group.

In addition to the basic need for new behavioral assessment instruments, individuals ascribing to behavioral assessment may regard the use of intelligence and achievement tests as unnecessary. From a behavioral viewpoint, we strongly believe that such an approach is equivalent to "throwing the baby out with the bathwater." As stated earlier, the determination of whether an instrument is a behavioral or traditional assessment technique is not inherent in the device itself, but a function of how it is applied. Information obtained from the IQ or achievement test can be extremely valuable as part of an entire behavioral assessment package. If the results of the individual's performance on the measure are not used to infer the presence or absence of hypothesized underlying processing mechanisms, and the conclusions drawn from the IQ or achievement tests are strictly based on the normative comparisons available,

IQ and achievement tests can be perceived as behavioral assessments of skills which have predictive validity concerning success in school. With the mentally retarded in particular, the inclusion of these measures as part of a psychological assessment battery is essential to assess identification/classification. It is our opinion that a complete assessment battery with the mentally retarded must include some measure of intelligence and current school achievement.

Adaptation of Behavioral Assessment Techniques to the Mentally Retarded

Once the mentally retarded are identified, assessment for the purpose of intervention/programming begins. Such assessment was noted to be strongly based on the principles and methods of behavioral assessment. Little attention has been given, however, to the incompatability of some strategies of behavioral assessment to the mentally retarded. Behavioral interviews and self-report measures, two of the most common techniques of behavioral assessment with the nonretarded, are subject not only to the problems inherent in the measure themselves, but may not be appropriate for use in their present forms with this group.

Although unquestionably there is reason to believe that the use of interview techniques with the mentally retarded would be highly unreliable, little effort has been made to adapt interview strategies that may be applicable for them. For example, since mentally retarded persons are often perceived as functioning intellectually and emotionally as younger than their age, it may be worthwhile to explore the use of structured-play interviews, similar to that used with children, as a means to assess specific reactions to social situations. One area in which this technique has been successfully used is in the assessment of social skills with the mentally retarded. Both Ross (1969) and the series of studies by Matson and his colleagues (Matson & Earnhardt, 1982; Matson & Stephens, 1978; Matson & Zeiss, 1979) provide examples of the potential for this type of behavioral assessment.

In the Ross (1969) study, doll play was used to assess social skills in educably mentally retarded children. Such a method provided an assessment of the child's social skills within a context a child could understand. With nonretarded children, social skills are typically assessed frequently lacking in the mentally retarded. By using doll play, a modality in which most mentally retarded children can relate, more accurate assessments of the child's reaction to social situations could be obtained. Such adaptations of play in assessing the social skills of mentally retarded children need to be researched further.

The studies of Matson and his colleagues demonstrate the type of adaptations necessary with mentally retarded adults in assessing social skills. In those studies, though a basic role-play format similar to that used with nonretarded adults was utilized, the behaviors assessed were specific to the types of behavioral excesses observed. Unlike assessments of social skills with nonretarded persons which often contain global ratings of assertiveness or heterosocial skills and/or the assessment of the subcomponents of these skills, the studies by Matson and his colleagues indicate that with mentally retarded persons assessments of social skills must include measures of overall socially acceptable behavior rather than the discrete social skill categories of assertiveness and/or heterosocial behavior.

Problems with Checklists and Rating Scales

The value of checklists and rating scales lies in the structure they add to the interview. Taken together, the checklist is viewed as the supplement to overall data collection and can provide some means of assessing individuals in a pre- and posttest format. However, the information gathered on checklists, such as the Vineland or ABIC, is typically provided in an interview with a knowledgeable informant. Because the informant is often unreliable, the data obtained through the checklist is no more valuable than behavioral interviews of the informant without a checklist. Essentially, the same information is obtained through checklists and interviews making the administration of both unnecessary. In this regard, we feel that unless the checklist can offer additional reliable and valid information, it does not really add to the assessment of the mentally retarded.

An exception to most interview format checklists with the mentally retarded is the ABS. This instrument is completed by knowledgeable informants. However, it is based on direct observation. In addition, the informant is not typically the referral source, as is the usual case with interview checklists such as the Vineland and ABIC, but an individual who can rate the behavior more objectively, such as a teacher or staff member of a residential living unit. Although such comparisons between the objectivity of different informants remains an empirical question yet to be tested, the necessity of objectivity in checklists is critical to their value. We therefore advocate that for data obtained on checklists and rating scales to be reliable and valid, they must be collected through direct observation. In such cases where this is impossible, it is acceptable to have objective, knowledgeable informants, other than the referral source, complete the checklists from memory.

An additional problem evident with checklists and rating scales is that the proliferation of available scales will indeed undermine the credibility of this method of assessment. The majority of the instruments are developed without standardization, provide poor selection of norms if norms are included at all, and generally ignore most well established psychometric properties of test construction, such as reliability and predictive validity. Time would be better spent if investigators developed standardized assessment instruments that would be applicable on a broader base and be recognized by such national organizations as the American Psychological Association (Division of Mental Retardation) and the Association for the Advancement of Behavior Therapy. The positive results of such an effort are clearly demonstrated by the success of the AAMD Adaptive Behavior Scale.

Problems with Methods of Direct Observation

Among all the methods of behavioral assessment, direct observation was found to show the most promise for assessing the mentally retarded. Although these methods provide a clear means for evaluating and monitoring the effectiveness of treatment programs, there has been a consistent lack of normative data from which conclusions could be drawn regarding the severity of identified behaviors. Behavior therapists interested in modifying behavior typically rely on their own or the judgment of a referral source to decide whether the target behavior is truly in need of remediation. We suggested that, rather than using such subjective measures to document the need for behavioral intervention, the behavioral excesses or deficits of target subjects and nontarget subjects be identified prior to beginning treatment of any behavior. Clinical decisions regarding the implementation of procedures should be made on the basis of the results of the data collection. For example, if a child is referred because of disruptive classroom behavior, a representative sample of the children in the class in addition to the target subject should be observed. Should all children exhibit similar levels of disruption, it would not be clinically nor ethically justified to change only the behavior of the subject who was selected for treatment.

Despite this need for more normative-based decision making regarding clinical treatment, direct observation is the most reliable and best method among the various behavioral assessment techniques for assessing the mentally retarded. It avoids the problems of interpretation and bias inherent in the use of knowledgeable informants in collecting data through interviews or checklists. Although other biases may be introduced depending on the direct observation technique that is chosen, such biases can be assessed and accounted for when the data are interpreted. A particularly important aspect of direct observation is the ability to match the most appropriate observation technique to the behaviors targeted for treatment so that the data obtained can be more meaningful to the assessor.

Unfortunately, observational systems are typically individualized to the specific behaviors under consideration for treatment. What is clearly needed is the development of an observational system which can be used to assess the same classes of behavior in different individuals across various settings. Such a system should include a normative base which permits comparisons with both mentally retarded and nonretarded individuals of various age groups. We strongly suggest that this type of effort should answer much of the call of investigators who, though consistently noting the need for normative comparisons in direct observation systems, have done little or nothing about it.

Use of Single-Subject Designs

Finally, it was noted that a number of single-case research designs are available for assessing the effectiveness of behavior change strategies. As a result, manipulations of independent variables to demonstrate the relationship between the treatment program and the target behavior are imperative in behavioral assessment for intervention/programming. Even though more elaborate designs such as the reversal or multiple baseline are desirable, such a quasi-experimental design as the A-B single-case methodology offers at least some evidence of credibility in the procedures. The availability of this technology places an important ethical burden of accountability on the behavioral therapist.

Behavioral assessment is the way of the future, because it offers a more standardized, objective, and credible means for assessing behavior of both retarded and nonretarded persons. Unfortuntely, the use of behavioral assessment strategies with the mentally retarded has not been considered as different from the assessment of other populations. Those researchers who have established themselves as authorities in the areas of mental retardation and behavioral assessment should now take the lead in developing and encouraging the use of behavioral assessment strategies for the mentally retarded. In this regard, it will be important to encourage increased reporting on the applied use of behavioral assessment with the mentally retarded.

References

Adams, H. E., Doster, J. A., & Calhoun, K. S. A psychologically based system of response classification. In A. R. Ciminero, K. S. Calhoun, & H. E. Adams (Eds.) *Handbook of behavioral assessment.* New York: Wiley, 1977.

Adams, J. Adaptive behavior and measured intelligence in the classification of mental retardation. *American Journal of Mental Deficiency,* 1973, 78, 77-81.

Adelson-Bernstein, N., & Sandow, L. Teaching buttoning to severely/profoundly retarded multi-handicapped children. *Education and Training of the Mentally Retarded.* 1978, 13, 178-183.

Arkowitz, H., Lichenstein, E., McGowen, K., & Hines, P. The behavioral assessment of social competence in males. *Behavior Therapy,* 1975, 6, 3-13.

Baer, D. M., & Guess, D. Receptive training of adjectivial inflections in mental retardates. *Journal of Applied Behavior Analysis,* 1971, 4, 129-139

Baer, D. M., Wolf, M. M., & Risely, T. R. Some current dimensions of applied behavior analysis. *Journal of Applied Behavior Analysis,* 1968, 1, 91-97.

Balthazar, E. E., *Balthazar scales of adaptive behavior II: Scale of social adaptation.* Palo Alto: Consulting Psychologist Press, 1973.

Bannister, D., Salmon, P., & Lieberman, D. M. Diagnosis-treatment relationships in psychiatry: A statistical analysis. *British Journal of Psychiatry,* 1964, 110, 726-732.

Barlow, D. H., & Hayes, S. C. Alternating treatments design: One strategy for comparing the effects of two treatments in a single subject. *Journal of Applied Behavior Analysis,* 1979, 12, 199-210.

Barton, E. S. Inappropriate speech in a severely retarded child: A case study of language conditioning and generalization. *Journal of Applied Behavior Analysis,* 1970, 3, 299-307.

Baumeister, A. A., & Forehand, R. Stereotyped acts. In N. R. Ellis (Ed.), *International review of research in mental retardation* (Vol. 6). New York: Academic Press, 1973.

Baumeister, A., & Muma, J. On defining mental retardation. *Journal of Special Education,* 1975, 9, 293-306.

Baumeister, A. A., & Rollings, J. P. Self-injurious behavior. In N. R. Ellis (Ed.) *International review of research in mental retardation* (Vol 9.) New York: Academic Press, 1976.

Bellack, A. S., Hersen, M., & Lamparski, D. Role-play tests for assessing social skills. Are they valid? Are they useful? *Journal of Consulting and Clinical Psychology,* 1979, 47, 335-342.

Bellack, A. S., Hersen, M., &Turner, S. M. Role-play tests for assessing social skills: Are they valid? *Behavior Therapy,* 1978, 9, 448-461.

Bellack, A. S., Hersen, M., & Turner, S. M. Relationship of role-playing and knowledge of appropriate behavior to assertion in the natural environment. *Journal of Consulting and Clinical Psychology,* 1979, 47, 670-678.

Berkson, G., & Mason, W. Stereotyped movements of mental defectives: IV. The effects of toys and the character of the acts. *American Journal of Mental Deficiency,* 1964, 68, 511-524.

Botterbusch, K. Hester evaluation system. In A. Sax (Ed.), Innovations in vocational evaluation and work adjustment. *Vocational Evaluation and Work Adjustment Bulletin,* 1975, 8, 62-65.

Botterbusch, K. D. *A comparison of four vocational evaluation systems.* Menomie, Wisc.: Materials Development Center, 1977.

Broden, M., Bruce, C., Mitchell, M. A., Carter, V., & Hall, R. V. Effects of teacher attention on attending behavior of two boys at adjacent desks. *Journal of Applied Behavior Analysis,* 1970, 2, 21-27.

Brown, A. *A first language.* Cambridge: Harvard University Press, 1973.

Butz, R. A., & Hasazi, J. E. The effects of reinforcement on perseverative speech in a mildly retarded boy. *Journal of Behavior Therapy and Experimental Psychiatry,* 1973, *4,* 167-170. (a)

Butz, R. A., & Hasazi, J. E. Developing verbal imitative behavior in a profoundly retarded girl. *Journal of Behavior Therapy and Experimental Psychiatry,* 1973, *4,* 389-393. (b)

Campbell, D. T., & Stanley, J. C. *Experimental and quasi-experimental designs for research.* Chicago: Rand McNally, 1966.

Carr, E. G. The motivation of self-injurious behavior: A review of some hypotheses. *Psychological Bulletin,* 1977, *84,* 800-816.

Carr, E. G., Binkoff, J. A., Kologinsky, E., & Eddy, M. Acquisition of sign language by autistic children. I: Expressive Labeling, *Journal of Applied Behavior Analysis,* 1978, *11,* 489-501.

Ciminero, A. R. Behavioral assessment: An overview. In A. R. Ciminero, K. S. Calhoun, & H. E. Adams (Eds.), *Handbook of behavioral assessment.* New York: Wiley, 1977.

Ciminero, A. R., Calhoun, K. S., & Adams, H. E. *Handbook of behavioral assessment.* New York: Wiley, 1977.

Ciminero, A. R., & Drabman, R. S. Current developments in the behavioral assessment of children. In B. B. Lahey & A. E. Kazdin (Eds.), *Advances in clinical child psychology* (Vol. 1), New York: Plenum Press, 1977.

Clausen, J. Quo Vadis, AAMD. *Journal of Special Education,* 1972, *6,* 51-60.

Cone, J. D. The behavioral assessment grid (BAG): A conceptual framework and a taxonomy. *Behavior Therapy,* 1978, *9,* 882-888.

Cone, J.D., & Hawkins, R. P. *Behavioral assessment: New directions in clinical psychology.* New York: Bruner/Mazel, 1977.

Coulter, W. A., & Morrow, H. W. A contemporary conception of adaptive behavior within the scope of psychological assessment. In W. A. Coulter & H. W. Morrow (Eds.), *Adaptive behavior: Concepts & measurements.* New York: Grune & Stratton, 1978. (a)

Coulter, W. A., & Morrow, H. W. A collection of adaptive behavior measures. In W. A. Coulter & H. W. Morrow (Eds.), *Adaptive behavior: Concepts and measurements.* New York: Grune & Stratton, 1978. (b)

Curran, J. P. Pandora's box reopened? The assessment of social skills. *Journal of Behavioral Assessment,* 1979, *1,* 55-71.

Darley, F. L. (Ed.) *Evaluation of appraisal techniques in speech and language pathology.* Reading, Mass.: Addison-Wesley, 1979.

Doll, E. A. *Vineland Social Maturity Scale.* Circle Pines, Minn.: American Guidance Service, 1965.

Dunn, L. M., & Markwardt, F. C. *Peabody individual achievement test.* Circle Pines, Minn.: American Guidance Service, 1970.

Eisler, R. M. The behavioral assessment of social skills. In M. Hersen & A. S. Bellack (Eds.), *Behavioral assessment: A practical handbook.* New York: Pergamon, 1976.

Eisler, R. M., Miller, P. M., & Hersen, M. Components of assertive behavior. *Journal of Clinical Psychology,* 1973, *29,* 295-299.

Evans, I. M., & Nelson, R. O. Assessment of child behavior problems. In A. R. Ciminero, K. S. Calhoun, & H. E. Adams (Eds.), *Handbook of behavioral assessment.* New York: Wiley, 1977.

Fjellstedt, N., & Sulzer, B. Reducing the latency of a child's responding to instructions by means of a token system. *Journal of Applied Behavior Analysis,* 1973, *6,* 125-130.

Forehand, R., & Baumeister, A. A. Deceleration of aberrant behavior among retarded individuals. In M. Hersen, R. Eisler, & P. M. Miller (Eds.), *Progresss in behavior modification* (Vol. 2). New York: Academic Press, 1976.

Foxx, R. M., & Azrin, N. H. *Toilet training the retarded: A rapid program for day and nighttime independent toileting.* Champaign: Research Press 1973.

Frank, G. *Psychiatric diagnosis: A review of research.* Oxford: Pergamon, 1975.

Glaser, R. Instructional technology and the measurement of learning outcomes: Some questions. *American Psychologist,* 1963, *18,* 519–521.

Goldfried, M. R., & Kent, R. N. Traditional versus behavioral personality assessment: A comparison of methodological and theoretical assumptions. *Psychological Bulletin,* 1972, *77,* 409–420.

Goldfried, M. R., & Linehan, M. M. Basic issues in behavioral assessment. In A. R. Ciminero, K. S. Calhoun, & H. A. Adams (Eds.), *Handbook of behavioral asssessment.* New York: Wiley, 1977.

Grossman, H. J. (Ed.) *Manual on terminology and classification in mental retardation.* Washington, D.C.: American Association on Mental Deficiency, 1977.

Guarnaccia, V. J. Factor structure and correlates of adaptive behavior in non-institutional retarded adults. *American Journal of Mental Deficiency,* 1976, *80,* 543–547.

Guess, D., Sailor, W., Rutherford, G., & Baer, D. M. An experimental analysis of linguistic development: The productive use of the plural morpheme. *Journal of Applied Behavior Analysis,* 1968, *1,* 299–306.

Gully, K. J., & Hosch, H. M. Adaptive Behavior Scale: Development as a diagnostic tool via discriminant analysis. *American Journal of Mental Deficiency,* 1979, *83,* 518–523.

Haring, N. G., & Pious, C. Future dimensions in work with severely and profoundly handicapped persons: An overview. In N. G. Haring & L. J. Brown, (Eds.), *Teaching the severely handicapped* (Vol. 1). New York: Grune & Stratton, 1976.

Hartmann, D. P. Considerations in the choice of interobserver reliability estimates. *Journal of Applied Behavior Analysis,* 1977, *10,* 103–116.

Hartmann, D. P., Roper, B. L., & Bradford, D. C. Some relationships between behavioral and traditional assessment, *Journal of Behavioral Assessment,* 1979, *1,* 3–21.

Hawkins, R. P., & Dobes, R. W. Behavioral definitions in applied behavior analysis: Explicit or implicit. In B. C. Etzel, J. M. Le Blanc, & D. M. Baer (Eds.), *New developments in behavioral research: Theory, methods, and applications. In honor of Sidney W. Bijou.* Hillsdale, N.J.: Lawrence Erlbaum, 1975.

Heber, R. A. A manual on terminology and classification in mental retardation. *American Journal of Mental Deficiency* (Monograph Supplement), 1961.

Heber, R. Mental retardation: Concept and classification. In E. P. Trapp & P. Himselstein (Eds.), *Readings on the exceptional child.* New York: Appleton-Century-Crofts, 1962.

Hersen, M. Historical perspectives in behavioral assessment. In M. Hersen & A. S. Bellack (Eds.), *Behavioral assessment: A practical handbook.* New York: Pergamon, 1976.

Hersen, M., & Barlow, D. H. *Single case experimental designs: Strategies for studying behavior change.* New York: Pergamon, 1976.

Hersen, M., & Bellack, A. S. *Behavior assessment: A practical handbook.* New York: Pergamon, 1976.

Hill, A. D., & Strain, P. S. The effects of teacher-delivered social reinforcement on the task persistent behavior of educable mentally retarded children. *Psychology in the Schools,* 1977, *14,* 207–212.

Hulzinga, R. J. The relationship of the ITPA to the Stanford-Binet, Form L-M and the WISC. *Journal of Learning Disabilities,* 1973, *6,* 53–58.

Hung, D. W. Teaching mute retarded children vocal imitation. *Journal of Behavior Therapy and Experimental Psychiatry,* 1976, *7,* 85–88.

JASTAK, J. F., & JASTAK, C. R. *The wide range achievement test*. Wilmington: Guidance Associates of Delaware, 1965.

KANFER, F. H., & SASLOW, G. Behavioral diagnosis. In C. M. Franks (Ed.), *Behavior therapy: Appraisal and status*. New York: McGraw-Hill, 1969.

KAZDIN, A. E. The effect of response cost in suppressing behavior in a pre-psychotic retardate. *Journal of Behavior Therapy and Experimental Psychiatry*, 1971, 2, 137–140.

Kazdin, A. E. The influence of behavior preceeding a reinforced response on behavior change in the classroom. *Journal of Applied Behavior Analysis*, 1977, 10, 299–310.

KAZDIN, A. E. *History of behavior modification: Experimental foundations of contemporary research*. Baltimore: University Park Press, 1978.

KAZDIN, A. E., & ERICKSON, L. M. Developing responsiveness to instructions in severely and profoundly retarded residents. *Journal of Behavior Therapy and Experimental Psychiatry*, 1975, 6, 17–21.

KAZDIN, A. E., & GEESEY, S. Simultaneous-treatment design comparisons of the effects of earning reinforcers for one's peers versus oneself. *Behavior Therapy*, 1977, 8, 682–693.

KAZDIN, A. E., & HARTMANN, D. P. The simultaneous treatment design. *Behavior Therapy*, 1978, 9, 912–922.

KAZDIN, A. E., & STRAW, M. K. Assessment of the behavior of the mentally retarded. In M. Hersen & A. S. Bellack (Eds.). *Behavioral assessment: A practical handbook*. New York: Pergamon, 1976.

KEANE, V. E. Incidence of speech and language problems in the mentally retarded. *Mental Retardation*, 1972, 10, 3–8.

KENT, R. N., & FOSTER, S. L. Direct observational procedures: Methodological issues in naturalistic settings. In A. R. Ciminero, K. S. Calhoun, & H. E. Adams (Eds.), *Handbook of behavioral assessment*. New York: Wiley, 1977.

KIRK, S. A., & KIRK, W. D. *Psycholinguistic learning disabilities: Diagnosis and remediation*. Urbana: University of Illinois Press, 1971.

KIRK, S. A., & KIRK, W. D. Uses and abuses of the ITPA. *Journal of Speech and Hearing Disorders*, 1978, 43, 58–75.

KIRK, S. A., MCCARTHY, J. J., & KIRK, W. D. *Examiner's manual: Illinois test of psycholinguistic abilities* (rev. ed.). Urbana: University of Illinois Press, 1968.

KLEIN, R. D. Modifying academic performance in the grade school classroom. In M. Hersen, R. Eisler, & P. M. Miller (Eds.), *Progress in behavior modification* (Vol. 8). New York: Academic Press, 1979.

KNAPCZYK, D. R., & LIVINGSTON, G. Learning economy: A practical approach to prevocational training of money management. *Research and the Retarded*, 1977, 4, 7–17.

LAMBERT, N. M. The adaptive behavior scale-public school version: An overview. In A. R. Coulter & H. W. Morrow (Eds.), *Adaptive behavior: Concepts and measurements*. New York: Grune & Stratton, 1978.

LAMBERT, N. M., & NICOLL, R. C. Dimensions of adaptive behavior of retarded and nonretarded public school children. *American Journal of Mental Deficiency*, 1976, 81, 135–146.

LAMBERT, N. M., WINDMILLER, M., COLE, L., & FIGUEROA, R. *AAMD adaptive behavior scale-public school version*. Washington, D.C.: American Association on Mental Deficiency, 1974.

LAZARUS, A. A. Multimodal behavior therapy: Treating the basic "id". *Journal of Nervous and Mental Disease*, 1973, 156, 404–411.

LAZARUS, A. A. *Multimodal behavior therapy*. New York: Springer, 1976.

LEE, D. Y. Evaluation of a group counseling program designed to enhance social adjustment of mentally retarded adults. *Journal of Counseling Psychology*, 1977, 24, 318–323.

LEFF, R. B. Teaching the TMR to dial the telephone. *Mental Retardation*, 1974, 12, 12–13.

Leff, R. B. Training TMR children and adults to dial the telephone. *Mental Retardation*, 1975, *13*, 9-11.

Leland, H., Nihira, K., Foster, R., Shellhaas, M., & Kagin, E. *Conference on measurement of adaptive behavior:* II. Parsons, Kansas: Parsons State Hospital and Training Center, 1968.

Leland, H., Shellhaas, M., Nihira, K., & Foster, R. Adaptive behavior: A new dimension in the classification of the mentally retarded. *Mental Retardation Abstracts*, 1967, *4*, 359-387.

Lewinsohn, P. M. The behavioral study and treatment of depression. In M. Hersen, R. M. Eisler, & P. M. Miller (Eds.), *Progress in behavior modification* (Vol. 1). New York: Academic Press, 1975.

Lewisohn, P. M., & Shaffer, M. Use of home observations as an integral part of the treatment of depression. *Journal of Consulting and Clinical Psychology*, 1971, *37*, 87-94.

Lewis, J. F., & Mercer, J. R. The system of multicultural pluralistic assessment: SOMPA. In W.A. Coulter & H. W. Morrow (Eds.), *Adaptive behavior: Concepts and measurements*. New York: Grune & Stratton, 1978.

Linden, E. *Apes, men and language*. New York: E. P. Dutton, 1974.

Linehan, M. M. Issues in behavioral interviewing. In J. D. Cone & R. P. Hawkins (Eds.), *Behavioral assessment: New directions in clinical psychology*. New York: Bruner/Mazel, 1977.

Lovaas, O. I., Litrownick, A., & Mann, R. Response latencies to auditory stimuli in autistic children engaged in self-stimulatory behavior. *Behavior Research and Therapy*, 1971, *9*, 39-49.

Lutzker, J. R., & Sherman, J. A. Producing generative sentence usage by imitation and reinforcement procedures. *Journal of Applied Behavior Analysis*, 1974, *7*, 447-460.

Malone, D. R., & Christian, W. P. Adaptive behavior scale as a screening measure for special education placement. *American Journal of Mental Deficiency*, 1974, *79*, 367-371.

Mann, R. A. Assessment of behavioral excesses in children. In M. Hersen & A. S. Bellack (Eds.), *Behavioral assessment: A practical handbook*. New York: Pergamon, 1976.

Marchetti, A., & Matson, J. L. Training skills for community adjustment. In J. L. Matson & J. R. McCartney (Eds.), *Handbook of behavior modification with the mentally retarded*, Plenum Press, 1981.

Matson J. L. A controlled group study of pedestrian skill training for the mentally retarded. *Behavioral Research and Therapy*, 1980, *18*, 99-106.

Matson, J. L., & Earnhardt, T. An analysis of the effects of self-monitoring on institutionalized adults. *Behavior Modification*, 1982, *2*.

Matson, J. L., Ollendick, T. II., & Adkins, J. A comprehensive dining program for mentally retarded adults. *Behavior Research and Therapy*, 1980, *18*, 107-112.

Matson, J. L., & Stephens, R. M. Increasing appropriate behavior of explosive psychiatric patients and a social skills training package. *Behavior Modification*, 1978, *2*, 61-65.

Matson, J. L., & Zeiss, R. A. Group training of social skills in chronically explosive, severely disturbed psychiatric patients. *Behavioral Engineering*, 1978, *5*, 41-51.

Matson, J. L., & Zeiss, R. A. The buddy system: A method for generalized reduction of inappropriate interpersonal behaviors of retarded psychiatric patients. *British Journal of Social and Clinical Psychology*, 1979, *18*, 401-405.

McFall, R. P., & Lillesand, D. B. Behavioral rehearsal with modeling and coaching in assertion training. *Journal of Abnormal Psychology*, 1971, *77*, 313-323.

Mercer, J. R. *Labeling the mentally retarded: Clinical and social system preparation on mental retardation*. Berkeley: University of California Press, 1973.

Mercer, J. R., & Lewis, J. F. *System of multicultural pluralistic assessment: SOMPA*. New York: Psychological Corporation, 1977.

Meyer, V., Liddell, A., & Lyons, M. Behavioral interviews. In A. R. Ciminero, K. S. Calhoun, & H. E. Adams (Eds.), *Handbook of behavioral assessment*. New York: Wiley, 1977.

Miller, A., & Miller, E. E. Cognitive-developmental training with elevated boards and sign language. *Journal of Autism and Childhood Schizophrenia*, 1973, *3*, 65-85.

Morganstern, K. P. Behavioral interviewing: The initial stages of assessment. In M. Hersen & A. S. Bellack (Eds.), *Behavioral assessment: A practical handbook*. New York: Pergamon, 1976.

Morrow, H. W., & Coulter, W. A. A survey of state policies regarding adaptive behavior. In W. A. Coulter, & H. W. Morrow (Eds.), *Adaptive behavior: Concepts and Measurements*. New York: Grune & Stratton, 1978.

Nelson, R. O., Gibson, F., & Cutting, D. S. Videotaped modeling: The development of three appropriate social responses in a mildly retarded child. *Mental Retardation*, 1973, *11*, 24-28.

Nelson, R. O., & Hayes, S. C. Some current dimensions of behavioral assessment. *Behavioral Assessment*, 1979, *1*, 1-16.

Nihira, K. Factorial dimensions of adaptive behavior in adult retardates. *American Journal of Mental Deficiency*, 1969, *73*,,868-878. (a)

Nihira, K. Factorial dimensions of adaptive behavior in mentally retarded children and adolescents. *American Journal of Mental Deficiency*, 1969, *74*, 130-141. (b)

Nihira, K. Factorial descriptions of the AAMD Adaptive Behavior Scale. In W. A. Coulter & H. W. Morrow (Eds.), *Adaptive behavior: Concepts and meausurements*. New York: Grune & Stratton, 1978.

Nihira, K., Foster, R., Shellhaas, M., & Leland, H. *American association on mental deficiency adaptive behavior scale*, 1975, revision. Washington, D.C.: American Association on Mental Deficiency, 1975.

O'Leary, K. D., Kaufman, K. F., Kass, R. E., & Drabman, R. S. The effects of loud and soft reprimands on the behavior of disruptive students. *Exceptional Children*, 1970, *37*, 145-155.

Osgood, C. E. (Ed.) *Contemporary approaches to cognition, a behavioristic analysis*. Cambridge: Harvard University Press, 1957.

Paraskevopoulos, J. N., & Kirk, S. A. *The development and psychometric characteristics of the revised Illinois test of psycholinguistic abilities*. Urbana: University of Illinois Press, 1969.

Piene, H. A., Gregersen, G. F., & Sloane, H. A program to increase vocabulary and spontaneous verbal behavior. *Mental Retardation*, 1970, *8*, 38-44.

Piller, R. P. The Micro-tower system. In A. Sax (Ed.), Innovations in vocational evaluation and work adjustment. *Vocational Evaluation and Work Adjustment Bulletin*, 1976, *9*, 50-53.

Pisauro, M. L. Comprehensive occupational assessment and training system In A. Sax (Ed.), Innovations in vocational evaluation and work adjustment. *Vocational Evaluation and Work Adjustment*, 1976, *9*, 39-45.

Repp, A. C., Roberts, D. M., Slack, D. J., Repp, C. F., & Berkler, M. S. A comparison of frequency, interval, and time-sampling methods of data collection. *Journal of Applied Behavior Analysis*, 1976, *9*, 501-508.

Risley, T. R., & Wolf, M. M. Established speech in echolalic children. *Behavior Research and Therapy*, 1967, *5*, 73-88.

Robertson, S. J., Simon, S. J., Pachman, J. S., & Drabman, R. S. Self-control and generalization procedures in a classroom of disruptive retarded children. *Child Behavior Therapy*, 1980, *1*, 347-362.

Robinson, N. M., & Robinson, H. B. *The mentally retarded child*. New York: McGraw-Hill, 1976.

Rosen, G. A. The VIEWS system. In A. Sax (Ed.), Innovations in vocational evaluation and work adjustment. *Vocational Evaluation and Work Adjustment Bulletin*, 1977, *10*(3), 50-51.

Ross, S. A. Effects of intentional training in social behavior on retarded children. *American Journal of Mental Deficiency*. 1969, *73*, 912-919.

Ryckman, D. B., & Wiergernik, R. The factors of the Illinois Test of Psycholinguistic Abilities: A comparison of 18 factor analyses. *Exceptional Children*, 1969, *36*, 107-113.

Santogrossi, D. A., O'Leary, K. D., Romanczyk, R. G., & Kaufman, K. F. Self-evaluation by adolescents in a psychiatric hospital school token program. *Journal of Applied Behavior Analysis*, 1973, *6*, 277-288.

Sattler, J. M. *Assessment of children's intelligence*. Philadelphia: W. B. Saunders, 1974.

Schreibman, L., & Carr, E. G. Elimination of echolalic responding to questions through training of a generalized verbal response. *Journal of Applied Behavior Analysis*, 1978, *11*, 453-463.

Shapiro, E. S., & Klein, R. D. Self-management of classroom behavior with retarded/disturbed children, *Behavior Modification*, 1980, *4*, 83-97.

Smith, C. H. Total communication using the simultaneous method. In M. P. Creedon, (Ed.), *Appropriate behavior through communication*. Chicago: Michael Reese Medical Center, Dysfunctioning Child Center Publishing, 1975.

Spreen, O. Language functions in mental retardation: A review, I. Language development, types of retardation, and intelligence level. *American Journal of Mental Deficiency*, 1965, *6*, 482-494.

Stimbert, V. E., Minn, J. W., & McCoy, J. F. Intensive feeding training with retarded children. *Behavior Modification*, 1977, *1*, 517-530.

Strain, P. S., & Pierce, J. E. Direct and vicarious effects of social praise on mentally retarded preschool children's attentive behavior. *Psychology in the Schools*, 1977, *14*, 349-352.

Stuart, R. B. *Trick or treatment*. Champaign, Ill.: Research Press. 1970.

Terman, L. M., & Merrill, M. A. *Measuring intelligence*. Boston: Houghton-Mifflin, 1937.

Terman, L. M., & Merrill, M. A. *Stanford-Binet intelligence scale*. Boston, Houghton-Mifflin, 1973.

Turkewitz, H., O'Leary, K. D., & Ironsmith, M. Producing generalization of appropriate behavior through self-control. *Journal of Consulting and Clinical Psychology*, 1975, *43*, 577-583.

Twardosz, S., & Baer, D. M. Training two severely retarded adolescents to ask questions. *Journal of Applied Behavior Analysis*, 1973, *6*, 655-661.

Ulmann, J. D., Sulzer-Azaroff, B. Multielement baseline design in educational research. In I. Ramp & G. Semb (Eds.), *Behavior analysis areas of research and application*. Englewood Cliffs, N.J.: Prentice-Hall, 1975.

U.S. Department of Labor, *The dictionary of occupation titles*, (3rd ed.). Washington, D.C.: Government Printing Office, 1965.

Walls, R. T., Werner, T. J., Bacon, A., & Zane, T. Behavior checklists. In J. D. Cone & R. P. Hawkins, (Eds.), *Behavioral assessment: New directions in clinical psychology*. New York: Bruner/Mazell, 1977.

Wechsler, D. *Manual for the Wechsler adult intelligence scale*. New York: Psychological Corporation, 1955.

Wechsler, D. *Manual for the Wechsler preschool and primary scale of intelligence*. New York: Psychological Corporation, 1967.

Wechsler, D. *Manual for the Wechsler preschool and primary scale of intelligence*. New York: Psychological Corporation, 1967.

WOLFF, W. T., & MERRENS, M. R. Behavior assessment: A review of clinical methods. *Journal of Personality Assessment*, 1974, *38*, 3-16.
WOLPE, J. *The practice of behavior therapy.* New York: Pergamon, 1973.
ZIMMERMAN, E. H., ZIMMERMAN, J., & RUSSELL, C. D. Differential effects of token reinforcement on instruction following behavior in retarded students instructed as a group. *Journal of Applied Behavior Analysis*, 1969, *2*, 110-112.

7 Trends and Issues in Behavioral Research on Training Feeding and Dressing Skills

Dennis H. Reid

Introduction

One of the first areas in which the efficacy of behavior modification procedures was demonstrated with mentally retarded persons was self-help skill training. Since the first demonstrations in the early 1960s that mentally retarded individuals could be taught self-help skills with behavioral procedures, a considerable amount of research has been conducted on the development, refinement, and evaluation of various self-help skill-training methods. Two specific self-help skills that have received much research attention are independent feeding and dressing. Just as in normal development, in which self-feeding and at least basic self-dressing skills are the first self-help behaviors to be acquired, so too, it is important to teach these two sets of behaviors to mentally retarded persons. Without such skills, mentally retarded persons can exert only minimal independence in their daily environments. The significance of these two skill areas is reflected also in the large number of commercially available training programs and curricula that were developed for use with the mentally retarded and that include both feeding and dressing components (Johnson & Werner, 1975; Shearer, Billingsley, Frohman, Hilliard, Johnson, & Shearer, undated; Watson, 1972; Westway & Apolloni, 1978).

Two general conclusions can be drawn from the behavioral research and training literature generated on feeding and dressing skills. First, considerable progress has occurred in the development and evaluation of behavioral procedures for teaching such skills to the mentally retarded. Few people familiar

---

Dennis H. Reid • Western Carolina Center, Morganton, North Carolina 28655 with the behavior modification and/or mental retardation literature are likely to argue with such a statement. Second, and perhaps a more debatable statement, is that despite the notable progress that has occurred, considerably more research is still needed in both the self-feeding and self-dressing training areas. This chapter will examine the basis of these two assertions and more specifically, will (1) summarize the behavioral research on training self-feeding and self-dressing skills to the mentally retarded, with an emphasis on the progress that has occurred in the research, and (2) discuss areas where continued or new research is needed.

In summarizing the research to date, no attempt will be made to review comprehensively all the behavioral research in the feeding and dressing skill areas. Sources that review or summarize the self-help training literature with the mentally retarded are available (Snell, 1978; Watson & Uzzell, 1980; Whitman & Scibak, 1979). A brief chronological description of key studies will be provided here to summarize the directions of the research and the accomplishments, as well as to present a framework indicating future research needs. Following this chronological description, separate chapter sections will discuss current research issues and suggested directions for future work. An attempt will be made to indicate, as alluded to elsewhere (Watson & Uzzell, 1980), that there are significant shortcomings with the use of current behavioral technologies for teaching independent feeding and dressing skills. Similarly, a discussion of the behavioral deficits and excesses characteristic of mentally retarded persons that are integrally related to the development of independent feeding and dressing skills, problems that have *not* been addressed to date in the behavioral research, will follow. Since research on teaching self-feeding skills has received more attention than that of self-dressing, the former will be discussed first.

Trends and Issues in Behavioral Research on Training Self-Feeding Skills

Chronological Summary of Studies

The systematic use of behavioral procedures in training self-feeding skills to mentally retarded persons began in this country in the early 1960s. At that time, research was conducted to demonstrate that behavioral training strategies, based primarily on operant conditioning, could be used to teach various self-help skills, including self-feeding (Bensberg, 1965; Bensberg, Colwell, & Cassel, 1965). Typically, the research methodology fell short of basic standards for applied behavioral research as described by Baer, Wolf, and Risley (1968) but, nevertheless provided support for the usefulness of behavior modification procedures in teaching self-help skills to mentally retarded individuals. Also, as noted elsewhere (Whitman & Scibak, 1979), the studies in the early 1960s were a significant impetus for the more rigorous research that occurred in the 1970s and 1980s.

After the initial reports in the early 1960s that suggested behavioral techniques could be used to teach self-help skills, three general targets of inquiry were pursued in the research involving self-feeding skills. The first studies focused, as expected, on developing and evaluating various *acquisition strategies* (i.e., assisting mentally retarded persons in acquiring independent feeding skills). Second, a relatively large number of studies focused on *deceleration strategies* for decreasing behaviors during the mealtimes that either interfered with independent feeding (such disruptions as throwing food), and/or were socially unacceptable (eating all foods with fingers). A smaller third set of investigations focused specifically on both *acquisition* and *deceleration* strategies simultaneously.

Acquisition Research with Self-Feeding Skills

Independent feeding has been considered one of the easier self-help skills to teach mentally retarded persons, provided severe neuromuscular disorders are not present that interfere with necessary motor skills (e.g., arm and hand movements necessary to bring food from the plate to the mouth, and the ability to chew and to swallow). Watson (1967) has discussed the factors that make self-feeding a relatively easy self-help skill to teach, including the fact that there is an inherent reinforcer (the food) involved, and that, generally, the shaping or chaining procedures used in training are straightforward. Typically, the behavioral procedures used to teach basic self-feeding skills involve a trainer physically guiding a client's hand through the feeding sequence, and then reducing the amount of guidance as the client demonstrates progress, while reinforcing successful attempts (O'Brien, Bugle, & Azrin, 1972). As also reported in the same study, there are two common methods for reducing the amount of guidance. One involves moving the hand of the trainer that provides the physical guidance gradually from the client's hand, to the client's forearm, elbow, and eventually, to the shoulder. In the second method, the trainer breaks the eating sequence into small steps, and as the client progresses from step to step, the trainer gradually eliminates the physical guidance from those steps at the end of the sequence. Most of the research on teaching independent feeding skills to the mentally retarded involves these procedures. However, as the research has evolved from the 1960s to the 1980s, the degree of sophistication in implementing these procedures has improved considerably.

Early data-based reports of programs designed specifically to teach independent feeding skills to mentally retarded persons typically indicated successful outcomes (i.e., participants became more independent during mealtimes). However, frequently there was insufficient information to allow for a thorough experimental evaluation of the procedures, such as a lack of reliability of measurements, or perhaps a lack of any objective, quantifiable data (Berkowitz, Sherry, & Davis, 1971; Zeiler & Jervey, 1968). Generally, the early training programs focused on rudimentary skills necessary for such independent feeding as eating foods with a spoon. Later research paid more attention to evaluation methodology from a behavioral research point of view, such as concern over reliability of the measurement system (O'Brien *et al.*, 1972), as well as expanding the type of skills taught. For instance, as opposed to teaching how to eat all foods with a spoon, the full array of utensils (knife, fork, and spoon) was included (Nelson, Cone, & Hanson, 1975). Recent research has continued to expand the types of self-feeding skills taught (multiple utensil usage, social manners, neatness) to approximate normal mealtime procedures more closely (Matson, Ollendick, & Adkins, 1980) and to include independent feeding skills in public dining places (Marholin, O'Toole, Touchette, Berger, & Doyle, 1979; van den Pol, Iwata, Ivancic, Page, Neef, & Whitley, 1981). In addition to expansion in the types of skills taught, there has been considerable elaboration in the types of training procedures used in the most recent research. Whereas early research taught skills during actual dining routines using the basic acquisition strategy described earlier, van den Pol *et al.* (1982) used a simulation training procedure with photo slides of a restaurant and a simulated counter to teach a generalizable set of public dining skills. Matson *et al.* (1980) also added novel procedures to feeding-training regimes, such as self-evaluation and peer feedback.

Deceleration Research with Feeding-Related Behavior

Although the research just discussed focused primarily on teaching appropriate self-feeding skills, at least as much research has been conducted to evaluate procedures for reducing behaviors that interfered with appropriate self-feeding. As noted earlier, the interference could be due to behaviors *incompatible* with self-feeding, such as playing with food. In addition, the interference could be due to behaviors that are not incompatible with self-feeding *per se*, but are *socially unacceptable* (e.g., eating very quickly or sloppily). Table I presents a wide variety of inappropriate behaviors that have been targeted in the literature for deceleration through different punishment procedures.

The early deceleration research on inappropriate mealtime behaviors is similar to early research on acquisition of self-feeding skills in that it generally reported favorable results but was not conducted in a manner that allowed for a thorough evaluation of the procedures (Hamilton & Allen, 1967; Henriksen & Doughty, 1967). Generally, the early research used reinforcers (such as praise) contingent on appropriate self-feeding and/or punishment procedures (such as removal of a person from the food, or vice versa) contingent on inappropriate eating to decrease undesirable mealtime behavior.

Similar to the trend in the acquisition research, improvements in the ex-

TABLE I
Samples of Target Behaviors and Punishment Procedures
Used for Mealtime Behaviors

Inappropriate behaviors targeted[a]	Punishment procedures	Reference
Throwing food, stealing food, moving from one table to another, "General disorderly conduct"	Termination of meal, via removing the client from the meal	Hamilton & Allen, 1967
Stealing food, rapidly eating, eating with hands, hitting persons, throwing food	Verbal reprimand, manual restraint	Henriksen & Doughty, 1967
Spilling food, yelling, eating with hands, playing with utensils	15-second removal of client from meal	Martin, McDonald, & Omichinski, 1971
Eating with hands, spilling, oversized bites, chewing napkin, drooling, putting napkin in food	Verbal reprimand, manual restraint, 30-second removal of food	O'Brien & Azrin, 1972
Eating with hands, stealing, mouth-to-plate eating	10-second removal of food	Christian, Hollomon, & Lanier, 1973
Eating with hands, stealing, screaming, throwing food	Permanent removal of client from meal	Albin, 1977
Rapidly Eating	Brief manual restraint	Favell, McGimsey, & Jones, 1980

[a] The behaviors and punishment procedures presented do not necessarily include all components involved in each study.

perimental rigor with which the deceleration research was conducted occurred in the later research. Generally, there was more concern for experimental designs, reliability of measurement systems, and specification of procedures in the later studies (Favell, McGimsey, & Jones, 1980; Martin, McDonald, & Omichinski, 1971; O'Brien & Azrin, 1972; Plummer, Baer, & LeBlanc, 1977). However, there were also later reports that were more of a general program–evaluation nature than an experimental nature in that reliable replications of treatment effects were not presented (Albin, 1977; Azrin & Wesolowski, 1974; Christian, Hollomon, & Lanier, 1973). A second trend in the later deceleration research was an expansion in the comprehensiveness with which dependent variables were investigated. For instance, attention was paid to the potential effects of punishment procedures on behaviors other than those on which punishers were contingent (Martin *et al.*, 1971), and to social validity estimates of observed behavior changes (O'Brien & Azrin, 1972).

Feeding Research Focusing on Acquisition and Deceleration Strategies

Several reports have included data from investigations that focused on increasing appropriate self-feeding behaviors and decreasing inappropriate behaviors. Most of the studies involving mealtime behaviors of the mentally retarded have addressed, in some fashion, concerns over both acquisition and deceleration strategies. However, relatively few studies presented *formal data* to evaluate increases in desirable self-feeding behaviors and decreases in undesirable mealtime behaviors. Such research occurred sporadically in the latter 1960s and early to mid-1970s and included program–evaluation–type reports (Groves & Carroccio, 1971) and more rigorously controlled applied behavioral research (Barton, Guess, Garcia, & Baer, 1970; Stolz & Wolf, 1969).

Among the studies that focused directly on both increases and decreases in various mealtime behaviors is an investigation by Azrin and Armstrong (1973) that probably stimulated more interest in training self-feeding skills to the mentally retarded than any other report, at least among caregivers. In an attempt to overcome various problems with previously reported training programs, Azrin and Armstrong developed an *intensive* training approach. The program was developed to be used with serious feeding deficits and was designed to be more effective and to work more quickly ("only a few days") than traditional training programs. It also included specific maintenance components and allowed the participants to eat in a manner indistinguishable from normal people. In order to accomplish the multitude of purposes, numerous procedures were combined into the intensive training program including minimeals (brief meals served hourly throughout the day as opposed to the standard three meals), manual guidance, separate training procedures for each utensil, physical interruption procedures for inappropriate behaviors, overcorrection for spilling errors, and the initial use of a 2:1 trainer-to-client ratio. Results of the program have suggested the superiority of intensive procedures over more traditional approaches in terms of overall amount of improvement in self-feeding skills (including drinking skills). Additional support for the use of intensive training programs has been reported with subsequent research (Stimbert, Minor, & McCoy, 1977), although the speed with which mentally retarded persons progress through the program has been more variable than that reported by Azrin and Armstrong (1973).

Specific Research Issues

The previous section provided a brief sketch of the directions behavioral research on training self-feeding skills to the mentally retarded has taken since the early 1960s. Clearly, a number of behavioral procedures have been developed and evaluated for teaching independent feeding skills as well as decreasing undesirable mealtime behaviors. However, as noted earlier, this does not mean that few research questions regarding the development of self-feeding skills by the mentally retarded remain. The success of the previous research has set the stage for more specific problems in current training regimes to be denoted, for more possibilities to be raised toward increased skill development, and, subsequently, for more research questions to be answered. This section addresses issues related to the teaching of self-feeding skills that are being currently researched and/or warrant future research attention.

Teaching Advanced Mealtime Skills

One of the most apparent trends in the feeding research to date is the focus on more advanced mealtime skills. For instance, target behaviors have progressed from spoon feeding (Zeiler & Jervey, 1968) to independent dining in public restaurants (van den Pol et al., 1981). This research trend is likely to continue for at least two reasons. First, the advances in teaching *basic* self-feeding skills (e.g., eating independently with a spoon and fork) derived through earlier behavioral research and subsequent program implementation have allowed many mentally retarded individuals to acquire the basic skills relatively quickly. The previous lack of such programs prohibited mentally retarded persons from participating in more *advanced* programs as the basic behaviors were prerequisites for acquiring the more advanced skills. Second, the national movement toward normalizing living environments and subsequent de-institutionalization has focused attention on the need to teach the mentally retarded the multitude of skills necessary to eat in normal ways and in noninstitutional environments.

The need to teach mentally retarded persons mealtime skills for noninstitutional settings is reflected in the rapidly growing body of research under the generic label of *community survival skills*. Several studies falling in this category involving mealtime skills in public restaurants have been noted already (Marholin et al., 1979; van den Pol et al., 1981). However, a wide variety of other skills warrant research attention regarding the development of effective and efficient acquisition strategies. For instance, teaching meal preparation skills such as cooking has been researched only minimally (Bellamy & Clark, 1977; Robinson-Wilson, 1977). Research attention is warranted for methods of teaching the skills necessary for purchasing foods that are nutritious as well as cost efficient. Eating in public dining places other than fast-food restaurants needs attention because food selection, purchasing, and consumption practices are relatively restricted in such restaurants. The consumption of alcohol and other legal drugs has not been addressed through programmatic research. That is, where mentally retarded persons have the legal right to purchase and consume such items, it seems desirable that they be taught to do so in socially acceptable ways as well as in ways that are not obviously detrimental from a medical perspective. In short, an almost infinite number of behaviors within the community survival skill area are important, but methods of teaching and maintaining the skills have not been researched.

Although the past trend and current emphasis toward teaching advanced self-feeding skills to the mentally retarded is most evident in the community survival skills research involving the mildly and moderately mentally retarded, similar directions, albeit on a less-advanced skill level, are apparent with the severely and profoundly mentally retarded in institutional settings. For instance, the involvement of numerous eating utensils versus using only a spoon has occurred in institutional settings. Similarly, a general movement toward normalization is apparent in the use of multiple food items served in normal preparations (Korabek, Reid, & Ivancic, 1981) as opposed to the use of food that was abnormally prepared, such as being intermixed "into the consistency of a lumpy paste" (Song & Gandhi, 1974). Also, the Matson et al. (1980) program that focused on such advanced self-feeding skills as social manners and neatness included severely and profoundly retarded participants in an institutional setting. Continued behavioral research on teaching and maintaining normal mealtime skills to the severely and profoundly retarded would be useful. For instance, research could be conducted on methods of teaching family-style dining (pouring drinks, passing, and serving food). Also, deceleration strategies could be developed and evaluated for reducing behaviors that detract from a normal self-feeding style but are more subtle than the obvioulsy inappropriate behaviors, such as food throwing and stealing, that were targeted in previous research. Such behaviors might include chewing without closing one's mouth or rapid self-feeding. The need for additional deceleration research is indicated in a report by Favell *et al.* (1980) in which the rapid eating habits of profoundly mentally retarded persons were targeted. The base rate of the participants in the Favell *et al.* (1980) program was approximately one bite every three seconds.

Training Persons with Physical Handicaps

Most research presented previously in this chapter did not include mentally retarded persons with serious physical handicaps that interfere with self-feeding. Specifically, physical disabilities that can seriously hinder the arm and hand movements necessary for self-feeding (e.g., severe spasticity or athetosis) or interfere with integral oral mechanisms (e.g., sucking and chewing processes) were not addressed. Although such disabilities have been discussed frequently in the mental retardation and occupational therapy literature, only minimal behavioral research has been conducted that focused on overcoming such problems. It is predicted, however, that attention paid to the feeding problems of the physically handicapped mentally retarded by applied behavioral researchers will increase. This prediction is based on two factors. First, the problems and subsequent remedial needs of this population have recently become widely recognized, both on a legal and professional/educational (see *The Journal of the Severely Handicapped*, Volumes 1–5) basis. Second, although relevant behavioral research has been scarce, results from available studies indicate that some physical problems which interfere with mealtime behaviors can be alleviated through a behavioral approach. For instance, Thompson, Iwata, and Poynter (1979) reduced the pathological tongue–thrust behavior of a mentally retarded child through contingent punishment of the tongue thrust and reinforcement of proper behavior.

Recently, Iwata, Riordan, Wohl, and Finney (1982) provided an overview of how a behavioral approach can be applied to eating problems considered to be physical in nature. Iwata *et al.* (1982) describe a number of problems that have been resolved, or conceivably could be resolved, through a proficient application of behavioral procedures, including food refusal and selectivity, obesity, pathological tongue thrust, and vomiting and rumination. Actually, although not restricted to mentally retarded persons with obvious physical handicaps, a considerable amount of behavioral research has been conducted on the specific problems of vomiting and rumination (see Davis & Cuvo, 1980, for a review).

In addition to the problem areas just noted, a number of other physically related problems could be approached behaviorally and warrant research attention. For instance, teaching physically handicapped mentally retarded persons how to use adaptive equipment (such as elbow supports for persons with deficient control of arm movements; built-up or specially shaped utensil handles for persons with poor grip control), and the subsequent fading of the use of the adaptive equipment is a needed line of research. Even though such equipment is used somewhat frequently in feeding regimes by caregivers (Snell, 1978), systematic research on the most proficient methods of its use is not readily available.

Using Mealtimes to Enhance Multiple Skill Development

The focus so far has been trends and issues in behavioral research related to teaching independent feeding skills, or to reducing physical problems or inappropriate behaviors that interfere with self-feeding. A somewhat related focus that has been addressed recently with the mentally retarded is using mealtimes to teach adaptive skills besides self-feeding (Halle, Marshall, & Spradlin, 1979; Schepis, Reid, Fitzgerald, Faw, van den Pol, & Welty, in press). More specifically, by expanding the incidental teaching approach of using normally occurring interactions between caregivers and clients to teach language skills to the clients (Hart & Risley, 1968, 1974, 1975), desirable communication behaviors of mentally retarded persons have been increased during mealtime activities. Halle *et al.* (1979) increased relevant vocalizations of moderately and severely mentally retarded persons during mealtimes by modeling appropriate requests for food and/or briefly delaying the delivery of food for 15 seconds. Schepis *et al.* (in press) used multiple procedures during mealtimes, including modeling, food delay, manual guidance, and contingent food presentation, to increase manual sign-language interactions of profoundly mentally retarded persons. Such incidental approaches appear to be a fruitful area for continued research for at least three reasons. First, as noted earlier, mealtime has an inherent reinforcer (the food) that conceivably could be used contingently to shape a variety of language behaviors without detracting significantly from the overall self-feeding process. Second, since mealtimes frequently involve a number of people in close proximity, such social-interaction skills as sharing could be taught. The social and interactional learning possibilities specifically related to mealtime activities have been noted in behavioral research with preschool children (McMahon & Forehand, 1978), but research with the mentally retarded has been minimal. Finally, as noted elsewhere with basic care activities involving persons with severe physical handicaps that prohibit independent self-care (Ivancic, Reid, Iwata, Faw, & Page, 1981), mealtimes involve consistent and frequent interactions with caregivers. Such consistency and frequency are characteristics desirable for behavioral training sessions.

Nutritional Concerns

The need to be concerned with the nutritional status of mentally retarded persons, especially the more seriously impaired, has been recognized frequently in the mental retardation and clinical dietery literature (Jaslow & Spagna, 1977; Laidler, 1976). Concerns over nutrition-related problems are especially relevant with the multihandicapped mentally retarded. For instance, specific nutrient deficiencies and growth delays are noted (Brown, Davis, & Flemming, 1979), as are constipation and regurgitation problems (Laidler, 1976). For these reasons, behavioral research that addresses mealtime procedures should attend to such problems where relevant. For instance, an investigation that evaluates methods of decreasing certain inappropriate self-feeding behaviors (such as finger feeding) should be equally concerned with demonstrating that overall food intake was not hampered significantly. Unfortunately, in most cases only decreases in certain mealtime behaviors were demonstrated during a behavioral program, with no data reported that would indicate that participants increased, or at least maintained, their original level of food intake (Christian et al., 1973; Henriksen & Doughty, 1967; Martin et al., 1971). Decreased food intake should be a special concern in programs where inappropriate behaviors are followed by a time-out procedure that involves removal of the person from the meal, during which time part or all of the meal is missed (see Table I for examples of time-out procedures during mealtime). On the other hand, where food portions are increased for program purposes, concerns over nonbeneficial weight gains should be addressed (Favell et al., 1980).

Recently, there have been two developments that indicate increased awareness of nutritional considerations when implementing behavioral approaches to alter mealtime performance. First, some researchers have included evaluative measures of physical well-being. They are, however, relatively gross measures, such as body weight during the behavioral programs (Albin, 1977; Barton et al., 1970; Favell et al., 1980). Other researchers have included precautionary steps, such as providing high-protein food following a meal that was partially missed due to time-out (Albin, 1977). Second, government regulatory standards have placed operational controls on how food can be deprived from a person as part of a training program (ACMRDD Standards, 1977). Such standards should help promote attention to nutritional concerns in future research endeavors.

Caregiver Training and Management

A significant concern in the general behavior modification literature has been the training of caregivers of the mentally retarded in the proficient use of behavioral training procedures (Gardner, 1973). Concern has also been expressed over the maintenance of caregiver usage of the procedures over periods of time (Kazdin, 1973). This concern also has been addressed recently in mealtime research involving mentally retarded persons (Korabek *et al.*, 1981). Basically, the concern is that where specialized procedures are needed to teach self-feeding skills or to overcome physical disabilities that interfere with eating, caregivers need additional training. The need for research on how to train caregivers such skills becomes more apparent when considering that many people (e.g., institutional attendants, parents) who are responsible for feeding training and/or care of retarded individuals do not have a professional background in behavioral training techniques. Perhaps more importantly, continued research is needed on methods of managing the continued use of behavioral training procedures during mealtimes by caregivers once they have learned how to use the procedures. That is, since even *intensive* procedures for teaching independent self-feeding skills can require training over an 8-week time span and cover over 200 meals to obtain success (Stimbert *et al.*, 1977), procedures are needed to help maintain proficient caregiver performance over those extended time periods. The need for research to develop effective caregiver management procedures during feeding–training regimes becomes more apparent when considering the general behavioral literature on caregiver performance. For instance, there is a vast amount of data showing that institutional staff performance frequently is not improved significantly when staff members are trained in a specific set of skills, but no explicit management procedures are employed in the actual job site where the skills are to be used (Greene, Willis, Levy, & Bailey, 1978; Iwata, Bailey, Brown, Foshee, & Alpern, 1976; Montegar, Reid, Madsen, & Ewell, 1977; Quilitch, 1975). More specific information on needed research in the caregiver management area will be presented in the corresponding section pertaining to the behavioral research on self-dressing.

Summary of Trends and Issues in Feeding Research

This section summarized the behavioral research on teaching independent feeding skills to mentally retarded persons and discussed areas where research is needed and likely to continue. Specific trends were noted, generally for both the acquisition and deceleration of mealtime behaviors of the mentally retarded, and included: the development of a wider variety of target behaviors as dependent variables, an expansion of the types of behavior-change strategies used, and an increased sophistication in the experimental methodologies used to evaluate training procedures. Areas in need of research include:

1. Teaching advanced and more normalized self-feeding skills
2. Teaching persons with physical handicaps that interfere with independent feeding
3. Using mealtime processes to enhance multiple skill development
4. Including nutritional safeguards in behavioral programs with mealtime behaviors
5. Developing effective caregiver training and management procedures specifically designed for mealtime procedures

Specific examples of research needs within each of the five general areas just noted were also provided. In the next section the trends and issues related to research on self-dressing skills will be discussed.

TRENDS AND ISSUES IN BEHAVIORAL RESEARCH ON TRAINING SELF-DRESSING SKILLS

Self-dressing skills are important to mentally retarded persons in much the same way as independent feedings skills. Being able to dress themselves allows individuals greater control over their environment than having to rely on a caregiver. Also, from a more pragmatic point of view for caregivers, independent dressing skills allow the caregivers to be free from the time-consuming task of dressing clients. In addition, there is a third benefit of functional dressing skills that is idiosyncratic to self-dressing. That is, every individual with whom a mentally retarded person comes into contact will most likely be affected by the appearance of that person, including how the person is dressed. Teaching the mentally retarded to dress independently and socially appropriately increases the probability that the effect their appearance has on other individuals will be beneficial. Although the specific impact appropriate dress has on social interactions has not been specifically addressed experimentally, there is general belief that clothing significantly affects a handicapped individual's interpersonal interactions (see Newton, 1976, for a summary). Similarly, the importance of dressing styles is reflected in the views of people who are in service–provision roles for the mentally retarded. For instance, a survey conducted among professionals and administrators from five southeastern states revealed that 94% believed that mentally retarded persons should be able to dress in accordance with popular fashion and 100% agreed that these individuals should not "stand out" because of unusual dress styles (Nutter & Reid, 1978).

A number of investigations have been conducted concerning methods of teaching independent dressing skills. A larger number of commercially available training programs and curricula designed for teaching self-dressing skills to the mentally retarded are available. However, the total amount of behavioral literature pertaining to training self-dressing skills is considerably less than that pertaining to self-feeding.

Chronological Summary of Studies

Overall, a chronological summary of the behavioral research on training independent dressing skills to mentally retarded persons indicates developmental trends similar to those in the behavioral research on training self-feeding skills. The teaching or acquisition strategy is basically the same for both sets of skills; that is, to evoke desired dressing behaviors, trainer instructions, and, if necessary, modeling, physical prompts, and/or manual guidance are provided. The physical guidance is then systematically faded, while target behaviors are reinforced. A description of the basic behavioral acquisition model for teaching dressing skills is provided by Watson and Uzzell (1980). A major difference between the two strategies for teaching self-feeding and self-dressing exists, however, in that there is not an inherent reinforcer (i.e., the food) involved in dressing as there is in successful feeding. Hence, a trainer must provide a reinforcing stimulus that is not normally present during self-dressing regimes. This need for reinforcers extrinsic to the normal dresssing process becomes a more significant training consideration when one focuses on advanced dressing skills in which terminal behaviors are not based on immediate functional utility (warmth provided by clothing) but on delayed social consequences according to social custom (not wearing striped garments with checkered ones). This latter point will be addressed in more detail later.

As with the research on self-feeding, the early behavioral research (i.e., early to mid 1960s) on self-dressing typically indicated that mentally retarded persons could become more independent in dressing and undressing themselves through participation in a behavioral program, but it lacked experimental components integral to applied behavioral research. Frequently, independent dressing was one of many targeted skill areas forming part of a multiple self-help skills training program, but detailed information on the procedures used with dressing *per se* was lacking (Bensberg, Colwell, & Cassel, 1965; Girardeau & Spradlin, 1964). Teaching very basic dressing and undressing skills, such as pulling pants up and down, also has been included in programs that were primarily concerned with toilet training (Mahoney, Van Wagenen, & Meyerson, 1971). However, as with the research on self-feeding, the early research on self-dressing provided the groundwork for the more advanced research that followed, although some of the more recent research is plagued with methodological deficiencies similar to those in the early studies. Such methodological problems include weak experimental designs, that is, no control groups and/or no experimental replications (Colwell, Richards, McCarver, & Ellis, 1973; Murphy & Zahm, 1978), no reliability estimates on measures of client progress (Brody, Esslinger, Casselman, McGlinchey, & Mitala, 1975; Cuvo, 1973) and insufficient procedural information to allow for experimental replication (Gray & Kasteler, 1969).

During the investigations directly targeting self-dressing skills in the 1970s, there were three trends that were similar to trends in the self-feeding research of the same period. However, in all, the thoroughness of the research on self-dressing was considerably less than that with self-feeding. The first of the three trends during the 1970s was the focus on a wider variety, and more advanced set, of self-dressing skills. For instance, whereas early research generally targeted a relatively small and simple set of self-dressing skills, such as putting on and taking off a shirt, pants, and socks (Minge & Ball, 1967), later research included such basic skills plus more complex ones, including tying shoes and fastening bras (Martin, Kehoe, Bird, Jensen, & Darbyshire, 1971). Samples of the types of dressing skills focused on in the 1960s and 1970s are presented in Table II. The second apparent trend was that the research in the 1970s expanded the types of training procedures used. Most noticeably, Azrin, Schaeffer, and Wesolowski (1976) developed an intensive training program for self-dressing that was similar in goals and methodology to the intensive training approach developed for self-feeding that was described earlier. Finally, the third trend in the research was an increase in experimental rigor in the investigations on teaching self-dressing skills. Indications of the increased attention paid to ex-

TABLE II
Samples of Types of Dressing Skills Targeted in Behavioral Research

Dressing skills	Reference
Removing shirt or dress, pants, socks; putting on shirt or dress, pants, socks	Minge & Ball, 1967
Putting on underpants, undershirt, bra, sweater, socks, shoes; lacing and tying shoes	Martin, Kehoe, Bird, Jensen, & Darbyshire, 1971
Putting on and removing socks, shoes, pants, shirt	Azrin, Schaeffer, & Wesolowski, 1976
Removing socks, shoes, shirt, pants (including unsnapping, zipping) and putting them away; getting new shirt, pants and putting them on	King & Turner, 1975
Selecting blouses that are color-coordinated with pants	Nutter & Reid, 1978

perimental methodology are reflected in almost every component of the research, ranging from the use of social validity procedures (Nutter & Reid, 1978) to long-term follow-up measures (Ball, Seric, & Payne, 1971).

Since the main emphasis was on demonstrating methods of teaching mentally retarded persons to dress and undress themselves independently, a somewhat related line of research was the demonstration of methods to reduce the frequency of mentally retarded persons' undressing inappropriately. That is, a problem that has been reported a number of times is the disrobing in public by an individual, frequently a severely or profoundly mentally retarded person living in an institutional setting. Because of the social undesirablility and potential health hazards involved in undressing in public (Durana & Cuvo, 1980), several behavioral procedures have been used to decrease such disrobing. Usually, differential reinforcement of other behavior (DRO) either by itself or with other procedures (e.g., time-out and response-cost) has been used with reportedly good success (Paul & Miller, 1971; Schaeffer & Martin, 1969; Thompson & Grabowski, 1972), however there has been some inconsistency in the effectiveness of DRO (Durana & Cuvo, 1980). Other deceleration strategies that have appeared successful in reducing disrobing in public include overcorrection (Foxx, 1976) and time-out with physical restraint (Hamilton, Stevens, & Allen, 1967). Outside of the research on undressing in public, there has not been the concern over decreasing the occurrence of behaviors that interfere with appropriate self-dressing skills as there has been with behaviors interfering with self-feeding.

Considerably less research has been conducted on methods of teaching self-dressing skills to mentally retarded persons than of teaching self-feeding skills. Generally, the research available allows for the conclusion that a technology exists for caregivers of the mentally retarded (at essentially all levels of retardation) for teaching basic self-dressing skills as well as related, but generally simpler (Snell, 1978), undressing skills. However, it is not clear if more elaborate conclusions, based on behavioral research with good internal and external validity, can be supported. We have only begun to answer the multitude of questions related to teaching totally independent dressing skills. Attempts to describe specifically what questions have not been answered and, correspondingly, those areas in need of research will be treated next.

Before discussing the *specific* areas in need of research related to self-dressing skills, further explanation on the *overall* need for research in this skill area seems warranted. Despite the existence of a technology for assisting mentally retarded persons in acquiring basic dressing and undressing skills, an indication that many dressing-related problems still exist can be obtained by observing a group of mentally retarded individuals in a residential setting, whether it be a group home, a halfway house, or (especially) an institution. Certainly, the vast majority of individuals will be dressed, although it would not be surprising to find at any given time at least a few individuals living in a state institution who are not completely clothed. However, besides being clothed (and it would not be apparent that each mentally retarded person had dressed independently), the similarity between how mentally retarded persons are dressed and how persons of normal intelligence and adaptive functioning are dressed begins to decrease. Typical differences in the dress of the mentally retarded include wearing clothes that are not fashionable (clothes of poor quality or different from popular style), wearing poorly fitting clothes or wearing clothing items that do not correspond to popular standards for color coordination or color patterns (two obviously different checkered patterns on a pair of pants and shirt), wearing clothes inadequately laundered (noticeably wrinkled blouses), and wearing clothing that may be fashionable and appropriately laundered but worn in a manner that is discrepant from peer group norms (pants not completely buttoned, a slip extending noticeably beyond a dress hemline). These examples are not intended to reflect the dressing styles of all mentally retarded persons, as that would be a gross misrepresentation.

However, the examples do represent a significant number of individuals based on this author's observations of literally thousands of retarded persons, especially among the severely and profoundly mentally retarded, in numeruous residential settings in different parts of the country. Such dressing patterns are somewhat surprising considering the vast array of commercially available programs for teaching a wide diversity of self-dressing skills as indicated earlier. Apparently, the programs are not being used by care-givers or the programs are not being used proficiently. A third explanation for the abnormal dressing style of many mentally retarded individuals is that the commercially available programs (most of which have not been experimentally evaluated) are not effective.

Specific Research Issues

Many of the specific areas warranting research in the self-dressing area are the same as those in the self-feeding domain. However, a number of different areas also exist.

Teaching Advanced Dressing Skills

As with the research on self-feeding, probably the most apparent of the recent trends in the behavioral research on self-dressing skills is the focus on teaching *advanced* skills. That is, recent research has focused on skills that are more releated to dressing in accordance with social customs as opposed to focusing on the basic skills necessary to ensure that an individual wears at least protective clothing—lower garment, upper garment, and footwear. Similarly, recent research has targeted skills that involve care and preparation of clothing items to make normal dressing behaviors possible. For instance, Cronin and Cuvo (1979) targeted clothing-care skills by training mending skills to mentally retarded persons; Thompson, Braam, and Fuqua (1982) targeted independent laundering skills; Nutter and Reid (1978) focused on socially appropriate dressing skills to train mentally retarded women to select clothing items based on popular fashions and color coordination. These studies represent additional examples of the growing emphasis on teaching community survival skills to the mentally retarded. It is likely that research on dressing skills to enhance community survival skills will continue along with research on self-feeding.

Numerous questions also arise when considering teaching dressing skills necessary for community living. Predominantly, the questions center on how to *teach* specific skills, and how to *define* and *measure* relevant behaviors in accurate, yet programmatically efficient, ways. Such questions might include how to teach mentally retarded individuals to determine the appropriate fit of clothing (appropriate tightness, length of garments, etc.,) and how to coordinate clothes for seasonal needs or social functions. Similarly, teaching additional skills for clothing care warrant research, such as the appropriate folding and hanging of garments, and the ability to determine which articles of clothing should be folded and stored in a drawer, versus those that should be hung in a closet. Teaching these persons how to purchase clothing that balances functional considerations (e.g., providing a comfortable degree of warmth during winter months), current fashion trends, and economic concerns would also be a useful line of research.

Although a basic premise of the community-survival skills research involving advanced self-dressing skills is to assist mentally retarded persons to live in community settings, this should not be interpreted to mean that there is minimal need to teach advanced dressing skills in institutional settings. As observations of dress styles during a quick tour of many institutions will indicate, there is a strong need to teach skills to institutionalized residents that will allow them to dress more independently and normally. Unfortunately, however, teaching more advanced self-dressing skills to the institutionalized mentally retarded is likely to be a formidable task because of traditional institutional operations. More specifically, many institutional operations do not allow for advanced dressing skills to develop. Industrial or mass-laundering procedures typically destroy color and fit of fashionable clothing items, for example, lack of sufficient storage space for individual clothes does not allow for appropriate clothing care, and residents receive relatively small amounts for clothing allowance per individual. Hence, in order to make significant advances in the types of dressing skills taught in institutional setttings, researchers will have to address their inquiry either directly or indirectly to methods of changing administrative and support-service (e.g., laundry) operations, as well as to the development of teaching strategies to mentally retarded clients.

Since institutional populations are becoming more concentrated with persons exhibiting the most serious skill deficiences—the severely and profoundly mentally retarded (Scheerenberger, 1976), teaching residents advanced self-dressing skills may be a difficult task. Overcoming such deficiencies in order to teach relatively complicated tasks involved in advanced self-dressing is likely to require extensive training. One potentially fruitful line of research in this area would be the development of prosthetic devices or, as referred to in vocational training, "jigs" (Gold & Barclay, 1973) that could be used to help mentally retarded persons to select appropriate clothing. For instance, simple coding designs could be labeled unobtrusively on the inside of garments to indicate which items would be color coordinated if worn together. In this manner, mentally retarded persons could match a small number of codes in order to color coordinate their clothing, as opposed to matching items from an infinite array of color-shade combinations. Similarly, unobtrusive markings could be placed on the middle of the bottom of a shirt and the inside midpoint of the waistband of a pair of pants in order to provide a cue for lining up the shirt with the pants, as opposed to having a shirttail hanging out or having the front of the pants twisted to the side. A number of such procedures are currently in use in residential settings, but systematic evaluation of how to use the procedures, as well as the eventual fading out of their use, has not been conducted or disseminated.

Developing Social Validity Components in Advanced Dressing Programs

As more advanced self-dressing skills become the target of behavioral research, special concern over social validity will be needed. Even though social validity is becoming a key issue in behavioral research in general, concern is especially needed for skills involved in advanced self-dressing; that is, much of normal dressing activities is based on what is considered to be fashionable or popular. The determination of what is popular, and therefore desirable to be taught to mentally retarded persons from a normalization perspective, can be considered a special case of determining the social validity (popularity, fashionableness, etc.) of the dressing behaviors targeted. Nutter and Reid (1978) recently addressed this point in their program that was designed to enable mentally retarded women to color coordinate garments according to popular fashion. To determine what the popular fashion was, Nutter and Reid observed the color combinations worn by 649 women in the local community and determined the 27 most popular combinations. Similar methods regarding the determination and specification of popular dressing behaviors are warranted for a variety of dressing skills. For instance, methods are needed for determining what type of garment is "in style" (e.g., a particular type of jeans) when purchasing clothing or selecting particular items to be worn on a given day. Thus, whenever clothes are chosen because of societal norms as opposed to protective functions, social validity-type questions are involved in determining the appropriateness of the garments. Therefore, a useful direction for future research would be to develop ways for care-givers to determine and incorporate popular dressing behaviors into programs for training self-dressing skills. Although the method described by Nutter and Reid (1978) provides one approach, their community observation system was time consuming and thus likely to have wide applicability to caregivers. For maximum utility, the procedures must not only be affective but also efficient.

Research is also needed on the development of methods to teach mentally retarded individuals how to determine for themselves popular and unpopular dressing behaviors. For instance, methods that nonretarded persons use to determine how to dress fashionably could be specified, and perhaps simplified, and then taught at least to persons with mild and/or moderate mental retardation. One such method might be to teach how to identify an appropriate peer group and to observe the dressing styles of the group (via *in vivo* observations, magazine pictures, television, etc.) in relation to different social activities such as going to school, going to a dance, and going on a picnic. Mentally retarded individuals could then attempt to match their dressing style to that of the peer group for a particular activity.

Training Persons with Physical Handicaps

The behavioral literature on teaching self-dressing skills to mentally retarded persons with physical handicaps is similar to the self-feeding literature in that there is a general paucity of experimental studies. A trend to conduct such research should occur because of the increased awareness of the educational rights of the physically handicapped mentally retarded, although the trend is not yet as apparent in the dressing research as it is with feeding.

Basically, the research aims with this population is the same for teaching self-feeding and self-dressing skills: to develop and evaluate methods to assist individuals in overcoming or circumventing (i.e., using adaptive equipment) physical disabilities that interfere with independent functioning. Differences exist in the two skill areas, however, in that specific types of physical disabilities must be addressed. Basic concerns in self-feeding are developing methods for overcoming the physical problems associated with oral processes involved in eating and with the specific arm and hand movements necessary for getting food from the plate to the mouth. On the other hand, primary concerns in self-dressing involve developing procedures for overcoming physical problems that interfere with specific fine motor skills idiosyncratic to dressing, such as buttoning, zipping, and tying. Also, concerns in self-dressing involve developing multiple gross-motor movements necessary for putting on and taking off pants, shirts, bras, and hats.

A second issue in the self-dressing area involving the physically handicapped mentally retarded that warrants attention is the teaching of self-dressing skills that minimize the abnormal appearances associated with physical anomalies (see Newton, 1976, for a discussion). Such research is needed to determine specific methods of dressing that will minimize unusual appearances as well as to determine procedures for training retarded persons to use those methods. Similarly, research attention should be given to using specially adapted clothing that appears normal and attractive yet makes provisions for irreversible handicaps that prohibit totally normal self-dressing (see Gay Apparels, undated). For instance, where an individual lacks sufficient manual dexterity for buttoning or zipping because of abnormally wide but short fingers, Velcro fasteners, which are visible only to the individual wearing the clothing, can be used. If such questions seem to be out of the realm of typical behavioral approaches, they are nevertheless integral to the development of independent dressing skills by mentally retarded persons with physical handicaps and, therefore, should be given serious consideration in future behavioral research.

Staff Management

Further research might center on the development of supervisory methods for insuring the proficient use, over periods of time, of training programs for caregivers responsible for teaching independent dressing to mentally retarded persons. The need for management strategies for caregiver performance is especially apparent when involving more seriously mentally retarded clients (i.e., severely and profoundly mentally retarded; physically handicapped mentally retarded). There are at least three reasons for the need for such research related to training self-dressing skills. First, despite a considerable amount of behavioral research on methods of caregiver training performance in mental retardation in general, there have been only a handful of studies that actually evaluated long-term effects of management interventions on caregiver behavior (see Ivancic *et al.*, 1981,for a discussion). Hence, there is little experimental data available regarding the effectiveness of procedures for maintaining desired staff behaviors. Second, training independent dressing skills to the most severely mentally retarded is frequently time consuming (Adelson-Bernstein & Sandow, 1978). Where caregivers (e.g., institutional staff) are expected to continue training procedures over long periods of time, reinforcers for caregivers are needed to maintain such endeavors. In some cases, client progress might provide such reinforcers. However, when the progress is slow, as is frequently the case with the severely and profoundly mentally retarded (Berkson & Landesman-Dwyer, 1977), such progress is not likely to function as a reinforcer (Kazdin, 1973; Panyan, Boozer, & Morris, 1970). A third reason for the need for specific procedures to maintain proficient staff-training performances is that the staff behavior (i.e., attention) is most likely the only reinforcer that will maintain client progress. That is, there is probably no immediately reinforcing consequence for maintaining independent dressing by clients except staff behavior. Hence, it is crucial that staff consistently provide necessary reinforcers to clients to maintain progress in self-dressing activities.

A research question which stems from the time-consuming characteristic of dressing programs with the seriously mentally retarded is determining the advantages and disadvantages of using intensive training procedures (Azrin *et al.*, 1976) versus more typical nonintensive ones vis-à-vis care-giver performance. More specifically, intensive training procedures that involve a large amount of staff time but encompass only a small amount of calendar time (e.g., 15 hours of training over three days) may have different effects on staff behavior than more traditional procedures that involve staff time encompassing longer calendar periods (e.g., 15 hours of training spread over 10 weeks). Research evaluating potentially differential effects of the two types of procedures, such as the amount of staff adherence to the specific training regimes, could prove useful for service providers.

Summary of Trends and Issues in Dressing Research

This section has focused on discussion of the behavioral research on teaching independent dressing skills to the mentally retarded as well as areas warranting additional research. Generally, the research that has occurred has followed the same trends as the behavioral research on self-feeding skills, although a considerably smaller amount of research has been directed toward self-dressing. Trends that have occurred since the early research in 1960s include an expansion in the types of dressing behaviors taught to retarded persons, an expansion in the types of training procedures used, and an overall but somewhat inconsistent increase in experimental rigor in conducting the investigations. Areas in need of additional research include:

1. Teaching advanced self-dressing skills
2. Using social validity components in the research on advanced self-dressing
3. Training mentally retarded persons with physical handicaps
4. Managing caregiver performance in training programs

General Summary

In this chapter we reviewed past trends and discussed relevant issues in behavioral research on training self-feeding and self-dressing skills to mentally retarded persons. Two general assertions about behavioral research in these two self-help skill areas were made: (1) that considerable advances have taken place since the early 1960s in the development and evaluation of behavioral procedures for training these skills to the retarded; and (2) despite the apparent progress, a larger number of questions still remain regarding training independent dressing and feeding skills, such that considerably more research is still needed.

Past reviews and summaries of self-help skill literature were cited to prove that significant progress has occurred in the development of behavioral training technologies for self-feeding and self-dressing. General research trends occurring in the two areas since the 1960s that reflect such progress were also discussed. Progress in the expansion in the types of skills targeted as well as the types of training procedures used has been noted, and in the increased experimental rigor with which the research has been conducted. Information from more than 20 studies targeting skills in each of the two self-help areas was used to exemplify these trends.

To support the second general assertion, that more research is needed, we discussed five general areas related to self-feeding research and four areas related to self-dressing research. We highlighted the importance of future research in each of these areas regarding the continuing need to improve the technologies for training truly independent feeding and dressing skills to the retarded. In many cases, we made optimistic predictions that future research would be conducted in specific areas. As with any predictions, the exact likelihood of the occurrence of such research is unknown. We hope, however, that this chapter will have the effect of increasing that likelihood.

Acknowledgments

Appreciation is expressed to Martin Ivancic for his assistance in obtaining relevant information; to Louis Burgio, Helen Reid, Maureen Schepis, and Gerry Faw for their comments on an earlier draft; and to Christine Trippel for manuscript preparation.

References

ACMRDD, *Standards for services for developmentally disabled individuals.* Chicago: Joint Commission on Accreditation of Hospitals, 1977.

ADELSON-BERNSTEIN, N., & SANDOW, L. Teaching buttoning to severely/profoundly retarded multihandicapped children. *Education and Training of the Mentally Retarded*, 1978, *13*, 178-183.

ALBIN, J. B. Some variables influencing the maintenance of acquired self-feeding behavior in profoundly retarded children. *Mental Retardation*, 1977, *15*, 49-52.

AZRIN, N. H., & ARMSTRONG, P. M. The "minimeal"—A method for teaching eating skills to the profoundly retarded. *Mental Retardation*, 1973, *11*, 9-13.

AZRIN, N. H., SCHAEFFER, R. M., & WESOLOWSKI, M. D. A rapid method of teaching profoundly retarded persons to dress by a reinforcement-guidance method. *Mental Retardation*, 1976, *14*, 29-33.

AZRIN, N. H., & WESOLOWSKI, M. D. Theft reversal: An overcorrection procedure for eliminating stealing by retarded persons. *Journal of Applied Behavior Analysis*, 1974, *7*, 577-581.

BAER, D. M., WOLF, M. M., & RISELY, T. R. Some current dimensions of applied behavior analysis. *Journal of Applied Behavior Analysis*, 1968, *1*, 91-97.

BALL, T. S., SERIC, K., & PAYNE, L. E. Long-term retention of self-help skill training in the profoundly retarded. *American Journal of Mental Deficiency*, 1971, *76*, 378-382.

BARTON, E. S., GUESS, D., GARCIA, E., & BAER, D. M. Improvement of retardates' mealtime behaviors by time-out procedures using multiple-baseline techniques. *Journal of Applied Behavior Analysis*, 1970, *3*, 77-84.

BELLAMY, G. T., & CLARK, G. Picture recipe cards as an approach to teaching severely and profoundly retarded adults to cook. *Education and Training of the Mentally Retarded*, 1977, *12*, 69-73.

BENSBERG, G. J. (Ed.). *Teaching the mentally retarded: A handbook for ward personnel*. Atlanta, Ga.: Southern Regional Education Board, 1965.

BENSBERG, G. J., COLWELL, C. N., & CASSEL, R. H. Teaching the profoundly retarded self-help activities by behavior shaping techniques. *American Journal of Mental Deficiency*, 1965, *69*, 674-679.

BERKOWITZ, S., SHERRY, P. J., & DAVIS, B. A. Teaching self-feeding skills to profound retardates using reinforcement and fading procedures, *Behavior Therapy*, 1971, *2*, 62-67.

BERKSON, G., & LANDESMAN-DWYER, S. Behavioral research on severe and profound mental retardation (1955-1974). *American Journal of Mental Deficiency*, 1977, *81*, 428-454.

BRODY, J. F., ESSLINGER, S., CASSELMAN, G., McGLINCHEY, M., & MITALA, R. The itinerant training team: Variations on a familiar concept. *Mental Retardation*, 1975, *13*, 38-42.

BROWN, J. E., DAVIS, E., & FLEMMING, P. L. Nutritional assessment of children with handicapping conditions. *Mental Retardation*, 1979, *17*, 129-132.

CHRISTIAN, W. P., HOLLOMON, S. W., & LANIER, C. L. An attendant operated feeding program for severely and profoundly retarded females. *Mental Retardation*, 1973, *11*, 35-37.

COLWELL, C. N., RICHARDS, E., McCARVER, R. B., & ELLIS, N. R. Evaluation of self-help habit training of the profoundly retarded. *Mental Retardation*, 1973, *11*, 14-18.

CRONIN, K. A., & CUVO, A. J. Teaching mending skills to mentally retarded adolescents. *Journal of Applied Behavior Analysis*, 1979, *12*, 401-406.

CUVO, A. J. Child care workers as trainers of mentally retarded children. *Child Care Quarterly*, 1973, *2*, 25-37.

DAVIS, P. K., & CUVO, A. J. Chronic vomiting and rumination in intellectually normal and retarded individuals: Review and evaluation of behavioral research. *Behavior Research of Severe Developmental Disabilities*, 1980, *1*, 31-59.

DURANA, I., & CUVO, A. J. A comparison of procedures for decreasing public disrobing of an institutionalized profoundly mentally retarded woman. *Mental Retardation*, 1980, *18*, 185-188.

FAVELL, J. E., McGIMSEY, J. F., & JONES, M. L. Rapid eating in the retarded: Reduction by nonaversive procedures. *Behavior Modification*, 1980, *4*, 481-492.

Foxx, R. M. The use of overcorrection to eliminate the public disrobing (stripping) of retarded women. *Behavior Research and Therapy*, 1976, *14*, 53-61.

Gardner, J. M. Training and trainers. A review of research on teaching behavior modification. In R. D. Rubin, J. P. Brady, & J. H. Henderson (Eds.), *Advances in behavior therapy* (Vol. 4). New York: Academic Press, 1973.

Gay Apparels Company, Inc. Special catalog for home care clients. Cotter, Arkansas: Author, undated.

Girardeau, F. L., & Spradlin, J. E. Token rewards in a cottage program. *Mental Retardation*, 1964, *2*, 345-351.

Gold, M. W., & Barclay, C. R. The learning of difficult discriminations by the moderately and severely retarded. *Mental Retardation*, 1973, *11*, 9-11.

Gray, R. M., & Kasteler, J. M. The effects of social reinforcement and training on institutionalized mentally retarded children. *American Journal of Mental Deficiency*, 1969, *74*, 50-56.

Greene, B. F., Willis, B. S., Levy, R., Bailey, J. S. Measuring client gains from staff-implemented programs. *Journal of Applied Behavior Analysis*, 1978, *11*, 395-412.

Groves, I. D., & Carroccio, D. F. A self-feeding program for the severely and profoundly mentally retarded. *Mental Retardation*, 1971, *9*, 10-12.

Halle, J. W., Marshall, A. M., & Spradlin, J. E. Time delay: A technique to increase language use and facilitate generalization in retarded children. *Journal of Applied Behavior Analysis*, 1979, *12*, 431-439.

Hamilton, J., & Allen, P. Ward programming for severely retarded institutionalized residents. *Mental Retardation*, 1967, *5*, 22-24.

Hamilton, J., Stephens, L., & Allen, P. Controlling aggressive and destructive behavior in severely retarded institutionalized residents. *American Journal of Mental Deficiency*, 1967, *71*, 852-856.

Hart, B. M., & Risley, T. R. Establishing use of descriptive adjectives in the spontaneous speech of disadvantaged preschool children. *Journal of Applied Behavior Analysis*, 1968, *1*, 109-120.

Hart, B. M., & Risley, T. R. Using preschool materials to modify language of disadvantaged children. *Journal of Applied Behavior Analysis*, 1974, *7*, 243-256.

Hart, B., & Risley, T. R. Incidental teaching of language in the preschool. *Journal of Applied Behavior Analysis*, 1975, *8*, 411-420.

Henriksen, K., & Doughty, R. Decelerating undesired mealtime behavior in a group of profoundly retarded boys. *American Journal of Mental Deficiency*, 1967, *72*, 40-44.

Ivancic, M. T., Reid, D. H., Iwata, B. A., Faw, G. D., & Page, T. J. Evaluating a supervision program for developing and maintaining therapeutic staff-resident interactions during institutional care routines. *Journal of Applied Behavior Analysis*, 1981, *14*, 95-107.

Iwata, B. A., Bailey, J. S., Brown, K. M., Foshee, T. J., & Alpern, M. A performance-based lottery to improve residential care and training by institutional staff. *Journal of Applied Behavior Analysis*, 1976, *9*, 417-431.

Iwata, B. A., Riordan, M. M., Wohl, M. K., & Finney, J. W. Pediatric feeding disorders: Behavioral analysis and treatment. In P. J. Accardo, (Ed.), *Failure to thrive in infancy and early childhood: A multidisciplinary approach to a common pediatric problem*. Baltimore: University Park Press, 1982.

Jaslow, R. T., & Spagna, M. B. Gaps in a comprehensive system of services for the mentally retarded. *Mental Retardation*, 1977, *15*, 6-9.

Johnson, V. M., & Werner, R. A. *A step-by-step learning guide for retarded infants and children*. Syracuse: Syracuse University Press, 1975.

Kazdin, A. E. Issues in behavior modification with mentally retarded persons. *American Journal of Mental Deficiency*, 1973, *78*, 134-140.

King, L. W., & Turner, R. D. Teaching a profoundly retarded adult at home by non-professionals. *Journal of Behavior Therapy & Experimental Psychiatry,* 1975, *6,* 117-121.

Korabek, C. A., Reid, D. H., & Ivancic, M. T. Improving needed food intake of profoundly handicapped children through effective supervision of institutional staff. *Applied Research in Mental Retardation,* 1981, *2,* 69-88.

Laidler, J. Nutritional assessment of common problems found among the developmentally disabled. *Mental Retardation,* 1976, *14,* 24-28.

Mahoney, K., Van Wagenen, R. K., & Meyerson, L. Toilet training of normal and retarded children. *Journal of Applied Behavior Analysis,* 1971, *4,* 173-181.

Marholin, D., O'Toole, K. M., Touchette, P. E., Berger, P. L., & Doyle, D. A. 'I'll have a Big Mac, large fries, large coke, and apple pie,"'... or teaching adaptive community skills. *Behavior Therapy,* 1979, *10,* 236-248.

Martin, G. L., Kehoe, B., Bird, E., Jensen, V., & Darbyshire, M. Operant conditioning in dressing behavior of severely retarded girls. *Mental Retardation,* 1971, *9,* 27-31.

Martin, G. L., McDonald, S., & Omichinski, M. An operant analysis of response interactions during meals with severely retarded girls. *American Journal of Mental Deficiency,* 1971, *76,* 68-75.

Matson, J. L., Ollendick, T. H., & Adkins, J. A comprehensive dining program for mentally retarded adults. *Behavior Research and Therapy,* 1980, *18,* 107-112.

McMahon, R. J., & Forehand, R. Nonprescription behavior therapy: Effectiveness of a brochure in teaching mothers to correct their children's inappropriate mealtime behaviors. *Behavior Therapy,* 1978, *9,* 814-820.

Minge, M. R., & Ball, T. S. Teaching of self-help skills to profoundly retarded patients. *American Journal of Mental Deficiency,* 1967, *71,* 864-868.

Montegar, C., Reid, D. H., Madsen, C. H., & Ewell, M. D. Increasing institutional staff-to-resident interactions through in-service training and supervisor approval. *Behavior Therapy,* 1977, *8,* 533-540.

Murphy, M. J., & Zahm, D. Effect of improved physical and social environment on self-help and problem behaviors of institutionalized retarded males. *Behavior Modification,* 1978, *2,* 193-210.

Nelson, G. L., Cone, J. D., & Hanson, C. R. Training correct utensil use in retarded children: Modeling vs. physical guidance. *American Journal of Mental Deficiency,* 1975, *80,* 114-122.

Newton, A. Clothing: A positive part of the rehabilitation process. *Journal of Rehabilitation,* 1976, *42,* 18-22.

Nutter, D., & Reid, D. H. Teaching retarded women a clothing selection skill using community norms. *Journal of Applied Behavior Analysis,* 1978, *11,* 475-487.

O'Brien, F., & Azrin, N. H. Developing proper mealtime behaviors of the institutionalized retarded. *Journal of Applied Behavior Analysis,* 1972, *5,* 389-399.

O'Brien, F., Bugle, C., & Azrin, N. H. Training and maintaining a retarded child's proper eating. *Journal of Applied Behavior Analysis,* 1972, *5,* 67-72.

Panyan, M., Boozer, H., & Morris, N. Feedback to attendants as a reinforcer for applying operant techniques. *Journal of Applied Behavior Analysis,* 1970, *3,* 1-4.

Paul, H. A., & Miller, J. R. Reduction of extreme deviant behaviors in a severely retarded girl. *Training School Bulletin,* 1971, *67,* 193-197.

Plummer, S., Baer, D. M., & LeBlanc, J. M. Functional considerations in the use of procedural time-out and an effective alternative. *Journal of Applied Behavior Analysis,* 1977, *10,* 689-705.

Quilitch, H. R. A comparison of three staff-management procedures. *Journal of Applied Behavior Analysis,* 1975, *8,* 59-66.

Robinson-Wilson, M. A. Picture recipe cards as an approach to teaching severely and profoundly retarded adults to cook. *Education and Training of the Mentally Retarded,* 1977, *12,* 69-73.

SCHAEFFER, H. H., & MARTIN, P. L. *Behavioral Therapy.* New York: McGraw-Hill, 1969.

SCHEERENBERGER, R. C. A survey of public residential facilities. *Mental Retardation,* 1976, *14,* 32-35.

SCHEPIS, M. M., REID, D. H., FITZGERALD, J. R., FAW, G. D., VAN DEN POL, R., & WELTY, J. Incidental teaching of sign language skills to autistic and profoundly retarded youth. *Journal of Applied Behavior Analysis,* in press.

SHEARER, D., BILLINGSLEY, J., FROHMAN, A., HILLIARD, J., JOHNSON, F., & SHEARER, M. *The Portage guide to early education: Instructions and checklist.* Portage, Wisc.: Cooperative Educational Service Agency, undated.

SNELL, M. E. (Ed.). *Systematic instruction of the moderately and severely handicapped.* Columbus, Ohio: Charles E. Merrill, 1978.

SONG, A. Y., & GANDHI, R. An analysis of behavior during the acquisition and maintenance phase of self-spoon feeding skills of profound retardates. *Mental Retardation,* 1974, *12,* 25-28.

STIMBERT, V. E., MINOR, J. W., & McCOY, J. F. Intensive feeding training with retarded children. *Behavior Modification,* 1977, *1,* 517-529.

STOLZ, S. B., & WOLF, M. M. Visually discriminated behavior in a "blind" adolescent retardate. *Journal of Applied Behavior Analysis,* 1969, *2,* 65-77.

THOMPSON, T., & GRABOWKSI, J. *Behavior modification of the mentally retarded.* New York: Oxford University Press, 1972.

THOMPSON, G. A., IWATA, B. A., & POYNTER, H. Operant control of pathological tongue thrust in spastic cerebral palsy. *Journal of Applied Behavior Analysis,* 1979, *12,* 325-333.

THOMPSON, T. J., BRAAM, S. J., & FUQUA, R. W. Training and generalization of laundry skills: A multiple-probe validation with multiply handicapped persons. *Journal of Applied, Behavior Analysis,* in press.

VAN DEN POL, R. A., IWATA, B. A., IVANCIC, M. T., PAGE, T. J., NEEF, N. A., & WHITLEY, F. P. Teaching the handicapped to eat in public places: Acquisition, generalization, and maintenance of restaurant skills. *Journal of Applied Behavior Analysis,* 1981, *14,* 61-69.

WATSON, L. S. Application of operant conditioning techniques to institutionalized severely and profoundly retarded children. *Mental Retardation Abstract,* 1967, *4,* 1-18.

WATSON, L. S. *How to use behavior modification with mentally retarded and autistic children: Programs for administrators, teachers, parents, and nurses.* Tuscaloosa, Al.: Behavior Modification Technology, Inc., 1972.

WATSON L. S., & UZZELL, R. Teaching self-help skills, grooming skills, and utensil feeding skills to the mentally retarded. In J. L. Matson & J. R. McCartney (Eds.), *Handbook of behavior modification with the mentally retarded.* New York: Plenum Press, 1980.

WESTWAY, A. M., & APOLLONI, T. (Eds.). *Becoming independent: A Living system.* Bellevue, Wash.: Edmark Associates, 1978.

WHITMAN, T. L., & SCIBAK, J. W. Behavior modification research with the severely and profoundly retarded. In N. R. Ellis, (Ed.), *Handbook of mental deficiency, psychological theory of research.* Hillsdale, N.J.: Lawrence Erlbaum, 1979.

ZEILLER, M. D., & JERVEY, S. S. Development of behavior: Self-feeding. *Journal of Consulting and Clinical Psychology,* 1968, *32,* 164-168.

8   A Critical Assessment of Overcorrection Procedures with Mentally Retarded Persons

RALPH P. FERRETTI AND ALBERT R. CAVALIER

INTRODUCTION

The last two decades have been a time of enormous change in the history of residential facilities for mentally retarded persons. These changes stand in stark contrast to the preceding period of neglect, during which "morons" were seen as "responsible to a large degree for many, if not all, of our social problems" (Goddard, 1915). The two most widely advocated solutions for these problems, sterilization and institutional segregation, arose from the common motivation to improve the genetic pool (Baumeister, 1970). Sterilization did not receive widespread support because of moral considerations, leaving segregation as the only viable method of control.

A major consequence of widespread segregation was that institutions became increasingly custodial, failing to fulfill their earlier educational mission. The appalling conditions which accompanied this isolation, the rise of advocacy groups, and President Kennedy's public expression of concern about the mentally retarded (President's Panel on Mental Retardation Report, 1962) served as the impetus for the emergence of the principle of normalization (Nirje, 1969) and the de-institutionalization movement. Two important effects

---

RALPH P. FERRETTI • Cognitive Studies, 406 Hall Health, GS-27, University of Washington, Seattle, Washington 98125.   ALBERT R. CAVALIER • National Research and Demonstration Institute, Association for Retarded Citizens, 2501 Avenue J, Arlington, Texas 70611. This work was in part supported by grant HD-124 from the National Institute of Child Health and Human Development while the authors were predoctoral Fellows in Mental Retardation at the University of Alabama, and grant HD-13029 from the National Institute of Child Health and Human Development to the Kansas Center for Mental Retardation and Human Development.

of this new advocacy (Kurtz, 1975) were the placement of the brightest, most competent mentally retarded persons in community and other noninstitutional settings, and a heightened sensitivity for the kinds and quality of treatment provided consumers of residential institutional services.

The single most important criterion for institutional placement is the client's level of mental retardation (Saenger, 1960). More than half of the institutionalized retarded persons are in the severe or profound range (Baumeister, 1970), so it is not surprising that most training programs in residential facilities are directed at self-help and behavior-management problems. In general, the most effective interventions combine, in various proportions, reinforcement for appropriate behavior and aversive consequences for inappropriate behavior. In those instances in which aggressive-disruptive, stereotyped or self-injurious behaviors are targeted for change, overtly punitive contingencies have often been used because the misbehavior effectively precludes the shaping of appropriate behavior (Koegel & Covert, 1972; Risley, 1968). Although many of these techniques have been shown to have immediate and durable effects (cf. Baumeister & Forehand, 1973), their use has been severely limited by legal constraints in most states (*Wyatt* v. *Stickney,* 1972, Middle District, State of Alabama). This has necessitated the development of treatment procedures that are effective but are perceptibly benign.

It is in this zeitgeist that a new set of procedures has emerged for managing the diversity of behavioral inadequacies of mentally retarded persons. These procedures have been generically described as *overcorrection* (OC), and in many instances have been shown to be effective alternatives to more traditional aversive procedures in reducing the likelihood of inappropriate behavior in the mentally retarded. These procedures have been most frequently used with institutionalized severely and profoundly retarded persons, although there have been several successful reports concerning persons of normal intelligence (cf. Murphy, 1978). Given the present attitudinal climate, OC procedures are particularly appealing because they sometimes function as punishers without raising the legal or ethical questions associated with traditional punishment techniques, and they are purported to be "educative," in the sense that they involve the repetitive practice of "appropriate" forms of the misbehavior (Foxx, 1976a). These reasons are sufficient to compel us to critically summarize the literature on OC procedures with respect to their effectiveness, generality, durability, and side effects for specific behavioral problems of the mentally retarded, as well as to evaluate these procedures in light of the characteristics which are thought to contribute to their effectiveness.

The rationale for OC procedures (Foxx & Azrin, 1973) is to correct the environmental effects of an inappropriate act to a vastly improved state and to intensively practice appropriate forms of the inappropriate behavior. The former component has been called *restitution* (R), while the latter has been termed *positive practice* (PP). For example, a person who has thrown a chair or overturned a table would be required not only to return the object to its correct position (R) but also to restore all other chairs and tables to their proper location, dust and polish them, and apologize to everyone affected by the misbehavior (PP). If a person steals food from a fellow client, he must return the food to its original owner (R) and secure another, similar item for the victim (PP). When no environmental disruption results from the misbehavior (e.g., stereotyped and self-injurious behaviors), R is inapplicable and only PP is used. For example, clients engaged in stereotyped bodyrocking would be required to maintain their shoulders in two postures: shoulders forward away from the chair, and shoulders back against the chair, as in the normal sitting position.

In principle, Foxx and Azrin (1972) state that the effectiveness of OC depends on these design characteristics: (1) OC should be directly related to the misbehavior lest it become arbitrary and punitive; (2) OC should be effected immediately after the misbehavior, thereby providing for the extinction of the misbehavior and reducing the likelihood of future misbehaviors since immediate negative consequences are more effecive than noncontiguous ones (Azrin & Holz, 1966); (3) OC should be extended in duration, precluding the client from reinforcing activities. Consequently, the restriction period constitutes a time-out from positive reinforcement; and (4) The client should be actively performing the OC without pausing. The expenditure of work and effort should have an inhibitory effect.

In sum, we have identified and summarized along a number of dimensions 54 published reports on OC procedures with mentally retarded persons, the results of which are presented in Table I. All the articles are empirical studies of the effectiveness of OC procedures for various behavioral problems of mentally retarded persons. Some are analytic with respect to the parameters of treatment effectiveness, others assess the effectiveness of OC relative to alternative treatments. These issues, and the papers which bear on them, will be discussed. For simplicity of exposition, we have organized these papers around the behavioral problems for which OC has been used. It should be noted that reports of the use of OC with clients of normal intelligence (Azrin & Nunn, 1973) and/or other diagnostic or behavioral characteristics without apparent intellectual involvement (Klinge, Thrasher, & Myers, 1975), as well as review and theoretical papers, are not included in Table I. These latter reports will be

TABLE I
Summary of Empirical Studies of Overcorrection with Retarded Persons

Author & year	Target behavior	Number subjects, institutionalized?	Diagnostic[a] group	IQ and/or Vineland Social Maturing Quotient[b]
Eating skills				
Azrin & Armstrong, 1973	Proper utensil use	22, Yes	P-MR	IQ = 15 VSMQ = 10
Azrin & Wesolowski, 1974	Stealing	34, Yes	S-MR, P-MR	IQ = 15
Stimbert, Minor, & McCoy, 1977	Correct (B_1), incorrect (B_2), & inappropriate (B_3) eating behaviors	6, No	Mod-, S-, P-MR	S_1: VSM age = .89 S_2: VSM age = 1.50 S_3: Cattel MA = 1.00 S_4: VSM age = 1.62 S_5: VSM age = 1.00 S_6: Cattel MA = .75
Toileting skills				
Azrin & Foxx, 1971	Enuresis & encopresis	9, Yes	P-MR	IQ = 14
Azrin, Sneed, & Foxx, 1973	Enuresis	12, Yes	P-MR	IQ = 12 VSMQ = 6.3
Butler, 1976	Toileting	1, No	Spina-bifida	?
Doleys & Arnold, 1975	Encopresis	1, No	Mod-MR	?
Freeman & Pribble, 1974	Toileting	1, Yes	Autistic	IQ = 52
Leon, 1975	Encopresis	1, Yes	Mild-MR	IQ = 58
Matson, 1977	Encopresis	1, Yes	Autism	?
Sadler & Merkert, 1977	Enuresis & encopresis	14, Yes	S-, P-MR	?
Smith, Britton, Johnson, & Thomas, 1975	Toileting	5, Yes	P-MR	VSM age = 18/12

Age[c]	Design[d]	Duration each overcorrection episode[a]	Total daily duration	Baseline rate[c,e]	Overcorrection treatment or posttreatment rates[c,e,f]	Follow-up
38	Pre & post (maintenance) assessment for MM & "best effort" control groups	?	2 hr 15 min	83% errors	6% errors	No
41	A(SC), B(TR)	?	30 min	19/day	0	No
6.25	A(BL), B(SR+, MM, and TO)	?	3-6 15 min sessions	$B_1 = 9.8$/session $B_2 = 3.3$/session $B_3 = 23.3$/session	$B_1 = 24$/session $B_2 = 5.3$/session $B_3 =$ near 0/session	12 mo, $B_1 = 24.7$/session $B_2 = 6.5$/session $B_3 = 8.5$/session
43	Pre & post (maintenance) assessment for OC & control groups	?	8 hr	2/day/resident	.15/day/resident	No
37	Successive treatments: BL, UA, DB	45 min	"All night"	50% of nights	4% of nights	No
4.5	DB training, maintenance	1 or 2 PP trials, emphasis on cleanliness responsibility	24 hr	?	10.5/wk	No
8	A(BL), B(OC)	?	24 hr	3/wk	Near 0	5 mo, 1/wk
5.5	A(BL), B(SR+ & OC)	15 min	24 hr	5/day	0/day	No
9	A(BL), B(OC & SR+)	?	24 hr	2.4/day	Near 0	1 mo, near 0
16	A(SR+), B(SR+ & SC)	10 min	24 hr	3.6/day	0	No
Range = 7-12	Pre & post (1 & 2) assessment for OC, no-training, & scheduling method groups	?	24 hr	.88/day	Post 1: .20/day Post 2: .05/day	No
Range = 25-26	A(BL), B(DB)	?	8 hr	Wetting: 76/wk Take self to toilet = 0/wk	Wetting: 20/wk Take self to toilet = 53/wk	7 mo, data not reported

Continued

TABLE I *(continued)*

Author & year	Target behavior	Number subjects, institutionlized?	Diagnostic[a] group	IQ and/or Vineland Social Maturity Quotient[b]
Aggressive-disruptive behaviors				
Azrin & Wesolowski, 1975(a)	Vomiting	1, Yes	P-MR	VSMQ = 2.6
Duker & Seys, 1977	Vomiting	1, Yes	P-MR	VSMQ = 6
Foxx, 1976a: Exp 1	Disrobing	1, Yes	P-MR	IQ = 16
Exp 2	Disrobing	1, Yes	P-MR	IQ = 12
Foxx & Azrin, 1972: Exp 1	Object-throwing	1, Yes	P-MR	IQ = 16
Exp 2	Physical attacks	1, Yes	P-MR	IQ = 8
Exp 3	Screaming	1, Yes	?	?
Martin & Matson, 1978	Vocalization	1, Yes	P-MR	Fairview Self-Help Scale = 21 mo
Shapiro, 1979	Paper tearing	1, No	Mod-MR	?
Webster & Azrin, 1973	Screaming, stripping, tantrums, etc.	8, Yes	Mod-, S-, P-MR	IQ = 27
Stereotyped Behaviors				
Azrin, Kaplan, & Foxx, 1973	Body-rocking, head-weaving, hand-movements, etc.	9, Yes	S-, P-MR	VSMQ = 9.3 IQ = 18
Azrin & Wesolowski, 1975b	Floor-sprawling	11, Yes	P-MR	VSM age = 1.5 MA = 1.5
Cavalier & Ferretti, 1980	Mouthing, object-manipulation	1, No	P-MR	?

Age[c]	Design[d]	Duration each overcorrection episode[a]	Total daily duration	Baseline rate[c,e]	Overcorrection treatment or posttreatment rates[c,e,f]	Follow-up
36	Sequential treatments: BL, RR, TO, PP, & self-correction	RR:2 hr PP:45–60 min	24 hr	2/day	RR: 2/day PP:0/day	12 mo, 0
19	A(DRO), B(DRO & OC), A, B, A, B	20 min	8 hr	5/day	Near 0	2 mo, near 0
52	A(TO), B(OC), A, B	30 min	16 hr	5/day	0/day	No
31	A(PR), B(OC), A, B	30 min	16 hr	8/day	0/day	No
50	A(SC & disapproval), B(SR$^+$ & HO)	30 min	24 hr	13/day	Near 0	No
22	A(TO & disapproval), B(SR, MA, OH)	30 min	24 hr	6/day	Near 0	No
56	A(disapproval), B(HO, SR, QT)	30 min	24 hr	10/day	Near 0	No
20	A(BL), B(OC & DRO), A, B, A	15 sec–10 min	1.5 hr	347.5/day	50/day	12 mo, (OC in effect) near 0
5.5	A(BL), B(OC), A, B	7 min	30 min	78% intervals	11% intervals	18 mo, 0% intervals
31	A(BL), B(RR)	2 hr	?	7/day	.45/day	No
31	A(BL), B(SR$^+$), A, C(SR$^+$ & AR)	20 min	10 hr	75% of time	.5% of time	No
35	A(SC), B(PP)	12 min	8 hr	11.8/day	0	6 mo, 0
5	MBL, reversal, across treatments, behaviors, & environments: BL, Slap, DRA, FM & DRA, Slap & DRA	5 min	30 min	67% of time	64% of time	No

Continued

TABLE I (continued)

Author & year	Target behavior	Number subjects, institutionalized?	Diagnostic[a] group	IQ and/or Vineland Social Maturity Quotient[b]
Stereotyped Behaviors (continued)				
Denney, 1980	Hand/finger-mouthing, hand-waving, hand-wringing	3, Yes	P-MR	?
Doke & Epstein, 1975:				
Exp 1	Thumbsucking	2, No	Culturally deprived	S_1:82 S_2:75
Exp 2	Thumbsucking	1, No	Culturally deprived	S_1 from Exp 1
Exp 3	Hand-in-mouth (B_1), Inappropriate object-manipulation (B_2) body-movements (B_3)	1, No	Culturally deprived	S_1 from Exp 1
Foxx & Azrin, 1973: Exp 1	Hand/object-mouthing	2, No	S-MR	S_1:VSMQ = 23 S_2:VSMQ = 28
Exp 2	Head-weaving, hand-clapping	4, No	S-MR autistic	S_1 & S_2 from Exp 1 S_3:VSMQ = 35
Lambert, Bruwier, & Cobben, 1975	Hand-clapping	1, No	P-MR	MA/Brunet-Lezine = 10-12 mo
Luiselli, Helfen, Pemberton, & Reisman, 1977	Masturbation	1, No	? - MR	VSM age = 5.2
Luiselli, Pemberton, & Helfen, 1978	Table-tapping	1, Yes	Mod-MR	VSMQ = 34
Marholin & Townsend, 1978	Hand/finger-movements	1, Yes	Autistic	VSMQ = 1.5

Age[c]	Design[d]	Duration each overcorrection episode[a]	Total daily duration	Baseline rate[c,e]	Overcorrection treatment or posttreatment rates[c,e,f]	Follow up
S_1:14 S_2:14 S_3:15	MBL, sequential treatments across subjects: BL, DRI, DRI, & FM	1 min	20 min	S_1:84% of time S_2:78% of time S_3:97% of time	Near 0 for all subjects	2 mo, near 0 for all subjects
4	A(BL), B(OH), A, B (for S_2)	2 min	30 min	S_1:18% S_2:58%	S_1:8% S_2:2%	No
4	A(SR+), B(OH), A, C (threat of OH)	2 min	30 min	60%	Near 0	1 mo, near 0
4	MBL, sequential treatments, across behaviors & treatments: SR+, threats, OH	15 sec	1 hr	B_1:89% B_2:12% B_3:20%	Near 0 for all behaviors	No
?	Sequential treatments across subjects: SR+ noncontingent SR+ Punishment, OC	2 min	30 min	S_1:120/hr S_2:105/hr	0 for both subjects	No
7.5	$S_{1,2,3}$:A(BL), B(OC), A, C (threat of OC), S_4:A(BL), B(OC), C(threat of OC)	S_1 & S_2 same as Exp 1, S_3:5 min increased to 20 min, S_4:5 min	6 hr	S_1:82% of time S_2:83% of time S_3:90% of time S_4:89% of time	0 for all subjects	No
13.5	MBL, reversal, across treatments & environments: BL, forced object-manipulation, physical contact, slap, DRO, FM	5 min	3 hr	80% of time	12% of time	No
8	A(SR+), B(SR+ & FM)	12 sec	36 min	58%	0	12 mo, 0
10	MBL, reversal, across treatments & behaviors: BL, SR+, SR+ & FM	1 min	21 min	32% of time	Near 0% of time	3.5 mo, near 0
10	A(SR+), B(3 min OC), C(5 min OC), B	3–5 min	20 min	79.3% of intervals	3.8% of intervals	No

Continued

TABLE I *(continued)*

Author & year	Target behavior	Number subjects, institutionalized?	Diagnostic[a] group	IQ and/or Vineland Social Maturity Quotient[b]
Stereotyped behaviors (continued)				
Martin, Weller, & Matson, 1977	Object-transferring	1, Yes	P-MR	?
Matson, Ollendick, & Martin, 1979	Object-transferring, object-throwing, nose-touching, hand-shaking, etc.	8, Yes	P-MR	Previously published reports
Ollendick, Matson, & Martin, 1978: Exp 1	Hand-shaking, nose-touching	2, Yes	S-MR	S_1:VSMQ = 2.80 S_2:VSMQ = 9.68
Exp 2	Laughing, head-weaving	2, Yes	S-MR	S_1:VSMQ = 4.40 S_2:VSMQ = 7.20
Roberts, Iwata, McSween, & Desmond, 1979	Mouthing (B_1), growling (B_2), table-hitting (B_3)	3, Yes	P-MR	?
Rollings, Baumeister, & Baumeister, 1977: Exp 1	Head-weaving	1, Yes	S-MR	?
Exp 2	Body-rocking	1, Yes	P-MR	?
Rusch, Close, Hops, & Agosta, 1976	Searching	1, No	S-, P-MR	?

Age[c]	Design[d]	Duration each overcorrection episode[a]	Total daily duration	Baseline rate[c,e]	Overcorrection treatment or posttreatment rates[c,e,f]	Follow up
27	A(BL), B(OC) A, B, A	5 min	2 hr	700/day	4/day (5–10 treatment days)	No
?	Particular designs previously published	—	—	S_1: 716 S_2: 20 S_3: 17 S_4: 9 S_5: 47 S_6: 25 S_7: 20 S_8: 26	2 0 1 1 0 0 1 0	12 mo, 675 1 3 7 39 22 29 17
S_1:24 S_2:40	A(BL), B(FM), A	5 min	45 min	S_1:12.8/day S_2:16.8/day	S_1:1/day S_2:/2 day	1.5 mo; S_1:1/day S_2: near 0
S_1:23 S_2:34	A(BL), B(FM), A: hand OC on topographically dissimilar behaviors	5 min	45 min	S_1:11/day S_2:5/day	S_1:2/day S_2:2/day	1.5 mo, S_1:7/day S_2:4/day
S_1:26 S_2:21 S_3:10	MBL, reversal, across behaviors & subjects	1–2 min	10–20 min	B_1—S_1: 96%, S_2: 100%, B_2—S_2:36%, B_3—S_3:50%	Near 0 for all subjects & behaviors	No
21	A(BL), B(FM) with alternating treatment & non-treatment phases during B	5 min	20 min	31/min	33/min (across all OC sessions)	No
35	MBL across behaviors: BL, FM with alternating treatment & non-treatment phases during FM	5 min	20 min	43/min	Near 0/min	6 mo, 27/min
39	MBL, reversal, across treatments & environments (En_1, En_2, En_3), BL, reprimands, OC	5–10 min	30–90 min	En_1:24% of time En_2:61% of time En_3:55% of time	Near 0 level for reprimands & OC for all environments	No

Continued

TABLE I *(continued)*

Author & year	Target behavior	Number subjects institutionalized	Diagnostic[a] group	IQ and/or Vineland Social Maturity Quotient[b]
Stereotyped behavior (continued)				
Wells, Forehand, & Hickey, 1977: Exp 1	Mouthing	2, No	S-MR	S_1:VSMQ = 38 S_2:VSMQ = 33
Exp 2	Mouthing	2, No	S-MR	Same as Exp 1
Wells, Forehand, Hickey, & Green, 1977	Object manipulation (B_1), mouthing (B_2), hand-movements (B_3), others (B_4)	2, No	S-MR	S_1:VSMQ = 38 S_2:VSMQ = 33
Self-injurious behaviors				
Azrin, Gottlieb, Hughart, Wesolowski, & Rahn, 1975	Head-hitting	11, Yes	S- P-MR	IQ = 13
Barmann, 1979	Nail-biting	1, No	Mod-MR	?
Barnard, Christophersen, & Wolf, 1976	Head-banging (B_1) & Mouthing (B_2)	2, No	S_1:?-MR S_2: S-MR	?
Clements & Dewey, 1979	Eye-poking (B_1), hand-biting (B_2), object-breaking (B_3)	1, Yes	S-MR	Griffith's Mental Development Scales MA = 3 yrs 1 mo
DeCantanzaro & Baldwin, 1978	Head-hitting	2, Yes	P-MR	?

Age[c]	Design[d]	Duration each overcorrection episode[a]	Total daily duration	Baseline rate[c,e]	Overcorrection treatment or posttreatment rates[c,e,f]	Follow-up
S_1:10 S_2:10	MBL across behaviors, sequential treatments across subjects: BL, OC warning	?	30 min	S_1:65% of time S_2:58% of time	S_1:5% of time S_2:28% of time	No
Same as Exp 1	MBL across behaviors, sequential treatments across subjects: BL, warning & OC	2.5 min	30 min of time	S_1:55% of time S_2:33% of time	S_1:10% of time S_2:5%	No
S_1:10 S_2:10	Sequential treatments, MBL across subjects & behaviors: BL, OC, OC & SR+	2.5 min	30 min	B_1— S_1:67% S_2:55% B_2— S_1:70% S_2:20% B_3— S_1:1.5% S_2:24% B_4— S_1:12% S_2:50%	Near 0 for all behaviors & subjects	No
30	A(BL), B(SR+ & OC (HC, RR))	RR:2 hr HC:20 min	24 hr	—	99% reduction of BL	No
9	A(BL), B(OC)	30 min	3 hr	75/wk	4/wk	2.5 mo, near 0
S_1:4 S_2:3	MBL, sequential treatment, across subjects: BL, medical assistance or OH	7 min	24 hr	B_1— S_1:2.9/hr B_2— S_2:30% of time	B_1— S_1:near 0 B_2— S_2:near 0	S_1:30 mo (OC in effect), near 0
11	MBL, sequential treatments, across behaviors: eye-poking, hand-biting, object-breaking	10 min	6 hr	B_1— 114.8/day B_2— 9.8/day B_3— 48/day	Near 0 for all behaviors	6 mo, near 0
S_1:8 S_2:12	MBL across subjects: BL, SR+, FM, PM, & SR+	S_1:3 repeats S_2:25 repeats of FM	?	S_1:60/min S_2:1.85/min	S_1:1.5/min S_2:.2/min	No

Continued

TABLE I *(continued)*

Author & year	Target behavior	Number subjects, institutionalized?	Diagnostic[a] group	IQ and/or Vineland Social Maturity Quotient[b]
Self-injurious behaviors (continued)				
Foxx & Martin, 1975:				
Exp 1	Coprophagy (B_1) & pica (B_2)	1, Yes	P-MR	?
Exp 2	Coprophagy & pica	2, Yes	P-MR	S_1:IQ = 16 S_2:IQ = 18
Exp 3	Scavenging	1, Yes	P-MR	?
Freeman, Graham, & Ritvo, 1975	Nail-picking	1, Yes	Aphasia	?
Harris & Romanczyk, 1976	Head-banging	1, No	Mod-MR	VSMQ = 45 IQ = 47
Kelly & Drabman, 1977a	Eye-poking	1, No	"High risk"	?
Kelly & Drabman, 1977b	Head-hitting	1, No	S-MR	IQ = 33 VSMQ = 55
Matson, Stephens, & Smith, 1978	Pica (B_1) & hair-pulling (B_2)	1, Yes	P-MR	?
Measel & Alfieri, 1976:				
Exp 1	Head-slapping	1, Yes	P-MR	?
Exp 2	Head-banging	1, Yes	P-MR	?
Steen & Zuriff, 1977	Biting (B_1) & scratching (B_2)	1, Yes	P-MR	?

Age[c]	Design[d]	Duration each overcorrection episode[a]	Total daily duration	Baseline rate[c,e]	Overcorrection treatment or posttreatment rates[c,e,f]	Follow-up
30	MBL across behaviors: Coprophagy & pica	30 min	"Waking hours"	B_1-8/day B_2-10/day	Near 0	No
S_1:31 S_2:20	A(BL), B(PR), C(OC) across subjects	30 min	"Waking hours"	S_1:4/day S_2:5.5/day	0	No
33	A(BL), B(OC), A, B	30 min	8 hr	100% of available trash	Near 0	No
6,5	A(BL), B(SR$^+$ & OC)	1 min	3 hr	18/day	0/day	No
8	A(BL), B(OC), across environments (En$_1$, En$_2$)	5 min	En$_1$:4.5 hrs, En$_2$: "waking hours"	En$_1$:32/day, En$_2$: 15.44/day	Near 0 in both environments	No
3	A(BL), B(FM & SR$^+$), A, B	12 repeats of FM	10 min	23.4/day	6/day (in generalization setting)	No
10	A(BL), B(SR$^+$ & FM, with successfully longer treatment sessions)	20 repeats of FM	1 min–? hr	27/min	Near 0 for all treatment session durations	Yes, near BL levels (no data)
57	MBL across behaviors: pica, hair-pulling	10 min	8 hr	B_1-15/day B_2-2/day	Near 0/day	3 mo, B_1- 3/day, B_2- 0/day
14	MBL across treatments: BL, SR$^+$, OC & SR$^+$	10 min	3 hr	5.15/min	Near 0	4 mo, near 0
16	A(BL), B(SR$^+$), C(SR$^+$ & OC)	10 min	3 hr	.9/min	15.3/min	No
21	A(BL), B(RR & SR$^+$)	?	10 trials	B_1-117/session, B_2- 88/session	Near 0 session for both behaviors	"Several wks," D_1 0/session, B_2-0/session

Continued

TABLE I *(continued)*

Author & year	Target behavior	Number subjects, institutionalized?	Diagnostic[a] group	IQ and/or Vineland Social Maturity Quotient[b]
Self-injurious behaviors (continued)				
Zehr & Theobold, 1978	Head-hitting, face-scratching	2, Yes	P-MR	S_1:VSMQ = 7.2 S_2:VSMQ = 7.0
Other Problem Behaviors				
Doleys, Wells, Hobbs, Roberts, & Cartelli, 1976	Compliance	4, Yes	Mild-, Mod-, S-MR, autistic	41
Foxx, 1976 (b)	Attendance	1, Yes	Mild-MR	IQ = 59
Foxx, 1977	Eye-contact	3, No	S_1:autistic S_2 & S_3: S-MR	S_2:VSMQ = 28

[a] Mild-MR: mild mental retardation; Mod-MR: moderate mental retardation; S-MR: severe mental retardation; P-MR: profound mental retardation.
[b] IQ: Intelligence Quotient (Stanford-Binet or Wechsler Scales); VSM age: Vineland Social Maturity Age; VSMQ: Vineland Social Maturity Quotient. Note: Individual data were reported if: (1) n for experiment <3, (2) different measures of the same psychological attribute were recorded. Otherwise, an average or range was reported.
[c] Note if n for an experiment <3, individual data were reported. Otherwise, an average or range was reported.

[d] AR: Austism Reversal Overcorrection
BL: Baseline
DB: Dry Bed Overcorrection
DRA: Differential Reinforcement of Alternative Behaviors
DRI: Differential Reinforcement of Incompatible Behaviors
DRO: Differential Reinforcement of Other Behaviors
FM: Functional Movement Overcorrection
HC: Hand Control Overcorrection
HO: Household Orderliness Overcorrection
MA: Medical Assistance Overcorrection
MBL: Multiple Baseline
MM: Mini-Meal Overcorrection
OC: Overcorrection
OH: Oral Hygiene Overcorrection
PP: Positive Practice
PR: Physical Restraint
QT: Quiet Training Overcorrection
RR: Required Relaxation Overcorrection
S: Subject
SC: Simple Correction
SP: Social Punishment
SR^+: Positive Reinforcement
TO: Time Out
TR: Theft Reversal Overcorrection
UA: Urine Alarm

Note: The order of treatment reads: A(Treatment 1), B(Treatment 2), etc.

[e] Baseline rate for behavior targeted with OC during all observation sessions of first available baseline period.
[f] Treatment rate for behavior targeted with OC during last three observation sessions of last OC treatment period.
[g] Percentage computed for OC episodes of longest duration.

Age[c]	Design[d]	Duration each overcorrection episode[a]	Total daily duration	Baseline rate[c,e]	Overcorrection treatment or posttreatment rates[c,e,f]	Follow-up
S_1:24 S_2:19	A(BL), B(FM), A, B	5 min	"Waking hours"	S_1:23/ 10 min S_2:0 min latency between self-injury	S_1:.38/ 10 min S_2:63 min latency between self-injury	No
10	MBL, reversal, across subjects & treatments: BL, SP, PP, TO	40 sec	30-40 min	S_1:100% S_2:95% S_3:100% S_4:93%	S_1:90% S_2:48% S_3:77% S_4:80%	No
31	MBL across environments (En_1, En_2): TO, OC	30 min	En_1:2 hr En_2:1 hr	En_1:22% En_2:32%	En_1:100% En_2:100%	No
S_1 & S_2:8 S_3:6	Simultaneous-treatments (SR^+, SR^+ & FM) & *either* changing criterion (S_1 & S_3) with reversal across experimenters (S_1) *or* MBL across experimenters (S_2)	S_1 & S_2: 2-5 min S_3:2 min	200 trials/day	S_1:23% S_2:33% S_3:47.75%	S_1:97%[g] S_2:95%[g] S_3:90%[g]	No

noted in those contexts in which they illuminate our discussion of the use of OC procedures with mentally retarded persons.

The principal dimensions along which the papers in Table I have been summarized are: (1) specific target behavior(s), (2) number of subjects, their institutional status, diagnostic classifications, levels of intellectual and social functioning, and chronological age, (3) experimental design, (4) duration of each OC treatment episode and total duration of each day's training sessions, and (5) baseline, treatment, and follow-up frequencies of the behavior targeted with OC. In the following section, we offer a description and explanation of these findings for the behavioral problems with which OC procedures have been most frequently used.

Efficacy and Durability

Toileting Skills

Perhaps the most burdensome and distasteful problem for parents and caretakers of mentally retarded children is chronic incontinence. No other behavioral problem is more disruptive of the normalization process because bowel and bladder control is often a precondition to public school enrollment (Eyman, Tarjan, & Cassady, 1970).

Reliable data on the proportion of toilet-trained, noninstitutionalized mentally retarded persons are not available, however, Eyman *et al.* (1970) reported compelling data on a relatively large number of institutionalized mentally retarded children. These data were organized according to the clients' chronological age (below 6, 6–12, above 12), level of intellectual functioning (above or below 30 IQ), and extent of bowel and bladder control (fully trained, partially trained, untrained). The vast majority of the youngest children were untrained, although more than 20% of those children with IQs above 30 were partially trained. Between the ages of 6 and 12, 50% of those clients with the lowest measured intelligence were as yet untrained, while more than 70% of those children with IQs greater than 30 were completely trained. By the age of 12, nearly all children with the higher IQs were fully trained. In marked contrast, only 50% of those with the lowest IQs were fully trained, and more than 20% remained untrained. Clearly, special technologies are needed to facilitate the acquisition of toileting skills in institutionalized severely and profoundly mentally retarded persons.

Azrin and Foxx's (1971) report of a complex toilet-training program for institutionalized, profoundly mentally retarded adults was the seminal work on OC procedures, although none of the nomenclature that has since become associated with OC appeared in the text. The specific procedures derive from a conception of toileting formulated by Ellis (1963), as a "complex and lengthy chain of responses that...requires strong positive and negative consequences for its maintenance in that chain, rather than considering it as a simple associative muscular reflex to internal stimuli" (Azrin & Foxx, 1971, p. 98). The specific components of the *cleanliness-training* program described in this report are prototypical of subsequent efforts to use OC to foster the acquisition of toileting skills. When accidents occurred, clients were required to shower, remove and rinse out their soiled clothing, change into clean clothing, and mop the training area. In addition to these core OC components, time-out procedures were used and social and edible rewards were given on a fixed-interval schedule for bowel and bladder control. The results were unambiguous. Training of voluntary control was accomplished in 3 days for all residents, and accidents were virtually absent by the fifth month of training.

Azrin, Sneed, and Foxx (1973b) compared *dry-bed* OC against a urine alarm procedure in controlling enuresis in a group of severely mentally retarded adults. In addition to cleanliness-training OC, a PP component, which involved repetitive trips to the bathroom from the bed, was included. The urine alarm procedure did not significantly reduce the occurrence of bed wetting in these clients. In contrast, the dry-bed OC required an average of 1¼ nights to achieve the following criteria of success: no more than one accident during a training night and correct toileting on at least 50% of all opportunities during the night. For 12 weeks thereafter, bed wetting rarely occurred.

Freeman and Pribble (1974) have reported equally impressive results using identical procedures with an autistic child who functioned at the moderately mentally retarded level of intelligence. The effects were immediate, and after five months of training, no further accidents occurred. Doleys and Arnold (1975) used *full-cleanliness* OC to control the encopresis of a moderately mentally retarded boy. Substantial suppression of toileting accidents at home and school was achieved after 14 weeks of training. However, accidents did occur, although infrequently, in both environments because of the mother's and the teacher's failure to apply the program consistently. Butler (1976) used cleanliness-training and PP procedures in an attempt to toilet train a spina bifida myelocele child. The client had partial paralysis of the buttocks that prohibited bowel control. As a consequence, the goals of the program were to insure bladder control and responsibility for cleaning bowel accidents. Baseline data on the frequency of bladder accidents were not given, although it was stated that the client was "continuously wet." Neither baseline nor treatment data on the client's efforts after bowel accidents were provided. Again, we have the author's assurance that responsibility was taken for these accidents. In any case, accidents continued to occur, but with less frequency, and these changes were maintained during 7 months of training.

Leon (1975) used R and reinforcement for cleanliness to establish bowel control in a 9-year-old mentally retarded child. The client had been admitted to an institution for short-term treatment of encopresis. During the first 8 days of treatment, there was a measurable increase in the frequency of soiling. On the 9th day, no accidents occurred. This was maintained for the final 13 days of training, at which time the client was returned to the community. Informal reports from a liaison worker showed only one occurrence of soiling during the first month following training. Smith, Britton, Johnson, and Thomas (1975) had relatively good success in controlling the enuresis of five severely mentally retarded adults with OC procedures. Substantial reductions in the frequency of accidents were observed, but these effects required 9 weeks of training. Follow-up data were not reported, but these changes were said to be maintained for 4 of the clients during a 30-day period. One client was reported to have regressed. However, the procedural recommendations of Azrin and Foxx (1971) were not strictly adhered to. Time-out periods were reduced, and cleanliness-training procedures were modified, in part because one client seemed to enjoy the graduated guidance. The authors speculated that these alterations may have slowed the reduction in toileting accidents and made relapses during training more likely.

Sadler and Merkert (1977) compared OC procedures against a scheduling method in toilet training a group of severely and profoundly mentally retarded children. The scheduling method's influence was inconstant, initially accelerating, and then reducing the frequency of bed wetting to a near-zero level. The authors also examined staff preferences for, and the amount of time required to effect, each treatment. On the average, OC procedures were seven times as lengthy as the scheduling method, and this expenditure of time was reflected in mixed staff reports. The results of the treatment were satisfying, but the heavy investment of effort was seen as a liability "which may require offsetting reinforcement and encouragement for the adults carrying out the...program" (p. 500). These concerns about the practical requirements of OC prompted Matson (1977) to use simple correction in treating the encopresis of an institutionalized, autistic boy. Simple correction after each accident requires that the child attempt to eliminate in the toilet for 2 min, change his clothing and clean himself, and properly dispose of his soiled clothing. Rapid elimination of soiling was achieved, and was maintained during a 3-month period.

In summary, OC procedures have proven to be effective in promoting toileting skills in mentally retarded children. These procedures are protracted, requiring from 20 to 40 min for each toileting accident. Many residential facilities with low staff/client ratios may require less time consuming procedures to insure proper toileting. Apparently, the effectiveness of OC procedures does not critically depend on strict compliance with the procedural recommendations of Azrin and Foxx (1971). Particular treatment components may be reduced in duration (cf. Smith *et al.*, 1975), or completely eliminated (cf. Matson, 1977) with little change in effectiveness. Unfortunately, it is not possible to draw strong conclusions about the effectiveness of OC relative to other procedures in toilet training mentally retarded children. No treatment comparisons of substance have been conducted to date.

Eating Skills

The mealtime behavior of institutionalized mentally retarded persons often adversely affects their social adaptation. The first serious programmatic efforts to train proper eating skills were hastened by the deplorable dining conditions in residential facilities for the mentally retarded during the 1960s (cf. Edwards & Lilly, 1966). The focus of these efforts has been either to increase or establish proficiency in the use of eating utensils (Berkowitz, Sherry, & Davis, 1971) or to eliminate inappropriate responses such as finger feeding or food stealing (Azrin & Wesolowski, 1974). Most programs depend on the intrinsically reinforcing properties of food by making access to it contingent on appropriate eating responses.

Azrin and Armstrong (1973) were first to describe a mealtime training program which embodied the OC rationale. The *mini-meal* training package is an assemblage of 18 specific components which include time-out, graduated guidance, fading, shaping, and PP for eating errors. Restitutional overcorrection, although compatible with the program, was not explicitly described in this report. The uniqueness of this approach derives in part from the division of each regular meal into three mini-meals, thereby more widely distributing training across the day. This program was compared against an unspecified *best-effort* control program for a group of profoundly mentally retarded adults. The control program was marginally effective, training only about one-third of its clients during an 18-day period. On the other hand, all mini-meal clients were completely trained within 12 days. Eating errors were maintained at a near-zero level during a 28-week maintenance period.

Stimbert, Minor, and McCoy (1977) modified the mini-meal method to train six children that were moderately, severely or profoundly mentally retarded. The procedural modifications restricted training to one utensil and cleanups to the training room, eliminated complex behaviors such as cutting meat, and divided each meal into two mini-meals. It was found that inappropriate responses were substantially reduced, but not eliminated, in all clients. Correct eating responses were accelerated for five children, and became much less variable for the remaining child. One child regressed during maintenance, but responded positively when graduated guidance was reintroduced. The influence of training on appropriate eating was still in evidence 8 months after the completion of training. There appeared, however, to be a greater number of inappropriate responses during the follow up as compared to the maintenance period.

Azrin and Wesolowski (1974) instituted a package of *theft-reversal* OC procedures to suppress food stealing during mealtime in a group of severely and profoundly mentally retarded adults. After each stealing incident, the thief was required not only to return the stolen item but also to obtain another identical item for the victim. This procedure was compared with simple correction, in which the thief simply returned the stolen item to its owner. Simple correction proved ineffective, but OC rapidly eliminated food stealing in these clients. These procedures were not passively accepted by these clients. It was reported that most of these people physically resisted the OC episodes.

The evidence to date suggests that OC procedures are useful for a variety of mealtime problems of mentally retarded persons. The resultant behavior change appears to be fairly rapid and stable over time. Again, it is not possible to assess the relative efficacy of different training procedures because the necessary comparative studies have not been conducted (Whitman & Scibak, 1979).

Aggressive-Disruptive Behaviors

Overtly aggressive and disruptive behaviors are common concomitants of the institutional experience of the mentally retarded (Hamilton, Stephens, & Allen, 1967). Residents displaying these behaviors are more likely to receive the reprobation of their caretakers, precluding access to privileged positions and programs within the institution, and reducing the likelihood of referral for noninstitutional placement (Abelson & Johnson, 1969). For these reasons, a variety of techniques for controlling these behaviors, including some derived from the OC rationale, has been developed (Whitman & Scibak, 1979).

In the most articulate statement of the OC rationale for aggressive and disruptive behaviors, Foxx and Azrin (1972) delineated a variety of OC procedures which were used in various combinations with two profoundly mentally retarded adults and one brain-damaged adult. Other techniques, including time-out, physical restraint, simple correction, electro-convulsive shock, inattention, and rewarding quiet periods, had limited success. The OC routines rapidly reduced the object throwing, physical attacks, and screaming of these clients, but were initially met with resistance that became less intense with continued training. Object throwing was at a zero level during the last month of the 14-week study, while attacks and screams were virtually eliminated for the last 11 training weeks.

Webster and Azrin (1973) used a *required-relaxation* OC procedure to control a variety of aggressive and disruptive behaviors in a group of severely mentally retarded adults. In theory, required relaxation is directed at the agitated emotional state that precedes the disruptive act, rather than at the act itself. The procedure requires that a disruptive client lie quietly in bed for a period of time during which no other activity is permitted. In this study, the introduction of OC was associated with a rapid, nearly complete reduction in the target behaviors, which continued at this level for 80 training days.

Shapiro (1979) used both R and PP to suppress the paper tearing of a moderately mentally retarded child. After each paper-tearing episode, the child was required to clean up the classroom and then practice reading without damaging the book's pages. The target behavior was promptly suppressed during the treatment period, and remained at a zero level during the 18-month follow-up period. Martin and Matson (1978) succeeded in drastically reducing the frequency of disruptive vocalizations of an institutionalized, profoundly mentally retarded client with PP OC. Disruptions rarely occurred during a 10-month maintenance period, but the end of training was associated with a resumption of these vocalizations, albeit less frequently than the pretreatment level.

Foxx (1976a) applied R and PP to the public disrobing of two profoundly mentally retarded women. Time-out, simple correction, differential reinforcement of other behavior (DRO), and physical restraint had been used unsuccessfully with the first client prior to this study. A sizeable reduction in the frequency of stripping was recorded on the first day of OC and was virtually eliminated for the final 62 days of treatment. However, verbal control over the PP behaviors was never established because the client passively resisted the trainer's instructions. In the second study, the effectiveness of OC was compared with that of contingent physical restraint. Restraint was ineffective, while OC virtually eliminated stripping during the final 17 days of treatment.

Azrin and Weslowski (1975a) compared PP and simple correction, rather than OC, with time-out and required relaxation in treating the habitual vomiting of a profoundly mentally retarded woman. Neither time-out nor required relaxation had an appreciable influence on the baseline level of vomiting, but the effect of PP and simple correction was gradual and constant. Vomiting was nearly eliminated by the second week of training and remained at that level during a 1-year postcheck. Similarly, Ducker and Seys (1977) used R to control vomiting in a profoundly mentally retarded woman. The frequency of vomiting was reduced to a low level and was maintained during two months of training.

These data suggest that OC procedures are generally effective for controlling a variety of aggressive-disruptive behaviors in the institutionalized mentally retarded. Again, the effects seem to be long lasting, save the notable exception of Martin and Matson (1978). Their findings attest to the necessity of carefully planned maintenance programs to insure durable treatment effects. These programs should include specific attempts to reinforce incompatible behaviors which are subject to naturally reinforcing consequences (Shapiro, 1979).

There appear to be client characteristics which place severe constraints on the effectivenes of required relaxation in controlling aggressive-disruptive behavior. Webster and Azrin (1973) reported that two aggressive clients were excluded from their study because of "difficulty in keeping them in bed without constant physical restraint." Azrin and Wesolowski (1975a) found that required relaxation made their client "resistive and incontinent." Therefore, required relaxation "seems best suited to individuals for whom it is undertaken willingly; otherwise, the intended function of calming seems to be thwarted" (Azrin & Wesolowski, 1975a, p. 147).

Stereotyped Behaviors

Stereotyped behaviors are among the most frequently observed attributes of the institutionalized mentally retarded. These behaviors are seen in nearly two-thirds of institutionalized severely mentally retarded residents (Berkson & Mason, 1963). Stereotypies are characteristically "highly consistent and repetitious motor posturing behaviors, the adaptive consequence of which, if any, are not immediately apparent" (Baumeister & Forehand, 1973, p. 56). Common examples are bodyrocking, swaying, handwaving, and pillrolling. The frequency of these behaviors, as well as their association with reduced responsiveness to environmental events (Koegel & Covert, 1972; Lovaas, Litrownik, & Mann, 1971), has led to sustained research attention.

Because their maintaining conditions are difficult to identify, a number of notions have been advanced to account for stereotyped behaviors. Often these interpretations emphasize the organism's internal organization of the controlling conditions, rather than simple associative mechanisms (Baumeister & Forehand, 1973; Berkson, 1967). One idea is that stereotyped behavior is a manifestation of frustration, anxiety, discomfort, or unsatisfied needs (Kaufman & Levitt, 1965). Some workers (Hutt & Hutt, 1965) believe that these behaviors occur in response to excessive stimulation, and others claim that stereotypies serve to induce stimulation for an otherwise stimulus-deprived organism (Berkson & Mason, 1964). A more general explanation posits that stereotyped behaviors are responses to a homeostatic imbalance from optimal stimulation (Baumeister & Forehand, 1973). Whenever stimulation exceeds, or is less than, the optimum, these "compensatory" behaviors will appear. This explanation accounts nicely for the findings that stereotypies tend to increase under conditions of heightened or reduced stimulation (Forehand & Baumeister, 1970; Kaufman & Levitt, 1965). This position is not without criticism, however, the most forceful of which is conceptual circularity (Baumeister & Forehand, 1973).

The first report of the use of the OC rationale for stereotyped behaviors was made by Foxx and Azrin (1973). In their first experiment, the effectiveness of OC in suppressing the hand and object mouthing of two severely mentally retarded children was compared with four other procedures: punishment by a slap, DRO, punishment by means of coating the skin with a distasteful solution, and noncontingent primary and secondary reinforcement. Neither noncontingent reinforcement nor DRO influenced the frequency of stereotyped behaviors. Slapping drastically decelerated the stereotype of one client, but was ineffective for the other, producing a strong emotional response. Overcorrection reduced the stereotypies of both clients to near-zero levels. In the second experiment, OC was applied to each episode of hand and object mouthing, headweaving, and handclapping of three severely mentally retarded children and one autistic child. For three of the children, the introduction of OC led to a rapid reduction in the rate of stereotyped behaviors. For the remaining child, the duration of OC had to be increased from 5 to 20 min before a near-zero level was observed. Following a return to baseline and reintroduction of OC, a verbal-warning condition, during which the stereotypies could occur no more than once without receiving OC, was started. During this condition, the frequency of stereotyped behaviors was near zero and this remained for more than a month.

Azrin, Kaplan, and Foxx (1973a) used an *autism-reversal* ward program in conjunction with reinforcement for appropriate classroom behavior for treating a variety of stereotyped behaviors of a group of 32 severely and profoundly mentally retarded adults. Despite the program's novel description, it directly reflects the PP rationale. The resident was required to use the body part involved in the stereotypy in an appropriate form of the inappropriate movement. Reinforcement alone reduced by half the baseline level of stereotypies, but the combined OC and reinforcement program produced a near-zero level within two weeks. This rate was maintained for all residents for 49 days thereafter.

Martin, Weller, and Matson (1977) were successful in eliminating the nonfunctional object transferring of a profoundly mentally retarded woman. The authors anecdotally reported that there seemed to be a decrease in object transferring and increases in appropriate behavior outside the OC environment which may, in part, have resulted from reinforcement for appropriate behavior. Azrin and Wesolowski (1975b) suppressed the floor sprawling of a group of profoundly mentally retarded adults with PP. Previous attempts to control this behavior with simple correction and positive reinforcement met with limited success. Within a week of starting OC, floor sprawling was substantially reduced and completely absent for the following 12 days of observation. Verbal warnings were sufficient to control the behavior after the fourth day of training. Reports from ward attendants after 6 months indicated that floor sprawling occurred infrequently.

Luiselli, Helfen, Pemberton, and Reisman (1977) used a combined reinforcement and *functional-movement* PP program to eliminate the classroom masturbation of an 8-year-old mentally retarded boy. Reinforcement for on-task academic work had little influence on the frequency of masturbation. However, the combined reinforcement and OC program eliminated the masturbation within 9 days, and for the following 20 days of treatment. At follow-up checks of up to 12 months, masturbation was still absent. In a similar vein, Luiselli, Pemberton, and Helfen (1978) used a combined reinforcement and functional-movement PP program to suppress the repetitive fingertapping of a moderately mentally retarded boy. Reinforcement for hands-on-lap behavior did not influence fingertapping. The joint program immediately reduced the target behavior to a near-zero level, and also suppressed other stereotypies that were observed as collateral responses. Withdrawal of these contingencies was not associated with increases in the frequencies of these behaviors, damaging the internal validity of the authors' conclusions. Follow-up observations after 3½ months did not reveal a single occurrence of these behaviors.

Denney (1980) compared differential reinforcement of toy playing (DRI) with a combined DRI and *wheelchair-mobility* PP program in controlling a variety of stereotyped behaviors of three profoundly mentally retarded, nonambulatory children. Differential reinforcement of toy playing induced a modest reduction in stereotyped responding, as well as a modest increase in appropriate toy play. The combination of DRI and PP brought about an immediate near-zero reduction in stereotypies and a swift acceleration in toy play. These changes were stable during a 2-month follow-up period. Despite the program's effectiveness in controlling the target behaviors, the clients did not achieve proficiency in the use of their wheelchairs.

The studies reviewed to this point have generally shown PP to be effective in controlling the stereotyped behaviors of mentally retarded persons. In principal, the PP behavior should be related to the misbehavior (cf. Foxx & Azrin, 1972), but in practice, procedures developed for one topographic class of stereotypies may be effective for a different class of behaviors. This possibility was first considered by Epstein, Doke, Sajwaj, Sorrell, and Rimmer (1974) with two schizophrenic children who engaged in foot stereotypies. They showed that a PP program designed for inappropriate hand movements was equally effective in controlling inappropriate vocalizations and foot movements. The practical implications of these findings are sizeable because they question the necessity of designing specific OC programs for the topographically varied stereotyped behaviors of mentally retarded persons.

Three clinical reports have since appeared that bear importantly on this issue. In the first of three experiments, Doke and Epstein (1975) used an *oral-hygiene* PP procedure to suppress the thumbsucking of a culturally deprived boy. The thumbsucking of a second child who witnessed these procedures, but was not treated himself, was also eliminated. The second experiment purported to show that the verbal warning that preceded each PP episode could suppress the thumbsucking of the untreated child from the first study before the target behavior was weakened by OC. In fact, threats to carry out OC did suppress this child's thumbsucking and this was maintained for a month after the cessation of threats. This finding is not surprising since observation of the treatment was sufficient to suppress the behavior. In the third experiment, the effects of verbal warnings and OC on the same child's thumbsucking and inappropriate body movements and object manipulation were assessed in a different training environment. The introduction of threats for thumbsucking immediately eliminated this behavior, replicating the second experiment, but led to marked increases in inappropriate body movements and the start of previously unobserved stereotypies. Threats of OC for both inappropriate body movements and object manipulation were ineffective. However, OC itself abruptly reduced all previously observed inappropriate behaviors. After the first week of treatment, all misbehaviors were eliminated. No generalization of these suppressive effects was seen during other times of the day.

Ollendick, Matson, and Martin (1978) conducted two experiments to further investigate the generality of OC in treating topographically similar and dissimilar behaviors. In the first experiment, the authors were able to suppress to near-zero levels the nosetouching and handshaking of two severely mentally retarded adults with functional-movement OC. However, withdrawal of the contingencies did not result in an increased frequency of stereotypies. Ollendick *et al.* (1978) then showed that the *same* OC procedure reduced the head-weaving and inappropriate laughing of two other severely mentally retarded adults by 60%. A return to baseline produced behavior levels comparable to pretreatment frequencies. The authors tentatively concluded that "the magnitude and permanence of overcorrection effects may depend upon a topographic match between the overcorrection procedure and the treated behaviors" (p. 402).

Roberts, Iwata, McSween, and Desmond (1979) designed OC activities topographically dissimilar from the targeted behaviors of three profoundly mentally retarded adults. In addition to observing changes in the targeted stereotypies, data were also recorded on the occurrence of the PP behaviors. For the first client, *clapping* OC rapidly reduced the target mouthing, but was associated with an increase in collateral grabbing and a decrease in the PP behavior. In the case of the second client, the likelihood of both growling and mouthing was reduced by *finger-movement* PP, but not to zero levels in the former instance. When OC was in effect for growling, mouthing was suppressed despite the fact that it had not as yet been treated. No clear pattern emerged for this child's PP behavior. Finally, tablehitting of the third client was nearly eliminated by the introduction of *grimace* OC. There seemed to be a modest decrease in the likelihood of grimacing when it was used as the PP behavior. The authors concluded that topographic similarity between the PP behavior and the misbehavior is not a critical component of treatment effectiveness, and that in the absence of specific positive consequences, the PP behavior is likely to decrease in frequency by virtue of its use in the OC program. The data of Ollendick *et al.* (1978) concur with this conclusion, but suggest that PP behavior which is topographically related to the target response may lead to greater suppression of the target response than unrelated behaviors.

The Roberts *et al.* (1979) study raises an important question about the influence of OC on the PP behaviors. In theory, PP should promote appropriate forms of the misbehavior (Azrin & Foxx, 1971), but their data suggest the contrary conclusion. Generally, suppression of stereotypies was associated with a reduction in the PP behavior. If corroborated by other data, this conclusion would violate a basic tenet of the OC rationale. Wells and her associates (Wells, Forehand, & Hickey, 1977; Wells, Forehand, Hickey, & Green 1977) investigated this problem. In their first experiment, Wells, Forehand, and Hickey (1977) studied the effects of verbal warnings on target mouthing as well as the collateral inappropriate object manipulation and appropriate toy play of two severely mentally retarded children. The mouthing of one child was nearly eliminated and that of the other child was moderately reduced by warnings. The frequency of inappropriate object manipulation increased concurrent with decreases in mouthing by both children. Toy play was maintained at a low level. Both children participated in the second experiment, during which *toy-play* PP was contingent on each occasion of mouthing. Positive practice reduced the mouthing of both children and most interestingly, brought about an increase in the appropriate toy play in one child. However, this increase in toy play was also associated with increased aggressive and escape behavior.

Wells, Forehand, Hickey, and Green (1977) used a toy-play PP procedure to successively suppress the inappropriate object manipulation, mouthing, hand movements, and other inappropriate behaviors of two severely mentally retarded children. Positive practice eliminated all inappropriate behaviors of both children, and resulted in a spontaneous increase in the appropriate toy play of one child. Increases in the toy play of the other child required the addition of verbal prompting and reinforcement. Finally, reductions in targeted stereotypies were associated with reductions in the collateral stereotypies of one child, and with increases in the stereotypies of the other. The authors concluded that in some instances, PP "may be sufficient to teach and motivate the increased occurrence of appropriate behaviors practiced during manual guidance" (p. 686).

Marholin and Townsend (1978) compared the effectiveness of 3 and 5 min of physical restraint in controlling the repetitive twiddling of an autistic/mentally retarded girl. Both durations of restraint were equally effective in suppressing twiddling to near-zero levels, but neither duration led to any reduction in a generalization environment. Moreover, neither duration seemed to produce changes in the client's approach or avoidance of her trainer. Rusch, Close, Hops, and Agosta (1976) compared a complete *hands-washing* PP package against the verbal reprimand component of the package in reducing the nonfunctional searching behavior of a severely mentally retarded adult. Verbal reprimands were sufficient to substantially reduce searching behavior, but no generalization occurred in environments where training was not provided. After withdrawal of the contingencies, PP was reintroduced and it further reduced the searching behavior to near-zero levels. Some generalization of the training effects was seen during daily nontraining sessions. After the behavior was eliminated, verbal reprimands were enough to maintain searching at a very low level.

There have been three published reports in which PP has had less auspicious outcomes on the stereotyped behaviors of mentally retarded persons. Lambert, Bruwier, and Cobben (1975) contrasted five treatments in reducing the gestural stereotypies of a severely mentally retarded boy: the availability of object for play, trainer-initiated physical contact, punishment by a slap, DRO, and functional-movement OC. The presentation of objects and physical contact reduced by more than half the frequency of the target behavior and resulted in a measurable increase in toy play and client-initiated contacts. The slap contingency promptly reduced the gestures to a zero level. This effect was maintained while the client remained in the presence of the trainers, but there was some slippage in their absence. Differential reinforcement of other behavior engendered little change in the target behavior. The introducton of PP somewhat reduced the inappropriate gestures, but these behaviors still occurred with great frequency. The child also exhibited violent emotional behavior during PP's administration. Neither fading of the manual guidance nor verbal control over the PP behavior was ever accomplished.

Rollings, Baumeister, and Baumeister (1977) applied functional-movement PP to the stereotyped headweaving and bodyrocking of two severely mentally retarded adults. The bodyrocking of one client was slowly decelerated during 2 weeks of OC and was correlated with an increase in the frequency of inappropriate head nods. During a 6-month follow-up session, the frequency of bodyrocking was lower than that of the original baseline, but much higher than at the end of training. The proximity of the trainer to the client influenced the frequency of bodyrocking, headnodding, and self-hitting. The greater the proximity, the higher the frequency of nodding and self-hitting and the lower the frequency of bodyrocking. These data suggest that distance from the trainer became discriminative for OC. The effects of OC on the headnodding of the second adult can be simply summarized: No change in its frequency occurred during three weeks of intensive OC.

Finally, Cavalier and Ferretti (1980) assessed the effects of four procedures (i.e., a mild slap to the forearm, differential reinforcement of an alternative behavior [DRA], functional-movement PP plus DRA, a mild slap plus DRA) on the stereotyped fingerdigging, appropriate object manipulation, and collateral self-injurious behaviors of a profoundly mentally retarded girl. The slap resulted in a rapid suppression of target and nontarget behaviors. During DRA, a slight increase in object manipulation was achieved, but no suppression of the other behaviors was evidenced. Overcorrection plus DRA proved relatively ineffective in suppressing fingerdigging and accelerating object manipulation. As in the report of Lambert *et al.* (1975), manual guidance was always required and verbal control over the PP behavior was never secured. The combined slap plus DRA program proved to be most effective. Near-zero suppression of fingerdigging was attained on the first day of use, collateral self-injurious behaviors were virtually eliminated, and object manipulation was substantially increased.

It should be concluded from most of these reports that the PP rationale has been the basis for a number of effective techniques in reducing a variety of stereotyped behaviors of mentally retarded persons. It must be said, however, that the effects of OC have not been rapid, effective and enduring in all instances. In many studies, the suppressive effects of OC were seen only after extended training. In three cases (Cavalier & Ferretti, 1980; Lambert *et al.*, 1975;

Rollings *et al.*, 1977), the effects were modest or negligible. Two studies in which substantial control over stereotyped behavior was obtained failed to show maintenance during follow-up periods (Ollendick *et al.*, 1978; Rollings *et al.*, 1977). Matson, Ollendick, and Martin (1979) collected 1 year follow-up data for 8 mentally retarded clients who had been treated with OC procedures for a variety of stereotyped behaviors. In all but two clients, the posttreatment behavior frequencies had returned to the pretreatment levels. No clear explanation of these results could be offered, but it was suggested that the reinforcement of an alternative or incompatible behavior following the suppression of the target stereotypy might enhance long-term maintenance of the treatment effects. The educative properties of PP have also been questioned by several investigators (Denney, 1980; Murphy, 1978; Roberts *et al.*, 1979). In fact, in only two cases have increases in the PP behavior, in the absence of specific reinforcing contingencies, been reported. However, these data are tentative since this parameter has not been systematically evaluated.

Finally, there have been several direct comparisons of alternative treatment approaches for suppressing stereotypies, but they all have limited generality across clients, are generally subject to the criticism of order effects, and invariably involve within-subject comparison with OC as the last intervention. In spite of these problems, OC is frequently at least as effective as most other programs, except for procedures that appear more overtly punitive, such as electric shock (Baumeister & Forehand, 1972).

Self-Injurious Behaviors

Undoubtedly, the most dangerous behaviors of mentally retarded persons are those which are self-injurious behaviors (SIB). These behaviors are "acts which are usually highly repetitive or stereotyped in character and which result in direct tissue damage to the person" (Baumeister & Rollings, 1976, p. 2). Self-injurious behavior, then, is a subclass of stereotyped behaviors that threaten the physical health and well-being of the client. The findings and conclusions drawn about treatments for and principles underlying stereotyped behaviors are generally applicable to SIB (cf. Baumeister & Forehand, 1973; Baumeister & Rollings, 1976). Common examples of SIB are scratching, eye gouging, head banging, and eye poking. The severe and often life threatening consequences of these behaviors, and their persistence in the face of these adverse consequences, have evoked much applied and theoretical work.

The occurrence of these behaviors is not exclusively restricted to the institutionalized mentally retarded. The prevalence of SIB in children of normal intelligence ranges from 3.6% (Kravitz, Rosenthal, Teplitz, Murphy, & Lesser, 1960) to 15.2% (Delissavoy, 1962) of the population. These behaviors are usually infrequent, occur during a limited time of childhood, and disappear by age 5 (Shentoub & Soulairic, 1967). Surprisingly, the prevalence of SIB among institutionalized mentally retarded persons is not markedly different from the aforementioned statistics for children of normal intelligence. In at least two published surveys, figures of about 9% have been reported (Schroeder, 1974; Smeets, 1971), but estimates have ranged as high as 12% (Ross, 1972). These behaviors are usually of great intensity, their frequency is inversely related to level of intelligence, and they occur throughout the lifetime of many mentally retarded persons.

The OC rationale was first used by Azrin, Gottlieb, Hughart, Wesolowski, and Rahn (1975) to suppress the SIB of an unselected sample of 10 severely and profoundly mentally retarded persons and one schizophrenic client from a variety of institutions. Their OC program was a modification of *autism-reversal, required-relaxation, hand-control,* and *hand-awareness* procedures (Azrin & Nunn, 1973), which was in effect against a background of reinforcement for outward-directed activities. Required relaxation was used with six clients but was positively reinforcing for three of them. A hand-control procedure was used for those people with whom required relaxation failed, as well as the remaining five clients. On the first day of treatment, self-injury was reduced 90% from the pretreatment level. By the third month of training, SIB were nearly eliminated.

Freeman, Graham, and Ritvo (1975) used the physical-restraint component of graduated guidance along with reinforcement for appropriate behavior to control the nailpicking of an aphasic child. Within 4 days after start of treatment, the frequency of nailpicking dropped to zero. Barmann (1979) modified the fingernail biting of a moderately mentally retarded, Down's syndrome child with both R and PP that were administered by the child's mother. For each episode of fingernail biting, the client was required to file, shape, and paint her fingernails and those of her mother, as well as repetitively bring both hands from her sides to her lips. The frequency of nailbiting was reduced to a very low level during the first week of training and was eliminated after 3 weeks of treatment. The target behavior remained at this low level for 10-weeks after treatment.

In the first of three experiments, Foxx and Martin (1975) compared the effects of admonitions and simple correction against a R and PP program in managing the coprophagy and pica of a profoundly mentally retarded woman. The combined admonition and simple-correction program did not alter the frequency of these behaviors, but the OC package reduced coprophagy, and then pica of two other profoundly mentally retarded persons. In both cases, physical restraint had a slight suppressive influence on the target behaviors, but not nearly of the same magnitude as OC. During the first week of OC, scavenging was reduced to less than one occasion per day and was nearly eliminated after 4 weeks of treatment. In the final study, the cigarette-butt scavenging of a profoundly mentally retarded man was eliminated with OC procedures, and remained at that level for more than a month of additional treatment. None of the clients in these experiments were reported to be combative during OC, and their appearance and grooming behaviors seemed to improve by virtue of this treatment. No data to support the anecdotal observations were provided.

Matson, Stephens, and Smith (1978) used the *oral-hygiene* OC Foxx and Martin (1975) and *hair-brushing* PP to control the pica and hairpulling of a profoundly mentally retarded woman. The client was required to brush her teeth with a mixture of lemon juice and hot sauce because she drank the prescribed mouthwash during pretreatment sessions. Pica was promptly suppressed by OC, but this change seemed to be associated with an acceleration in the as yet untreated hairpulling behavior. The introduction of OC for hairpulling decelerated it to a near-zero level, where it remained during a 3-month postcheck. A small increase in the frequency of pica was noted during the follow-up period. The authors reported that there seemed to be a spontaneous increase in the PP behavior as a consequence of the treatment regimen.

Harris and Romanczyk (1976) used functional-movement OC to control the head and chinbanging of a moderately mentally retarded, rubella child. The application of OC at home and in the classroom nearly eliminated these behaviors in both environments, and these levels were maintained over 5 months of training. Steen and Zuriff (1977) were able to suppress the fingerbiting and scratching of a profoundly mentally retarded woman by fading physical restraints and shaping relaxation behavior with reinforcement procedures. The client was taught to relax both her arms and hands and this produced a solid reduction in the target SIB by day 76 of treatment. Staff reports one year later indicated that these behaviors remained at low levels without the use of physical restraints.

DeCantanzaro and Baldwin (1978) compared the influence of functional-movement OC, DRO, and OC plus DRO on the headhitting of two profoundly mentally retarded boys. Both children had been continuously held in restraints to prevent physical damage. Overcorrection was sufficient to bring about a rapid, but nonzero, reduction in the frequency of self-injury. Differential reinforcement of other behavior also had a marked suppressive effect on the self-hitting of one client, but was not used for the other client because previous applications met with little success. The combined OC plus DRO program was most successful, eliminating the SIB of both children within 20 training sessions. Once the program's success was established, control over its execution was transferred to the regular ward staff. The behaviors stayed at a near-zero level for the remainder of the study.

Kelly and Drabman (1977a) used functional-movement OC on the eyepoking of a child who had been identified as being at risk during infancy. After 7 days of OC, eyepoking occurred infrequently in the training environment. Response suppression was also observed in a generalization environment where no contingencies were in effect. Clements and Dewey (1979) studied the effects of functional-movement and a variety of other OC procedures on the eyepoking, handbiting, and object breaking of a severely mentally retarded boy. Each of these behaviors was successively eliminated in short order by its particular OC program, and was absent during a 6-month follow-up period. However, a dramatic acceleration in a variety of previously unseen stereotyped behaviors was noted. Although no data were reported, these stereotypies were said to occur as frequently as 1000 times a day.

Zehr and Theobald (1978) assessed the influence of the graduated-guidance component of functional-movement OC on the headhitting and facescratching of two profoundly mentally retarded women. Different measures of OC effectiveness were used for these two clients. A frequency measure was used for the first client, but the latency between the release from restraints and self-injury was used for the second client because of the frequency and intensity of the target behavior. The headhitting of the first client was eliminated within 5 hr of treatment with graduated guidance, and the latency of self-injury in the second client was markedly increased relative to baseline conditions. However, SIB continued to occur about once every 45 min. On the basis of these findings, it was concluded that manual guidance is the effective ingredient in the OC package.

Functional-movement OC was used by Kelly and Drabman (1977b) to prevent the headhitting of a severely mentally retarded girl. Restraint, scolding, and DRO had all been used without success in the past. Overcorrection gradually reduced the frequency of head hits, which yielded a criterion of 1 min without self-injury on the 12th training day. The training sessions were then extended in duration from 1 min through 2 hr. Low frequencies of self-injury were maintained through the 1-hr sessions, but over 90 head hits were recorded during each of the first 2 days of the 2-hr treatment. At this point, the staff discontinued the program because it interfered with other instructional activities. A 6-month follow-up revealed that the frequency of self-injury had returned to the pretreatment level.

In the first of two experiments, Measel and Alfieri (1976) contrasted the effects of DRI and functional-movement OC plus DRI on the headslapping of a profoundly mentally retarded boy. No change in the frequency of headslaps could be attribtued to DRI, but the combined OC plus DRI program produced an immediate and durable suppression of the target behavior. Four months later, headslapping was still absent. In the second experiment, these interventions were used to treat the headbanging of another profoundly mentally retarded child. Both DRI and OC plus DRI induced an acceleration in the rate of headbanging that was so extreme that it was necessary to discontinue training for fear of endangering the child's life. Similar findings were reported by Barnard, Christophersen, and Wolf (1976). They trained the parents of four children, two of whom were intellectually delayed, in the use of OC procedures for headbanging and handbiting SIB. Of the three children who were treated for headbanging, OC produced an immediate, near-zero level of self-injury in two cases. The headbanging of these clients rarely occurred during follow-up checks as long as 30 months after training. Overcorrection accelerated the rate of headbanging in the third client despite attempts to improve the effectiveness of the treatment by increasing its duration. The results for both children who were treated for handbiting were more favorable. Handbiting was nearly eliminated at home, and generalization of the training effects was seen during classroom hours.

Our conclusions about the efficacy of OC procedures for SIB mirror those drawn for other behavioral aberrations of mentally retarded persons. In general, OC procedures reduce the occurrence of SIB, in most cases to near-zero levels. These procedures have proven to be robust in spite of the wholesale omission of major components of the prescribed treatment regimen (Freeman et al., 1975; Zehr & Theobald, 1978). Often these effects are maintained over extended periods of time; sometimes they fail to persist. Suppression of the target behavior is sometimes accompanied by increases in collateral stereotyped and self-injurious behaviors (Clements & Dewey, 1979). In two cases (Barnard et al., 1976; Measel & Alfieri, 1976) OC was demonstrably ineffective. In one instance, OC was abandoned despite its effectiveness because of the considerable cost it exacted on the training staff (Kelly & Drabman, 1977b). Finally, although there have been few comprehensive treatment comparisons, the data generally suggest that OC is a reasonably effective alternative to other treatment procedures, with the exception of punishment by electric shock (Azrin et al., 1975).

Other Problem Behaviors

There remain three published reports on the use of OC for problems that do not neatly fit any previous behavior categories. In the first of these papers, Doleys, Wells, Hobbs, Roberts, and Cartelli (1976) compared the influence of social punishment (i.e., a verbal reprimand and silent glare), time-out, and PP on the noncompliance of four mentally retarded children. The assessment procedure consisted of a command to play with a collection of toys, followed by the application of one of the contingencies for failures to comply with the command. It was found that social punishment was the most effective treatment in reducing the frequency of noncompliance in every child. In two cases, noncompliance was reduced to near-zero levels. Time-out was minimally effective, yielding a negligible reduction in the noncompliance of one client and a modest reduction in the other. No effect was seen in two of the three clients for whom PP was used. The occurrence of noncompliance was reduced by half in the remaining client. The authors speculated that the brevity of OC or the absence of a verbal reprimand may have diminished OC's effectiveness.

Foxx (1976b) used OC to increase a mildly retarded woman's attendance at self-care and special education classes. Treatment was begun in the grooming class. Whenever the client failed to attend class, she was required to groom a group of profoundly mentally retarded women. Within a month of the start of OC, regular attendance of the grooming class was established. However, no change in her poor attendance at the special education class was seen until she was threatened to have to tutor other clients. Perfect attendance was established without using OC. It was noted that OC first met with combative behavior which was treated effectively with required relaxation.

In a novel application of the OC rationale, Foxx (1977) used a functional-movement PP and reinforcement program to shape eye contact in an autistic child and two severely mentally retarded children. It was reasoned that commands to the child to look at the trainer should acquire discriminative avoidance properties by virtue of its association with OC for failures to respond. This treatment package was contrasted with reinforcement for discriminative eye contact. Reinforcement alone was nominally effective in increasing eye contact, never raising it on average to more than 55% of the time. On the other hand, the OC plus reinforcement quickly produced more than

90% attention in all three children. Different durations of OC were required to elevate the occurrence of eye contact in these children. For one child, 2 min of OC sufficed, but 5 min were needed for the other children. All three showed some negative emotional and escape behaviors at the beginning of PP that extinguished within a few sessions.

General Summary

The conclusion from the large volume of data reviewed is that OC is an effective treatment alternative for a wide variety of behavior problems of mentally retarded persons. Overcorrection is not, however, a universal panacea. Many instances of limited effectiveness have been reported, and the magnitude of behavior change depends in part on the particular target behavior. To date, there have been no systematic attempts to "unpackage" the OC procedure. It may be that specific components, or combination of components, are most efficacious for particular behavior problems. The findings on the durability of treatment effects are equivocal, in many cases inducing lasting alterations in the target behaviors, and in some instances bringing about only transient changes. Negative side effects commonly associated with the application of other punishment procedures occur with OC. Few investigations contrasting alternative treatment approaches within the same experiment have been done, and those that are available have limited generality across clients. These issues, which comprise the substance of our discussion, will be elaborated in subsequent sections.

GENERALIZATION AND SIDE EFFECTS

It is critically important in the evaluation of a new treatment to assess the degree of stimulus and response generalization it affords. The client who receives the intervention usually manifests a complex of aberrations in addition to the targeted behavior. Likewise, the persons who implement the intervention and the situations in which the client behaves are likely to be numerous and diverse. Thus, it seems wise for the researcher to evaluate as many of the observable effects of the training procedure as possible. Unfortunately, many findings that bear on these issues in the punishment literature (Gardner, 1969) have been rather unsystematic and impressionistic in nature. This situation also characterizes much of the OC literature.

In many of the published reports, multiple-behavior problems of a single client were treated with OC procedures, but no independent measures of changes in the specific behaviors were taken. For example, Azrin, Sneed, and Foxx (1973) reported that four clients engaged in more than one stereotypy and specific OC procedures were applied to the behaviors as they occurred. Only the overall effect of OC on the incidence of stereotyped behaviors was recorded. Similarly, Stimbert et al. (1977) recorded the number of inappropriate eating responses of six mentally retarded children. Overcorrection was contingent on the occurrence of any of these behaviors and only overall changes were reported. From a practical standpoint, it was most efficient to treat these behaviors concurrently. However, a sequential analysis design (Sherman & Baer, 1969) would have allowed these authors to assess the generality of OC across behaviors while allowing each of the behaviors to be treated. In sum, only 10 of the above reviewed reports used a sufficiently analytic design to permit scrutiny of generalization of treatment effects across behaviors. Two of these studies report limited evidence of concurrent reductions in collateral misbehaviors (Luiselli et al., 1978; Roberts et al., 1979). The remaining studies showed either no change or an increase in the occurrence of collateral misbehaviors (Cavalier & Ferretti, 1980; Doke & Epstein, 1975; Foxx, 1976b; Foxx & Martin, 1975; Matson et al., 1978; Roberts et al., 1979; Rollings et al., 1977; Wells, Forehand, & Hickey, 1977; Wells, Forehand, Hickey, & Green, 1977). It seems that the effects of OC do not usually generalize to untreated misbehaviors. It should be noted that in these 10 studies the collateral and target responses were stereotyped behaviors. Thus, the generality of this conclusion for other collateral misbehaviors of mentally retarded persons is uncertain.

Similar analytic problems beset attempts to assess the generality of treatment effects across trainers and environments. The majority of the observations are anecdotal, and in may cases trainers are confounded with environments. For example, Butler,(1976) reports that his client continued to have toileting accidents at school despite a reduction in accidents at home. A teacher administered the program at school and the parents administered the program at home. This problem arises for at least three other studies that anecdotally report clients' discrimination of training effects (Doke & Epstein, 1975; Foxx & Azrin, 1973; Stimbert et al., 1977). A number of other workers have noted the stimulus specificity of OC effects (DeCantanzaro & Baldwin, 1978; Foxx, 1976b; Foxx & Azrin, 1972; Martin & Matson, 1978; Martin et al., 1977). In fact, generalization of training effects across stimuli has been anecdotally reported in only two papers (Azrin & Foxx, 1971; Foxx, 1976a), and in both cases multiple trainers were used. In effect, generalization was programmed by this procedure. In the entire OC literature with mentally retarded persons, only six studies provide sufficiently detailed information from which we can draw confirmable conclusions about the situational specificity of the effects of OC. In four of these six studies (Foxx, 1976b; Harris & Romanczyk, 1976; Marholin & Townsend, 1978; Rollings et al., 1977) discrimination of trainers or environments occurred. In the remaining two studies (Barnard et al., 1976; Kelly & Drabman, 1977a), generalized suppression in nontraining settings was seen. Although the generalization literature is not completely consistent, most of the empirical evidence compels us to conclude that OC, along with other punishment procedures, shares in the failure to consistently transfer its inhibitory effects to other trainers and situations (Birnbrauer, 1968). The Rusch et al. (1976) study is particularly instructive about the conditions likely to bring about generalization. They investigated changes in the frequency of a stereotyped behavior after the successive application of OC in two environments. No generalized suppression in a nontraining setting was seen until the client was treated in both environments. It appears, then, that for a stimulus class to acquire aversive properties, training must occur with at least two exemplars of the class (Stokes & Baer, 1977).

There have been a number of reports of favorable side effects associated with the use of OC with mentally retarded persons. The suppression of misbehaviors with OC has been said to produce greater social responsiveness (Azrin et al., 1975; Foxx & Azrin, 1972; Martin et al., 1977; Rusch et al., 1976), improvements in personal hygiene and physical appearance (Azrin & Wesolowski, 1975a; Foxx, 1976a; Foxx & Martin, 1975), an increase in the number and kinds of foods accepted by clients (Stimbert et al., 1977), and to permit the resumption of self-help and academic training and participation in other ward activities (Foxx, 1976b; Harris & Romanczyk, 1976; Webster & Azrin, 1973).

Overcorrection has also been associated with negative side effects, and they have been of three varieties. The most frequently cited side effect is emotional, escape, and resistive behavior (Azrin & Wesolowski, 1974; Doleys & Arnold, 1975; Foxx, 1976a,b, 1977; Foxx & Azrin, 1972, 1973; Lambert et al., 1975; Rollings et al., 1977; Wells, Forehand, & Hickey, 1977). In most cases, these responses are short-lived, occurring at the start of training and decreasing in intensity and frequency over time. There have been reports, particularly regarding the use of required relaxation, in which the behaviors were so severe that treatment was curtailed or avoided (Azrin & Wesolowski, 1975a; Webster & Azrin, 1973). The next most common complaint is that the suppression of the target behavior is associated with an acceleration of collateral or previously unseen misbehaviors. To the host of the above mentioned reports, we add two other anecdotal observations of this correlation (Clements & Dewey, 1979; Martin & Matson, 1978). Findings like these led Dunham (1971) to propose that punishment "defines a version of Sidman avoidance contingency for all other responses in the organism's repertoire" (p. 61). Finally, OC has been reported to be positively reinforcing to clients on two occasions (Measel & Alfieri, 1976; Smith *et al.*, 1975). In Measel and Alfieri's study, the rate of self-injury was so greatly accelerated that treatment was stopped for fear of loss of life.

Overcorrection procedures are not without influence on the training staff that implement them. Only one study reported direct measures of staff impressions of OC. Webster and Azrin (1973) had staff members respond to a questionnaire about their reactions to required relaxation relative to time-out and "other" treatment procedures. Required relaxation was preferred by 74% of the respondents for the principal reason that it was more attractive to visitors. A number of other investigators have casually commented about positive staff responses to OC. Azrin and Foxx (1971) indicated that before the toilet training program was begun, the ward staff were pessimistic about its effectiveness, but after completetion, viewed it quite favorably. In three other studies (Azrin *et al.*, 1975; Foxx & Azrin, 1972; Foxx & Martin, 1975), OC was said to be preferred by staff over time-out or restraint.

There have been a number of other workers who have expressed some apprehension about the effects of OC on training personnel. The consensus is that OC is most appropriate for residential environments in which staff limitations do not disrupt other programmatic efforts (Clements & Dewey, 1979; Duker & Seys, 1977; Sadler & Merkert, 1977; Smith *et al.*, 1975). In one study (Luiselli *et al.*, 1977), the duration of OC had to be reduced because it interfered with other teacher responsibilities. The magnitude of the training effort demanded by the OC rationale has worked to the detriment of clients on two occasions (Kelly & Drabman, 1977b; Zehr & Theobald, 1978). Effective treatment had to be discontinued because of the inability of staff to maintain both OC and other training duties. These concerns have led workers to make wholesale alterations in, or reduce the duration of, major components of OC as originally prescribed by Azrin and Foxx (1971).

Overcorrection has been successfully used with schizophrenic, brain-damaged, and all intellectual levels of mentally retarded persons. We believe that this treatment rationale has great generality within the population of intellectually impaired persons. We would, however, hope to see the rationale extended to a wider range of behavioral problems so that the boundary conditions of treatment effectiveness can be more firmly established. As we noted above, adult clients were explicity excluded from treatment in two studies (Azrin, Kaplan, & Foxx, 1973; Webster & Azrin, 1973) because of "severe behavior problems," thus limiting the scope of the problems that are amenable to treatment with OC. Required relaxation has already been determined to be best suited for compliant clients (Azrin & Wesolowski, 1975a).

Implicit in most of the studies that we have discussed is that OC, as a sound rationale and effective procedure, is applicable to the greater population of nonintellectually impaired persons. This reaches its most explicit statement in the study on theft-reversal OC by Azrin and Wesolowski (1974); therefore, we will discuss their reasons for using mentally retarded persons. Mentally retarded persons were studied because their failure to conceal their thefts permitted the theft intervention program to be more easily evaluated. We question whether the results of this or other OC studies are readily generalizable to the population at large given the knowledge available to date. Azrin and Wesolowski cite four reasons which they believe account for the effectiveness of their treatment: (1) termination of reinforcement by withdrawing the stolen item; (2) negative reinforcement of nonstealing by the effort required; (3) time-out from positive reinforcement; and (4) reeducation, in providing experience in the act of giving. They then conclude "on a theoretical basis, the theft-reversal procedure can be expected to be effective with nonmentally retarded persons, since the same reasons noted above for the effectiveness of the procedure apply to normal persons" (p. 580).

First, it seems doubtful that termination of reinforcement would deter nonretarded people from stealing, as they would lose nothing in the attempt and the pay off would probably be on a powerful variable-ratio schedule. Second, evidence suggests that response cost and negative reinforcement for nonstealing, as it is presently used in the judicial system (i.e., effort and fines), is not overwhelmingly successful. Third, time-out from positive reinforcement alone has not met with complete success with profoundly mentally retarded persons (e.g., Barton, Guess, Garcia, & Baer, 1970) and is the mainstay of the present, partially effective penal system. Fourth, much of the available evidence supports the conclusion that OC alone does not promote increases in the PP behavior, raising serious doubts about the "educative" properties of OC. Thus, there seems to be little reason to believe that these components of questionable efficacy should be successful when used in combination. Logic alone will not suffice to establish the generality of these OC procedures. Further research will settle the question.

Parameters and Procedural Components of OC

It is impossible to evaluate the generality of the OC procedure because it is a rationale from which numerous procedures are derived. When a specific OC procedure fails, others are implemented. Distinctively different OC procedures are used for each class of behavior problems. Each OC procedure is comprised of different components, any one or combination of which may be effective. There have been no systematic efforts to date to sort out the confounded treatment variables.

Required relaxation has been used in a number of studies, both alone and in combination with other procedures. Foxx and Azrin (1972) used required relaxation in conjunction with *social* and *household* OC for composite durations of 30 min. Webster and Azrin (1973) made a 2-hr episode of required relaxation alone contingent on each misbehavior. In both cases, the treatment was effective in suppressing the target misbehavior. Similar findings have been obtained for other categories of misbehaviors. Each OC episode has ranged in length from 1 min (e.g., Roberts et al., 1979) to 30 min (Foxx & Azrin, 1972) with no apparent reduction in the effectiveness of treatment for stereotyped behaviors. There has been only one study that assessed the efficacy of different OC durations (Marholin & Townsend, 1978), and 3 min of the physical restraint component of OC was found to be as effective as 5 min in suppressing stereotyped behavior. Thus, there is no evidence of a systematic relationship between the length of each OC episode and treatment effectiveness. Nevertheless, there have been instances in which increases in the duration of OC have brought about behavior change not realized with briefer applications (Foxx, 1977; Foxx & Azrin, 1973). In both cases, the initial and subsequent durations were within the range of effectiveness established in other successful reports. The practical conclusion to draw from these findings is that a first failure with a brief application of OC should be followed with longer durations. However, no absolute criterion for the continuation of treatment with OC can be reasonably applied. Practical considerations, such as the availability of treatment resources, must be the overriding determinants in the decision-making process.

As Azrin (1977) has stated, OC typically entails a number of factors, including extinction, time-out from positive reinforcement, response prevention, physical restraint, prompting, and DRO. We recognize that it is not a central concern of the practitioner to determine which components function as the active ingredients, but we believe that the knowledge afforded by a thorough analysis will greatly benefit understanding and application in a burgeoning field. Deitz (1978) has made this point most cogently in his discussion of changing attitudes of applied behavior analysts. The historic focus in the field has been on the independent variables that control socially important behaviors. Thus, the methods and philosophy of applied behavior analysis were consistent with, and a specific extension of, those of the experimental analysis of behavior. Most recently, some applied behavior analysts (Azrin, 1977) have advocated a shift from the formulation of laws that govern socially relevant behaviors (i.e., analysis) to the application of known laws to practical problems (i.e., outcome). Dietz discussed two dangers associated with this change. First, our knowledge of laws from which the technologies emerge is wholly inadequate, so our technologies cannot be fully satisfactory. Second, a preoccupation with "cures" may lead to the abandonment of those methods that inform our theories of behavior. In other words, the change may limit what is discovered. Of course, we cannot divorce our practical and analytic purposes, but there most be a healthy balance in our pursuit of both. In the case of OC procedures, the potential savings in time and effort alone will be sufficient rewards for such a pursuit. Unfortunately, little data is available, and much of it is conflicting.

Time-out and physical restraint have been used as independent OC components in a number of studies and have not met with much success (Azrin & Wesolowski, 1975a; Foxx, 1976a; Foxx & Azrin, 1972; Foxx & Martin, 1975). However, three studies exist in which either of these components has been effective (Doleys et al., 1976; Freeman et al., 1975; Marholin & Townsend, 1978). Physical restraint was so potent in the Freeman et al. study that the authors concluded that it is the effective component of the OC package. In 14 studies, reinforcement procedures (i.e., DRA, DRI, or DRO) have been compared with OC for controlling a veritable multitude of misbehaviors, and in each case reinforcement has fared poorly (e.g., Cavalier & Ferretti, 1980; Denney, 1980; Duker & Seys, 1977). Increases in the PP behavior have been infrequently reported, so it is unlikely that the suppressive effects of OC are attributable to the development of behaviors that are incompatible with the misbehavior. A number of studies (Azrin & Wesolowski, 1974, 1975b; Foxx & Azrin, 1972) have evaluated the use of simple correction for a number of behavior problems, and all except one have found it to be ineffective. The lone exception was reported by Matson (1977). Verbal warnings or admonitions have been successfully used to control the stereotypes of mentally retarded persons in five studies. In three of these reports, warnings were used to maintain the treatment effects induced by OC (Doke & Epstein, 1975; Foxx, 1976b; Foxx & Azrin, 1973). In the remaining two studies, warnings alone were sufficient to control the target behavior (Rusch et al., 1976; Wells, Forehand, & Hickey, 1977). In the former studies, the warnings may have acquired discrminative aversive properties by virtue of their association with OC, and in the latter cases, the warnings must have acquired these properties before experimentation. As we have already noted, warnings have been used for stereotyped behaviors, so their effects may be problem specific.

It appears that in those studies in which the discernible components of OC have been compared against the entire OC package, the specific components have not been generally effective. Of course, there have been many studies in which the effectiveness of these isolated procedures has been demonstrated for a variety of behavior problems (e.g., Repp, Deitz, & Deitz, 1976; Salzberg & Napolitan, 1974; White, Neilson, & Johnson, 1972). Perhaps there are individual behavioral characteristics that predispose a given client to the effects of a specific component or combinations of components. It may also be that these components interact when used in combination. The critical features of the treatment effectiveness of OC can be established only through systematic component analyses.

Methodological Considerations

The experimental designs used in evaluating the effectiveness of OC procedures appear to depend in part on the nature of the misbehavior. When the potential for inflicting severe damage on one's person or on the environment exists, an A–B design is utilized, baseline data are limited, and recording procedures are variable.

Often the failure to withdraw effective treatment contingencies or to return to less effective ones weakens conclusions about the degree of control afforded by OC. Azrin and Wesolowski (1974) compared simple correction, which was in effect during the baseline period, against theft-reversal OC in a within-subjects design. A non-intervention condition was not included because it would have permitted the victim to be deprived of his possessions. However, reintroduction of simple correction with subsequent readaministration of OC would have both satisfied this ethical consideration and strengthened the authors' conclusions. Similar concerns are germane to a number of other studies. In the first of three experiments, Foxx and Azrin (1972) used both simple correction and social disapproval during the baseline period, followed by R. In the second experiment, time-out and social disapproval were operative prior to R, and in the third experiment, social disapproval preceded R. Azrin and Wesolowski (1974, 1975b) compared OC against simple correction, which was operative during baseline. Webster and Azrin (1973) applied OC after a baseline which was void of any treatment. Although the authors report that the reliability of recordings was assured by having two attendants agree that a disruption occurred, the number of disagreements was not reported. The results were replicated across many clients, but we feel that a withdrawal and readministration of OC was needed since all clients participated at the same time, in the same setting, and were subject to the same influences.

Freeman et al. (1975) used a combined reinforcement and OC program following baseline observations of an autistic child's nailpicking. The reliability of their measures was not reported. Harris and Romanczyk (1976) used OC first at the school and then at the home of a self-injurious child. Baseline recordings preceded treatment in each environment. The authors reported that there was no change in self-injury at home while treatment was in effect at school, but baseline at home was recorded after the completion of training at school. The design would have been more compelling if baseline data had been collected at home prior to or during treatment at school. No reliability was reported. Kelly and Drabman (1977b) used OC, which was successively lengthened in duration, after a baseline period without treatment. Marholin and Townsend (1978) alternated 3 and 5 min of OC after a brief baseline session. Withdrawal of OC of a given duration before application of OC with a different duration might have revealed differences in the effects of both durations. It is not surprising that 5 min of OC maintained the effects established with 3 min of OC. Finally, the threat of self injury compelled Steen and Zuriff (1977) to abbreviate baseline recording and begin training with OC. Reliability was not determined because of the obviousness of the target behavior.

Azrin et al. (1975) recorded baselines of SIB by observing clients for as long as feasible. The extent of the observation period varied widely across clients, ranging from only 10 min to 8 hr per day for 12 days. Different response measures were employed, depending on the spacing and duration of the various behaviors. Moreover, day-to-day variability across subjects was obscured by merely reporting frequency of self-injury during baseline. Finally, a unitary function was reported for subjects receiving different treatments (i.e., required-relaxation or hand-control training). This prohibits the independent evaluation of these separate procedures. Given these facts, the reporting of group data seems tenuous. However, the authors report that the ward staff unanimously agreed that the recorded frequency was representative of the usual frequency of the clients. In their first experiment, Measel and Alfieri (1976) alternated reinforcement alone with OC and reinforcement after brief baseline observations of a mentally retarded child's headslapping. The target behavior occurred infrequently during the combined reinforcement and OC program. However, a steady decline to a near zero level was observed during the baseline period, during which no treatment was in effect. Reinforcement alone brought about an initial increase, and then a steady decrease in headslapping. The combined program was started while the behavior was decelerating under the influence of the reinforcement program. No treatment should have been undertaken until stable behavior levels had been achieved.

In the absence of ethical considerations, methodological and interpretive problems exist in many of the studies. In the Azrin and Wesolowski (1975a) case report, the last week of time-out, which preceded OC, brought about a sizeable reduction in vomiting. Therefore, it is impossible to determine whether the continuance of time-out would have brought about the suppression attributed to OC. A return-to-baseline condition would have avoided this confounding. Barmann (1979) used OC after baseline recordings of the nail-biting of a mentally retarded child. No procedures were used to insure experimental control, despite the fact that the child's mother began administering the program a week after the start of treatment with a different trainer. Baseline recordings in the presence of the mother could have been made during the first week of training. In four studies (Doleys & Arnold, 1975; Leon, 1975; Matson, 1977; Smith *et al.*, 1975), OC was used to toilet train mentally retarded persons after baseline observations. It is unlikely that an alternative design could have been used in the second and third reports because of the nature of the problem and the fact that a single subject participated in both experiments. Given the relatively large number of subjects, Smith *et al.* (1975) may have been able to use a multiple baseline, successive treatment-across-subjects design. Doleys and Arnold (1975) could have made multiple baseline recordings at home and school rather than reporting the total number of toileting accidents in both settings. No reliability was reported by Doleys and Arnold, or by Leon, or by Matson; Smith *et al.* had poor reliability.

In the Azrin, Kaplan, and Foxx (1973) experiment, the sequence of procedures consisted of nonreinforcement for 6 days, reinforcement alone for 8 days, a return to nonreinforcement for 5 days, and the combined reinforcement plus autism-reversal program for a minimum of 70 days. The reinforcement program reduced self-stimulation to about ⅓ of its baseline level, whereas reinforcement plus autism reversal reduced self-stimulation by about 85% during the last week of application. First, it should be noted that the return to baseline resulted in an increase in self-stimulation that was reliably below the previous nonreinforcement level. Apparently, there was a residual suppression of self-stimulation attributable to the reinforcement contingencies. Second, there were vast differences in the duration of the reinforcement (8 days) and the combined reinforcement plus autism-reversal program (70 days). Extension of the reinforcement program may have resulted in suppression effects similar to those resulting from the combined program. Repp, Deitz, and

Speir (1974) nearly eliminated stereotyped responding in three mentally retarded people by making social reinforcement (a praise and hug) contingent on the absence of the behavior. Finally, statistical analyses were reported on the following comparisons: baseline-reinforcement, baseline-combined program, and the two baseline conditions. No analysis was reported on the comparison of the two treatment conditions. Perusal of the data suggest a greater suppression under the combined program, but this may not have been borne out statistically.

In the Foxx and Azrin (1973) study, the superiority of OC relative to punishment by slapping in the case of the first client may have been confounded by the withdrawal of noncontingent reinforcement. The resident received the various procedures in the following sequence: (1) free reinforcement, (2) reinforcement for nonmouthing, (3) punishment by a slap, (4) free reinforcement, and (5) OC. The free reinforcement procedure was reinstated to provide a more uniform baseline before applying OC. The termination of free reinforcement was contiguous with the institution of OC, thus the suppression attributed to OC may have resulted from the interaction of OC and the withdrawal of the noncontingent reinforcement. The resident in question self-stimulated 80% of the time during baseline. Reinforcement delivered noncontingently would in fact be highly correlated with the occurence of self-stimulation. The withdrawal of noncontingent reinforcement might be frustrating, with the effect of suppressing the response. This effect, when compounded with the aversive properties of OC, may have produced the greater suppresion relative to the punishment contingency. Repp et al. (1976) appreciably reduced both the frequency and variability of stereotyped behavior of mentally retarded children in a classroom setting using DRO schedules alone. They also indicated that the failure of DRO by Foxx and Azrin (1973) was most likely attributable to selecting too large of an initial DRO interval. In Study 2, a reversal design was employed with four mentally retarded self-stimulators, and unequivocal support for the suppressive effects of OC was obtained. Additionally, data were reported for only the last three sessions of each condition. This disallows evaluation of the variability of these data across the various treatments. Finally, the duration of each of the treatments was not reported. These data are important when we consider that the clinical utility of a punishment procedure is in part determined by the strength, immediacy, and durability of the resulting behavior change (Epstein et al., 1974).

The Rollings et al. (1977) procedures may account for their failure to obtain any suppressive effects with OC in study 1. Given the brief daily session and OC durations, only two OC episodes could have been administered during a training session, even if we assume that the termination of OC was maximally contiguous with the next episode of headweaving. This infrequent application of OC may not have provided sufficient opportunities for the client to learn the contingencies. Additionally, the duration of each OC incident may not have been sufficiently long to produce the desired suppressive effect. Finally, during the baseline conditions within each training session, both observers were 8 ft. behind the subject. This may have provided a discriminative cue for the subject signaling a safe period. When the cues were eliminated in Study 2, suppression of the contingent response was achieved.

Butler (1976) reported only the number of enuretic episodes during the bladder-training program. Baseline data were not reported, the reliability of his measures was not established, and data to support his contention that the client took responsibility for toileting accidents were not forthcoming. Luiselli et al. (1977) used OC to eliminate the in-class masturbation of a mentally retarded boy after initial baseline observations. The authors reasoned that a reversal design was inappropriate because the absence of the contingency would not have been discriminable once the behavior was eliminated. A multiple baseline across settings was rejected because masturbation was restricted to class. However, training was done during three distinct periods throughout the day, allowing for a multiple-baseline-across-sessions (cf. Rusch et al., 1976). Luiselli et al. (1978) used a reversal, multiple-baseline-across-behaviors design to compare the effectiveness of reinforcement alone against reinforcement and OC in controlling a variety of misbehaviors. Unfortunately, the combined program induced a generalized suppression in all behaviors, and the rates never recovered to pretreatment levels.

Doleys et al. (1976) used a reversal design in contrasting the effects of time-out, OC, and social punishment on the noncompliance of four children. In two of the four clients, the effects of social punishment persisted during return-to-baseline conditions. The same trainer administered the commands to play during each treatment and he may have become discriminative for social punishment. This problem may have been avoided by including an additional trainer for whom failures to comply were not followed with any treatment (cf. Foxx, 1977). In the first of two experiments, Ollendick et al. (1978) used a withdrawal design to check the influence of an OC procedure topographically related to the targeted stereotyped behaviors of two children. The return-to-baseline conditions did not result in increases in the target behavior of either child. In the second study, OC was topographically unrelated to the stereotypies, and increases in these behaviors were seen during the return-to-baseline period. The authors argued that the extended suppression seen in the first study, and the failure to observe it in the second experiment, was determined by the topographic similarity between OC and the targeted behavior. It is possible that the findings of the first study reflect the failure to establish experimental control over the target stereotypies. These alternatives could have been evaluated if the second client in each study had been used as a multiple-baseline control for the first client and the treatment had been reversed after achieving a low frequency.

There are a number of investigators who have provided support for the efficacy of OC but failed to establish the reliability of their measurements (Clements & Dewey, 1979; DeCatanzaro & Baldwin, 1978; Duker & Seys, 1977; Sadler & Merkert, 1977). We recognize that there are situations in which the introduction of a second observer can prove disruptive to the measurement process (e.g., Clements & Dewey, 1979), but we feel that it is otherwise essential to insure independent verification of behavioral observations.

A series of studies are methodologically sound, have demonstrated measurement reliability, and result in conclusive support for the efficacy of OC. These studies used either multiple-group comparisons (Azrin & Armstrong, 1973; Azrin & Foxx, 1971; Azrin, Sneed, & Foxx, 1973); multiple-baseline-designs across subjects (Barnard et al., 1976; Denney, 1980; Foxx & Martin, 1975; Stimbert et al., 1977; Wells, Forehand, & Hickey, 1977; Wells, Forehand, Hickey, & Green, 1977), across behaviors (Doke & Epstein, 1975; Foxx, 1976b; Foxx & Martin, 1975; Matson et al., 1978; Roberts et al., 1979; Wells, Forehand, & Hickey, 1977; Wells, Forehand, Hickey, & Green, 1977); across trainers (Foxx, 1977); across environments (Foxx, 1976b; Rusch et al., 1976), or reversal designs (Doke & Epstein, 1975; Foxx, 1976a; Kelly & Drabman, 1977a; Martin & Matson, 1978; Martin et al., 1977; Shapiro, 1979; Zehr & Theobald, 1978).

Despite the methodological and interpretative difficulties in many of the above mentioned studies, we feel that OC has been shown to be effective for a variety of behavior problems of mentally retarded persons. The gravest problems exist in those studies designed to compare directly the treatment alternatives. Most outstanding was the failure to provide control for order effects. In all but one of the comparative studies (Cavalier & Ferretti, 1980), OC was the last treatment effected. In every case, we feel that there is suggestive evidence for the operation of order effects. We would like to see more research in which OC precedes other contingencies. Future work should be cognizant of counterbalancing procedures when comparing multiple intervention programs.

Finally, OC has usually been employed in a context of externally imposed positive reinforcement for more suitable alternative behaviors. Such an alternative response situation is thought to result in maximum response suppression (Azrin & Holz, 1966). As Gardner (1969) eloquently states: "Although desirable as a treatment strategy, such a procedure does, however, confound the contributions of punishment and positive reinforcement in subsequent behavior except in those studies which utilize a precise functional analysis design" (pp. 88–89).

Practicality

In many clinical and institutional settings, workers must often make a choice of treatment programs which are demonstrably effective for the problems with which they are confronted. In this situation, factors other than effectiveness must necessarily enter into the decision process. These factors are: the compatibility of the intervention program with existing programmatic efforts, financial and manpower limitations, ease of implementation, the rapidity with which change is effected and the acceptability to the general public. The following discussion will consider OC in light of each of these criteria.

Overcorrection appears to be most fruitfully employed in a context of positive reinforcement for suitable alternative behaviors. Despite the above mentioned interpretive problems inherent in this plan, it appears necessary to insure successful suppression of undesirable responses and acquisition of more appropriate behavior. This situation is generally true of any treatment which is aversive or punishing in nature (Gardner, 1969). Moreoever, OC is most likely to be effective in settings with an interested staff and a large staff–resident ratio because this insures rapid detection and interruption of the inappropriate behavior. Azrin, Kaplan, and Foxx (1973) report that two instructors were required during the first few days of autism-reversal training as each resident was added to the program. Only three residents were present at the beginning of training. Foxx and Azrin (1973) state that a high ratio of teachers to children (1 : 3) enabled the children to receive frequent instruction in appropriate behavior during the course of OC for self-stimulatory behavior. Azrin and Wesolowski (1975b) assigned two special trainers to their floor-sprawling OC program, which after 6 months was maintained by ward attendants. For the first two or three days of SIB OC training in the Azrin *et al.* (1975) study, two special instructors continually observed the client for 12-hr per day. Ward staff assisted during the first few days and were taught and supervised by the instructors.

The mini-meal program of Azrin and Armstrong (1973) required that two trainers per client be present until the client could be easily managed by one trainer.

Special supervision and large staff–resident ratios were not always necessary, however, as normal ward staff was sometimes sufficient for effective program implementation (e.g., Azrin, Sneed, & Foxx, 1973; Azrin & Wesolowski, 1975a; Webster & Azrin, 1973). When a large ratio is required, we feel that this would place a considerable demand on most public residential institutions, which are generally overcrowded and understaffed. Given the choice between two treatment programs when funds and energies are limited, we believe that the ease with which they can be implemented must be of prime importance. We wish to emphasize that the general conditions operative at residential institutions at the time of intervention serve to limit both the number of alternatives and the effectiveness of programmatic efforts. In our opinion, these considerations have two obvious implications: (1) the program which is easier to implement should be chosen, or (2) the resources which institutions have at their disposal should be increased.

Many behaviors, particularly those that have potential for inflicting severe damage, demand rapid suppression. Overcorrection has been used to produce fairly quick suppression of a variety of behaviors (e.g., Azrin, Kaplan, & Foxx, 1973; Azrin, Sneed, & Foxx, 1973; Azrin et al., 1975; Azrin & Foxx, 1971; Azrin & Wesolowski, 1974; Azrin & Wesolowski, 1975a,b; Epstein et al., 1974; Foxx, 1976a,b; Foxx & Azrin, 1972; Webster & Azrin, 1973), and consequently, we believe that the Azrin et al. (1975) conclusion about the speed of suppression of SIB by OC is generalizable to a wide range of behaviors and intervention settings. They say: "the present method appears at least as rapid as has been reported for the alternative methods but far less rapid than the almost instantaneous benefit obtained in most reports of shock" (p. 110).

Ultimately, the treatment alternatives available to staff will be defined by their acceptability to the public. Procedures which are overtly punitive have come under great scrutiny, resulting in both public vexation and legal strictures. For example, a recent court ruling (*Wyatt* v. *Stickney*, 1972, Middle District, State of Alabama) placed specific restrictions on the use of shock as a behavioral management technique. Given this attitudinal climate, programs must be developed which are relatively effective and perceptibly benign. In many respects, OC appears to be just such a program. Its most attractive feature is that it is purported to be reeducative. This emphasis on constructive, rather than merely punitive consequences, is timely.

Public sentiment must continue to play a role in treatment policy, but it should not be the guiding force in program development. Gardner's (1969) statement adequately reflects our convictions:

> Most clinical treatment personnel categorically reject the use of punishment procedures as legitimate behavior change approaches. Punishment procedures are typically viewed as inhumane, deplorable, unethical and nonprofessional.... In general, it appears that punishment is frequently rejected as a treatment procedure, not on the basis of an objective evaluation of scientific data, but rather on the basis of ethical, philosophic, and sociopolitical considerations. (pp. 87-88)

A recent survey of public facilities for the mentally retarded (Wallace, Burger, Neal, van Brero, & Davis, 1976) revealed that in those not using aversive conditioning procedures, 62% of the chief psychologists stated that these procedures would be beneficial for treating some of their residents. In those using the procedures, no legal action was necessary for misusing them.

However, two facilities reported cases in which legal action was threatened by parents if contingent shock were to be discontinued with their children. The authors concluded:

> In a general sense, therapy should result in the least amount of pain to the patient, and sometimes this will mean that the administration of a few harmless but painful stimuli may be more desirable than chemical or mechanical restraints which often leave a patient in a state of even greater or recurrent punishment. If through the appropriate use of aversive conditioning techniques we can help keep certain mentally retarded individuals awake and untied, then this controversial treatment has a place in treatments for the mentally retarded. (p. 18)

In our opinion, psychologists, in an objective search for knowledge, should assume active responsibility to demythologize public conceptions about punishment. This will ultimately benefit both the discipline and the recipients of its services.

Theoretical and General Considerations

The theory upon which OC is based emphasizes two components: punishment and education. However, the germane literature is not always clear as to what is punitive, what is educative, and what has been taught. For example, OC procedures designed for stereotyped and self-injurious behaviors are educative because clients learn specific movements to specific commands with the extremities involved in the behavior. However, whether learning to extend ones arms to the words "arms out" has any functional utility would seem dependent on whether a client can generalize to more practical commands, such as "come here" or "bring that here." Moreover, if practicing "overly correct forms of relevant behavior" is a necessary component of the

OC procedure, what can account for the finding that OC procedures designed for stereotyped hand movements were as effective in suppressing stereotyped foot movements as procedures designed specifically for the foot behavior (e.g., Epstein et al., 1974)? Moreover, the PP behavior has been reported to increase in only isolated cases (i.e., Wells, Forehand, & Hickey, 1977; Wells, Forehand, Hickey, & Green, 1977). In fact, the association of PP with the entire OC program may result in its suppression (Roberts et al., 1979). These data suggest that the *specific* educational component contributes relatively little to the overall effectiveness of OC.

The punitive element of OC has been variously stated as being both the physical effort required in R and PP (of which the desired behavior is a part) and the initially administered physical guidance. Curiously, Azrin et al. (1975) state "the present method appears to be more acceptable as a treatment than either shock or time out seclusion, in that no physical punishment is used" (p. 110). If OC is a punishment procedure, but is not physically punitive, we wonder in what way OC *is* punitive. Further adding to this confusion, Azrin and Wesolowski (1975a) state:

> The self-correction procedure seemed easier to carry out than the previously reported overcorrection procedure ... where the subject would have had to overcorrect to a far greater extent than simply cleaning up the vomit from her clothes, bed or the floor; these activities are all too easily interpreted by the trainee and the trainer as punitive rather than reeducative. (p. 147)

It is also unclear as to what maintains the PP behavior, as it appears to be a component of the aversive contingency. At first glance, it would appear that it is maintained by negative reinforcement obtained by avoiding the physical guidance. However, the client could avoid *both* the positive behavior and physical guidance, by not emitting the target response. With the suppression of the target response, conditions necessary for the maintenance of the PP behavior are absent. Both the suppression of the target response and the establishment of overly correct forms of the behavior are the goals of OC, but the latter is incompatible with the theoretical effects of the avoidance contingency. It may be that the often noted use of a context of positive reinforcement for appropriate behavior may offset the effects of the avoidance contingency and maintain the PP behavior.

We realize that these theoretical vagaries are not of central concern to the applied researcher. However, as previously stated, consideration of them may possess heuristic value for future researchers and offer a substantial savings in time and effort. More precise understanding of the principles underlying the OC procedures would allow for more effective implementation of them.

As has been noted, there is some theoretical ambiguity as to what is the effective component or components in the OC package. We suggest for consideration that a modified *response cost* (RC) element may be the active ingredient. The notion of RC was initially formulated to denote that the physical or monetary cost of a response affects the rate with which that response is exhibited (Weiner, 1962). However, the great majority of laboratory and applied investigations has focused on the removal of conditioned reinforcers contingent on a response, as opposed to physical cost or effort (Kazdin, 1972). For example, in laboratory studies, Weiner (1962, 1963, 1964, 1969) employed point loss as the RC and found it effectively suppressed reinforced responding. Nevertheless, Azrin (1958) found that physical cost (increased effort) reduced high rates of unreinforced responding. For the purpose of drawing the analogy between RC and OC, it may be helpful to conceptualize the client as having time and effort "in his pocket" and OC as withdrawing from these possessions. While this notion is largely speculative, there are parallels between the findings with OC and RC (e.g., Elliott & Tigue, 1968; Kazdin, 1973; Phillips, 1968; Phillips, Phillips, Fixsen, & Wolf, 1971; Schmauk, 1970; Siegel, Lenske & Broen, 1969). There may be heuristic value in a marriage of the available knowledge on both sets of procedures, followed by direct investigations. It is possible that Azrin and his associates have revived the initial formulation of response-produced physical cost, added supplementary components, and couched the package in publicly acceptable terminology.

It is apparent from the increasing number of studies employing OC that interest in this procedure is skyrocketing. We are both impressed and disconcerted with the general approach of Azrin and his associates; impressed because of the difficulty and importance in capturing public support, disconcerted because at times their descriptive terminology connotes more than is defined. Terms like *autism reversal* or *habit reversal* suggest the eradication of some past problem, when all that is meant is a reduction in the future probability of a specific behavior called an autism or habit. Another example is *medical assistance for physical aggression* which suggests that the aggressor will acquire the competencies necessary to assist in medical treatment of the victim. Doke and Epstein (1975) have recommended "that technologists maintain a clear distinction between the rational 'packaging' that makes overcorrection easier to sell and the physical parameters of overcorrection procedures that determine their effectiveness and generality" (p. 510). This use of euphemisms may inadvertently create unwarranted public optimism before this set of procedures is well documented. The immediate gains, in the form of public support, produced by this approach may not balance against the potential long range disenchantment resulting from unfulfilled expectations.

CONCLUSIONS

Overcorrection, a procedure with punitive and educative components, has been used to suppress a variety of behaviors among intellectually impaired persons in laboratory and clinical settings. An analysis of OC's effectiveness and durability, generalization and side effects, parameters and procedural components, methodologies, practicality, and theory were presented. It was concluded that: (1) OC appears to be generally effective across many misbehaviors among the intellectually impaired, (2) the durability of treatment effects is equivocal, and may depend upon the inclusion of incompatible responses which are maintained by naturally occurring reinforcement, (3) OC appears to share many of the same positive and negative side effects with other aversive conditioning procedures, that is, trainer, situation, and response specificity, increased attention and social interaction, etc., (4) although OC is a multi-component procedure, no systematic efforts have been made to determine the effective component(s) to date, (5) the choice of OC over other alternatives as an intervention program must be dependent upon multiple considerations, and (6) the rationale underlying the effectiveness of OC procedures is in need of further clarification. The paucity of studies bearing on durability, component analysis, side effects, and effectiveness relative to other treatment procedures make any of the conclusions about these factors tentative. We feel the promise of OC is that a single rationale may provide for the resolution of a multitude of behavior problems typically observed in mentally retarded persons. It is hoped that researchers will design maximally effective intervention technologies by designing studies which are more analytic relative to independent variables that control and modify these problem behaviors.

ACKNOWLEDGMENTS

The authors owe a debt of gratitude to Tom Heffernan for assistance in the initial literature search, to Pam Hudson for typing the manuscript, and to Emily Ellis for her English translation of the report of Lambert et al. (1975). Thanks are also due to Dr. A. A. Baumeister and Dr. N. R. Ellis for their comments on the paper.

References

Abelson, R.B., & Johnson, R. C. Heterosexual and aggressive behaviors among institutionalized retardates. *Mental Retardation*, 1969, *7*, 28–30.

Azrin, N.H. Some effects of noise on human operant behavior. *Journal of the Experimental Analysis of Behavior*, 1958, *1*, 183–200.

Azrin, N. H. A strategy for applied research: Learning based but outcome oriented. *American Psychologist*, 1977, *32*, 140–149.

Azrin, N. H., & Armstrong, P. M. The "mini-meal": A method for teaching eating skills to the profoundly retarded. *Mental Retardation*. 1973, *11*, 9–13.

Azrin, N. H., & Foxx, R. M. A rapid method of toilet training the institutionalized retarded. *Journal of Applied Behavior Analysis*, 1971, *4*, 89–99.

Azrin, N. H., & Holz, W. C. Punishment. In W. K. Honig (Ed.). *Operant behavior: Areas of research and application*. New York: Appleton-Century-Crofts, 1966.

Azrin, N.H., & Nunn, R. G. Habit-reversal: A method of eliminating nervous habits and tics. *Behaviour Research and Therapy*, 1973, *11*, 619–628.

Azrin, N. H., & Wesolowski, M.D. Theft refersal: An overcorrection procedure for eliminating stealing by retarded persons. *Journal of Applied Behavior Analysis*, 1974, *7*, 577–581.

Azrin, N. H., & Wesolowski, M. D. Eliminating habitual vomiting in a retarded adult by positive practice and self-correction. *Journal of Behavior Therapy and Experimental Psychiatry*, 1975, *6*, 149–152. (a)

Azrin, N. H., & Wesolowski, M. D. The use of positive practice to eliminate persistent floor sprawling by profoundly retarded persons. *Behavior Therapy*, 1975, *6*, 627–631. (b)

Azrin, N. H., Kaplan, S. J., & Foxx, R. M. Autism reversal: Eliminating stereotyped self-stimulation of retarded individuals. *American Journal of Mental Deficiency*, 1973, *78*, 241–248.

Azrin, N. H., Sneed, T. J., & Foxx, R. M. Dry bed: A rapid method of eliminating bedwetting (enuresis) of the retarded. *Behaviour Research and Therapy*, 1973, *12*, 147–156.

Azrin, N. H., Gottlieb, L., Hughart, L., Wesolowski, M. D., & Rahn, T. Eliminating self-injurious behavior by educative procedures. *Behaviour Research and Therapy*, 1975, *13*, 101–111.

Barmann, B. C. The use of overcorrection with artificial nails for the treatment of chronic fingernail biting. *Mental Retardation*, 1979, *17*, 309–311.

Barnard, J. D., Christophersen, E. R., & Wolf, M. M. Parent-mediated treatment of children's self-injurious behavior using overcorrection. *Journal of Pediatric Psychology*, 1976, *1*, 56–61.

Barton, E. S., Guess, D., Garcia, E., & Baer, D. M. Improvements of retardates' mealtime behaviors by time out procedures using multiple baseline techniques. *Journal of Applied Behavior Analysis*, 1970, *3*, 77–84.

Baumeister, A. A. The American residential institution: Its history and character. In A. A. Baumeister & E. C. Butterfield (Eds.), *Residential facilities for the mentally retarded*. Chicago: Aldine, 1970.

Baumeister, A. A., & Forehand, R. Effects of contingent shock and verbal command on body rocking of retardates. *Journal of Clinical Psychology*, 1972, *28*, 586–590.

Baumeister, A. A., & Forehand, R. Stereotyped acts. In N. R. Ellis (Ed.), *International review of research in mental retardation* (Vol. 6). New York: Academic Press, 1973.

Baumeister, A. A., & Rollings, J. P. Self-injurious behavior. In N. R. Ellis (Ed.), *International Review of Research in Mental Retardation* (Vol. 8). New York: Academic Press, 1976.

Berkovitz, S., Sherry, P. J., & Davis, B. A. Teaching self-feeding skills to profound retardates using reinforcement and fading procedures. *Behavior Therapy*, 1971, *2*, 62–67.

BERKSON, G. Abnormal stereotyped motor acts. In J. Zubin & H. F. Hunt (Eds.), *Comparative psychopathology—Animal and human*. New York: Grune & Stratton, 1967.

BERKSON, G., & MASON, W. Stereotyped movements of mental defectives: III. Situation effects. *American Journal of Mental Deficiency*, 1963, *68*, 409-412.

BERKSON, G., & MASON, W. Stereotyped behaviors of chimpanzees: Relation to general arousal and alternative activities. *Perceptual and Motor Skills*, 1964, *19*, 635-652.

BIRNBRAUER, J. S. Generalization of punishment effects: A case study. *Journal of Applied Behavior Analysis*, 1968, *1*, 201-211.

BUTLER, J. F. Toilet training a child with spina bifida. *Journal of Behavior Therapy and Experimental Psychiatry*, 1976, *7*, 63-65.

CAVALIER, A. R., & FERRETTI, R. P. Stereotyped behavior, alternative behavior, and collateral effects: A comparison of four intervention procedures. *Journal of Mental Deficiency Research*, 1980, *24*, 219-230.

CLEMENTS, J., & DEWEY, M. The effects of overcorrection: A case study. *Behaviour Research and Therapy*, 1979, *17*, 515-518.

DECANIANZARO, D. A., & BALDWIN G. Effective treatment of self-injurious behavior through a forced arm exercise. *American Journal of Mental Deficiency*, 1978, *82*, 133-439

DEITZ, S. M. Current status of applied behavior analysis: Science versus technology. *American Psychologist*, 1978, *33*, 805-814.

DELISSAVOY, V. Headbanging in childhood. *Child Development*, 1962, *33*, 43-56.

DENNEY, M. Reducing self-stimulatory behavior of mentally retarded persons by alternative positive practice. *American Journal of Mental Deficiency*, 1980, *84*, 610-615.

DOKE, L. A., & EPSTEIN, L. A. Oral overcorrection: Side effects and extended applications. *Journal of Experimental Child Psychology*, 1975, *20*, 496-511.

DOLEYS, D. M., & ARNOLD, S. Treatment of childhood encopresis: Full cleanliness training. *Mental Retardation*, 1975, *13*, 14-16.

DOLEYS, D. M., WELLS, K. C., HOBBS, S. A., ROBERTS, M. W., & CARTELLI, L. M. The effects of social punishment on noncompliance: A comparison with time out and overcorrection. *Journal of Applied Behavior Analysis*, 1976, *9*, 471-482.

DUKER, P. C., & SEYS, D. M. Eliminaton of vomiting in a retarded female using restitutional overcorrection. *Behavior Therapy*, 1977, *8*, 255-257.

DUNHAM, P. J. Punishment: Method and theory. *Psychological Review*, 1971, *78*, 58-70.

EDWARDS, M., & LILLY, R. T. Operant conditioning: An application to behavioral problems in groups. *Mental Retardation*, 1966, *4*, 18-20.

ELLIOTT, R., & TIGHE, T. Breaking the cigaret habit: Effects of a technique involving threatened loss of money. *Psychological Record*, 1968, *18*, 503-513.

ELLIS, N. R. Toilet training the severely defective patient: An S-R reinforcement analysis. *American Journal of Mental Deficiency*, 1963, *68*, 98-103.

EPSTEIN, L. H., DOKE, L. A., SAJWAJ, T. E., SORRELL, S., & RIMMER, B. Generality and side effects of overcorrection. *Journal of Applied Behavior Analysis*, 1974, *7*, 385-390.

EYMAN, R. K., TARJAN, G., & CASSIDY, M. Natural history of acquisition of basic skills by hospitalized retarded patients. *American Journal of Mental Deficiency*, 1970, *75*, 120-129.

FOREHAND, R., & BAUMEISTER, A. A. The effect of auditory and visual stimulation of stereotyped body rocking behavior and general activity of severe retardates. *Journal of Clinical Psychology*, 1970, *26*, 426-429.

FOXX, R. M. The use of overcorrection to eliminate the public disrobing (stripping) of retarded women. *Behavior Research and Therapy*, 1976, *14*, 53-61. (a)

FOXX, R. M. Increasing a mildly retarded women's attendance at self-help classes by overcorrection and instruction. *Behavior Therapy*, 1976, *7*, 390-396. (b)

Foxx, R. M. Attention training: The use of overcorrection avoidance to increase the eye contact of autistic and retarded children. *Journal of Applied Behavior Analysis*, 1977, *10*, 489-499.
Foxx, R. M., & Azrin, N. H. Restitution: A method of eliminating aggressive-disruptive behavior of retarded and brain damaged patients. *Behaviour Research and Therapy*, 1972, *10*, 15-27.
Foxx, R. M., & Azrin, N H. The elimination of autistic self-stimulatory behavior by overcorrection. *Journal of Applied Behavior Analysis*, 1973, *6*, 1-14.
Foxx, R. M., & Martin, E. D. Treatment of scavenging behavior (coprophagy and pica) by overcorrection. *Behavior Research and Therapy*, 1975, *13*, 153-162.
Freeman, B. J., & Pribble, W. Elimination of inappropriate toileting behavior by overcorrection. *Psychological Reports*, 1974, *35*, 802.
Freeman, B. J., Graham, V., & Ritvo, E. R. Reduction of self-destructive behavior by overcorrection. *Psychological Reports*, 1975, *37*, 446.
Gardner, W. I. Use of punishment procedures with the severely retarded: A review. *American Journal of Mental Deficiency*, 1969, *6*, 399-406.
Goddard, H. H. The possibilities of research as applied to the prevention of feeblemindedness. *Proceedings National Conference of Charities and Correction*, 1915, 307-312.
Hamilton, J., Stephens, L., & Allen, P. Controlling aggressive and destructive behavior in severely retarded institutionalized residents. *American Journal of Mental Deficiency*, 1967, *71*, 852-856.
Harris, S. L., & Romanczyk, R. G. Treating self-injurious behavior of a retarded child by overcorrection. *Behavior Therapy*, 1976, *7*, 235-239.
Hutt, C., & Hutt, S. Effects of environmental complexity on stereotyped behavior of children. *Animal Behaviour*, 1965, *13*, 1-4.
Kaufman, M. E., & Levitt, H. A. A study of three stereotyped behaviors in institutionalized mental defectives. *American Journal of Mental Deficiency*, 1965, *69*, 467-473.
Kazdin, A. E. Response cost: The removal of conditioned reinforcers for therapeutic change. *Behavior Therapy*, 1972, *3*, 533-546.
Kazdin, A. E. The effect of response cost and aversive stimulation in suppressing punished and nonpunished speech disfluencies. *Behavior Therapy*, 1973, *4*, 73-82.
Kelly, J. A., & Drabman, R. S. Generalizing response suppression of self-injurious behavior through an overcorrection punishment procedure: A case study. *Behavior Therapy*, 1977, *8*, 468-472. (a)
Kelly, J. A., & Drabman, R. S. Overcorrection: An effective procedure that failed. *Journal of Clinical Child Psychology*, 1977, *6*, 38-40. (b)
Klinge, V., Thrasher, P., & Myers, S. Use of bedrest overcorrection in a chronic schizophrenic. *Journal of Behavior Research and Experimental Psychiatry*, 1975, *6*, 69-73.
Koegel, R. L., & Covert, A. The relationship of self-stimulation to learning in autistic children. *Journal of Applied Behavior Analysis*, 1972, *5*, 381-387.
Kravitz, H., Rosenthal, V., Teplitz, Z., Murphy, J. B., & Lesser, R. E. A study of headbanging in infants and children. *Diseases of the Nervous System*, 1960, *21*, 203-248.
Kurtz, R. A. Advocacy for the mentally retarded: The development of a new social role. In M. J. Begab & S. A. Richardson (Eds.), *The mentally retarded and society: A social science perspective*. Baltimore: University Park Press, 1975.
Lambert, J. L., Bruwier, D., & Cobben, A. La reduction d'un compartment stereotype chez un enfant arriere mental profond: Comparison de cinq methods. *Revue Suisse de Psychologie Pure et Appliquee*, 1975, *34*, 1-18.
Leon J. The use of overcorrection to eliminate functional encopresis: A case study. *Research and the Retarded*, 1975, *2*, 1-5.

Lovaas, O. I., Litrownik, A., & Mann, R. Response latencies to auditory stimuli in autistic children engaged in self-stimulatory behavior. *Behaviour Research and Therapy*, 1971, *9*, 39-49.

Luiselli, J. K., Helfen, C. S., Pemberton, B. W., & Reisman, J. The elimination of a child's in-class masturbation by OC and reinforcement. *Journal of Behavior Therapy and Experimental Psychiatry*, 1977, *8*, 201-204.

Luiselli, J. K., Pemberton, B. W., & Helfen, C. S. Effects and side-effects of a brief overcorrection procedure in reducing multiple self-stimulatory behavior: A single case analysis. *Journal of Mental Deficiency Research*, 1978, *22*, 287-293.

Marholin II, D., & Townsend, N. M. An experimental analysis of side effects and response maintenance of a modified overcorrection procedure. *Behavior Therapy*, 1978, *9*, 383-390.

Martin, J., & Matson, J. L. Eliminating the inappropriate vocalizations of a retarded adult by overcorrection. *Scandinavian Journal of Behavior Therapy*, 1978, *7*, 203-209.

Martin, J., Weller, S., & Matson, J. Eliminating object-transferring by a profoundly retarded female by overcorrection. *Psychological Reports*, 1977, *40*, 779-782.

Matson, J. L. Simple correction for treating an autistic boy's encopresis. *Psychological Reports*, 1977, *41*, 802.

Matson, J. L., Stephens, R. M., & Smith, C. Treatment of self-injurious behavior with overcorrection. *Journal of Mental Deficiency Research*, 1978, *22*, 175-178.

Matson, J. L., Ollendick, T. H., & Martin, J. E. Overcorrection revisited: A long-term follow-up. *Journal of Behavior Therapy and Experimental Psychiatry*, 1979, *10*, 11-13.

Measel, C. J., & Alfieri, P. A. Treatment of self-injurious behavior by a combination of reinforcement for incompatible behavior and overcorrection. *American Journal of Mental Deficiency*, 1976, *81*, 147-153.

Murphy, G. H. Overcorrection: A critique. *Journal of Mental Deficiency Research*, 1978, *22*, 161-173.

Nirje, B. The normalization principle and its human management implications. In R. B. Kugel & W. Wolfensberger (Eds.), *Changing patterns in services for the mentally retarded*. Washington, D. C.: President's Committee on Mental Retardation, 1969.

Ollendick, T. H., Matson, J. L., & Martin, J. E. Effectiveness of hand overcorrection for topographically similar and dissimilar self-stimulatory behavior. *Journal of Experimental Child Psychology*, 1978, *25*, 396-403.

Phillips, E. L. Achievement place: Token reinforcement procedures in a homestyle rehabilitation setting for "pre-delinquent" boys. *Journal of Applied Behavior Analysis*, 1968, *1*, 213-223.

Phillips, E. L., Phillips, E. A., Fixsen, D. L., & Wolf, M. M. Achievement place: Modification of the behaviors of pre-delinquent boys within a token economy. *Journal of Applied Behavior Analysis*, 1971, *4*, 45-59.

President's Panel on Mental Retardation. *A proposed program for national action to combat mental retardation*. Washington, D. C.: U. S. Government Printing Office, 1962.

Repp, A. C., Deitz, S. M., & Deitz, D. E. D. Reducing inappropriate behaviors in classrooms and in individual sessions through DRO schedules of reinforcement. *Mental Retardation*, 1976, *14*, 11-15.

Repp, A. C., Deitz, S. M., & Speir, N. C. Reducing stereotypic responding of retarded persons by differential reinforcement of other behaviors. *American Journal of Mental Deficiency*, 1974, *79*, 279-284.

Risley, T. The effects and side effects of punishing the autistic behaviors of a deviant child. *Journal of Applied Behavior Analysis*, 1968, *1*, 21-34.

ROBERTS, P., IWATA, B. A., McSWEEN, T. E., & DESMOND, E. F. An analysis of overcorrection movements. *American Journal of Mental Deficiency,* 1979, *83,* 588-594.

ROLLINGS, J. P., BAUMEISTER, A. A., & BAUMEISTER, A. A. The use of overcorrection procedures to eliminate the stereotyped behaviors of retarded individuals: An analysis of collateral behaviors and generalization of suppressive effects. *Behavior Modification,* 1977, *1,* 29-46.

ROSS, R. T. Behavioral correlates of levels of intelligence. *American Journal of Mental Deficiency,* 1972, *76,* 515-519.

RUSCH, F., CLOSE, D., HOPS, H., AGOSTA, J. Overcorrection: Generalization and maintenance. *Journal of Applied Behavior Analysis,* 1976, *9,* 498.

SAENGER, G. Factors influencing the institutionalization of mentally retarded individuals in New York City. Albany: New York State Interdepartmental Health Resources Board, 1960.

SADLER, O. W., & MERKERT, F. Evaluating the Foxx and Azrin toilet training procedure for retarded children in a day training center. *Behavior Therapy,* 1977, *8,* 499-500.

SALZBERG, B., & NAPOLITAN, J. Holding a retarded boy at a table for 2 minutes to reduce inappropriate object contact. *American Journal of Mental Deficiency,* 1974, *78,* 748-751.

SCHMAUK, F. J. Punishment, arousal, and avoidance learning in sociopaths. *Journal of Abnormal Psychology,* 1970, *76,* 325-335.

SCHROEDER, S. R. *The analysis of self-injurious behavior: Pathogenesis and treatment.* Unpublished study, University of North Carolina and Murdock Center, 1974.

SHAPIRO, E. S. Restitution and positive practice overcorrection in reducing aggressive-disruptive behavior: A long-term follow-up. *Journal of Behavior Therapy and Experimental Psychiatry,* 1979, *10,* 131-134.

SHENTOUB, S., & SOULAIRAC, A. L'Enfant auto-matilateur. Cited in A. A. Green, *Archives of General Psychiatry,* 1967, *17,* 234-244.

SHERMAN, J. A., & BAER, D. M. Appraisal of operant techniques with children and adults. In C. M. Franks (Ed.), *Assessment and status of the behavior therapies and associated developments.* New York: McGraw-Hill, 1969.

SIEGEL, G. M., LENSKI, J., & BROEN, P. Suppression of normal speech disfluencies through response cost. *Journal of Applied Behavior Analysis,* 1969, *2,* 265-276.

SMEETS, P. M. Some characteristics of mental defectives displaying self-mutilative behaviors. *Training School Bulletin,* 1971, *68,* 131-135.

SMITH, P. S., BRITTON, P. G., JOHNSON, M., & THOMAS, D. A. Problems involved in toilet-training profoundly mentally handicapped adults. *Behaviour Research and Therapy,* 1975, *13,* 301-307.

STEEN, P. L., & ZURIFF, G. E. The use of relaxation in the treatment of self-injurious behavior. *Journal of Behavior Therapy and Experimental Psychiatry,* 1977, *8,* 447-448.

STIMBERT, O. E., MINOR, J. W., & McCOY, J. F. Intensive feeding training with retarded children. *Behavior Modification,* 1977, *1,* 517-529.

STOKES, T. F., & BAER, D. M. An implicit technology of generalization. *Journal of Applied Behavior Analysis,* 1977, *10,* 349-367.

WALLACE, J., BURGER, D., NEAL, H. C., VAN BRERO, M., & DAVIS, D. E. Aversive conditioning use in public facilities for the mentally retarded. *Mental Retardation,* 1976, *14,* 17-19.

WEBSTER, D. R., & AZRIN, N. H. Required relaxation: A method of inhibiting agitative-disruptive behaviour of retardates. *Behaviour Research and Therapy,* 1973, *11,* 67-78.

WEINER, H. Some effects of response cost upon human operant behavior. *Journal of the Experimental Analysis of Behavior,* 1962, *5,* 201-208.

WEINER, H. Response cost and the aversive control of human operant behavior. *Journal of the Experimental Analysis of Behavior,* 1963, *6,* 415-421.

WEINER H. Response cost effects during extinction following fixed-interval reinforcement in humans. *Journal of the Experimental Analysis of Behavior,* 1964, 7, 333-335.
WEINER, H. Controlling human fixed-interval performance. *Journal of the Experimental Analysis of Behavior,* 1969, 12, 349-373.
WELLS, K. C., FOREHAND, R., & HICKEY, K. Effects of a verbal warning and overcorrection on stereotyped and appropriate behaviors. *Journal of Abnormal Child Psychology,* 1977, 5, 387-403.
WELLS, K. C., FOREHAND, R., HICKEY, K., & GREEN, K. D. Effects of a procedure derived from the overcorrection principle on manipulated and nonmanipulated behaviors. *Journal of Applied Behavior Analysis,* 1977, 10, 679-687.
WHITE, G. D., NEILSON, G., & JOHNSON, S. M. Time out duration and the suppression of deviant behavior in children. *Journal of Applied Behavior Analysis,* 1972, 5, 111-120.
WHITMAN, T. L., & SCIBAK, J. W. Behavior modification research with the severely and profoundly retarded. In N. R. Ellis (Ed.), *Handbook of mental deficiency, Psychological theory and research* (2nd ed.). Hillsdale, N. J.: Lawrence Erlbaum, 1979.
Wyatt v. Stickney, 344 F. Supp. 373, 387 (M. D. Ala. 1972), Aff'd in part, modified in part sub nom. *Wyatt v. Aderholt,* 503 F 2d 1305 (5th cir. 1974).
ZEHR, M. D., & THEOBALD, D. E. Manual guidance used in a punishment procedure: The active ingredient in overcorrection. *Journal of Mental Deficiency Research,* 1978, 22, 263-272.

9 Training Parents of Developmentally Disabled Children

KARL ALTMAN AND MARY MIRA

INTRODUCTION

There have been several reviews of the literature on training parents to apply behavioral techniques (Baker, 1976; Berkowitz & Graziano, 1972; Forehand & Atkeson, 1977; Gardner, 1976; Johnson & Katz, 1973; McMahon & Forehand, 1980; O'Dell, 1974); however, only Baker (1976) has focused on parents of children with developmental disabilities. These parents deserve special consideration because their children frequently require special training over a long period of time. Although it is not clear whether behavior problems are more prevalent among developmentally disabled children, the skill deficits which define this population suggest the need for trained parents who could offset some of the deficit by providing supplementary home training. Similarly, a developmentally disabled child with behavior problems may require a more highly trained parent because of slower learning rates and a need for a more structured learning situation.

This chapter develops several issues related to the training of parents of developomentally disabled children. The first section presents a rationale for training such parents in behavioral principles and procedures. Next, the types of problem behaviors and skills these parents have handled is described, followed by a description of the roles they have played in the treatment/training of their children. The next sections describe methods by which parents of developmentally disabled children are trained, the content of the parent training programs, and what procedures have been used to assure parent compliance and progress. This is followed by a section dealing with the effectiveness of parent training programs in terms of the generality of trained parent

KARL ALTMAN AND MARY MIRA • Children's Rehabilitation Unit, University of Kansas Medical Center, Kansas City, Kansas 66103. Salary support for this project was provided by grant MCT-000944 from the Office of Maternal and Child Health.

and child behaviors across time, as well as behaviors, settings, people, and cost. The final section presents an exemplary methodology of program development.

Rationale

There exists a substantial rationale for training parents to function as teachers of skills and as therapists for problem behaviors. Those reasons common to all parents will be mentioned first, followed by reasons specific to parents of developmentally disabled children.

General Rationale

Parenthood

Parents can achieve the status of parenthood with little or no training but some parents, especially those with handicapped children, have inadequate repertoires for carrying out that role.

> Perhaps to no other major role in our lives do we bring such a dearth of explicit knowledge. Most of us, like pioneers following a windblown trail, are forced to rely on trial and error, the "common sense" wisdom of our elders and friends, or upon popular magazines. (Kozloff, 1973, p.v)

The recognition that many parents do not have the capability to prevent behavior problems or to train skills prompted Hawkins (1971) to suggest a "Universal Parenthood Training" program which would be part of compulsory education and serve a primary prevention role. Although Hawkin's proposal did not single out parents of developmentally disabled children, it is relevant to them. There is some evidence that the special needs of certain children dictate special parental skills. For example, Fraiberg, Smith, and Adelson (1969) described how parents of some blind infants do not hold or talk to their children until they are shown how. Hayden (1976) also describes the unpreparedness of the handicapped child's parents who recount feeling most useless from not knowing what to do after their child was referred to, but did not as yet enter, a school program. In one of the few published empirical demonstrations Koegel, Glahn, and Nieminen (1978) found that mothers of autistic children were unable to train skills until they were provided with a demonstration.

A typical reaction to the lack of preparedness for parenthood has been an excessive reliance on professionals. This reliance and its support by professionals has been termed *professional preciousness* (Heifetz, 1977b). An alternative view is that parents have the major moral, legal and ethical responsibility for their children which they should not be forced to relinquish during treatment. Rather, the therapist should help them be more effective in carrying out their responsibilities (Graziano, cited in Berkowitz & Graziano, 1972). Special educators have also minimized parents' roles as teachers and the influence of the home on the child's learning (Bricker, Bricker, Iacino, & Dennison, 1976; O'Connell, 1975). A more enlightened view envisions parents and teachers joined in a working partnership and sharing responsibility for training new skills (McConnel & Jeffree, 1975). This view is corroborated by others who note that the professional is transient and should not be the dominant authority in constructing and implementing the child's program (Hobbs, 1975; Warfield, 1975).

Personnel Shortage

Lindsley (cited in Baker, Heifetz, & Brightman, 1972) reported the ratios of professionals to mentally retarded children in this country as one psychiatrist for every 5,000 mentally retarded children; one child psychologist per 2,500 mentally retarded children; and one special education teacher per 500 mentally retarded children. Considering the advantages of parents in terms of a 1 or 2 : 1 ratio, around-the-clock availability and low cost (Barrett, 1969), it is not surprising that there has been an increasing reliance on parents as change agents for their own children (Bernal & North, 1978).

Prevention

There is a preventative value in involving parents in the child's training. Since the child develops within a network of interactions along physical, temporal, and social dimensions, a problem exists not only within the child but within this network (Gardner, 1976). Prevention of significant disorders requires intervention programs which change the pattern of the child's interactions, especially with the parents. Left alone the parents may unwittingly fall into what Wahler (1976) has called "trap" situations which maintain deviant child behavior. Thus, since the parents shape and maintain behavior, problems can be prevented by teaching them to apply basic behavior-modification procedures more systematically (O'Dell, 1974).

Even though some parents are able to manage behavior so as to prevent problems, there is an additional preventive concern to maximize learning and to minimize delay. The learning rates of developmentally disabled children almost double when parents apply behavioral procedures in home programming (Fredricks, Baldwin, & Grove, 1976). Training parents of developmentally disabled children to recognize and reinforce developmental gains may prevent further delay. Wahler (1976) found that without training, parents and siblings of developmentally disabled children often fail to reinforce developmental change.

Proximity

American parents spend large amounts of time with their children (Green, Budd, Johnson, Lang, Pinkston, & Rudd, 1976; Goldstein & Lanyon, 1971) and are viewed as the primary influence in shaping child behavior during the early years (McConkey & Jeffree, 1975). The potency of parents themsleves as reinforcers has been indicated (Atkeson & Forehand, 1979; Green *et al.*, 1976; Redd & Birnbrauer, 1970; Risley, 1968; Shearer & Shearer, 1972; Terdal & Buell, 1969). Parent praise, in some cases, may be more potent than other commonly sought motivators such as ice cream (Risley, 1968).

As primary sources of reinforcement, parents who dispense reinforcement contingently will acquire stimulus control over the child's behavior (Watson & Bassinger, 1974). Such stimulus control over target behaviors is essential for treatment effects to generalize to, and be maintained in, the natural environment. The value of directly training parents to produce general and durable child behavior change has been suggested by several investigators (Bernal & North, 1978; Harris, 1975; Johnson & Katz, 1973; Fredericks *et al.*, 1976; Moore & Bailey, 1973; Risley & Wolf, 1968; Shearer & Shearer, 1972). Since parents can observe the child's behavior in its natural setting over extended periods of time, they, more than professionals, are in an ideal position to assess their child's behavior (Frankel, 1979; Jeffree, McConkey, & Hewson, 1977; McConkey & Jeffree, 1975). Occasionally, parents's firsthand knowledge of the child's behavioral and medical history (Barrett, 1969) has even allowed professionals to suggest interventions without ever having seen the child (Galloway & Galloway, 1971; Lindsley, 1966; Mira, 1970).

Rationale Specific to Parents of Developmentally Disabled Children

Disability-Imposed Requirements

There are several problems in training developmentally disabled children which require programming the child's environment more carefully for maximal development to occur. One problem arises because generally useful reinforcing stimuli are not effective with some developmentally disabled children, for example, severely handicapped deaf/blind children (Mira & Hoffman, 1974) and autistic children (Lovaas, Koegel, Simmons, & Long, 1973).

A second training problem derives from the need for special procedures to promote maintenance outside the clinical training setting. Lovaas *et al.* (1973) found that treatment effects were maintained only with children whose parents could duplicate the training environment in the home. Watson and Bassinger (1974) also report that if the controlling stimuli in the social environment do not resemble those in the training environment, the developmentally disabled child will not maintain, and may even lose, acquired skills.

Another disability-related problem arises because the circumscribed social lives of developmentally disabled children result in reduced opportunity for incidental and peer-mediated learning. This restrictive situation emphasizes the need to program more dimensions of the child's environment, including the home.

A fourth disability-related reason for training parents is that the persistent nature of most disabilities requires long-term training of new skills if the children are to function with maximal independence (Ambrose & Baker, 1979; Heifetz, 1977b). The use of parents as trainers could provide a sizeable block of training time.

Parental Stresses and Need for Information

Parents with developmentally disabled children have concerns about the social acceptability of their children. Problematic behavior may be viewed differently by the parent (or by others) when displayed by an obviously developmentally disabled child. The provision of information about specific skills for dealing with problem behavior has an "anxiety-reducing" effect (Heifetz, 1977a; Tavormina, 1975). Heifetz's (1977a) results also suggest that parent training increases parents' feelings of confidence in their ability to evaluate services offered to their children.

A related issue is the difficulty that parents of developmentally disabled children experience in gaining information about developmental outcomes. Traditional evaluative diagnostic procedures are of limited use in projecting future performances. However, parents who are involved in child training programs which generate data about the child's behavioral improvement have some basis for formulating their expectations (Salzinger, Feldman, & Portnoy, 1970).

Parents of developmentally disabled children have special informational needs about the child's disability and training requirements which are related to the roles parents are being asked to play in their child's training. Also, these parents are being given a greater advocacy role than parents with non-developmentally disabled children via participation on consent boards and in Individualized Educational Plan (IEP) conferences. This increasing responsbility requires that they have extensive information about developmental disabilities and their children's skills (Hobbs, 1975).

Parent–Child Interactions

One of the major factors determining developmental competence is the interaction between parent and child, particularly the contingent responsiveness of the parent (Beckwith, 1976). Since it has been shown that the patterns of interactions between parent and handicapped child differ from those of parent and nonhandicapped child, that is, in ways less encouraging to development (Kogan & Tyler, 1973; Kogan, Wimberger, & Bobbitt, 1969; Marshall, Hegrenes, & Goldstein, 1973; Terdal, Jackson, & Garner, 1976), it is important that professionals be attentive to this interaction and help change it when indicated.

Summary

Among the reasons for training parents to teach new skills or to deal with problem behaviors are their availability, their potency as sources of reinforcement, and their ability to prevent additional deficits and problems. Other reasons that are unique to parents of developmentally disabled children relate to the fact that the children's training needs are long-term and often require that more dimensions of the environment be programmed.

The next section elaborates the target behaviors parents of developmentally disabled children share with other parents as well as those that are unique to them.

PROBLEM BEHAVIORS AND SKILLS TRAINED BY PARENTS AND TECHNIQUES FOR SELECTION

Diagnostic or Behavioral Characteristics of the Population Served

Parents of many types of disabled children have been trained. Some programs include parents of children with a variety of disabilities in the same training group (Ambrose & Baker, 1979; Mira, 1970; O'Dell, Flynn, & Benlolo, 1977;

Walder, Cohen, Brieter, Datson, Hirsch, & Leibowitz, 1969). Often studies indicate that subjects had received several diagnostic labels from the list which included mentally retarded, emotionally disturbed, autistic, and brain injured (Lovaas et al., 1973; Nordquist & Wahler, 1973; Salzinger et al., 1970). Since diagnostic labels may be used differently by different agencies and may not convey clear information about the child's behavior, the present authors and others have made a plea for sufficiently detailed descriptions of subjects' behavior to allow comparions across studies and replication of procedures (Patterson, McNeal, Hawkins, & Phelps, 1967).

Another characteristic of many of the developmentally disabled children described in the studies is that they display multiple behavioral problems, combining difficulties relating to their activity level, social interactions, compliance, verbal behavior, and abusiveness (Christophersen & Sykes, 1979; Hawkins, Peterson, Schweid, & Bijou, 1966; Johnson, Whitman, & Barloon-Noble, 1978; Patterson et al., 1967; Salzinger et al., 1970). An issue that relates to this characteristic is that of selecting the order in which to manage problem behaviors. (See the guidelines that are described on pp. 310-312.)

Common Target Behaviors

Parents of developmentally disabled children have dealt with a range of problem behaviors, many of which are similar to behaviors reported for children without disabilities: noncompliance (Budd, Green, & Baer, 1976; Forehand, Chaney, & Yoder, 1974), tantrums (Mira, 1972; Salzinger et al., 1970; Terdal & Buell, 1969), problems of attention, play or social interaction (Mash & Terdal, 1973; Patterson et al., 1967), sleep disturbances (Salzinger et al., 1970), high activity rates (Frazier & Schneider, 1975) and destructive or aggressive acts (Christophersen & Sykes, 1979; Krupsaw & Altman, 1980).

Parents of developmentally disabled children have also worked on behaviors not generally reported among children without disabilities: shaping eye contact (Benassi & Benassi, 1973; Watson & Bassinger, 1974), self-injurious behavior (Altman, Haavik, & Cook, 1978; Barnard, Christophersen, & Wolf, 1976; Harris & Romanczyk, 1976; Merbaum, 1973), self-stimulation and stereotypic behaviors (Christophersen & Sykes, 1979; Cook, Altman, Shaw, & Blaylock, 1978; Herbert & Baer, 1972; Johnson et al., 1978), response to rehabilitative procedures and use of prostheses (Hoover, 1970; Mira, 1972; Wolf, Risley, & Mees, 1964), and a somewhat new area—the treatment of somatic disorders (Gentry, 1976; Haavik, Altman, & Woelk, 1979).

In addition to managing problem behaviors, parents of developmentally disabled children have trained a variety of behaviors in many skill areas. These areas include: preacademic skills (Holmberg, 1977; Hunt & Sulzer-Azaroff, 1974; Seitz & Marcus, 1976), motor skills (Mathis, 1971; Watson & Bassinger, 1974), self-help skills such as toileting (Barrett, 1969; Haus & Thompson, 1976), feeding (Inglis, 1977; Longin, Cone, & Longin, 1975; Miller, Patton, & Henton, 1971), weight measurement (Altman, Bondy, & Hirsch, 1978; Rotatori, Fox, & Switzky, 1979), and social skills (Moore & Bailey, 1973). Despite the caution that speech is harder to work with than behavior problems (Kozloff, 1973), parents have conducted a number of successful language training programs. Schumaker and Sherman (1978) present an excellent review of parents as intervention agents for language training which lists empirically derived suggestions for parents.

Sequencing Parent-Training Targets

For developmentally disabled children there is no empirically based rationale for determining the order in which to work on problem behaviors. For skill building, the existing information on the sequence of emerging behavioral skills has led to programs based on these developmental sequences.

For behavior problems, there are few guidelines for selecting the order of treatment although some practices are evident in the literature. Several programs have trained parents to manage problem behaviors before teaching skills to their children. An inclusive training package developed by Watson and Bassinger (1974) starts by training parents to eliminate undesirable behaviors and to shape compliance before going on to train self-help, language, social, motor, and academic skills. Hoover (1970) and Mira (1972) found that some parents of deaf children needed to deal with such problem behaviors as gaze-aversion before working on lip-reading skills.

It is generally recommended that self-stimulating, stereotypic, and self-injurious behaviors be given priority over other behavior problems or skills when treating children, not only because of their potential danger to the child, but because they interfere with acquisition of other behaviors (Lovaas *et al.,* 1973; Lovaas & Newsom, 1976).

Several authors advocate teaching parents to gain compliance before dealing with either specific problem behaviors or skill deficits (Forehand *et al.,* 1974; Mash, Lazere, Terdal, & Garner, 1973; Watson & Bassinger, 1974). This approach is generally used with parents of very young children (Mira & Cairns, 1978; Peed, Roberts, & Forehand, 1977; Terdal & Buell, 1969). It was also used by Patterson et al., (1967) who trained a set of parents to increase their use of positive social reinforcement and to initiate more social interaction before training other behaviors.

There is also the consideration that parents who are learning child-management skills would best be served by starting with a likely success (Gardner, 1976). Lindsley (1966) began his parent-training groups by teaching a simple procedure to decelerate a common problem encountered in the home. Parents placed all items left lying around during the day into a box which they could retrieve only on the following Sunday. This "Sunday Box" procedure started parents on a program in which they would eventually deal with complex problems of their developmentally disabled children by giving them an effective management technique that had a high probability of rapid success.

Some trainers have chosen not to teach parents to deal with one problem behavior at a time but rather to group a child's problem behaviors into one class labeled *inappropriate behavior*, and to label other behaviors approriate behavior, and respond to each instance of a behavior in the class in an identical way. Frazier and Schneider (1975) taught a set of parents to respond positively to their hyperactive child when he engaged in appropriate mealtime behaviors and to respond to any one of more than 10 specific misbehaviors by placing the child in a time-out chair. Hawkins et al. (1966) grouped a large number of a boy's undesirable behaviors of varying topographies into one class termed *objectionable behavior*. The mother was taught to respond to each instance of any behavior in that class in the identical way. Experimental support showing the validity of this practice for certain behaviors is provided by Wahler (1975) who found that stable clusters of behavior were a predictable covariant with other behaviors in that response class.

Surveying parent opinion is another way which has been suggested for describing the order of target behaviors. A recent survey (Sparling, Lowman, Lewis, & Bartel, 1978) produced the following hierarchy of parent-training curricula, ranked from most to least important: (1) promoting health; (2) identifying community resources; (3) family coping; (4) promoting learning and development; (5) social-emotional development; (6) continuing child development; and (7) nontraditional parenthood. Their findings indicate that promoting learning and development become important only after the health of the child and the functioning of the family are assured, and after community resources have been contacted. Lance and Koch (1973) surveyed parents from local and state day and residential schools as to what specific behaviors should be programmed. Toileting was the most important self-help skill, followed by eating and dressing, respectively. Taking parent priorities into account may produce greater parent attendance and cooperation at training sessions as well as facilitate acquisition and maintenance of programming.

Summary

The findings discussed in this section indicate that there is a great variability in diagnostic labels applied to children of parents participating in training programs. To make across-study comparisons more reliable, it is important that each study provide a detailed description of child behavior. Parents of developmentally disabled children have remedied a wide range of problem behaviors and trained a variety of skills, including many that traditionally were the province of specialists. There is no single rationale for ordering target problem behaviors, although knowledge about skill sequences gives some guidelines for selecting the order in which to train new skills. A variety of tactics have been suggested in the literature for sequencing targets, such as dealing with problem behavior before skill building, building compliance first, starting with a guaranteed success, or surveying parents first. As target behaviors become more complex, we would expect that parents' roles and responsibilities in training their children would likewise change. In the next section we survey the roles parents are playing.

How Trained Parents Have Functioned

Before the development of behavior-management procedures to modify children's problem or deficit behaviors, parents of developmentally disabled children were viewed by professionals as either subjects for study or as patients in need of treatment, perhaps to the child's disadvantage (Baker, 1976). Baker reports that parents who had previously been taught to take a passive role in their child's training, functioning as patients in a parents' group or merely as observers, were poorer teachers of their children than parents without previous experiences of passivity (Baker, 1976). The roles that parents of mentally retarded children are filling now are varied and require a range of child-training skills. Gardner (1976) describes four levels of parent functioning based on skills trained:

1. *Applicator.* The parent supplies rewards under very limited and specified conditons and is required to make only minimal decisions about programming.

2. *Technician.* The parent applies behavior modification techniques under very limited conditions and is required to make only minimal decisions about programming.
3. *Generalist.* The parent applies principles and techniques of behavior modification to a wide variety of problems. This skill is the most appropriate one for parents, and is generally the target level in most programs.
4. *Consultant.* The person trained at this level teaches others the principles and procedures of behavior modification. Parents seldom function as consultants and, with a few exceptions, programs to train them at this level do not exist.

The roles that trained parents have played are described below, giving consideration to Gardner's (1976) skill levels.

Supplement Training Occurring in School or Clinic

The rationale for supplemental home training is to increase the opportunities for the child to experience new stimuli or contingencies. It is a role particularly suited to skill building activities. In general, supplementary training is not a role of parents dealing with problem behaviors. Benassi and Benassi (1973) advocate involving persons in the client's natural environment to enhance the benefits of clinic–rehabilitation therapy. Longin, Longin, and Cone (1975) using a multiple baseline across subjects design demonstrated that parents' home sessions which supplemented school speech sesssions produced "accelerated expressive language skills with growth continuing past the completion of the training program" (p. 2). Hunt and Sulzer-Azaroff (1974) also documented the effectiveness of parents who provide supplementary training. For some skills, such as toileting, it is practically impossible to gain complete control by training solely at school (Fredricks *et al.*, 1976).

Conduct Generalization Probes

A few studies have had parents witness training of their child in the clinic by professionals, and who then tried to elicit the same behavior themselves, in the clinic or in the home. An example of this is the study of Altman, Haavik, and Cook (1978) in which self injurious behavior was treated in a clinic by aversive procedures. In their study, a multiple baseline across settings was used. Once an effective treatment procedure was demonstrated in the clinic, the parent measured the behavior at home to determine if generalization was occuring. Failure to find generalization revealed the need to implement the treatment package in the home setting as well.

In a study by Handleman (1979) parents conducted home probes of verbal responses trained at school. For some children, training in varied school locations by the therapist was necessary before generalization to the home was observed. Use of home probes is a sophisticated procedure which could be used to determine if school training has reached a more functional level, and therefore, if it will transfer. Thus, home probes may provide a more sensitive measure of skill acquisition than periodic report cards. The involvement of the parents may be minimal, but essential. If the parent only records the behavior in the home, the skill level required of the parent would not be very advanced. Although the trend has not as yet been reported in the literature, it is conceivable that parents, functioning as generalists, could conduct probes in the home and, on the basis of data obtained, could implement appropriate training procedures independently.

Maintaining Behaviors Taught Elsewhere

Training parents to maintain behavior taught elsewhere is vital for developmentally disabled children. The children's failure to generalize newly acquired behaviors to new environments is a central feature of their learning disability (Campione & Brown, 1977), unless the program specifically trains for it (Borkowski & Cavanaugh, 1979). The evidence is clear that, without the trained parent using the same procedures in the home, treatment effects frequently do not generalize from the clinic to other settings or from the therapist to other persons. A classic example of this is in the treatment of autistic children. Lovaas and colleagues (Lovaas & Newsom, 1976), demonstrated that, with their population, the only children who maintained gains in play, social skills, and communication were those whose parents applied the same procedures in the home as the professionals did in the hospital.

The necessity of training parents to carry out similar treatment procedures in the home to those applied in the clinic has been demonstrated for the treatment of self-injurious behaviors by aversive procedures (Altman, Haavik, & Cook, 1978; Harris & Romanczyk, 1976; Merbaum, 1973) and for the treatment of public masturbation by aversive procedures (Cook, Altman, Shaw, & Blaylock, 1978). In none of these studies was home treatment delayed sufficiently to determine if generalization would eventually occur, because, when target behaviors are self-injurious there is questionable ethical justification for delaying the home treatment. Although the target behaviors were highly dangerous to the child, the parents' skill level included only the application of a specific procedure following the occurrence of a specified behavior. In terms of Gardner's level of skill classification, the parents functioned as technicians or applicators, since they were not required to make independent decisions. The training parents received was also restricted to the use of a single procedure.

The importance of parents in assuring maintenance of trained behaviors has also been shown for building such skills as independent standing and self-feeding (Miller et al., 1971) and toilet training (Mahoney, Van Wagener, & Meyerson, 1971). Although specific data are not provided, Kysela, Daly, Doxsey-Whitfield, Hillyard, McDonald, McDonald, and Taylor (1979) describe a well-sequenced parent-training program in which parents begin their training by learning to maintain behaviors already trained at school.

Managing Problem Behaviors Not Treated Elsewhere

In many parent-training programs the professional works primarily with the parents who then assume major responsibility for working with the child in the home. To assume this role as primary therapist, Gardner (1976) states that parents should be trained as generalists who would be able to go beyond the specific problem on which they were trained and to generalize procedures to new problems and environments.

A common model of parent training is exemplified by those programs which have as their goal the training of parents at the generalist level, and the teaching in the clinic of those principles of learning- and behavior-management procedures that are necessary to implement programs independently in the home (O'Dell et al., 1977; Salzinger et al., 1970; Tavormina, 1975; Terdal & Buell, 1969; Walder et al., 1969). Although some programs taught parents principles of learning, one study found that theoretical lectures on learning principles did not assist parents as much as the procedure-oriented workshop sessions (O'Dell et al., 1977).

Occasionally professionals have gone into the home to train parents in the skills to deal with problem behaviors which occur there. In some of the home programs the parents have been taught to function as generalists by applying treatment procedures beyond the target behavior (Christophersen & Sykes, 1979), while in other programs the parents functioned only as behavioral technicians (Frazier & Schneider, 1975; Johnson et al., 1978) by applying procedures designed by the professional.

Using parents as principle therapist has not been restricted to problems of only moderate severity but has been applied to the treatment of children engaging in self-injury (Barnard *et al.*, 1976).

Another example of programs which are designed to train parents to be the primary manager of the child's problem behavior are those which train parents, generally with the child present, to alter their interaction with the child in the home soas to elicit greater compliance. Although behavior changes may occur in both parent and child at the clinic during training sessions, the major treatment occurs in the home with clinic visits used primarily to train the parent (Forehand *et al.*, 1974).

Another model of parents who function as primary therapists is the use of home-based reinforcement for problems occurring in the classroom. There are several advantages in this procedure, including parental access to more of the child's reinforcers, bypassing the ethical issues involved in the application of control procedures in the school, and freeing the teacher to spend more time on skill building. Giving the parent the responsibility for part of the child's educational plan also may increase cooperation between school and home. Despite the fact that this tactic for treating school behavior problems is generally effective (Atkeson & Forehand, 1979), it has been used primarily with non-developmentally delayed children.

Thus, it appears that many researchers have recognized that parents can carry out programs at home, but to do so requires them to have a range of skills to enable them to function independently.

Train New Skills

There is justification for preparing parents of developmentally disabled children to be able to continue new programs with their children after completion of a training program. Since these parents are not dealing with a few isolated behavior problems, they are better served by more comprehensive training at a level which will prepare them to function independently (Heifetz, 1977a).

Some programs have sought to give parents a comprehensive behavioral repertoire to enable them to train new skills at home (e.g., Baker *et al.*, 1972; Ramey, Collier, Sparling, Loda, Campbell, Ingram, & Finkelstein, 1976; Revill & Blunden, 1979; Shearer & Shearer, 1976). Baker (1977) and colleagues used a series of manuals covering such areas as self-help, language, behavior problems, and play activities to train parents of mentally retarded children.

> Each manual is designed to be self-contained and includes sections on choosing a target skill, setting the stage for teaching sessions, behavioral principles, data-keeping procedures, and answers to questions frequently raised by parents. (Heifetz, 1977a, p. 196)

A number of these comprehensive training programs advocate a sit-down-and-train approach (e.g., Shearer & Shearer, 1976; Watson & Bassinger, 1974), while others reflect the shift to an interactional training model noted by Berkowitz and Graziano (1972). An example of the interactional approach is the Parent Involvement Project described by McConkey and Jeffree (1975). Although there are specific objectives and a number of activities to facilitate learning, all teaching situations

> are designed to fit easily into an on-going parent-child relationship at home and are based upon toys or pieces of apparatus that are easily available to parents Throughout training the emphasis is on learning through play and parents are discouraged from creating an "artificial" teaching situation. (McConkey & Jeffree, 1975, p. 14).

Eventually the parents learn to plan their own teaching situations and to formulate their own objectives. The parent-child interaction has been utilized to train language (Seitz & Marcus, 1976; Seitz & Riedell, 1974; Whitehurst, Novak, & Zorn, 1972). The more nautural and less formal training approach has merit in that it requires less training time, uses natural consequences, and does not require special sessions or generalization to the primary setting.

Despite the recognition that parents of developmentally disabled children should be trained to develop and conduct management programs for problem behaviors on their own after completion of training, there are no programs described that specifically prepare parents for a level of competence. Most studies focus on parent performance and child behavior change *during* the treatment program rather than emphasizing what happened to parent and child behaviors *after* the initial training target is achieved.

Preventing Developmental Deficits and Behavior Problems

One anticipated impact of a cadre of trained parents would be the prevention of future disorders. Berkowitz and Graziano (1972) state that by providing nonprofessionals, including parents, with skills to deal with future problems, "behavior therapy has moved one focus of treatment several steps closer to a *prevention* model of mental health service" (p. 299). Gelfand and Hartmann

(1977) state, "If effective parenting skills can be widely taught . . . and if the skills can be actually applied in child rearing, many child behavior disorders could be prevented" (p. 372).

Most preventive efforts have been directed at children who are at risk for the future expression of developmental delays. These programs have attempted to give parents the child-rearing skills that would encourage normal development. The controversial "Milwaukee Project" carried out by Heber and Garber (1975) represents one attempt to demonstrate that mental retardation can be prevented in high-risk populations. Many simultaneous manipulations were performed besides attempts to train parents at home. Consequently, it is difficult to determine which program components were responsible for the child-skill gains. A number of other methodological shortcomings have been discussed (Page, 1972). However, the magnitude of the programs' effect warrants investigation of such salient components as the school program and the use of the parent–child interaction to train skills.

Some early intervention programs focus on altering the interactions of parents with their children in a way that encourages the child's development. Ramey, responding to evidence that mental retardation is associated with specific parenting behavior and also evidence that children's development can be enhanced by environmental manipulations, designed a program, Project CARE, which used family educators to train mothers in the home to modify their responsiveness to their infants (Ramey & Gowen, 1979). Their preliminary data indicate that mothers' behavior could be altered toward interactive patterns that are associated with normal development.

Mira and Cairns also trained mothers of high-risk children to alter their interactions with the children (Cairns & Mira, 1979; Mira, 1978; Mira & Cairns, 1978). Using a program of demonstration, behavioral rehearsal, and feedback based on a parent-training program developed by Hanf and Kling (1973) and modified by Forehand and colleagues (Forehand & Peed, 1979; Peed et al., 1977), they taught mothers to increase contingent positive responses to play and vocal behavior in clinical play situations. They then trained the parents in the home to respond similarly during caretaking activities. The short-term effect of the program has been demonstrated on physical and developmental changes in a failure-to-thrive child (Mira & Cairns, 1981). The long-term effects of intervention in parent–interaction on children's behavioral development have yet to be documented.

Another effect was carried out by Mash and Terdal (1973) who trained parents to encourage the development and maintenance of nondeviant classes of behaviors. They trained mothers of developmentally delayed children with no behavior problems to play effectively with their children in order to give the child experience initiating social interactions and influencing responsiveness of the environment. Children learned to respond more appropriately to their mothers' behaviors in the play situation.

Training Other Parents and Children

Parents Train Other Parents

Gardner (1976) pointed out the value of parents teaching other parents. First, they provide a model of something that *parents can do* and also provide dramatic documentation that change is possible. Secondly, parents can *identify* more easily with other parents than with professionals, and are less likely to reject the fact that they control behavior when the information is presented by "someone who has been there." In addition to corroborating the above, Hall, Grinstead, Collier, and Hall (1978) noted that personal testimonials by parents generated enthusiasm and encouraged open discussion and participation in training groups.

Perhaps the best example of a program in which parents train other parents to work with their own developmentally disabled children is the *Early Intervention Project* (Frangia & Reisinger, 1979). The mainstay of the early intervention project is time repayment for individual services received. Parents learn to manage their child's behavior by differentially reinforcing appropriate interactions and, if necessary, using contingent time-out. A concurrent hierarchical preschool program in which some parents serve as aides provides skill training. Frangia and Reisinger (1979) provided impressive data indicating that the cost of their program is rather low. Hayden (1976) also described a program in which parents encouraged other parents to work with their own children although no information regarding the specific nature of the training program nor its effectiveness is provided in the study. If it can be demonstrated that such programs are effective and inexpensive, then "parents training other parents" would seem a worthwhile direction for future training programs.

Parents Training Other Children

Although professionals commonly train parents to train their own children, in some instances it may be advantageous for parents to first learn to apply a procedure with another child. This is suggested by the work of Risley (1968) who found that for some parents who are resistant to changing their interaction style a "cross-fostering" approach may be a helpful intermediate training strategy. When parents trained their own children, their skill in praising appropriate behavior increased rapidly, but not to a level sufficient for training, and their tendency to nag and threaten persisted. When mothers trained a different child first, they praised that child more liberally and almost never nagged and threatened. The simultaneous manipulation of several variables such as unfamiliar training material and amount of praise cautions that more research is needed to determine the specific circumstances under which cross-fostering can be recommended.

Advocates, Advisors, and Decision Makers

There are new areas in which parents are being asked to function in informed ways. First, they are assigned major consent roles in the planning of educational programs along new guidelines for education of the handicapped (Public Law 94-142). Carrying out this role requires parents to have information about how their children learn and how to assess effects of different teaching efforts, and secondly, ethical considerations in the use of aversive treatment have led to the development of ethics committees which include parents (Cook, Altman, & Haavik, 1978). For parents to function effectively on such committees or even to give informed consent to use aversive treatment with their own children requires a knowledge of how to select target behaviors, limits and benefits of alternative-treatment procedures, an understanding of behavioral records, side effects, and an ability to weigh beneficial side effects and time constraints.

Hobbs (1975) described a number of other roles parents should play in making decisions about their developmentally disabled children. He suggests that parents be given the primary responsibility for acquiring the skills to assume the major decision-making role for their children, and he offers suggestions on how to go about getting needed information. Despite parents' emerging roles as advocates and decision makers, there are few programs which are training them to function this way.

The only program formally training parents to assume advisor-functions is the Regional Intervention Project (Ora & Reisinger, 1971). The program trains parents of young behavioral and developmentally delayed children to function in all phases of the treatment program. The few professionals are resource consultants to a service delivery system completely implemented by parents and volunteers; parents operate all advisory and evaluation boards, and the program is accountable to the trained-parent consumers.

Hayden (1976) appears to train parents informally as advocates and advisors. Parents of children in the Experimental Educational Unit School have served in a variety of roles. They are used to reassure new enrollees and counsel new parents about available resources. They assist in getting support for "Education for All" legislation, help establish new programs in the community, and extend special services of the public schools. They have helped to change legislation requiring insurance companies to provide coverage for children with birth defects.

Summary

Parents of developmentally disabled children are assuming more active, varied, and complex roles in the training of their children. They provide supplemental training, program home environments to assure that new skills be maintained, and, very commonly, manage behavior problems that are not being treated elsewhere. Parents are being trained with the hope of being able to teach new skills to their children and to prevent new problem behaviors from developing. In a few programs, parents conduct generalization probes and teach other children or parents. There is a growing emphasis on parents functioning as decision makers and educated advocates for their children. There is an emphasis on giving parents the skills to design, carry out, and evaluate child training programs, instead of serving merely as applicators of a program designed and monitored by a professional. In the next section we will discuss some of the techniques with which parents learn the skills to teach and manage their developmentally disabled children.

METHODS OF TEACHING

There are two general approaches being used to train parents of developmentally disabled children. With the first, parents receive instruction in principles and procedures of child management and training via lectures, media presentations, and possibly, demonstration. Parents then apply what they have learned in the home and return to the clinic to discuss the results and receive feedback from professionals and occasionally peers in groups. Generally, parents do not demonstrate to the professional what they are learning; effects of training are determined by reported or observed changes in the child's behavior.

In the second approach, parents are taught directly and are required to demonstrate the procedures either with their child or by role playing in simulated situations. Desired changes in parent (and child) behavior occur initially in the training sessions with the professional. In this direct approach, emphasis is placed on the techniques of modeling and supervised behavioral rehearsal. In actual practice, many training programs use combinations of specific teaching techniques from both approaches. Rather than weigh the relative merits of a primarily direct versus a primarily indirect parent-training methodology, we will discuss the features of some of these specific teaching techniques which have been used either as primary or supplemental tools with parents of developmentally disabled children.

Media

Manuals

Training programs for parents of developmentally disabled children have made extensive use of manuals, primarily in combination with other methods. Often these are manuals designed for general child management such as *Living With Children* (Patterson & Guillion, 1968), which may be used intact or may serve as a guide from which sample teaching plans are prepared (Thompson & Young, 1977). Tavormina (1975) used *Parents Are Teachers* (Becker, 1971) as the weekly lesson plan for the parents in his behaviorally oriented group. O'Dell *et al.* (1977) used material from three parent-training manuals (Becker, 1971; Hall, 1971; Patterson & Guillon, 1968) to prepare material including a programmed text for the pretraining in the behavior principle phase. Benassi and Benassi (1973) used sections of two parent-training manuals (Valett, 1969; Williams & Jaffa, 1971) but cautioned that because of differing parental education levels, trainers must present new material to parents initially at a very elementary level and then continuously test their comprehension as the concepts are developed at more complex levels.

Some training programs developed their own manuals (Salzinger *et al.*, 1970). Kozloff organized weekly meetings of parents of autistic children around chapters of *Educating Children with Learning and Behavior Problems* (Kozloff, 1974). The book covers topics on designing programs and sequences in seven skill areas. Also included is a behavior scale parents can use to evaluate their children before and after training (Kozloff, 1979). The book alone was found to be less effective than a more comprehensive multimethod program for parents of autistic children, although parents receiving training solely by means of the book improved their teaching (Kaufman, Villani, Bakalor, Price, Prinz, Paradise, & Tyson, 1977).

Watson developed a programmed text for parents to use in the academic training component of his program (Watson & Bassinger, 1974). Using popular language it presented concepts of reinforcement, shaping, stimulus control, application of the concepts and data collection, and included self-administered tests to check comprehension. After completion of the academic training phase, parents received another programmed text in the practicum phase. The second text contained programs for skill building and the elimination of undesired behavior (Watson, 1972).

There has been considerable evaluation of the contribution of manuals and other written instructional material to parent training; however, only one study focusing on parents of developmentally disabled children was found, namely, Heifetz (1977a). This researcher compared the effectiveness of the READ Project manuals used alone and in combination with parent-training programs encompassing differing levels of professional assistance — including telephone consultation, training groups, and training groups plus home visits. Manuals used included those addressing self-help skills, behavior problems, toileting, and language. "The manuals-alone format was as effective as the more expensive training formats in producing gains in children's self-help skills and fostering knowledge of behavioral principles in mothers" (Heifetz, 1977a, p. 194). When compared with the no-treatment control condition, only the manuals-alone condition showed significantly greater improvement on untargeted self-help skills. Considering the cost of professional consultations, Heifetz's (1977a) findings tempt us to advise use of the economical manuals. However, the average educational level of the mothers in this study was 13.4 years, and of fathers, 14.3 years. The results may not have been the same had the study been done with parents of lesser education.

McMahon and Forehand (1980) present an extensive review of parent training manuals as self-contained teaching methods. They conclude that design limitations, variations in targets and populations, among other things, preclude general statements about the value of manuals as being completely self-contained treatments. However, there is evidence for the success of manuals used in combination with minimal amounts of assistance by therapists. And, a few studies indicate that for specific problems or populations the manuals are effective alone. Bernal and North (1978) surveyed parent-training manuals and presented a detailed description of the characteristics of each. They concluded that the more useful manuals for parents were those that dealt with circumscribed problems. As the target problems increased in complexity or involved more settings, parents required more help from professionals.

Before judging whether a given manual should be recommended for parent training, we need to specify more carefully the prerequisite parent skills for successful use. For example, the parent must at least be able to follow written instructions such as those in the manual. Manuals could be prepared which would rely on complex or simple written instructions, pictorial illustrations, or sample situations. It is conceivable that some parents may learn more easily from one mode/level of presentation, for example, simple sentences with pictorial representations. Parents might then be grouped according to entry skills and outcome studies could be conducted to determine which manuals would be more effective with parents who have certain prerequisite skills.

Manuals as teaching aids are attractive from an intervention standpoint because they are inexpensive and readily available. From a research standpoint, they offer a standardized treatment condition allowing comparison and revision as well as specification of prerequisite skills and target behaviors.

Curriculum Guides

There are no curriculum guides designed specifically to remedy problem behaviors that are directed to those who work with parents of developmentally disabled children. One of the most thoroughly researched methods of parent training has been refined by Forehand and associates (Forehand & King 1977; Peed *et al.*, 1977) from a program described in an unpublished manuscript (Hanf & Kling, 1973). Recently they have published a detailed description of the training program (Forehand & Peed, 1979).

Mira and Cairns (1979) have adapted the above procedures for training parents of high-risk infants and children to interact with their children in a way that encourages development. They have prepared a curriculum guide designed to supplement a workshop to train front-line professionals to teach parents. The guide describes assessment procedures and the training sequence, and includes a series of scripts for role playing various parent-child interactions which provide practice in recording parent and child behaviors.

Curriculum guides have been developed specifically to train skill building in parents of high-risk, mentally retarded children (Baker *et al.*, 1972; Shearer & Shearer, 1976), and autistic children (Kozloff, 1973). Although both the Shearer & Shearer (1976) and Kozloff (1973) guides have been shown to be effective, only the READ manuals (Baker *et al.*, 1972) have proven effective when used alone.

Films

Several training programs use films as a method of teaching parents to deal with problem behaviors (O'Dell *et al.*, 1977; Walder *et al.*, 1969). Kozloff (1979) uses videotapes showing previously trained parents working with their children as "hard evidence" of the effectiveness of the program. If appropriate tapes are lacking, he uses commercially produced films on the management of children in general.

Watson and Bassinger (1974) used films to supplement practicum training of parents. The film presented techniques for teaching the same skills which were covered by a programmed text. For three parents, however, seeing a film of someone else training a child was not as effective for the development of skills as was watching parents demonstrate and receive feedback (Watson & Bassinger, 1974).

Demonstration and Practice

Role Playing

Several training programs for parents of developmentally disabled children include role playing as part of the curriculum. Parents act out the skills they are learning with the therapist or with other parents, with parents reversing from child to parent roles. Gardner (1976) suggests that a positive aspect of role playing is that parents can practice a skill to gain proficiency in a nonthreatening situation. He cautions that it may result in only minimal generalization to the natural environment because of different stimulus conditions. He recommends that after role playing the parent be given a chance to practice the skills while receiving immediate feedback via an electronic bug-in-the-ear technique. Another advantage of role playing is the enhanced learning provided by the active involvement of the training group members through role playing (Benassi & Benassi, 1973). Walder *et al.* (1969) not only gave parents a chance to practice shaping a behavior of another parent, but also had them shape the behavior of animals in a lab to study the effects of intermittent reinforcement on extinction.

The contribution of role playing to the total parent-training package has not been assessed. The comparative effectiveness of role playing was evaluated by Flanagan, Adams, and Forehand (1979) who found that it was a better instructional technique than videotaped modeling, written instruction or lecture-presented instruction on the use of time-out in a simulated child-problem situation.

Modeling

Modeling is a common component of training parents to deal with behavior problems. The therapist may model a procedure with the parents (Forehand *et al.*, 1974; Mira & Cairns, 1979), the group leader may demonstrate shaping the behavior of a group member (Walder *et al.*, 1969), other specialists such as speech therapists may demonstrate a new concept by modeling with each other (Benassi & Benassi, 1973), or the trainer may model a procedure to deal with one of the parent's presenting problems (Tavormina, 1975). Gardner points out the advantages of having parents watch an experienced trainer model a procedure: it gives parents a model of a successful application of a procedure which they can duplicate, and provides a dramatic demonstration that control of a deviant response is possible. If the model is an experienced parent, the demonstration is even more powerful since a naive parent will be more likely to identify with another parent than with a professional (Gardner, 1976).

Mash *et al.* (1973) documented the effect of modeling in eliminating problem behaviors. A group of three mothers were taught to respond differentially to their developmentally disabled children's compliant and noncompliant behavior. The program used instruction by professionals, modeling by a fourth mother who demonstrated procedures by interacting with her own child, and group discussion of the demonstration. The three observer mothers had no supervised practice in the clinic, and were getting feedback only from changes in their children's behavior at home. The demonstration mother had previously been in a training program without modeling. The observer mothers were able to solicit greater compliance from their children in a command situation following training. They decreased their use of commands and questions, stopped using negative interactions following compliance, and stopped responding positively to competing behavior. Two of the three observer mothers increased positive attention for compliance and gained greater compliance in a play situation. The demonstration mother did not show the gains that the observer mothers did. She had participated in the same discussions; the only difference was that she had not had a chance to observe someone working with a child.

A few authors have also used modeling to teach parents to train new skills. Lovaas and Newsom (1976) described an unpublished thesis by Glahn which demonstrated that mothers of "psychotic" children "were unable to produce measurable improvement until after they were given training which consisted of watching an experienced therapist teach a given behavior to a child" (Glahn, cited in Lovaas & Newsom, 1976, p. 350). However, the mothers improved only the skill they had observed being trained. A second training program which included training parents to recognize correct and incorrect use of instructions, prompts, shaping, consequation, and intertrial intervals was necessary before parents could train a variety of skills.

Koegel *et al.* (1978) replicated the finding that a brief demonstration to parents of autistic children was sufficient to permit their children to perform the target behaviors. However, as with Lovaas and Newsom (1976) generalization to new target behaviors did not occur until they supplemented training with a videotape teaching general behavioral principles by examples.

Thus, live and video modeling of training procedures have been used to successfully train parents to modify problem behaviors and train new skills. There is some evidence (Koegel *et al.*, 1978; Lovaas & Newsom, 1976) that generalized training skill is acquired if the modeled behaviors demonstrate general principles rather than focus on a specific skill.

Behavioral Rehearsal

Another technique of parent training is to have the parent practice in the treatment setting the behavior(s) that will have to be performed in real life, receiving immediate therapist feedback about the performance. This supervised practice, often combined with demonstration by the therapist and reciprocal role playing by parent and therapist, is a major training tool of some treatment approaches (Peed *et al.*, 1977). Feedback to the parent may be presented in a variety of ways. It may be delivered immediately and directly by the trainer who remains in the room and communicates verbally or by prearranged hand signals; it may be presented remotely via a bug-in-the-ear system; or the feedback may be delayed until the practice is completed.

Direct training in a hands-on setting has advantages for training parents of at-risk children who come from lower socioeconomic groups, and who themselves have inadequate parenting histories and skill deficits (e.g., Ayllon & Roberts, 1975; Risley, 1968). These parents may be unfamiliar with receiving information from didactic lectures and written instructions. Their verbal repertories may be restricted, which limits their ability to comment verbally on their child's activities. Thus, it may be necessary to not only teach the parents to be more contingent in attending to their child, but to improve the parents' verbal labeling skills. Also, directed practice with the child allows the trainer to observe how the parents' behavior is changing over sessions, offering a chance to monitor actual parent behavior rather than parents' reports about their behavior.

Mira and Cairns advocate a training program which recognizes the above difficulties with indirect training programs for mothers of children who are at-risk for neglect, abuse, or developmental delay. They train parents with a minimum of didactic instruction, relying on demonstration, role playing, and directed rehearsal with the parents as they play with their children in the clinic or when they administer daily care or training in the home (Mira & Cairns, 1979).

Only rarely has the differential effect of practice and feedback been studied. Doleys, Doster, and Cartelli (1976) assessed the contribution of practice and self-recording to a program that also included reading, lecture, and role playing. Five mothers of children with learning disabilities were trained first to increase their rate and variety of positive responses and to decrease commands and questions during five training sessions involving lectures, discussion of reading material, modeling, and role playing. In the second training phase, lasting three sessions, each mother interacted with her child, while other mothers remotely observed, recorded, and heard trainer's comments. Each mother then recorded audio tapes of her interaction and got feedback from the trainer. The lecture-modeling-role playing produced some changes in mother's interactions, but changes after practice and feedback were greater.

One additional aspect of parent training formats has received some attention in the literature, namely, group versus individual training. Group training appears to have the advantages of cost savings and amenability to a structured curriculum using, for example, films, and group problem solving (Baker, 1976). In one of the reviews of the parent-training literature, O'Dell (1974) described group and individual parent-training formats and stated: "Conclusions concerning which approach or combination of approaches are best in certain training situations must remain tentative because of the lack of controlled comparative research" (O'Dell, 1974, pg. 423). A controlled comparison of group and individual training formats for parents of mentally retarded children was conducted by Brightman, Baker, Clark, and Ambrose (1978). Parents were individually ($n = 16$) or group-trained ($n = 38$) to teach self-help skills and manage problem behaviors or were assigned to a delayed training ($n = 13$) control group. Pre- and postdependent measures included parents' knowledge of behavior modification, a behavioral sample of parent teaching, and children's self-help skills and behavior problems. Although both training groups were superior to the controls for all dependent measures, no differences between individuals and group formats were observed at posttest or 6-month follow-up. Thus, in training self-help and problem behavior management skills, effectiveness does not seem to be an issue. However, considering that Brightman *et al.* (1978) found group training to demand only about one-half the professional time, the cost factor would favor a group format. If replicated, these findings support a shift toward group training for parents of developmentally disabled children.

CONTENT OF PARENT-TRAINING PROGRAMS

The training content ideally should be related to parents' long-term needs. Even though, in general, parents of children may seek assistance initially for a circumscribed behavior problem, parents of developmentally disabled children may be concerned about broader, long-term goals. However, in determining the content of the training program for such parents, professionals must take into account whether the parents understand the extent of the child's learning deficits, the parents' personal investment in direct training, and the parents awareness of their potential as trainers (Thompson & Young, 1977). Initially, parents of developmentally disabled children may not be ready to be trained for a life-long problem but may only be able to consider their own or their child's short-term needs for training.

Some long-range goals for parent-training endeavors have been as extensive as total family rehabilitation, including preparation of the parent for employment, improving home-making skills (Heber & Garber, 1975; Levitt & Cohen, 1976), and locating health and social services (Levitt & Cohen, 1976). One short-term goal especially appropriate for parents of the developmentally disabled person is the provision of normative information regarding growth and development (Haus & Thompson, 1976). Such information can help parents understand the extent of delay and provide them a rationale for enlisting parent assistance in direct child training.

The next section discusses several points about the content of training programs. Topics covered include the breadth of current training content, those components parents are learning to handle, and the specific intervention techniques they are being taught. The value of training parents in general principles of learning, in addition to specific techniques, is also discussed. The section concludes with a description of recommended components of a comprehensive package to train parents in general principles.

Breadth of Training

As parent training technology developed, there has been a trend away from teaching a single technique to deal with a specific behavior problem toward a focus on changing the parent-child interaction. There has also been an increase in the sophistication of methods taught to parents (Berkowitz & Graziano, 1972). Parents of developmentally disabled children are learning to apply complex procedures, are being taught programs involving multiple steps, and are dealing with behaviors once considered the domain of specialists treating children in clinics.

When parents are taught one procedure for one problem, these treatment plans may be drawn up as a means of individualizing for parents who are simultaneously learning a broader range of principles and procedures (Salzinger *et al.*, 1970; Thompson & Young, 1977). These individually designed programs serve not only to tailor a broad spectrum curricula for an individual family's requirements but also to demonstrate to parents ways in which the basic concepts of behavioral analysis and the principles of learning apply to their own problems.

About the only instance in which parents of the developmentally disabled are trained in only one procedure for only one problem behavior is in the application of an aversive procedure to deal with an alarming behavior. Parents have successfully learned these procedures and have been able to maintain treatment effects from a clinic program. In some cases the parents have taken total responsibility for applying the program in the home. These techniques have included response-contingent application: of shock to extend treatment effects for self-injurious behavior from school to home (Merbaum, 1973); of aromatic ammonia to obtain setting generality in the treatment of self-injurious behavior from clinic to home (Altman, Haavik, & Cook, 1978); and lemon juice to achieve generalization of treatment for public masturbation (Cook, Altman, Shaw, & Blaylock, 1978). Parents have also learned to apply overcorrection procedures for self-injurious behavior initially treated by professionals in the clinic (Harris & Romanczyk, 1976) and solely in the home with the mother as the therapist (Barnard *et al.*, 1976).

Selecting and Describing Intervention Goals

For problem behaviors the parents, rather than professionals, typically select the intervention targets (e.g., Altman, Haavik, & Cook, 1978), Teaching parents to describe the child's problem behavior in a way that can be agreed on and measured was stressed by parent trainers using the precision teaching model (Galloway & Galloway, 1971; Hoover, 1970; Lindsley, 1966; Mira, 1970, 1972). Salzinger *et al.*, (1970) trained parents to describe the target problem behaviors clearly and found that the ability to do this characterized their most successful parents.

For skill building, parents typically have not been asked to assess the child, break tasks down into components, or to select short-term goals. Parent training starts after the professional has selected the training tasks (Fredricks *et al.*, 1976). Hayden (1976) describes this step of task analysis as the most difficult, yet the most important. In some programs, however, parents do select the skills to be trained. Frankel (1977) has recently developed an assessment instrument for use by parents of moderately mentally retarded youngsters. Parents learned to transfer their observations to the assessment instrument and then to plan skill-building activities in the indicated areas. Although Frankel (1979) stresses that the instrument is most effective when parent and clinician work together, the parent is definitely taking a more active part in the selection of targets for skill building. In a program described by Altman, Haavik, and Woelk (1978), the clinician identifies the deficit skills and seeks parent consultation for corroboration of the deficit in child behavior at home. Next, parents assist in selecting those deficit skills that seem most necessary for daily living. Other programs also have parents participate in task selection, but the specific amount of involvement is not clear (Shearer, 1976).

Specific Intervention Skills

A frequent skill taught to parents is the contingent use and withdrawal of attention (the latter frequently via time-out). Time-out is a common procedure taught to parents for dealing with problem behavior (Budd *et al.*, 1976; Frazier & Schneider, 1975; Johnson *et al.*, 1978). In learning to deal with problem behaviors, parents have also learned how to use specific consequation procedures, such as overcorrection (Barnard *et al.*, 1976) and use of such aversive procedures as shock (Merbaum, 1973) and aromatic ammonia (Altman, Haavik, & Cook, 1978). In general, for dealing with problem behavior, parents have learned primarily how to manipulate the consequences of that behavior.

Parents have learned other dimensions of consequation, and this is particularly true for skill building. Aspects of the use of consequences have included fading from tangible to social reinforcers (Kozloff, 1974), the most effective ways of applying consequences (Barrett, 1969; Gardner, 1976; Koegel *et al.*, 1978) and how to vary reinforcement schedules to maximize acquisition and maintenance (Nordquist & Wahler, 1973; Risley & Wolf, 1967).

Other intervention skills taught to parents include how to present stimuli (Koegel *et al.*, 1978), how to build responses via prompting and shaping (Koegel *et al.*, 1978; Kozloff, 1974), fading (Arnold, Sturgis, & Forehand, 1977; Haus & Thompson, 1976; Mock, 1977; Nordquist & Wahler, 1973), and chaining, use of successive approximations, and effective sequencing of shaping steps (Kozloff, 1974).

It appears that parents learning to train new skills are being taught a more comprehensive repertoire than those in programs focusing on eliminating problem behaviors. The operational definition and measurement of the broad range of techniques derived from general principles has only begun to occur. The Training Proficiency Scale (Watson, 1972) and the parent target behaviors described in Koegel *et al.* (1978) are a step in the direction of pinpointing essential techniques for training parents to build skills. Only after the necessary skills are well defined can outcome studies be conducted.

Evaluation of Effectiveness

For the most part, evaluation of program effectiveness has been left to the professional. However, there are instances in which parents have been trained to evaluate the results of their intervention and make program changes on the basis of the outcome data. Hall, Axelrod, Tyler, Grief, Jones, and Robertson (1972) demonstrated that parents could modify problem behaviors and use research designs to document that they had done so. Frangia and Reisinger (1979) describe a program in which parents of mentally retarded children demonstrate a reversal design for other parents to show stimulus control of oppositional behavior. Parents conduct a 4-day contingency reversal which is used to convince them of the necessity of contingent parental attention in controlling oppositional behavior.

Haavik *et al.* (1979) trained parents of a severely mentally retarded boy to use a reversal design to determine whether a diet was effective in controlling seizures. The initial reversal was crucial in convincing parents of the need to rigidly adhere to the diet to suppress seizures. The parents later systematically added and removed foods on their own, showing that they had learned to employ a reversal design to evaluate the effects of intervention.

Thus, although program evaluation by parents is not prevalent in the literature, there are indications that parents can be trained to do so. Also, in one area of child training (the planning of individualized educational plans mandated by PL 94-142), parents are being encouraged to take a more active part in the evaluation and planning of their children's programs. It seems warranted at this time to study the effects of training parents in program evaluation on their skills in teaching their children.

Training in General Principles of Learning

Many trainers recognize that parents of developmentally disabled children must function as generalists in the home environment. Operating on the belief that an understanding of learning principles will help parents formulate and carry out individual child-training programs, these trainers teach parents using a broad curriculum whose goal includes verbal understanding of both principles of learning and common procedures based on these principles (Benassi & Benassi, 1973; Patterson et al., 1967; Walder et al., 1969; Watson & Bassinger, 1974). However, we do not yet have enough evidence to determine whether knowledge of learning principles enables parents to function as better trainers than if their training only emphasized procedures. Principles of learning and procedures are presented in the same training package, or, even if presented sequentially, often there is no measure of their differential effects. Another problem in determining the value of learning principles is that they are taught by didactic means, whereas the procedures are often taught via modeling and directed practice.

Three studies have looked at the value of training in behavioral principles in contrast to training focused upon specific procedures (Koegel et al., 1978; Longin et al., 1975; O'Dell, Flynn, & Benlolo, 1977).

O'Dell et al. (1977) trained parents of exceptional children under one of three conditions: theoretical pretraining in behavioral principles followed by a practical workshop on procedures taught via descriptions, modeling, and rehearsal; enrollments in a pretreatment placebo group teaching general information about exceptional children followed by the workshop; or, enrollment in the workshop only.

A variety of measures were taken following the workshop and at a 1-month follow-up. The three groups did not differ in acquisition of behavioral skills, in attendance or participation, or in attitudes toward the training of their children. Those pretrained in behavioral principles did not show an advantage in the number of successful projects completed at the time of training or the percentage of projects which were successful. The obvious conclusion is that pretraining in theoretical behavioral principles did not help skill acquisition, nor were parents put off by going directly into a workshop that could have been viewed as "mechanistic" in approach. Also, those who had verbal pretraining did not do as much home implementation as those without pretraining, suggesting that teaching parents to talk about behavioral principles may have led them to do more talking than managing of their children's behavior problems. The authors suggest that parents may lose their enthusiasm for working on their children's problems during the extra time spent in the pretraining.

Longin et al. (1975) had four mothers of nonambulatory mentally retarded children read *Living with Children* (Patterson & Guillon, 1968). They did not validate that parents actually read the book or assess their mastery of the information. Three weeks later, two mothers were given three sessions of didactic training in basic principles of behavior modification, including defining and counting behavior, reinforcement, and techniques for increasing or decreasing target behavior. Next, mothers were given specific instructions for feeding, which included a task analysis and strategies for shaping and maintaining behavior. Modeling, rehearsal, direct feedback, and discussion sessions were also used. To complete the multiple-baseline design, the other two mothers were given the same treatments staggered in time.

The outcome measures were verbal commanding and praising, physical prompting, and "clutter" plus generalization measures. Results showed that two of the four mothers increased and generalized their training skills, but only after specific techniques were taught. This study suggests that pretraining in principles alone did not teach mothers to shape or maintain their children's behavior. Training of specific procedures was necessary for the mothers to become effective trainers. A problem with interpretation of this study is that the length of training in each phase may not have been adequate (4½ hours) and that training occurred in the clinic, but outcome measures were made in the home.

In the third of the studies looking at the value of teaching principles, Koegel *et al.* (1978) gave parents of autistic children a brief training program aimed at teaching the child a specific behavior and a subsequent general training to teach them principles and a general set of skills not specific to one behavior. In the training on one task, parents were given a brief (10-15 min) demonstration of how to deliver an instruction, use edibles as consequents, ignore incorrect responses, reinforce approximations, and prompt and shape. This demonstration was sufficient for parents to learn to train that specific behavior; however, they did not generalize the training to teaching new behaviors. In the subsequent general training, the parents received lectures and video presentations about principles and how to train the same skills, but the training was not directed at any specific child behavior. This subsequent general training was effective in training the parents to teach new behaviors to their children. There are problems with drawing firm conclusions about the value of training in general principles from this study. The general training occurred only subsequent to the demonstration of how to teach specific skills. Also, the general training lasted longer than that directed at a specific skill (164 min vs. 10-15 min).

Two studies (Longin *et al.*, 1975; O'Dell *et al.*, 1977) examined the effects of teaching parents general principles versus teaching general principles supplemented with specific procedures. O'Dell *et al.* (1977) found the two procedures to be equally effective while Longin *et al.* (1975) found the supplementary training to be essential for those parents who increased parent-training skills. The studies differ in a number of major ways: whether analyses were group or single subject, the content nature of the principle-training and procedure-training components, and the kinds of outcome measures. The reasons for discrepencies in outcome will become clear only when studies use comparable analysis which do not mask the effects of individual subjects; when the kind of training given for principles and procedures is more standardized across studies; and when similar outcome criteria are used to assess the effects.

Both the Koegel *et al.* (1978) and Longin *et al.* (1975) studies examined the effects of training principles and procedures on generalization to untrained child behavior. Despite the many differences between the two studies, it appears that training principles or procedures alone do not produce generalization. Parents will generalize their training to new child target behaviors only when *both* principles and procedures have been taught.

Comprehensive Training Package

If understanding of, and ability to apply, general principles of learning is valuable in training parents as generalists, it would be important to have available a comprehensive program for this training. There seems to be agreement that the following steps should be part of a comprehensive parent training program (Kozloff, 1979; Shearer, 1976). Such a program would begin by teaching parents to specify and operationally define the target behavior(s). For problem behaviors, they would learn to measure base rates. For skill deficits, once the target behavior is identified and defined, they would learn to analyze it into components. These components are often a "best guess" of the successive approximations which ultimately lead to the target behavior. Parents would then learn to select short-term goals and write prescriptions. The next step — implementation — requires that parents have the techniques necessary to train new skills and eliminate problem behaviors. Having implemented a behavior change program, they would then learn to evaluate the program's effectiveness. Next they would learn to use evaluation results to make decisions about continued revising or selecting a new goal because criteria had been met, the goal was found to be inappropriate, or could not be achieved efficiently under current technology or training situation.

Despite the agreement that the above components of a training program are important, the specific set of parent behaviors required for all these procedural steps has yet to be identified and the evidence documenting if and how to train them is for the most part not available.

Summary

Training programs for parents of developmentally disabled children are focusing less on the teaching of a specific procedure to deal with a problem behavior or training a new skill, and more on information about a broader array of topics. Parents are currently learning multiple-step programs, are being taught task analysis and the many parameters of effective use of consequences, and how to accurately evaluate the effects of their training. Self-injurious behavior is the one behavior problem for which the training focus remains highly specific.

Although there is general agreement that parents of developmentally disabled children must learn to function as generalists after training is completed, and that learning about principles of learning will aid them in generalizing their training, there are very few studies that document the actual contribution of general training supplementing training in specific procedures, and very few programs that were described offer parents such training in a comprehensive manner.

Engaging, Maintaining, and Insuring Progress of Parents during Training

It has been demonstrated that a technology for parent training exists and is effective for altering problem behaviors and skill deficits. What remains to be done is to find a means to get that technology to those it will benefit. This entails not only identification of the target populations, but also engaging and maintaining them in training programs, insuring acquisition of training skills, and maintaining the use of those skills after training.

Engaging Parents

Many parents referred for training never enter into a program. Mira (1970) reported that 16% of parents referred never showed up. Weinrott, Bauske, and Patterson (1979) lost 30% of their parents during baseline. An important consideration before engaging parents of developmentally disabled children in training is the degree of acceptance of their child's delay. Thompson and Young (1977) point out that, in the initial phase of having to deal with a developmentally disabled child, parents are not ready to make use of training that emphasizes their own long-term role in aiding their child's development.

Kozloff (1979) also addresses the issue of parents' readiness to begin working on their child's behavior. His guide for assessing families' strengths and problems is a list of prerequisite parent skills, attitudes, and interactions necessary for parent training to be successful. By way of example, a set of parents just receiving confirmation that their child is developmentally delayed and displaying "autistic-like" behaviors will need time and assistance to move from the level of asking, "Is it true and why did it happen?" to the point of "What can we do about it." Parents in this position would probably not be ready to meet the Lovaas and Newsom (1976) criteria of a successful parent: namely, to be willing to use strong consequences, to dedicate a major part of their life to training their child and keeping a contingent house, and to be able to deny that their child is ill, thus giving their child some responsibility for his or her behavior.

Another factor mitigating against entering into parent training is illness of the child. Developmentally disabled children with medical complications may have life-threatening needs which diminish the importance of a parent-training program. Indeed Altman, Haavik, and Cook (1978) report that parents discontinued a successful treatment program for hairpulling when the child's seizures required more of their attention.

Some families may have significant survival-oriented concerns which would take priority over learning to train their child. This may be a reason why low socioeconomic status (SES) has been prognostic of failure in some parent-training programs (Chilman, 1973). Considerations of these survival concerns has led some investigators to provide free food (Ramey, Starr, Pallas, Whitten, & Reed, 1975), job training (Heber & Garber, 1975), child care and transportation (Badger, 1972). Attending to such survival-oriented priorities before or during parents training may improve the chances of training low SES parents.

It should be noted that associations between low SES and failure in parent training has been salient only under specific circumstances. Hunt and Sulzer-Azaroff (1974) and Ayllon and Roberts (1975) have successfully trained such parents. The inconsistency between their reported success and others' reported failure may be explained by the fact that a number of training programs which have been successful with low SES parents have not relied on written or lecture-presented instructions (e.g., Ayllon & Roberts, 1975; Heber & Garber, 1975; Hunt & Sulzer-Azaroff, 1974), but rather on direct feedback and modeling. Attending to low SES parents' more pressing needs, plus tailoring the method of instruction so as to be less foreign to them, may improve our ability to engage these parents in their children's training.

It has been suggested that assembling parents of developmentally disabled children in groups will help them see the rationale for training. Fredricks *et al.* (1976) begin their parent-training program with a parent group meeting designed to

> sell the idea of participating in a program to the parents. Two major "selling" points have been found to be successful. First, the accelerated rate at which a child can acquire skills should be demonstrated to the parent by specific examples. Second, the necessity for the generalization from center to home of the child's learning, especially in the areas of self-help skills, toilet training, and language acquisition, should be stressed. (p. 109)

Maintaining Parents

Methods of maintaining parents' involvement during training have received more attention than initial engagement. A wide variety of tactics have been used to maintain parents in training. Some trainers have relied exclusively on the assumption that child behavior change will be one of the most effective reinforcers for maintaining parent-training behavior (Kozloff, 1974; Risley, 1968). Others, however, do not support this view (Baker, 1976; Wahler, 1976). What may be happening is that the large child behavior changes that occur with initial applications of basic procedures "do seem to strengthen the parents' use of those procedures, increase parents' interest in learning more procedures, and produce optimistic statements from parents regarding their child's future" (Kozloff, 1974, p. 211). However, with the sustained parental efforts required to deal with behavior problems and to program increasingly more complex skills, additional incentives appear to be required (Baker, 1976; Kozloff, 1974). In teaching more complex skills parents may "go through many extinction trials for precious little reinforcement from the child" (Kozloff, 1974, p. 211).

One way to capitalize on the apparently weak and/or transient reinforcement parents receive from child behavior changes is to deliberately program for continued reinforcement. Gardner (1976) states that behaviors associated with being able to control one's environment will increase because of the reinforcement value of the control. He recommends producing some behavior change immediately, teaching the parents to recognize the relationship between the intervention and that behavior change, and then attempting to modify a problem behavior with which they would have a low probability of success. This system of teaching parents what they need to solve the presenting problem and starting with easy problems provides some built-in insurance that parents' problems will be solved.

Another tactic for programming early success involves a high density of therapist contact. Weinrott *et al.* (1979) maintained 70% of their clients who entered training by using daily phone calls during the first 6 weeks. Carefully programming parent success followed by a very gradual increase in training time and task difficulty and finally, gradual fading of consultant contact may provide a successful maintenance technique. It is no different from the shape, prompt, reinforce, and fade strategy that is applied to the training of many other behaviors.

Many programs have not recognized that it is necessary to rely, at least temporarily, on consequences other than child behavior change even though such consequences may be less "natural." Consequences which have been employed or suggested to maintain parents in training programs have been varied. Incentives have included contingency contracts and fee rebates (Benassi & Benassi, 1973; Walder *et al.*, 1969), access to prosthetics or continuation in treatment (Harris & Romanczyk, 1976; Hoover, 1970; Mira, 1972; Terdall & Buell, 1969), child care during training (Badger, 1972), and self-reinforcement in the form of positive self-statements (Kazdin, 1973; Wells, Griest, & Forehand, 1980). Another tactic termed *contingent professional resources* by Baker (1976) makes admission to training sessions contingent on completing homework assignments (Mira, 1970; Walder *et al.*, 1969).

There have been a few suggestions to assist maintenance by strategies other than incentives. By arranging for parents to be trained with other parents, support groups and friendships have emerged. Hayden (1976) and Brightman *et al.* (1978) view these relationships as helpful for maintaining the training efforts of parents of developmentally disabled children. Similar logic seems behind the notion that parents relate to, and learn from, paraprofessionals more easily than professionals (Levitt & Cohen, 1976).

A related strategy has been that of Hall and Nelson (1980). Responding to evidence that single parents have higher drop-out rates and the least consistent participation in the programs, Baker *et al.* (1972) and Hall and Nelson (1980) shifted the training site to a community "single-parent" site and found an increase in single-parent involvement.

As with single parents, where interpersonal support is minimal, cases in which the relationship between the two parents is poor may not bode well for training efforts (Kozloff, 1974; Mealiea, 1976); however, with special effort some success has been reported. Mealiea (1976) reports that when a child's behavior reflects deviant family patterns, altering the behavior problem without tending to the pathological family system will have only minimal impact. The treatment goal must be a change in family system. He suggests starting with the behavior problem and teaching parents to modify it, then shifting the focus to the parents and their interactions.

Whereas a number of failures to maintain parent-training behavior may be traced to such programming tactics as increasing time demand on parents too rapidly, or simply asking more than the "traffic would bear" (Hamilton, 1977; Inglis, 1977; Mahoney et al., 1971), some successful efforts have relied on more deliberate programming with close monitoring and troubleshooting (Mathis, 1971) and gradual fading of consultant contact (Fabry & Reid, 1978; Foreyt & Parks, 1975; Moore & Bailey, 1973). Watson and Bassinger (1974) presented a well-paced systematic parent-training program in which they were able to get parents to spend 2 to 3 hours per day training their children.

Despite the fact that many methods for maintaining parents in training have been mentioned in the literature, research specifically studying the effectiveness of these methods is limited.

Eyberg and Johnson (1974) compared a parent-training program with contracted refundable deposit for attendance, as well as contingent telephone and training time to one without maintenance incentives. The incentive condition resulted in completion of more assigned data recordings, treatment of more child-problem behaviors, and a higher staff rating for cooperation. Hunt and Sulzer-Azaroff (1974) examined the effectiveness of feedback on return of homework assignments by parents of mentally retarded children. Feedback, phone calls or notes, graphs of child behavior kept by parents, and graphs of parent behavior prepared by the experimenters resulted in a higher percentage of returned homework assignments than no feedback or faded feedback conditions. One study has assessed the effects of prompting parents to attend training sessions. At a center-based program, Allyon and Roberts (1975) demonstrated that finding and reminding parents to attend training sessions improved the percentage of parents in attendance from 8% to 77%.

The studies by Eyberg and Johnson (1974) and Hunt and Sulzer-Azaroff (1974) support the notion that response-contingent consequences for parent-training behaviors do produce better maintenance during training. Ayllon and Roberts (1975) add the finding that prompting may also be helpful. Thus far, the area of insuring maintenance of parent behavior during training has received very little empirical attention.

Insuring Progress

An issue closely related to maintaining parents in training programs is insuring progress during the training. The only procedure for insuring progress that has been examined is a programmed sequence with success criteria for each step. Gardner (1976) presented a lecture series for training verbal skills to four groups of trainers, one group of which were mothers of autistic children. Requiring that each person earn a 90% score on one unit before going on to the next improved learning for the three nonparent groups. The mothers learned at a high level throughout the program and their performance was not enhanced by the contingent condition. Watson and Bassinger (1974) also made parents' progress through the training program dependent on their test scores, but provided no information on the comparative effect of a contingent program pace. Mindell and Budd (1977) directly measured several parent behaviors (e.g., pointing, praising, use of verbal and physical prompts, use of tangibles, number of repetitions) in efforts to reduce child noncompliance. Using a multiple baseline design across parent behaviors, these authors were able to document parent progress at each step of the training program although they did not specify criteria for each step. Thus, combining direct measurement of parent behavior with a sequential training program provides a way of assessing parent progress during training. The effectiveness of parent-training programs would be better understood and perhaps enhanced by adding direct measurement of parent progress and arranging training to fit multiple baseline designs.

Summary

In summary, successful recruiting of parents for training requires careful assessment of the family living situation, acceptance of their child's disability, an expressed willingness to use training techniques, and an adequate health status of the child. In general, low socioeconomic status parents have been poor risks, as have those who do not recognize their affiliation with other group members. Once parents have been recruited, maintaining participation in the training program becomes an issue. Many training programs have relied on child progress to maintain parents in training programs. With children who learn slowly and have behavior problems, child progress does not appear to be a sufficient maintenance strategy. Strategies which have been cited as successful include: starting with targets with a high probability of success; training parents in the company of other parents who will provide support and encouragement; fading contact with professionals gradually; and establishing behavioral contracts with incentives, for example, providing rebates for parent compliance. What little research has been done suggests that parents will stay in training programs longer when provided with response-contingent consequences (e.g., performance feedback).

An area that has received very little attention has been insuring progress during training. Documenting progress with direct measures of parent behavior and the use of specific success criteria for training program components are the bare essentials for insuring parent progress in training programs.

Effectiveness of Parent-Training Programs

The issue of the short- and long-range effectiveness of parent-training efforts is probably the most crucial of this field. We must assess whether our training efforts have a significant effect on important dimensions of the behavior of developmentally disabled children, not just during the time of training but over a longer portion of their lives. Likewise, we must know whether the changes we effect in parents' behavior enable them to function as trainers after we leave. Can they generalize their training to other of their child's behaviors, to dealing with their child in other settings or to training other children? A remaining question in assessing the effectiveness of parent training is how the programs in which trained parents work with their children compare in terms of cost-effectiveness to other strategies for training the child.

Do Trained Parents Change Behavior?

An earlier section of this chapter cited a wide variety of problem behaviors and skills successfully trained by parents of developmentally disabled children. Although the majority of those citations were case studies, a number of more extensive controlled investigations have also demonstrated that trained parents do change child behavior. A few examples will be described.

In the Portage Project, an extensive study including 103 multiply handicapped preschool-age children, parents were taught (in the home) a "prescriptive, precision teaching approach using positive reinforcement" (Penistone, 1972, p. 1). Home trainers made weekly visits to instruct parents in what and how to teach, what to reinforce, and how to observe and record behavior (Shearer, 1976). Portage Project children were compared to randomly selected preschool children before and after home training on a number of developmental scales. The Portage Project children made significantly greater gains on cognitive academic, language, and social measures than the control group (Shearer & Shearer, 1976).

Revill and Blunden (1979) replicated the Portage Project in England and in Wales with 19 families having developmentally disabled children. A multiple baseline design across two geographic areas was used to demonstrate the effectiveness of the Portage model. It was found that the rate at which Portage items were learned increased after training, thereby replicating the original program's effectiveness.

The READ project is another parent-training program which has evaluated the effectiveness of trained parents in changing the behavior of developmentally disabled children. Heifetz (1977a) randomly assigned 160 families to three experimental conditions differing in amount of professional assistance provided parents. The 20-week program emphasized child self-help skills. Children of experimental group mothers showed significantly larger gains than did control children. Thus, it appears that after training, parents are able to effect behavior change in their developmentally disabled children.

Durability of Change

Durability of Parent Behavior

Although numerous studies have demonstrated that parents can learn to effectively decrease problem behavior and build skills, there is less documentation that they continue to use these procedures after training. The issue of durability, or temporal generality, is perhaps even more significant for the developmentally disabled population than other groups because of their life-long deficits.

Three studies have examined the durability of parent-training efforts after program termination. In each instance there were no continued consultations or other attempts to program temporal generality. O'Dell et al. (1977) separated parents of exceptional children into three pretraining groups, namely, didactic pretraining in basic behavioral principles, placebo, and no pretraining. All parents then attended a 6-session workshop training skills, including defining, recording, graphing, differential attention, and breaking complex behaviors into smaller units. A number of contingencies were used to encourage attendance, but none were in effect for maintenance. Follow-up questionnaires were mailed, of which 58% were returned. At 1-month follow-up, 35% of the group pretrained on basic principles, 17% of the placebo pretraining, and 66% of the no pretraining group reported continuing to use graphing and recording. The proportionately higher percentage maintaining in the no pretraining group may be owing to a "burn out" effect induced by pretraining. The poor return and questionnaire measures render these results tentative.

Baker (1977) conducted a 14-month follow-up of 95 of the 100 families who participated in the READ Project. Follow-up information was gathered in the home through structured interviews. A 20-week parent-training program examined the effects of a manual alone, a manual plus telephone contact, the preceding plus a training group, the preceding combined with a home visit, versus a delayed treatment control group. All conditions were more effective than the no-treatment control group, but did not differ among themselves. Follow-up retesting of parents' knowledge of behavior principles indicated maintenance with no additional gains. However, the major concern here is with what happened to parent-training efforts. Fifty-one percent continued a "useful degree of regular teaching for these skills to the criterion of formal sessions of three or more per week, for longer than one month, or regular incidental teaching continued as necessary" (Baker, 1977, p. 215). With respect to those parents targeting behavior problems, 69% made some effort to continue; however, only 29% carried out the program to satisfactory completion. Again the questionnaire measures temper the validity of these data. However, assuming parents would wish to impress the interviewer and overreport, it seems that at least half of the parents do not maintain their efforts without explicit follow-up contingencies.

Ambrose and Baker (1979) conducted a 6-month follow-up of 88 families who completed a 10-session training course designed to help parents teach their developmentally disabled children. Using the same measurement techniques as in Baker (1977), described above, they found that 75% of the parents who selected skill-building targets continued programs formally or incidentally for at least one month or until mastery. Incidental training efforts accounted for the majority of effort. For parents targeting behavior problems, less than 66% made some effort to continue training. Of these, only 49% met the criterion for "good continuation," that is, at least one program with a substantial decrease in the target behavior.

The studies by O'Dell *et al.* (1977), Baker (1977), and Ambrose and Baker (1979) represent initial attempts to assess whether trained parents continue to use their skills after training programs have ended. Indeed, in many cases they did not use the newly trained skills. These studies point out the need to (1) directly assess whether the results of parent-training efforts maintain after training, and (2) to develop and evaluate strategies which will promote greater maintenance.

Durablity of Child Behavior

A related issue is whether child behavior is durable irrespective of parent-training efforts. Baker (1977) reported that children's *Behavioral Assessment*

Manual scores indicated they had maintained the gains in self-help skills achieved during training 14 months earlier. Moore and Bailey (1973) brought the child and mother back to the clinic 1, 4, and 7 months after the last training session to determine whether the mother maintained previously acquired control over the child's preacademic and social behavior. The control was maintained for preacademic behaviors and enhanced for social behaviors. These few follow-up investigations (Baker, 1977; Moore & Bailey, 1973) indicate that the child-behavior change achieved by trained parents can be durable.

Generalization across Behaviors

Parent Behavior

Once parents have been trained to alter specific target behaviors, can they then use these techniques to train other deficit skills or to deal with different problem behaviors? Fourteen-month follow-up data from the READ Project indicated that while only 14% of the families reported beginning new "formal" training programs involving regular sessions for repeated practice of a skill, 76% reported new incidental training programs incorporating teaching into the daily routine (Baker, 1977).

Ambrose and Baker (1979) using the same assessment procedures as Baker (1977) conducted a 6-month follow-up of 88 families who completed the UCLA Parents as Teachers program. Thirty-two percent of the parents reported implementing new formal training programs for at least 1 month or until mastery. However, 60% of the parents reported incidental training of a new behavior for at least 1 month or until mastery. These studies (Ambrose & Baker, 1979; Baker, 1977) show that some parents trained by the READ Project procedure report continuing to train new target behaviors after completion of the program. The percentage of parents who apparently can and do train new behaviors is highest for incidental training efforts. Ambrose and Baker (1979) also found that parents who had more behavioral sophistication at follow-up also seemed to carry out more new programs. However, determinations of sophistication and generalization were based upon parent report, and may both reflect some other dimension, for example, motivation to please the interviewer.

Other studies indicate that parent-training techniques may differ in producing different parental competencies and subsequent generalization to new targets. Two studies examining parent-training program components found that generalization of parent-training techniques to new targets occurs only under certain conditions. Glahn (cited in Lovaas & Newsom, 1976) and Koegel *et al.* (1978) both found that training in teaching a specific skill produced parents who were unable to teach other behaviors. Supplemental general training in behavioral principles (via videotapes portraying correct and incorrect use of techniques applicable to teaching a variety of behaviors) was effective in teaching parents to train new child behaviors.

The studies by Baker (1977) and Ambrose and Baker (1979) address the important question of use of trained skills by parents with new child behaviors *after* training. Glahn (cited in Lovaas & Newsom, 1976) and Koegel *et al.* (1978) also addressed the question of generalization to other child behaviors but only *during* training. These studies suggest that parents can and do train new child target behaviors but may do so only after receiving certain kinds of training or only through more informal means.

Child Behavior

A related question is whether there is generalization of the effects of parent training to child behaviors that did not receive attention during the training program. Baker (1977) reported that there were further gains in unprogrammed self-help skills after program termination. However, he did not include an untreated control group, and one treatment group even showed declines. Generalization of child behavior was assessed only indirectly by a single administration of the *Behavioral Assessment Manual*. One study used direct and continuous measurement of parent and child behavior and assessed generalization of both. Riner and Budd (1977) taught a parent techniques to improve child compliance to specific instructions. Generalization of parent-training techniques and child compliance to spontaneous instructions was assessed. It was observed that

> Even though the mother showed limited generalization of parent-training skills to spontaneous instructions, the child's compliance evidenced clear-cut generalized improvements from training instructions to spontaneous instructions. (Riner & Budd, 1977, p. 7)

The above study points out that in assessing generalization to new targets, it is important to directly measure both parent and child behavior since child behavior may generalize even though parent behavior does not. Since few studies have directly measured both parent and child behaviors, conclusions regarding the significance of generalization across behaviors are not yet warranted.

Generalization across Settings

Parent Behavior

Skills taught to parents or children will be of little value if they are not used outside of the training setting. Studies which have evaluated this dimension of training indicate that generalization to natural settings does not occur automatically. Miller and Sloane (1976) trained five parents of nonverbal children to modify antecedents and consequences of child vocalizations. Measures of parent behavior were taken in two home-training settings and one generalization setting. "Increases in parent prompting and reinforcing their children's vocalizations generalized only minimally to a new setting in the home where parent training had not occurred" (Miller & Sloane, 1976, p. 355).

Mindell and Budd (1977) also investigated the generalization of parent training skills across settings. Informing parents that their newly acquired skills "would be useful" in other settings was sufficient to obtain generalization from a structured laboratory to a structured home setting, but not to unstructured laboratory or home settings.

Embry, Kelley, Herbert-Jackson, and Baer (1979) examined the effects of a "practical parenting" course on parent-child interactions in free-play and instructional training settings. Parents generalized their use of differential attention only to the free-play setting. The addition of individualized feedback (in-home graphic and verbal feedback, plus self-recording of parent attention) substantially increased the amount of appropriate parent-training behavior in both generalization settings. These results replicate the effect of feedback (Hunt & Sulzer-Azaroff, 1974) and self-recording (Herbert & Baer, 1972) on maintenance of parent behavior during training.

Reisinger, Frangia, and Hoffman (1976) examined the effects of a clinic toddler-management training program on the in-home parent management of children's oppositional behavior. All mothers demonstrated their ability to use intervention techniques in the clinic and showed some evidence of generalization to the home. However, when mothers were divided in terms of presence or absence of marital difficulty, those with such difficulty evidenced less generalization. With respect to generalization of parent behavior across settings, it appears that such factors as setting similarity, instruction to generalize, feedback, and marital discord affect the outcome.

Child Behavior

Does child behavior generalize across settings? Handleman (1979) trained children to respond to common questions in two school settings and probed for generalization at home. Only one of four children generalized these skills to the home when trained in a cubicle, seated, facing the tutor. The three additional children generalized responses to the home setting after school training was done in a number of different locations with the tutor standing in front of the child.

Longin *et al.* (1975) trained parents at home to facilitate the expressive language of their severely mentally retarded children. A multiple-baseline design across children revealed that gains in words spoken in school were not observed until after parent training was begun at home. Thus, child behavior trained by parents at home generalized from home to school. Hall and Broden (1977) also documented the effect of home training on school behavior. Tutoring by the mother at home improved spelling-test performance in school.

Miller and Sloane (1976) studied the generalization of parent training across stimulus settings. Minimal generalization was found from home training to a school free-play setting while only one of five children generalized a vocalization trained at home to a school speech session. However, child behavior did generalize to a new home setting. It is interesting to note that parent-training behavior did not generalize to the new home setting even though child behavior did generalize. However, Embry *et al.* (1979) found generalization of children's behavior to be related to concomitant use of training techniques by parents. Mindell and Budd (1977) also found that some measures of child response indicated generalization of child behavior across settings only when changes in parent behavior were also observed.

Thus, it appears that child behaviors do generalize from school to home and home to school under certain circumstances. Generalization of parent behavior is not always necessary for the child's behavior to generalize. The number and nature of training settings as well as the application of trained parent behaviors in those settings seem to be important variables to examine in assessing the setting generality of child behavior.

Generalization across People

Parent Behavior

Skills that parents learn in the clinic will, in some cases, generalize to their management of untreated children in the home. This has been documented for families trained to deal with behavior problems of children without developmental disabilities (Humphreys, Forehand, McMahon, & Roberts, 1978). There are only a few studies of generalization of trained behaviors across untreated siblings of developmentally disabled children. Anecdotal evidence from the Portage Project (Shearer, 1976) and another large-scale intervention program (Gray & Klaus, 1970) indicate that some parents do generalize newly acquired skill-building techniques to other family members. Ayllon and Roberts (1975), using a more limited sample, also documented that mothers could generalize skills needed to teach "cognitive" skills to other children within the experimental setting.

Child Behavior

The issue of generalization across people is also relevant for the developmentally disabled child. If behaviors newly trained by parents are restricted to the presence of the parent, training my be of limited value. The few studies in which generalization from home to school occurred also provide evidence that generalization across people does occur with developmentally disabled children (Hall & Broden, 1977; Longin et al., 1975). There is no way to determine to what extent settings or people were responsible for the generalization in those studies. No other controlled studies could be found which demonstrate that behaviors trained by parents occur in the presence of other people.

Suggestions for Enhancing Generality

The field of parent training for children in general, not only those with developmental disabilities, is only now moving to the study of broader issues such as durability and extent of behavior change. The few efforts that have been made have been fraught with methodological problems. Many of these inadequacies may be traced to what Mash and Terdal (1977) have designated as the treatment-termination model of follow-up: that is, give people a training program, leave them alone, and look later to see what they are doing. What is needed is a recognition that generalization requires careful, more standardized assessment, and usually also requires deliberate programming. Mash and Terdal (1977) suggest viewing follow-up assessment as *"ongoing measurement of behavior and relevant context over extended periods of time* rather than the measurement of effects following treatment" (p. 1291).

Despite the primitive state of our technology a number of techniques for enhancing generalization have been demonstrated by the various parent-training programs. In the next section a number of these potentially successful strategies for training generalization are described with reference to selected studies illustrating their application. The categories which follow are credited to Stokes and Baer (1977).

When a program is first being tested, the "train-and-hope" strategy may be appropriate. The new training program is first conducted, then a follow-up is done to assess the extent of generality. An analysis can then be performed to identify variables which may promote generalizations of the program. The train-and-hope strategy is exemplified by the studies of Baker (1977) and Ambrose and Baker (1979). Their analysis of follow-up results indicate that those parents who continued to program for their children at the time of follow-up had better proficiency at the end of training. Out of Baker's work came several recommendations for helping parents persist in teaching their children. The recommendations included acknowledging the value of incidental teaching and programming for it, giving parents a follow-through plan when training is over, and arranging periodic follow-up meetings to support parents' continued efforts (Baker, 1977). With the train-and-hope strategy, rather than programming beforehand for generalization, we evaluate if, and under what conditions, generalization has occurred and put those conditions into effect in future developments of that training program.

A second strategy for achieving generalization, and one which may involve the parents in the generalization training, uses sequential modification. When checks for generalization are conducted and generalization is found to be lacking or insufficient, procedures are systematically applied with each setting, person, or response. An example of this strategy for programming generalization is provided by the study of Altman, Haavik, and Cook (1978). Self-injury was suppressed in the clinic but no generalization was observed at home with the parents, in the grandparents' home, or at school until the contingencies were systematically applied in each setting.

Another strategy for training generalization is called *training sufficient exemplars*. As with sequential modification, training is conducted for each of a number of stimulus conditions or responses; however, with sufficient exemplars, the training is not conducted for all stimulus conditions or responses. An excellent example was reported by Stokes, Baer, and Jackson (1974).

> They established that training and maintenance of retarded children's greeting responses by one experimenter was not usually sufficient for the generalization of the responses across experimenters. However, high levels of generalization to over 20 members of the institution staff (and newcomers as well) who had not participated in the training of the responses were recorded, after a second experimenter trained and maintained the response in conjunction with the first experimenter. Thus, when generalization did not prevail after the training of one stimulus exemplar, it was programmed by training a greater diversity of stimulus (trainer) conditions. (Stokes & Baer, 1977, p. 355)

Another strategy derives from findings that indiscriminable contingencies may facilitate generalization. When reinforcement is not forthcoming for every response, a child may be unable to discriminate responses which are never reinforced because they are carefully interspersed among responses that are reinforced. A study in progresss indicates that in generalization settings when unreinforced probe stimuli are interspersed with reinforced stimuli and thereby rendered indiscriminable, developmentally disabled children continue to respond correctly (Haavik, Spradlin, & Altman, 1980). When the unreinforced probe stimuli are not interspersed, rendered discriminable, correct responding decreases and variability increases. Response decrements were most obvious in the setting (home) most dissimilar from the training setting (school). These findings imply that one way to increase responsiveness in the home setting is to set up a situation at home using the parents as trainers wherein reinforced training for certain tasks is interspersed throughout a number of daily parent-child experiences. Other tasks trained and reinforced in different settings (e.g., school) might then be interspersed with those already being trained and reinforced at home. In this way, a response trained and reinforced at school might generalize to the home environment without ever having to directly reinforce it in that environment.

The final strategy suggested by Stokes and Baer (1977) for encouraging generalization of parent training prescribes that all relevant environments be arranged so that there are common stimuli present. Several authors have reported successful generalization when this technique was used. Hall and Broden (1977) trained parents to teach correct spelling at home, but closely approximated school test conditions in the home training. Under these conditions the home training transferred to spelling test performance at school. Mindell and Budd (1977) demonstrated that a parent-training program coupled with a suggestion that the treatment could generalize to the home was sufficient to facilitate generalization of a mother's behaviors related to gaining her child's compliance; however, generalization occurred only from a structured clinic setting in which a mother delivered a set of prespecified instructions to a similarly structured activity setting using similar materials in the home. There was no generalization from the structured activity setting in the clinic to unstructured play settings in either clinic or home.

Another way of facilitating generalization may be by building an additional reinforcement system for parental persistence. This has been suggested by Baker (1976) who proposed planning for family members to reinforce each other for continuing the training of the child. Kazdin (1973) suggests that generality may be enhanced if parents are taught methods of self-reinforcement for continuing the child's training once a behavior modification program is withdrawn. Although not specifically dealing with parents of the developmentally disabled, the study of Wells *et al.* (1980) confirms the value of self-control procedures for encouraging continued parental involvement in children's training. They trained mothers in self-recording, conseqence selection, and self-reinforcement, following a parent-training program. On follow-up, the children whose mothers were trained in self-control procedures performed more favorably on target behaviors than untrained mothers, indicating the value of self-control training for parents to program maintenance.

Generality may also be encouraged by reducing the parents' identification with professionals during training. The designers of Project RIP, a program in which parents carry major responsibility for selecting and carrying out the management program for their preschool behavior-disordered children, advocate that, particularly for lower class families, it is necessary to build a system that will be supported by the consumer population by involving the consumers in all phases of the program (Reisinger, Ora, & Frangia, 1976). Some of the evidence from this program suggests that continued use of trained skills may be the result of the amount of independence parents had from professionals during the training program (Reisinger *et al.*, 1976).

Another strategy to promote temporal generality is to insure a high level of training proficiency before termination and to provide additional intensive training if parents do not meet exit criteria at the end of training. Ambrose and Baker (1979) found that parents who continued child programming after training were those who were more proficient in the use of behavioral skills at the time their training terminated.

A two-fold strategy makes use of gradual fading of training plus instructing parents to follow a reimplementation criterion. Hirsch and Altman (1981) described a parent-operated weight-control program for developmentally disabled adolescents. For one family, therapist contact was gradually faded over a 14-month period. The family was to reinstitute the weight-control program whenever a prespecified criterion was reached. Criteria for again terminating the program were also prearranged. Gradual fading of therapist contact permitted problems associated with independent program management to be resolved with minimal assistance. Setting up explicit criteria for reinstituting the treatment program established the realistic expectation that behaviors may never be totally eliminated and effective programs need to be reimplemented.

It is hoped that these suggestions will enhance efforts to program generalization of parent and child behaviors. These are, however, only interim suggestions. Ultimately, only more extensive research efforts will determine an efficient, effective technology for generalization.

Cost-Effectiveness

Although it has often been stated that training parents is a cost-effective strategy for training developmentally disabled children (Baker, 1976; Hayden & Pious, 1979), there is little documentation of this assertion. Little has changed since Johnson and Katz's (1973) review of the parent training literature pointed out that the cost of parent-training programs had been largely ignored. Some studies have indicated a dollar cost of their training programs, for example, $1000 per child per year (Watson & Bassinger, 1974), $600 per child (Frangia & Reisinger, 1979). Others specify the cost not in dollars but in training time, for example, circa 480 hours plus driving time to train four families (Kozloff, 1974). Perhaps the most complete cost-effectiveness data are in studies contrasting various training techniques. Such studies typically indicate number of hours to train parents to some criterion under each training condition (Worland, Carney, Milich, & Grame, 1980) or simply describe the conditions and indicate the number of hours for each training format (Brightman et al., 1978).

It is only recently that accountability has caused the helping professions to examine cost-effectiveness more carefully. There has been little systematic work done with the result that there is no clear definition of the components that must necessarily be studied. In the following discussion, cost-effectiveness is discussed in terms of three components; assessing effectiveness, cost, and the relationship of these two dimensions.

Effectiveness

The determination of effectiveness requires definition of program goals and selection of valid and reliable dependent measures. For behaviorally oriented parent-training programs the definition of goals has not been a problem. For the most part, target behaviors have been clearly specified. However, the selection of outcome measures and the data-collection process have been more difficult.

The outcome measures chosen are, in large part, determined by the objectives of training. Some programs focus primarily upon training the parent and looking for changes either in parent knowledge of behavioral principles or in parent behavior in simulated (O'Dell et al., 1977) or actual training situations. Other studies have used child behavior change as a measure of an adequately trained parent (Mash & Terdal, 1973; Nordquist & Wahler, 1973; Terdal & Buell, 1969). Since we do not have clear guidelines for the most appropriate outcome measure, it seems that multiple measures must be taken. Parents' knowledge of principles and direct measurement of parent and child behavior change seem an appropriate minimum.

Another important consideration is the adequacy of the data collection. In determining effectiveness, some studies rely exclusively on parents for data collection (Cooke, Altman, Shaw, & Blaylock, 1978). Sometimes parents are poor recorders (Herbert & Baer, 1972), and sometimes they are accurate recorders (Hall, Cristler, Cranston, & Tucker, 1970). The safest strategy supplements parent recording with independent observers until accuracy is documented. Care must be taken to find ways of *independently* validating the recording procedure. Numerous studies (Fabry & Reid, 1978; Moore & Bailey, 1973; Reisinger & Ora, 1977) suggest that independent observers entering the natural setting and directly recording behavior result in reactive measures. As Johnson and Lobitz (1974) have shown, parents can make their child look "bad" or "good" if instructed. When the demand characteristics of the situation lead the parents to make their child and themselves look good, as in home follow-up, we cannot be certain of the validity of our measures. Indeed Reisinger and Ora (1977) found that parents felt "pressured to perform" when observers were in the home. The pursuit of more unobtrusive home measurement systems, for example, randomly recorded audio tapes, seems warranted (Arnold *et al.*, 1977).

Cost

Cost can be defined in terms of money or time and should include all costs related to increasing effectiveness (Gross, 1977). Both money and time may be spent by those doing and those receiving training. The labor of the trainer, trainee, and volunteers, as well as the costs of facilities, equipment, and materials must be included in an adequate cost-effectiveness analysis (Yates, 1977). Parents are sometimes considered valuable trainers because they are available and free, but this is an incorrect assumption. The loss in parent income and/or time necessitated by training programs is a "hidden" cost that should be considered. It may be one reason that some investigators consider it extraordinary to have more than 60% of parents, whose children are in a school setting, also participate in a home program on a continuing basis (Fredricks *et al.*, 1976).

Relationship of Cost to Program Effectiveness

Once appropriate dependent measures are identified and the costs, implicit and explicit, are calculated, the cost-effectiveness of a program can be determined. This determination may be done according to a particular formula. Gross (1977) proposed a formula which includes cost per unit of time, for example, days divided by the estimated effectiveness. Effectiveness is rated on a scale of 1 to 5 with 5 being highly effective. Thus, a program which cost $20 per day (including cost of program operation and parents donated time) that was rated 5 (highly effective) would have a cost-effectiveness rating of 20 ÷ 5 = 4.0. Another program with the same cost but a lesser effectiveness rating, 2 for example, would be rated 10. Thus, the higher the rating, the lower the cost-effectiveness. The formula allows comparison between different programs and hence may make program selection more data-based; however, the effectiveness rating remains somewhat subjective.

A good example of a program doing a comprehensive assessment of cost-effectivness is Kovitz (1976). Cost measures included cost to the client in terms of money and time as well as cost to the trainer in contact time and extra time. Parent-training progress measures included attendance, punctuality, and assignments completed. Outcome measures included a test of parents' knowledge of behavioral principles, children's report of parent behavior, development assessment, direct measures of child target behavior, and a satisfaction rating. If direct measures of parent-training behaviors are added, the program described by Kovitz (1976) exemplifies a comprehensive measurement system for a cost-effectiveness analysis.

Summary

The first concern with the effectiveness of training programs for parents of developmentally disabled children is whether parents can change child behavior. It appears that they can, and do. The second question is the durability of this change for both child and parent behavior. Although direct measures of parent behavior are usually lacking, it does appear that approximately one-half of the parents continue some form of training of their childen. Sometimes child behavior changes seem to be durable in spite of parents' failure to continue training.

The third concern is whether parent and child behaviors generalize to other settings, child behaviors, and people. Setting generality for both parent and child behaviors sometimes occurs but cannot be assumed. There is indication that setting generality is enhanced by training it and giving parents feedback about their performance and specific instruction to generalize. One factor implicated in lack of setting generality is admitted marital difficulty.

Transfer of child behavior from school to home and home to school has been reported. Important factors appear to be the number and nature of the training settings, and whether parents also apply training contingencies in other settings.

There is little evidence to indicate whether parents of developmentally disabled children will use their newly acquired training techniques with other children. There is some indication that they do but we have little information about conditions under which they are likely to do so. The children do appear to perform their newly acquired behaviors in the presence of people not present in the training settings.

The best procedures for assessing the cost-effectiveness of programs have not as yet been determined. However, we can specify some of the factors that must be considered. Evaluation of effectiveness requires designation of adequate outcome measures which for parent training include knowledge of principles, direct measurement of parent and child behavior, and extent of parent and, where possible, child satisfaction with the program. Cost requires consideration of not only cost to parent and professional in terms of money and time spent but also of such hidden costs as overhead, program preparation, and parent loss of income by taking time away from work.

Program-Development Methodology

Methodological critiques of the parent-training literature have appeared in a number of literature reviews (Baker, 1976; Johnson & Katz, 1973; McMahon & Forehand, 1980; O'Dell, 1974). Most of these are valid for developmentally disabled children. Rather than repeat those criticisms this section will present a description of an exemplary program-development effort incorporating selected research efforts which have addressed the various components.

A model for the first stage of the development of a parent-training program is provided by the sequence used by Clark, Greene, Macrae, McNees, David, and Risley (1977) for program development and evaluation. They developed and evaluated a parent advice package for family shopping trips. The first step documented an effective procedure in a controlled environment with two families. Direct measures of a number of parent and child behaviors were included. Next, the effective treatment procedures were integrated into a written manual and tested in the natural environment with four families. Close supervision was available and helped to identify problems with the manual. The manual was found to be usable and effective in the natural setting when supplemented with some experimenter redirecting. A third study with four additional families validated the adequacy of the manual used without professional assistance. The durability of behavior change was assessed by direct measurement during later shopping trips. Questionnaires given to parents and children addressed the social validity of the manual and indicated the parents were pleased. The program was found to be usable, effective, and well received by parents and children.

The next step of an exemplary program involves dissemination to a larger group of parents and comparison with control groups. Baker (1977) and his colleagues have conducted the largest tightly controlled evaluation of a commercially available manual (McMahon & Forehand, 1980). The manual has been tested and found effective with large groups of parents. An assessment of the UCLA training program which includes the manual revealed that parents increased their knowledge of behavior principles and teaching proficiency relative to a non-treatment control group (Baker, 1977). The training-program format, group versus individual, was studied. Both formats were superior to non-treatment controls but did not differ from one another. Thus, the group approach with its lesser cost would appear more attractive (Brightman et al., 1978). The effectiveness of the manual with and without supplementary services was also assessed (Heifetz, 1977a). Supplementary services were found to be unnecessary, and the manual alone appeared to be the most cost-effective program for some parents.

Two additional avenues have been pursued by the UCLA project. One direction has been to examine the durability of parent-training efforts through 6- (Ambrose & Baker, 1979) and 12-month follow-up studies (Baker, 1977). These investigations examined maintenance of parent-training efforts and child-behavior gains, and generalization to new training efforts by parents and to skills for children.

Another line of inquiry for the UCLA project has been a more detailed study of parents who have difficulty acquiring and/or maintaining trained skills. Using primarily interview data and post hoc analyses, a number of parent characteristics have been identified which, given the basic training program, appear prognostic of an unsuccessful parent trainer. The intent is to maximize the effectiveness of the basic training program by early or preidentification of those who need different or supplementary training (Clark & Baker, 1979). Indeed preliminary work has shown that additional more extensive training is of benefit for some families (Ambrose & Baker, 1979). Such attempts to identify salient parent behaviors may also permit separation of parents who are not yet ready to begin a parent-training program, for example, because of more pressing survival needs or lack of recognition of the child's problems. Thus, the studies by Baker and colleagues have shown that their program is effective in comparison with untreated controls; that cost-effectiveness of supplementary services and training formats may be estimated; that certain global parent characteristics may be prognostic of failure and indicate a need for a different training program; and that the durability of parent-training efforts in part depends on such variables as the skill level of the parents, the nature of the continued training (formal vs. incidental), and whether the targets were skills or behavior problems.

Another recent methodological advance is the attempt to carefully specify the necessary and sufficient behaviors for achieving acquisition and generalization of child behavior. Koegel et al. (1978) found some training procedures which resulted in acquisition but no generalization and others that produced both. Similar efforts have been conducted by Miller and Sloane (1976) and Handleman (1979). In order for training programs to effect long-term as well as initial behavior change and be efficient, detailed behavioral analyses are essential. Similarly, if programs are not universally effective, we need to clearly specify with whom and under what circumstances they are effective. Koegel et al. (1978), Miller and Sloane (1976), and Handleman (1979) provide a beginning for specifying the circumstances. Thus far, however, attempts to designate the population for which programs are effective have only focused on global characteristics, for example, socioeconomic status, and these have been indirectly assessed. We will eventually need to identify the specific parent *behaviors* that are prerequisites for a particular training program.

To summarize, in the development of parent-training programs the first step must be to document effectiveness, short- and long-term, under tightly controlled circumstances using multiple measures. The next step is to apply the program in more natural situations, but only on a limited basis. If effectiveness, usefulness, and lack of side effects are documented at this point, the program may be packaged and tried on a larger population. Efforts are then directed at pinpointing the population and circumstances under which the program is effective. Supplementary and/or branching programs may be developed for those parents without the requisite behaviors to benefit from the standard treatment package. Finally, a component analysis is conducted, the essential elements are determined, and the package is refined for use by the consumer.

Summary and Conclusions

There are many reasons for training parents of developmentally disabled children. A number of these reasons are shared with all parents, reasons related to availability, potency as sources of reinforcement and ability to prevent additional deficits and problems. Other reasons, unique to parents of developmentally disabled children, relate to the fact that the training needs of their children are long term and often require that more dimensions of the environment be programmed. Also, the expanding role of parents of developmentally disabled children as advocates, decision-makers, and enlightened consumers of child care services dictates that they have more sophistication about training methods.

There are target behaviors that parents of developmentally disabled children share with other parents, but there are also target behaviors that are unique. Parents of developmentally disabled children have remedied a wide range of problem behaviors and trained a variety of skills, including many that traditionally were the province of specialists. When multiple targets are present, there is no single rationale for ordering target-problem behaviors, although knowledge about skill sequences gives some guidelines for selecting the order of new skills to train. There have been a variety of tactics presented for selecting initial target behaviors, such as starting with the easiest, the most interfering, or surveying parent opinion. The limits of what parents can teach are continually expanding. As these behaviors become more complex, we would expect that parents' roles and responsibilities in training their children would likewise change.

Parents of developmentally disabled children are assuming more active, varied, and complex roles in the training of their children. No longer are they passive recipients of services. They provide supplemental training, program home environments to assure maintenance of skills and, very commonly, correct problems not being treated elsewhere. Parents train new skills and learn to prevent new problem behaviors from developing. Less commonly, parents conduct generalization probes and teach other children or parents. There is a greater emphasis being placed on the function of parents as decision makers and educated advocates for their children. There is an increased effort to give parents skills to enable them to design, carry out, and evaluate child-training programs instead of serving merely as applicators of a program designed and conducted by a professional. For some kinds of child problems, the parent-trainer is required to make an extensive commitment to the child's program. What is not addressed in the literature is whether professionals may not sometimes ask a greater commitment from parents than they ask of teachers or therapists, and whether they are justified in doing so. Training these parents to be self-sufficient teachers and therapists reflects the recognition that the problems and deficits of developmentally disabled children are long lasting.

Parents are being taught by a variety of methods, either individually or in groups, apart from the child, and also, directly interacting with the child. In both indirect and direct training, various teaching tools are used. The indirect method has the advantage of lending itself to the use of media and group training. The direct training methods (modeling, rehearsal, and feedback) have advantages with certain parents who are not oriented to didactic methods of information exchange. There are no clear-cut answers about the relative values of the various teaching methods: the best parent-training method will vary with the type of client and whether the primary criterion is effectiveness or efficient use of professional time.

A limitation of the methods by which most parent training occurs is that there is little attention paid to the fact that the behavior of an individual is supported by a family system. In most parent-training programs usually only one family member (generally the mother) is trained to alter the behavior of one child in the family by manipulating contingencies which may not be the major contingencies operating within that family. Patterson and colleagues are among the few who describe programs that get at the child's behavior by altering the relationship between the child's and family's behavior (Patterson, Reid, Jones, & Conger, 1975).

The content of parent training programs should be related to the parent's long-term objective. Some programs have emphasized training specific procedures, while others have focused on general principles. Some preliminary research suggests that training specific procedures is effective but does not produce generalization. Thus, long-term objectives which require generalization of training efforts would necessitate training more general principles. (Note: what consititutes training of general principles varies from program to program. Our remarks are based on the program of Koegel et al., 1978.)

There is a trend toward training efforts which emphasize the parent–child interaction, more complex child behaviors, and multiple-step programs. Self-injurious behavior is the major target for which the training focus remains highly specific.

Parents have been taught to do a variety of tasks including assessment (i.e., describe target behavior and evaluate developmental level), consequation, presention of stimuli, prompting, shaping, and even evaluating the effectiveness of training techniques. Recent research efforts are beginning to specify parent-training behaviors more precisely. For example, use of consequation was further specified into such subcomponents as whether it was immediate, effective, unambiguous, and/or contingent by Koegel et al. (1978). Such precise specification is essential for the standardization, replication, and evaluation of parent-training programs.

Successful recruiting of parents for training requires careful assessment of the family-living situation and the parents' present training skills. In general, we know which broad classes of parents, that is, single parents and those of low socioeconomic status, have been poor risks. However, such information is too general for making clinical decisions. Identification of specific parent entry skills and careful assessment of family situations may permit individually tailored programs with higher success rates.

Once parents have been recruited, maintaining participation in the training program becomes an issue. Many training programs have relied on child progress to maintain parents in training programs. With children who learn slowly and have extensive behavior problems, child progress does not appear to be sufficient to maintain parent behavior. A number of strategies have been cited for aiding maintenance of parent behavior. These include starting with problems that have a high probability of success, training parents with others who will provide support and encouragement, fading contact with professionals gradually, and providing additional incentives, for example, rebates, for parent compliance. What little research has been done suggests that parents will stay in training programs longer when provided with response-contingent consequences, for example, performance feedback.

An area that has received very little attention has been insuring progress during training. Documenting progress with direct measures of parent behavior and the use of specific success criteria for training-program components are the bare essentials for insuring parent progress in training programs.

There are a number of concerns when considering the effectiveness of parent-training programs. The initial one is whether parents can change child behavior. It appears that they can. The second question concerns durability. Although direct measures of parent behavior are usually lacking, it appears that approximately one-half of the parents continue some form of training. Child behavior changes seem to be durable sometimes in spite of the parents' failure to continue training. Since durability of child and parent behavior are not perfectly covariant, it is important to directly measure both.

The third concern about effectiveness is whether parent and child behaviors generalize to other settings, child behaviors, and people. Generalization across these three dimensions does occur, but cannot be assumed. The literature to date only documents a few of the many factors which will either enhance or impede generalization. However, it appears that generalization is more likely to occur when the training includes deliberate programming for it.

A number of potentially valuable techniques for promoting generalization are suggested. These include sequential modification of settings and responses by several trainers, use of sufficient examplars, use of indiscriminable contingencies, provision of stimuli common to training and generalization settings, incorporation of explicit instructions to use procedures across settings, training in self-monitoring techniques, giving direct reinforcement for parental persistence, and gradually fading parent dependence on professionals.

The issue of cost-effectiveness is not well developed in the parent-training literature as yet, although the field has addressed many of the component questions, such as the considerations required to judge effectiveness. There is indication that formulas for determining program cost are being developed which may, in the future, be usefully applied to parent-training efforts.

In place of a methodological critique, which seems premature, we present the following strategy for developing an effective parent-training program. Initially the short- and long-term effectiveness of the program must be documented under tightly controlled circumstances using multiple measures. Next, the program is applied in more natural situations, but still on a limited basis. If effectiveness, usefulness, and lack of side effects are documented, the program is packaged and tried on a larger scale. Analyses are then directed at pinpointing the population and circumstances for which the program is effective. Supplementary and/or branching programs are developed for those without requisite behaviors to benefit from the standard treatment package. Finally, a component analysis is conducted to determine the essential elements, and the package is refined for use by the consumer.

Acknowledgments

The authors wish to thank Ms. Sandy Hoffman for her invaluable assistance in the preparation of this manuscript.

References

Altman, K., Bondy, A., & Hirsh, G. Self-monitoring combined with contingency contracting in weight reduction programs for retarded adolescents with Prader-Willi syndrome. *Journal of Behavioral Medicine*, 1978, *1*, 403–413.

Altman, K., Haavik, S., & Cook, J. W. Punishment of self-injurious behaviour in natural settings using contingent aromatic ammonia. *Behaviour Research and Therapy*, 1978, *16*, 85–96.

Altman, K., Haavik, S., & Woelk, C. Retarded children: An update for physicians on program alternatives. *The Journal of the Kansas Medical Society*, 1978, *79*, 62–63.

Altman, K., Hobbs, S., Roberts, M., & Haavik, S. Control of disruptive behavior by manipulation of reinforcement density and item difficulty subsequent to errors. *Applied Research in Mental Retardation*, 1980, *1*, 193–207.

Ambrose, S. A., & Baker, B. L. Training parents of developmentally disabled children: Follow-up outcome. *Maintenance of treatment effects following behavioral family therapy*. Paper presented at the meeting of the American Psychological Asociation, New York, September 1979.

Arnold, S., Sturgis, E., & Forehand, R. Training a parent to teach communication skills: A case study. *Behavior Modification*, 1977, *1*, 259-276.

Atkeson, B. M., & Forehand, R. Home-based reinforcement programs to modify classroom behavior: A review and methodological evaluation. *Psychological Bulletin*, 1979, *86*, 1298-1308.

Ayllon, T., & Roberts, M. D. Mothers as educators for their children. In T. Thompson & W. S. Dockens (Eds.), *Applications of behavior modification*. New York: Academic Press, 1975.

Badger, E. D. A mother's training program — a sequel article. *Children Today*, 1972, *36*, 7-11.

Baker, B. L. Parent involvement in programming for the developmentally disabled child. In L. L. Lloyd (Ed.), *Communication assessment and intervention*. Baltimore, Md.: University Park Press, 1976.

Baker, B. L. Support systems for the parent as therapist. In P. Mittler, (Ed.), *Research to practice in mental retardation: Care and intervention* (Vol. 1). Baltimore, Md.: University Park Press, 1977.

Baker, B. L., Heifetz, L. J., & Brightman, A. J. *Parents as teachers*. Cambridge, Mass.: Behavioral Education Projects, 1972.

Barnard, J. D., Christophersen, E. R., & Wolf, M. M. Parent-mediated treatment of children's self-injurious behavior using overcorrection. *Pediatric Psychology*, 1976, *1*, 56-61.

Barrett, B. H. Behavior modification in the home: Parents adopt laboratory-developed tactics to bowel-train a 5½ year old. *Psychotherapy: Theory, Research and Practice*, 1969, *6*, 172-176.

Becker, W. C. *Parents are teachers*. Champaign, Ill.: Research Press, 1971.

Beckwith, L. Caregiver-infant interaction as a focus for therapeutic intervention with human infants. In R. N. Walsh & W. T. Greenough (Eds.) *Environments as therapy for brain dysfunction*. New York: Plenum Press, 1976.

Benassi, V. A., & Benassi, B. An approach to teaching behavior modification principles to parents. *Rehabilitation Literature*, 1973, *34*, 134-137.

Berkowitz, B. P., & Graziano, A. M. Training parents as behavior therapists: A review. *Behaviour Research and Therapy*, 1972, *10*, 297-317.

Bernal, M. E., & North, J. A. A survey of parent training manuals. *Journal of Applied Behavior Analysis*, 1978, *11*, 533-544.

Borkowski, J. G., & Cavanaugh, J. C. Maintenance and generalization of skills and strategies by the retarded. In N. R. Ellis (Ed.), *Handbook of mental deficiency, psychological theory and research* (2nd ed.). Hillsdale, N. J.: Lawrence Erlbaum, 1979.

Bricker, D., Bricker, W., Iacino, R., & Dennison, L. Intervention strategies for the severely and profoundly handicapped. In N. G. Haring & L. J. Brown (Eds.), *Teaching the severely handicapped* (Vol. 1). New York: Grune & Stratton, 1976.

Brightman, R. P., Baker, B. L., Clark, D. B., & Ambrose, S. A. *Effectiveness of alternative parent training formats*. Paper presented at the meeting of the Western Psychological Association, San Francisco, April 1978.

Budd, K. S., Green, D. R., & Baer, D. M. An analysis of multiple misplaced parental social contingencies. *Journal of Applied Behavior Analysis*, 1976, *9*, 459-470.

Cairns, G., & Mira, M. *Parent training consultation in a rural community*. Unpublished manuscript, 1979. (Available from Mary Mira, Ph. D., Department of Psychology, Children's Rehabilitation Unit/University Affiliated Facility, University of Kansas Medical Center, 39th and Rainbow Boulevard, Kansas City, Kansas 66103).

Campione, J. C., & Brown, A. L. Memory and metamemory development in educable retarded children. In R. V. Kail, Jr., & J. W. Hagen (Eds.), *Perspectives on the development of memory and cognition*. Hillsdale, N.J.: Lawrence Erlbaum, 1977.

CHILMAN, C. S. Programs for disadvantaged parents: Some major trends and related research. In B. M. Caldwell & H. N. Ricciuti (Eds.), *Review of child development research*. Chicago: University of Chicago Press, 1973.

CHRISTOPHERSEN, E. R., & SYKES, B. W. An intensive, home-based family training program for developmentally delayed children. In L. A. Hammerlynck (Ed.), *Behavioral systems for the developmentally disabled: I. School and family environments*. New York: Brunner/Mazel, 1979.

CLARK, D. B., & BAKER, B. L. Training parents of developmentally disabled children: Prediction of follow-up outcome. In *Maintenance of treatment effects following behavioral family therapy*. Paper presented at the meeting of the American Psychological Association, New York, September 1979.

CLARK, H. B., GREENE, B. G., MACRAE, J. W., MCNEES, M. P., DAVID, J. L., & RISLEY, T. R. A parent–advice package for family shopping trips: Development and evaluation. *Journal of Applied Behavior Analysis*, 1977, *10*, 605–624.

COOK, J. W., ALTMAN, K., & HAAVIK, S. Consent for aversive treatment: A model form. *Mental Retardation*, 1978, *16*, 47–51.

COOK, J. W., ALTMAN, K., SHAW, J., & BLAYLOCK, M. Case histories and shorter communications: Use of contingent lemon juice to eliminate public masturbation by a severely retarded boy. *Behaviour Research and Therapy*, 1978, *16*, 131–134.

DOLEYS, D. M., DOSTER, J., & CARTELLI, L. M. Parent training techniques: Effects of lecture-role playing followed by feedback and self-recording. *Journal of Behavior Therapy and Experimental Psychiatry*, 1976, *7*, 359–362.

EMBRY, L. H., KELLEY, M. L., HERBERT-JACKSON, E., & BAER, D. *Group parent training: An analysis of generalization from classroom to home* (ECI Document 116). Lawrence, Ks.: Kansas Research Institute for Early Childhood Education of the Handicapped, 1979.

EYBERG, S. M., & JOHNSON, S. M. Multiple assessment of behavior modification with families: Effects of contingency contracting and order of treated problems. *Journal of Consulting and Clinical Psychology*, 1974, *42*, 594–606.

FABRY, P. L., & REID, D. H. Teaching foster grandparents to train severely handicapped persons. *Journal of Applied Behavior Analysis*, 1978, *11*, 111–123.

FLANAGAN, S., ADAMS, H. E., & FOREHAND, R. A comparison of four instructional techniques for teaching parents to use time-out. *Behavior Therapy*, 1979, *10*, 94–102.

FOREHAND, R., & ATKESON, B. M. Generality of treatment effects with parents as therapists: A review of assessment and implementation procedures. *Behavior Therapy*, 1977, *8*, 575–593.

FOREHAND, R., & KING, H. E. Noncompliant children: Effects of parent training on behavior and attitude change. *Behavior Modification*, 1977, *1*, 93–108.

FOREHAND, R., & PEED, S. Training parents to modify noncompliant behavior of their children. In A. J. Finch, Jr., & P. C. Kendall (Eds.), *Treatment and research in child psychopathology*. New York: Spectrum, 1979.

FOREHAND, R., CHANEY, T., & YODER, P. Parent behavior training: Effects on the non-compliance of a deaf child. *Journal of Behavior Therapy and Experimental Child Psychiatry*, 1974, *5*, 281–283.

FOREYT, J. P., & PARKS, J. T. Behavioral controls for achieving weight loss in the severely retarded. *Journal of Behavior Therapy and Experimental Psychiatry*, 1975, *6*, 27–29.

FRAIBERG, S., SMITH, M., & ADELSON, E. An educational program for blind infants. *Journal of Special Education*, 1969, *3*, 121–140.

FRANGIA, G. W., & REISINGER, J. J. Parent implementation of a preschool intervention system. *Journal of Clinical Child Psychology*, 1979, *8*, 64–68.

FRANKEL, R. Parents as evaluators of their retarded youngsters. *Mental Retardation*, 1979, *17*, 40-42.

FRAZIER, J. R., & SCHNEIDER, H. Parental management of inappropriate hyperactivity in a young retarded child. *Journal of Behavior Therapy and Experimental Psychiatry*, 1975, *6*, 246-247.

FREDRICKS, H. D., BALDWIN, V. L., & GROVE, D. A home-center based parent training mode. In D. L. Lillie, F. L. Trohanis, & K. W. Goin (Eds.), *Teaching parents to teach*. New York: Walker, 1976.

GALLOWAY, C., & GALLOWAY, K. C. Parent classes in precise behavior management. *Teaching Exceptional Children*, 1971, *3*, 120-128.

GARDNER, J. M. Training parents as behavior modifiers. In S. Yen & R. W. McIntire (Eds.), *Teaching behavior modification*. Kalamazoo, Mich.: Behaviordelia, 1976.

GELFAND, D. M., & HARTMANN, D. P. The prevention of childhood behavior disorders. In B. B. Lahey & A. E. Kazdin (Eds.), *Advances in clinical child psychology* (Vol. 1). New York: Plenum Press, 1977.

GENTRY, W. D. Parents as modifiers of somatic disorders. In E. J. Mash, L. C. Handy, & L. A. Hamerlynck (Eds.), *Behavior modification approaches to parenting*. New York: Brunner/Mazel, 1976.

GOLDSTEIN, S. B., & LANYON, R. I. Parent-clinicians in the language training of an autistic child. *Journal of Speech and Hearing Disorders*, 1971, *36*, 552-560.

GRAY, S. W., & KLAUS, R. A. The early training project: A seventh year report. *Child Development*, 1970, *41*, 909-924.

GREEN, D. R., BUDD, K., JOHNSON, M., LANG, S., PINKSTON, E., & RUDD, S. Training parents to modify problem child behaviors. In E. J. Mash, L. C. Handy, & L. A. Hamerlynck (Eds.), *Behavior modification approaches to parenting*. New York: Brunner/Mazel, 1976.

GROSS, A. M. The use of cost-effectiveness analysis in deciding on alternative living environments for the retarded. In P. Mittler (Ed.), *Research to practice in mental retardation: Care and intervention* (Vol. 1). Baltimore: University Park Press, 1977.

HAAVIK, S., SPRADLIN, J., & ALTMAN, K. *Programming generalization of developmental skills of retarded children across trainers, school and home settings*. Unpublished manuscript, 1980. (Available from Karl Altman, Ph. D., Department of Psychology, Children's Rehabilitation Unit/University Affiliated Facility, University of Kansas Medical Center, 39th and Rainbow Boulevard, Kansas City, Kansas 66103.)

HAAVIK, S., ALTMAN, K., & WOELK, C. Effects of the Feingold diet on seizures and hyperactivity: A single subject analysis. *Journal of Behavioral Medicine*, 1979, *2*, 365-374.

HALL, M. C., GRINSTEAD, J., COLLIER, H., & HALL, R. V. *Responsive parenting: A preventative program which incorporates parents training parents*. Paper presented at the meeting of the Association for the Advancement of Behavior Therapy, Chicago, December 1978.

HALL, M. C., & NELSON, D. J. *Responsive parenting: An economical approach for teaching single-parenting skills*. Unpublished manuscript, 1980. (Available from Marilyn Clark Hall, Ph. D., Responsive Parenting Program, Crestview Elementary School, 6101 Craig Road, Shawnee Mission, Kansas 66202.)

HALL, R. V. *Managing behavior* (Vol. 2). Lawrence, Ks.: H. & H. Enterprises, 1971.

HALL, R. V., & BRODEN, M. Helping teachers and parents to modify behavior of their retarded and behavior-disordered children. In P. Mittler (Ed.), *Research to practice in mental retardation: Education and training* (Vol. 2). Baltimore: Univeristy Park Press, 1977.

HALL, R. V., CRISTLER, C., CRANSTON, S. S., & TUCKER, B. Teachers and parents as researchers using multiple-baseline designs. *Journal of Applied Behavior Analysis*, 1970, *3*, 247-255.

HALL, R. V., AXELROD, S., TYLER, L., GRIEF, E., JONES, F. C., & ROBERTSON, R. Modification of behavior problems in the home with a parent as observer and experimenter. *Journal of Applied Behavior Analysis*, 1972, *5*, 53-64.

HAMILTON, D. C. The treatment of enuresis. In S. M. O'Neil, B. N. McLaughlin, & M. B. Knapp (Eds.), *Behavioral approaches to children with development delays*. St. Louis: C. B. Mosby, 1977.

HANDLEMAN, J. S. Generalization by autistic-type children of verbal responses across settings. *Journal of Applied Behavior Analysis*, 1979, *12*, 273–282.

HANF, C., & KLING, J. *Facilitating parent–child interaction: A two stage training model*. Unpublished manuscript, 1973. (Available from the University of Oregon Medical School, Portland, Oregon 97201.)

HARRIS, S. L. Teaching language to nonverbal children with emphasis on problems of generalization. *Psychological Bulletin*, 1975, *82*, 563–580.

HARRIS, S. L., & ROMANCZYK, R. G. Treating self-injurious behavior of a retarded child by overcorrection. *Behavior Therapy*, 1976, *7*, 235–239.

HAUS, B. G., & THOMPSON, S. The effect of nursing intervention on a program of behavior modification by parents in the home. *Journal of Psychiatric Nursing and Mental Health Services*, 1976, *14*, 9–16.

HAWKINS, R. P. Universal parenthood-training: A proposal for preventive mental health. *Educational Technology*, 1971, *11*, 28–35.

HAWKINS, R. P., PETERSON, R. F., SCHWEID, E., & BIJOU, S. W. Behavior therapy in the home: Amelioration of problem parent–child relations with the parent in a therapeutic role. *Journal of Experimental Child Psychology*, 1966, *4*, 99–107.

HAYDEN, A. H. A center-based parent-training model. In D. L. Lillie, P. L. Trohanis, & K. W. Goin (Eds.), *Teaching parents to teach*. New York: Walker, 1976.

HAYDEN, A. H., & PIOUS, C. G. The case for early intervention. In R. L. York & E. Edgar (Eds.), *Teaching the severely handicapped* (Vol. 4). Seattle: American Association for the Education of the Severely/Profoundly Handicapped, 1979.

HEBER, R., & GARBER, H. The Milwaukee project: A study of the use of family intervention to prevent cultural-familial mental retardation. In B. Z. Friedlander, G. M. Sterritt, & G. E. Kirk, (Eds.), *Exceptional infant: Assessment and intervention* (Vol. 3). New York: Brunner/Mazel, 1975.

HEIFETZ, L. J. Behavioral training for parents of retarded children: Alternative formats based on instructional manuals. *American Journal of Mental Deficiency*, 1977, *82*, 194–203. (a)

HEIFETZ, L. J. Professional preciousness and the evolution of parent-training strategies. In P. Mittler, (Ed.), *Research to practice in mental retardation: Care and intervention* (Vol. 1). Baltimore: University Park Press, 1977. (b)

HERBERT, E. W., & BAER, D. M. Training parents as behavior modifiers: Self-recording of contingent attention. *Journal of Applied Behavior Analysis*, 1972, *5*, 139–149.

HIRSCH, G., & ALTMAN, K. Maintenance of programmed weight loss in Prader-Willi syndrome patients. In V. Holm, S. I. Sulzbacher, P. L. Pipes, & M. J. Steffes (Eds.), *The Prader-Willi syndrome*. Baltimore: University Park Press, 1981.

HOBBS, N. The parent and the professional, Appendix A. *The Futures of Children*. San Francisco: Josey-Bass, 1975.

HOLMBERG, N. J. Mark learns to imitate after behavioral interferences are reduced. In S. M. O'Neill, B. N. McLaughlin, & M. B. Knapp (Eds.), *Behavioral approaches to children with developmental delays*. St. Louis: C. B. Mosby Co., 1977.

HOOVER, L. Teaching behavior modification techniques to parents of hearing handicapped children. In J. B. Miller (Ed.), *A demonstration home training program for parents of preschool deaf children*. Kansas City, Ks.: University of Kansas Medical Center, 1970. (ERIC Document Reproduction Service No. ED 058 697.)

HUMPHREYS, L., FOREHAND, R., MCMAHON, R., & ROBERTS, M. Parent behavioral training to modify child noncompliance: Effects on untreated siblings. *Journal of Behavior Therapy and Experimental Psychiatry*, 1978, *9*, 235–238.

Hunt, S., & Sulzer-Azaroff, B. *The effect of verbal and graphic feedback on parent consistency in running homework sessions with their children.* Paper presented at the meeting of the American Psychological Association, New Orleans, August 1974.

Inglis, S. The effects of maternal attitudes on a home management program. In S. M. O'Neil, B. N. Mclaughlin, & M. B. Knapp (Eds.), *Behavioral approaches to children with developmental delays.* St. Louis: C. B. Mosby, 1977.

Jeffree, D. M., McConkey, R., & Hewson, S. A parental involvement project. In P. Mittler (Ed.), *Research to practice in mental retardation: Care and intervention* (Vol. 1). Baltimore: University Park Press, 1977.

Johnson, C. A., & Katz, R. C. Using parents as change agents for their children: A review. *Journal of Child Psychology and Psychiatry*, 1973, *14*, 181-200.

Johnson, M. R., Whitman, T. L., & Barloon-Noble, R. A home-based program for a preschool behaviorally disturbed child with parents as therapists. *Journal of Behavior Therapy and Experimental Psychiatry*, 1978, *9*, 65-70.

Johnson, S. M., & Lobitz, G. K. Parental manipulation of child behavior in home observations. *Journal of Applied Behavior Analysis*, 1974, *7*, 23-31.

Kaufman, K. F., Villani, T. V., Bakalor, J., Price, G. H., Prinz, R. J., Paradise, B., & Tyson, R. *Systematic evaluation of comprehensive training for parents of autistic children.* Paper presented at the meeting of the American Psychological Association, San Francisco, August 1977.

Kazdin, A. E. Issues in behavior modification with mentally retarded persons. *American Journal of Mental Deficiency*, 1973, *78*, 134-140.

Koegel, R. L., Glahn, T. J., & Nieminen, G. S. Generalization of parent-training results. *Journal of Applied Behavior Analysis*, 1978, *11*, 95-109.

Kogan, K. L., & Tyler, N. Mother-child interactions in young physically handicapped children. *American Journal of Mental Deficiency*, 1973, *77*, 492-497.

Kogan, K. L., Wimberger, H. C., & Bobbitt, R. A. Analysis of mother-child interaction in young mental retardates. *Child Development*, 1969, *40*, 799-812.

Kovitz, K. E. Comparing group and individual methods for training parents in child management techniques. In E. J. Mash, L. C. Handy, & L. A. Hamerlynck (Eds.), *Behavioral modification approaches to parenting.* New York: Brunner/Mazel, 1976.

Kozloff, M. A. *Reaching the autistic child: A parent training program.* Champaign, Ill.: Research Press, 1973.

Kozloff, M. A. *Educating children with learning and behavior problems.* New York: Wiley, 1974.

Kozloff, M. A. *A program for families of children with learning and behavior problems.* New York: Wiley, 1979.

Krupsaw, R., & Altman, K. *Suppressing the aggressive-destructive behavior of a retarded adolescent by a delayed overcorrection procedure.* Paper presented at the meeting of the Association for Behavior Analysis, Dearborn, Michigan, May 1980.

Kysela, G. M., Daly, K., Doxsey-Whitfield, M., Hillyard, A., McDonald, L., McDonald, S., & Taylor, J. The early education project. In L. A. Hamerlynck (Ed.), *Behavioral systems for the developmentally disabled: School and family environments* (Vol. 1). New York: Brunner/Mazel, 1979.

Lance, W. D., & Koch, A. C. Parents as teachers: Self-help skills for young handicapped children. *Mental Retardation*, 1973, *11*, 3-4.

Levitt, E., & Cohen, S. Educating parents of children wtih special needs. Approaches and issues. *Young Children*, 1976, *31*, 263-272.

Lindsley, O. R. An experiment with parents handling behavior at home. *Johnstone Bulletin*, 1966, *9*, 27-36.

Longin, N. S., Cone, J. D., & Longin, H. E. Training behavior modifiers: Parents' behavioral and attitudinal changes following general and specific training. *Mental Retardation*, 1975, *13*(5), 42. (Abstract)

Longin, N. S., Longin, H. E., & Cone, J. D. *Training parents to facilitate expressive language in their severely retarded children.* Paper presented at the meeting of the Association for the Advancement of Behavior Therapy, San Francisco, December 1975.

Lovaas, O. I., & Newsom, C. D. Behavior modification with psychotic children. In H. Leitenberg (Ed.), *Handbook of behavior modification and behavior therapy.* Englewood Cliffs, N.J.: Prentice-Hall, 1976.

Lovaas, O.I., Koegel, R., Simmons, J. Q., & Long, J. S. Some generalization and follow-up measures on autistic children in behavior therapy. *Journal of Applied Behavior Analysis*, 1973, *6*, 131-166.

Mahoney, K., Van Wagener, R. K., & Meyerson, L. Toilet training of normal and retarded children. *Journal of Applied Behavior Analysis*, 1971, *4*, 173-181.

Marshall, N. R., Hegrenes, J. R., & Goldstein, S. Verbal interactions: Mothers and their retarded children vs. mothers and their nonretarded children. *American Journal of Mental Deficiency*, 1973, *77*, 415-419.

Mash, E. J., & Terdal, L. Modification of mother-child interactions: Playing with children. *Mental Retardation*, 1973, *11*, 44-49.

Mash, E. J., & Terdal, L. G. After the dance is over: Some issues and suggestions for follow-up assessment in behavior therapy. *Psychological Reports*, 1977, *41*, 1287-1308.

Mash, E. J., Lazere, R., Terdal, L., & Garner, A. Modification of mother-child interactions: A modeling approach for groups. *Child Study Journal*, 1973, *3*, 131-143.

Mathis, H. I., Training a "disturbed" boy using the mother as therapist: A case study. *Behavior Therapy*, 1971, *2*, 233-239.

McConkey, R., & Jeffree, D. M. Partnership with parents. *Special Education: Forward Trends*, 1975, *2*, 13.

McMahon, R. J., & Forehand, R. Self-help behavior therapies in parent training. In B. B. Lahey & A. E. Kazdin (Eds.), *Advances in clinical child psychology* (Vol. 3). New York: Plenum Press, 1980.

Mealiea, W. L., Jr. Conjoint-behavior therapy: The modification of family constellations. In E. J. Mash, L. C. Handy, & L. C. Hamerlynck (Eds.), *Behavior modification approaches to parenting.* New York: Brunner/Mazel, 1976.

Merbaum, M. The modification of self-destructive behavior by a mother-therapist using aversive stimulation. *Behavior Therapy*, 1973, *4*, 442-447.

Miller, H. R., Patton, M. E., & Henton, K. R. Behavior modification in a profoundly retarded child: A case report. *Behavior Therapy*, 1971, *2*, 375-384.

Miller, S. J., & Sloane, H. N., Jr. The generalization effects of parent training across stimulus settings. *Journal of Applied Behavioral Analysis*, 1976, *9*, 355-370.

Mindell, C., & Budd, K. S. *Issues in the generalization of parent training across settings.* Paper presented at the meeting of the American Psychological Association, San Francisco, August 1977.

Mira, M. Results of a behavior modification training program for parents and teachers. *Behavior Research and Therapy*, 1970, *8*, 309-311.

Mira, M. Behavior modification applied to training young deaf children. *Exceptional Children*, 1972, *39*, 225-229.

Mira, M. Facilitation of development in high risk children. In *Pediatrics: Focus on developmental disabilities.* Symposium presented at the University of Kansas College of Health Sciences, Department of Continuing Education, Kansas City, Kansas, March 1978.

Mira, M., & Cairns, G. *Caregiver/child interaction: A target for intervention.* Paper presented at the meeting of the American Association of Mental Deficiency, Denver, May 1978.

Mira M., & Cairns, G. *A handbook of positive parenting*. Kansas City, Missouri: Child Behavior and Development Consultants, 1979.

Mira, M., & Cairns, G. Intervention in the interaction of a mother and child with nonorganic failure to thrive. *Pediatric Nursing*, 1981, 7, 41–46.

Mira, M., & Hoffman, S. Educational programming for multihandicapped deaf–blind children. *Exceptional Children*, 1974, 40, 513–514.

Mock, L. Dave learns to dress himself. In S. M. O'Neil, B. N. Mclaughlin, & M. B. Knapp (Eds.), *Behavioral approaches to children with developmental delays*. St. Louis: C. B. Mosby Co., 1977.

Moore, B. L., & Bailey, J. S. Social punishment in the modification of a pre-school child's "autistic-like" behavior with a mother as therapist. *Journal of Applied Behavior Analysis*, 1973, 6, 497–507.

Nordquist, V. M., & Wahler, R. G. Naturalistic treatment of an autistic child. *Journal of Applied Behavior Analysis*, 1973, 6, 79–87.

O'Connel, C. Y. The challenge of parent education. *Exceptional Children*, 1975, 41, 554–556.

O'Dell, S. Training parents in behavior modification: A review. *Psychological Bulletin*, 1974, 81, 418–433

O'Dell, S., Flynn, J., & Benlolo, L. A comparison of parent training techniques in child behavior modification. *Journal of Behavior Therapy and Experimental Psychiatry*, 1977, 8, 261–268.

Ora, J. P., & Reisinger, J. J. *Preschool intervention: A behavior service delivery system*. Paper presented at the meeting of the Amerian Psychological Association, Washington, D. C., September 1971.

Page, E. B. Miracle in Milwaukee: Raising the IQ. *Educational Researcher*, 1972, 1, 434–446.

Patterson, G. R., & Guillion, M. E. *Living with children*. Champaign, Ill.: Research Press, 1968.

Patterson, G. R., McNeal, S., Hawkins, N., & Phelps, R. Reprogramming the social environment. *Journal of Child Psychology and Psychiatry*, 1967, 8, 181–195.

Patterson, G. R., Reid, J. B., Jones, R. R., & Conger, R. E. *A social learning approach to family intevention*. (Vol. 1). *Families with aggressive children*. Eugene, Or.: Castalia Publishing, 1975.

Peed, S., Roberts, M. W., & Forehand, R. Evaluation of the effectiveness of a standardized parent training program in altering the interaction of mothers and their noncompliant children. *Behavior Modification*, 1977, 1, 223–250.

Penistone, E. *An evaluation of the Portage project*. Unpublished manuscript, 1972. (Available from The Portage Project, Cooperative Educational Service Agency No. 12, Portage, Wisconsin.)

Ramey, C. T., Collier, A. M., Sparling, J. J., Loda, F. A., Campbell, F. A., Ingram, D. L., & Finkelstein, N. W. The Carolina abecedarian project: A longitudinal and multidisciplinary approach to the prevention of developmental retardation. In T. D. Tjossem (Ed.), *Intervention strategies for high risk infants and young children*. Baltimore: University Park Press, 1976.

Ramey, C. T., & Gowen, J. W. *Maternal characteristics and intellectual development: Implications for parent education to prevent sociocultural mental retardation*. Paper presented at the meeting of the American Psychological Association, New York, September 1979.

Ramey, C. T., Starr, R. H., Pallas, J., Whitten, C. F., & Reed, V. Nutrition, response-contingent stimulation, and the maternal deprivation syndrome: Results of an early intervention program. *Merrill-Palmer Quarterly*, 1975, 21, 45–53.

Redd, W. H., & Birnbrauer, J. S. Adults as discriminative stimuli for different reinforcement contingencies with retarded children. In R. Ulrich, T. Stachnik, & J. Mabry (Eds.), *Control of human behavior* (Vol. 2). Glenview, Ill.: Scott, Foresman, 1970.

REISINGER, J. J., FRANGIA, G. W., & HOFFMAN, E. H. Toddler management training generalization and marital status. *Journal of Behavior Therapy and Experimental Psychiatry*, 1976, 7, 335-340.

REISINGER, J. J., & ORA, J. P. Parent-child clinic and home interaction during toddler management training. *Behavior Therapy*, 1977, 8, 771-786.

REISINGER, J. J., ORA, J. P., & FRANGIA, G. W. Parents as change agents for their children. A review. *Journal of Community Psychology*, 1976, 4, 103-123.

REVILL, S., & BLUNDEN, R. A home training service for preschool developmentally handicapped children. *Behaviour Research and Therapy*, 1979, 17, 207-214.

RINER, L. S., & BUDD, K. S. Generalized improvements in child compliance following parent training. In *Generalization issues in behavioural parent training*. Paper presented at the meeting of the Association for the Advancement of Behavior Therapy, Atlanta, November 1977.

RISLEY, T. R. Jenny Lee: Learning and lollipops. *Psychology Today*, 1968, 1, 28-31; 62-65.

RISLEY, T. R., & WOLF, M. M. Experimental manipulation of autistic behaviors and generalization into the home. In S. W. Bijou & D. M. Baer (Eds.), *Child development readings in experimental analysis*. New York: Appleton-Century-Crofts, 1967.

RISLEY, T., & WOLF, M. Establishing functional speech in echolalic children. In H. N. Sloane, Jr., & B. D. Macaulay (Eds.), *Operant procedures in remedial speech and language trainning* Boston: Houghton Mifflin, 1968.

ROTATORI, A. F., FOX, R., & SWITZKY, H. A parent-teacher administered weight reduction program for obese Down's syndrome adolescents. *Journal of Behavior Therapy and Experimental Psychiatry*, 1979, 10, 339-341.

SALZINGER, K., FELDMAN, R. S., & PORTNOY, S. Training parents of brain-injured children in the use of operant procedures. *Behavior Therapy*, 1970, 1, 4-32.

SCHUMAKER, J. B., & SHERMAN, J. A. Parent as intervention agent. In R. L. Schiefelbusch (Ed.), *Language intervention strategies*. Baltimore: University Park Press, 1978.

SEITZ, S., & MARCUS, S. Mother-child interactions: A foundation for language development. *Exceptional Children*, 1976, 42, 445-449.

SEITZ, S., & RIEDELL, G. Parent-child interactions as the therapy target. *Journal of Communication Disorders*, 1974, 7, 295-304.

SHEARER, D. E., & SHEARER, M. S. The Portage project: A model for early childhood intervention. In T. D. Tjossem (Ed.), *Intervention strategies for high risk infants and young children*. Baltimore: University Park Press, 1976.

SHEARER, M. S. A home-based parent-training model. In D. L. Lillie, F. L. Trohanis, & K. W. Goin (Eds.) *Teaching parents to teach*. New York, Walker, 1976.

SHEARER, M. S., & SHEARER, D. E. The Portage project: A model for early childhood education. *Exceptional Children*, 1972, 36, 210-217.

SPARLING, J., LOWMAN, B., LEWIS, I., & BARTEL, B. *What parents say about their information needs*. Progress report to ACYF (Administration for Children, Youth, and Families), 1978.

STOKES, T. F., & BAER, D. M. An implicit technology of generalization. *Journal of Applied Behavior Analysis*, 1977, 10, 349-367.

STOKES, T. F., BAER, D. M., & JACKSON, R. L. Programming the generalization of a greeting response in four retarded children. *Journal of Applied Behavior Analysis*, 1974, 7, 599-610.

TAVORMINA, J. B. Relative effectiveness of behavioral and reflective group counseling with parents of mentally retarded children. *Journal of Consulting and Clinical Psychology*, 1975, 43, 22-31.

TERDAL, L., & BUELL, J. Parent education in managing retarded children with behavior deficits and inappropriate behaviors. *Mental Retardation*, 1969, 7, 10-13.

TERDAL, L., JACKSON, R. H., & GARNER, A. M. Mother-child intractions: A comparison between normal and developmentally delayed groups. In E. J. Mash, L. A. Hamerlynck, & L. C. Handy (Eds.), *Behavior modification and families*. New York: Brunner/Mazel, 1976.

Thompson, T., & Young, A. Behavioral counseling of the parents of retarded children. In T. Thomspon & J. Grabowski (Eds.), *Behavior modification of mentally retarded*. New York: Oxford University Press, 1977.

Valett, R. E. *Modifying children's behavior: A guide for parents and professionals*. Belmont, Calif.: Fearon, 1969.

Wahler, R. G. Some structural aspects of deviant child behavior. *Journal of Applied Behavior Analysis*, 1975, *8*, 27–42.

Wahler, R. G. Deviant child behavior within the family: Developmental speculations and behavior change strategies. In H. Leitenberg (Ed.), *Handbook of behavior modification and behavior therapy*. Englewood Cliffs, N.J.: Prentice-Hall, Inc., 1976.

Walder, L. O., Cohen, S. I., Breiter, D. E., Datson, P. G., Hirsch, I.S., & Leibowitz, J. M. Teaching behavioral principles to parents of disturbed children. In B. G. Guerney (Ed.), *Psychotherapeutic agents: New roles for nonprofessionals, parents and teachers*. New York: Holt, Rinehart & Winston, 1969.

Warfield, G. J. Mothers of retarded children review a parent education program. *Exceptional Children*, 1975, *41*, 559–562.

Watson, L. S. *How to use behavior modification with mentally retarded and autistic children: Programs for administrators, teachers, parents and nurses*. Columbus, Ohio: Behavior Modification Technology, Inc., 1972.

Watson, L. S., & Bassinger, J. F. Parent training technology: A potential service delivery system. *Mental Retardation*, 1974, *12*, 3–10.

Weinrott, M. R., Bauske, B. W., & Patterson, C. R. Systematic replication of a social learning approach to parent training. In P. Sjoden, S. Bates, & W. S. Dockens, III (Eds.), *Trends in behavior therapy*. New York: Academic Press, 1979.

Wells, K. C., Griest, D. L., & Forehand, R. The use of a self-control package to enhance temporal generality of a parent-training program. *Behaviour Research and Therapy*, 1980, *18*, 347–353.

Whitehurst, G. J., Novak, G., & Zorn, G. A. Delayed speech studied in the home. *Developmental Psychology*, 1972, *2*, 169–177.

Williams, J. L., & Jaffa, E. B. *Ice cream, poker chips, and very goods: A behavior modification manual for parents*. College Park, Md.: Maryland Book Exchange, 1971.

Wolf, M., Risley, T., & Mees, H. Application of operant conditioning procedures to the behavior problems of an autistic child. *Behaviour Research and Therapy*, 1964, *1*, 305–312.

Worland, J., Carney, R., Milich, R., & Grame, C. Does in-home training add to the effectiveness of operant group parent training? A 2-year evaluation. Unpublished manuscript, 1980. Washington University, School of Medicine, St. Louis, Missouri.

Yates, B. T. A cost–effectiveness analysis of a residential treatment program for behaviorally disturbed children. In P. Mittler (Ed.), *Research to practice in mental retardation: Care and intervention* (Vol. 1). Baltimore: University Park Press, 1977.

10 Socioecological Programming of the Mentally Retarded

Michael L. Jones, James E. Favell, and Todd R. Risley

The 1970s have been referred to as the "decade of litigation" (Anderson, Greer, & Dietrich, 1976) in describing the reforms mandated by court rulings (most notably, *Wyatt* v. *Stickney,* 1972) and subsequent federal law (e.g., Education for all Handicapped Children Act of 1975), providing for the care and treatment of the mentally retarded. One solution has been a move toward deinstitutionalization, as evidenced by a steady growth in the number of community-based treatment programs over the past decade (Lent, 1978; Zigler & Balla, 1977). However, these programs are typically limited to the less handicapped because of entrance requirements (e.g., self-help skills, absence of problem behaviors) and the need for specialized services (e.g., frequent medical monitoring) for the more handicapped, which may not be readily available in the community.

Although it is not theoretically essential or preferred, continued institutionalization is currently the only alternative for most of the profoundly mentally retarded (Birnbrauer, 1976; Miller, 1975), and especially for those profoundly mentally retarded persons who exhibit multiple physical, sensory and/or neurological impairments (Berkson & Landesman-Dwyer, 1977; Miller, 1976). With continued improvements in medical care, an increased number of these profoundly multiply handicapped individuals survive beyond infancy and childhood (Landesman-Dwyer, 1974) to enter institutions. Moreover, there has been a steady decline in the mortality rate of these individuals residing in institutions (Conley, 1973). As a result, the proportion of profound-

---

Michael L. Jones, James E. Favell, and Todd R. Risley • Western Carolina Center, Morganton, North Carolina 28655. This research was supported by Grant HD 10953 from the National Institute of Child Health and Human Development.

ly multiply handicapped clients in institutions has increased, and this trend is likely to continue.

Although the mandate to provide habilitative programming for *all* mentally retarded persons is clear, the goals of habilitation for the profoundly multiply handicapped and the technology for attaining these goals are much less apparent (Landesman-Dwyer & Sackett, 1978). The fact remains, however, that habilitative programming must be provided, and in the majority of cases, habilitation must be attempted within the context of an institutional environment.

The Institution as a Habilitative Environment

Every man-made environment is designed for a specific purpose. The ecology is planned to evoke certain behaviors and to provide access to certain experiences. Educational environments for students at all levels have been well researched (e.g., Gump, 1974; Krantz & Risley, 1977; Lot & Sommer, 1967; Montes & Risley, 1975), and are designed to facilitate the acquisition of skills by promoting behaviors that are essential to learning.

For example, the educational preschool setting is equipped with childsize furniture and rugs for playing on the floor. Windows are low to facilitate looking outside, and entertaining materials are presented on low, open shelves to encourage selection and play (Montes & Risley, 1975). In short, the physical environment is designed to optimize exploration and the initiation of interactions—behaviors that promote new learning (Hart & Risley, 1976). During activities that call for increased attending (e.g., demonstration projects) the environment may be organized to enhance attending by the arrangement of children's desks or chairs (Krantz & Risley, 1977).

The ecology of an educational setting is complimented by the selection and sequencing of activities which will facilitate learning. For the preschooler, story time sets the occasion to acquire and practice attending skills; structured play activities provide opportunities to improve fine and gross motor skills. Periods of structured instruction are interspersed with ample periods of free time, during which opportunities to explore and interact with the environment and to socialize with peers are available. This free time is characterized as educational because children have the opportunity to elaborate and generalize skills through self-initiated practice (Hart & Risley, 1976). The teacher may also utilize these child-initiated activities as incidental-teaching opportunities (Hart & Risley, 1975). Similarly, the sequencing of vigorous and sedentary activities may be arranged to facilitate attending during instructional periods and to reduce the disruption of transition between activities (Krantz & Risley, 1977).

The institutional environment to which many profoundly multiply handicapped persons are confined is also designed for a specific purpose—to promote ongoing health care, not learning. In fact, these clients are frequently prohibited from exploring and interacting with the environment for their own health and safety and to facilitate the staff's ability to provide health care. Clients are confined to bed or wheelchairs during much or all of the day; toys and materials, if present at all, are kept safely out of reach to prevent the possibility of breakage and subsequent injury to the client.

Because of the limited number of staff and the extent of health care often required, the majority of staff time is spent providing basic care, feeding clients, dispensing medical treatments, and generally maintaining a hospital-like order to the environment. Socialization between staff and clients is minimal, in part due to the low ratio of staff to clients, but also because of the general lack of intrinsic reinforcement provided from working with these clients. Interactions with clients, when they occur, are usually characterized by staff performing some activity for clients, rather than encouraging independent behavior.

Habilitative programming is typically provided by specialists (e.g., physical, occupational or recreational therapists, special education teachers or teacher's aides) rather than caregivers, and involves removing the client from his residential environment (where opportunities for learning are virtually nonexistent) to an "enriched" treatment or classroom. Here, the client is put through a prescribed training sequence and returned to the residential environment, to spend his "free time" until the next habilitative or health care activity is administered. Frequently, the enriched habilitative environment varies little from the residential setting in that opportunities to explore and interact remain limited. Instead, the client is required to follow instructions or passively participate in the ongoing treatment, and the opportunity to practice those behaviors being trained is denied.

The end result is that client habilitation is attempted in a totally nonhabilitative environment. Unfortunately, this is the approach adopted by many institutions when pressed to provide habilitative services. It is understandable that developmental gains among clients are insignificant, transient, or nonexistent, that training activities become ritualistic and are continued for the sole benefit of complying with regulatory standards, and ultimately, that some professionals have concluded the profoundly mutliply handicapped may be incapable of learning functional skills (Ellis, 1979; Professional Advisory Committee, 1979).

Thus, the problems with habilitation for the profoundly multiply handicapped as it has been attempted in the institutional environment should be apparent. The solution, as we perceive it, is twofold; in addition to research investigating specific treatment techniques for this population, there is clearly a need for research investigating the optimal environment within which to apply these techniques.

This chapter will focus on the latter areas of research. Our intent is to delineate those environmental factors which affect the quality of habilitative services and to describe some of our efforts directed toward establishing a technology for manipulating these variables to improve the quality of services. We should stress from the onset that the work presented here is by no means definitive; this remains a very dynamic area of research. Our research is presented only as an example, and with the hope that it will serve as a stimulus for continued development of this technology.

A Socioecological Approach to Service Delivery

For the past five years, we have been involved in a project to develop a habilitative training model for profoundly multiply handicapped clients in an institutional setting. This work represents an extension of previous research conducted by the Living Environments Group (Risley, 1977), which has investigated educational environments for infants, toddlers and preschoolers, recreational environments for underprivileged youth and nursing-care environments for the aged.

Our model is based on the premise that the success of any service delivery system, regardless of orientation, depends on the support provided by the physical and social dimensions of the client's living environment. Berkson and Landesman-Dwyer (1977) refer to the physical and social characteristics of the environment as the social ecology; thus, the manipulation of these environmental variables to improve services may be termed *socioecological programming*. It is important to stress that socioecological programming refers exclusively to the physical and social aspects of the environment, and their effect on service delivery by staff and client habilitation. In this chapter, we will be concerned only with the environmental *context* of service delivery and will omit any discussion of service *content* (e.g., specific treatment techniques or curricula). The technology of socioecological programming is applicable to the habilitative process, regardless of its content.

The institutional living environment must provide support for a number of concurrently existing (and often conflicting) needs of both client and caregiver. Boles and Bible (1978) noted that minimally, the living environment serves as school, hospital, home, work setting, community, and laboratory for the client, who is expected to behave as student, patient, family member, employee, friend, and subject. Whereas the caregiver must fill the role of teacher, nurse's aide, family member, work supervisor, friend, and researcher, depending on the activities occurring in the environment. Simply stated, the goal of socioecological programming is to maintain a balance between these various needs, to provide an optimal service environment for both clients and caregivers (Boles & Bible, 1978).

The social ecology of habilitation can be conceptualized as a triadic relationship between the physical environment, the client and the caregiver, as illustrated in Figure 1. Beyond basic concerns for health and safety, the environment must offer a maximum of learning opportunities to the client. It should be maximally stimulating and engaging, by providing an abundance of entertaining materials. Clients should have ample opportunities to explore and interact with the environment and to practice and generalize skills. In addition, the environment must be sufficiently demanding to encourage continued development and independence.

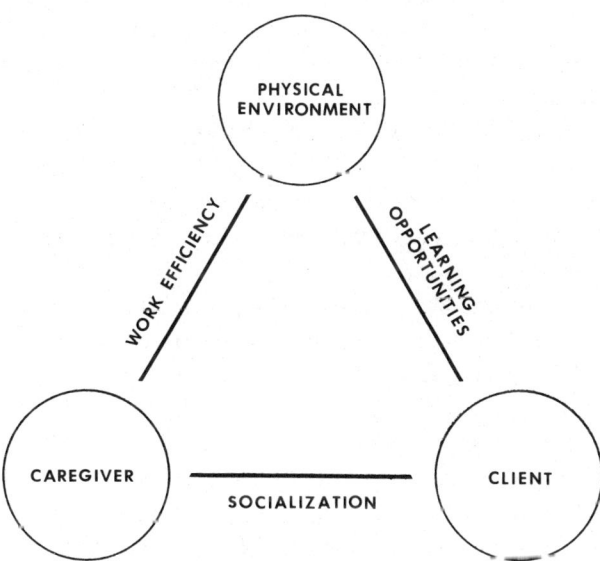

FIGURE 1. The relationship between clients, caregivers, and the physical environment in socioecological programming.

For the caregiver, the environment should be arranged to maximize work efficiency, both in the accessibility of equipment and materials, and in the organization of staff and activities. Finally, the environment should foster appropriate socialization between caregivers and clients. For instance, nonclient activities (e.g., housekeeping duties) should be organized for maximum speed and efficiency, so caregivers can spend more time in client-related activities. These client-related activities should be organized to maximize socialization, allowing staff time to prompt and reinforce appropriate (i.e., independent) behavior by clients, to respond to client's needs, and to monitor client's interactions with the environment.

The environment must also provide the client some measure of control over the actual environment itself and those who provide services (Skinner, 1972). The environment should facilitate the client's ability to indicate needs, to initiate learning activities with caregivers, and to select among the "motivational variables" that are available (Hart & Risley, 1978).

Evaluating the Quality of a Habilitative Environment

In order to improve the socioecological dimensions of a service system, we must first be able to objectively evaluate the quality of the *living environment*. This objective measurement is essential to identify inadequacies in the environment and to maintain quality through repeated evaluation and subsequent feedback to managers and caregivers.

One central issue in the evaluation of living environments is the identification of those variables or measures which accurately reflect the quality of services. Perhaps the most extensive compilations of measures on the quality of services are the regulatory standards used in licensing treatment programs for the mentally retarded (i.e., Accreditation Council, 1978; U.S. D.H.E.W., 1974). Crosby (1976) used these particular regulatory standards to outline the essential requirements of active programming. In reference to the environment for programming, he suggests that this environment must approximate the normal setting in the community as closely as possible; specifically, the environment should offer a homelike atmosphere, and clients should be divided into small, familylike groups for programming. Unfortunately, Crosby's interpretation of these standards offers little in the way of a quantifiable basis for evaluating the environment; others have observed that the regulatory standards are concerned primarily with "product" measures (e.g., building construction, client records, etc.), to the exclusion of direct observations of the "process" of habilitation (Repp & Barton, 1980).

Regulatory standards, as they are currently used to evaluate and license treatment programs, have also been criticized for their lack of representatives and accuracy. Because of the schedule of reviews (annually or semiannually) and the fact that reviews are announced in advance, they tend to be quite reactive, and as Bible and Snead (1976) demonstrated, the level of active programming may be atypically high during the review process. In reference to the validity of licensing, Repp and Barton (1980) found essentially no difference in direct observations of programming activities (client and staff behavior), between licensed and unlicensed wards, within the same institution.

Several researchers have argued that the quality of the environment is best evaluated through direct measures of client and staff behavior. For instance, Cataldo and Risley (1974) developed a system called the *Resident Activity MANIFEST*, which focuses on client behavior to determine the extent to which clients are: stimulated by the environment (i.e., exhibit movement, vocalize, attend to external stimuli), interacting with the environment, and/or participating in organized activities in the environment. One advantage of this system noted by the authors is that it allows for the quantification of differences between environments in which little or no active programming is provided.

Boles and Bible (1978) developed what is called the *Student Service Index* which involves direct observations of staff/client interactions, client programming, distribution of staff among clients, cleanliness of clients and the environment, and accuracy of completing recording forms used on the ward. Similarly, Repp and Barton (1980) observed both client and staff behavior, to determine the extent to which each group was involved in habilitative programming. Staff behaviors were in two major categories—interaction and noninteraction with clients; client behaviors included on and off task in a training situation, no training, self-stimulation and self-aggression, and aggression directed toward others.

The discussion above should serve to illustrate the diversity of measures and methodologies that have been used to evaluate the quality of institutional environments for the mentally retarded. Based on our own experience over the past five years, and on an extensive review of regulatory standards and the research literature, we have identified four socioecological variables which are conducive to direct observation, and which we consider reflective of the quality of a habilitative environment. These variables are by no means all-inclusive and represent only a portion of the measures that are currently obtained as part of an in-house, facility-wide evaluation system used at our facility. Further, these measures are concurrently obtained through a variety of observation protocols (e.g., observations by "external," administrative staff *and* observations by "internal," direct-line supervisors). Therefore, the following descriptions present only the general characteristics of each variable.

Material/Activity Availability

This variable is concerned with the extent to which appropriate entertainment materials (e.g., toys, games, instructional materials, T.V.) and/or structured activities (e.g., training, recreation, health care) are provided for clients. This measure varies depending on the developmental level and extent of physical/sensory handicaps of the clients in a given location. For example, materials for nonambulatory, multiply handicapped clients must be located within arm's reach to be scored as available. This measure is typically assessed by determining the proportion of clients who could be engaged with the available materials in a given location. For instance, if 5 toys were observed in a room in which 10 clients were present, material availability would be scored for 5 clients (or 50%).

Client Engagement with Materials/Activities

This measure assesses the extent to which clients are actually using available materials or are appropriately participating in structured activities. Again, this variable is typically assessed as the percentage of clients present who are engaged.

Staff Behavior with Clients

In almost all instances, staff interactions with clients should be characterized as social in a positive or appropriately corrective manner. Whenever possible, the caregiver should be attempting to engage the client(s) in the ongoing activity or with materials, and reinforcing participation by the client(s). Again, the criterion for this measure varies according to the developmental level of the client. For example, less assistance and prompting should be used with less handicapped clients.

Staff Behavior in Nonclient Activities

When caregivers are involved in nonclient activities (e.g., housekeeping, clerical), they should be working as efficiently, thoroughly, and safely as possible. Our experience suggests that caregivers often spend an inordinate amount of time involved in nonclient activities. Therefore, we have tried to maximize efficiency in these activities, so that caregivers are free to spend as much time as possible with clients. Safety is stressed for the benefit of the caregiver, and also for the client in that the caregiver should not create environmental hazards (e.g., leave cleaning fluids out in the presence of clients) when performing nonclient activities.

As mentioned, these socioecological variables are assessed by a variety of measurement techniques, all of which incorporate direct observations. These measures are used to evaluate the effects of all attempts to improve the environment through socioecological programming. Research is currently ongoing to establish the social validity of these variables, as judged by client representatives, that is, parent groups, human rights committees, and client advocates (Silverman, 1980).

The Technology of Socioecological Programming

As stated earlier, the goal of socioecological programming is to manipulate the living environment so as to maintain a balance between the various needs or demands of both clients and caregivers. Our efforts have been directed toward establishing a technology of *socioecological programming* that can be applied to a variety of problems within the institutional environment. The following are some guiding principles we have adopted in developing this technology.

Client Needs

First and foremost, the needs of the client should supersede those of the caregiver and the institution. King, Raynes, and Tizard (1971) emphasized the need for *client-centered* rather than *institution-centered* care practices, and found the orientation of care practices to be the primary determinant of the quality of life provided for clients. Indeed, any attempt to modify the living environment should be for the clear and primary benefit of the clients. This should be reflected in both the care and treatment procedures with clients and in the policies and philosophy of the institution.

Most institutions lack the resources to concurrently address all of the client's needs all of the time. For example, training activities are rarely conducted seven days a week, because of limited staff on weekends. When services must be limited, quality should not be sacrificed for quantity; it is best to provide fewer services at a consistent level of quality than to attempt to provide many services in a slipshod fashion. To the extent necessary, client needs should be prioritized. Essential basic care and medical treatments should have the highest priority, especially for more handicapped clients. Likewise, training activities for the maintenance of existing skills (e.g., opportunities for practice, physical therapy sessions) should take precedence over activities addressing the acquisition of new skills (e.g., one-to-one skill-training activities.

A final consideration of client needs relates to the flexibility of the environment. The environmental design must be flexible enough to address the needs of the clients individually, rather than as a group (Crosby, 1976).

Staff Characteristics

Several researchers (e.g., Boles & Bible, 1978; Risley & Favell, 1979) have lamented the problems with institutional staff, for example, low pay, poor motivation, high turnover, and little specific or extensive training in the care and treatment of the mentally retarded. Ensuring quality programming with this type of staff requires attention to many socioecological variables, such as environmental design, material selection, activity organization, and the development of staff training and evaluation systems (Risley, 1977). There have been ample demonstratons that the manipulation of these and other motivational variables can impact institutional staff performance (see Boles & Bible, 1978).

Our experience suggests that the following considerations should be made when manipulating socioecological variables to improve staff performance. First, the demands placed on caregivers should not outstrip their ability to meet them. It is essential that each new procedure or manipulation be thoroughly evaluated, and its practicality demonstrated before it is incorporated into the ongoing program. In many cases, it may be helpful to solicit staff feedback to evaluate the effectiveness of such changes.

Even when the feasibility of a procedure is beyond question, staff should be held accountable only to the extent that their responsibilities are explicitly and objectively stated. Each step of a work routine must be clearly delineated so staff understand what is expected of them, and so supervisors have an objective basis for evaluating their performance.

Open Environment Design

We have stressed the importance of providing clients with opportunities to explore and interact with their environment. However, when clients are given this opportunity, staff should always be in a position to monitor and supervise their activity to provide assistance and reinforcement, to prevent possible injury, and with more handicapped clients, to intervene in the event of a medical emergency (e.g., seizures). It is equally important that the direct-line supervisor is capable of monitoring the work activity of all staff to ensure appropriate conduction of activities, intervene when a problem arises, and provide for direct assistance as needed.

Research by the Living Environments Group has found that these conditions can best be ensured with an *open environment;* that is, an environment having a minimum of visual and physical barriers, with most or all activities conducted within a single, large room (Twardosz, Cataldo, & Risley, 1974). This research (conducted with normal infants and toddlers, but applicable to the living environment for mentally retarded clients as well) demonstrated that an open environment does not interfere with the conduction of small-group, training activities, or other activities (i.e., nap periods) which require a minimum of distractions. Further, the open environment was shown to greatly improve caregivers' ability to monitor and supervise children and the supervisor's ability to monitor caregivers.

Zone versus Man-to-Man

A typical method of assigning staff to provide care for clients involves giving each caregiver the responsibility of a specific group of clients. This method is frequently referred to as the *family-group,* or *man-to-man* approach (LeLaurin & Risley, 1972), because the clients participate in each activity as a group, and the caregiver is solely responsible for providing each activity to each client. When the first client has completed an activity, he or she waits until the last client has completed it, before moving to the next activity; when the last client is finished, the caregiver then presents the next activity.

Proponents of this method argue that it is preferable because individualized attention can be given to each client according to his or her needs (e.g., Crosby, 1976). In reality, clients spend much of their time waiting for other members of the group to complete an activity, and since the caregiver must continually supervise the entire group, there is little time available to spend with each client individually.

It has also been argued that the man-to-man approach fosters a strong one-to-one relationship between the caregiver and the clients in his or her group. Although this may be true, it should be emphasized that a particular caregiver, who generally works a 40-hour week, is actually with the clients less than half of their awake hours. Even then, the caregiver is or should be distributing his or her time among all members of the group.

An alternative approach to staff assignment of care responsibilities is referred to as the *zone* method, where staff are assigned the responsibility for a specific activity area or zone, and supervise that activity with each client passing into the zone (LeLaurin & Risley, 1972). As each client finishes an activity, he or she can be sent directly to another activity and caregiver or to a central, supervised "holding activity." Since clients arrive at each zone singly, the caregiver can immediately provide individual attention to engage them in the new activity. This method of staff assignment was shown to reduce the disruption created by children transitioning between activities, and resulted in higher levels of participation in these activities, when compared to the man-to-man procedure (LeLaurin & Risley, 1972).

Opponents of the zone approach often contend that this method is too mechanistic and liken it to an industrial assembly-line, arguing that caregivers may neglect the personal aspects of the job, that they cannot be held accountable for or take pride in the care of the individual client, etc. However, *any* organizational approach may become mechanistic when the demands on staff are unrealistically high and, more importantly, when there is no method for frequently monitoring and providing feedback to staff on the quality of their performance. As described in a later section, a comprehensive quality assurance system has been incorporated into our program to ensure that clients receive thorough and humane care at a consistently high level.

Generalist versus Specialist

A final consideration in socioecological programming concerns the variety of work responsibilities required of institutional staff. Earlier, we noted that the client's needs dictate that the caregiver assume a number of roles to meet them. The *Specialist* approach has been to hire specialized staff to provide each service to clients; for example, teacher's aides provide education, P.T. aides provide physical therapy exercises, nurse's aides provide medical services, etc. Each type of specialized staff is supervised by the appropriate professional, and the quality of each service is ultimately determined by the quality of supervision.

In contrast, our approach as been to prepare staff as *Generalists* who are capable of meeting almost all of the clients' needs. The most obvious advantage to this method is that all services are monitored by a single line of supervision, thus improving coordination and ensuring consistent quality across services.

Since all staff are capable of providing a variety of services, there is maximum flexibility for the supervisor to regulate the timing and quantities of various services to fit the residents' needs at any particular time. Unlike the specialist model, in which the absence of the P.T. specialist would mean that P.T. would be omitted during her absence, the generalist model allows all services to continue regardless of the absence of any particular employee. Also, at times of severe staff shortage (e.g., bad weather) all available staff can be deployed into the high-priority duties (e.g., basic health care) rather than having to deploy staff according to their specialty areas regardless of client needs. Finally, the generalist model (referred to as *Transdisciplinary* by Crosby, 1976) promotes a natural integration of services not characteristic of the specialist model—since the staff who are providing basic care also understand the basic methods of education, P.T., etc., it is more likely that these services will be delivered with greater consistency and coordination; for example, while a resident is being bathed, the caregiver can simultaneously give proper attention to correct body positioning, range of motion, and basic self-help training.

In the generalist model, professional staff function primarily as consultants. They prescribe services and design specific programs for clients, provide training and follow-up to caregivers, and when highly sophisticated services are required, provide therapy directly to clients. Thus, they are freed from the responsbility of supervision to practice the skills for which they were trained.

The simplified management structure also serves to buffer caregivers from concurrent demands by the various professionals. Input from each discipline is directed to the program supervisor, who in turn assigns work responsibilities to caregivers. As a result, greater integration of services is achieved.

Applications of Socioecological Programming

The application of socioecological programming to a particular problem begins with observing staff and clients in the activity as it is usually conducted. The observer should note the behavior of staff and clients, the amount and flow of traffic, and the materials and equipment used in the activity. Based on this observation, methods for improving interactions and learning opportunities for clients, improving staff efficiency, reducing the amount of traffic, and making materials/equipment more accessibile or usable can be identified. It is important, however, that any possible modifications in the environment or activity are clearly for the benefit of the clients. Although some modifications (e.g., building in learning opportunities) directly affect the client, others may have an indirect benefit; for example, reducing the time staff spend preparing for an activity results in more time to spend working with clients.

The next step is to discuss possible changes with staff, to determine why the activity is conducted the way it is conducted, and to ensure that all necessary components are incorporated into modifications of the activity. It is also important to provide a rationale to staff for making the proposed changes.

The modifications should then be implemented on a trial basis to identify and correct any problems which may have been overlooked and to demonstrate that the changes do indeed improve the quality of service. Staff responsibilities should be delineated by developing an objective description of procedures for conducting the activity, and the modifications should be incorporated into the program. Once implemented, it is important that adequate follow-up occur to ensure that the modified activity continues to operate effectively.

In our work, socioecological programming has been successfully applied to numerous areas of service delivery. The following examples show how changes in the physical environment and the restructuring of activities can positively impact services.

Restructuring the Environment

One housekeeping responsibility that our staff perform is washing and making beds. Once a week, each client's bed is stripped, washed, and refurnished with clean linen. We found that by simply using a fitted bottom sheet instead of a flat sheet to make beds, the amount of time required for a caregiver to complete this activity can be reduced by half. Although this represents a relatively modest timesaving, it means that caregivers can now be deployed to work directly with clients during this time, instead of performing housekeeping duties.

Another example of an environmental change to improve services involved the modification of the bathing activity, in which each client participates everyday. We modified the surface for giving baths, by stretching a mesh hammock over the existing porcelain bathing slab, as shown in Figure 2. As a result, the bathing experience is much more pleasant and safer for clients—no more lying on a cold, hard slab, with risks of bumped heads and limbs. Because this bathing net holds little water, it allows staff to conduct the entire bathing activity—undressing, bathing, drying and dressing—all in one place, rather than lifting the client to a dressing table for drying and dressing. By reducing the number of lifts (by one-third), the net saves staff time, energy, and the risk of

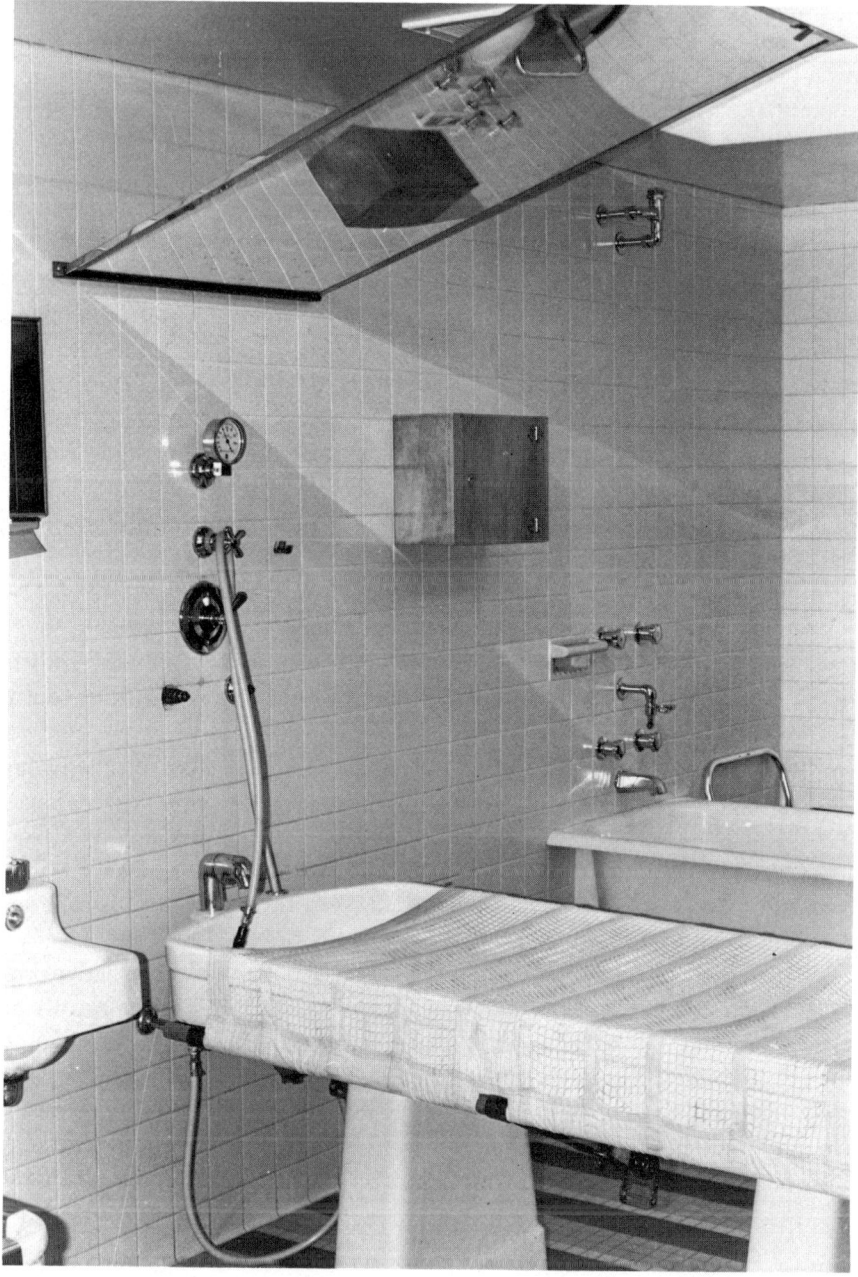

FIGURE 2. A mesh hammock stretched over the existing porcelain slab improves comfort and safety for clients and reduces lifting for staff. Mirror over bathing surface allows clients to observe and participate in bathing.

back injuries. It also minimizes disruptions to caregivers outside the bathing areas who were frequently called in to help lift heavier clients. It is important to note that the time saved by using the bathing net is *not* used to reduce the amount of bath time, but rather to allow bathing to be a more relaxing experience for clients and staff. Caregivers can spend this extra time prompting clients to actively participate in the bath, as a means of learning new skills, and practicing or refining existing skills.

We have already stressed the importance of an open environment to improve supervision of clients and caregivers. The environment should have a minimum of visual barriers, and physical barriers (when needed to define activity zones) should be low and portable (to allow flexibility in arranging the environment). Another characteristic of the open environment is the centralization of activity zones. In the ideal arrangement, clients would spend the majority of the day in a central activity area, from which they would move to various activity zones (e.g., feeding, bathing, gross motor play, skills training, etc.) located on the perimeter.

In our program, achieving an open environment required literally redesigning an existing ward, as illustrated in Figure 3. Initially, this ward for 20 clients was arranged as shown in Figure 3A. Clients spent much of their day in the living area and were transported to and from the training area for education, structured leisure activities, etc. Figure 3B shows how we modified the ward arrangement to centralize activity areas. The wall between the Living Area and Bedroom A was removed, resulting in a large, open space in which a variety of activities could operate concurrently. As a result, the time and effort required to monitor and supervise clients and staff was greatly reduced. This centralization of activity zones also reduced the time required and disruptions resulting from transitioning clients between activities.

Even in the best organized program, clients are not involved in active programming all the time; they are frequently confronted with an abundance of "free time", during which staff are not always available to provide stimulating leisure activities. Productive use of this free time is important to the maintenance of developing skills, and in some cases, may prohibit the development of undesirable behaviors (e.g., self-stimulation); but, profoundly multiply handicapped clients are characterized by low rates and limited capability to independently participate in productive leisure activities.

One application of socioecological programming is represented by our evaluation of leisure materials (i.e., toys) in an effort to improve the ability of these clients to use their free time productively. We have found for example, that many profoundly multiply handicapped clients show distinct preferences

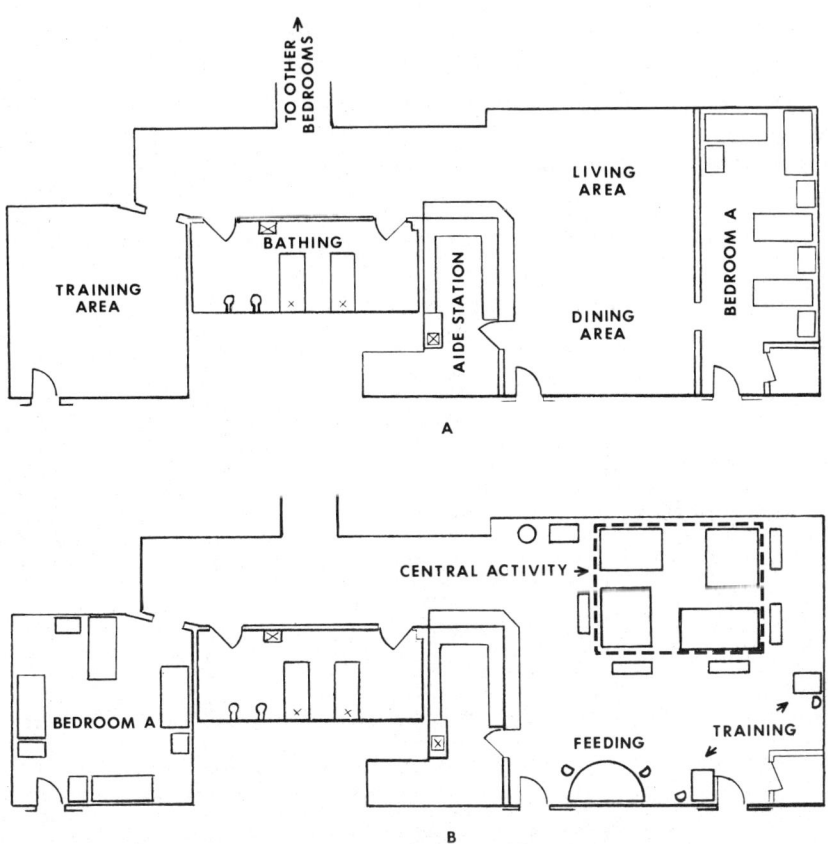

FIGURE 3. Floor plan of ward for 20 clients before (A) and after (B) redesigning, which resulted in a more open environment and the centralization of activity zones.

for certain toys. Unlike normal children, who show common or group preferences (Quilitch, Christophersen, & Risley, 1977), preferences among these clients tend to be idiosyncratic (Jones, Cannon, & Favell, 1978). It has been demonstrated with severely mentally retarded clients that simply making more preferred (vs. less preferred) toys available can increase levels of play (Favell & Cannon, 1977). We have also noted that higher densities of toys (i.e., providing two or three toys instead of one) can increase levels of independent play (Jones et al., 1978).

Another application has involved modifying commercially available toys so they can be used by multiply handicapped persons with minimal assistance from caregivers. Figure 4 illustrates a toy which has been modified in this manner. The toy is a "Busy Mobile" (manufactured by Kohner Brothers, Inc.), that is originally designed to fasten to an infant's crib. The toy is operated by winding a spring-driven mechanism, that when activated, turns the windmill-shaped mobile. The toy was modified by replacing the spring drive with a small electronic timer and electric motor, and adding a music box so a tune is produced when the mobile is activated. A joystick manipulator was constructed which allows a handicapped person to activate the toy (for an interval set by the timer) by applying a slight pressure to the manipulator.

Our research has also shown that the manner in which toys are presented

FIGURE 4. Commercial toy that has been modified by replacing spring drive with electric motor and adding a music box and joystick manipulator so it can be independently operated by a client.

to clients can affect levels of play, and can be used to increase or decrease specific behaviors (e.g., increased midline play; reduced mouthing of toys). As a result, we have developed a variety of "toy holders" for presenting toys, which can be attached directly to clients' wheelchairs, thus ensuring continuous toy availability. Two examples of these specialized toy holders are illustrated in Figure 5A and Figure 5B (see pages 392 and 393).

Based on our research, we have developed a methodology for evaluating toys and toy play, on a individual client basis. This evaluation allows us to select (and/or develop) the most suitable toys(s) for a given client, and to determine the best method (i.e., toy holder) for presenting toys to the client during free time. We have successfully applied this methodology to increase levels of independent play among the clients of our program (Jones, 1980).

For example, we observed one sample of 13 clients in their wheelchairs during periods of free time. In one condition, toys were made available to staff to provide to clients and prompt toy play; in a second condition, each client's wheelchair was equipped with a specially designed toy holder (similar to those in Figure 5) on which selected toys were fastened, based on individual client evaluations.

We observed an increase in independent toy play from 15% to 43% of our observatons when toys were provided as described in the latter condition. This method also ensured that clients always had toys available for play; we noted an increase in toy availability from 32% when staff were relied on to provide toys, to 100% when the toy holders were used to provide toys to clients.

There was some speculation that the use of these toy holders would reduce the frequency of interactions between staff and clients, because they might physically interfere with caregivers' ability to contact clients; and/or since clients would always have toys available, staff might be less likely to contact them to present toys, etc. To the contrary, staff showed a slight increase in the frequency of contacting clients when the toy holders were used.

Finally, when staff were asked to comment on the utility and desirability of this method of providing toys to clients, they were in unanimous agreement that the toy holders improved toy availability and levels of toy play, that they did not interfere with staff/client interactions, and that they should by used throughout the profoundly multiply handicapped unit of the facility. Follow-up observations conducted three months later showed that the toy holders were still being used consistently (toy availability was still 100%), and increases in independent toy play were still maintained.

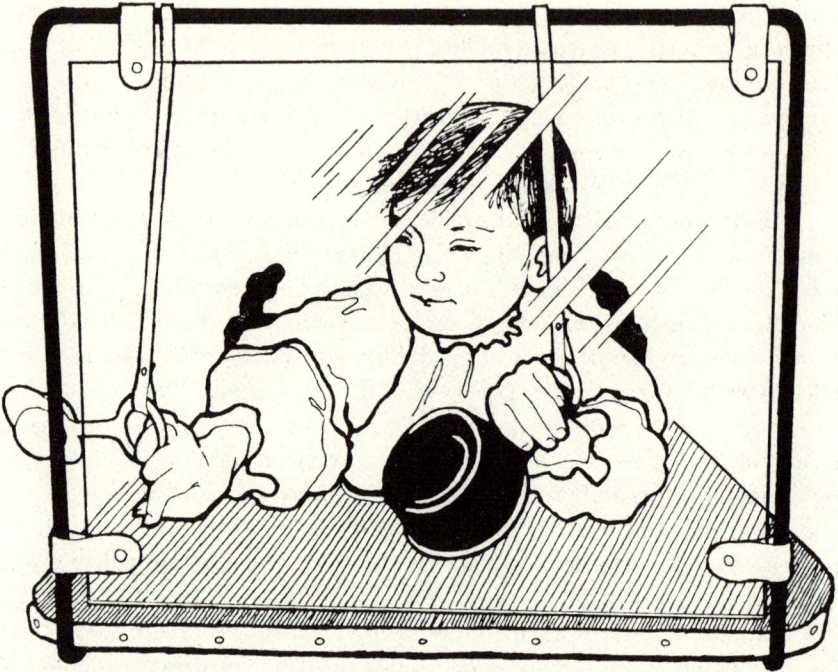

FIGURE 5. Toy holders: (A) Holders used with wheelchair tabletops consist of metal rod frames which are attached to the underside of the tabletops. Toys may be positioned at any point along the horizontal frame to encourage midline or lateral arm or head movement. A plexiglas panel prevents toys from moving out of reach when the client attempts to grasp, and does not create a

Reorganizing Care Activities

Basic to socioecological programming is the division of clients' activities and staff responsibilities into functional activity "zones," such as feeding, bathing, skill training, recreation, etc. In organizing activities, we have found it useful to conceptualize each activity as three distinct "sub-routines."

Set-up

The first caregiver assigned to manage the activity is responsible for gathering and preparing all necessary materials *before* the first client enters the zone. This is done to ensure that a caregiver does not have to interrupt the activity or leave a client unattended, while he or she locates materials. In setting up for an activity, we have found it useful to prepare many of the materials needed a day in advance. For example, half of our clients are given a

visual barrier. Toys may also be fastened directly to the plexiglas panel; (B) Toy holder attached directly to adaptive wheelchair. This holder allows positioning of toys to encourage bilateral midline plan, for clients with more severe physical limitations.

spongebath in bed each morning: each client is awakened, assisted with sponging and dressing, and escorted to the next activity (e.g., breakfast). The clothes for each client are selected the day before and placed at the foot of each bed so they are readily available when the caregiver arrives to provide the spongebath. All other materials needed for the activity (e.g. soap, washclothes, towels, deodorant, tissues, etc.) are on a spongebathing cart, which can be wheeled from bed to bed as clients are contacted. In preparing for this activity, the caregiver adds whatever is needed to the cart (i.e., fills a wash pail and a rinse pail with warm water), checks the cart to make sure everything is present, then contacts the first client.

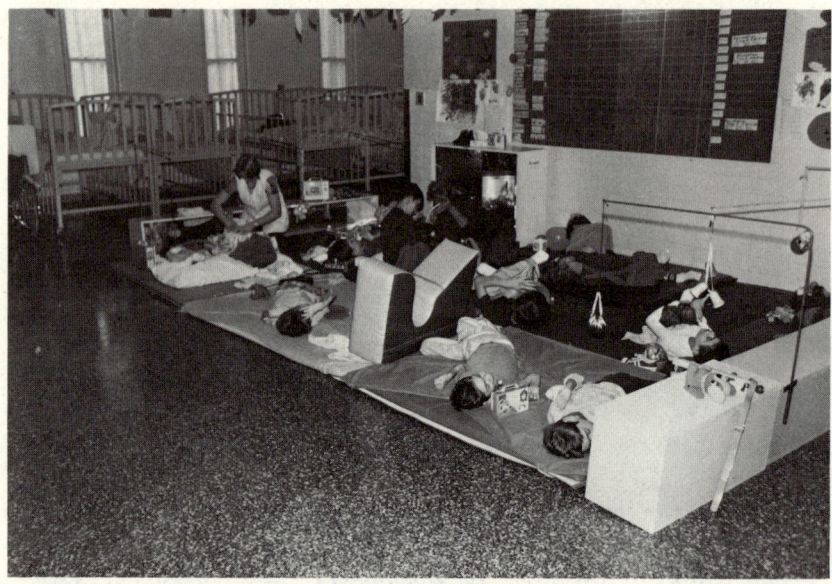

FIGURE 6. The Central Activity Area which is set up first each morning and maintained throughout the day. Clients are positioned on mats or beanbag chairs, and are provided with a variety of play materials and given considerable caregiver attention.

Conduct the Activity.

In almost all activity zones, only one client is present at a time, for each caregiver, therefore ensuring individual attention. As each client enters the zone, the caregiver greets him or her and then conducts the activity as prescribed for that particular client, including specific training activities, positioning considerations, etc. The caregiver records the relevant training and/or health information, transfers the client to the next activity, and prepares for the next client.

Clean-Up

Once the last client has completed the activity, the area is cleaned up, all materials and equipment are replenished and stored, and all recording forms are completed and turned in to the supervisor. In the example of spongebathing, the cart is cleaned and restocked then stored for the next morning; clients' clothes are selected and placed on their beds.

Clients are rarely involved in habilitative activities all day long; in many programs, clients spend a good part of the day waiting between activities, with little or nothing to do. One manner in which we addressed this problem was to establish a *Central Activity Area* (shown in Figure 6), which serves as a "holding activity" to occupy clients between other scheduled activities.

Instead of waiting in bed or wheelchairs between activities, clients are positioned on mats or in bean bags on the floor to facilitate creeping, crawling, or independent sitting, thus maximizing opportunities to explore and interact with the environment and providing frequent changes in position. This zone is stocked with an abundance of entertaining toys, selected for safety and durability, to promote toy play; the zone is *always* managed by at least one caregiver who has the sole responsibility of circulating around the area contacting each client. These contacts include greeting the client, attending to any physical need (e.g., wiping noses and faces, diapering, etc.), repositioning him or her as needed, conducting a specific training activity, and prompting the client to play with a toy, before moving to the next person.

By monitoring the number of clients in the area at any time of the day, additional staff can be assigned as needed to ensure that each client is contacted at least once every 15–20 minutes. As more staff are available, additional activities can be conducted in this zone, so at times, clients may also participate in physical therapy exercises, structured recreation activities, and other practice exercises while waiting between scheduled activities. Of course when staff shortages occur, some activities must be limited (e.g., training activities), but at a minimum, this zone ensures each client's basic care needs are met, and that each receives a minimally adequate level of quality interactions with staff and ample opportunities to explore and interact with the environment.

With this organizational plan, schedules for clients and staff can be logically developed, and clients can be moved individually from one activity to another without the long waits associated with group transitions. One of the "tools" we have found essential to this organization is the *Activity Schedule Board*, which serves as a visual prompt to staff and the supervisor and a guide for what needs to be done in each activity zone, throughout the day. The utility of these schedule boards was demonstrated in a study by LeLaurin (1974). In an infant day care center where all children were on individual parent-established schedules of feeding, children were often not fed on time and usually cried before being fed. Each child's schedule was listed on an individual instruction sheet. However, when each child's feeding schedule was prominently displayed on a large board in the feeding area, there was a dramatic increase in

FIGURE 7. The Master Schedule Board lists each client's activities, in half-hour blocks, throughout the day. Minor schedule changes are made by removing or replacing coded tags; major changes (e.g., client is in the Infirmary, visiting at home, etc.) are noted in the "Status" column.

CLIENT	STATUS	7	8	9	10	11	12	1	2	3	4	5	6	7
Susie		B	M CA	FG FG	PT ST	CA CA	M CA	Nap CA	RT CA	CA CA	CA CA	CA	M CA	CA SB
Betty Jo		CA	CA	M CA	CA CA	CA CA	CA	M	PT	ST CA	RT CA	CA	CA	M CA
Teresa		SB	B	FG FG	RT DB	DB OT	CA	CA	CA	CA CA	CA CA	CA	M	CA B
Tommy		CA	M	M CA	CA FG	CA CA	CA	M	CA	ST CA	CA CA	RT	CA	CA M CA
Darren		SB	PD	CA CA	ST FG	CA PD	PD	CA	FG	FG CA	CA CA	CA	CA	CA B
Jeff		CA	M	CA CA	CA CA	CA PT	CA	M	CA	ST CA	CA CA	CA	M	CA B
Amy		SB	SB	FG FG	ST RT	CA OT	CA	Nap	RT	CA CA	CA CA	CA	CA	CA CA
Stacey		CA	M	CA CA	CA CA	CA CA	CA	CA	ST	PT CA	CA CA	CA	M	M CA B
Frances		CA	B	M CA	M CA	CA CA	CA	CA	CA	CA CA	CA CA	RT	CA	M CA
Jerry	home today	CA	SB	CA PT	CA CA	CA FG	CA	M	PT	ST CA	CA CA	CA	PT	CA CA
Elizabeth		SB	CA	CA CA	CA FG	FG CA	CA	Nap	CA	ST CA	CA CA	CA	CA	CA B
Tracy		CA	CA	CA CA	ST FG	CA CA	PD	CA	M	CA CA	CA CA	CA	CA	CA M
Chris		CA	SB	M CA	CA FG	CA CA	PD	M	Nap	CA CA	CA CA	CA	CA	M CA M
Laura		CA	SB	CA CA	ST FG	PT FG	PD	CA	ST	CA CA	CA CA	CA	CA	CA CA
Rhonda		CA	B	M CA	CA FG	FG CA	CA	CA	M	CA CA	PT CA	CA	CA	CA CA
Iris		CA	M	CA CA	CA CA	FG CA	CA	M	ST	CA CA	CA CA	CA	M	CA CA
Connie		B	M	B CA	ST CA	FG FG	M	CA	M	CA CA	CA CA	CA	M	M CA CA SB
Ricky		CA	CA	CA PT	CA ST	CA CA	CA	CA	ST	CA CA	CA CA	CA	CA	CA M
Kim		CA	B	FG FG	FG CA	CA CA	M	Nap	CA	CA CA	CA CA	RT	M	CA CA
Timmy		CA	M	B PD	PT ST	CA CA	M	CA	CA	RT CA	CA CA	CA	M	CA CA

Socioecological Programming

CLIENT	EQUIPMENT	FEEDING INSTRUCTIONS	MAINTENANCE ACTIVITY	RESPONSE
Susie	small coated spoon	Must eat everything on her tray	Hold out spoon in open hand	Touches spoon within 5 sec
Betty Jo	blue scoop dish	See feeding program; must sit upright	Assist to push spoon into food	Brings spoon to mouth; holds spoon
Teresa	coated spoon; scoop dish	Conduct feeding program; encourage her to eat slowly	Place spoon in her hand	Holds spoon for 5 sec
Tommy	coated spoon	Make sure he's in upright position; feed slowly to avoid gagging	Present cup 5 in. from hand	Reaches for and touches cup
Darren	coated spoon; sleek seat	Grasp head firmly at chin to reduce head movement	Slowly move spoon in front of eyes	Tracks spoon for 12 in.
Jeff	coated spoon; spouted cup	NO MILK. Feed slowly; stop meal if he begins to seizure	Place spoon in hand; assist to scoop & bite	Holds onto spoon for 5 sec.
Amy	built up spoon; yellow bowl	Conduct feeding program; encourage to sit erect	Assist to hold spoon; scoop and take bite	Holds spoon 3-5 sec.
Stacey	built up spoon; scoop dish	Conduct feeding program; save finger foods for last	Present cup	Grasps and drinks from cup
Frances	coated spoon	Must eat everything on tray. Use liquid to reinforce eating	Place cup in hand	Holds cup for 2-3 sec.
Jerry		Encourage to sit with head up	Present spoon 5 in. from his hand	Reaches and touches spoon
Elizabeth	small coated spoon; small cup	Feed slowly; encourage her to open her mouth for food	Request to open mouth	Opens mouth within 5 sec.
Tracy	coated spoon	Feed slowly; must eat everything	Talk softly during meal	Looks toward trainer briefly
Chris	Coated spoon	Feed slowly; make sure he keeps his head erect	Request to close mouth after bite	Closes mouth within 5 sec.
Laura	Coated spoon	Feed very slowly; encourage holding head erect	Ask her to look at you	Looks for 5 sec.
Rhonda	Coated spoon	Place food on back of tongue to prevent tongue thrust	Place cup in hand	Drinks from cup
Iris	Coated spoon	Feed 3/4 food on tray; talk softly to encourage chewing	Move spoon from midline to right	Tracks for 12 in
Connie Sue	Coated spoon; spouted cup	Inhibit self stimulation; make sure her head is erect	Place spoon in hand	Holds for 5 sec.
Kim		Encourage to sit erect	Slowly move spoon across eyes	Tracks for 5 in.
Ricky	Coated spoon	Feed slowly; talk softly to him during meal	Place empty cup in hand	Holds cup for 2-3 sec.

FIGURE 8. The activity board used in feeding, lists prosthetic equipment, special feeding instructions, and training information for each client. Clients are fed in the order listed on the activity board.

the percentage of children fed on schedule and a significant decrease in the level of prefeeding crying.

For our clients, two types of activity boards are used.

1. The *Master Schedule Board* (shown in Figure 7) lists in half-hour blocks the designated activity for each client. This board is located over the Central Activity Area and prompts staff to prepare clients for scheduled activities. Activities are represented by coded tags which can be removed or replaced to indicate daily changes in each client's schedule.

2. Each zone has an *Activity Board* (or in some cases an *Activity Sheet*) which lists information for each client on how the activity should be conducted; this includes the sequence in which clients should participate in the activity, health and training information, positioning considerations, special prosthetic equipment to be used, etc. An example of the Activity Board posted for feeding is given in Figure 8.

Equally important to this organization and the smooth conduct of client activities is the scheduling of staff work responsibilities. For example, Quilitch (1975) found that an administrative directive and an instructional workshop on leading recreational activities were insufficient to prompt institutional staff to conduct recreational activities with mentally retarded clients. The number of clients participating in recreational activities was significantly increased only when individual staff were specifically scheduled to conduct these activities and given feedback on the number of clients participating.

Similarly, we have found that staff time must be tightly scheduled if caregivers are to perform effectively and clients are to receive the services they need throughout the day. Therefore, the supervisor's first responsibility each morning is to assign each caregiver an individual schedule of work activities. The development of staff schedules is no easy task, but we have established some guidelines which are useful in effectively assigning work responsibilities.

The first step in developing efficient schedules is to conceptualize the arrangement of the activity zones. Throughout the day, various activities will be ongoing simultaneously; the sequencing and duration of each will depend on a variety of factors (e.g., number of staff present). High-priority activities, such as basic health care (e.g., feeding), must occur at or about the same time every day, and the same amount of time must be scheduled for these activities each day, to ensure consistent quality. The scheduling of lower-priority activities (e.g., environmental maintenance, some training activities) may be less consistent, since these might have to be curtailed when staff shortages occur. In scheduling zones, it is helpful to diagram the various activities in half-hour blocks as shown in Figure 9, beginning with the higher priority activities, then

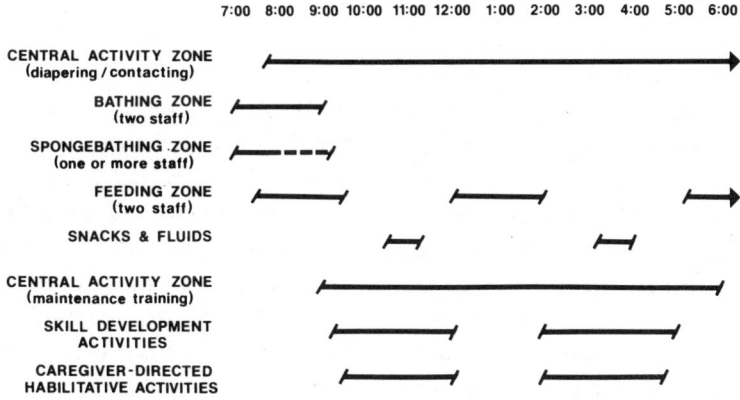

FIGURE 9. Schedule of activity "zones" throughout the day. Note that some zones require two staff members.

scheduling in lower priority activities where extra time is available.

To determine the amount of time that should be allotted for each activity, the first step is to determine approximately how much time is required to conduct the activity thoroughly with each client. For example, we found it takes about 20 min to bathe a client, including ample training opportunities, proper positioning, transferring the client to and from the activity, etc. If 10 clients are to be bathed, 200 min should be allotted for the bathing activity.

Next, the number of staff assigned to the zone concurrently should be determined, based on the characteristics of the activity and the zone, and the need for staff elsewhere to manage other zones. In bathing, we found that it was best to always have two caregivers assigned, because we have two bathing surfaces available, and because staff often assist each other in lifting the heavier clients. Finally, ample time must be scheduled for set-up and clean-up, before and after the activity. Again using the example of bathing, we found that it requires 5 min each for two caregivers to set up the bathing zone and 15 min each for them to clean up after the routine is completed.

Once the parameters of each zone are established, staff schedules can be developed accordingly. Starting with the highest priority activities, staff should be deployed, in half-hour blocks, to manage the various zones. To the extent possible, workloads should be equalized among staff so that no single caregiver is assigned an inordinate amount of very strenuous work. It is generally preferable to schedule a caregiver for no more than one continuous hour in the same activity and to intersperse rigorous, demanding activities (e.g., bathing) with more relaxed activities (e.g., feeding). It is also advisable to alternate staff in and out of activity zones at natural breaks in the activity (e.g., the beginning or end of an activity).

As illustrated in Figure 9, varying numbers of staff will be needed throughout the day to manage the activity zones; for example, as many as six caregivers are required to operate all zones at 7:30 A.M., whereas only three or four staff would be needed later in the morning and in the afternoon. If possible, part-time staff should be used to meet the demands of high-activity periods. This will ensure that sufficient staff are available when they are needed, and that there is no surplus of staff when only a few zones are operating. Using part-time staff will reduce the amount of staff training required (i.e., they need only be trained for the activities in which they are needed) and does not require scheduling these staff for lunch breaks.

For full-time staff, lunch breaks should be scheduled as close to normal mealtimes as possible. Although the middle of the day may be one of the busiest times, it is important to staff morale that they eat at a normal time, not at 10:30 A.M. or 2:00 P.M. For example, lunch breaks can be scheduled between 11:00 and 12:00 and still provide adequate coverage for the clients' lunch. Coffee breaks must also be worked into the schedule; this allows each caregiver a break (coffee or lunch) at approximately 2-hour intervals, throughout an 8-hour shift. We have found it best to schedule staff for breaks in groups, allowing half to break while the other half continue activities with clients. Staff are required to take their breaks outside of the ward, so they do not distract staff who are working with clients and so they can enjoy their entire break without being asked to assist with ward activities.

Ample time must be scheduled each day for housekeeping duties and time will also have to be worked in for staff meetings, charting and other clerical work, and general environmental maintenance. The latter activities are typically not required on a daily basis, so it is advisable to plan ahead and schedule these on different days throughout the week or month. For example, time can be scheduled each Wednesday for staff meetings and each Friday for clerical work. When scheduling these activities necessitates sacrificing client services, low priority activities should be omitted first.

In developing staff schedules, we have found it useful to design a basic schedule for each number of staff that may be present on a given day. Each morning, the supervisor determines the number of staff present, selects the corresponding basic schedule, makes any necessary adjustments for the day's activities, and assigns each caregiver a work schedule. Figure 10 shows the basic schedule used for five caregivers.

Socioecological Programming

Date: _____   Ward: Magnolia   Shift: FIRST

SCHEDULE FOR 5 STAFF

(1) Time	Activ	(2) Time	Activ	(3) Time	Activ	(4) Time	Activ	(5) Time	Activ	(6) SV Time	Activ	(7) Time	Activ
7:00	B	7:00	B	7:00	SB	7:00	SB	7:00	SB	7:00		7:00	
7:30	B	7:30	B	7:30	SB	7:30	F	7:30	F	7:30	MM	7:30	
8:00	F	8:00	F	8:00	SC/CD	8:00	B	8:00	B	8:00	MM	8:00	
8:30	F	8:30	F	8:30	CD	8:30	B/BC	8:30	B/BC	8:30	MM	8:30	
9:00	Ⓑ/F	9:00	Ⓑ/F	9:00	Ⓑ/CD	9:00	F/Ⓑ	9:00	F/Ⓑ	9:00	MM	9:00	
9:30	FC	9:30	CD	9:30	CM	9:30	ST	9:30	ST	9:30		9:30	
10:00	FL	10:00	CD	10:00	CM	10:00	ST	10:00	ST	10:00		10:00	
10:30	CD	10:30	ST	10:30	ST	10:30	CM	10:30	CM	10:30		10:30	
11:00	Ⓑ	11:00	Ⓑ	11:00	Ⓑ	11:00	CD	11:00	CM	11:00		11:00	
11:30	CD	11:30	CM	11:30	CG/MP	11:30	Ⓑ	11:30	Ⓑ	11:30		11:30	
12:00	CD	12:00	CM	12:00	MM	12:00	F	12:00	F	12:00		12:00	
12:30	CM	12:30	CD	12:30	MM	12:30	F	12:30	F	12:30		12:30	
1:00	MM	1:00	F	1:00	F	1:00	CM	1:00	CD	1:00		1:00	
1:30	Ⓑ/F	1:30	Ⓑ/F	1:30	F/Ⓑ	1:30	F/Ⓑ	1:30	CD/Ⓑ	1:30	MM	1:30	
2:00	CM	2:00	FC	2:00	ST	2:00	ST	2:00	CD	2:00		2:00	
2:30	ST	2:30	CM	2:30	CG	2:30	CD	2:30	CP	2:30		2:30	
3:00	ST	3:00	ST	3:00	CD	3:00	FL	3:00	CM	3:00		3:00	
3:30	ST/WC	3:30	ST/WC	3:30	WC	3:30	CD/WC	3:30	WC	3:30		3:30	

CODE

- B — Bathing
- Ⓑ — Staff Break
- BC — Bathing Area Clean-Up
- CD — Central Activity Zone - Diapering and Basic Care
- CG — Caregiver Directed Habilitative Activities
- CM — Central Activity Zone - Maintenance Training
- CP — Cart Preparation
- F — Feeding
- FC — Feeding Area Clean-Up
- FL — Fluids and Snacks
- MM — Meal Manager
- SB — Spongebathing
- SC — Spongebathing Clean-Up
- ST — Skill Development Training
- WC — Ward Clean-Up

FIGURE 10. Basic schedule for five caregivers and a supervisor. The supervisor makes schedule changes and comments and assigns one schedule to each caregiver. This schedule does not include part-time caregivers.

Now that we have outlined the method of organizing and managing an activity as a zone, it would be worthwhile to illustrate how socioecological programming has been applied to improve the quality of an activity. Mealtimes for profoundly multiply handicapped persons have great potential as learning activities. Meals set the occasion to learn and practice a variety of self-help skills, such as holding a spoon, cup or toothbrush, taking a bite or drink, selecting among reinforcers (i.e., food items), etc. However, mealtimes can also be a very aversive experience for these persons (many of whom have difficulty in chewing and swallowing) when they are not allowed to participate at their own pace, and when staff consider feeding an arduous chore that is best gotten over with (Roberts, 1977).

The reorganization of mealtimes began with observing the method by which this activity was normally conducted. We noted that as the mealtime approached, all staff stopped whatever activity they were conducting, prepared all the clients and the environment for feeding, and then each caregiver began feeding a client. Typically, only five staff were available to feed 20 clients, so at any given time, five clients were eating while the remaining 15 were either waiting to be fed or waiting for the remaining clients to eat so other activities could resume. Since caregivers were responsible for supervising all the clients, they had little undivided attention to provide to the clients they were feeding; when clients did receive individual attention, others were neglected. As a result, staff attempted to rush through feeding so activities could again resume with all clients. Once the meal was completed, all staff again rushed to clean-up and brush the teeth of clients and clean up the environment.

The activity was modified by first assiging one person to set up the feeding zone before the meal began. While other staff continue activities with clients, this person prepares all the materials needed for feeding, clean-up, and toothbrushing; this setup is facilitated by prearranging many of the materials on activity carts. Once the zone is ready, two staff are assigned to assist clients with eating while a third serves as the *Meal Manager*, who prepares clients' food trays, assists clients who are finished eating with cleaning up and brushing teeth, and transfers clients to and from the activity areas. The two staff who are feeding concentrate only on feeding, so they have time to provide individual attention to each client, to ensure proper positioning of the client, to conduct training activities and prompt independent responding, and to interact with the client in a relaxed manner. Thus the meal can be conducted at a desirable pace with each client.

Meanwhile, the clients who are not eating remain in the Central Activity

Area, where staff continue basic health care and training activities throughout the meal. When the meal is completed, one caregiver is assigned the responsibility of cleainng up the feeding zone and restocking the carts for the next meal.

Maintaining Improvements in Service Delivery

We have described how the institutional environment may be organized to emphasize activity and client habilitation rather than custodial care. Once these improvements have been made, the crucial issue becomes one of maintaining them over time. In many cases, increased demands have been placed on staff to provide better services for clients. Our experience has been that without explicit maintenance procedures, these reforms would eventually fade. To prevent this from occurring, we have developed a formal system for both training new staff and maintaining quality performances after they are trained.

As each activity is developed, the procedures for conducting it are formalized, by writing a detailed description. This description becomes part of a *Caregiver Manual* that includes every ward responsibility for which staff are responsible. In addition to this written procedure, a checklist is developed that outlines each step in the activity. These checklists (an example is presented in Figure 11) are used by the supervisor to evaluate staff's performance in each activity, as described below.

The first step for a new employee during training is to read the *Caregiver Manual*, concentrating on one activity at a time. The trainee then observes the activity as it is conducted by a trained caregiver and asks questions to clarify any details of the procedure. After understanding how to perform the activity, the trainee is given the opportunity to practice it while the supervisor observes. Using the checklist as a guide, the supervisor points out any problems (i.e., missed items on the checklist) and emphasizes any good points in the trainee's performance.

If necessary, the trainee is asked to read the procedure again in the manual and/or again observe another caregiver conduct the activity. The trainee then attempts the activity again, while the supervisor observes and scores the performance. The process is repeated as needed until the trainee receives a perfect score on the checklist. The trainee is then "certified" in that activity and is allowed to conduct it independently. In this manner, the trainee is eventually certified to perform each of the many activities conducted in the program; the trainee is not allowed to manage any activity independently until he or she is certified to do so.

```
                                                            RR-3
                                                            3/80
DIAPERING CHECKLIST

Monitoring: Observe caregiver throughout          Caregiver: _____
            diapering routine, complete
            checklist, and provide feedback
            before end of shift.
Routing:    Record necessary supervisory forms and
            place in caregiver's personnel file.
Score:      3 = Exceptionally good performance
            2 = Satisfactory performance (or yes)
            1 = Performance needs improvement
            0 = Unsatisfactory performance (or no)
            NA = Not Applicable
```

	DATE:				
Did the caregiver:	TIME:				
1. Wash hands after each diapering was completed?					
2. Greet client appropriately, check client to see if he is wet or soiled?					
3. Gather necessary materials and assemble within an arm's reach of the client?					
*4. Assist client in removing all soiled/wet clothing; close diaper pins when taken off?					
5. Place soiled/wet clothing out of reach of other clients in a manner that prevented wetting or soiling of a clean area?					
*6. Assist client in rinsing stomach, legs, genitals and bottom, in that order, with soapy washcloth?					
*7. Assist client in rinsing stomach, legs, genitals and bottom, in that order, with wet washcloth?					
*8. Assist client in putting on clean diaper?					
9. Pin the diaper by placing one hand between the client and the diaper, replacing the pin in an outward and upward position?					
*10. Assist client in redressing?					
11. Position client according to specified positioning instructions?					
*12. Allow the client to practice an incidental learning activity at some time during the routine?					
13. Make sure client is properly dressed and has a toy before leaving the area?					
14. Record/report information, as needed?					
15. Sort and place soiled linen in appropriate receptacles?					
16. For each item with an asterisk (*): a. Tell the client what she was going to do, and politely ask him to assist? b. Wait briefly for the client to respond; enthusiastically praise the client for any assistance (even small efforts)? c. Assist the client to complete the task, providing the least possible physical assistance? d. Insure that the task is thoroughly completed?					
COMMENTS:	Items passed:				
	Items rated:				
	Points earned:				
	Points possible:				
	Employee's initials:				

FIGURE 11. Example of activity which is used for training staff and for continual monitoring of staff performance. All caregivers are expected to reach and maintain 100% accuracy (i.e., a score of 2 or 3 on each item), and each caregiver is checked once a month on all activities.

Once staff have been trained to the required criterion of performance (100%), it is essential to have explicit procedures for maintaining this level of quality. For some activities, caregivers monitor their own performance. For example, after bathing is completed, a caregiver is responsible for cleaning up the bathing zone. The caregiver uses a clean-up checklist, which lists each step of the procedure (e.g., mopping the floor, restocking the linen cabinet, etc.). The checklist serves several functions: it visually prompts the caregiver to perform each step, indicates which steps are completed (checked), and provides feedback on any steps that are neglected (not checked). It also provides a continuous public record of which steps have been completed and which steps remain to be done, in the event a different caregiver has to take over the activity.

Although a limited amount of self-recording and feedback is possible, the supervisor regularly checks the accuracy of this self-monitoring and performs the major portion of daily performance monitoring and feedback. Two types of supervisory monitoring, *process* and *product measures*, are used. For some activities, the supervisor inspects the quality of *performance products* and gives feedback to the responsible staff. Examples include bedmaking, assembling and organizing materials and cleaning activities. After the activity is completed, the supervisor reviews the product and completes a checklist to indicate if it was done correctly, and deficiencies are immediately brought to the responsible caregiver's attention.

In many cases, product measures are preferred because of their validity. For example, monitoring the process of an activity might indicate superficially good performance, while undetected deficiencies fail to produce the desired result. Also, since product monitoring does not involve direct observation of staff performance, it has a less reactive effect on their performance, thereby resulting in a more accurate measure of their typical performance. Product measures are also more convenient and less time-consuming because they can be performed at the supervisor's convenience, whereas process measures require that the supervisor schedule a specific time to observe preformance and remain until the activity is completed.

However, some activities require *process measures* in addition to, or instead of, product measures: (1) In some cases it is difficult or impossible to observe the product of an activity. For example, it is impossible to evaluate the quality of a caregivers verbal interaction with a client without directly observing the interaction; it is much easier and more reliable to observe a caregiver washing his or her hands before feeding a client than attempting to inspect hands for cleanliness. (2) Frequently, a bad product can be so disastrous that it is essential to avoid it by detecting and correcting an undesirable performance as it occurs. For example, leaving a client unattended in bathing may eventually result in someone's falling off of the bathing surface. The supervisor must correct such a poor perfomance *before* this "product" results. (3) Other products may take a long time to produce, or may be determined jointly by the performance of many caregivers (e.g., client gains resulting from training activities), thus making it difficult to evaluate the quality of the product before taking corrective action.

Therefore, staff's performance in most activities (especially those involving clients) is evaluated by observing the process as it occurs. The procedure for evaluating performance is identical to that used for training new staff. Once a caregiver is certified to conduct an activity, the supervisor observes his or her performance once a month, using the activity checklist to evaluate and provide feedback on the performance. All staff are expected to maintain 100% accuracy in performing activity; if a caregiver falls below this criterion, the supervisor points out any deficiencies, explains how to correct the problem, or refers the caregiver to the activity description in the manual and then performs another check at the next opportunity (usually the following day). These checks are continued until the caregivers performance is corrected, and then the monthly schedule of evaluating his or her performance is resumed.

With both product and process measures, it is important that the supervisor discuss the results with the caregiver promptly after conducting the check. This allows the supervisor to compliment the caregiver's good performance and explain where improvements are needed. After each check, the caregiver initials the checklist to indicate that this feedback was provided.

In addition to monitoring specific activities performed by staff, the supervisor also conducts two types of general monitoring of performance. On a quasi-random schedule, the supervisor observes each caregiver once a week, using the General Activity Checklist. This check is conducted reardless of the caregiver's activity and evaluates the following dimensions of his or her work: (1) If not working with clients, is the caregiver clearly involved in a work activity? (2) If working with clients, is the caregiver socially interacting with them in an appropriate manner by attempting to engage the client(s) in the activity or with materials? Is the caregiver adequately providing activities/materials for client(s), and distributing attention among as many clients as possible or appropriate? (3) Is the caregiver in the assigned location, conducting the assigned activity, as indicated on the work schedule? As with specific activity checks, the supervisor reviews the evaluation with the caregiver, and provides positive and/or corrective feedback.

The supervisor also conducts a general quality check each week on a quasi-random, time-sampling basis. The supervisor notes: (1) the percentage of clients who have materials or activities available; (2) the percentage of clients who are engaged in appropriate activities or with materials; (3) whether each caregiver is in the assigned location and conducting the assigned activity (according to the daily schedule); and (4) the specific work activity of each caregiver (i.e., appropriately interacting with clients, appropriately performing nonclient activities, or off-task). These general checks keep the attention of the supervisor and the staff focused on the dimensions of the program that are essential to the maintenance of quality, that is, adherence to work schedules, appropriate interactions with clients, and appropriate engagement of clients with the environment. As with all performance checks, staff are given immediate feedback on these dimensions of quality.

The supervisor's monitoring and feedback to staff is the major influence on the quality of services they provide. However, it is important to support and verify the supervisory monitoring procedures with an *external* evaluation system. This external system ensures that the supervisor continues to perform a managerial role, rather than becoming too involved in assisting staff to provide services. Because the supervisor is in such close and frequent contact with staff, it is easy to come under their social control, which may influence the supervisor's ability to provide objective (especially negative) feedback. To overcome this problem, external evaluations are performed by a consultant, who represents (or is) the supervisor's boss, and who is socially and administratively separated from the caregivers. The consultant performs a number of important functions in the program. This person conducts intermittent quality checks similar to those performed by the supervisor, thus imposing an external criterion of quality. This is important because it demonstrates to staff that the supervisor is accountable to an external authority for maintaining specific standards, rather than arbitrarily establishing and enforcing personal standards.

In addition, the consultant meets with the supervisor weekly to review all data collected during the week (by caregivers, and quality assurance data by the supervisor and consultant). This meeting is used to review the program's operation, to discuss any problems with certain aspects of the program (including staff and clients), and to compare the supervisor's and consultant's quality assurance data to ensure that the standards of quality are maintained.

Some Issues Related to Socioecological Programming

The applications of socioecological programming outlined above have greatly improved the quality and consistency of services for our clients. Modifications of the physical environment have made staff's work easier, more efficient, and more effective, and have improved the ability of clients to independently interact with their environment. The reorganization of activities for both clients and staff has increased the amount of time staff is able to spend with clients, instead of performing housekeeping and other duties, and has increased learning opportunities for clients. The development of objective and effective methods of training and monitoring staff performance has maintained the quality of care and treatment provided.

It is important to note that these reforms were accomplished in an institutional setting. However, the extent to which similar improvements can be replicated in other institutions is uncertain. A major determinant of our success has been the continual support of the administration of the facility, which is firmly committed to improved habilitative services. The successful replication of this technology in other settings will certainly depend on the availability of similar commitment and support. Yet, even with this support, many of the problems we have encountered are attributable to the characteristic shortcomings of institutions (e.g., ineffective use of resources, poor communications, resistance to change, bureaucratic practices, etc.). It is reasonable to assume that this technology might be more effective in alternative treatment settings where these problems may be less manifest.

It should also be noted that this technology is by no means complete; continued development and refinement of these techniques is essential, as is empirical validation of their effectiveness in other settings. The following issues are related to future research and development in the area of socioecological programming.

Designers have traditionally emphasized durability and serviceability in the construction of institutions, often to the exclusion of the clients' and staff's needs or best interests. For example, terrazzo floors and tiled walls common to institutions are easy to clean and last indefinitely, but are uncomfortable to walk on, acoustically bad, and dangerous to clients with poor motor skills who may fall easily.

Although efforts to overcome the impersonal atmosphere of institutions have been attempted, success is frequently limited. Often the original conception of an environment that will be pleasant and habilitative is lost in the translation from planning to finished structure. Rivlan and Wolfe (1979) traced the development of a children's psychiatric hospital from original conception to final construction and use. Much of the original plan for a therapeutic environment was lost after subjection to government regulations, building codes, architect's interpretation, etc. Attempts to furnish living environments have met with similar difficulty; Cheek, Maxwell, and Weisman (1969) described the problems encountered in carpeting units for geriatric residents. In one unit, carpeting was poorly received: direct-line staff viewed it as a wasteful expenditure when other essentials (e.g., hygiene items for clients) were in short supply; housekeeping staff complained about the problems in maintaining cleanliness because of the type of carpet selected and the lack of appropriate equipment and procedures for cleaning the carpet. However, carpeting in a second setting was well received because sufficient planning had gone into the decision to use carpeting; for example, the housekeeping staff assisted in the selection of the carpet by evaluating samples for ease of maintenance and durability; and equipment and procedures for cleaning the carpet were available at the time it was installed.

These examples illustrate the importance of more thorough and better coordinated planning in the design and development of living environments. Research is needed to identify designs and materials that meet both the needs of clients and staff as well as the pragmatics of providing services.

With the shift from custodial care to active treatment for the mentally retarded, several perspectives have emerged on the best environment and organization for providing treatment. Canter and Canter (1979) described the following models of service delivery for handicapped clients: (1) the *prosthetic model*, in which programming and the environment should be arranged to compensate for the client's disabilities; (2) the *normalization* model, in which all aspects of the client's program (e.g., home life, school, or work) should be as close to that found among the normal population as possible; (3) the *enhancement* model, in which a maximum of stimulation and support should be provided to the client; and (4) the *personal growth* model, in which programming must allow each client to reach his or her full potential, incorporating any components from the above models that may be necessary (e.g, more enhancement and prosthetics for more handicapped clients).

As Canter and Canter noted, we currently have no way of assessing each client's potential, but this is all the more reason to specify and emphasize the opportunities which are provided for each client's individual development. For example, the prosthetic aspects of our toy research (e.g., toy holders for nonambulatory clients) would not be applicable and probably should not be used with ambulatory or semiambulatory clients. Instead, their environment should be planned to promote independent exploration for and selection of entertainment materials. Since profoundly multiple handicapped clients are not capable of independently traveling between home and school, the normalized model of education occurring in a classroom separate from the home environment may be less applicable to them and much of their time would be spent in transition or waiting. The most relevant opportunities for learning the practical skills they need (e.g., self-help, communication of needs) occur in their living environment. Clearly, additional research is needed to examine the rationale for each model of service delivery and to determine the extent to which the characteristics of each are applicable to different handicapped populations.

Finally, research is needed to establish valid standards and norms for qualitative services. Presently, we are faced with attempting to improve what, in many cases, are grossly inadequate environments and services. Although these conditions may be improved, there is currently no valid criterion for an optimal level of services. Regulatory standards offer some guidelines, but as we have already noted, facilities which are licensed to provide habilitative services (i.e., meet these standards) do not necessarily offer consistent, qualitative treatment (e.g., Repp & Barton, 1980).

In order to establish more accurate standards of service, future research should be more concerned with collecting normative data on environmental, client, and staff related variables and examining the degree to which various parameters of institutional service differ from the experiences available in the normal environment. For example, Reuter, Archer, Dunn, and White (1980) observed that profoundly multiply handicapped clients in a licensed mental retardation facility receive interactions with adults only about 10% of the time they are awake, whereas normal infants reared at home receive nearly four times as much adult contact. If consistent developmental gains are to be achieved with the mentally retarded, we must, at the very least, offer them the same opportunities as normal children. Beyond this, future research must determine the extent to which services for the mentally retarded must surpass normalcy to achieve optimal development.

ACKNOWLEDGMENTS

The authors are grateful to Meda J. Smith for her assistance in preparing the manuscript.

References

ACCREDITATION COUNCIL FOR SERVICES FOR THE MENTALLY RETARDED AND OTHER DEVELOPMENTALLY DISABLED PERSONS. *Standards for services for developmentally disabled individuals.* Chicago: Joint Commission on Accreditation of Hospitals, 1978.

ANDERSON, R. M., GREER, J. G., & DIETRICH, W. L. Education and training programs: Overview and perspectives. In R. M. Anderson, J. G. Greer, & R. E. Smith (Eds.), *Educating the severely and profoundly retarded.* Baltimore: University Park Press, 1976.

BERKSON, G., & LANDESMAN-DWYER, S. Behavioral research on severe and profound mental retardation (1955-1975). *American Journal of Mental Deficiency,* 1977, *81*(5), 428-454.

BIBLE, G. H., & SNEAD, T. J. Some effects of an accreditation survey on program completion at a state institution. *Mental Retardation,* 1976, *14*(5), 14-15.

BIRNBRAUER, J. S. Mental retardation. In H. Leitenburg (Ed.), *Handbook of behavior modification and behavior therapy.* Englewood Cliffs, N.J.: Prentice-Hall, 1976.

BOLES, S. M., & BIBLE, G. H. The student service index: A method for managing service delivery in residential settings. In M. S. Berkler, G. H. Bible, S. M. Boles, D. E. D. Deitz, & A. C. Repp (Eds.), *Current trends for the developmentally disabled.* Baltimore: University Park Press, 1978.

CANTER, S., & CANTER, D. Building for therapy. In D. Canter & S. Canter (Eds.), *Designing for therapeutic environments: A review of research.* New York: Wiley, 1979.

CATALDO, M. F. & RISLEY, T. R. Evaluation of living environments: The MANIFEST description of ward activities. In P. O. Davidson, F. W. Clark, & L. A. Hamerlynck (Eds.), *Evaluation of social programs in community, residential and school settings.* Champaign, Ill.: Research Press, 1974.

CHEEK, F. E., MAXWELL, R., & WEISMAN, R. Carpeting the ward: An exploratory study in environmental psychiatry. *The American Journal of Psychiatry,* 1969, *125,* 1056-1062.

CONLEY, R. W. *The Economics of Mental Retardation.* Baltimore: The Johns Hopkins University Press, 1973.

CROSBY, K. G. Essentials of active programming. *Mental Retardation,* 1976, *14*(2), 3-9.

EDUCATION FOR ALL HANDICAPPED CHILDREN ACT OF 1975, Public Law 94-142, 94th Congress, S-6, Nov. 29, 1975.

ELLIS, N. R. The Partlow case: A reply to Dr. Roos. *Law and Psychology Review,* 1979, *5,* 15-49.

FAVELL, J. E., & CANNON, P. R. Evaluation of entertainment materials for severely retarded persons. American Journal of Mental Deficiency, 1977, *81*(4), 357-361.

GUMP, P. V. Big schools—small schools. In R. H. Moos & P. M. Insel (Eds.), *Issues in social ecology: Human milieus.* Palo Alto, Calif.: National Press Books, 1974.

HART, B. M., & RISLEY, T. R. Incidental teaching of language in the preschool. *Journal of Applied Behavior Analysis,* 1975, *8,* 411-420.

HART, B. M., & RISLEY, T. R. Environmental programming: Implications for the severely handicapped. In J. H. Prehm & S. J. Deitz (Eds.), *Early intervention for the severely handicapped: Programming and accountability.* University of Oregon: Severely Handicapped Learner Program Monograph No. 2, 1976.

JONES, M. L. *The analysis of play mtaterials for the profoundly retarded, multi-handicapped.* Unpublished Masters thesis, University of Kansas, 1980.

JONES, M. L., CANNON, P. R., & FAVELL, J. E. *Adapting toys to the population: Toys for profoundly retarded, multihandicapped individuals.* Symposium presentation at the Annual

Meeting of the Association for the Advancement of Behavior Therapy, Chicago: November 1978.

KING, R. D., RAYNES, N. V., & TIZARD, J. *Patterns of residential care: Sociological studies in institutions for handicapped children.* London: Routledge & Kegan Paul, 1971.

KRANTZ, P. J., & RISLEY, T. R. Behavioral ecology in the classroom. In K. D. O'Leary & S. G. O'Leary (Eds.), *Classroom management: The successful use of behavior modification* (2nd Ed.). New York: Pergamon Press, 1977.

LANDESMAN-DYWER, S. *Application and modification of the behavior of nonambulatory, profoundly mentally retarded children.* Unpublished doctoral dissertation, University of Washington, 1974.

LANDESMAN-DWYER, S., & SACKETT, G. P. Behavior changes in nonambulatory, mentally retarded individuals. In C. E. Meyers (Ed.), *Quality of life in severely and profoundly mentally retarded people: Research foundations for improvement.* Washington, D.C.: American Association on Mental Deficiency, 1978.

LELAURIN, K. *The organization of day care environments: An examination of the duties of supervisor in a day care center for children under walking age.* Unpublished doctoral dissertation, University of Kansas, 1974.

LELAURIN, K., & RISLEY, T. R. The organization of day-care environments: "Zone" versus "man-to-man" staff assignments. *Journal of Applied Behavior Analysis,* 1972, 5, 225-232.

LENT, J. R. Organizing service delivery for the severely retarded: A futurist's view. In M. S. Berkler, G. H. Bible, S. M. Boles, D. E. D. Deitz, & A.C. Repp (Eds.), *Current trends for the developmentally disabled.* Baltimore: University Park Press, 1978.

LOTT, D. F., & SOMMER, R. Seating arrangement and status. *Journal of Personality and Psychology,* 1967, 7(1), 90-95.

MILLER, C. R. Deinstitutionalization and mortality trends for the profoundly mentally retarded. In C. C. Cleland & L. W. Talkington (Eds.), *Research with the profoundly retarded.* Published proceedings of the Western Research Conference, 1975, 1-8.

MILLER, C. R. Subtypes of the P.M.R.: Implications for placement and progress. In C. C. Cleland, J. D. Swartz, & L. W. Talkington (Eds.), The profoundly mentally retarded. Second Annual Conference Proceedings, Western Research Conference, 1976, 57-61.

MONTES, F., & RISLEY, T. R. Evaluating traditional day care practices: An empirical approach. *Child Care Quarterly,* 1975, 4, 208-215.

PROFESSIONAL ADVISORY COMMITTEE. A note on professional testimony and opinions in the Partlow case. *Mental Retardation,* 1979, 17(3), 165-166.

QUILITCH, H. R. A comparison of three staff management procedures. *Journal of Applied Behavior Analysis,* 1975, 8, 59-66.

QUILITCH, H. R., CHRISTOPHERSEN, E. R., & RISLEY, T. R. Evaluation of children's play materials. *Journal of Applied Behavior Analysis,* 1977, 10, 501-502.

REPP, A. C., & BARTON, L. E. Naturalistic observations of institutionalized retarded persons: A comparison of licensure decisions and behavioral observations. *Journal of Applied Behavior Analysis,* 1980, 13, 333-341.

REUTER, J., ARCHER, F., DUNN, V., & WHITE, C. Social milieu of a residential treatment center for profoundly handicapped young children. *American Journal of Mental Deficiency,* 1980, 84, 367-372.

RISLEY, T. R. The ecology of applied behavior analysis. In A. Rogers-Warren & S. F. Warren (Eds.), *Ecological Perspectives in Behavior Analysis.* Baltimore: University Park Press, 1977.

RISLEY, T. R., & FAVELL, J. E. Constructing a living environment in an institution. In L. A. Hamerlynck (Ed.), *Behavioral systems for the developmentally disabled: II. Institutional, clinic and community environments.* New York: Brunner/Mazel, 1979.

RIVLAN, L., & WOLFE, M. Understanding and evaluating therapeutic environments for children. In D. Canter & S. Canter (Eds.), *Designing for therapeutic environments: A review of research.* New York: Wiley, 1979.

ROBERTS, E. V. Mealtimes in an institution: A disabled person's experiences. In R. Perske, A. Clifton, B. McClean, & J. I. Stein (Eds.), *Mealtimes for severely and profoundly handicapped persons: New concepts and attitudes.* Baltimore: University Park Press, 1977.

SILVERMAN, B. A. *A management system for improving and maintaining quality living environments for developmentally disabled persons.* Unpublished masters thesis, University of Kansas, 1980.

SKINNER, B. F. Compassion and ethics in the care of the retarded. In B. F. Skinner (Ed.), *Cumulative record: A selection of papers.* New York: Appleton-Century-Crofts, 1972.

TWARDOSZ, S., CATALGO, M. F., & RISLEY, T. R. Open environment design for infant and toddler day care. *Journal of Applied Behavior Analysis,* 1974, 7, 529–546.

UNITED STATES DEPARTMENT OF HEALTH, EDUCATION, AND WELFARE. Regulations for intermediate care facility services for the mentally retarded. *Federal Register,* 1974, 39, 2220–2235.

Wyatt v. Stickney, 344 F. Supp. 387, 395-407, Middle District of Alabama, 1972.

ZIGLER, E., & BALLA, D. A. Impact of institutional experience on the behavior and development of retarded persons. *American Journal of Mental Deficiency,* 1977, 82(1), 1–11.

11 A Review of Behavior Modification Procedures for Treating Social Skill Deficits and Psychiatric Disorders of the Mentally Retarded

JOHNNY L. MATSON, THOMAS M. DILORENZO,
AND FRANK ANDRASIK

INTRODUCTION

Initially, behavior modification with mentally retarded persons involved the utilization of learning principles established in the animal laboratory. As a result, early studies were aimed at analyzing the effectiveness of different types of reinforcement schedules with this group. One of the primary goals of such research was to establish the universality of learning principles between laboratory animals and humans. Examples of this early work follow.

The research of Ellis, Barnett, and Pryer (1960), which typifies this early trend, was concerned with the effect of alternating schedules of reinforcement on rates of bar pressing of mentally retarded subjects. The majority of the subjects were sensitive to schedule changes (e.g., continuous reinforcement switched to fixed-ratio reinforcement schedules). Interval and ratio schedules produced distinct records similar to Ferster and Skinner's (1957) work with rats and pidgeons.

Similarly, Spradlin, Girardeau, and Corte (1965) used shaping to establish an operant knob-pulling response in 15 mentally retarded persons, in the

JOHNNY L. MATSON • Department of Learning and Development, Northern Illinois University, DeKalb, Illinois 60115.   THOMAS M. DILORENZO • Department of Psychology, West Virginia University, Morgantown, West Virginia 26506.   FRANK ANDRASIK • Department of Psychology, State University of New York at Albany, Albany, New York 12203.

severe and profound range, so that the effects of fixed and interval reinforcement schedules could be tested. Typical fixed-ratio behavior with high rates of responding and pauses after reinforcement were noted; however, fixed-interval schedules yielded low rates of responding.

Early studies, such as these typify results of a series of studies in which knowledge about the laws of learning as they apply to mentally retarded persons were the topic of investigation. Initially, the findings proved to be the foundation for a large number of operant studies of ameliorating behavior problems; later, the studies were the basis for investigating the training of self-help skills to the mentally retarded. These studies were conducted in the institutional setting, which was, almost exclusively, the site of early behavior modification research with the mentally retarded.

The next step for behaviorists was to apply the knowledge gained from these early studies. At first, studies were directed at controlling behavioral excesses, such as aggression, disruption, and stereotyped movements. Forehand and Baumeister (1976) posed several reasons for researchers to begin focusing on this class of behaviors. First, aberrant behavior can be harmful to the individual himself or to his environment. This increased disruption often interferes with ongoing activities. Forehand and Baumeister (1976) further state that aberrant behavior reduces the individual's interaction with his environment which in turn makes the mentally retarded individual less responsive to environmental events (Kogel & Covert, 1972; Lovaas, Litrownik, & Mann, 1971).

Aberrant behaviors with high frequency or duration must be decelerated before the mentally retarded person will be able to increase his responsiveness to the environment. After increasing responsiveness through decelerating aberrant behavior with behavior modification techniques, the research turned to address more pragmatic concerns such as toilet training (Lohmann, Eyman, & Lask, 1967), self-feeding (Edwards & Lilly, 1966), and independent dressing (Ellis, 1963; Martin, Kehoe, Bird, Jensen, & Darbyshire, 1971). The trend away from studying laws of learning to studying pragmatic treatment issues occurred within a few years.

This rapid growth may be attributed to the successes achieved by behavior modifiers which are demonstrated, in perhaps the most striking fashion, by Azrin and his colleagues (Ayllon & Azrin, 1968; Azrin & Foxx, 1971; O'Brien & Azrin, 1972). The majority of these studies, which focused on training of self-help skills, were conducted with severe and profoundly mentally retarded persons in institutional settings. Experimentation with this segment of the mentally retarded population was popular because these pragmatic skill deficits were generally viewed as the most pressing and difficult treatment concerns of hospital staff (Ayllon & Azrin, 1968).

Additionally, it was assumed that basic learning principles developed in the laboratory could be applied more readily and more appropriately with persons having more limited cognitive ability than with individuals judged to be moderately or mildly mentally retarded. Teaching adaptive behaviors to the institutionalized severely and profoundly mentally retarded is still the primary emphasis of treatment research. This continued trend has caused some professionals to express concern about the declining interest in research with the mentally retarded persons in the mild and moderate ranges (Haywood, 1979).

Within the last decade the impetus for community placement of the mentally retarded has greatly accelerated (Wolfensberger, 1971). Given this trend, the identification of problem areas and development of procedures to ensure successful adjustment of these less-impaired people (cognitively) must be addressed. In studies on community adjustment of the mildly and moderately mentally retarded individuals, several variables which contribute to successful community placement have been suggested. The most important factor—and one which has been infrequently researched—is social skills competency, a problem which can result in a greater incidence of psychopathology (Kolstoe & Shafter, 1961; Zigler & Phillips, 1960). This problem is pervasive among the mentally retarded since social inadequacy is one of the defining characteristics of mental retardation (Doll, 1941; Grossman, 1977).

Another highly important variable, researched even less frequently, is the amelioration of various types of psychopathology displayed by mentally retarded individuals. The assumption that treatment of psychological disorders exhibited by these persons is necessary for proper community adaptation is amply supported by Sarason and Gladwin (1958). These authors have noted that the types of psychopathology exhibited and the complexity of these problems are greater for the mentally retarded than for persons of normal intelligence.

The high incidence of these clinically relevant problems is further exacerbated by attitudes of community members who frequently dislike, distrust, and fear the mentally handicapped (Rabkin, 1979). Community members resist the placement of such individuals in hotels and boarding houses so much that passage of municipal ordinances to prohibit the existence of various types of group and transitional homes has resulted (Segal & Aviram, 1976). Such an atmosphere hardly lends itself to the establishment of a supportive environment for the community-bound resident or the mentally retarded person currently living in the community. Undoubtedly, these community attitudes extend the already existing pathology of many individuals.

Besides the lack of focus on social skill deficits and related psychopathology of the mentally retarded, a frequent assumption among professionals working with the mentally retarded is that behavior modification approaches are less applicable for those who display higher cognitive functioning (mildly and moderately mentally retarded) (Aanes & Haagenson, 1978; Zaharia, 1975). We take the position that this assumption is incorrect, since endorsement of such a model would result in an even greater de-emphasis on needed treatment of the mental health problems of the majority of mentally retarded people. As Aanes and Haagenson (1978) note, this approach to treatment is based on the assumption that being around people who act in normal ways is sufficient to make higher functioning mentally retarded persons normal. This approach confuses normalization as a goal or outcome of treatment by categorizing it as treatment. Despite the fact that no study has been conducted to directly support or refute normalization as treatment, considerable indirect support has documented the necessity of planning and implementing specific treatment prodecures (Stokes, Baer, & Jackson, 1974). It is our contention that compelling reasons exist for increasing the emphasis on treating social deficits and various forms of psychopathology. This position has been long-standing and has been voiced by others (Sarason & Gladwin, 1958); yet, it has not become popular. Doubros (1966), argued that the goals of behavior therapy with high-level institutionalized mentally retarded adolescents should be to increase socially acceptable behavior and to generate skills for self-control. Even with such encouragement, the empirical treatment data which would make these clinically relevent treatment goals a reality have rarely appeared.

Thus, despite the considerable emphasis on community placement of the mentally retarded, major deficit areas for coping in the community, such as pathological behavior and lack of social skills, have generally been ignored. To assume that such behaviors can be ameliorated simply by being in the general proximity of "normal people" seems oversimplified. In addition, there may be persons with severe pathology who live in the community (both retarded and nonretarded individuals). Thus, being in this environment will not ensure that the mentally retarded person will model behaviors of "normal" people. In fact, without sufficient support services and treatment, it is likely that a mentally retarded person may end up in an environment that is not a great deal better than what had been provided in large, overcrowded institutions. The purpose of the present review is to analyze and critically evaluate the limited number of studies that have appeared on treating social skills deficits and various forms of psychopathology. In doing so, directions for future research will be identified and discussed.

Social Skills

Social skills have been defined in a number of ways. The most widespread definition currently in use, though, is provided by Hersen and Bellack (1977):

> We therefore emphasize an individual's ability to express both positive and negative feelings in the interpersonal context without suffering consequent loss of social reinforcement. Such skill is demonstrated in a large variety of interpersonal contexts... and involves the coordinated delivery of appropriate verbal and nonverbal responses. In addition, the socially skilled individual is attuned to the realities of the situation and is aware when (s)he is likely to be reinforced for his/her efforts. Thus, at times, the socially skilled individual may have to forego the expression of "hostile" assertiveness if such expression is likely to result in punishment or social censure. (p. 512)

Typically, targeted behaviors in social skills training have included eye contact, appropriate content of speech, and appropriate assertion. Teaching speech, play behavior, and self-help skills have generally been excluded from the current definition, although such behavior has frequently been included in broader definitions of social skills (Boruchow & Espenshade, 1976; Whitman, Mercurio, & Caponigri, 1970).

Justification for treating social skills deficits of mentally retarded persons comes from several sources. Not only has it been demonstrated that mentally retarded persons are especially deficient in interpersonal skills (McDaniel, 1960; Wiess & Weinstein, 1967), but, as previously mentioned, it has been shown that the possession of social skills is related to successful community adjustment (Schalock & Harper, 1978). Another important reason for training social skills is that deficits in this area serve to enhance and maintain various types of psychopathology evidenced by the mentally retarded based on DSM III definitions (both Axis I and II) of mental disorders (The Committee on Nomenclature and Statistics of the American Psychiatric Association, 1980). In many cases, behaviors targeted as social deficits overlap a number of mental disorders and may constitute aspects of the disorders. For example, social withdrawal, an important aspect of schizophrenia and depression, to name just two, may be due in part to a lack of skills in social adaptation. Also, as adaptive functioning is now additionally evaluated on Axis V in DSM-III, mentally retarded individuals will likely be found deficient in this respect as well.

Kelly, Wildman, Urey, and Thurman (1979) provided a further rationale for the remediation of social/conversational skill deficits in the mentally retarded prior to their entry into "nonretarded" settings. First, skill-deficient mentally retarded individuals may be actively avoided by others who find them sufficiently unrewarding. This would result in restricted opportunities for interaction which would reduce the probabilities of obtaining environmental reinforcement for skill improvement. Second, since knowledge can be gained through social discourse, intellectual development and growth may be hampered. Lastly, without intervention, a mentally retarded individual placed among peers will likely be unable to benefit from observational learning.

Research has been conducted which demonstrates that psychotic individuals are more likely to adjust adequately to the community when they are trained in appropriate social responding (Hersen & Bellack, 1976b). Although no data currently exist, it would seem that other types of mental deficiencies might be favorably altered by enhanced social functioning. However, despite agreement on the importance of interpersonal functioning for mentally retarded persons (Engel, 1958; McDaniel, 1960), there has been little research conducted in this area.

Rationales such as those mentioned above would seem to support the importance of adaptive social skills among the mentally retarded. At least three studies provide objective data to substantiate the claim that social skills are related to success in the community after placement. In one study, subjects successfully and unsuccessfully placed in the community were compared (Krisheft, Reynolds, & Stunkard, 1959). Eighty-one percent of the successfully placed individuals were rated as possessing adequate social skills, while only 31% of the unsuccessful cases possessed these skills. In a second study, Charles and McGrath (1962) found significant correlations between staff and peer ratings of social competence of successful and unsuccessful community placements and levels of adjustment. Additional evidence about the importance of appropriate social skills was provided by Skaarbrevik (1971), who found that a negative correlation occurred between the presence of social handicaps and success in the community.

Several methods have been proposed for the teaching of social skills. In chronological order, they are simple contingency programs, social skills training (a social-learning oriented treatment package) and self-monitoring. We will now provide a critical review and analysis of these three treatment procedures that are used to facilitate the acquisition of social skills with the mentally retarded. Papers which provide narrative descriptions of results of training programs without mentioning specific experimental methodology (e.g., Boruchow & Espenshade, 1976) will not be reviewed.

Simple Contingency Programs

In one of the earliest simple contingency programs tested, Brodsky (1967) studied two mentally retarded females, both of whom rarely initiated social contact and did not respond to other residents' attempts to speak with them. Social behavior was recorded in both a controlled experimental and a naturalistic setting before and during treatment. One of the subjects was reinforced for initiating verbal interactions on the ward or on the lawn in front of the unit. This treatment resulted in increased appropriate verbal responding. The second subject was reinforced for emitting appropriate social statements in a series of interviews with no programming to the natural environment. In the latter case, no generalization across settings resulted.

Using a similar procedure, Deutsch and Parks (1978) modified the inappropriate conversational speech of a 14-year-old moderately mentally retarded male. The target behavior, conversational speech, was defined as making verbalizations which were relevant to experimental questions and which were made in a "normal," intelligible tone of voice. Although the subject was able to speak in a socially appropriate manner, he typically failed to do so. Music, as contingent reinforcement, proved to be successful for training socially appropriate responding. Similar successful results have been reported with the use of primary, token, and social reinforcement to increase verbal and social interactions of the mentally retarded (Barton, 1973; Doljanac, Schrader, & Christian, 1977; Luiselli, Colozzi, Donellon, Helfen, & Pemberton, 1978; Paloutzian, Hasazi, Streifel, & Edgar, 1971; Wehman, Karan, & Rettie, 1976).

A less positive, but nonetheless successful, approach to the treatment of inappropriate social behavior was conducted by Schutz, Wehman, Renzaglia, and Karan (1978). Their study was conducted with two mentally retarded adults who had been institutionalized for over 10 years. Treatment was conducted in an experimental workshop of a large university, which was housed in a residential facility. The target behaviors were jabbering, singing, and grunting to themselves. These behaviors were successfully suppressed during work time by employing social disapproval that was contingent on the occurrence of these target behaviors. The content of the therapist's disapproving statements about elicited responses that were incorrect (e.g., "Talking while you're working is disturbing to others"; "Work time is quiet time") proved to be particularly important in giving specific descriptive information to the subjects.

Whitman, Burish, and Collins (1972) have also taught adaptive conversational speech by using tangible reinforcers paired with information feedback. These authors trained four mentally retarded adolescents who each had relatively long histories of institutionalization. Treatment consisted of giving explicit instructions to the subjects that they could earn a reward only by speaking to each other appropriately. (Training was done in pairs.) Since both subjects were already familiar with a token–reward system, token marks, in addition to verbal praise, were used to reinforce appropriate verbalizations. From the results, the authors concluded that instructions and reinforcement were effective techniques for eliciting and increasing interpersonal language interactions. In addition, it was reported that some generalization to play sessions resulted from training. It should be noted, however, that the generalization data consisted of measures of verbal behavior based on a continued game-playing situation versus actual classroom performance. From this standpoint, the issue of generalization to a live classroom cannot be answered from these data.

These studies, aimed at training social skills, utilized only three types of behavior modification techniques: information feedback, social disapproval, or reinforcement. An assumption is made that the training was successful in these cases because subjects already possessed correct social responses. The treatment goal, therefore, was to increase the frequency of appropriate social responding rather than to teach these responses. Since the acquisition of new social skills in mentally retarded persons has not been demonstrated by using reinforcement, by information feedback, or by social disapproval, alone or in combination, the applicability of such a method is limited. There are data to support its use as a motivational technique following skill acquisition.

Social Learning Approach

The components of structured learning therapy have been hypothesized to be particularly appropriate for a mentally retarded learner (Perry & Cerreto, 1977). This assumption has been supported by previous research demonstrating that moderately and severely retarded individuals can learn new skills from models (Seitz & Hoekenga, 1974; Stephan, Stephano, & Talkington, 1973; Talkington, Hall, & Altman, 1973). Reinforcement and modeling as a package have also proven to be an effective technique in the acquisition of verbal and motor skills among the mentally retarded (Whalen & Henker, 1969, 1971).

Correlational studies have been conducted which employ an extensive set of experimental measures to assess the role of social cognition in interpersonal behavioral repertoires. In one of the first studies, Affleck (1975a) observed social deficits of 16 mentally retarded young men by presenting four structured "role plays" on social conflict using a nonretarded adult as the role model prompter. This prompter was provided with a precise description of the roles to be enacted and specific guidelines for providing systematic responses to various categories of subject behavior (e.g., recognition of a second person's expressed feelings and intents, and conceptualization of a conflict). Ratings of the videotaped sessions suggested that role taking is related to the tendency to recognize the other's feelings and intents during social encounters. In a similarly designed study (Affleck, 1975b), 50 mentally retarded children were paired and assessed as to their interpersonal skills while playing a two-person card game. Children with greater ability to assume different interpersonal roles exhibited greater interpersonal skills during the contrived game. Assessments were made by categorizing each response emitted by the children. Results were later replicated using the same procedures with a different mentally retarded population (Affleck, 1976). It was found that social role-taking ability was associated with the tactics for assessing needs, motivation, or expectations of others.

A major problem with the Affleck studies was the imprecise manner in which target behaviors were defined and measured. Similarly, the procedures were not sufficiently defined to allow replication of the study. This lack of specificity markedly impairs the applicability of the findings of these reports in terms of evaluating what was measured and how training was carried out.

The first study which utilized a number of treatment procedures to train social skills with discrete operationally defined behaviors was performed by Gibson, Lawrence, and Nelson (1976). They taught appropriate cooperation, verbalizations, and recreational activities to three mentally retarded adult residents of a short-term, behaviorally oriented treatment facility. Target behaviors were trained using instructions, modeling, and feedback with preselected situations as the stimuli for conversation. Various combinations of these training components were compared: (1) social reinforcement and modeling; (2) social reinforcement, instructions, and performance feedback; and (3) social reinforcement, instructions, modeling and performance feedback. All three procedures resulted in positive changes, with the latter being the most effective combination.

In a controlled group study by Perry and Cerreto (1977), another interesting and highly pertinent approach to social skills training was conducted. They taught appropriate mealtime verbal behavior and appropriate peer conversational skills to 30 mentally retarded adults. One group of 10 subjects was taught social skills by utilizing modeling, role play, and social reinforcement. The second group was trained with a discussion format, while the remaining group served as a no-treatment control. The treatment package of modeling, role play, and social reinforcement was found to be the best technique for effecting change.

A third system of treating social skills deficits involves a "package" of treatment procedures. This technique was developed by Twentyman and McFall (1975) for training assertive skills with college students. The package has also been used with chronic schizophrenics for treating a broader range of social deficits including eye contact, making socially appropriate requests of others, and tone of voice (Hersen & Bellack, 1976a; Jaffe & Carlson, 1976). Social skills training, as these procedures are referred to by Hersen and Bellack (1976a) and Jaffe and Carlson (1976), differs from the procedures of Affleck (1975a,b, 1976) and Gibson *et al.* (1976) in that the behaviors treated and the procedures utilized are defined more discretely. The explicit behavioral definitions have been assessed in a manner that has been proven reliable. These units of behavior, as a result, can be more accurately pinpointed and treated than those behaviors previously determined by imprecise methods of criterion selection and definition (e.g., the Affleck studies).

Matson and Stephens (1978) were the first to use the social skills training package described by Hersen and Bellack (1976a) with mentally retarded clients. They treated inpatients with a mixed diagnosis of chronic psychosis and mental retardation for frequent arguing and fighting. Target behaviors within training sessions were tailored for each subject on the basis of pretreatment observations and included interruptions, irrelevant comments, inappropriate laughter, inappropriate requests, and frequent inattention. Social skills training sessions ranged from 10 to 40 minutes. Feedback concerning appearance was given at the beginning of each session, and consisted of praise for appropriate grooming and dress and instructions to improve appearance.

Feedback on appearance was followed by six role-played scenes presented by a "narrator." For example, the narrator might say, "You are sitting in a table in the lunchroom; a patient comes up and says. . . ." At this point, another therapist, the role model prompt, would say, "Give me your bread." Based on the response made by the subject, the narrator therapist would provide feedback concerning the adequacy of the response and instruct the subject on more appropriate ways to respond. This was followed by modeling of the response by the trainer. Feedback was given after each scene for each target behavior being treated. If improvement was evident, the narrator might say, "That's better, Ann; you looked right at him when you spoke." Depending on the quality of the response, the therapist would (1) represent the same scene; (2) instruct the role model to demonstrate appropriate responding; or (3) present and narrate the next scene in the sequence. All target behaviors were reviewed at least once for each scene, and social praise was provided for appropriate responding. Effectiveness was assessed across behaviors and subjects with a multiple-baseline design. Trained skills generalized to the ward setting, and arguing and fighting were markedly reduced. Some deterioration in trained behaviors was observed during the 3 months of formal follow-up with rapid deterioration of trained skills thereafter.

Another successful application of the social skills training package to the mentally retarded was reported by Turner, Hersen, and Bellack (1978). Using a treatment strategy similar to Matson and Stephens (1978), these researchers treated prosocial behaviors (e.g., number of words spoken, eye contact, and smiles) with a 19-year-old mentally retarded male. Six months following initial treatment, booster sessions were used to enhance initial training effects. All treated behaviors improved initially, decreased over the 6 months of no treatment, then improved again with the reinstatement of booster sessions.

Matson and Zeiss (1978), using the social skills treatment package approach, conducted a study utilizing a group format. They trained four groups of three mentally retarded psychotic subjects who displayed numerous aggressive behaviors. Two groups sat and discussed problem situations while the other two groups acted out the problems on the ward. Skills training was effective for all groups, although patients trained with *in vivo* role playing improved more quickly. This study extended the limited knowledge of social skills training with the mentally retarded by demonstrating that behaviors could be trained in a small group format with extremely aggressive patients who evidenced an extreme lack of social and hygienic skills. Generalization from the training procedures to nontherapy situations had equally good results (e.g., physical appearance improved; frequency of lying, fighting, and arguing decreased). Furthermore, gains were maintained for 10 weeks by using booster training sessions once or twice per week.

One of the most elaborate package treatment programs was employed by Rychtarik and Bornstein (1979). In this investigation, three mentally retarded workshop employees were treated for three target conversation skills (eye contact, questioning, and positive feedback). Training, implemented in lagged fashion across behaviors, consisted of instructions, modeling, coaching, behavioral rehearsal, video-feedback, corrective feedback, and social reinforcement. The above were accomplished in three 1½-hour training sessions. Training effects were evaluated by having the subjects engage in a series of 4-minute conversations with undergraduate university students. Substantial improvement was shown for two of the three subjects. Ratings of overall conversational ability, performed by independent raters, revealed minimal improvement, however. The authors speculate that the limited training procedure and/or the measurement scale itself (used by the independent raters), may account for these results in part.

In addition to these initial studies demonstrating the efficacy of the social skills package for treating the mentally retarded, several studies have been designed to address the issues of programming generalization and maintenance of target behaviors more directly. Such studies are necessary because previous social skills training experiments with mentally retarded individuals have shown that gains frequently do not maintain or generalize to the natural environment in an optimal fashion. (Matson & Stephens, 1978).

Using the "standard" instructions, feedback, and modeling-treatment package, Kelly, Furman, Phillips, Hathorn, and Wilson (in press) have addressed the generalization problem in training social skills to the mentally retarded. They used a structured conversation format with a nonretarded peer partner to train answering questions, asking the partner questions, and offering social invitations. Conversational skills were successfully trained and generalized to interactions that subjects had with peers of normal intelligence, and to interactions during the free play. Results were maintained at a 3-week follow-up.

Kelly *et al.* (1979) followed the above study with an investigation designed to evaluate the effectiveness of group-administered training for remediating conversational skills deficits in 10 mentally retarded adolescents. Treatment consisted of instructions, modeling (film of two socially skilled high school students who were not mentally retarded), group discussion, and rehearsal. Skill training was implemented in a multiple-baseline fashion across the various target behaviors. Generalization probes were performed while subjects interacted with unfamiliar individuals who were not cognitively impaired. Skill improvement was observed both during training and generalization tests; these improvements were still evident at a 1-month follow-up. Thus, the utility of a group training approach was again demonstrated.

Wortmann and Paluck (1979) also found significant generalization of assertive verbal responses trained to five mentally retarded females. Component behaviors were taught to the subjects with modeling plus role playing (Friedman, 1971); modeling plus instructions (Hersen, Eisler, Miller, Johnson, & Pinkston, 1973); and behavior rehearsal plus performance feedback (McFall & Marston, 1970).

Another method of programming generalization and maintenance of social skills (Matson & Zeiss, 1979) that has proved to be effective is to add a

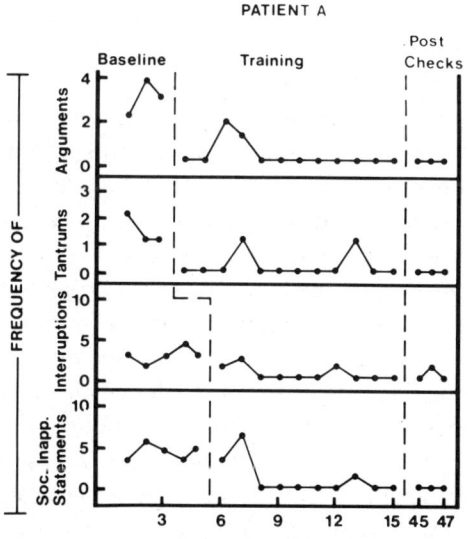
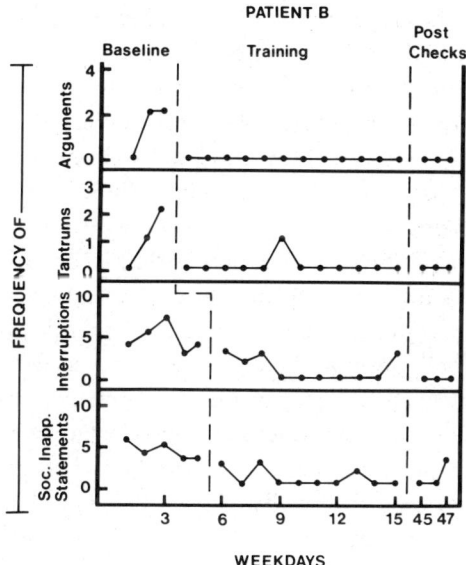

FIGURE 1. Mean frequencies recorded by the two patients. (From "The Buddy System: A Method for Generalized Reduction of Inappropriate Interpersonal Behavior of Retarded Psychiatric Patients" by J.L. Matson and R.A. Zeiss *British Journal of Social and Clinical Psychology*, 1979, 18, 401-406.

component for monitoring target behaviors by patients to the standard social skills training procedures (e.g., training scenes, instructions, modeling, and reinforcement). Two mildly mentally retarded psychotic patients (florid psychotic symptomatology was not present during the study) monitored their partner's behaviors (e.g., tantrums, arguments) and provided social reinforcement, prompts, and information feedback to the "buddy" directly in the living environment. As can be seen in Figure 1, the procedure was effective in teaching appropriate social behaviors on the ward as well as in the therapy sessions. Treatment effects were maintained at the 6-week follow-up.

A more active attempt to study the issue of generalization of trained social skills to the natural environment was made by Matson and Earnhart (1981). These researchers treated four adult females in the moderate and severe range of mental retardation with self-monitoring, information feedback, role playing, and social reinforcement in daily training room sessions. The social skills training plus patient monitoring (see Matson & Zeiss, 1979) provided in the therapy room was compared to treatment room sessions plus performance feedback and instructions provided immediately after an instance of a target behavior on the ward (e.g, talking too loudly, pestering staff). Monitoring was done daily during 1-hour ward observations. It was found that on-ward training, in addition to treatment in the therapy room, was necessary for establishing correct performance of target behaviors in the natural environment. Once socially inappropriate behaviors had been decelerated for several days, gains were maintained by prompting subjects on the ward, without therapy-room sessions.

Matson, Zeiss, Zeiss, and Bowman (1980), in one of the few multiple-group comparison studies, investigated the differential efficacy of a skills training package (instructions, feedback, modeling, and role playing) versus contingent attention for appropriate behavior. Various social skills behaviors were targeted for treatment including appearance, compliance, mannerisms, and affect. Both treatments were introduced in lagged fashion across behaviors. Improvement was assessed by probe sessions and ward observations. Although the skills training procedure resulted in substantial improvement for the treated behaviors on the ward (which was maintained at 1-month follow-up), gains were also evident for the attention-only condition. Generalization to untreated behaviors was minimal for both procedures. The target behaviors selected for the present study were those which staff were most willing to reinforce; it is likely that this procedural step accounted, in large part, for the strong treatment generalization effects. Secondly, the fact that attention-only produced some improvement suggests that performance factors, as well as acquisition factors, need to be given attention in interventions. Further investigation of both these issues seems desirable.

In the previous section, a number of studies were described in which basic contingency programs were used to modify the conversational skills of residents. Alternative treatment procedures for promoting conversational skills have been investigated in a series of studies reported by Matson and Andrasik (1982). These authors conducted three separate, single-case experiments (each employing a multiple-baseline-across-subjects design with withdrawal phases included in the last experiment) to investigate the effectiveness of attention, self-reinforcement, modeling, and social skills training combined with self-reinforcement. Although improvement occurred with some of the individual interventions for some of the treated behaviors, treatment effects were optimized when skill training was combined with self-management procedures. The self-management intervention was designed to promote a more active form of subject involvement, as it required subjects to self-monitor and self-reinforce in the actual ward environment. This procedure, which enhanced the overall treatment effect, is judged desirable because it first of all reduces staff involvement, and secondly it increases patient involvement (and somewhat lessens the typical criticisms of coercion). Replication of these effects, plus extension to other target problems, awaits further study.

The last investigation discussed here is novel in approach and focus. Matson (1980) describes one project in which mentally retarded individuals were used as assistants in the training of other mentally retarded subjects. Prior to initiation of training of others, the two moderately mentally retarded individuals selected to serve as trainers received instructions on how to function as role model prompts. Once trained, the assistants were observed for their performance of both appropriate and inappropriate conversational skills emitted during a leisure time period. This period of baseline assessment was followed by a noncontingent attention phase, and then by social skills training (in which they served as trainers). Substantial improvement in conversational skills was not evident in the resident assistants until they began to serve as trainers during social skills training. These results suggest that observational learning was chiefly responsible for the improvements noted. These findings are encouraging and suggest a number of directions for future research, which include determining how to maximize these observational learning effects and investigating the generality of these effects for differing classifications of mental retardation.

From the studies reviewed in the social learning section, the authors note three progressions in treatment. First, studies have been made increasingly more sound from a methodological point of view. This has been accomplished by providing operationally defined target behaviors and procedures which make the studies more reliable and easier to replicate. Second, oversimplified treatment strategies have been replaced by more complex package treatment procedures which have been more successful in effecting change. And third, important pragmatic issues, such as generalization and maintenance of treatment gains, have become the focus of the most recent studies. These studies are important as they seem to have the most direct implications for community placement.

Self-Monitoring

A procedure which has proven widely applicable in treating numerous clinically relevant problems is self-monitoring (Mahoney, 1977; Nelson, 1977). The procedure may vary on a number of dimensions but in the typical situation the patient tallies on a data sheet whether he or she either exhibited, or failed to exhibit, an operationally defined behavior. Typical behaviors successfully treated include multiple tics (Hutzell, Platzek, & Logue, 1974), maternal attention to appropriate child behavior (Herbert & Baer, 1972), and smoking (McFall, 1970). As with the other procedures described for treating clinical problems of the mentally retarded, there is a paucity of data demonstrating successful treatment. However, what has been reported is encouraging with respect to the potentially wide applicability of the technique with the mentally retarded.

Zegiob, Klukas, and Junginger (1978) have studied the reactivity of self-monitoring with two adult females, one in the mild and one in the moderate range of mental retardation. Behaviors selected for treatment were socially inappropriate excesses, nose- and mouth-picking, and head-shaking. The subjects were asked to record each occurrence of the target behaviors on cards given to subjects each day at the beginning of the self-monitoring period. No comments were made regarding self-monitoring. Reactive changes in the target behaviors were reported; however, the subjects' accuracy in recording was quite low. This study was of value for demonstrating that self-monitoring of negative (decelerative) responses may serve as an effective treatment procedure due to reactive effects even when accuracy in self-recording is low. The experimenters suggest that the low rates of accurate self-recording may have been due to the method in which the treatment procedures were used, such as enforcing extended time periods during which self-recording was to be conducted and making available few cues for self-recording during these time periods.

Excesses in inappropriate social skills have also been successfully treated with self-monitoring. Matson (1979) trained a 28-year-old moderately mentally retarded female to refrain from negative statements, another social deficit frequently present with the mentally retarded. Treatment was divided into two phases, a one-to-one trainer-subject meeting in a therapy room, and training on the ward. Emphasis in the training room consisted of teaching how to record negative comments in the living area. Training included examples of appropriate recording procedures using real life events of the subject and the treatment components of instruction, feedback, and modeling provided by staff. Treatment effects proved to be stimulus specific to the extent that negative statements decreased only when treatment was in effect, but increased rapidly to baseline levels when treatment was discontinued. Data were promising because it was demonstrated that a moderately mentally retarded person could accurately record a high-frequency behavior in an unstructured living area. These data differed from the Zegiob *et al.* (1978) data perhaps because of differences in the amount and structure of the training.

These few studies suggest that successful application of self-monitoring procedures with the mentally retarded is possible. However, future research in this area is necessary before any definitive conclusions can be drawn about how these procedures can best be utilized with different behaviors and subpopulations of mentally retarded individuals.

Summary

The initial reports of social skills training with reinforcement procedures were designed to increase the use of previously acquired social skills responses. Although reinforcement is sufficient with some mentally retarded persons living in the community, most of these persons do not possess a full repertoire of appropriate social behaviors. People who do not know how to perform in socially adequate ways required more complex training with procedures, such as instructions, feedback, and modeling.

Several conclusions can be drawn from the early social skills studies as compared to later comprehensive package-treatment studies. For example, Affleck's studies do not include precisely defined target behaviors, nor is the methodology detailed sufficiently to allow replication. Similarly, the behaviors assessed seem to be selected more for the purpose of addressing a theoretical question than for solving a pragmatic clinical issue. Reversing the order in which theoretical versus pragmatic topics are addressed warrants considerable attention given the need for useful treatment procedures. We support a more pragmatic approach during initial development of a treatment strategy, an approach argued convincingly by Brooks and Baumeister (1977).

The problem of generalization has been addressed in several social skill studies (Kelly *et al.*, in press; Matson, 1980; Matson & Andrasik, 1982; Matson & Earnhart, 1981; Matson & Zeiss, 1979; Wortmann & Paluck, 1979), either by treating the behavior in the natural environment, or by training skills that are more likely to generalize to the natural setting (e.g., self-monitoring and using peer role models). Similarly, booster sessions have been successfully employed to enhance the maintenance of treatment gains (Matson & Zeiss, 1979; Turner *et al.*, 1978). Critical variables, such as determining which mentally retarded individuals can adequately learn to self-monitor, the effects of related patient characteristics, and investigating which procedures are most staff efficient, are yet to be adequately evaluated.

An additional advantage of some techniques for promoting generalization and maintenance (e.g., self-monitoring) is that mentally retarded persons are taught to assume some responsibility for their own treatment. This goal is important, since a relatively common feature of mentally retarded persons is a disproportionate amount of dependence on parents and helping professionals for even the simplest activities (Mahoney & Mahoney, 1976.) It should be recognized from the data on generalization and maintenance that additional components will probably be required in at least some cases to ensure the more effective and efficient treatment of social skills.

Defining what constitutes appropriate social skills for different subpopulations within mental retardation is another area which urgently needs to be addressed. This research is essential, since it is obvious that what skills can be realistically taught and the order of priorities would vary greatly between a severely mentally retarded institutionalized person and one who is mildly mentally retarded and lives in the community. The behaviors to be trained should lend themselves to ease of observation and the natural environment and should be those which are prevalent among the mentally retarded. An analysis based on adaptation to the natural environment (e.g., community living) should be an essential criterion to determine which types of behavior are most frequent and problematic for this population.

Phobias

Another area in the behavior modification literature frequently researched with persons of normal intelligence, but largely ignored for mentally retarded persons, is phobias. Zigler (1966) and Bijou (1966) are among those who suggest that avoidance behavior is characteristic of the mentally retarded person, a problem seen as interfering with their adaptive abilities. It has been hypothesized that desensitizing the mentally retarded individual to aversive/feared consequences may enhance positive adaptation. Such a rationale is pertinent, given present trends in mental retardation treatment which call for placing persons in the "least restrictive" environment, a situation likely to arouse a variety of fears, many of which revolve around living in strange surroundings. The development of treatment procedures which will ensure an easy transition from the institution to community seems a high priority.

Among the few controlled published studies on fear reduction with mentally retarded persons is an article by Peck (1977), who treated 20 mildly mentally retarded persons for fears of either rats or high places. Subjects were randomly assigned to (1) contact desensitization; (2) vicarious symbolic desensitization; (3) systematic desensitization; (4) placebo-attention control; and (4) no-treatment groups. Although the number of subjects assigned to each condition was small and variable (a range of 4 to 8 patients), some initial conclusions about the effectiveness of these procedures could still be drawn. Contact desensitization was the most effective procedure, and, according to the author, the acting out of situations by the subjects, rather than merely imagining them, was a factor which contributed to these positive results. The design of the experiment makes this assumption difficult to confirm, however, as none of the other methods differed in effectiveness and all were of minimal utility.

Matson (1981) studied 24 mildly and moderately mentally retarded adults who were paired by level and type of fear. One member of each pair was then randomly assigned to a no-treatment control group or to participant modeling. The behavior selected for treatment was fear of going to public places, such as a movie theatre or grocery store. This clinical problem was considered particularly important for treatment, since ameliorating these behaviors is consistent with the concept of normalization. Significant differences in fear levels were present between subjects after 3 months of treatment, and at the 4-month follow-up. Findings were consistent with Peck's (1977) data in that the participant modeling procedure which was similar to Peck's contact desensitization procedure proved to be a highly effective treatment.

Matson (1980) has also treated fear of interpersonal behavior (unwillingness to speak to adults) with three moderately mentally retarded children between 8 and 10 years of age. Subjects who were treated with participant modeling in a multiple-baseline fashion across subjects improved markedly, and results were maintained at the 6-month follow-up. This study extended several ways. First, children were matched on age, sex, and level of mental retardation

TABLE I
Behavioral Hierarchy Used in Ascending Intensity of Fear Elicitation[a]

B. Baseline—No systematic therapy.
19. Talking to therapist in office about cars.
18. Talking to therapist in building lobby, pointing to cars.
17. Talking to therapist outside of building, looking at cars.
16. Talking to therapist sitting in front of car.
15. Talking to therapist and pointing out various parts of the car.
14. Talking to therapist leaning on the car.
13. Talking to therapist with car door open.
12. Talking to therapist with car door open and therapist inside.
11. Talking to therapist with car door open and both inside.
10. Talking to therapist with both inside and motor running.
9. Talking to therapist with both inside, motor running and doors closed.
8. Taking short ride around entrance mall.
7. Taking short ride around parking lot.
6. Taking ride for 10-min toward workshop.
5. Taking ride for 15-min toward workshop.
4. Taking ride for 20-min toward workshop.
3. Taking ride for 25-min toward workshop.
2. Taking ride to outside workshop all the way.
1. Regular placement and travel to outside workshop.

[a] From "Eliminating Fear in a Mentally Retarded by Behavioral Hierarchies and Operant Techniques" by I. J. Mansdorf, *Journal of Behavior Therapy and Experimental Psychiatry*, 1976, 7, 189–190. Reproduced by permission.

with persons who were judged to evidence normal levels of fear on the dependent variables. These control children were also assessed, thus establishing a criteria for successful treatment with phobias for the first time. Additionally, this study was the first in which mentally retarded children were treated for excessive fears, and in which a family member served as a therapist.

Mansdorf (1976), in a single-case study, treated a 35-year-old mildly mentally retarded woman who experienced fear of riding in a car. The experimenter used a modified systematic desensitization technique which consisted of combining a hierarchy of anxiety-inducing stimuli paired with token reinforcement (typically, relaxation is paired with the hierarchy). The hierarchy used is contained in Table I. Treatment proved to be effective for eliminating the patient's reluctance to ride in a car within 11 weeks, as graphically illustrated in Figure 2. These gains were maintained for one year.

Fear of heights (acrophobia) has also been treated with the mentally retarded using desensitization (Guralnick, 1973). A 21-year-old mongoloid male was treated by stacking blocks on top of each other to increase the height at which he could stand. Food and social approval were given as contingent reinforcers for successful performance. Forty-two sessions of 30 minutes each

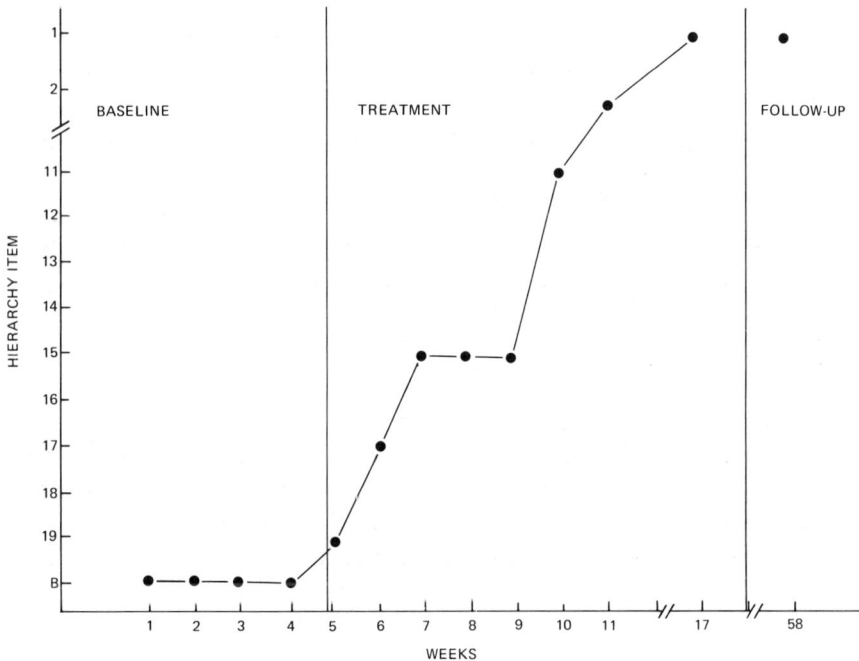

FIGURE 2. Hierarchy item completed and weeks in treatment. (From "Eliminating Fear in a Mentally Retarded Adult by Behavior Hierarchies and Operant Techniques" by I.J. Mansdorf, *Journal of Behavior Therapy and Experimental Psychiatry*, 1976, 7, 189-190. Reproduced by permission.)

minutes each were needed to achieve the treatment goal (the subject was able to stand on a chair that was 20 inches high. As with the other studies published on the treatment of phobias with the mentally retarded, these results are encouraging.

Summary

It is apparent that considerable research needs to be conducted in the area of phobias with the mentally retarded. Generally, it has been found that conventional clinical interventions can be effective in reducing fears of the mentally retarded without making substantial modifications in the treatment procedures. This finding is encouraging, and it certainly may make the bridge from treating persons of normal intelligence to treating mentally retarded persons easier.

Peck's (1977) finding that contact desensitization procedures were more effective than procedures requiring a higher degree of such abstract cognitively oriented procedures as imagery are not surprising. This result was predictable, since the use of contrived rather than real-life experiences has proven to be difficult to implement without considerable training (Matson, 1981). As a result, procedures with less cognitive imagery may achieve a higher level of generalization across populations receiving treatment. Certainly this issue deserves further study. However, an even more important area for study is the establishment of different behavior modification procedures to treat different fear responses for the varied subpopulations of mentally retarded persons.

Other Psychiatric Disorders

In addition to fears and a general lack of essential social skills, which are part of, or precursors to, many psychiatric illnesses, there are a number of other significant mental health problems in the mentally retarded. Among the disorders effectively treated and experimentally evaluated are psychotic speech, depression, temper outbursts, compulsive behavior, hyperactivity, exhibitionism, and public masturbation.

Psychotic Speech

One of the most prevalent mental health problems of the mentally retarded is schizophrenia, particularly with persons in the mild and moderate ranges. In one successful treatment program, Kazdin (1971) modified the conversational speech of a moderately mentally retarded 29-year-old psychotic female who blurted out socially inappropriate statements during working hours. The subject was told each morning that when the target response occurred, she would lose a token. For the first three weeks of the response-cost period, one token was lost each time she blurted out a socially inappropriate statement. During the second three weeks, two tokens were forfeited. Tokens retrieved by the staff as a penalty for inappropriate statements were those earned by the subject for production on the job. Response cost was effective in decreasing "psychotic talk" and effects were maintained over time (at 4-weeks follow-up).

Three studies have been performed on patients with dual diagnoses of mental retardation and psychosis. The first two studies, which were discussed in a previous section (Matson & Stephens, 1978; Matson & Zeiss, 1978), targeted social skill deficits in subjects whose psychotic symtoms were controlled in large part by medication. The third study investigated the efficacy of a package training procedure for dually diagnosed individuals whose psychotic symptoms were not controlled by medication. (This study is discussed in detail below.)

Stephens, Matson, Westmoreland, and Kulpal (1979) conducted a series of investigations which attempted to change verbal behaviors related to the hallucinations and delusions evidenced in four psychotic, mentally retarded individuals. All four individuals were on maintenance dosages of psychotropic medication but had responded minimally to this medication. Three separate single-case experiments (two employing a multiple-baseline, and one employing a reversal design) were utilized to assess the effectiveness of the social skill package for improving social skills component behaviors and decreasing inappropriate verbalizations.

At the end of the respective treatments, all subjects displayed significant improvement; a 2-month follow-up conducted on two of the individuals revealed maintenance of initial effects. Generalization effects were found for probe scenes conducted on the ward as well. These results, which support the efficacy of skill training paired with medication, are encouraging. In addition to producing a favorable outcome, the results provided initial evidence that the more aversive procedures previously used may not always be necessary for modifying overt psychotic communication skill deficits. Given the limited number of treated cases and follow-up, further research clearly seems warranted.

Depression

The first reports describing the existence of affective symptoms in the mentally retarded appeared in the late 1800s (Clouston, 1883; Hurd, 1888). Although several authors have since argued that affective disorders do not exist or cannot be diagnosed in the mentally retarded (Craft, 1959; Earl, 1961; Payne, 1968), a large number of case reports and large-scale epidemiologic studies have appeared which support the contention that affective symptoms do occur in the mentally retarded (e.g., Adams, Kivowitz, & Ziskind, 1970; Carlson, 1979; Heaton-Ward, 1977; Herskovitz & Plesset, 1941; Reid, 1972; Reid & Naylor, 1976.) The following conclusions about affective disorders and the mentally retarded seem most supported by the existing studies:

1. Clinical symptoms of depression and mania, as described in DSM-III, do occur in the mentally retarded.
2. Affective features become less typical and more difficult to diagnose as one moves to increasingly lower levels of mental retardation.

3. The limited available data suggest that prevalence rates of affective disorders in the mentally retarded approach those evident in the non-mentally retarded.

Despite the long-standing attention devoted to the study of affective disorders in the mentally retarded, treatment has consisted almost solely of pharmacological and other medical means (e.g., Reid, 1976; Rivinus & Harmatz, 1979; Roith, 1961). Recently, one case report which describes success at alleviating symptoms of depression in a mentally retarded subject by use of a nonmedical treatment procedure has appeared (Matson, Dettling, & Senatore, 1981). The subject, a former long-term institutionalized male in his mid-thirties, was treated for frequent suicidal threats, extreme social isolation, and constant ruminating about past events. Treatment, which consisted of self-evaluation, monitoring, reinforcement, instructions, feedback, and modeling by the therapist, performed over 5 months of weekly meetings, was effective in establishing more frequent and appropriate social contacts and in enhancing the frequency of positive versus negative statements about his life. Further investigation of nonpharmacological treatments for affective disorders of the mentally retarded is warranted from these encouraging preliminary findings.

Temper Outbursts

Harvey, Karan, Bhargava, and Morehouse (1978) have successfully applied relaxation training, cue conditioning, and cognitively oriented procedures to establish self-control of temper outbursts in a moderately mentally retarded female. This treatment package resulted in a decrease from an average of three outbursts a week to less than one outburst monthly. Therapeutic gains were maintained for 1 year. Follow-up was terminated at this point, and, as a result, it is not clear if further maintenance of treatment effects resulted.

Compulsive Behavior

Cuvo (1976) treated an institutionalized mentally retarded female adult for repeatedly going up and down stairs, running back and forth on the sidewalk, running in circles, and related behaviors. These responses, which were described as compulsive in nature, had occurred for approximately 40 years.

To eliminate repetitive walking and running to a knitting class, a program was instituted to reinforce competing incompatible behavior (Foxx & Azrin, 1973). It was found that reinforcement was functionally related to a decrease in walking time to the woman's class. In an earlier study, Mulhern and Baumeister (1969) obtained similar results by reducing rocking in two severely mentally retarded persons by reinforcing "sitting still."

Hyperactivity

In a study with a mentally retarded, hyperactive 3-year-old girl, Stoudenmire and Salter (1975) used primary reinforcers (M & M candies) to increase prosocial behaviors defined as *immobile* and *attending* behaviors. Although no instructions were given, the child was shaped in eight sessions. Utilizing an ABAB design, immobile behavior and attending to objects were shown to be under the control of reinforcers.

Exhibitionism

Lutzker (1973) treated a profoundly mentally retarded institutionalized male by reinforcing any behavior other than exhibitionism (the target behavior was displayed 30% of the time during which observations were made). The procedure was effective within a few weeks. Long-term effects were not reported.

Public Masturbation

In the final study to be reviewed, Cook, Altman, Shaw, and Blaylock (1978) successfully eliminated instances of public masturbation by a severely mentally retarded boy. This treatment consisted of squirting lemon juice into the subject's mouth contingent on initiating masturbation. The procedure was effective in a period from 13 to 16 days both in the home and at school.

Summary

The few studies presented here are promising. All the behavior therapy techniques employed in these studies have been used to treat these same problems in a much more extensive manner with populations of normal intelligence. Techniques used include systematic desensitization, behavior rehearsal, relaxation training, covert therapies, cognitive restructuring, and self-control strategies (Harvey, 1979). Despite the fact that very few studies have been published on the effective use of these techniques with the mentally retarded (Peck, 1977), the available information is sufficient to suggest that further investigation should be made on a wider variety of psychiatric problems.

Conclusions

The focus of most behavior modification research with the mentally retarded has been training self-help skills, such as dressing, feeding, and toileting. Other deficit areas of mentally retarded persons which have received considerable attention are shaping speech and suppressing or eliminating self-stimulatory, self-injurious, and aggressive disruptive behaviors. Although treatment in these areas should unquestionably be of a high priority, there is a need for behavior modifiers to address more rigorously clinical problems traditionally associated with this population. The need for such work is apparent, given that the majority of mentally retarded persons are in the mild or moderate range of retardation. It can be implied from current thinking that if these mentally retarded persons are not presently in the community, it is highly probable that they soon will be. Since the community is a much more discriminating environment with respect to deviant social behavior when compared to the institution, deviant social behavior is much less likely to be tolerated in the community environment.

Problems such as social skills deficits, fears, and psychotic behaviors of the mentally retarded have rarely been addressed, as evidenced by the small number of published studies. Future experimentation using single-subject designs to treat these and other problems, such as psychosomatic disorders, addictive behaviors, bereavement, and obsessive-compulsive disorders would be of value. Also, a number of additional techniques which are commonly employed with persons of normal intelligence might be evaluated. Systematic desensitization, flooding, implosive therapy, self-control procedures, thought stopping, and biofeedback are just a few of the methods that might prove applicable.

Although the literature addressing pragmatically important treatment issues of the mentally retarded appears quite promising, the research reviewed suffers from problems frequently observed in the behavior modification literature (or treatment literatures using other theoretical orientations) where a few exploratory studies have been published. Conclusions regarding clinical utility are limited owing to a general lack of experimental rigor. In order to assess the design integrity of the studies summarized in this chapter, a series of tables have been prepared which list key design features, consisting of sample size, mental retardation classification, treatment strategy utilized, target behaviors treated, setting in which the intervention was conducted, utilization of follow-up, and adequacy of the experimental design. Criteria for judging design adequacy were those proposed by Atkeson and Forehand (1979).

According to these authors, there are three types of designs considered adequate to conclude that results are due to the experimental manipulations: (1) ABA designs, or some variation thereof, with baseline and reversal; (2) multiple-baseline designs, and (3) group designs with appropriate control groups.

Tables II, III, and IV summarize the studies which have been devoted to the treatment of social skills deficits, phobias, and other psychiatric disorders, respectively.

As can be seen from the tables, the treatment studies are quite variable. Upon examination of the measures summarized, each study differs on the number of subjects, their mental retardation classification, treatment strategy, behaviors treated, and setting. Over 56% of the studies have no follow-up. Not only have demographic variables and dependent measures varied, but the experimental designs of the studies reviewed have not been adequate in over 18% of the cases. One may conclude that results are owing to the treatment intervention rather than confounding variables. Consequently, comparing findings across studies must be done cautiously.

Our review indicates that large group studies, generalization, and maintenance are all issues for further investigation. Another difficulty apparent in the literature is that sufficient detail about subjects is not always provided. Rarely are adaptive behavior level and IQ both reported, although the policy of the American Association for Mental Deficiency has been that both are necessary for properly determining mental status (Grossman, 1977). Also, compliance of the individual, fitness of response by the mentally retarded person to various reinforcers, type of living environment, and a brief description of other behavioral assets and deficits (e.g., hygiene skills, social skills) are important for understanding the treatment needs of mentally retarded persons.

Evidence of the applicability of behavior modification procedures to treat clinical problems with the mentally retarded, traditionally reserved for persons of normal intelligence, is encouraging. The documentation of these successful treatments and the prevalence of behavioral deficits among the mentally retarded which impede community adjustment makes such deficits a high priority for further study. However, without well developed treatment programs that are systematically assessed, the goal of better adaptation with the mentally retarded is not likely to occur. Hopefully, more research and study on these important clinical problems will soon be performed.

TABLE II
Summary of Social Skills Studies

Author	N	MR classification	Treatment strategy[a]	Behaviors treated[b]	Setting	Follow-up	Adequate design
Sample contingency programs							
Barton (1973)	3	Profound	Token reinforcement	Conversation skills	Therapy room	No	Yes
Brodsky (1967)	2	No data	Token reinforcement	Conversation skills	Lab & playground	No	Yes
Deutsch & Parks (1978)	1	Moderate	Music reinforcement	Conversation skills	Playroom	No	Yes
Doljanac et al. (1977)	8	Borderline to moderate	Token reinforcement	Conversation skills	Institution	No	No
Luiselli et al. (1978)	1	Moderate	Tokens & shaping procedures	Conversation skills	Classroom	No	Yes
Paloutzian et al. (1971)	20	Severe	Reinforcement	Motor behavior	Institution	No	Yes
Schultz et al. (1978)	2	Severe	Social disapproval	Inappropriate verbal	Experimental workshop	No	Yes
Wehman et al. (1976)	3	Severe	Social reinforcement	Cooperative play	Sheltered workshop	No	Yes
Whitman et al. (1970)	4	Moderate	Token & social reinforcement	Conversation skills	Playroom	No	Yes

Social learning approach

Afleck (1975a)[c]	16	Mild & Moderate	—	—	—	—
Affleck (1975b)[c]	50	Mild	—	—	—	—
Affleck (1976)[c]	50	Mild	—	—	—	—
Gibson et al. (1976)	3	Borderline to moderate	Package	Peer interactions	Residents' Cottage	No	Yes
Kelly et al. (in press)	10	Borderline to moderate	Package	Conversation skills	Institution	1 mo.	Yes
Kelly et al. (in press)	2	Moderate to severe	Package	Conversation skills	Therapy room	3 wk.	Yes
Matson et al. (1980)	8[d]	No data	Package versus continuous attention	Social skills	Institution	1 mo.	Yes
Matson (1980)	2	Moderate	Package[e]	Conversation skills	Institution	No	Yes
Matson & Andrasik (1982)							
Experiment 1	2	Moderate	Self-reinforcement	Conversation skills	Institution	No	Yes
Experiment 2	3	Mild & moderate	Package & self-management	Conversation skills	Institution	No	Yes
Experiment 3	3	Mild	Package & self-management	Conversation skills	Institution	No	Yes

Continued

TABLE II (continued)

Author	N	MR classification	Treatment strategy[a]	Behaviors treated[b]	Setting	Follow-up	Adequate design
Social learning approach (continued)							
Matson & Earnhart (1982)	4	Moderate & severe	Package	Social behavior	Institution	4 mo.	Yes
Matson & Stephens (1978)	4	No data	Package	Social skills	Institution	12 wk.	Yes
Matson & Zeiss (1978)	12	No data	Package	Social skills	Institution	10 wk.	Yes
Matson & Zeiss (1979)	2	Mild	Package	Interpersonal behavior	Institution	6 wk.	Yes
Perry & Cerreto (1977)	30	Borderline to severe	Package	Social behavior	Cafeteria/ living room	No	Yes
Rychtarik & Bornstein (1979)	3	Mild	Package	Conversation skills	Sheltered workshop	No	Yes
Seitz & Hoekenga (1974)	4	Severe	Modeling	Communication skills	Clinic	No	No
Stephan et al. (1973)	33	Borderline & mild	Modeling	Telephone usage	Classroom	No	Yes
Talkington et al. (1973)	75	Severe	Modeling	Communication skills	School	No	Yes

Social learning approach (continued)

Study	N	Severity	Technique	Behavior	Setting	Follow-up	Generalization
Turner et al. (1978)	1	No data	Package	Social skills	Laboratory	6 mo.	Yes
Whalen & Henker (1969)	6	Moderate to profound	Modeling & reinforcement	Social behavior	Institution	No	Yes
Whalen & Henker (1971)	15	Mild & moderate	Modeling & reinforcement	Social behavior	Institution	6 mo.	Yes
Wortman & Paluck (1979)	5	Moderate & severe	Package	Assertion	Institution	6 mo.	No
Self-Monitoring Approach							
Matson (1979)	1	Moderate	Self-monitor	Negative statements	Institution	No	Yes
Zegiob et al. (1978)	2	Mild & moderate	Self-monitor	Stereotypic behavior	Institution	6 mo.	Yes

[a] "Package" refers to the combination of treatment techniques employed by Hersen and Bellack (1976a) and Jaffe and Carlson (1976). The studies above utilized several or all of the following procedures: modeling, role playing, instructions, feedback, behavioral rehearsal, self-monitoring, and reinforcement.
[b] "Social Skills" refers to the discrete behaviors developed from Hersen and Bellack's (1977) definition. Typical behaviors used as dependent measures in these studies were: eye contact, response duration, and appropriate content of speech.
[c] Affleck's studies (1975a, 1976) were correlational in design as opposed to treatment studies.
[d] Twelve subjects were included in this investigation; 4 were diagnosed as mentally retarded, 4 were diagnosed as mentally retarded and psychotic, and data on the 4 remaining patients, diagnosed as schizophrenic, are not summarized here.
[e] Subjects served as training assistants.

TABLE III
Summary of Phobia Studies

Author	N	MR classification	Treatment strategy	Behaviors treated	Setting	Follow-up	Adequate design
Guralnick (1973)	1	Severe	Systematic desensitization	Acrophobia	Gymnasium	Yes[a]	No
Mansdorf (1976)	1	Mild	Systematic desensitization	Fear of riding in cars	Car	58 wk.	No
Peck (1977)	20	Mild	Desensitization	Fear of rats or acrophobia	Varied settings	No	Yes
Matson (1980a)	24	Mild & moderate	Participant modeling	Fear of going into community stores	Shelter workshop & community stores	4 mo.	Yes
Matson (1980b)	3	Moderate	Participant modeling	Fear of adults	Clinic & home	6 mo.	Yes

[a] The follow-up period was not specifically outlined.

TABLE IV
Summary of Studies for Other Psychiatric Disorders

Author	N	MR classification	Treatment strategy	Behaviors treated	Setting	Follow-up	Adequate design
Inappropriate psychotic verbalizations							
Kazdin (1971)	1	Moderate	Response cost	Inappropriate verbalization	Sheltered workshop	4 wk.	No
Stephens et al. (1979)							
Experiment 1	1[a]	Moderate	Package	Social skills	Institution	No	Yes
Experiment 2	1[a]	Mild	Package	Social skills & psychotic talk	Institution	No	Yes
Experiment 3	2[a]	Moderate & severe	Package	Social skills & inappropriate verbalization	Institution	2 mo.	Yes
Depression							
Matson et al. (1982)	1	Moderate	Social learning techniques	Verbal statements	Clinic	8 mo.	Yes
Temper Outbursts							
Harvey et al. (1978)	1	Moderate	Relaxation training	Temper tantrums	Workshop nursing home	6 wk.	Yes

Continued

TABLE IV (continued)

Author	N	MR classification	Treatment strategy	Behaviors treated	Setting	Follow-up	Adequate design
Compulsive Behavior							
Cuvo (1976)	1	Mild	Primary & social reinforcement	Repetitive behavior	Institution	No	Yes
Mulhern & Baumeister (1969)	2	Severe	Primary reinforcement	Stereotypic behavior	Experimental chamber	No	No
Hyperactivity							
Stoudenmire & Salter (1975)	1	No data	Primary reinforcement	Attention	Clinic	No	No
Exhibitionism							
Lutzker (1973)	1	Profound	Social reinforcement	Exhibitionism	Institution	3 wk.	Yes
Public Masturbation							
Cook et al. (1978)	1	Severe	Contingent lemon juice	Public masturbation	Home & school	6 mo.	Yes

[a] Subjects were additionally diagnosed as schizophrenic.

REFERENCES

AANES, D., & HAAGENSON, L. Normalization: Attention to a conceptual disaster. *Mental Retardation*, 1978, *16*, 55-56.

ADAMS, G. L., KIVOWITZ, J., & ZISKIND, E. Manic depressive psychosis, mental retardation and chromosal rearrangement. *Archives of General Psychiatry*, 1970, *23*, 305-309.

AFFLECK, G. G. Role-taking ability and interpersonal conflict resolution among retarded young adults. *American Journal of Mental Deficiency*, 1975, *80*, 223-236. (a)

AFFLECK, G. G. Role-taking ability and the interpersonal competencies of retarded children. *American Journal of Mental Deficiency*, 1975, *80*, 312-316. (b)

AFFLECK, G. G. Role-taking ability and the interpersonal tactics of retarded children. *American Journal of Mental Deficiency*, 1976, *80*, 667-670.

ATKESON, B. M., & FOREHAND, R. Home-based reinforcement programs to modify classroom behavior: A review and methodological evaluation. *Psychological Bulletin*, 1979, *86*, 1298-1308.

AYLLON, T., & AZRIN, N. *The token economy: A motivational system for therapist rehabilitation.* New York: Meredith, 1968.

AZRIN, N. H., & FOXX, R. M. A rapid method of toilet training the institutionalized retarded. *Journal of Applied Behavior Analysis*, 1971, *4*, 89-99.

BARTON, E. S. Operant conditioning of appropriate and inappropriate social speech in the profoundly retarded. *Journal of Mental Deficiency Research*, 1973, *17*, 183-191.

BIJOU, S. W. A functional analysis of retarded development. In N. R. Ellis (Ed.), *International review of research in mental retardation.* New York: Academic Press, 1966.

BORUCHOW, A. W., & ESPENSHADE, M. E. A socialization program for mentally retarded young adults. *Mental Retardation*, 1976, *14*, 40-42.

BRODSKY, G. The relation between verbal and nonverbal behavior change. *Behaviour Research and Therapy*, 1967, *5*, 182-191.

BROOKS, P. H., & BAUMEISTER, A. A. A plea for consideration of ecological validity in the experimental psychology of mental retardation: A guest editorial. *American Journal of Mental Deficiency*, 1977, *81*, 407-416.

CARLSON, G. Affective psychoses in mental retardates. *Psychiatric Clinics of North America*, 1979, *2*, 499-510.

CHARLES, D. C., & MCGRATH, K. The relationship of peer and staff ratings to release from institutionalization. *American Journal of Mental Deficiency*, 1962, *67*, 414-417.

CLOUSTON, T. S. *Clinical lectures on mental diseases.* London: J. & A. Churchill, 1883.

COOK, J. W., ALTMAN, K., SHAW, J., & BLAYLOCK, M. Use of contingent lemon juice to eliminate public masturbation by a severely retarded boy. *Behaviour Research and Therapy*, 1978, *16*, 131-134.

CRAFT, M. Mental disorder in the defective: A psychiatric survey among inpatients. *American Journal of Mental Deficiency*, 1959, *63*, 829-934.

CUVO, A. J. Decreasing repetitive behavior in an institutionalized mentally retarded resident. *Mental Retardation*, 1976, *14*, 22-25.

DEUTSCH, M., & PARKS, L. A. The use of contingent music to increase appropriate conversational speech. *Mental Retardation*, 1978, *16*, 33-36.

DOLJANAC, R. F., SCHRADER, S. J., & CHRISTIAN, J. G. *Development of verbal interaction skills in the mentally retarded.* Paper presented at the Association for Advancement of Behavior Therapy, Atlanta, November 1977.

DOLL, E. The essentials of an inclusive concept of mental deficiency. *American Journal of Mental Deficiency*, 1941, *46*, 211-219.

DOUBROS, S. G. Behavior therapy with high level, institutionalized, retarded adolescents. *Exceptional Children*, 1966, *12*, 229-233.

EARL, C. J. C. *Subnormal personalities: Their clinical investigation and assessment.* London: Balliere, Tindal & Cox, 1961.

EDWARDS, M., & LILLY, R. T. Operant conditioning: An application to behavioral problems in groups. *Mental Retardation,* 1966, *4,* 18-20.

ELLIS, N. R. Toilet training the severely defective patient on S—R reinforcement analysis. *American Journal of Mental Deficiency,* 1963, *68,* 98-103.

ELLIS, N. R., BARNETT, C. D., & PRYER, M. W. Operant behavior in mental defectives: Exploratory studies. *Journal of Experimental Analysis of Behavior,* 1960, *3,* 63-69.

ENGEL, A. M. Employment of the mentally retarded. In *Vocational rehabilitation of the mentally retarded.* Washington, D. C.: U.S. Department of Health, Education and Welfare, 1958.

FERSTER, C. B., & SKINNER, B. F. *Schedules of reinforcement.* New York: Appleton-Century-Crofts, 1957.

FOREHAND, R., & BAUMEISTER, A. A. Deceleration of aberrant behavior among retarded individuals. In M. Hersen, R. M. Eisler, & P. M. Miller (Eds.), *Progress in behavior modification* (Vol. 2). New York: Academic Press, 1976.

FOXX, R. M., & AZRIN, N. H. The elimination of autistic self-stimulatory behavior by overcorrection. *Journal of Applied Behavior Analysis,* 1973, *6,* 1-14.

FRIEDMAN, P. H. The effects of modeling and role playing on assertive behavior. In R. D. Rubin, H. Fensterheim, A. A. Lazarus, & C. M. Franks (Eds.), *Advances in behavior therapy.* New York: Academic Press, 1971.

GIBSON, F. W., LAWRENCE, S. P., & NELSON, R. O. Comparison of three training procedures for teaching social responses to developmentally disabled adults. *American Journal of Mental Deficiency,* 1976, *81,* 379-387.

GROSSMAN, H. (Ed.) *Manual on terminology and classification in mental retardation.* Washington: American Association on Mental Deficiency, 1977.

GURALNICK, M. J. Behavior therapy with an acrophobic mentally retarded young adult. *Journal of Behavior Therapy and Experimental Psychiatry,* 1973, *4,* 263-265.

HARVEY, J. R. The potential of relaxation training for the mentally retarded. *Mental Retardation,* 1979, *17,* 71-76.

HARVEY, J. R., KARAN, O. C., BHARGAVA, D., & MOREHOUSE, N. Relaxation training and cognitive behavioral procedures to reduce violent temper outbursts in a moderately retarded woman. *Journal of Behavior Therapy and Experimental Psychiatry,* 1978, *9,* 347-351.

HAYWOOD, H. C. What happened to mild and moderate mental retardation? *American Journal of Mental Deficiency,* 1979, *83,* 429-431.

HEATON-WARD, A. Psychosis in mental handicap. *British Journal of Psychiatry,* 1977, *130,* 525-533.

HERBERT, E. W., & BAER, D. M. Training parents as behavior modifiers: Self-recording of contingent attention. *Journal of Applied Behavior Analysis,* 1972, *5,* 139-149.

HERSEN, M., & BELLACK, A. S. A multiple-baseline analysis of social skills training in chronic schizophrenics. *Journal of Applied Behavior Analysis,* 1976, *9,* 239-245. (a)

HERSEN, M., & BELLACK, A. S. Social skills training for chronic psychiatric patients: Rationale, research findings and future directions. *Comprehensive Psychiatry,* 1976, *17,* 559-580. (b)

HERSEN, M., & BELLACK, A. S. Assessment of social skills. In A. R. Ciminero, K. S. Calhoun, & H. E. Adams (Eds.), *Handbook for behavioral assessment.* New York: Wiley, 1977.

HERSEN, M., EISLER, R. N., MILLER, P. M., JOHNSON, M. B., & PINKSTON, S. G. Effects of practice, instructions and modeling on components of assertive behavior. *Behaviour Research and Therapy,* 1973, *11,* 443-451.

HERSKOVITZ, H. H., & PLESSET, M. R. Psychoses in adult mental defectives. *Psychiatric Quarterly,* 1941, *15,* 574-588.

HURD, H. M. Inbecility with insanity. *Journal of Insanity,* 1888, *45,* 263-371

HUTZELL, R. R., PLATZEK, D., & LOGUE, P. E. Control of symptoms of Gilles de la Tourette syndrome by self-monitoring. *Journal of Behavior Therapy and Experimental Psychiatry,* 1974, 5, 71-76.

JAFFE, P. G., & CARLSON, P. M. Relative efficacy of modeling and instructions in eliciting social behavior from chronic psychiatric patients. *Journal of Consulting and Clinical Psychology,* 1976, 44, 200-207.

KAZDIN, A. E. The effect of response cost in suppressing behavior in a pre-psychotic retardate. *Journal of Behavior Therapy and Experimental Psychiatry,* 1971, 2, 137-140.

KELLY, J. A., FURMAN, W., PHILLIPS, J., HATHORN, S., & WILSON, T. Teaching conversational skills to retarded adolescents. *Child Behavior Therapy,* in press.

KELLY, J. A., WILDMAN, B. G., UREY, J. J. R., & THURMAN, C. Group skills training to increase the conversational repertoire of retarded adolescents. Paper presented at the meeting of the Southeastern Psychological Association, New Orleans, March 1979.

KOEGEL, R. L., & COVERT, A. The relationship of self-stimulation to learning in autistic children. *Journal of Applied Behavioral Analysis,* 1972, 5, 381-387.

KOLSTOE, O. P., & SHAFTER, A. J. Employability prediction for mentally retarded adults: A methodological note. *American Journal of Mental Deficiency,* 1961, 66, 287-289.

KRISHEFT, C. H., REYNOLDS, M. C., & STUNKARD, C. L. A study of factors related to rating post-institutional adjustment. *Minnesota Welfare,* 1959, 11, 5-15.

LOHMANN, W, FYMAN, R. K., & LASK, E. Toilet training. *American Journal of Mental Deficiency,* 1967, 71, 551-557.

LOVAAS, O. I., LITROWNIK, A., & MANN, R. Response latencies to auditory stimuli in autistic children engaged in self-stimulatory behavior. *Behaviour Research and Therapy,* 1971, 9, 39-49.

LUISELLI, J. K., COLOZZI, G., DONELLON, S., HELFEN, C. S., & PEMBERTON, B. W. Training and generalization of a greeting exchange with a mentally retarded language-deficient child. *Education and Treatment of Children,* 1978, 1, 23-30.

LUTZKER, J. R. Reinforcement control of exhibitionism in a profoundly retarded adult. *Proceedings of 81st Annual Convention, American Psychological Association,* 1973, 925-926.

MAHONEY, M. J. Some applied issues in self-monitoring. In J. D. Cone & R. P. Hawkins (Eds.), *Behavioral assessment: New directions in clinical psychology.* New York: Brunner/Mazel, 1977.

MAHONEY, M. J., & MAHONEY, K. Self-control techniques with the mentally retarded. *Mental Retardation,* 1976, 14, 338-340.

MANSDORF, I. J. Eliminating fear in a mentally retarded adult by behavioral hierarchies and operant techniques. *Journal of Behavior Therapy and Experimental Psychiatry,* 1976, 7, 189-190.

MARTIN, G. C., KEHOE, B., BIRD, E., JENSEN, V., & DARBYSHIRE, M. Operant conditioning in dressing behavior of severely retarded girls. *Mental Retardation,* 1971, 9, 27-31.

MATSON, J. L. Decreasing inappropriate verbalizations of a moderately retarded adult by a staff assisted self-control program. *The Australian Journal of Mental Retardation,* 1979, 5, 242-245.

MATSON, J. L. Acquisition of social skills by mentally retarded adult training assistants. *Journal of Mental Deficiency Research,* 1980, 24, 129-135.

MATSON, J. L. A controlled outcome study of phobias in mentally retarded adults. *Behaviour Research and Therapy,* 1981, 19, 101-108.

MATSON, J. L. Assessment and treatment of clinical phobias in mentally retarded children. *Journal of Applied Behavior Analysis,* 1981, 14, 145-152.

MATSON, J. L. Preventing home accidents: A training program for the retarded. *Behavior Modification,* 1980, 4, 397-410.

MATSON, J. L., & ANDRASIK, F. Training leisure-time social interaction skills to mildly mentally retarded. *American Journal of Mental Deficiency,* 1982, 86, 533-542.

Matson, J. L., & Earnhart, T. Programming treatment effects to the natural environment: A social learning procedure for training institutionalized retarded adults. *Behavior Modification*, 1981, 5, 27-38.

Matson, J. L. & Stephens, R. M. Increasing appropriate behavior of explosive chronic psychiatric patients with a social skills training package. *Behavior Modification*, 1978, 2, 61-75.

Matson, J. L., & Zeiss, R. A. Group training of social skills in chronically explosive, severely disturbed psychiatric patients. *Behavioral Engineering*, 1978, 5, 41-50.

Matson, J. L., & Zeiss, R. A. The buddy system: A method for generalized reduction of inappropriate interpersonal behavior of retarded psychiatric patients. *British Journal of Social and Clinical Psychology*, 1979, 18, 401-405.

Matson, J. L., Zeiss, A. M., Zeiss, R. A., & Bowman, W. A comparison of social skills training and contingent attention to improve behavioral deficits of chronic psychiatric patients. *British Journal of Social and Clinical Psychology*, 1980, 19, 57-64.

Matson, J. L., Dettling, J., & Senatore, V. Treating depression of a mentally retarded adult. *The British Journal of Mental Subnormality*, 1981, 16, 86-88.

McDaniel, J. Group action in the rehabilitation of the mentally retarded. *Group Psychotherapy*, 1960, 13, 543.

McFall, R. M. The effects of self-monitoring on normal smoking behavior. *Journal of Consulting and Clinical Psychology*, 1970, 35, 135-142.

McFall, R. M., & Marston, A. R. An experimental investigation of behavior rehearsal in assertive training. *Journal of Abnormal Psychology*, 1970, 76, 295-303.

Mulhern, T., & Baumeister, A. A. An experimental attempt to reduce stereotypy by reinforcement procedures. *American Journal of Mental Deficiency*, 1969, 74, 69-74.

Nelson, R. O. Methodological issues in assessment via self-monitoring. In J.D. Cone & R.P. Hawkins (Eds.)., *Behavioral assessment: New directions in clinical psychology*. New York: Brunner/Mazel, 1977.

O'Brien, F., & Azrin, N. H. Developing proper mealtime behaviors of the institutionalized retarded. *Journal of Applied Behavior Analysis*, 1972, 5, 389-399.

Paloutzian, R. F., Hasazi, J., Streifel, J., & Edgar, C. L. Promotion of positive social interaction in severely retarded young children. *American Journal of Mental Deficiency*, 1971, 75, 519-524.

Payne, R. The psychotic subnormal. *Journal of Mental Subnormality*, 1968, 34, 25-34.

Peck, C. L. Desensitization for the treatment of fear in the high level adult retardate. *Behaviour Research and Therapy*, 1977, 15, 137-148.

Perry, M. A., & Cerreto, M. C. Structured learning training of social skills for the retarded. *Mental Retardation*, 1977, 15, 31-34.

Rabkin, J. G. Criminal behavior of discharged mental patients: A critical appraisal of the research. *Psychological Reports*, 1979, 44, 1-27.

Reid, A. H. Psychoses in adult mental defectives: I. Manic depressive psychosis. *American Journal of Psychiatry*, 1972, 120, 205-212.

Reid, A. H. Psychiatric disturbances in the mentally handicapped. *Proceedings of the Royal Society of Medicine*, 1976, 69, 509-512.

Reid, A. H., & Naylor, G. J. Short-cycle manic depressive psychosis in mental defectives: A clinical and physiological study. *Journal of Mental Deficiency Research*, 1976, 20, 67-76.

Rivinus, T. M., & Harmatz, J. S. Diagnosis and lithium treatment of affective disorder in the retarded: Five case studies. *American Journal of Psychiatry*, 1979, 136, 551-554.

Roith, A. I. Psychotic depression in a mongol. *Journal of Mental Subnormality*, 1961, 7, 45-47.

Rychtarik, R. G., & Bornstein, P. H. Training conversational skills in mentally retarded adults: A multiple baseline analysis. *Mental Retardation*, 1979, 17, 289-293.

Sarason, S. B., & Gladwin, T. The severely defective individual. *The Journal of Nervous and Mental Disease*, 1958, 126, 64-96.

Schalock, R. L., & Harper, R. S. Placement from community-based mental retardation pro-

grams: How well do clients do? *American Journal of Mental Deficiency*, 1978, *83*, 240-247.
Schutz, R., Wehman, P., Renzaglia, A., & Karan, O. Efficacy of contingent social disapproval on inappropriate verbalizations of two severely retarded males. *Behavior Therapy*, 1978, *9*, 657-662.
Segal, S., & Aviram, V. Community-based sheltered care. In P. Ahmed & S. Plot (Eds.), *State mental hospitals*. New York: Plenum Press, 1976.
Seitz, S., & Hoekenga, R. Modeling as a training tool for retarded children and their parents. *Mental Retardation*, 1974, *12*, 28-31.
Skaarbrevik, K. J. A follow-up study of educable mentally retarded in Norway. *American Journal of Mental Deficiency*, 1971, *75*, 560-565.
Spradlin, J. E., Girardeau, F. L., & Corte, E. Fixed ratio and fixed interval behavior of severely and profoundly retarded subjects. *Journal of Experimental Child Psychology*, 1965, *2*, 340-353.
Stephan, C., Stephano, S., & Talkington, L. W. Use of modeling in survival skill training with educable mentally retarded. *The Training School Bulletin*, 1973, *70*, 63-68.
Stephens, R. M., Matson, J. L., Westmoreland, T., & Kulpal, J. Social skills training with chronic retarded-psychotic patients. *Journal of Mental Deficiency Research*, 1981, *25*, 187-197.
Stokes, T. F., Baer, D. M., & Jackson, R. L. Programming the generalization of a greeting response in four retarded children. *Journal of Applied Behavior Analysis*, 1974, *7*, 599-610.
Stoudenmire, J., & Salter, L. Conditioning prosocial behaviors in a mentally retarded child without using instructions. *Journal of Behavior Therapy and Experimental Psychiatry*, 1975, *6*, 39-42.
Talkington, L. W., Hall, S. M., & Altman, R. Use of peer modeling procedure with severely retarded subjects on a basic communication response skill. *The Training School Bulletin*, 1973, *69*, 145-149.
The Committee on Nomenclature and Statistics of the American Psychiatric Association. *DSM-III: Diagnostic and Statistical Manual of Mental Disorders* (3rd ed.) Washington, D.C.: American Psychiatric Association, 1980.
Turner, S. M., Hersen, M., & Bellack, A. S. Use of social skills training to teach prosocial behaviors in an organically impaired and retarded patient. *Journal of Behavior Therapy and Experimental Psychiatry*, 1978, *9*, 253-258.
Twentyman, G. T., & McFall, R. M. Behavioral training of social skills in shy males. *Journal of Consulting and Clinical Psychology*, 1975, *43*, 384-395.
Wehman, P., Karan, O., & Rettie, C. Developing independent play in three severely retarded women. *Psychological Reports*, 1976, *39*, 995-998.
Weiss, D., & Weinstein, E. A. Interpersonal tactics among mental retardates. *American Journal of Mental Deficiency*, 1967, *72*, 267-271.
Whalen, C. K., & Henker, B. A. Creating therapeutic pyramids using mentally retarded patients. *American Journal of Mental Deficiency*, 1969, *74*, 331-337.
Whitman, T. L., Burish, T., & Collins, C. Development of interpersonal language responses in two moderately retarded children. *Mental Retardation*, 1972, *10*, 40-45.
Whitman, T. L., Mercurio, J. R., & Caponigri, V. Deveolopment of social responses in two severely retarded children. *Journal of Applied Behavior Analysis*, 1970, *3*, 133-138.
Wolfensberger, W. Will there always be an institution? Part I: The impact of epidemiological trends. *Mental Retardation*, 1971, *9*, 14-20.
Wortmann, H., & Paluck, R. J. Assertion training with institutionalized severely retarded women. *Behavior Therapist*, 1979, *2*, 24-25.
Zaharia, R. *Behavior modification and normalization: A process of checks and balances*. Paper presented at Region VIII AAMD Conference, October 1975.
Zegiob, L., Klukas, N., & Junginger, J. Reactivity of self-monitoring procedures with retarded adolescents. *American Journal of Mental Deficiency*, 1978, *83*, 156-163.

ZIGLER, E. Research on personality structure in the retardate. In N.R. Ellis (Ed.), *International review of research in mental retardation*. New York: Academic Press, 1966.

ZIGLER, E., & PHILLIPS, L. Social effectiveness and symptomatic behaviors. *Journal of Abnormal Social Psychology*, 1960, *61*, 231-238.

12 Psychoactive Drugs in Mental Retardation

MICHAEL G. AMAN

INTRODUCTION

Psychopharmacology, or the use of drugs to modify behavior, received its real birth in the 1950s with the introduction of chlorpromazine which was synthetically produced (Caldwell, 1978). In the three decades which have since intervened, there has been an explosive development in the variety of drugs manufactured and in the rate of psychotropic drug prescription in virtually every type of mental disorder. The area of mental retardation is no exception and indeed the prescription of psychoactive drugs has reached exceptionally large proportions in this population.

With this in mind, a knowledge of the psychoactive drugs is very important to those involved in treatment of the mentally retarded. This chapter will attempt to review prevailing attitudes toward psychoactive medication, the prevalence of drug prescription among the mentally retarded, and the scientific evidence attesting to the usefulness of these agents. Some shortcomings of past research will be identified, accompanied by suggested trends for the future. This will be followed by a discussion of ethical issues surrounding psychotropic drug treatment.

In this chapter, the term *psychoactive drug* will be used to refer to any substance which produces behavioral, emotional, or cognitive changes, and *psychotropic drug* will be used somewhat more restrictively to refer to psychoactive drugs which are administered for the express *purpose* of producing such changes. The drugs discussed in this chapter, their respective classes, and trade names are presented in the Appendix.

MICHAEL G. AMAN • Department of Psychiatry, School of Medicine, University of Auckland, P. B., Auckland, New Zealand. Preparation of this manuscript was supported by a grant from the Medical Research Council and the Child Health Research Foundation of New Zealand to Professor J.S. Werry

Attitudes toward Psychopharmacolgy and Its Role

Pharmacotherapy has received a variable reception, depending in part on the discipline of the person involved. Historically, some psychotherapists, particularly those with a psychodynamic orientation, spurned the use of psychotropic drugs in the belief that such treatment would interfere with patient-therapist interactions and modify symptoms before their role was understood (see Freeman, 1970b). Furthermore, the prechlorpromazine era saw the use of many ineffective and even toxic substances, and this soured the medical profession toward psychotropic agents in general (Caldwell, 1978).

Elsewhere, many nonmedical specialists see the use of pharmacotherapy as an insidious means for defining mental retardation as a "medical domain," and thus as a way of infringing on professional territory which is "rightfully" theirs. Others liken drug treatment to a "chemical straitjacket" which suppresses symptoms but does nothing to assist, and may even retard, the person in his development.

In the past, there has also been considerable debate about what results could be obtained through the use of drugs. At one time serious attempts were actually made to reverse intellectual deficits through the use of substances such as glutamic acid, pituitary extract, and Vitamin B_1 (see Freeman, 1970a; Louttit, 1965; Share, 1976). This has been referred to as the "magic bullet" theory (Yannet, 1957; Wolfensberger & Menolascino, 1968).

However, today pharmacotherapy is usually employed in the hopes of diminishing pathological behavior and of ultimately encouraging the development of adaptive behavior. The problem is that knowledge of the effects of many psychoactive drugs is based more on medical lore than on a solid and well-developed empirical base. It is important to remember that psychoactive drugs provide nothing which is not already possessed by the person concerned. As pointed out by Hollis and St. Omer (1972) "drugs can merely accelerate or decelerate behaviors which are already in the subject's repertoire or change the probability of their occurence" (p. 403). Assuming that the direction of change is known beforehand, medication could provide a powerful therapeutic adjunct. Since psychotropic drugs are almost always given for treatment of behavior problems in this population, it is appropriate to take a brief look at the nature of behavior problems in the mentally retarded.

Behavior Problems in the Mentally Retarded

This topic is covered in much greater depth in other chapters of this book (see Chapter 9). The incidence of certain behavior problems is apparently much greater among the mentally retarded than among the general population. Payne, Johnson, and Abelson (1969, cited in Gadow, 1979) conducted a massive survey encompassing more than 24,000 residents. Ward personnel were asked to rate the residents on a 4-point scale, ranging from "never" to "frequently". The most common maladaptive behaviors rated as "frequently" were hyperactivity, aggressivity, running, and self-destructiveness. Twenty-one percent of the residents were described as occasionally hyperactive and/or aggressive. Rutter (1975) found that, as assessed by parent and teacher scales, behavioral problems in mentally retarded children are in the range of 30% to 40%—several times the rate of that in the general population. He also pointed out that three disorders and one symptom tend to occur more commonly among the mentally retarded: autism, disintegrative psychosis, hyperkinetic syndrome, and stereotyped repetitive movements.

Philips and Williams (1975) studied 100 consecutive mentally retarded referrals to a child psychiatric clinic. Thirty-eight of these children were found to have psychotic symptoms, and 49 had nonpsychotic disorders. The most commonly occurring problems were: aggression, poor social relations, developmental lags, "neurotic" traits, and school problems. The authors took pains to point out that this pattern differed little from nonretarded children referred for emotional problems, but it is clear that their *incidence* is greatly inflated. In a subsequent report, Philips and Williams (1977) examined the incidence of hyperactivity from the above sample. Of the 62 nonpsychotic children, 19 (or 31%) were categorized as hyperactive (DSM II); of the 38 psychotic children, 20 (or 54%) were hyperactive. Although the authors pointed out that hyperactivity was not an *inevitable* concomitant of mental retardation, their figures certainly suggest a strong association.

Schroeder, Schroeder, Smith, and Dalldorf (1978) conducted a survey of *self-injurious behavior* (SIB) over three years in a large institution for the mentally retarded. Their results showed that approximately 10% of cases were identified as having SIB at each of three intervals, a result similar to other investigations in the area (Maisto, Baumeister, & Maisto, 1978). Self-injurious behavior tended to occur more commonly among the more severely retarded, those who were institutionalized longer, and among younger cases.

Gardner (1967) presented contrasting arguments as to why the mentally retarded might be expected to have either higher or lower levels of depressive illness. The four pertinent epidemiological studies cited found a range of incidence of about .3% to 1.1%. Although Gardner concludes that the area requires more research, these studies are consistent in suggesting that the incidence of depressive illness in mental retardation is fairly low.

It must be remembered that studies such as the above render only rough figures, since many of the disorders have not been sufficiently operational to render unequivocal diagnosis, because of referral biases, and because some of the investigations did not employ control groups. Nevertheless, by sheer force of numbers, these investigations make it clear that there is a substantially higher incidence of behavior problems among the mentally retarded, especially those who are institutionalized. Prominent among these behavior problems are psychotic behavior, hyperactivity, and stereotyped movements; depressive illness, however, is probably not found in large proportions among the mentally retarded.

Prevalence of Psychoactive Drug Treatment

In Institutions

There have been a number of surveys attempting to assess the incidence of psychotropic drug prescription among the mentally retarded. These are presented in Table I. Prevalences of psychotropic and anticonvulsant drugs are presented separately since psychotropic drugs are generally prescribed specifically for a behavioral problem, whereas anticonvulsants are usually (but not always) given for a seizure disorder. However, it should be noted that regardless of *intent* behind prescription of these drugs, anticonvulsants are increasingly being regarded as definitely having psychoactive effects (Stores, 1978).

When prevalence of psychotropic drugs is examined in Table I, it can be seen that, in general, between 40% and 50% of institutionalized patients receive such medications. Approximately 25% to 35% of residents receive anticonvulsant medications. Of those studies reporting both psychotropic and anticonvulsant medication (Bullmore, cited in Kirman, 1975; Cohen & Sprague, 1977; Hughes, 1977; Pulman, Pook, & Singh, 1979; Silva, 1979; Spencer, 1974; Tu, 1979), the range varied from 50% to 68%, indicating that *more than half* of institutionalized patients can be expected to be on psychoactive medication at any one time. Thus, it can readily be seen that psychoactive drug treatment holds a prominent (although unproven) place in institutions for the mentally retarded.

Lipman's (1970) study, which is often quoted, is an interesting case. Lipman conducted a comprehensive survey in which questionnaires were sent to 160 institutions for the mentally retarded. He found that 51% of all residents had been or were being treated with psychotropic medication. Thioridazine (Mellaril) and chlorpromazine (Thorazine) accounted for 58% of all drug usage. The institutions involved also reported that roughly 25% of patients

TABLE I
Prevalence of Drug Treatment in the Mentally Retarded

Authors	Number of patients surveyed	% receiving psychotropic medication	% receiving anticonvulsant drugs	Total percentage[a]	Most common drugs prescribed
Lipman, 1970	Residents of 109 state and private institutions	51%[b]	Not reported	Not reported	Thioridazine, chlorpromazine, trifluoperazine, diazepam, chlordiazepoxide
Spencer, 1974	585	22% + (antipsychotics only surveyed)	24%	51% +	Phenobarbitone, haloperidol, chlorpromazine, phenytoin, thioridazine
Bullmore (cited in Kirman, 1975)	617	?	27%	60%	Not reported
Sewell & Werry, 1976	254	40%	Not reported	Not reported	Thioridazine, chlorpromazine, methotrimeprazine, nitrazepam
Cohen & Sprague, 1977	1,924	51%	36%	66%	Thioridazine, chlorpromazine, phenobarbital, diazepam, primadone, mesoridazine
Hughes, 1977	219	Not reported	Not reported	68%	Phenobarbital, phenytoin, diazepam (usually as an anticonvulsant), chlorpromazine, thioridazine, haloperidol

Continued

TABLE I (*continued*)

Authors	Number of patients surveyed	% receiving psychotropic medication	% receiving anticonvulsant drugs	Total percentage[a]	Most common drugs prescribed
Pulman, Pook, & Singh, 1979	435	46.9%	34.3%	60%	Phenytoin, diazepam, carbamazepine, trimeprazine, haloperidol, phenobarbitone, promethazine
Silva, 1979	260	?	24.2%	65.8%	Phenytoin, phenobarbital, thioridazine, hydroxyzine, primadone
Tu, 1979	2,238	42%	27%	58%	Thioridazine, chlorpromazine, mesoridazine, diazepam, thioxanthene
Gadow, 1979 (noninstitutionalized children)	3,306	7%	12%	18%	Phenytoin, phenobarbital, methylphenidate, primadone, thioridazine, diazepam

[a]Since there is overlap (some patients received *both* psychotropic and anticonvulsant drugs), the two component percentages will not necessarily sum to equal the total percentage.

[b]This figure may represent an overestimate of drug incidence since the survey asked how many patients had been, or were currently being, treated with psychotropic medication.

typically received these drugs for 4 or more years. Furthermore, Lipman noted that a number of drugs were often given in dosages that *exceeded* the manufacturer's recommendations. This occurred in particular with the antipsychotic and benzodiazepine drugs, which are known to have depressant or sedative effects.

Tu and Smith (1979) examined the association between rate of medication in institutions for the mentally retarded and various patient characteristics. In the population of over 2,000 patients studied, it was found that (1) females were given more drugs than male residents, (2) there was far greater drug use in *small* institutions than in large ones, and (3) there was far greater drug use among psychotic than nonpsychotic patients. However, age and degree of subnormality were *not* related to the frequency of drug prescription.

With Noninstitutionalized Retardates

At the time of writing, only one survey exists of drug usage in noninstitutionalized mentally retarded persons. Gadow (1979, 1981) surveyed all programs for the trainable mentally handicapped in the State of Illinois. He found that 7% of these children were receiving psychotropic medication for behavioral/emotional problems, and 11% were receiving anticonvulsant drugs. Therefore, a total of 18% were receiving psychoactive treatment.

Summary

Thus, large percentages of institutionalized patients receive psychoactive drugs as part of their treatment. Although the 18% prevalence figure reported for noninstitutionalized mentally retarded persons is lower on a percentage basis, the absolute number of such children affected is still large, perhaps even larger than those so treated in institutions. The implications are obvious. The professional involved with treatment of the mentally retarded, regardless of his professional affiliation, cannot afford to be ignorant of the uses and abuses, as well as the risks, involved with psychoactive treatment of these persons.

LITERATURE REVIEW

Background and Scope

Previous Reviews

For the interested reader, there are several excellent drug reviews which may also be consulted to augment the present chapter. The reviews by Freeman (1970a) and by Sprague and Werry (1971) are probably the most comprehensive. Freeman's paper is notable because of its thorough clinical detail, whereas that by Sprague and Werry studies the area from a rigorous methodological stance.

Other good reviews include a chapter by Freeman (1970b) which is directed to physicians and stresses general principles of management and drug administration. Lipman, DiMascio, Reatig, and Kirson (1978) have prepared an up-to-date and thorough examination of the antipsychotic and stimulant drug literature. Sprague and Baxley (1978) have incisively explored the philosophical implications of prescribing psychotropic drugs, as well as the ethical and legal aspects of such treatment. A chapter by Werry and Sprague (1972) is valuable because of the distinctive perspective (drug companies, physicians, government, and public) offered of drug treatment. Finally, Wolfensberger and Menolascino (1968) have presented an excellent discussion of principles involved in evaluating the ability of drugs to improve cognitive development.

Methodological Considerations

Before proceeding to the literature survey, it is appropriate to examine a number of considerations which bear strongly on the scientific merit of any drug investigation. Sprague and Werry (1971) outlined six minimal criteria which should be observed when conducting such a study. These include provision of placebo control, random assignment to drug groups, "blind" evaluation of drug effects to minimize bias, standardized dosages, standardized evaluations, and appropriate statistical analysis. Aman and Singh (1980) added another criterion; namely, that the trials should be free of other, confounding drugs. Although this last requirement would seem to be self-evident, it is startling to note how often it is violated, rendering a substantial percentage of studies in this area uninterpretable. When Sprague and Werry (1971) reviewed this area, they noted with dismay that few of the studies with the mentally retarded actually fulfilled all these criteria. We shall return at the end of the literature review to see if there have been significant improvements over the last 10 years.

Scope of This Review

The review which follows will present a sample of the best research conducted up to 1970 (a period comprehensively reviewed by Sprague and Werry, 1971, and by Freeman, 1970a). Research completed during the last decade will be covered if it was published in English, was conducted with mentally retarded subjects, and stressed behavioral, cognitive, or emotional changes. Studies emphasizing side effects and physiological effects are generally not covered. This selectivity, stressing the most recent work and presenting only the best of earlier work, may give the false impression that this body of research is of a higher caliber than is in fact the case. The reader should be warned of this bias in reporting, but it seemed most useful to summarize the best material rather than to present an endless array of bad studies just to prove a point.

Major Tranquilizers: Antipsychotics, Neuroleptics

As shown in Table I, this class of drugs has been the major one used in the treatment of behavioral problems in mentally retarded persons. No doubt part of the initial popularity of this group was based on the apparent similarity of some maladaptive behaviors in the mentally retarded to the symptoms of nonretarded psychotic patients, presumably making these behaviors amenable to antipsychotic drug treatment. Of course such logic is not necessarily valid. Three drugs from this category account for the majority of antipsychotic drug usage: chlorpromazine and thioridazine, which are classified as phenothiazines, and haloperidol which is a butyrophenone.

Phenothiazines

Chlorpromazine. Chlorpromazine (Largactil, Thorazine, Megaphen) is one of the oldest and most extensively used psychotropic drugs in mental retardation. Because of its popularity among clinicians, it has served as the comparison drug in numerous studies examining the relative effects of two or more drugs.

Ison (1957) conducted a relatively well-controlled study in which the effects of chlorpromazine and placebo on intelligence were compared. The WISC (Wechsler Intelligence Scale for Children) or the WAIS (Wechsler Adult Intelligence Scale) were used according to the subject's ability. The results of this trial indicated that, of a total of 14 statistical comparisons, only two subtests (Comprehension and Digit Symbol) showed significant drug effects, in both cases in the direction of improvement. This study was unique, not only because it fulfilled all the experimental criteria outlined earlier, but because an effort was made to examine the response of diagnostic subgroups. Subjects characterized as brain damaged seemed to show a better response to chlorpromazine than the other groups, but this finding needs replication before it can be accepted as a reliable phenomenon.

Adamson, Nellis, Runge, Cleland, and Killian (1958) compared the effects of chlorpromazine, reserpine, chlorpromazine-plus-reserpine, and placebo. Subjects received each drug for 60 days in a crossover design (i.e., each subject served as his own control). The results suggested problem behaviors were reduced most by chlorpromazine, then by reserpine, and least by placebo. Unfortunately, the statistical analysis used was not entirely satisfactory so that these descriptive results could not be confirmed inferentially. It was especially notable that a placebo response was observed in 40% to 70% of subjects and lasted up to 6 weeks. This nonspecific drug response is a phenomenon that all too many researchers choose to ignore, shrugging off the need for untreated controls as unethical or "unnecessary."

Wardel, Rubin, and Ross (1958) examined the effects of chlorpromazine, reserpine, and placebo in behaviorally disturbed women. Measures of outcome included clinical global impressions, plus observations of five behavioral dimensions. The results were essentially nonsignificant, with neither of the drugs producing appreciable benefit. However, the strength of these negative conclusions is mitigated somewhat by low interobserver reliabilities and substantial data loss.

Moore (1960) adopted a novel approach to the assessment of drug effects. The subjects were 90 mentally retarded women who had been chronically treated with chlorpromazine. In half of the subjects, the drug was removed and replaced by placebo, whereas the remainder continued to receive their usual medication. The results indicated that the *placebo* group made greater gains than the chlorpromazine group on the Stanford Achievement Tests, although three other categories (Stanford Binet IQ, ratings of behavior, and ratings of academic progress) showed no drug-related differences. This study is alarming in that it suggests that chlorpromazine actually may have been *suppressing* achievement.

Hollis and St. Omer (1972) conducted an extremely involved study in which four standardized doses of chlorpromazine were compared to a no-drug condition under several types of operant control (discriminative stimulus, fixed ratio schedule, variable interval schedule, and extinction). Unfortunately, the results were reported graphically, selectively, and without inferential statistical analysis. The drug reportedly reduced operant responding and this effect was directly related to dose. Extinction of a lever response was apparently quickened by chlorpromazine, but so also was extinction of a rocking response which may be analogous to stereotypic movements. Such measures challenge easy interpretation, but the results can be construed as suggesting both diminished performance under drug (reduction of learned responses) as well as the promotion of improvement (rapid extinction of the rocking).

McConahey (1972) employed a double blind, crossover design to compare placebo to chlorpromazine. The unique aspect of this study was that the drug was being evaluated against the backdrop of a behavior-modification program which was implemented in the mornings only, with afternoons serving as control periods. The results indicated that chlorpromazine yielded no benefit as compared with placebo. Unfortunately, the analysis used was unidimensional in the sense that it allowed an evaluation of drug therapy and behavior modification in isolation. The appropriate analysis would have allowed an assessment of the *additive* effects of drug and behavior modification as well. This methodological flaw is particularly distressing since this was one of only two studies that could be located in which drug and behavioral treatment in the mentally retarded were compared.

Väisänen, Kainulainen, Paavilainen, and Viukari (1975) compared chlorpromazine, sulpiride (an antipsychotic), and placebo in 60 "restless" residents. The design was that of a double blind, placebo-controlled, crossover trial. Measures of change included ratings of six behavioral categories, two evaluations of sleep, and clinical global impressions. The only variable to show any changes was global impressions, with sulpiride (but not chlorpromazine) significantly better than placebo. There was also a tendency for sulpiride to surpass chlorpromazine, but this was nonsignificant.

Marholin, Touchette, and Stewart (1979) evaluated the effects of withdrawal of chlorpromazine, using a reversal design procedure, in five chronically treated residents. Objective measures of change were obtained, but the results are difficult to assess because of the small number of subjects and the limited number of crossovers in this study. Response to the drug was highly variable, but in some cases the drug apparently resulted in the worsening of both ward and workshop behaviors.

Sprague and Werry (1971) and Freeman (1970a) cite approximately 20 other studies examining chlorpromazine, most of which were poorly controlled or totally uncontrolled. Almost without exception these studies showed a drug-induced reduction in problem behavior. Such problem behaviors typically included aggressiveness, self-injury, stereotyped movements, and hyperactivity. However, conclusions of such research must be tempered by the outcome of better controlled studies such as those outlined above.

Despite chlorpromazine's well-entrenched place in the pharmacological treatment of behavior disorders in the mentally retarded, these earlier, well-controlled studies, and recent studies challenge its position. Regardless of the already massive volume of data, research of high calibre is still required to examine the effects of chlorpromazine on specific cognitive and behavioral functions and also in well-defined subgroups.

Thioridazine. Thioridazine (Mellaril) is another drug used extensively in the treatment of behavioral problems. Aman and Singh (1980) comprehensively reviewed studies of this drug in childhood disorders (including mental retardation, hyperactivity, "emotional" disorders, and epilepsy). Twenty-four studies were located, and these were evaluated according to the six methodological criteria outlined earlier. Only six of these studies fulfilled all the criteria satisfactorily. Furthermore, evaluations tended to be of the global, "better/worse" variety rather than of a standardized form which could reveal meaningful qualitative changes resulting from the drug. Also, only four of these 24 studies addressed themselves to the cognitive effects of this drug, and two of these suggested that thioridazine tends to impair intellectual performance. Two of the earlier studies and all those appearing since 1970 will be examined here.

Alexandris and Lundell (1968) conducted a double-blind assessment of thioridazine, amphetamine, and placebo in 21 hyperactive residents. The children were rated for drug changes on 14 behavioral dimensions, and their performance was assessed on the WISC, the Bender Visual Motor Gestalt Test, and the Goodenough Draw-A-Person Test. The results indicated that thioridazine caused the greatest social improvement, with 11 of the 14 behavioral categories showing a significant benefit over placebo. Most of these changes were in the area of hyperactivity, attention span, and aggressiveness. Amphetamine produced only two behavioral changes (improved concentration and work interest), but the dose was exceedingly high (mean of 52 mg/day) so that this was probably not an appropriate assessment of this drug. None of the psychological tests showed significant changes.

Davis, Sprague, and Werry (1969) carried out a double-blind, crossover trial comparing thioridazine, methylphenidate (Ritalin), and placebo. Subjects were nine severely retarded residents selected for high rates of stereotypy. Indices of drug change included amount of stereotypy, nonstereotyped behavior, gross body movement, rocking, and complex hand movements. Thioridazine caused a significant reduction in stereotyped movements, but no changes in other behaviors. Methylphenidate caused no significant changes. This was a model study, concentrating not only on possible positive changes but also on whether or not a reduction occurred in other, adaptive behaviors as well.

In a poorly controlled trial, Le Vann (1970) compared thioridazine, chlorprothixene (Tarasan), and placebo. Both drugs produced a reduction in problem behaviors (hostility, overactivity, sleep problems) with chlorprothixene rendering the greatest improvement.

Davis (1971) carried out a second study examining the effects of thioridazine, methylphenidate, and placebo. Subjects were taught to perform a rocking and a bar-pressing response in the presence of specified discriminative stimuli. The results were essentially nonsignificant with no drug-related changes; however, there was some evidence that the drugs caused greater *variability* in performance.

Heistad and Zimmerman (1979) reported an investigation in which, owing to a court order, all patients had to be taken off medication for a trial period, presumably to determine whether the drug was warranted in individual cases. They exploited the occasion to derive empirical data by substituting placebo when thioridazine was terminated. The design was double blind but with a single crossover (i.e., drug was always given *first,* placebo second). Measures of drug effect included a nurses' rating scale, plus an observational, time-sampling technique which rendered 10 categories. Positive changes favoring thioridazine were found on "self-stimulation," a "net adaptive," and two composit categories. The nurses' scale was essentially negative, but there was a significant effect for the combined positive dimensions.

Singh and Aman (1981) withdrew 19 severely retarded residents from their former thioridazine treatment and stepped them through a trial comparing a low standardized dose of thioridazine, the residents' previous individual doses, and placebo. Measures of outcome included physiological indices, motor development, instruction following, behavior observations, and behavior ratings. Results showed that few of the measures were actually influenced by the drug conditions. However, where changes did occur, these generally indicated that benefit was derived from the drug (reduced self-stimulation, hyperactivity, and bizarre behavior, and increased social behavior). Even more important though, was the finding that the standardized dose (which was less than half the mean former dose for these residents) was equally beneficial to outcome.

Finally, in a recent study, Wysocki, Fuqua, Davis, and Breuning (1981) reported a discrimination learning study with this drug. The subjects were four mentally retarded adults who were withdrawn from thioridazine on a multiple-baseline schedule. They were required to match the color of a stimulus by selecting one of two test stimuli after various delays. The results, presented graphically, suggested that the limit of delay (or the longest delay at which the subject could respond correctly) increased following reductions in thioridazine dose. The authors interpreted the results as indicating impairment of discrimination because of the drug.

In summary, there is some convincing evidence attesting to thioridazine's usefulness in altering certain maladaptive behaviors. However, it is important to note that, even when positive changes have occurred, these were usually outnumbered by the dimensions of social behavior showing no change. Only a few studies have examined the cognitive effects of this drug, but there is growing evidence that it may depress learning performance. Overall, the evidence with thioridazine appears more positive than the evidence with chlorpromazine, but this may reflect a biased sample of chlorpromazine investigations.

Other Phenothiazines. Mesoridazine (Serentil) was evaluated in two uncontrolled trials (Lacny, 1973; Zaleski, 1970). Both suggested improvement on the majority of behavioral dimensions assessed.

Arnold and Maginn (1967) reported good results from using fluphenazine (Anatensol, Sevinol), but, once again, the design was unsatisfactory. La Veck and Buckley (1961) in a well-controlled study were unable to demonstrate any benefit due to the drug.

Kurland and Goldberg (1970) reported the use of peracetazine (Quide) in a nonblind, poorly controlled trial. Aspects of behavior were said to improve, but learning as assessed by subtests of the WISC, showed no changes.

Tischler, Patriasz, Beresford, and Bunting (1972) looked at pericyazine (Neuleptil) in children presenting difficult management problems. Control in this study was unsatisfactory; results suggested some behavioral improvement from use of the drug, and no effects on learning.

Butyrophenones

After chlorpromazine and thioridazine, the other major tranquilizer used extensively in the mentally retarded is haloperidol. Recent research reflects (or perhaps has encouraged) this popularity.

Haloperidol (Haldol, Serenace). Burk and Menolascino (1968) compared haloperidol to placebo in a double-blind study. The results, expressed exclusively in terms of global clinical improvement, suggested that the drug produced significant benefit. Grabowski (1973a), reporting a totally uncontrolled trial, concluded that haloperidol produced a number of therapeutic changes in children and adolescents. In another investigation of similar quality, Grabowski (1973b) again reported a reduction in hyperactivity, and improvement in social behavior, concentration, and "emotion" because of the drug.

Le Vann (1971) compared the effects of haloperidol to chlorpromazine in children. Haloperidol was significantly superior as assessed by global impressions, and ratings of various behavioral dimensions also suggested superiority of the butyrophenone.

Two other studies (Claghorn, 1972; Ucer & Kreger, 1969) comparing haloperidol with thioridazine in mentally retarded children showed a general, although often not significant, superiority of the butyrophenone in controlling behavior.

Thus, there is some evidence that haloperidol may surpass the established phenothiazines in certain respects. However, this is difficult to establish since such differences could be attributable to the particular dosages employed, or may be specific to certain subpopulations. Unfortunately, most of the comparative studies did not incorporate a placebo so that the degree of absolute improvement is impossible to assess. Furthermore, the earliest studies of a drug such as this tend to reflect the enthusiasm of the investigators involved, and as history has shown, subsequent trials are often less optimistic.

Other Butyrophenones. Pipamperone (Dipiperon) was assessed in one well-controlled study (van Hemert, 1975) and another totally uncontrolled trial (Haegeman & Duyck, 1978). The former found drug-related improvements on fits of anger, aggressiveness, sleep disorders, and manageability. The latter found improvement on the same categories, as well as hyperactivity and self-mutilation.

Rauwolfia Alkaloids (Reserpine)

Reserpine (Rauloydin, Raurine, Rau-sed, Reserpoid, Sandril, Serfin, Serapsil, Serpate, Vio-serpin) is one of the oldest psychotropic drugs in existence. It is native to India and neighboring countries, where crude preparations have been used for centuries for a variety of medical conditions (Goodman & Gilman, 1965). Although once a widely used psychiatric drug, this agent has largely been replaced by the phenothiazines because of unpredictability of response and the production of endogenous depression (Goodman & Gilman, 1965).

Two studies of this drug have already been mentioned during the discussion of chlorpromazine. Adamson *et al.* (1958) demonstrated that reserpine produced a beneficial behavioral effect midway between chlorpromazine and placebo, but there were no changes noted for psychometric and social maturity tests. Wardell *et al.* (1958), who also compared reserpine to chlorpromazine and placebo, were able to show few drug related changes, with the exception of possible improvement due to reserpine on a dimension relating to self-care during bath time, one of six indices employed.

Rosenblum, Callahan, Buoniconto, Graham, and Deatrick (1958) examined reserpine in relation to placebo in "disruptive" children of borderline IQ. Twelve categories of adjustment, plus a Manifest Anxiety Scale, were used to assess drug effects. There was a somewhat equivocal reduction in aggression for these children, but other dimensions of behavior were essentially unimproved by reserpine, and occasionally the placebo group made superior gains.

Thus, reserpine does not appear to be an effective drug in counteracting the behavior problems associated with mental retardation. It is interesting to note that controlled studies of the drug's usefulness in treating psychotic behavior in nonretarded patients have also been discouraging (Goodman & Gilman, 1965). Although the current discussion has been highly selective, more extensive surveys (Freeman, 1970a; Sprague & Werry, 1971) also support this negative conclusion.

Major Tranquilizers—Conclusions

The phenothiazine drugs are among the most studied for use in mental retardation. Despite the volume of research, much of it is uninformative because of poor experimental controls and failure to assess specific functions. Nevertheless, thioridazine appears to improve certain maladaptive behaviors, whereas the usefulness of chlorpromazine is open to challenge. Haloperidol, which has been investigated relatively recently, appears to be valuable in reducing hyperactive, aggressive, and stereotyped behavior. There is little research commending the use of reserpine.

Anticonvulsants

Some readers may be surprised to see this class of drugs included in a chapter devoted to psychoactive drug effects. However, there has been increasing appreciation, especially over the last decade, of the psychoactive properties of these drugs. Schain (1979) has noted that, by definition, antiepileptic drugs act upon the brain and therefore can be expected to affect mental functions under certain circumstances.

Most of the research for this section will be derived from studies of nonretarded subjects. Thus far there simply has not been much research regarding use of this drug group with the mentally retarded, although, as shown in Table I, 24% to 36% of the retarded persons in institutions are so treated.

Anticonvulsants as "Psychotropic" Drugs

Although today the anticonvulsants are used largely in the control of epilepsy, there was a period when they were advocated for behavior problems in children and for specific learning problems. This was based on the observation that large proportions of children with behavior disorders seemed to have equivocal or abnormal electroencephalogram (EEG) patterns[1] (Gross & Wil-

---
[1] The evidence attesting to a direct association between brain damage and behavior disorders is somewhat weak, and a direct association with EEG abnormalities has been hotly contested (Werry, 1979).

son, 1964; Lindsley & Henry, 1941; Millichap, Egan, Hart, & Sturgis, 1969; Walker & Kirkpatrick, 1947). Thus a number of investigators have viewed children with behavior problems as having a kind of "epileptic equivalent" as the primary source of their behavioral difficulty. Following on this logic, it has been argued that since anticonvulsants are effective in suppressing *clinical* seizures, they may also be effective in cases of subclinical, abnormal discharges. However, the evidence in support of this position is extremely weak.

A number of uncontrolled studies have suggested that antiepileptic drugs, most notably phenytoin, have beneficial behavioral effects in children, especially those described as aggressive and prone to temper outbursts. Selection criteria have frequently included the requirement that subclinical EEG activity be present, but this appears to have made no real difference to outcome. Four studies (Baldwin & Kenny, 1966; Lindsley & Henry, 1941; Walker & Kirkpatrick, 1947; Zimmerman, 1956) reported beneficial changes from use of phenytoin. Another (Baldwin & Kenny, 1966) suggested that phenobarbital (Gardenal) is also useful, although Lindsley and Henry (1941) concluded the exact converse. Two reports (Gross & Wilson, 1964; Putnam & Hood, 1964) claimed a benefit from an assortment of anticonvulsant drugs. Millichap, Egan, Hart, and Sturgis (1969) evaluated the usefulness of phenytoin in children having specific learning disorders. The results were mixed, with a test of auditory perception showing improvement, but three tests of visual motor perception indicated no changes. Once again, none of the above studies was satisfactorily controlled. Some of the reports were literally anecdotal accounts, and their conclusions must be treated with caution.

Another group of uncontrolled reports have obtained negative results. Three studies (Cohn & Nardini, 1958; Green, 1961; Pasamanick, 1951) assessed phenytoin, phenobarbital, and other antiepileptic drugs, either separately or in combination. The children were variously described as having personality problems, aggressive behavior, and hyperactivity. All three studies described their results as disappointing.

Only three properly controlled studies of anticonvulsants could be located, all of which looked at the effects of phenytoin. Goldberg and Kurland (1970) compared the drug to placebo in mildly mentally retarded children. The children were observed over an 8-week period. Three measures of learning, plus eight factors on a rating scale, were measured. The results indicated that one rating scale dimension, distractibility, was improved. Although the authors tried to highlight other positive drug-related changes, it is worth remarking that this variable alone, out of at least 13 dependent measures, showed significant effects related to the drugs. The two remaining investigations studied delinquent boys (Conners, Kramer, Rothschild, Schwartz & Stone, 1971) and children characterized as having periodic temper outbursts (Looker & Conners, 1970). A variety of standardized rating scales as well as psychometric tests were used, but no differences could be demonstrated between phenytoin and placebo.

Thus it would appear that the usefulness of anticonvulsants for treating behavior and learning problems is rather doubtful, even in nonepileptic children showing abnormal "subclinical" EEGs. This would appear to be particularly true for phenobarbital and phenytoin, the drugs which have received the most attention in the past. It is possible that other drugs, such as carbamazepine (see Dalby, 1975; Stores, 1975) or sulthiame (see Conners & Werry, 1979; Stores, 1975) will eventually be shown to have useful psychotropic properties. However, at present this is conjectural and must await the outcome of future research.

Anticonvulsants in Treatment of Epileptic Conditions (Psychoactive Effects)

Anticonvulsants have always found their greatest usage, of course, among epileptic conditions, which tend to be much more prevalent among the mentally retarded than in the general population. Recently, there have been a number of reports in the medical literature claiming a decline (or occasionally improvement) in mental function owing to various antiepileptic drugs (see Stores, 1975; Trimble, 1979; Vallarta, Bell, & Reichert, 1974). These have been accompanied by a number of investigations attempting to assess the cognitive, psychological, and motor effects of the anticonvulsants.

This area of research is faced with massive problems of control and interpretation. First, it is difficult if not impossible to institute a placebo control group in epileptic patients owing to ethical/clinical considerations. Second, any derived cognitive changes are difficult to interpret since they may be a direct effect of the *drug* under investigation or a secondary consequence of improved or worsened *seizure control*. Third, epileptic conditions can be associated with degenerative disorders, making interpretation of concomitant drug effects extremely risky. Predictably, the best studies in this area tend to be with nonepileptic volunteers, but difficulties arise here as well, because extrapolation to the response of clinical populations is hazardous. With these cautions in mind, we shall review the available evidence. Unfortunately, there are very few studies looking at mentally retarded persons, so the evidence to be presented here is based largely on nonretarded populations.

Studies of the cognitive, psychological, and motor effects of anticonvulsants are presented in Table II. Four of the most intensively studied drugs

TABLE II
Studies of Phenytoin, Phenobarbital, Ethosuximide, and Carbamazepine

Authors	Drugs	Subjects	Design[a]	Results	Controlled	Serum levels	Group size (per drug)	Duration
Wapner, Thurston, & Holowach, 1962	Phenobarbital	Epileptic children (7–11 years)	Between	No changes on picture vocabulary test, Stanford Binet IQ, or maze task.	Yes	No	36	42 days
Guey, Charles, Coquery, Roger, & Soulayrol, 1967	Ethosuximide (in combination with barbiturates)	Epileptic children (6–17 years)	Single crossover	Initially a decline on WISC Verbal Scale, Benton Visual Retention, and Rorschach. At second follow-up, no significant decline.	No	No	25	6 months
Hutt, Jackson, Besham & Higgins, 1968	Phenobarbital	Normal adults	Correlational	Reaction time, vigilance, and verbal learning declined. Spontaneous speech increased.	?	Yes	4	22 days
Smith, Philippus, & Guard, 1968	Ethosuximide	Children with 14 and 6/sec positive spikes on EEG	Crossover	Significant increase in WISC Verbal Scale. No changes on WISC Performance Scale, Ravens Matrices, Rorschach.	Yes	No	10	21 days
Goldberg & Kurland, 1970	Phenytoin	Mentally retarded boys	Between	Distractibility on rating scale improved. At least 12 other learning and behavior indices unchanged.	Yes	No	25	8 weeks

Continued

TABLE II (continued)

Authors	Drugs	Subjects	Design[a]	Results	Controlled	Serum levels	Group size (per drug)	Duration
Idestrom, Schalling, Carlquist, & Sjoqvist, 1972	Phenytoin	Normal adults	Crossover	Movement time slowed (reaction-time task) and self ratings worsened.	Yes	Yes	15 & 20	Acute doses
			Correlational	Concentration and sedation (psychophysiological measures) worsened with increasing serum levels.				
Smith & Lowrey, 1972	Phenytoin	Normal adults	Crossover	Increase in WAIS Verbal and Performance scales.	Yes	No	20	21 days
Reynolds & Travers, 1974	Combinations of phenytoin and phenobarbital	Epileptic adolescents and adults	Correlational	Intellectual deterioration, psychiatric illness, and (less so) psychomotor slowing at higher serum levels at both drugs.	Partially	Yes	57	Chronic treatment
Browne, Dreifuss, Dyken, Goode, Penry, Porter, White, & White, 1975 Collaborative Study	Ethosuximide	Children with absence seizures	Crossover	Improvement on Halstead Reitan Battery.	Yes	No	37	8 weeks

Dekaban & Lehman 1975	Combinations of phenytoin, primadone, and phenobarbital	Normal and epileptic adolescerts and adults	Crossover	Apparent worsening on vigilance, reaction time, free recall and memory as dosage was increased.	?	No	15	7 days
Dodrill, 1975	Phenytoin	Epileptic adults	Correlational	Impairment on 8 tests with a heavy motor component (Halstead Neuropsychological Battery) at higher serum levels.	Yes	Yes	70	60 days
Matthews & Harley, 1975	Combinations of phenytoin, phenobarbital, primadone	Epileptic "patients"	Between	Poorer performance on WAIS Coding, Seashore Rhythm Test, Knox Cube Test, and motor steadiness tests at higher serum levels.	Partially	Yes	37 & 28	?
Schain, Riehl, & Ward, 1975	Carbamazepine	Epileptic children	Single crossover	Improvement on 2 indices of cognitive style.	No	No	9	4 months
Stores & Hart, 1976	Phenytoin, other mixed anticonvulsants	Children with focal and generalized seizures	Between	Reading scores depressed on phenytoin.	No	No	9	4 months
Schair, Ward, & Guthrie, 1977	Carbamazepine	Epileptic children	Single crossover	Improvement on 3 indices of cognitive style, WISC, Ravens Matrices, and ratings of attention.	No	?	45	4 to 6 months

Continued

TABLE II (continued)

Authors	Drugs	Subjects	Design[a]	Results	Controlled	Serum levels	Group size (per drug)	Duration
Macleod, Dekaban, & Hunt, 1978	Phenobarbital	Epileptic adult males	Crossover	Decline in short-term memory, but no change in long-term memory.	Yes	Yes	19	5 days
Camfield, Chaplin, Doyle, Shapiro, Cummings, & Camfield, 1979	Phenobarbital	Children having febrile convulsions	Between	No effects	Yes	Yes	35	8–12 months
			Correlational	Deficit on memory concentration scores of Stanford Binet at higher serum levels.				
Trimble & Corbett (cited in Trimble, 1979)	Phenytoin primadone, phenobarbital, carbamazepine	Epileptic children	Correlational	Decline in IQ with higher serum levels of phenytoin and primadone; similar trend with phenobarbital.	No	Yes	312 total	1 year

[a] Correlational implies that serum levels were obtained and that these were related to outcome.

(phenytoin, phenobarbitol, carbamazepine, and ethosuximide) are summarized. Since these studies were carried out in nonretarded populations, and because any psychoactive effect is incidental rather than the usual object of treatment, these investigations will be summarized only briefly here.

Phenytoin (diphenylhydantoin, DPH, Dilantin). This drug, one of the cornerstones of antiepileptic drug treatment, has recently come under attack for causing possible mental and psychomotor deterioration in patients on long-term treatment. In one study (Smith & Lowrey, 1972), an increase in IQ due to phenytoin was observed. However, in a number of other studies (Dekaban & Lehman, 1975; Dodrill, 1975; Idestrom, Schalling, Carlquist, & Sjoqvist, 1972; Matthews & Harley, 1975; Stores & Hart, 1976; Trimble & Corbett, cited in Trimble, 1979) deterioration because of the drug was found. Such worsening included decrements on reaction time and vigilance tasks, lowered self-ratings, sedative effects as measured by psychophysiological measures, reductions in free-recall and memory, depressed reading scores, increased motor tremor, psychiatric illness, and actual intellectual deterioration as measured on IQ tests (see Table II). However, it is important to note that most of these changes have not been replicated across studies and further, it is possible that in some instances the deterioration was due to inadequate seizure control or degenerative processes.

It will also be observed that the studies showing most deterioration were those designated as "correlational." These studies employed the strategy of relating performance to the actual level of drug in the blood stream. The significance of these studies is that deterioration has usually been noted *within the range which is generally regarded as therapeutic and "nontoxic."* This has led a number of authors (Simmons, Tymchuk, & Valente, 1975; Trimble, 1979; Trimble & Reynolds, 1976) to recommend that it may be better to risk a few seizures than produce oversedation with higher doses.

Phenobarbital (phenobarbitone, Gardental). One study (Wapner, Thurston, & Holowach, 1962) was unable to show any changes due to phenobarbital in epileptic children (Table II). However, a group of other investigations (Camfield, Chaplin, Doyle, Shapiro, Cummings, & Camfield, 1979; Dekaban & Lehman, 1975; Hutt, Jackson, Belsham, & Higgins, 1968; MacLeod, Dekaban, & Hunt, 1978; Matthews & Harley, 1975; Reynolds & Travers, 1974; Trimble & Corbett, cited in Trimble 1979) did document adverse effects. Among these were deterioration on tests of attention span, memory, and verbal learning. Intellectual deterioration and psychiatric illness increased with larger serum levels. Again, the warning about risking sedative effects at upper "therapeutic" levels appears very appropriate.

Parenthetically it should be mentioned that this drug is reputed to cause hyperactivity in some children (Ounsted, 1955; see also Schain, 1979), and an association with aggression and hyperactive behavior has often been noted in the clinical literature. One of the few studies which has examined this issue was unable to document a hyperkinetic reaction due to phenobarbital (Camfield et al., 1979). However, Wolf and Forsythe (1978), who conducted a large-scale investigation, found that 35% of children treated with phenobarbital displayed hyperactivity, whereas only 13% of a control group showed the behavior pattern. It is important, therefore, that clinicians and others directly involved with such children be aware of the possible association between phenobarbital treatment and behavior disturbance.

Carbamazepine (Tegretol). Thus far, carbamazepine has not been found to cause decline of cognitive performance at ordinary clinical doses. Although Trimble and Corbett (cited in Trimble, 1979) noted adverse effects from the sedative-type anticonvulsants and phenytoin, they could demonstrate no such effects from carbamazepine. Schain and his associates (Schain et al., 1975; Schain, Ward, & Guthrie, 1977) observed actual *improvements* in cognitive style and IQ when children were switched from their previous medication to carbamazepine. However, this may well reflect a suppression of cognitive function by the previously used sedative drugs rather than a genuine improvement due to carbamazepine.

Ethosuximide (Zarontin). Results with this drug have been mixed. Guey, Charles, Coquery, Roger, and Soulayrol (1967) found that performance on various WISC subtests, as well as on a test of visual perception, worsened. However, others (Browne, Dreifuss, Dyken, Goode, Penry, Porter, White, & White, 1975; Smith, Philippus, & Guard, 1968) noted a pattern of no-change mixed with improvement. It is very possible that improvements with this drug are due to its effects on *seizure activity*. Ethosuximide is commonly used in the treatment of absence (or petit mal) seizures which can substantially interfere with cognitive performance. Hence, improved cognitive function may reflect better seizure control rather than a direct effect on learning-related skills.

Psychoactive Effects of Anticonvulsants—Summary

The above review has been only a skeleton summary of possible psychoactive properties of the antiepileptic drugs. This area has not been extensively researched, particularly in children, and serious problems of control have already been outlined. However, there is strong evidence that phenytoin may impair certain cognitive and motor fucntions, especially at higher serum levels. Similar effects have been noted for phenobarbital and primidone (Mysoline).

However, Table II did not show all the variables studied, and in some cases only a small minority of measures showed drug related changes. Furthermore, there has been a failure for any clear pattern of decline to emerge from these studies, and, therefore, without such replication, any conclusions must be tentative.

What *is* clear from Table II, however, is that studies which link psychometric outcome to serum levels of the drugs are much more likely to show a statistical relationship. This is because there is a poor correspondence between dosage and blood levels, thereby rendering many "drug/no drug" comparisons crude from a methodological point of view. The inverse relationship between performance levels and serum levels suggests that clinicians should aim for the lowest clinically effective dose. Where very high doses are required to obtain seizure control, clinicians should consider changing the medication or alternatively consider the merits of chancing a few seizures rather than risk oversedation at higher doses.

This raises a related problem of particular importance with the mentally retarded. When blood levels of these drugs reach a certain magnitude, toxic effects commonly set in. Such effects can include tremor, blurring of vision, slurring of speech, incoordination, drowsiness, and mental confusion. Because of poor communication skills, many mentally retarded persons would find it impossible to relate the presence of these side effects. Such toxic effects might easily be miscontrued by others as part of that person's intellectual or neurological handicap. This suggests that those working with mentally retarded persons should be particularly mindful of the problem, and it further indicates the *necessity* for periodic serum assays and neurological assessment.

In summary, the antiepileptic drugs are important agents in the treatment of the mentally retarded not merely because of their seizure suppressing potential. The evidence that these drugs are useful psychotropic agents is dubious. However, where a clinical seizure disorder does exist, it is possible (although still unproven) that added behavioral benefit may be derived from certain drugs such as carbamazepine or sulthiame. The research on cognitive and psychological aspects suggests that phenytoin and phenobarbital may have adverse effects, although these drugs may have come in for more attention owing to their lengthy history of use in epilepsy. It was also observed that adverse effects can occur at serum levels not generally regarded as toxic. Finally, the danger of toxic effects being undetected or misconstrued as symptoms of mental retardation was discussed, and it was pointed out that personnel should be aware of this possibility and that periodic serum assays should be ordered to ensure against it.

Stimulants

Background

The stimulants include the amphetamines, methylphenidate (Ritalin), deanol (Deaner), and pemoline (Cylert, Ronyl). Historically, they are an interesting class since they are probably the most extensively researched pyschotropic drug group for use with children.

The stimulants received major recognition as a therapeutic tool following a widely cited study by Bradley (1937). In that investigation, a mixed group of children of normal IQ was treated with the amphetamine, Benzedrine. The children had presented with a wide variety of behavior disorders, extending from specific educational disabilities, through withdrawal, to highly aggressive behavior. However, following amphetamine treatment the children were described as being more "subdued', as having mood swings, with aggressive, noisy, and domineering behavior being greatly diminished, and with what Bradley termed a "paradoxical" reduction in excessive motor activity.

Subsequent investigations of the amphetamines and methylphenidate showed that drugs caused marked social improvements in hyperactive or minimally brain dysfunctioned (MBD) children (see Conners & Werry, 1979). Furthermore, it has now been widely established that these drugs, when administered to hyperactive/MBD children, often cause improvement in such cognitive functions as attention span, cognitive style, short-term memory, and so forth, particularly in the short-term (Aman, 1978, 1980; Barkley & Cunningham, 1978; Sroufe, 1975). However, there is little evidence that these drugs change the long-term *educational* prospects despite the evidence from the short-term laboratory tests (Aman, 1978, 1980; Barkley & Cunningham, 1978).

Recent studies have challenged the notion that the stimulants have a specific effect in hyperactive/MBD children which could be characterized as "calming" or "paradoxical." The concept was apparently compounded on the false belief that "normal" children would respond to the stimulant drugs with *greater* physical activity and *poorer* psychological organization. Investigations with nonhyperactive children (Rapoport, Buchsbaum, Weingartner, Zahn, Ludlow, Mikkelsen, Langer, & Bunney, 1980; Werry & Aman, in press) have shown that they also respond with reduced physical activity and superior cognitive performance, the most notable aspect of which is, again, improved concentration span.

Thus, enhancement of attention span and reduction of motor activity appear to be more-or-less general reactions to methylphenidate and the amphetamines. Furthermore, hyperactive and MBD children have been shown to have a particular deficit on tests of attention span (Anderson, Halcomb, & Doyle, 1973; Sykes, Douglas, & Morgenstern, 1972; Sykes, Douglas, Weiss, & Minde, 1971) and this has been widely perceived as the cause for many of the other problems encountered by these children. Hence, their special responsiveness to the stimulants may not be *paradoxical* at all, but instead probably reflects a predictable response to the stimulating properties of these drugs.

Stimulants in the Mentally Retarded

Despite their popularity elsewhere, the stimulants are not widely used with mentally retarded persons. In his nation-wide survey, Lipman (1970) found that fewer than 3% of residents were so treated, and similarly Cohen and Sprague (1977) found the prevalence to be between 2% and 3%. A number of writers (Freeman, 1970a; Lipman, 1970; Lipman et al., 1978; Sprague & Werry, 1971) have commented on this low prevalence and have expressed surprise that these drugs have not replaced some of the more sedative types such as the phenothiazines. Theoretically, at least, the stimulants might be expected to improve various types of disruptive behavior, and, at the same time, to have the possible added advantage of improving various cognitive functions.

However, the available evidence does not support this view. Studies of the stimulants in the mentally retarded are presented in Table III. With the exception of one report (Anton & Greer, 1969) all used double-blind, placebo-controlled designs and the methodology was generally good. Nevertheless, the response to these drugs was largely negative. Nine studies examined behavioral dimensions, but only five (Alexandris & Lundell, 1968; Anton & Greer, 1969; Christensen, 1975; Blacklidge & Ekblad, 1971; Spencer, 1970) showed even minimal improvements. It is important to note that most of these studies incorporated a wide variety of measures and that only a small minority of variables actually showed benefit. From a cognitive/learning point of view the situation is even worse. Of the six studies examining this dimension, four (Alexandris & Lundell, 1968; Blacklidge & Ekblad, 1971; Christensen, 1975; Morris, MacGillivray, & Mathieson, 1955) found essentially no change, whereas two (Bell & Zubek, 1961; Lobb, 1968) found *worsening* of performance while subjects were on the stimulants. Thus the general pattern of response under the stimulants is one of nonimprovement.

Two of these studies deserve further mention. The investigation by Lobb (1968) is unique because it is the only one which examined drug effects on the acquisition of a conditioned response. Given the nature of mental retardation,

TABLE III
Studies of Stimulant Drug Effects on Behavior and Learning

Authors	Drug	Dose	Duration	Number/group	Variables	Results
Morris, MacGillivray, & Mathiesson, 1955	Amphetamine	15 mg/day	4 weeks	25	IQ (3 tests), paired associate learning (4 measures), number sorting, voluntary attention (6 tests), memory (2 tests), level of aspiration (3 measures)	Drug group improved more on one index of voluntary attention. Control group improved more on a paired associate measure.
Clausen, Fineman, Henry, & Wohl, 1960	Deanol	15 mg/day	8 weeks	20	Simple and delayed reaction time, mirror drawing, critical flicker fusion, span of apprehension, WISC and WAIS subtests, teacher and ward rating scale	No changes
Bell & Zubek, 1961	Deanol, amphetamine	50 mg, BID	8 weeks	25	WAIS, coding, Porteus Mazes, digit span, number concepts, word matching, behavior rating forms	IQs depressed in amphetamine and deanol groups.
McConnell, Cromwell, Bailer, & Son, 1964	Dextroamphetamine	7.5 mg/day 15 mg/day	6 days	57	Activity measured by ballistographic chair, activity assessed by rating scale	No drug effects on activity.

Lobb, 1968	Amphetamine	0.2 mg/kg	Acute	160	GSR, response during adaptation, conditioning and extinction trials	Poorer conditioning and *less persistence of* response in drug group.
Alexandris & Lundell, 1968	Amphetamine	Mean dose = 52 mg/day	6 months	6 & 8	Ratings of 14 behavioral dimensions, WISC, Bender Visual Motor Gestalt Test, Goodenough Draw-A-Person	Ratings of comprehension and work interest improved on drug. All other measures unchanged.
Anton & Greer, 1969	Dextroamphetamine	10 mg/day	21 days	6	Subjective impressions of behavioral change	2 children showed "increased awareness of stimuli," less random activity, increase in vocalization.
Davis, Sprague, & Werry, 1969	Methylphenidate	0.44 mg/kg	Acute	9	Standardized observations of stereotypy, total other behavior, body-rocking, complex hand movements, electronic recording of head movement	No significant changes (see also thioridazine discussion).
Spencer, 1970	Pemoline (Ronyl)	60 mg/day	13 weeks	12	Subjective global assessment of "progress"	8 of 12 subjects showed improvement, difference between ratings marginally significant ($P < .07$)

Continued

TABLE III (continued)

Authors	Drug	Dose	Duration	Number/group	Variables	Results
Blacklidge & Ekblad, 1971	Methylphenidate	10 mg, BID	4 months	31	Parent and teacher rating scale, WRAT arithmetic, Gray's oral reading test, Porteus Mazes	Teachers' ratings of behavior improved due to drug.
Davis, 1971	Methylphenidate	0.5 mg/kg	Acute	10	Rocking or bar pressing in response to a discriminative time stimulus	Essentially no changes.
Christensen, 1975	Methylphenidate	0.3 mg/kg	4 weeks	13	12 categories of standardized observations, seat activity, teacher ratings of hyperactivity, academic productivity, academic accuracy	2 of 12 observational categories showed improvement (nondeviant behavior and vocalization). No other changes.

one would expect a variety of drug studies looking at basic theoretical areas, such as altered rates of conditioning and cognitive processes. However, these fundamental issues have hardly been addressed at all, let alone answered. The negative effects of amphetamine on conditioning observed by Lobb only seem to highlight the need for more research of this kind.

Christensen's (1975) study is also unusual since this is one of very few investigations (see also McConahey, 1972) to look at the effects of drug treatment in combination with other feasible treatments. In this study, drug and behavior modification treatments did not combine to render additive gains, largely because the behavior–modification program was so successful that there was little room for further improvement. However, in an earlier study with nonretarded, emotionally disturbed children, Christensen and Sprague (1973) found that the combination of methylphenidate with behavior modification did produce better results than either used in isolation.

Why are stimulants relatively ineffective in mentally retarded persons when they have found such extensive use in other groups, such as MBD, hyperactive, and conduct-disordered children? Robbins and Sahakian (1979) have reviewed the animal literature on psychomotor stimulants and related this to drug actions in man. They argue from this evidence that behavior tends to become progressively constricted and uniform with increasing dose "as though the organism was attending to a restricted range of stimuli" (p. 943). They also argue that stimulants may encourage perseveration of thought and stereotyped movements in children.

Of course, the high incidence of stereotypic movements is already well documented in the mentally retarded (Baumeister & Forehand, 1973; Schroeder et al., 1978). Further, there is strong evidence that mentally retarded persons may display a constricted "breadth of attention," most cogently demonstrated in the studies of Zeaman and his associates (Fisher & Zeaman, 1973; see also Ullman, 1974). Other investigators (Lovaas, Koegel, & Schreibman, 1979) have noted *stimulus overselectivity*, (the tendency to focus on a reduced portion of the environment), in related clinical populations, and they have pointed to evidence of this in the mentally retarded as well. If it is true that mentally retarded persons have a narrower field of attention, then it is possible, as pointed out by Robbins and Sahakian (1979), that this field is constricted still further by stimulants, resulting in essentially no change or even worsening in some cases. This is a hypothesis which should be tested, as it has obvious clinical implications.

In summary, the evidence is not completely available, but there is currently no compelling proof that the stimulants have a major role to play in the treatment of the mentally retarded. More research is needed to investigate dosage ranges and appropriate subject characteristics and to determine if certain subjects do show a beneficial response.

Anxiolytic Drugs

Anxiolytic drugs are used extensively with the mentally retarded. Lipman (1970) found the usage of benzodiazepines with the mentally retarded to be around 8%, whereas Cohen and Sprague (1977) found the incidence to be around 5%. Hughes (1977) reported that diazepam (Valium) alone accounted for 23% of drug usage in one institution, but it was being employed mainly as an antiepileptic. However, there is not much research on the anxiolytics in this population.

Antihistamines

The antihistamines are structurally very similar to the phenothiazine tranquilizers. However, because of their frequent use as sedatives, they have been grouped with the anxiolytics.

Diphenhydramine (Benadryl). Freeman (1970a) reported that no well-designed study had established the clinical usefulness of diphenhydramine in promoting behavioral change in disturbed mentally retarded persons. This situation remains unchanged today.

Hydroxyzine (Atarax). Craft (1957) conducted a well-controlled crossover study of hydroxyzine in severely mentally retarded aggressive and destructive residents. To measure drug effects, a rating scale was devised to evaluate activity, aggression, and social behavior separately. No differences were found between placebo and active drug treatments.

Maladjusted, educationally subnormal children were treated with hydroxyzine in another blind, placebo-controlled study (Segal & Tansley, 1957). Teacher ratings of activity, application, and progress in the basic subjects apparently revealed no drug effects. However, impressions of global improvement suggested that more children in the active drug group benefited, apparently becoming less restless, less distractible, and evidenced fewer psychosomatic manifestations.

Gianinni (1964) carried out a poorly controlled study in behavior problem children presenting with hyperactivity, shortened attention span, and irritability. The results suggested substantial improvement due to hydroxyzine particularly in the youngest subjects.

Benzodiazepines

Chlordiazepoxide (Librium). La Veck and Buckley (1961) treated behavior problem children in a well-designed study incorporating objective measures. The results suggested that chlordiazepoxide actually *increased* undesirable behavior (nonsignificantly so), as assessed by behavior checklists. The study also showed that, as determined by timed samples of playroom activity, children on the drug engaged in less constructive play, changed toys more, and became more overactive although it is not clear whether these were statistically significant changes.

In an uncontrolled trial, Krakowski (1963) treated emotionally disturbed children, some of whom were mentally retarded, with chlordiazepoxide. Remission of symptoms was described as substantial in this diagnostically mixed group, but the subgroup of children with mental deficiency was less improved than the remainder of the group.

Diazepam (Valium). Zrull, Westman, Arthur, and Rice (1964) compared diazepam to d-amphetamine and placebo in a mixed group which included mentally retarded children. The subjects were selected for evidence of hyperactivity, distractibility, impulsivity, and emotional instability. As assessed by clinical global impressions, diazepam resulted in *less* improvement than either d-amphetamine or placebo, but the dose of diazepam (10 mg, twice daily) may well have been too high for a realistic appraisal of the drug.

Diazepam was also evaluated in a totally uncontrolled trial which employed moderately and severely mentally retarded adults presenting with symptoms of agitation, self-injury, uncooperativeness, withdrawal symptoms, and loss of appetite (Galambos, 1965). It was reported that behavior generally improved on the drug, but it is unclear how change was measured and there was no statistical summary of results.

Related Drugs. Ucer (1968) assessed another benzodiazepine derivative, identified simply as RO 5-4556, in emotionally disturbed mentally retarded children. The drug was reported to decrease hyperactivity and anxiety, and the children were described as more alert and better able to communicate on treatment. However, the study was completely uncontrolled, and there was no statistical analysis of the results.

In a well-controlled study (Walters, Singh, & Beale, 1977), lorazepam (Ativan) was evaluated in hyperactive residents. The subjects were observed using a time-sampling technique, and behavior was categorized as appropriate, hyperactive, or inactive. Inactive behavior and appropriate behavior were unaffected by the drug, whereas the proportion of hyperactivity was actually significantly *increased* under lorazepam.

Meprobamate (Equanil, Miltown, Trelmar)

Although there have been enthusiastic reports about this drug in uncontrolled trials (e.g., Kugelmass, 1956), there is little evidence relating to the effectiveness of meprobamate. In a well-controlled investigation, Craft (1958) evaluated the effects of meprobamate on aggression, activity, and social behavior in severely mentally retarded residents. Craft concluded that the drug was of no value to the subjects, but his data actually indicate significant *improvements* in activity level and social behavior, although there were order effects relating to the *sequence* in which the subjects received the drug conditions.

The only other controlled trial of meprobamate assessed it in combination with promazine, a phenothiazine (La Veck & Buckley, 1961).

Anxiolytics — Summary

It should be clear that all three drug categories (antihistamines, benzodiazepines, and meprobamate) deserve further study before they are accepted as effective modifiers of problem behavior in the mentally retarded.

The research with hydroxyzine is inconsistent, but there is some indication that modest benefit may accompany treatment. Unfortunately, but predictably, the poorest controlled study showed the best results.

The benzodiazepines (chlordiazpoxide, diazepam, and lorazepam) are apparently not effective in the control of acting-out behaviors. The three best-controlled studies of these drugs (La Veck & Buckley, 1961; Walters *et al.*, 1977; Zrull *et al.*, 1964) not only failed to find improvement but actually showed *deterioration* in comparison with placebo. Children were employed in all three of these studies, which suggests that these drugs are contraindicated in young mentally retarded persons with acting-out behaviors.

There have not been enough controlled trials of meprobamate in the mentally retarded to even guess what its behavioral effects might be.

Antidepressant/Antimanic Drugs

Antidepressants

Other than their role in treating depression in nonretarded adults, the antidepressants (most notably imipramine) have been used successfully to treat such problems as restlessness, hyperactivity, conduct disorders, and aggressiveness in *nonretarded* children (Rapoport, 1965; Waizer, Hoffman, Polizos, & Bailer, 1977). One of the most established uses of the tricyclic antidepressants is in the treatment of nocturnal enuresis. Blackwell and Currah (1973) have comprehensively reviewed this literature, encompassing over 30 controlled studies, and they conclude that the case for *cure* of enuresis by tricyclic drugs is not proven. Although it is clear that these agents do *suppress* nighttime wetting in varying degrees, most children resume wetting when medication is stopped.

These drugs are virtually unstudied with respect to their behavioral effects in the mentally retarded (see also Freeman, 1970a). Carter (1966) reported two trials comparing nortriptyline (Allegron, Aventyl, Nortab) to phenobarbital, chlorpromazine, and (in one instance only) placebo. Nortriptyline was found not to differ from the other active drugs, but all agents surpassed placebo in production and duration of "tranquilization." The major problem with this study is in accepting the investigator's assessment of improvement, which was couched in terms of "quietness" and sleep onset, responses which are *not* universally regarded as desirable.

Most of the other reports of the tricyclics are either anecdotal accounts or evaluations of their effects on incontinence.

Obviously any conclusions about the behavioral effects of the antidepressants would be premature at this time.

Lithium Carbonate

During recent years lithium carbonate (Lithicarb, Lithium Phasal, Priadel) has been used in the treatment of bipolar (i.e., manic-depressive) and unipolar affective disorders. However, research on the possible effects of this drug in the mentally retarded has been quite prominent during the last decade, particularly for treating hyperactive and aggressive behavior.

Three uncontrolled studies (Dostal & Zvolsky, 1970; Micev & Lynch, 1974; Mullerova, Novotna, Rehan, & Skula, 1974) selected subjects randomly or for the presence of hyperactive, aggressive, and self-injurious behavior. All claimed that the drug produced improvement, including increased "adaptability" and reduced aggressiveness, motor activity, restlessness, and self-injury.

Naylor, Donald, Le Poidevin, and Reid (1974) carried out a carefully controlled trial of lithium carbonate in adult residents having mood swings or "recurrent behavioural changes." Results, which were assessed over 1-year treatment periods, indicated that the mean number of weeks ill while on lithium was significantly less than while on placebo. However, the mean number of "episodes" for the group while on lithium did not differ significantly from the number of episodes on placebo.

Mentally retarded adults with depressive symptoms were treated in another trial of lithium carbonate which was partially controlled (Rivinus & Harmatz, 1979). Although inappropriately analyzed, the data did suggest substantial reduction in symptoms of manic depressive illness under lithium treatment.

Finally, adult subjects were selected for presence of aggressive behavior in a further trial of lithium (Worral, Moody, & Naylor, 1975). Significant reduction in aggression was derived from the active drug, but the results were analyzed inappropriately, and it is unlikely that the correct analysis would have shown any effect.

The shortage of good studies with lithium carbonate makes this a difficult drug to evaluate. The best studies (Naylor *et al.*, 1974; Rivinus & Harmatz, 1979) employed subjects having affective symptoms, and these suggested modest improvements. It is still too early to determine whether lithium has beneficial effects on aggression, hyperactivity, and conduct disorders. In any case, this drug should be used conservatively, and only with the expectation of considerable therapeutic benefit, since it is suspected that irreversible kidney damage can sometimes result from such treatment.

Miscellaneous

This section was included to present some of the less conventional approaches to treating problems in mental retardation. No claim is made for comprehensive coverage since the area of mental retardation has witnessed the use of many highly unusual treatments. The drugs mentioned in the following section are offered as samples of these less common approaches.

Glutamic Acid

This drug was included largely as a historical note since a major controversy was waged surrounding glutamic acid in the 1950s and 1960s. Glutamic acid was apparently first used in mental retardation because of studies which indicated enhanced performance in animals and also because of a study in a petit mal epilepsy which suggested improvement in areas other than seizure control. There have been over 50 studies of this compound in the mentally retarded, attesting to the amount of interest in the drug. Probably the major reason for this intense interest is that the drug was actually reputed to increase intelligence.

In 1960, Astin and Ross reviewed this literature from a methodological stance. They demonstrated that the majority of controlled studies produced negative results, whereas the preponderance of positive studies were uncontrolled. Furthermore, Astin and Ross demonstrated that there has been insufficient attention devoted to control of environmental stimulation and dietary history, and also that cues may have been given to the drug's identity due to taste and side effects, particularly in the positive reports. Predictably, they concluded that a beneficial effect of glutamic acid had not been convincingly demonstrated.

More recently, Vogel, Broverman, Draguns, and Klaiber (1966) reviewed the literature on glutamic acid. They sifted through uncontrolled as well as controlled trials in search of factors signaling positive results. A number of possible factors associated with a positive response were identified and Vogel and his colleagues concluded that the drug may well have a role in improving intellectual performance. However, many of their arguments have an *ad hoc* ring about them, and it seems that they did not satisfactorily counter the major criticism of Astin and Ross; namely, that most studies showing benefit due to glutamic acid were poorly controlled or totally uncontrolled. Research on (and apparently also usage of) glutamic acid has died out over the last dozen years and little is heard of this controversy today.

5-Hydroxytryptophan

In the mid-1960s, reports appeared which claimed that the serotonin levels in the blood of children with Down's syndrome were substantially depressed below normal levels. Serotonin (or 5-hydroxytryptamine) is a neurotransmitter known to regulate sleep, body temperature, and, more controversially, affective states.

Based on the logic that these children were suffering from a serotonin deficit, Bazelon, Paine, Cowie, Hunt, Houck, and Mahanand (1967) tried treating infants with Down's syndrome with the immediate precursor of serotonin, 5-hydroxytryptophan (5-HTP). Administration of the compound did not elevate serotonin levels, but 5-hydroxyinidoles (end products of serotonin breakdown) were markedly increased. Bazelon *et al.* reported positive neurological changes, most noticeably an increase in muscle tone and reduced tongue protrusion. However, they also warned against drawing inferences regarding the effects of 5-HTP on intelligence, although this inevitably did occur.

Later, a more systematic evaluation of 5-HTP administration was undertaken by Partington, MacDonald, and Tu (1971). Twelve children were evaluated in a double-blind, placebo-controlled, crossover design with two dosage levels of the compound. Following 5-HTP therapy, there was no concomitant increase in serotonin levels, nor were there any changes in behavior ratings, neurological signs, or motor activity which was objectively recorded. Another study, which was partially controlled, evaluated 5-HTP treatment over a period of less than one year to over four years (Weise, Koch, Shaw, & Rosenfeld, 1974). The results were essentially negative, although the treated group did show an equivocal 3-point gain on the Gesell Developmental Schedule.

Thus, although the observation of reduced serotonin levels suggested a promising form of treatment, it is clear from these two recent studies that 5-HTP is not an important treatment for Down's syndrome.

Adrenocorticotropic Hormone

Lately there has been increased research activity revolving around the pituitary hormones and the area of mental retardation has not escaped invovlement. The primary role of adrenocorticotrophic hormone (ACTH) has classically been regarded as stimulation of the adrenal gland to secrete other hormones in times of stress. However, Sandman and his associates (Sandman, George, Walker, & Nolan, 1976; Walker & Sandman, 1979), claim that the neuroendocrine hormones play an essential role in regulating the central nervous system (CNS) as well. Animal experiments have suggested delayed extinction of learned responses and improved performance on aspects of discrimination learning. Studies with man have suggested an enhancement of visual memory and visual discrimination, and prolonged attention (Gaillard & Sanders, 1975; Sandman, George, Nolan, Van Riezen, & Kastin, 1975).

Sandman and his associates have reported two studies of the adrenocorticotropic hormones (ACTH) in mentally retarded adults. In the first trial (Sandman *et al.*, 1976), MSH/ACTH 4-10 was evaluated for its effects on an orienting response, discrimination learning, visual memory, and neuropsychological performance. The results suggested superior performance because of ACTH on the orienting response and on intradimensional and extradimensional shifts within a discrimination learning task. The second study (Walker & Sandman, 1979) assessed ACTH 4-9 on essentially the same battery of tests described above. This time there was no change in orienting response, but reversal and intradimensional shift problems were learned faster in the ACTH group. Thus, the pattern of drug-induced change was not consistent across these investigations; furthermore, the statistical analyses were often unsatisfactory, and lack of improvement characterized the majority of dependent measures.

Rapoport, Quinn, Copeland, and Burg (1976) assessed the effects of ACTH 4-10 on cognitive performance, psychological ratings, and behavioral adjustment of *nonretarded* learning-disabled children. The results were inadequately analyzed, but there was no suggestion of any beneficial drug effect.

In summary, there is little solid evidence to justify the use of ACTH in the mentally retarded. If these compounds do have useful CNS effects, they are probably of an arousal/motivational nature rather than of a learning enhancement type.

Other Agents

Drug research with the mentally retarded has gone in almost every conceivable direction. Louttit (1965) and Share (1976) have reviewed a variety of agents not covered here including vitamins, pituitary extract, and siccacell therapy. Kershner (1978) has presented a devastating critique of megavitamin therapy. Springer and Fricke (1975) present a useful discussion of nutrition as it relates to drug therapy.

Methodological Critique

The general lack of methodological rigor in this literature has made it virtually impossible to arrive at definitive conclusions. Even from a rudimentary point of view, the majority of drug studies in the mentally retarded can only be described as crude, and the research is sorely lacking in terms of the simple methodological principles outlined earlier.

Experimental control was often nonexistent. Wolfensberger and Menolascino (1968) have suggested that this betrays an acceptance of a disease model on the part of investigators. If mental retardation and its associated problems are viewed as a static, "incurable condition" which will yield only to a "magic bullet" therapy, then no control is *needed*. However, this is obviously an unreasonable assumption. Studies showing a pronounced placebo response lasting up to 6 weeks (e.g., Adamson et al., 1958) show the absurdity of the position that lack of control can be justified.

All the other principles mentioned earlier were violated with disconcerting regularity. The use of placebo was often dispensed with as being "unnecessary" or unethical, even though the value of the treatment in question had not been established. Drug confounding (i.e., the use of the trial drug in conjunction with previous maintenance drugs) was commonplace. This was especially true in the case of epileptic mentally retarded persons. Furthermore, standardized and specific measures have generally been eschewed in favor of global impressions of improvement. The problem with this, of course, is that it is impossible to establish what features characterize "improvement" for the person doing the evaluations.

The single most commonly violated principle in this area has been the proper application of statistical techniques. The majority of studies have avoided statistical procedures, unwittingly violated their assumptions, or simply misinterpreted their meaning, thereby frequently arriving at false conclusions. The use of statistics is often viewed as a highly esoteric way of proving what is already obvious or, worse still, of distorting the truth. However, it is clear that some standard is needed to evaluate drug effects, and appropriate statistical analysis is the best such yardstick that we have.

There is still much to be learned about even the most common drugs used with the mentally retarded. There is surprisingly little documentation, for example, that chlorpromazine results in benefit for the majority of mentally retarded persons so treated. This is also true of most other psychopharmacologic agents. There is even less information regarding the precise nature of drug-induced changes. It is clear that more information is needed relating to the psychoactive drugs if they are to be regarded as a truly viable form of treatment. It is also clear that we cannot continue to blunder along as previously, but that future research must be more scientifically sound.

Major Issues in Need of Study

In the course of preparing the above review it became clear that a number of important issues impinging directly upon the use of drugs have been largely or totally ignored. Some of these are discussed below.

Dosage Levels

The most common procedure for adjusting dosage in drug trials is by titration.[2] This technique has a number of disadvantages as well as obvious advantages. The greatest advantage is that, since people do not respond uniformly to drugs, this theoretically allows the investigator to maximize each person's response. However, from a research stance, there are a number of serious disadvantages. First, titration results not in one treatment but in a

---

[2] Titration usually involves the systematic increase of dosage (on an individual basis) until side effects begin to interfere with therapeutic effect. Dosage is then marginally decreased and maintained at that slightly reduced level.

multitude of treatments. Second, there is no assurance that any two investigators would titrate to similar levels, making comparions across studies and between drugs an impossible task. Third, and most importantly, the use of titration is tantamount to prejudging the nature of drug-induced changes. It assumes that the investigator will be able to *forecast* reliably the optimal level before having access to the results of the study. This, of course, is tautological and is scientifically unacceptable.

The use of standardized dosages, that is, based on the subject's body weight is, in the writer's opinion, more favorable. (Of course, there are times when this is inappropriate, such as when standardization by blood levels is possible.) Usage of standardized dosages enables comparisons to be made reliably across studies and between drugs. It also eliminates the issue of human judgment as a major factor in such studies. Finally, it makes objective and practical information available to others about what doses are likely to be most beneficial.

In a recent study, Singh and Aman (1981) compared a low standardized dose of thioridazine to the previous (usually much higher) titrated doses in a group of residents. Both doses produced improvements, but there was very little difference in therapeutic effects between the two regimens, suggesting that dosages used clinically are higher than necessary. If such a practice is commonplace it means that the individuals so treated are unnecessarily exposed to increased risk of undesirable effects.

Sprague and Sleator (1973, 1975, 1977) carried out an important series of dosage experiments in nonretarded hyperactive children. They found that as dosage of methylphenidate (Ritalin) was increased up to a maximum level, social behavior improved likewise. However, learning performance improved up to a moderate dosage, declined thereafter, and was actually *worsened* at the higher doses. This highlights an important issue, namely assessment of the whole person, not just problem behaviors. Had Sprague and Sleator examined drug effects on social behavior only, they would have been forced to conclude that "the more drug given, the better the response." However, inclusion of the learning measures revealed that the nature of the drug response is complex and that gains in one sphere can come at the expense of another.

In summary, the issue of dosage is virtually unstudied in the mentally retarded. Dosage studies have been unpopular with investigators because they are unusually cumbersome, time consuming, and because they implicitly question the long accepted notion of titration. However, it is clear that if drugs are to be prescribed rationally and knowledgeably, then more of this type of information is needed. Furthermore, we need to know not only what dosages are optimal for social adjustment, but also about the various other spheres of functioning affected. Given that a number of the most commonly used drugs have sedative properties, and that these drugs are not without some risk, we cannot afford to be administering doses which are potentially too high.

Follow-up Research

There has been a near absence of follow-up studies to assess the long-term effects of drugs in mental retardation, despite the fact that they are frequently administered over a period of several years. This is a serious omission because long-term effects do not always mirror those observed during shorter periods of administration. Thus, even if behavioral improvement is noted at the beginning of treatment, we have no guarantee that benefit will be maintained in the long run.

Since the drugs used most commonly in mental retardation are known to have sedative effects, it therefore appears essential to determine whether there are adverse effects on learning when drugs are administered over prolonged periods. In fact there have been isolated reports which suggest that suppression of learning may occur with certain drugs. In a retrospective study of children on phenothiazines, McAndrew, Case, and Treffert (1972) noted that three children showed marked increases on the Stanford Achievement Tests after discontinuation of thioridazine. The study by Moore (1960), cited earlier, suggested possible suppression in achievement due to chlorpromazine. Cordes (1973) described a case where the measured IQ of a girl was apparently depressed on anticonvulsant drugs. The association of depressed performance with drug treatment could have been coincidental in two of these accounts (Cordes, 1973; McAndrew et al., 1972) but together the three reports underline the need for more information on the topic.

Drugs with Other Treatments

The problems presented by the retarded can be massive as well as extremely refractory to *any* form of treatment. Therefore, it is necessary to look for the most powerful techniques available for dealing with these problems.

Two of the most commonly used techniques in the retarded are special education and behavior modification. Yet there have been very few evaluations of the possible interactive or additive effects of psychoactive drugs in combination with these interventions. This would seem to be a logical and potentially powerful approach to dealing with behavior and learning problems.

Two studies which attempted to assess this dual approach in the retarded have already been mentioned. McConahy's (1972) study of behavior modification in combination with chlorpromazine unfortunately did not analyze to determine whether the two treatments produced additive benefits. Christensen (1975) was unable to show much additional benefit when methylphenidate was added to a behavior-modification program. (This latter negative finding may have been due to a general lack of effect of stimulants in this population, as discussed earlier.) However, in studies of nonretarded, but emotionally disturbed or hyperactive children, psychotropic drugs have been shown to produce substantial additional benefits when added to behavioral programs (Christensen & Sprague, 1973; Gittelman-Klein, Klein, Abikoff, Katz, Gloisten, & Kates, 1976).

Two other studies have recently become available. One investigation (Breuning, O'Neill, & Ferguson, 1980) evaluated a token reinforcement program with and without neuroleptic drug treatment. It was found that when the drugs were *withdrawn*, significant and substantial improvements occurred due to the behavioral program used in isolation. Another study (Breuning & Davidson, 1981) examined the IQ's of residents under both standard and reinforcement conditions. It was found that the IQ scores rose dramatically under the reinforcement condition but only when medication (a mixed group of nueroleptics) was withdrawn. Based on these findings, Breuning and his associates have suggested that the drugs may have been actively interfering with the rehabilitative program of these residents. This is a serious accusation and one with possible legal implications for the use of psychoactive drugs. It underlines the need for more research in this important area of interactive effects between drug treatment and other therapies.

Lack of Learning-Related Measures

Mental retardation is first and foremost a disorder of learning, and when other aspects such as aggressiveness, hyperactivity, and bizarre behavior are present, they must be regarded as secondary, albeit important components of the problem. Never has a lack of interdisciplinary cooperation been so obvious as in this field. Measures of drug effect are too often dominated by vacuous clinical global impressions to the virtual exclusion of such theoretically meaningful indices as classical and operant conditioning and discrimination learning. As a result, the area of drug effects in this population is almost totally devoid of theoretical underpinning. For example, only one study was located which examined drug effects on acquisition of a conditioned response, this being an investigation by Lobb (1968) which examined drug effects on the rate of classical conditioning. Other well-recognized measures of cognitive function, such as discrimination learning tasks and vigilance tasks, are only rarely reported in this literature. Indices of learning employing standardized tests appear spasmodically, but even here it is difficult to establish a pattern.

It is not being argued that drugs should alter the retarded state of these persons, but it is absolutely essential that gains in the behavioral sphere do not come at the *expense* of cognitive abilities. However, as the area now stands, it is virtually impossible to make even an educated guess regarding the effects of most drugs on learning without resorting to the literature on other clinical populations.

Other Issues

Diagnostic Indicators

Some authors have commented that the existence of mental retardation in itself should not be reason for expecting a qualititatively different drug response from the nonretarded population. Obviously the IQ label *per se* attached to a person will not affect his response to pharmacotherapy. However, the incidence of brain damage, epilepsy, neurological handicap, and metabolic disorder is so greatly increased in the mentally retarded population that these may alter the nature of the responses.

Unfortunately, proportionately few studies have reported the composition of their samples in terms of neurological, biochemical, or standardized behavioral descriptors. The number of studies which have begun with well-defined subgroups to test the significance of carefully formulated diagnostic factors is miniscule. There is a great need for this kind of information if pharmacotherapy is to be applied on the basis of known diagnostic relationships, rather than on a mere hit-or-miss basis as is currently the case.

Onset of Drug Effect

It is commonplace for authors in this field to speculate that their results would have been stronger if higher doses and longer drug periods had been employed. This is based on the clinical observation that there is often a characteristic delay of therapeutic onset for many psychoactive drugs. However, there is very little systematically gathered evidence on this issue. This is unfortunate and difficult to understand because such information could be gathered at little or no extra cost and without jeopardizing other objectives in most investigations.

Summary of Issues

Literally hundreds of drug trials have been conducted with the mentally retarded and yet we have surprisingly little concrete information about basic issues. There are currently no hard data available relating to optimal dose ranges for various spheres of functioning. Follow-up reports have been haphazard, but those which have appeared have provided cause for concern about effects on intellectual performance. There has also been surprisingly little attention to the combination of drugs with other interventions. The usage of learning indices directly pertinent to mental retardation has been minimal. Attention to diagnostic indicators has been hit-and-miss, so that we still do not know which persons are likely to benefit, and if so, from which drugs. Finally there has been an inexplicable absence of research directed to the issue of latency of therapeutic onset.

Clearly we have barely scratched the surface in evaluating the psychoactive drugs in mental retardation. It is hoped that future research will address basic issues such as these rather than routinely promoting still more drugs in what is an already oversupplied field.

ETHICAL ISSUES

This topic is also discussed in Chapter 2, where legal and ethical issues in behavior modification, many of which are relevant to the current topic, are reviewed.

Unestablished Benefit

For most drugs used with the mentally retarded, the production of benefit to the person treated remains unproven. Certain drugs, such as thioridazine and haloperidol, probably do suppress such maladaptive behaviors as hyperactivity, stereotypic movements, and aggressiveness. However, even here the equation remains incomplete, and little is known about long-term outcome or about the effects of these agents on other adaptive behaviors such as learning. Some commonly used drugs such as chlorpromazine have strikingly little evidence attesting to their usefulness, either to the person treated or those immediately around him. Other drug classes, including the stimulants and minor tranquilizers, simply have not been shown to benefit the mentally retarded and, in some cases, appear to cause behavioral deterioration.

It is my belief that this partly reflects our total lack of sophistication in tailoring treatments to appropriately selected clinical subgroups rather than a genuine lack of therapeutic potential for many of these drugs. However, the simple fact remains that at this time psychopharmacological treatment in the mentally retarded is often of unestablished value and even when known beneficial effects do exist, other possible effects on adaptive functioning are poorly understood.

Physiological Risk

In the past, psychoactive drugs were largely viewed as benign or innocuous agents, often "worth a try" even if they were not necessarily *expected* to produce improvement. However, this attitude is no longer defensible.

Tardive Dyskinesia

In recent years there has been concern about the appearance of tardive dyskinesia following prolonged treatment with major tranquilizers. Tardive dyskinesia is a drug-induced movement disorder manifested by involuntary, repetitive and rhythmic movements of the tongue, lips, and facial muscles. These are sometimes accompanied by involuntary spasmodic movements of the extremities. The disorder is not life threatening, but the symptoms can obviously interfere with adaptive functioning. The symptons sometimes disappear with discontinuation of the drug, but they are often irreversible (Charalampous & Keepers, 1978; Gonzalez, 1979; Turek, Kurland, Hanlon, & Bohm, 1972). Tardive dyskinesia is set apart from other untoward drug effects because it is frequently first manifested upon reduction in dosage or discontinuation of the drug. This, of course, makes the disorder difficult to detect in its early stages since the drug seems to mask the very symptoms it causes.

The incidence of tardive dyskinesia is difficult to ascertain with estimates ranging from 1% to 41% of subjects treated with major tranquilizers (Shepherd & Watt, 1977). McAndrew *et al.* (1972) found that 14% of 74 children with behavior disorders developed tardive dyskinesia when abruptly withdrawn from neuroleptics. Paulson, Rizvi, and Crane (1975) observed that 21 (or 20%) of 103 mentally retarded youngsters on long-term phenothiazine therapy developed some degree of tardive dyskinesia. Obviously the risk of developing this disorder is considerable when mentally retarded persons are treated for protracted periods with neuroleptic drugs.

Other Drug-Induced Disorders

Other long-lasting or permanent neurological disorders have recently been documented as occurring consequent to treatment with psychoactive drugs. For example, Heistad and Zimmerman (1979) reported that when 60 patients were withdrawn from thioridazine, two who were previously seizure-free developed serious and repeated seizures. Vallarta *et al.* (1974) described progressive neurological deterioration as a result of chronic phenytoin intoxication. Elsewhere, ocular changes have been noted following long-term treatment with the neuroleptics (Charalampous & Keepers, 1978; McAndrew *et al.*, 1972).

Physiological Risk—Conclusions

My purpose in the foregoing discussion was not to employ scare tactics where medication is concerned but to portray the very real physiological risks that accompany such treatment. Given the existence of these risks, there should always be a reasonable expectation of benefit before psychoactive drugs are used. Unfortunately, the neuroleptics, which are the best documented drugs for producing beneficial change, have also come in for considerable attention insofar as undesirable aftereffects are concerned.

Other Problems with Drug Treatment

The possibility that certain psychoactive drugs may suppress cognitive development was discussed earlier. In addition to this, many people have expressed concern that inappropriate use of these drugs will make it easier to abuse the true function of our institutions for the mentally retarded, namely, to promote the acquisition of adaptive life skills. Instead, drugs are often viewed as serving the convenience of staff rather than needs of the residents, thereby helping to promote a "warehouse" role for the institution.

Mentally retarded persons present unique ethical difficulties for the administration of psychoactive drugs. First, they are usually the passive recipients of such treatment and are likely to be so treated regardless of their own wishes. Second, unlike most other populations, many mentally retarded persons would find it impossible to communicate the presence of side effects or other untoward reactions. Finally, because of their limited communicative ability, many mentally retarded individuals may misconstrue the *reasons* for such treatment, regarding it instead as a form of punishment imposed by staff.

Legal Developments

In the United States there have been significant legal developments in recent years which impinge directly on the area of drug treatment. These events would take us beyond the scope of the present chapter, but they are especially relevant to those concerned with psychoactive drugs and treatment of the mentally retarded. The interested reader is referred to Gadow (1979), Lockhart (1977), Sprague (1978a,b), and Sprague and Baxley (1978).

The Ethics of Drug Research

Given the uncertainties surrounding pharmacotherapy, the issue of research naturally arises. In recent years there has been a growing reaction against the research enterprise in general (Haywood, 1976) and against pharmacological research in particular (Sprague, 1978a). Many of these cries have been to the effect that drug research is *ipso facto* unethical in the mentally retarded. This is an unfortunate and sadly misplaced sentiment, for it often directly works *against* the interests of the very individuals likely to be treated with psychoactive drugs (see Lockhart, 1977). There is a variety of important medical, ethical, and legal questions revolving around the use of these agents and only by good and vigorous research can these issues be resolved so that the proper role of pharmacotherapy is understood.

Ethical Issues—Summary

There is a lack of solid evidence that the psychoactive drugs produce sustained benefit for persons so treated. The situation is complicated further by recent reports indicating that some drugs can have serious and permanent physical side effects. Also, the reduced ability of the mentally retarded to communicate verbally often places them at additional risk because the likelihood is increased that untoward reactions can go undetected. Finally, if these drugs are misapplied, albeit unintentionally, then their ultimate impact may actually be to *undermine* the habilitative role of our institutions. There have been a number of court cases over the last few years which have set explicit standards for the use of drugs as well as for other prominent modes of treatment. The most appropriate way of resolving many of these troubling issues is to seek answers through vigorous and attentive research of a high caliber.

Overall Conclusions

Knowledge of drug effects in the mentally retarded is of immense importance, if only because of the high incidence of psychoactive treatment in this population. However, past drug research in this area has been dominated by efforts lacking in proficiency. This can be seen in many studies which have been poorly controlled or totally uncontrolled, by measures bereft of theoretical (and often practical) import, and by a lack of systematic attack on basic issues. The result is a near lack of information on most drug classes.

At the same time there is a genuine need to be informed about the precise therapeutic value (or lack thereof) of psychoactive drugs, for the problems faced in the habilitation of some mentally retarded persons can be massive. Therefore, a concerted research effort is needed to attack fundamental theoretical and practical issues as they pertain to this group. Only in this way will it be possible to resolve the many psychological, medical, ethical, and legal questions which inevitably arise in relation to the use of drugs.

Acknowledgments

The author would like to acknowledge the assistance of Joan Mayhew for her exhaustive search for relevant library materials and her (as usual) meticulous typing. He is grateful to Nirbhay Singh, Ph.D., and Marina Vamos, MB, Ch.B., for their very helpful critical comments.

Appendix

Psychoactive Drugs, Their Respective Classes and Trade Names

Drug	Trade Name(s)
MAJOR TRANQUILIZERS	
Phenothiazines	
chlorpromazine	Largactil, Thorazine, Megaphen
thioridazine	Mellaril
mesoridazine	Serentil
fluphenazine	Anatensol, Sevinol
peracetazine	Quide
pericyazine	Neulactil
promazine	Sparine

APPENDIX *(continued)*

Drug	Trade Name(s)
Thioxanthenes	
chlorprothixene	Taractan, Tarasan
Butyrophenones	
haloperidol	Haldol, Serenace
pipamperon	Dipiperon
Rauwolfia Alkaloids	
reserpine	Rauloydin, Raurine, Rau-sed, Reserpoid, Sandril, Serfin

ANTICONVULSANTS

Drug	Trade Name(s)
phenytoin (diphenylhydantoin, DPH)	Dilantin
phenobarbital (phenobarbitone)	Gardenal
primidone	Mysoline
carbamazepine	Tegretol
ethosuximide	Zarontin
sulthiame	Ospolot

STIMULANTS

Drug	Trade Name(s)
amphetamine	Benzedrine
dextroamphetamine	Dexedrine
methylphenidate	Ritalin
deanol	Deaner
pemoline	Cylert, Ronyl

ANXIOLYTICS

Drug	Trade Name(s)
Antihistamines	
diphenhydramine	Benadryl
hydroxyzine	Atarax
Benzodiazepines	
chlordiazepoxide	Librium
diazepam	Valium
RO 5-4556	
lorazepam	Ativan
Other	
meprobamate	Equanil, Miltown, Trelmar

APPENDIX *(continued)*

Drug	Trade Name(s)
ANTIDEPRESSANT/ANTIMANIC DRUGS	
nortriptyline	Allegron, Aventyl, Nortab
imipramine	Tofranil, Imipramine, Imiprin
lithium carbonate	Lithicarb, Lithium Phasal, Priadel
MISCELLANEOUS	
glutamic acid	
5 hydroxytryptophan (5HTP)	
adrenocorticotrophic hormone (ACTH) neuropeptides	

References

Adamson, W. C., Nellis, B. P., Runge, G., Cleland, C., & Killian, E. Use of tranquilizers for mentally deficient patients. *American Journal of Diseases of Children*, 1958, *96*, 159–164.

Alexandris, A., & Lundell, F. W. Effect of thioridazine, amphetamine, and placebo on the hyperkinetic syndrome and cognitive area in mentally deficient children. *Canadian Medical Association Journal*, 1968, *98*, 92–96.

Aman, M. G. Drugs, learning and the psychotherapies. In J. S. Werry (Ed.), *Pediatric pyschopharmacology: The use of behavior modifying drugs in children*. New York: Brunner/Mazel, 1978.

Aman, M. G. Psychotropic drugs and learning problems—A selective review. *Journal of Learning Disabilities*, 1980, *13*, 87–96.

Aman, M. G., & Singh, N. The usefulness of thioridazine for treating childhood disorders—Fact or folklore? *American Journal of Mental Deficiency*, 1980, *84*, 331–338.

Anderson, R. P., Halcomb, C. G., & Doyle, R. B. The measurement of attentional deficits. *Exceptional Children*, 1973, *39*, 534–540.

Anton, A. H., & Greer, M. Dextroamphetamine, catecholamines, and behavior. *Archives of Neurology*, 1969, *21*, 248–252.

Arnold, E., & Magnin, D. W. Fluphenazine ("Anatensol") in the treatment of disturbed mentally retarded children. *The Medical Journal of Australia*, 1967, *1*, 758–760.

Astin, A. W., & Ross, S. Glutamic acid and human intelligence. *Psychological Bulletin*, 1960, *57*, 429–434.

Baldwin, R. W., & Kenny, T. J. Medical treatment of behavior disorders. In J. Hellmuth (Ed.), *Learning disorders* (Vol. 2). Seattle: Special Child Publications, 1966.

Barkley, R. A., & Cunningham, C. E. Do stimulant drugs improve the academic performance of hyperkinetic children? A review of outcome research. *Clinical Pediatrics*, 1978, *17*, 85–92.

Baumeister, A. A., & Forehand, R. Stereotyped acts. In N. R. Ellis (Ed.), *International review of research in mental retardation* (Vol. 6). New York: Academic Press, 1973.

BAZELON, M., PAINE, R. S., COWIE, V. A., HUNT, P., HOUCK, J. C., & MAHANAND, D. Reversal of hypotonia in infants with Down's syndrome by administration of 5-hydroxytryptophan. *Lancet*, 1967, *1*, 1130–1133.

BELL, A., & ZUBEK, J. P. Effects of deanol on the intellectual performance of mental defectives. *Canadian Journal of Psychology*, 1961, *15*, 172–175.

BLACKLIDGE, V. Y., & EKBLAD, R. L. The effectiveness of methylphenidate hydrochloride (Ritalin) on learning and behavior in public school educable mentally retarded children. *Pediatrics*, 1971, *47*, 923–926.

BLACKWELL, B., & CURRAH, J. The psychopharmacology of nocturnal enuresis. In I. Kolvin, R. McKeith, & S. Meadow (Eds.), *Bladder control and enuresis*. Clinics in Developmental Medicine, Nos. 48/49. London: Heinemann, 1973.

BRADLEY, C. The behavior of children receiving benzedrine. *American Journal of Psychiatry*, 1937, *94*, 577–585.

BREUNING, S. E., & DAVIDSON, N. A. Effects of psychotropic drugs on intelligence test performance of institutionalized retarded adults. *American Journal of Mental Deficiency*, 1981, *85*, 575–579.

BREUNING, S. E., O'NEILL, J., & FERGUSON, D. G. Comparison of psychotropic drug, response cost, and psychotropic drug plus response cost procedures for controlling institutionalized retarded persons. *Applied Research in Mental Retardation*, 1980, *1*, 253–268.

BROWNE, T. R., DREIFUSS, F. E., DYKEN, P. R., GOODE, D. J., PENRY, J. K., PORTER, R. J., WHITE, B. G., & WHITE, P. T. Ethosuximide in the treatment of absence (petit mal) seizures. *Neurology*, 1975, *25*, 515–524.

BURK, H. W., & MENOLASCINO, F. J. Haloperidol in emotionally disturbed mentally retarded individuals. *American Journal of Psychiatry*, 1968, *124*, 1589–1591.

CALDWELL, A. E. History of psychopharmacology. In W. G. Clark & J. Del Giudice (Eds.), *Principles of Psychopharmacology (2nd Ed.)*. New York: Academic Press, 1978.

CAMFIELD, C. S., CHAPLIN, S., DOYLE, A., SHAPIRO, S. H., CUMMINGS, C., & CAMFIELD, P. R. Side effects of phenobarbital in toddlers; behavioral and cognitive aspects. *Journal of Pediatrics*, 1979, *95*, 361–365.

CARTER, C. H. Nortriptyline HCl as a tranquilizer for disturbed mentally retarded patients: A controlled study. *The American Journal of the Medical Sciences*, 1966, *251*, 465–467.

CHARALAMPOUS, K. D., & KEEPERS, G. A. Major side effects of antipsychotic drugs. *Journal of Family Practice*, 1978, *6*, 993–1002.

CHRISTENSEN, D. E. Effects of combining methylphenidate and a classroom token system in modifying hyperactive behavior. *American Journal of Mental Deficiency*, 1975, *80*, 266–276.

CHRISTENSEN, D., & SPRAGUE, R. Reduction of hyperactive behavior by conditioning procedures alone and combined with methylphenidate (Ritalin). *Behaviour Research and Therapy*. 1973, *11*, 331–334.

CLAGHORN, J. L. A double-blind comparison of haloperidol (Haldol) and thioridazine (Mellaril) in outpatient children. *Current Therapeutic Research*, 1972, *14*, 785–789.

CLAUSEN, J., FINEMAN, M., HENRY, C. E., & WOHL, N. The effect of Deaner (2-dimethylaminoethanol) on mentally retarded subjects. *Training School Bulletin*, 1960, *57*, 3–12.

COHEN, M. N., & SPRAGUE, R. L. *Survey of drug usage in two midwestern institutions for the retarded*. Paper presented at the Gatlinburg Conference on Research in Mental Retardation, Gatlinburg, Tennessee, March 1977.

COHN, R., & NARDINI, J. E. The correlation of bilateral occipital slow activity in the human EEG with certain disorders of behavior. *American Journal of Psychiatry*, 1958, *115*, 44–48.

CONNERS, C. K., & WERRY, J. S. Pharmacotherapy of psychopathology in children. In H. C. Quay & J. S. Werry (Eds.), *Psychopathological disorders of childhood*. New York: Wiley, 1979.

Conners, C. K., Kramer, R., Rothschild, G. H., Schwartz, L., & Stone, A. Treatment of young delinquent boys with diphenylhydantoin sodium and methylphenidate. *Archives of General Psychiatry*, 1971, 24, 156-160.

Cordes, C. K. Chronic drug intoxication causing pseudoretardation in a young child. *Journal of the American Academy of Child Psychiatry*, 1973, 12, 215-222.

Craft, M. Tranquillizers in mental deficiency: Hydroxyzine. *Journal of Mental Science*, 1957, 103, 855-857.

Craft, M. Tranquillizers in mental deficiency: Meprobamate. *Journal of Mental Deficiency Research*, 1958, 2, 17-20.

Dalby, M. A. Behavioral effects of carbamazepine. In J. K. Penry & D. D. Daly (Eds.), *Advances in neurology* (Vol. 11). New York: Raven Press, 1975.

Davis, K. V. The effect of drugs on stereotyped and nonstereotyped operant behaviors in retardates. *Psychopharmacologia (Berl.)*, 1971, 22, 195-213.

Davis, K. V., Sprague, R. L., & Werry, J. S. Stereotyped behavior and activity level in severe retardates: The effect of drugs. *American Journal of Mental Deficiency*, 1969, 73, 721-727.

Dekaban, A. S., & Lehman, E. J. B. Effects of different dosages of anticonvulsant drugs on mental performance in patients with chronic epilepsy. *Acta Neurologica Scandinavica*, 1975, 52, 319-330.

Dodrill, C. Diphenylhydantoin serum levels, toxicity, and neuropsychological performance in patients with epilepsy. *Epilepsia*, 1975, 16, 593-600.

Dostal, T., & Zvolsky, P. Antiaggressive effect of lithium salts in severe mentally retarded adolescents. *International Pharmacopsychiatry*, 1970, 5, 203-207.

Fisher, M. A., & Zeaman, D. An attention-retention theory of retardate discrimination learning. In N. R. Ellis (Ed.), *International review of research in mental retardation* (Vol. 6). New York: Academic Press, 1973.

Freeman, R. D. Psychopharmacology and the retarded child. In F. J. Menolascino (Ed.), *Psychiatric approaches to mental retardation*. New York: Basic Books, 1970. (a)

Freeman, R. D. Use of psychoactive drugs for intelectually handicapped children. In N. R. Bernstein (Ed.), *Diminished people: Problems and care of the mentally retarded*. Boston: Little, Brown, 1970. (b)

Gadow, K. D. *Children on medication: A primer for school personnel*. Virginia: The Council for Exceptional Children, 1979.

Gadow, K. D. Prevalence of drug treatment for hyperactivity and other childhood behavior disorders. In K. D. Gadow & J. Loney (Eds.), *Psychosocial aspects of drug treatment for hyperactivity*. Boulder, Co.: Westview Press, 1981.

Gaillard, A. W. K., & Sanders, A. F. Some effects of ACTH 4-10 on performance during a serial reaction task. *Psychopharmacologia*, 1975, 42, 201-208.

Galambos, M. Long term clinical trial with diazepam on adult mentally retarded persons. *Diseases of the Nervous System*, 1965, 26, 305-309.

Gardner, W. I. Occurrence of severe depressive reactions in the mentally retarded. *American Journal of Psychiatry*, 1967, 124, 142-144.

Giannini, M. J. Hydroxyzine hydrochloride in treatment of behavioral disturbances in mentally retarded children. *New York State Journal of Medicine*, 1964, 64, 1721-1723.

Gittelman-Klein, R., Klein, D. F., Abikoff, H., Katz, S., Gloisten, A. C., & Kates, W. Relative efficacy of methylphenidate and behavior modification in hyperkinetic children: An interim report. *Journal of Abnormal Child Psychology*, 1976, 4, 361-379.

Goldberg, J. B., & Kurland, A. A. Dilantin treatment of hospitalized cultural-familial retardation. *Journal of Nervous and Mental Disease*, 1970, 150, 133-137.

Gonzalez, E. R. For mental patients, the "cure" may be worse. *Journal of the American Medical Association*, 1979, 242, 220-231.

GOODMAN, L. S. & GILMAN, A. (Eds.). *The pharmacological basis of therapeutics* (3rd ed.). New York: Macmillan, 1965.

GRABOWSKI, S. W. Haloperidol for control of severe emotional reactions in mentally retarded patients. *Diseases of the Nervous System*, 1973, *34*, 315-317. (a)

GRABOWSKI, S. W. Safety and effectiveness of haloperidol for mentally retarded behaviorally disordered and hyperkinetic patients. *Current Therapeutic Research*, 1973, *15*, 856-861. (b)

GREEN, J. B. Association of behavior disorder with an electroencephalographic focus in children without seizures. *Neurology*, 1961, *11*, 337-344.

GROSS, M. D., & WILSON, W. C. Behavior disorders of children with cerebral dysrhythmias. *Archives of General Psychiatry*, 1964, *11*, 610-619.

GUEY, J., CHARLES, C., COQUERY, C., ROGER J., & SOULAYROL, R. Study of psychological effects of ethosuximide (Zarontin) on 25 children suffering from petit mal epilepsy. *Epilepsia*, 1967, *8*, 129-141.

HAEGEMAN, J., & DUYCK, F. A retrospective evaluation of pipamperone (Dipiperon) in the treatment of behavioral deviations in severely mentally handicapped. *Acta Psychiatrica Belgica*, 1978, *78*, 392-398.

HAYWOOD, H. C. The ethics of doing research...and of not doing it. *American Journal of Mental Deficiency*, 1976, *81*, 311-317.

HEISTAD, G. T., & ZIMMERMANN, R. L. Double-blind assessment of Mellaril in a mentally retarded population using detailed evaluations. *Psychopharmacology Bulletin*, 1979, *15*, 86-88.

HOLLIS, J. H., & ST. OMER, V. V. Direct measurement of psychopharmacologic response: Effects of chlorpromazine on motor behavior of retarded children. *American Journal of Mental Deficiency*, 1972, *76*, 397-407.

HUGHES, P. S. Survey of medication in a subnormality hospital. *British Journal of Mental Subnormality*, 1977, *23*, 88-94.

HUTT, S. J., JACKSON, P. M., BELSHAM, A., & HIGGINS, G. Perceptual-motor behavior in relation to blood phenobarbitone level: A preliminary report. *Developmental Medicine and Child Neurology*, 1968, *10*, 626-632.

IDESTROM, C. M., SCHALLING, D., CARLQUIST, U., & SJOQVIST, F. Acute effects of diphenylhydantoin in relation to plasma levels. *Psychological Medicine*, 1972, *2*, 111-120.

ISON, M. G. The effect of 'Thorazine" on Wechsler Scores. *American Journal of Mental Deficiency*, 1957, *62*, 543-547.

KERSHNER, J. R. Leeches, quicksilver, megavitamins, and learning disabilities. *Journal of Special Education*, 1978, *12*, 7-16.

KIRMAN, B. Drug therapy in mental handicap. *British Journal of Psychiatry*, 1975, *127*, 545-549.

KRAKOWSKI, A. J. Chlordiazepoxide in treatment of children with emotional disturbances. *New York State Journal of Medicine*, 1963, *63*, 3388-3392.

KUGELMASS, I. N. Psychochemotherapy of mental deficiency in children. *International Record of Medicine and General Practice Clinics*, 1956, *169*, 323-338.

KURLAND, A. A., & GOLDBERG, J. B. Piperacetazine (Quide) in the management of behavioral disorders in mildly retarded institutionalized boys. *Current Therapeutic Research*, 1970, *12*, 798-804.

LACNY, J. Mesoridazine in the care of disturbed mentally retarded patients. *Canadian Psychiatric Association Journal*, 1973, *18*, 389-391.

LAVECK, G. D., & BUCKLEY, P. The use of psychopharmacologic agents in retarded children with behavior disorders. *Journal of Chronic Diseases*, 1961, *13*, 174-183.

LEVANN, L. J. Clinical experience with Tarasan and thioridazine in mentally retarded children. *Applied Therapeutics*, 1970, *12*, 30-33.

LEVANN, L. J. Clinical comparison of haloperidol with chlorpromazine in mentally retarded children. *American Journal of Mental Deficiency,* 1971, *75,* 719-723.

LINDSLEY, D. B., & HENRY, C. E. The effect of drugs on behavior and the electroencephalograms of children with behavior disorders. *Psychosomatic Medicine,* 1941, *4,* 140-149.

LIPMAN, R. S. The use of psychopharmacological agents in residential facilities for the retarded. In F. J. Menolascino (Ed.), *Psychiatric approaches to mental retardation.* New York: Basic Books, 1970.

LIPMAN, R. S., DIMASCIO, A., REATIG, N., & KIRSON, T. Psychotropic drugs and mentally retarded children. In M. A. Lipton, A. DiMascio, & K. F. Killam (Eds.), *Psychopharmacology: A generation of progress.* New York: Raven Press, 1978.

LOBB, H. Trace GSR conditioning with Benzedrine in mentally defective and normal adults. *American Journal of Mental Deficiency,* 1968, *73,* 239-246.

LOCKHART, J. D. Pediatric drug testing: Is it at risk? *Hastings Center Report,* 1977, *7,* 8-10.

LOOKER, A., & CONNERS, C. K. Diphenylhydantoin in children with severe temper tantrums. *Archives of General Psychiatry,* 1970, *23,* 80-89.

LOUTTIT, R. Chemical facilitation of intelligence among the mentally retarded. *American Journal of Mental Deficiency,* 1965, *69,* 495-501.

LOVAAS, O. I., KOEGEL, R. L., & SCHREIBMAN, L. Stimulus overselectivity in autism: A review of research. *Psychological Bulletin,* 1979, *86,* 1236-1254.

MACLEOD, C. M., DEKABAN, A. S. & HUNT, E. Memory impairment in epileptic patients: Selective effects of phenobarbital concentration. *Science,* 1978, *202,* 1102-1104.

MAISTO, C. R., BAUMEISTER, A. A. & MAISTO, A. A. Analysis of variables related to self-injurious behavior among institutionalized retarded persons. *Journal of Mental Deficiency Research,* 1978, *22,* 27-36.

MARHOLIN, D., TOUCHETTE, P. F., & STEWART, R. M. Withdrawal of chronic chlorpromazine medication: An experimental analysis. *Journal of Applied Behavior Analysis,* 1979, *12,* 159-171.

MATTHEWS, C. G., & HARLEY, J. P. Cognitive and motor-sensory performances in toxic and non-toxic epileptic subjects. *Neurology,* 1975, *25,* 184-188.

MCANDREW, J. B., CASE, Q., & TREFFERT, D. A. Effects of prolonged phenothiazine intake on psychotic and other hospitalized children. *Journal of Autism and Childhood Schizophrenia,* 1972, *2,* 75-91.

MCCONAHEY, O. L. A token system for retarded women: Behavior modification, drug therapy, and their combination. In T. Thompson & J. Grabowski (Eds.), *Behavior modification of the mentally retarded.* New York: Oxford University Press, 1972.

MCCONNELL, T. R., CROMWELL, R. L., BIALER, I., & SON, C. D. Studies in activity level: VII. Effects of amphetamine drug administration on the activity level of retarded children. *American Journal of Mental Deficiency,* 1964, *68,* 647-651.

MICEV, V., & LYNCH, D. M. Effect of lithium on disturbed severely mentally retarded patients. *British Journal of Psychiatry,* 1974, *125,* 110.

MILLICHAP, J. G., EGAN, R. W., HART, Z. H., & STURGIS, L. H. Auditory perceptual deficit correlated with EEG dysrhythmias. Response to diphenylhydantoin sodium. *Neurology,* 1969, *19,* 870-872.

MOORE, J. W. The effects of a tranquilizer (Thoraxine) on the intelligence and achievement of educable mentally retarded women. *Dissertation Abstracts,* 1960, *20,* 3200.

MORRIS, J. V., MACGILLIVRAY, R. C., MATHIESON, C. M. The results of the experimental administration of amphetamine sulfate in oligophrenia. *Journal of Mental Science/British Journal of Psychiatry,* 1955, *101,* 131-140.

MULLEROVA, S., NOVOTNA, J., REHAN, V., & SKULA, E. Lithium treatment of behavioral disturbances in patients with defective intellect. *Activitus Nervosa Superior (Praha),* 1974, *16,* 196.

NAYLOR, G. J., DONALD, J. M., LE POIDEVIN, D., & REID, A. H. A double-blind trial of long-term lithium therapy in mental defectives. *British Journal of Psychiatry*, 1974, *124*, 52–57.

OUNSTED, C. The hyperkinetic syndrome in epileptic children. *Lancet*, 1955, *2*, 303–311.

PARTINGTON, M. W., MACDONALD, M. R. A., & TU, J. B. 5-Hydroxytryptophan (5-HTP) in Down's syndrome. *Developmental Medicine and Child Neurology*, 1971, *13*, 362–372.

PASAMANICK, B. Anticonvulsant drug therapy of behavior problem children with abnormal electroencephalograms. *Archives of Neurology and Psychiatry*, 1951, *65*, 752–766.

PAULSON, G. W., RIZVI, C. A., & CRANE, G. E. Tardive dyskinesia as a possible sequel of long-term therapy with phenothiazines. *Clinical Pediatrics*, 1975, *14*, 953–955.

PAYNE, D., JOHNSON, R. C., & ABELSON, R. B. *Comprehensive Description of Institutionalized Retardates in Western United States*. Boulder Co: Western Interstate Commission for Higher Education, 1969.

PHILIPS, I., & WILLIAMS, N. Psychopathology and mental retardation: A study of 100 mentally retarded children: I. Psychopathology. *American Journal of Psychiatry*. 1975. *132*, 1265–1271.

PHILIPS, I., & WILLIAMS, N. Psychopathology and mental retardation: A statistical study of 100 mentally retarded children treated at a psychiatric clinic: II. Hyperactivity. *American Journal of Psychiatry*, 1977, *134*, 418–419.

PULMAN, R. M., POOK, R. B., & SINGH, N. N. Prevalence of drug therapy for institutionalized mentally retarded children. *Australian Journal of Mental Retardation*, 1979, *5*, 212–214.

PUTMAN, T. J., & HOOD, O. E. Project Illinois: A study of therapy in juvenile behavior problems. *Western Medicine*, 1964, *5*, 231–233.

RAPOPORT, J. Childhood behavior and learning problems treated with imipramine. *International Journal of Neuropsychiatry*, 1965, *1*, 635–642.

RAPOPORT, J. L., QUINN, P. O., COPELAND, A. P., & BURG, C. ACTH 4-10: Cognitive and behavioral effects in hyperactive, learning-disabled children. *Neuropsychobiology*, 1976, *2*, 291–296.

RAPOPORT, J. L., BUCHSBAUM, M. S., WEINGARTNER, H., ZAHN, T. P., LUDLOW, C., MIKKELSEN, E. J., LANGER, D., & BUNNEY, W. E. Dextroamphetamine: Cognitive and behavioral effects in normal and hyperactive children and normal adults. *Archives of General Psychiatry*, 1980.

REYNOLDS, E. H., & TRAVERS, R. D. Serum anticonvulsant concentrations in epileptic patients with mental symptoms. *British Journal of Psychiatry*, 1974, *124*, 440–445.

RIVINUS, T. M., & HARMATZ, J. S. Diagnosis and lithium treatment of affective disorder in the retarded: Five case studies. *American Journal of Psychiatry*, 1979, *136*, 551–554.

ROBBINS, T. W., & SAHAKIAN, B. J. "Paradoxical" effects of psychomotor stimulant drugs in hyperactive children from the standpoint of behavioral pharmacology. *Neuropharmacology*, 1979, *18*, 931–950.

ROSENBLUM, S., CALLAHAN, R. J., BUONICONTO, P., GRAHAM, B., & DEATRICK, R. W. The effects of tranquillizing medication (reserpine) on behavior and test performance of maladjusted, high-grade retarded children. *American Journal of Mental Deficiency*, 1958, *62*, 663–671.

RUTTER, M. L. Psychiatric disorder and intellectual impairment in childhood. *British Journal of Psychiatry*, 1975, Special Publication no. 9, 344–348.

SANDMAN, C. A., GEORGE, J. M., NOLAN, J. D., VAN RIEZEN, H., & KASTIN, A. J. Enhancement of attention in man with ACTH/MSH 4-10. *Physiology and Behavior*, 1975, *15*, 427–431.

SANDMAN, C. A., GEORGE, J., WALKER, B. B., & NOLAN, J. D. Neuropeptide MSH/ACTH 4-10 enhances attention in the mentally retarded. *Pharmacology Biochemistry and Behavior*, Supplement 1, 1976, *5*, 23–28.

SCHAIN, R. J. Problems with the use of conventional anticonvulsant drugs in mentally retarded individuals. *Brain and Development*, 1979, *1*, 77–82.

Schain, R. J., Kiehl, J. P., & Ward J. Analysis of cognitive effects of withdrawal of sedative anticonvulsants in epileptic children. *Pediatric Research*, 1975, *9*, 384.

Schain, R. J. Ward, J. W., & Guthrie, D. Carbamazepine as an anticonvulsant in children. *Neurology*, 1977, *27*, 476-480.

Schroeder, S. R., Schroeder, C. S., Smith, B., & Dalldorf, J. Prevalence of self-injurious behaviors in a large state facility for the retarded: A three-year follow-up study. *Journal of Autism and Childhood Schizophrenia*, 1978, *8*, 261-269.

Segal, L. J., & Tansley, A. E. A clinical trail with hydroxyzine (Atarax) on a group of maladjusted educationally subnormal children. *Journal of Mental Retardation*, 1957, *103*, 677-681.

Sewell, J., & Werry, J. S. Some studies in an institution for the mentally retarded. *New Zealand Medical Journal*, 1976, *84*, 317-319.

Share, J. B. Review of drug treatment for Down's Syndrome persons. *American Journal of Mental Deficiency*, 1976, *80*, 388-393.

Shepherd, M., & Watt, D. C. Long-term treatment with neuroleptics in psychiatry. In W. B. Essman & L. Valzell (Eds.), *Current developments in psychopharmacology* (Vol. 4). New York: Spectrum Publications, 1977.

Silva, D. A. The use of medication in a residential institution for mentally retarded persons, *Mental Retardation*, 1979, *17*, 285-288.

Simmons, J. Q., Tymchuk, A. J., & Valente, M. Treatment considerations in mental retardation. *Current Psychiatric Therapies*, 1975, *15*, 15-24.

Singh, N. N., & Amen, M. G. Effects of thioridazine dosage on the behavior of severely mentally retarded persons. *American Journal of Mental Deficiency*, 1981, *85*, 580-587.

Smith, W. L., & Lowrey, J. B. The effects of diphenylhydantoin on cognitive functions in man. In W. L. Smith (Ed.), *Drugs, development and cerebral function*. Springfield, Ill.: Charles C Thomas, 1972.

Smith, W. L., Philippus, M. J., & Guard, H. L. Psychometric study of children with learning problems and 14-6 positive spike EEG patterns, treated with ethosuximide (Zarontin) and placebo. *Archives of Disease in Childhood*, 1968, *43*, 616-619.

Spencer, D. A. Ronyl (pemoline) in overactive mentally subnormal children. *British Journal of Psychiatry*, 1970, *117*, 239-240.

Spencer, D. A. A survey of the medication in a hospital for the mentally handicapped. *British Journal of Psychiatry*, 1974, *124*, 507-508.

Sprague, R. L. Principles of clinical trials and social, ethical and legal issues of drug use in children. In J. S. Werry (Ed.), *Pediatric psychopharmacology: The use of behavior modifying drugs in children*. New York: Brunner/Mazel, 1978. (a)

Sprague, R. L. Psychopharmacology of the retarded: Present and future. *Psychopharmacology Bulletin*, 1978, *14*, 63-65. (b)

Sprague, R. L., & Baxley, G. B. Drugs for behavior management, with comment on some legal aspects. *Mental Retardation and Developmental Disabilities*, 1978, *10*, 92-129.

Sprague, R. L., & Sleator, E. K. Effects of psychopharmacologic agents on learning disorders. *Pediatric Clinics of North America*, 1973, *20*, 719-735.

Sprague, R. L., & Sleator, E. K. What is the proper dose of stimulant drugs in children? *International Journal of Mental Health*, 1975, *4*, 75-118.

Sprague, R. L., & Sleator, E. K. Methylphenidate in hyperkinetic children: Differences in dose effects on learning and social behavior. *Science*, 1977, *198*, 1274-1276.

Sprague, R. L., & Werry, J. S. Methodology of psychopharmacological studies with the retarded. In N. R. Ellis (Ed.), *International review of research in mental retardation* (Vol. 5) New York: Academic Press, 1971.

SPRINGER, N. S., & FRICKE, N. L. Nutrition and drug therapy for persons with developmental disabilities. *American Journal of Mental Deficiency*, 1975, *80*, 317-322.

SROUFE, L. Drug treatment of children with behavior problems. In F. Horowitz (Ed.), *Review of child development research* (Vol. 4). Chicago: University of Chicago Press, 1975.

STORES, G. Behavioral effects of anti-epileptic drugs. *Developmental Medicine and Child Neurology*, 1975, *17*, 647-658.

STORES, G. Antiepileptics (Anticonvulsants). In J. S. Werry (Ed.), *Pediatric psychopharmacology: The use of behavioral modifying drugs in children*. New York: Brunner/Mazel, 1978.

STORES, G., & HART, J. Reading skills of children with generalized or focal epilepsy attending ordinary school. *Developmental Medicine and Child Neurology*, 1976, *18*, 705-716.

SYKES, D., DOUGLAS, V., WEISS, G., & MINDE, K. Attention in hyperactive children and the effect of methylphenidate (Ritalin). *Journal of Child Psychology and Psychiatry*, 1971, *12*, 129-139

SYKES, D. H., DOUGLAS, V. I., & MORGENSTERN, G. The effect of methylphenidate (Ritalin) on sustained attention in hyperactive children. *Psychopharmacologia*, 1972, *25*, 262-274.

TISCHLER, B., PATRIASZ, K., BERESFORD, J., & BUNTING, R. Experience with pericyazine in profoundly and severely retarded children. *Canadian Medical Association Journal*, 1972, *106*, 136-141.

TRIMBLE, M. The effect of anti-convulsant drugs on cognitive abilities. *Pharmacology and Therapeutics*, 1979, *4*, 677-685.

TRIMBLE, M., & REYNOLDS, E. Anticonvulsant drugs and mental symptoms. *Psychological Medicine*, 1976, *6*, 169-178.

TU, J. A survey of psychotropic medication in mental retardation facilities. *Journal of Clinical Psychiatry*, 1979, *40*, 125-128.

TU, J. B., & SMITH, J. T. Factors associated with psychotropic medication in mental retardation facilities. *Comprehensive Psychiatry*, 1979, *20*, 289-295.

TUREK, I., KURLAND, A. A., HANLON, T. E., & BOHM, M. Tardive dyskinesia: Its relation to neuroleptic and antiparkinson drugs. *British Journal of Psychiatry*, 1972, *121*, 605-612.

UCER, E. Pilot study with RO 5-4556 in emotionally disturbed retarded children. *Current Therapeutic Research*, 1968, *10*, 187-195.

UCER, E., & KREGER, C. A double blind study comparing haloperidol with thioridazine in emotionally disturbed retarded children. *Current Therapeutic Research*, 1969, *11*, 278-283.

ULLMAN, D. G. Breadth of attention and retention in mentally retarded and intellectually average children. *American Journal of Mental Deficiency*, 1974, *78*, 640-648.

VAISANEN, K., KAINULAINEN, P., PAAVILAINEN, M. T., & VIUKARI, M. Sulpiride versus chlorpromazine and placebo in the treatment of restless mentally subnormal patients—a double-blind cross-over study. *Current Therapeutic Research*, 1975, *17*, 202-205.

VALLARTA, J. M., BELL, D. B., & REICHERT, A. Progressive encephalopathy due to chronic hydantoin intoxication. *American Journal of Diseases of Children*, 1974, *128*, 27-34.

VAN HEMERT, J. C. Pipamperone (Dipiperon, R3345) in troublesome mental retardates: A double-blind placebo controlled cross-over study with long-term follow-up. *Acta Psychiatrica Scandinavica*, 1975, *52*, 237-245.

VOGEL, W., BROVERMAN, D. M., DRAGUNS, J. G., & KLAIBER, E. L. The role of glutamic acid in cognitive behaviors. *Psychological Bulletin*, 1966, *65*, 367-382.

WAIZER, J., HOFFMAN, S. P., POLIZOS, P., & ENGELHARDT, D. M. Outpatient treatment of hyperactive school children with imipramine. *American Journal of Psychiatry*, 1974, *131*, 587-591.

WALKER, B. B., & SANDMAN, C. A. Influences of an analog of the neuropeptide ACTH 4-9 on mentally retarded adults. *American Journal of Mental Deficiency*, 1979, *83*, 346-352.

WALKER, C. F., & KIRKPATRICK, B. B. Dilantin treatment for behavior problem children with abnormal electroencephalograms. *American Journal of Psychiatry*, 1947, *103*, 484-492.

WALTERS, A., SINGH, N., & BEALE, I. L. Effects of lorazepam on hyperactivity in retarded children. *New Zealand Medical Journal*, 1977, 86, 473-475.

WAPNER, I., THURSTON, D. L., & HOLOWACH, J. Phenobarbital: Its effect on learning in epileptic children. *Journal of the American Medical Association*, 1962, 182, 937.

WARDELL, D. W., RUBIN, H. K., & Ross, R. T. The use of reserpine and chlorpromazine in disturbed mentally deficient patients. *American Journal of Mental Deficiency*, 1958, 63, 330-344.

WEISE, P., KOCH, R., SHAW, K. N., & ROSENFELD, M. J. The use of 5-HTP in the treatment of Down's syndrome. *Pediatrics*, 1974, 54, 165-168.

WERRY, J. S. Organic factors. In H. C. Quay & J. S. Werry (Eds.), *Psychopathological disorders of childhood* (2nd ed.). New York: Wiley, 1979.

WERRY J. S., & AMAN, M. G. Methylphenidate in hyperactive and enuretic children. In B. Shopsin & L. Greenhill (Eds.), *The Psychology of childhood: Profile of current issues*. Jamaica, N.Y.: Spectrum Publications, 1982.

WERRY, J. S., & SPRAGUE, R. L. Psychopharmacology. In J. Wortis (Ed.), *Mental retardation* (Vol. 4). New York: Grune & Stratton, 1972.

WERRY, J. S., AMAN, M. G., & DIAMOND, E. Methylphenidate and imipramine in hyperactive children. *Journal of Child Psychology and Psychiatry*, 1980, 21, 27-35.

WOLF, S. M., & FORSYTHE, A. Behavior disturbance, phenobarbital, and febrile seizures. *Pediatrics*, 1978, 61, 728-731.

WOLFENSBERGER, W., & MENOLASCINO, F. Basic considerations in evaluating ability of drugs to stimulate cognitive development in retardates. *American Journal of Mental Deficiency*, 1968, 73, 414-423.

WORRALL, E. P., MOODY, J. P., & NAYLOR, G. J. Lithium in non-manic depressives: Antiaggressive effect and red blood cell lithium values. *British Journal of Psychiatry*, 1975, 126, 464-468.

WYSOCKI, T., FUQUA, W., DAVIS, V., & BREUNING, S. E. Effects of thioridazine (Mellaril) on titrating delayed matching-to-sample performance of mentally retarded adults. *American Journal of Mental Deficiency*, 1981, 85, 539-547.

YANNET, H. Research in the field of mental retardation. *Journal of Pediatrics*, 1957, 50, 236-239.

YEPES, L., BALKA, E., WINSBERG, B., & BIALER, I. Amitriptyline and methylphenidate treatment of behaviorally disordered children. *Journal of Child Psychology and Psychiatry*, 1977, 18, 39-52.

ZALESKI, W. A. A clinical evaluation of mesoridazine in mentally retarded patients. *Canadian Psychiatric Association Journal*, 1970, 15, 319-322.

ZIMMERMAN, F. T. Explosive behavior anomalies in children on an epileptic basis. *New York State Journal of Medicine*, 1956, 56, 2537-2543.

ZRULL, J. P., WESTMAN, J. C., ARTHUR, B., & RICE, D. L. A comparison of diazepam, d-amphetamine and placebo in the treatment of the hyperkinetic syndrome in children. *American Journal of Psychiatry*, 1964, 121, 388-389.

13 Devices and Instrumentation for Skill Development and Behavior Change

JAMES A. MULICK, FRANK D. SCOTT, RONALD F. GAINES, AND BRIAN M. CAMPBELL

INTRODUCTION

> Children are not retarded. Only their *behavior* in average environments is sometimes retarded. In fact, it is modern science's ability to design suitable environments for these children that is retarded. We design environments to maintain life, but not to maintain dignified behavior. The purpose of this paper is to suggest techniques of designing *prosthetic* environments for maximizing the behavioral efficiency of exceptional children who show deficits when forced to behave in average environments. (O.R. Lindsley, 1964, p. 62)

In the time since Lindsley made these comments to begin his paper on the uses of the operant analysis of behavior and environmental engineering in mental retardation, there have been significant changes in the overall level of our technological sophistication and in the societal context in which services are provided. On the one hand, electromechanical relay circuit controls have been replaced with inexpensive solid-state electronics with miniaturization and increased complexity of control systems and appliances as a result. Handheld calculators and interactive electronic toys are commonplace, and microcomputers—while not readily available—are becoming accessible to the general public for private use.

JAMES A. MULICK • Child Development Center, Rhode Island Hospital, Brown University, Providence, Rhode Island 02903.   FRANK D. SCOTT • School Psychology Program, University of Rhode Island, Kingston, Rhode Island 02881.   RONALD F. GAINES • Palo Alto Veterans Administration Hospital, Palo Alto, California 94304.   BRIAN M. CAMPBELL • Department of Psychology, Nova University, Fort Lauderdale, Florida 33314.

Similarly, the operant analysis of behavior is no longer quite so unusual in applied settings. There have been impressive demonstrations of the use of operant principles in the successful teaching of useful skills (Barrett, 1977; Birnbrauer, 1976; Westling & Murden, 1978; Whitman & Scibak, 1979) and of improved management approaches for behavioral excesses and deficits with the mentally retarded (Mulick & Schroeder, 1980; Schroeder, Mulick, & Schroeder, 1979).

On the other hand, it is no longer as necessary as it once was to marshall our facts and sharpen our ethical arguments to justify providing handicapped persons with an opportunity to develop (Gardner, Long, Nichols, & Iagulli, 1980). Societal awareness and regulatory standards have undergone extensive revision in the last decade. Public Law 94-142 (The Education for all Handicapped Children Act of 1975) requires that all children are entitled to a free appropriate public education in the least restrictive environment regardless of their handicap. The Rehabilitation Act of 1973, Section 504, forbids discrimination on the basis of handicap, with far reaching effects on the concept of acceptable design of public and vocational environments. Title XIX requires facilities receiving federal reimbursement as Intermediate Care Facilities to set and follow standards for professional involvement, accountability, active treatment, and client rights. The need for objective assessment of progress toward goals, for careful planning, and for providing specialized services has been explicitly recognized in these regulations and laws. The 1978 revision of the Developmental Disabilities Act actually defines its target population in functional terms: individuals needing extended intervention prior to age 22 to ameliorate substantial functional limitation in three or more areas. These areas are self-care, language, learning, mobility, self-direction, independent living, and economic self-sufficiency. These standards have in part reflected, and have also served to promote a philosophy of normalization (Wolfensberger, 1972) that seeks to diminish the cultural and institutional differences which have characterized the separate environments inhabited by handicapped persons in the past.

Thus, efforts to understand the retardation of behavioral development in functional terms (Bijou, 1966; Lindsley, 1964) have led to a technology of teaching that improves their prospects for skill acquisition beyond the degree thought possible by many experts a generation ago. Along with this, efforts to reduce the burden of work for all of us have led to improvements in our technologies for communication, control, and information processing. While applications of these technologies are neither universal nor especially characteristic of mental retardation service settings, their existence gives renewed meaning to Lindsley's (1964) call for the use of *prosthetic strategies*. Accordingly, prosthetic devices compensate for sensory, motor, and skill deficits; prosthetic training calls for specialized teaching practices and specialized teaching objectives; and prosthetic environments are designed to support behavioral progress in such ways that the individual's existing response capabilities are made functional, and the need for deficient behavior is reduced. The societal changes of the past decade make prosthetic strategies more feasible by explictly mandating many of them, and by providing an expanded base of public financial support.

There remains a gap, however, between our technological knowledge and our actual standards of service delivery. Instructional as well as engineering technologies are disseminated gradually, and probably reflect respective market demand factors. Additionally, our experience with routine practices affects the level of our goal setting. Goals infrequently exceed past experience with a particular practice, and this fact probably sets the pace of dissemination of new approaches. Ironically, the philosophy of normalization actually occasions a process of radical change. These changes must be supported by a variety of innovative and unusual alterations of both the environment which supports the behavior of the handicapped (Barrett, 1979) and the social and cultural environment of the nonhandicapped. Prosthetic strategies, if successful in normalizing aspects of the behavior of the mentally retarded, will lead to success in community settings, and this may in turn recalibrate the cultural standards of the wider community.

Professionals seemingly require the experience of demonstration in order to change their practices. Demonstration is, fortunately, facilitated by the professional's success in solving an applied problem, and devices that assist in solutions can thereby achieve repeated and wider use. For example, wearing hearing aids is fairly commonplace and accepted. Teaching programs have now been devised to promote the use of such prostheses among the handicapped (e.g., Tucker & Berry, 1980). One wonders whether the general use of a device is actually a prerequisite for people to come to view its use by obviously exceptional persons as a self-evident goal.

We have been comparing the technology of teaching with that of engineering implicit in the use of instrumentation. Developments in both areas are probably often related. The development of new laboratory apparatuses and measurement devices helped to set the stage for the operant analysis of behavior (Skinner, 1956). The theoretical orientation of investigators interested in single-organism environment interactions led some to examine the effects of providing individuals with information on the dynamic status of physiological variables, which has now led to increasing availability of biofeedback devices. The development of computers and computer science appears to have influenced some theories about intelligence (Goldenberg, 1979; Kantor, 1978) and about the structure of language (Chomsky, 1965; von Glasersfeld, 1974). Computers, along with the fruits of functional analysis (Catania, 1972), may contribute to advances in language remediation with the handicapped (Goldenberg, 1979; Rumbaugh, 1977; Rumbaugh & Savage-Rumbaugh, 1978). Even the very concept of handicap may be related to the effectiveness of our prosthetic strategies—wearers of corrective lenses do not usually think of themselves as handicapped, although many would be quite handicapped without them.

Adequate development of the topic of instructional technology is beyond the scope of this chapter (see Catania & Brigham, 1978). Instead we concentrate primarily on the usefulness of devices to extend the performance and learning capabilities of persons with retarded development. The review is not exhaustive, as relevant assistive devices are described in a variety of disparate sources including engineering and computer science journals, rehabilitation and medical publications, occupational and physical therapy publications, and the behavioral literature. Our purpose has been to point out the value of instrumentation in facilitating behavior change and its measurement, to point out significant areas for behavioral research, and hopefully to challenge those interested in either instrumentation or behavioral habilitation to develop collaborative research and development programs. The materials are organized around areas of application, and yet there is a necessary overlap in some sections because many devices yield to consideration in more than one area.

Environmental Design Considerations

The prominence of normalization approaches in the field of mental retardation highlights the impact of general environmental characteristics on behavioral development. If handicapped persons are to be integrated into community settings, these settings will have to become, to some extent, prosthetic in terms of their needs. That is, they will have to be designed in ways that will minimize needs arising in important classes of deficient behavior. For some, this is accomplished through stimulus–substitution techniques (Lindsley, 1964). Thus, some communities provide a bell in addition to the traffic light so that blind pedestrians will know when it is safe to cross at an intersection. The distinctive color and shape of common road signs in the United States, and the

European system of international road signs, allows an alternative means of providing critical information to motorists who cannot read the printed words. Color blind individuals also benefit from this, and from the standardized position of the red, yellow, and green signals used on traffic lights. As previously noted, elimination of significant environmental barriers to successful integration for handicapped persons is an important requirement of Section 504 of the Rehabilitation Act of 1973.

Most efforts to eliminate architectural barriers to integration have concentrated on accessibility for persons with physical disabilities (see Bednar, 1977). This often involves effector substitution techniques (Lindsley, 1964), but may involve other factors too. Ramps for access by persons in wheelchairs are provided at roadside curbs and building entrances. Handrails to facilitate transfer are provided in restrooms and are placed in hallways for guidance. The height or shape of handles, latches, switches, and fixtures is frequently modified to make them accessible. Public transportation vehicles often need alterations such as portable ramps or elevators. Many of the changes are, in fact, required to accommodate the handicapped person who uses prosthetic equipment.

Orelove and Hanley (1979) have provided a useful checklist for public school officials to use in assuring the accessibility of their schools to severely handicapped students. The checklist includes considerations such as accentuated cueing (e.g., contrasting colors), architecture and building design, availability of adaptive equipment, design of interior building fixtures, and availability of appropriate instructional materials. The authors point out that prosthetic devices that impose particular spatial topographies on an individual's movement like wheelchairs or wrist splints determine the range of movement that should be allowed for in the environment. These factors influence the need for the spacing of objects and their height of placement. An individual's physical strength and manipulative ability is another factor that influences the design of items like doors and windows. Again, the use of bulky prosthetic devices requires consideration of their dimensions in allocating total room space, and even for the scheduling of times for student use of hallways. Finally, construction materials should be selected in consideration of the wear patterns that many prosthetic devices made of hard or heavy materials may impose over time. These guidelines are helpful. However, they are supported primarily on the basis of their substantial face validity, as there seems to be little systematic behavioral research on either the behavior of developmentally handicapped individuals who must learn to function in suitably altered community environments, or on the social interaction they have with nonhandicapped peers as a function of their placement in such environments.

From our point of view, the most important aspect of environmental design takes into account the extent the handicapped person is able to functionally interact with people and objects. This must necessarily involve stimulus and effector substitutes, but also seems to require substitutions of the typical reinforcing consequences of behavior in average settings; that is, provisions for shaping poorly developed behavioral repertoires and maintenance strategies must be considered. These factors include the rules followed by staff and caretakers governing social interaction. They also include the environmental organization of a setting, such as the design of rooms and their contents. Finally, the client's location and cosmetic appearance are important factors.

Prosocial responses among severely handicapped persons may be so minimal that they are not recognized by persons with average education and training who care for them (Mayhew, Enyart, & Anderson, 1978). This requires that environments must not only provide accessible rooms and settings designed for both learning and practicing community adaptive skills, but that they must also have explicit staff–client interaction guidelines, staff–management guidelines, and formal supervision arrangements. Lent, LeBlanc, and Spradlin (1970) reported one such therapeutic environment established for mentally retarded adolescent girls. The physical setting was modified to provide rooms and equipment similar to middle class homes in the community. Training was provided to the staff so that the resident's behavior could be appropriately changed and maintained, the staff's responsibilities could be monitored, and so that a system of record keeping could provide an indication of the girls' progress. Finally, the instructional goals were set to approximate average community standards. Obviously, if the goal of a program is community placement, it does no good to teach behaviors that are relevant only to isolated institutional wards equipped with unusually constructed devices and constituents (e.g., rubber chairs and padded walls). Beyond training conditions, however, program management practices must include specific standards for maintenance of reinforcing contingencies so that the behavioral gains made by clients will endure (see Martin & Pallotta-Cornick, 1979).

Devices that aid staff to teach programs include data systems and devices that cue staff members to change activities or when to interact with clients. Timers and alarms are often used in habilitative programs to alert staff that it is time to provide a scheduled reinforcer, provided the client is performing the targeted response (see Figure 1). Romanczyk, Colletti, and Kashinsky (1980) have recently experimented with the use of a microcomputer system arranged to assure the smooth daily management of a classroom for autistic youngsters.

FIGURE 1. Staff in this sheltered workshop use a commercially purchased calculator/timer with a continuously recycling countdown-timing function and 8-second beeping alarm. The recycling timer eliminates tedious resetting, and cues periodic data recording and fixed-interval reinforcement of clients. Courtesy of the Behavioral Treatment Unit, Dr. Joseph H. Ladd Center, North Kingstown, Rhode Island.

They report that the system allows rapid access by the teachers to each child's past records and present program without their having to leave the classroom or consult others. Because the computer can also incorporate new behavioral data into its records, cue teachers when scheduled events are to occur, and can provide an excellent record of ongoing events for administrative purposes, a considerable amount of routine paperwork has virtually become obsolete. This leaves teachers with more time to teach and to devise new ways of assuring that students will interact with the instructional program.

Appropriate engagement with the external environment is an important goal in its own right. Engagement is facilitated by the provision of attractive objects and materials. Recreational materials are of particular importance in this regard. Appropriate engagement in leisure time activities can reduce stereotyping and maladaptive behavior (Favell, 1973; Mulick, Hoyt, Rojahn, & Schroeder, 1978), encourage social play (Ferrara & Hill, 1980; Quilitch & Risley, 1973), and probably provides an avenue for practice and elaboration of cognitive skills that contribute to overall intellectual development. However, it is not enough just to have toys available. Mentally retarded individuals must have reliable access to them and know where to find them (Mulick et al., 1978). The materials must be carefully selected and often must be modified for individual needs (Favell & Cannon, 1977). Wehman (1979) comprehensively reviews the topic of leisure time programming for the mentally retarded, and suggests several points for making design alterations that modify recreational materials and promote engagement in general. Such considerations include (1) modifications to improve object stability; (2) enlargement of part or entire objects to minimize required fine motor skills (e.g., size may be gradually altered); (3) additions of prosthetic controls (e.g., added handles); (4) reductions in response requirements (e.g., shortening required movements to match the users range of motion); (5) altered discriminative cues (e.g., use of familiar objects, elimination of abstract instructions, removal of extraneous cues, strengthening important cues); and (6) improvements regarding safety and durability under the expected conditions of use.

Another aspect of environmental design involves adaptive clothing. Clothing may be modified by adding snaps or velcro fasteners to help individuals with motor handicaps learn to dress themselves. Clothes may also be designed to promote or discourage specific behavioral outcomes (see Hoffman & Morris, 1979). However, there seem to have been few studies of the effects of special clothing on the behavior of mentally retarded persons or of those who come into contact with them. This is a fruitful area for further study. Some recent findings may serve to illustrate the range of possible inquiry. Confinement in self-protective clothing and restraints may contribute, over time, to physical deformities and severe forms of maladaptive behavior like self-injury and self-restraint (Favell, McGimsey, & Jones, 1978; Lovaas & Simmons, 1969). Further, self-protective clothing appears to alter the stimulus properties of mentally retarded individuals such that the care-giving practices of staff change, even when only a facial mask is involved and manual or gross motor movements are not directly restrained (Rojahn, Schroeder, & Mulick, 1980; Schroeder, Rojahn, & Mulick, 1978). Conversely, maladaptive behaviors and the relative frequencies of occurence among different maladaptive response topographies appear to change when clothing is altered in some individuals (Rojahn, Mulick, McCoy, & Schroeder, 1978). Additional studies about how clothing alters the relative probabilities of different classes of behavior, and about the reactive and interactive effects of clothing and other adaptive devices in a social context are sorely needed.

Adaptive Equipment

It is not possible to build redundancy into average environments so that all handicaps can be accommodated. Yet, there is social pressure to encourage the movement of handicapped persons into average or nearly average environmental contexts. This process is facilitated by the use of adaptive devices which compensate for behavioral deficits and allow the handicapped to behave normally in average environments. Eyeglasses, hearing aids, and wheelchairs were examples used earlier. Lindsley (1964) included cosmetics, notebooks, watches, computers, and just about any tool used by humans, in the category of prosthetic devices. We have confined our discussion in this section to devices in three categories only: general control systems that may be used to operate both commonly used appliances and those especially designed for the handicapped, devices that correct problems with position and mobility, and devices that are useful in accomplishing some activities of daily living.

Control Systems

Much of our normal behavior in the modern world involves using control systems. These can be described simply as the interface between the individual and a device. This may be no more than regulating the transition from the state *on* to the state *off*. The device that accomplishes this is called a transducer because it converts one form of energy to another. It is accomplished on most mechanical and electronic devices with a simple mechanical lever switch. A switch stops or releases the energy that makes a device function. In spite of this simplicity of function there are many varieties with useful applications for persons with limited motor function or response repertoires. Some authors have even devised elaborate classification systems for switches (e.g., Silverman, 1980). Pressure activated switches either remain in the on or off position until moved again, or return to the resting state when pressure is removed by spring action. Variations on this theme include wobblesticks that activate a single switch when moved in any direction, and joysticks that activate one switch or another, up to about 8, depending on the direction it is moved. Mercury switches are another kind of mechanical switch that can register position or orientation; a small drop of mercury is placed in a tube such that if it is allowed to roll to the end where the circuit is interrupted by a space between two ends of the wire, it completes the circuit because it is a good conductor of electricity. Mercury switches are often called tilt switches because they operate through the action of gravity on the drop of mercury depending on the spatial orientation of the enclosing tube. These and other switches including pneumatic switches (air pressure), touch switches, and photoelectric cells provide only digital information. But other mechanical transducers such as potentiometers, strain gauges, microphones, variable capacitors, and variable inductors can be used to provide analogue information (Rugh & Schwitzgebel, 1977). For example, radio volume controls use potentiometers which alter the electrical resistance of the circuit. The continuously variable control provided by these transducers is essential for regulating many devices, such as the speed of an electric motor. Both digital and analogue transducers may be directly attached to the housing of a device, or may be used with a remote control linked to the appropriate device by cords or telemetry.

The importance of the user/device interface was illustrated in a recent study by Lawrence and Horne (1979). Twelve kinds of input modes were used by physically handicapped persons to operate an electronic modular environmental control aid (MECON aid) that was designed for interface studies. The task was typing a familiar sentence, and although the intelligence of the subjects was not specified, reading and spelling skills were prerequisite. Speed and accuracy measures established a hierarchy of both performance and subject preference among the 12 modes. Another important finding was that results of trials with nonhandicapped users produced different hierarchies and were therefore not applicable to handicapped users. The authors concluded that the availability of multiple-control input options is valuable in finding an optimal mode for individual handicapped users.

The selection of a control system depends on an adequate assessment of the user and the type of device to be controlled. Silverman (1980) suggests a number of useful criteria. The least sophisticated mechanism is the most preferable. The more complex mechanisms are likely to malfunction more often and to be more delicate than simpler ones. They are also likely to be more costly. If complex control systems are needed because of the nature of the information to be transduced (e.g., voice volume) then extra backup devices should be available. Another criterion is that the response required of the user should need little prerequisite differentiation (i.e., new learning) before control of the devices is possible. Handicapped users should be able to achieve functional control as immediately as possible. Further response differentiation can be required later. The control mechanism should require as little effort by the user as possible. Great effort or high response requirements will result in less use of the device, and identical outcomes that can be attained by means requiring less effort will be preferred. The dependence on others for help instead of independent action is a frequently observed example. Another consideration is that the control mechanism should interfere with other activities as little as possible. A pointer attached to a forehead band is an example of a simple gestural control mode that could interfere with visual scanning and impose an impediment to smooth interaction with the environment. This technique may be appropriate for quadriplegic individuals, but would not be preferred for a person with adequate arm control. Finally, the device may require a type of control that is more easily attained with particular control mechanisms. Pneumatic suck or puff activated controls may not be as good as touch or pressure activated controls for a device that requires sustained input for operation. Systems using spatial arrangement of signals (i.e., keyboards) often necessitate different control mechanisms than those designed to respond to the timing of inputs (i.e., scanners). As Lawrence and Horne (1979) demonstrated, selection of control systems should be based on thorough functional evaluation of the client during trial use of a device.

Adaptive Equipment for Positioning

Devices for positioning are used both for functional and structural (or physical) reasons. Individuals with severe motor handicaps must often be purposely positioned by care-takers to assure that access to environmental stimuli and to prosthetic control systems is as efficient as possible. Physical reasons include the presence of deformities, abnormal reflex and/or movement patterns, and disordered postural tone, which may all result in the prevention of voluntary movement and the long-term development of progressive deformities (Holt, 1963; Low, 1972).

An understanding of some of the physical problems involved is useful. Persons lacking significant voluntary motor control are subject to progressive fixed anatomical deformities, which in turn further limit mobility. For example, a spastic person who does not achieve the ability to walk is likely to develop hip deformities which occur because normal structural development of the hip joint requires the influence of the continually changing forces associated with normal mobility. Without these mechanical influences, growth is abnormal. Hence, one basic principle is that positioning systems should be selected so as to facilitate maximal usable joint function. Further, the presence of weak muscles may necessitate support. Those with weak trunk muscles often benefit from trunk support. If an individual consistently slumps involuntarily to one side or the other, the soft tissue including tendons and ligaments become stiff and contracted. The forces associated with the contractures and the continuing effects of gravity can affect bone growth so that fixed bone deformities occur. Supportive equipment can slow this process. Physical support may also be necessary in cases of structural deformity. For example, in cases of hydrocephalus, voluntary neck movement is possible, but the head is so heavy that it is not supported well enough without help. Finally, some support systems may be designed so that they provide particular kinds of sensory stimulation conditions. Such a system could be used to provide conditions which tend to facilitate muscles that are antagonistic to hypertonic muscles or inhibit abnormal stretch reflexes (Christopher, 1974). Physical and occupational therapy publications frequently provide descriptions and building plans for such devices (e.g., Bergen, 1974, 1975). An excellent parent oriented manual by Finnie (1975) on cerebral palsied children provides a discussion of a variety of adaptive aids that can be constructed in the home as well as nontechnical structural and functional rationales for their use.

Functionally, positioning devices can serve to complete the feedback loops prerequisite for learning: for example, the face is forward, the neck muscles are relaxed and in position for effective turning of the head to follow visual or auditory stimuli, the arm is positioned for maximal freedom of movement, and so forth. However, there may be a distinction between concepts of support and positioning as derived from a physiotherapist's viewpoint and those from a behavior analyst's perspective. Do braces, head supports, and special chairs designed to inhibit abnormal movement patterns improve long-term performance on specific tasks? Is there a physical development versus functional or social development cost/benefit ratio for the use of various devices with individuals (cf. Rojahn et al., 1980)? Have appropriate teaching strategies been introduced or modified to take into account the new positioning strategies? These and other functional questions are rarely asked when such devices are described in the rehabilitation literature. Future studies could address these questions by measuring the speed and accuracy of performance on specific tasks (Lawrence & Horne, 1979), the subject's social interaction (Rojahn et al., 1980), visual fixation (Schroeder, 1976), permanent product output, and other behavioral variables.

Mobility Devices

Whereas positioning devices permit the user to interact with the environment while minimizing the deforming effects of a movement disorder, mobility aids increase the range of possible interaction. Independent mobility and improved travel skills have been goals of behavioral intervention (e.g., O'Brien, Azrin, & Bugle, 1972). Mobility aids range from support devices designed to alter proprioceptive feedback and posture during ambulation and movement (Christopher, 1974), crutches and walkers (Carter, 1979; Horner, 1971), posture altering and supportive additions to tricycles and other mobility mechanisms (Bergen, 1974, 1975), to individually designed mobility prostheses including wheelchairs, adapted golf carts, and automobiles with special control systems (see Figure 2).

Therapeutic exercise programs are often used to help increase the general physical well being, muscle strength, and control of the physically handicapped. These programs have often been facilitated through the use of automated response detection, recording equipment, and automated delivery of sensory and tangible reinforcement (Ball, Combs, Rugh, & Neptune, 1977; Ball, McCrady, & Hart, 1975; Freidlander, Kamin, & Hesse, 1974; Griffin, Patterson, Locke, & Landers, 1975). Automation of these programs can be helpful in freeing therapists from the necessity of providing constant manual guidance and social reinforcement during treatment sessions. Clever auditory and visual reinforcers that are more effective than praise or tangibles for some individuals may be arranged.

Activities of Daily Living

Training in routine self-care activities has been the subject of many studies using operant methods (Westling & Murden, 1978). Interest in this area has been fairly strong because helping the mentally retarded gain independence in basic activities like dressing, washing, eating, and toileting is of value to the persons who care for them. Caregivers are more likely to cooperate with teaching programs devoted to fostering independent self-care skills. They often perceive the successful outcome as an opportunity to engage in more interesting or less demanding activities. Mentally retarded individuals may benefit from a sense of relative independence as a result of acquiring these skills and usually present a more socially attractive aspect to others when they do. This in turn may cause increased social interaction that would promote the acquisition of social skills. In addition, the routine nature of these self-care skills assures the presence of persons who can do the teaching. Finally, many of the activities have built-in reinforcement. Thus, the acquisition of self feeding at mealtime usually follows a period of relative food deprivation. The consumatory response of eating would tend to reinforce the response of indepen-

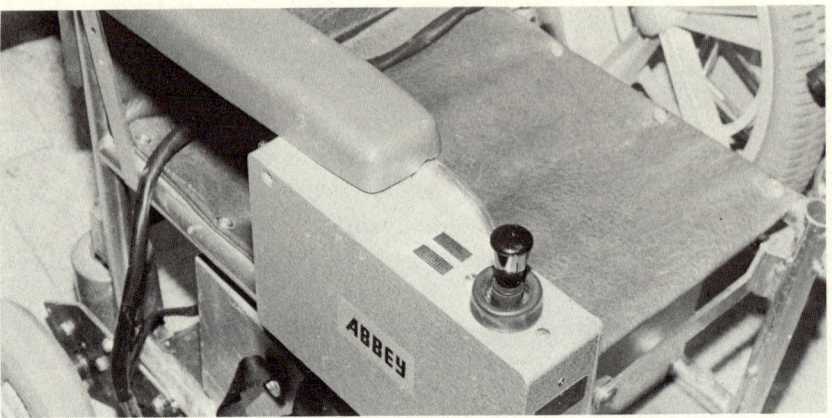

FIGURE 2. A joystick control system on a motorized wheelchair. Courtesy of W.M. Motloch, Rehabilitation Engineering Center, Children's Hospital, Palo Alto, California.

dently bringing the food to the mouth. Similarly, the natural physical and social consequences of incontinence may be uncomfortable to the learner, and providing positive consequences for successful toileting may seem quite natural to many care-givers.

The basic teaching strategy has been to select a skill for training and then to analyze the usual behavioral sequence. The behavioral sequence is broken down into small easily accomplished steps which represent the accomplishment of the entire task when completed (i.e., task analysis). Teaching usually begins with the last step, because accomplishing it leads immediately to reinforcement. Backward chaining is the major teaching approach used to foster independent self-help skills. Forward chaining is possible (Horner & Keilitz, 1975), but this requires continually altering the response followed by reinforcement as new behaviors are added at the end of the chain. In any case, if any link in the complete behavioral chain is made too difficult or is prevented by a physical handicap or a poorly differentiated response repertoire, reinforcement may be prevented or delayed too long for learning to occur. Adaptive equipment is frequently used to facilitate responding in such cases.

One approach is to alter the stimulus materials so that their discriminative properties are more effective. For example, Siegel (1977) used a floating target placed in the toilet to teach males to direct their urine stream more accurately. Another approach is to alter training materials so that less skilled motor responses are functionally effective. Snaps and velcro fasteners are substituted for buttons to enable mentally retarded or motor-handicapped persons to fasten their own clothing without the need for the same degree of fine-motor control required in buttoning. Alternatively, larger buttons can be used at first, and then gradually decreased in size as execution of the movements improves.

A variety of simple alterations of everyday utensils has been introduced to facilitate self-feeding in persons with movement disorders. Enlarged handle grips are added to utensils for persons with a poor grip, and utensils may be altered in shape to compensate for deformities or abnormal movement patterns (Popovitch & Kilfoil, 1978). Trefler, Westmoreland, and Burlinger (1977) describe a feeding spatula which is unlikely to stimulate infantile rooting, suck-swallow, gag, and bite reflexes which may persist in some motor delayed youngsters. For some individuals, conventional metal spoons may be unsatisfactory for a variety of reasons. The depth of the bowl may be too great to allow lip closure, too much food may be scooped each time, the size of the spoon may prevent reliable placement in the mouth, and the metal can have painful consequences when the bite reflex is stimulated. The mechanical feeding device shown in Figure 3 is designed for individuals who cannot scoop with a spoon. It is operated by using simpler alternative movements directed at the knobs. Bracing and support for the body, and stabilizing the plate or cup with a nonslip mat are also used to facilitate self-feeding.

Successful drinking can be promoted by using cups with protective tops to prevent spilling. Meal interruptions that prompt care-givers to clean up spills are avoided and do not impede training. Cups and glasses with sections cut out of the rim are sometimes used to avoid needing to tip the head back, or are used with individuals having poor lip closure. Gertenrich (1970) described a drinking device for use with clients having head and neck control, but who lack hand-arm control. It consists of a ring suspended on a bar, with a wide shallow cup placed through the ring. The ring suspension can swivel on the bar, and the cup and ring can rotate on the suspension.

Similar modifications can be made to facilitate washing and grooming. For example, handles can be added to scrub brushes, hair brushes, toothbrushes, combs, and razors. Electric toothbrushes and razors are used widely because fewer skilled movements are required.

Positioning may influence learning independent toileting in the same way that was described earlier for the general facilitation of functional behavior in motor handicapped individuals. Modification of the toilet seat to provide support required for inhibition of interfering involuntary movements and to promote relaxation are basic concerns (Bergen, 1974; Ottenbacher, Malter,

FIGURE 3. Mechanical feeding device which allows alternative motor responses to function in self-feeding for persons unable to perform the conventional scooping and arm raising response topography. Courtesy of W.M. Motloch, Rehabilitation Engineering Center, Children's Hospital, Palo Alto, California.

& Weckwerth, 1979). For persons in wheelchairs the toilet seat may be built up to reach the level of the wheelchair so as to permit easier transfer (Bortner, 1979). Wall-mounted handrails provide a stable source of leverage, and these are now common fixtures in barrier-free public toilet facilities. For more severe handicaps, there are wheelchairs available with partially removable seats. When positioned over a toilet, the wheelchair itself permits appropriate toileting. Thus, depending on the functional limitations imposed by a handicap, adaptive equipment can often be introduced to permit normalized toileting. There are, however, few reports of teaching programs used in conjunction with the above devices.

There are two related devices that have been used extensively in toilet training programs: a device to signal inappropriate wetting and a device to signal appropriate toileting. Foxx and Azrin's (1973) manual on toilet training the mentally retarded describes an extremely comprehensive approach to training and indicates the usefulness of signaling devices. Their purpose is to alert trainers to the occurrence of responding so that immediate reinforcement (or corrective action) can be provided. Electronic devices usually involve battery-operated alarms or buzzers. Two leads are separated by a short distance and mounted on a nonconductive material (training pants, a toilet insert, a mat placed under the bed sheet). Wetness from elimination saturates the material which completes the electronic circuit and sounds the alarm. Because consequences can be provided relatively quickly in naturalistic settings, faster and more reliable learning generally occurs through a straightforward application of operant principles.

Biofeedback Applications

The use of sophisticated instrumentation to aid in the modification of behavior is perhaps nowhere better seen than in the area of biofeedback. For all the complexity of the instrumentation that has become associated with it, the basic idea is fairly simple. To paraphrase Paskewitz (1975), providing information to the client about the dynamic status of biological systems should enable their voluntary control. Accordingly, a biofeedback system involves the detection and display of some physiological variable, such that the subject is placed in a feedback loop with information that has been detected, transduced, amplified, and processed, so that it is made perceptable through an alternative sensory pathway. Although this area has been conceptually linked with the development of electronic instrumentation used to render skin temperature, moisture, or synaptic electrical potentials detectable, simpler mechanical systems fall within the same category. For example, body weight has conventionally been monitored mechanically and processed for visual display with the common bathroom scale, and tactile information available through wearing nonelastic clothing provides direct—albeit sometimes painful—feedback over time about changes in body volume. Some of the adaptive skill training equipment noted earlier fits into this category as well (e.g., wetness and elimination detectors; Mowrer & Mowrer, 1938).

Separation of the reinforcing function of feedback from the effects of information alone has proven theoretically problematic in the biofeedback literature. However, the use of biofeedback with young children or mentally retarded clients often requires the arrangement of known reinforcing stimuli (e.g., tokens or operation of appliances) along with, or instead of, feedback to produce learned changes in the physiological variable being measured.

Sometimes the physiological variable itself is not of primary interest, but rather it is its known correlation with the occurrence of another overt behavior. In these cases the biofeedback device serves as a cueing function to the therapist during intervention (e.g., Schroeder, Peterson, Solomon, & Artley, 1977). Biofeedback instrumentation may be used to monitor a variety of physiological variables to aid in the diagnosis or in the validation of an overt behavioral characteristic (Cataldo, Russo, & Freeman, 1979), and can then be considered to represent an assessment tool (Rugh & Schwitzgebel, 1977; Russo, Bird, & Masek, 1980).

As technology develops and improved instrumentation becomes available, potential users face the dilemma of selecting devices to meet their needs from an increasing array of commercial products. Considerations for the selection of biofeedback equipment have been suggested elsewhere (Girdano, 1976; Rugh & Schwitzgebel, 1977), but many novel applications will almost certainly require some collaboration with engineering or technical experts who can judge the usefulness of equipment or modify them for specific functions. Already available systems make possible the reliable measurement and control of subtle and isolated variables such as the behavior of individual muscle groups or brain electrical activity. These allow the client to improve functions that would otherwise be confounded with normal or pathological activities and their feedback. The measurement specificity that biofeedback devices make possible can aid in communication and personal independence through their linkage to control systems and prosthetic devices (Goldenberg, 1979). At the present time, such applications are limited by the engineering problems involved in portability and durability of the equipment. Many products are bulky and delicate and few portable biofeedback products would stand up to long-term field applications even when their size would allow the retarded client to wear them freely. However, such design specifications are not insurmountable. The durability of a prototype portable EMG unit with audio feedback was demonstrated to a colleague when the design engineer picked up the unit and threw it against the wall (Schroeder, personal communication). This unit continued to function, but many commercial products would not have. Some areas of application, such as those involving brief laboratory training sessions, would not require this degree of durability.

Differential control of some portions of the human EEG spectrum through biofeedback and operant conditioning has been demonstrated (Lynch & Paskewitz, 1971), and work on the modification of epileptic seizures is beginning. Seifert and Lubar (1975) reported an attempt to alter activity in the 12-14 Hz band width over the sensorimotor cortex with biofeedback in six patients with uncontrolled seizures. Three of their subjects were classified as mentally retarded. All showed a decrease in seizures by the end of the three to four month series of training sessions, except for the youngest subject (12-years old) who was also mildly mentally retarded. The addition of a slide projector as heightened visual sensory reinforcement failed to improve the performance of the latter subject. The study employed sophisticated recording and processing equipment to filter and integrate the signals recorded from the subjects. Unfortunately, the design of the experiment does not allow for unequivocal attribution of the decrease in seizures to the biofeedback training. Cataldo et al., (1979) showed that the occurence of myoclonic seizures in a 5-year-old girl varied as a function of environmental setting and could be reduced by contingent time-out. In this study, the validity of a behavioral observation system to record seizures was established through the use of "observer calibration" sessions. Observational data were shown to be highly correlated with electrophysiological records of seizure activity. The use of psychophysiological recording instruments to validate observers' behavioral judgements is an important application, especially with phenomena requiring routine field observation.

Biofeedback has been used experimentally to aid in motor training with cerebral palsied individuals (Fernando & Basmajian, 1978). Finley and his coworkers have used a laboratory based EMG biofeedback system to demonstrate that reducing the voltage of the frontal EMG could result in children with primarily athetoid and spastic components learning to improve speech and motor skills (Finley, Niman, Standley, & Ender, 1976; Finley, Niman, Standley, & Wansley, 1977). It is assumed that relaxation of the frontal EMG can lead to general relaxation, and that once relaxed, a variety of adaptive movements and their accurate proprioceptive monitoring by the subject are easier. Finley et al., (1977) used a reversal design to demonstrate experimental control, and also employed a universal feeder to dispense material reinforcers to subjects upon reduction of cumulative integrated frontal EMG voltage to a criterion level. Cataldo, Bird, and Cunningham (1978) reported successful modification of EMG voltage at more than one location with two mentally retarded cerebral palsied clients using biofeedback. Their report is noteworthy because the experimental design allowed assessment of the therapeutic contribution of biofeedback itself, as well as of evidence for the generalization of effects to other muscle groups.

Motor control with cerebral palsied individuals can also be facilitated by providing information on head or joint position to the client. Wooldridge and Russell (1976) developed a mercury switch device capable of providing children with auditory or visual feedback, or with the operation of electronic toys and appliances as feedback for head position. Although the authors found that some children showed improved head control and head position awareness, the effects of training tended not to persist to times when the apparatus was not in use. Ball et al., (1975) used a position-activated mercury switch to turn on a radio when the head of their client was in an up-right position. Macurik (1979) provided contingent music to severely retarded nonambulatory clients in order to improve their seated posture. A photosensor fixed to the back of a chair ensured that correct head position would obstruct a light beam. The beam operated a relay that controlled a portable tape recorder. Grove, Dalke, Fredericks, and Crowley (1975) achieved an upright sitting position in their clients by using a lightweight cloth collar with position-sensing mercury switches. These authors suggested that automatic posture control devices might prove more beneficial than passive adaptive devices like braces, or the usual therapeutic exercise program, because they require active movement (unlike the brace), can be used continuously (unlike exercises), and selectively promote the desired postural outcome. Lack of durability of training effects remains a pervasive problem unless a permanent prosthesis is considered to be a desirable outcome. Similar feedback or control systems can be developed to provide information on joint position by using mechanical linkages, for example, to turn the shaft of a potentiometer (Brown, DeBacher, & Basmajian, 1979); however there is as yet limited experimental evidence for the value of position detectors in the acquisition of functional control of the extremities (Goldenberg, 1979; Wooldridge, Leiper, & Oston, 1976), and there are relatively few examples of their systematic use in the behavior modification literature.

Control of excessive motor activity is another area where instrumentation may allow flexibility in monitoring and intervention strategies. EMG-assisted relaxation training would be an obvious approach (e.g., Hampstead, 1979), although this does not seem to have been extensively employed with mentally retarded clients.

Schulman, Stevens, Suran, Kupst, and Naughton (1978) described an apparatus called a biomotometer which uses mercury switches and microprocessors to record data and deliver contingent auditory feedback through an earphone to hyperactive children. When contingent reinforcement is also provided for increases or decreases in activity counts, children's behavior in the classroom has been shown to change accordingly. However, auditory feedback signals provided to already distractible youngsters may be counterproductive, depending on the setting demands. Ball and Irwin (1976) described a mercury switch and timing device that provided feedback for in-seat behavior that reached fixed criterion intervals of time. The device's portability allowed its use in the classroom, and in-seat behavior was reinforced with money. Probably because the authors were careful to transfer control from the device to other more common controlling stimuli—first a kitchen timer and then a wall clock—clinical improvement occurred. In another report (Ball, McCrady, & Texeira, 1978), stereotypy was decreased in a severely mentally retarded adult by use of a mercury switch signaling and timing device and contingent negative social reinforcement. The same device was later used to signal sustained postural change for the purpose of increasing standing behavior in a hypoactive mentally retarded client. The circuitry for most of these instruments is simple, and some designs are provided in the articles or are said to be available from authors. Applications for their use with a variety of gross movement disorders are clear.

Self-injurious behavior is usually treated through contingency management procedures and is usually detected through direct observation of behavior (Schroeder, Schroeder, Rojahn, & Mulick, 1980). One problem with designing treatment programs around observed self-injurious responses is that the risk of allowing an uncontrollable episode to begin is greater. The possibility of controlling such responses would be greater if the behavior were detected early in the response chain. EMG biofeedback was used in two cases to detect self-injurious responses early, and to provide a degree of validity for observational ratings of the clients' behavior. Schroeder et al., (1977) measured voltage increases in the right trapezius muscle that seemed to predict headbanging in two mentally retarded boys. The programmed consequences for headbanging was contingent manual restraint, and the frequency of self-injury was ultimately reduced. The authors suggested that the EMG feedback signal was of use as an early warning system to therapists. Similarly, Lang and Melamed (1969) recorded EMG signals from under the chin and from the throat muscles of the neck of a 4-year-old chronic ruminative vomiter. The EMG tracings obtained on a polygraph provided an excellent record for discerning vomiting from other response patterns (e.g., crying). The EMG record was used to confirm the presence of the target vomiting response, and contingent electrical stimulation to the calf paired with a tone eliminated the behavior in six sessions.

Acoustic signals may also be used to operate feedback devices. Instrumentation may range from the relatively simple voice operated relay (VOR) to sophisticated microprocessor instrumentation designed to filter and integrate speech sounds for the purpose of focusing on isolated aspects of voice quality. Fletcher (1970) developed a complex instrument to detect, quantify, and display nasalization in connected speech. Daly and Johnson (1974) utilized this instrumentation system, the TONAR (The Oral Nasal Acoustic Ratio), to reduce hypernasality in the speech of three mentally retarded youngsters. Visual feedback with gradually adjusted nasality ratio thresholds and occasional social reinforcement served to bring the nasality of the subjects within or near the normal range during therapy sessions with standardized spoken material. Additional research is required to determine the effects of such training on conversational speech outside of the therapy setting. Strang and George (1975) used a VOR and group contingencies to reduce the noise level in a normal first-grade classroom. Their apparatus had a light display on a smiling clown face which provided feedback on the children's success at not being noisy. A similar system could well be used in some group settings for the mentally retarded where a reduction in noise level would be desirable (e.g., workshops and classrooms).

The studies reviewed in this section illustrate a variety of applications of biofeedback devices. This information may be provided to clients directly, combined with an automated reward system, or used to cue the behavior of a therapist. Biofeedback recording techniques may also be used to validate observational data systems with hard to discriminate or early components of clinically relevant behaviors. Lack of generalization and lack of durability of the effects of biofeedback training remain problems, but several strategies could be employed in future applied research. Stimulus control of the target behavior could be systematically faded to variables available in the natural environment as was done by Ball and Irwin (1976). Alternatively, permanent prosthetic devices may be developed for some problems so that the feedback need not be necessarily withdrawn. Greater portability and durability of devices would tend to increase generalization of behavior improvements, especially if the devices could be used in natural environments where behavioral improvements would tend to become incorporated into more complex setting-controlled behavioral repertoires. Finally, the careful selection of functional behaviors would tend to increase the chances that the natural consequences of behavioral improvements (e.g., inhibition of interfering movements during self-feeding) would help to maintain them.

Instructional Devices

The use of mechanical devices and programmed instruction for educating students was stimulated by Skinner (1954, 1958, 1961). He argued persuasively that the systematic application of basic operant conditioning principles could be more effective than traditional educational methods. Further, teaching machines were seen as having advantages over human teachers in several respects including: (1) untiring immediacy of feedback and programmed consequences following student responses; (2) increased flexibility in setting the frequency of opportunities for reinforcement; (3) the opportunity for individualizing the pace of instruction; (4) confirmation of student attention and hard evidence of learning by requiring overt responses as opposed to passive listening; (5) greater opportunity to evaluate teaching practices and curriculum through the analysis of student response records; and (6) reducing the teachers' time in repetitive drill activity. While originally proposed for use with a normal student population, many devices have been successfully designed for mentally retarded children and adults (see reviews by Greene, 1966; Malpass, 1967; Stolurow, 1960a, 1961).

The requirements of a Skinnerian teaching machine include: opportunity to record discrete, observable responses performed by the subject, immediate reinforcement, a record of subject responses, and a capability for altering stimuli and instructional programs in order to shape responses. Devices which meet these criteria are identified here as teaching machines. However, most devices, although designed to operate within an operant paradigm, usually do not incorporate each of the above requirements. Therefore, they will be termed instructional devices rather than teaching machines. It should also be noted that many devices discussed in other sections can also be viewed as instructional devices, but are covered elsewhere in order to emphasize other characteristics or applications.

Increasing On-Task Behaviors

In order to receive maximum benefit from educational programming, students should not be distracted by responses that compete with academically relevant responses and disturb their ability to attend to academically relevant stimuli. Examples frequently cited by teachers include out-of-seat behaviors, aggressiveness, tantrums, irrelevant or excessive verbalizations, and distractible behaviors (i.e., attending to irrelevant visual or auditory stimuli). The use of common timing devices has been reported by McLaughlin and his associates to improve classroom behaviors. A stopwatch and positive feedback through teacher praise was used to reduce the latency of on-task behavior following teacher instructions (Burnett, McLaughlin, & Hunsaker, 1978). McLaughlin, Brown, Malaby and Dolliver (1977) used a standard kitchen timer to cue reinforcement of on-task behavior of students when the bell sounded. The timer was set at intervals varying around an average of 5 minutes to reduce the predictability of the bell. The procedure was effective in increasing on-task behavior, but did not serve to increase the amount of correctly solved mathematics problems. A later study (McLaughlin, Dolliver, & Malaby, 1979) indicated that similar procedures increased work output, but accuracy data were not reported. Abramson and Crocker (1978) modified a kitchen clock so it could be stopped by a line switch. The clock was stopped by the teacher in response to excessive out-of-seat behavior, which represented temporal response cost to students: recess, lunch, and dismissal times were determined by this clock.

Noise-intensity levels of classrooms are modifiable through more sophisticated devices. Wilson and Hopkins (1973) provided popular music contingent upon quiet behavior. However, when noise-intensity levels exceeded a criterion level, a voice-operated relay switched off the radio. Tiller, Masek, and Walker (1974) utilized devices which measured noise-intensity duration in an EMR classroom. Excessive noise levels resulted in visual feedback, (i.e., lights). Students earned recess time on the basis of infrequent illuminations. The authors were successful in reducing noise levels and fading the use of the equipment from the classroom.

Devices have been used to facilitate the reduction of competing behaviors in the classroom. Firestone (1976) describes the use of Timex activity watches to compare activity levels of children. Jackson (1979) provided positive feedback through a lighted bulb to increase visual attention of a mentally retarded adult during a vocational training activity. The bulb was illuminated by means of a microswitch operated by an observer. A radio transmitter was used by Patterson, Jones, Whittier, and Wright (1965) to deliver an auditory stimulus to a brain-injured, hyperactive boy. The stimulus was provided on appropriate attending behavior and signified the accumulation of rewards. Edelson and Sprague (1974) were able to reduce in-seat movement through a cushion that measured stability/activity and a blinking red light to indicate reinforcement contingent on reduced activity. One difficulty with these devices is that the stimuli used to provide positive feedback are themselves distracting, and another is that the cues provided are difficult to fade.

Another application of instrumentation is worth mentioning. Rincover, Cook, Peoples, and Packard (1979) hypothesized that high-rate stereotyped behavior could, in fact, be self-stimulating—as it is so often described—in that it might represent behavior maintained by its own sensory consequences. Thus, masking the relevant sensory feedback of the behavior should result in extinction. One child's stereotyped handwaving decreased when proprioceptive feedback was presumably masked as a result of taping a small vibrator to the back of the hand. Another child required masking of both proprioceptive and visual feedback to produce a decrease in handwaving. Continued reduction in handwaving was promoted by training the children to play with toys, which also served as an alternative way for them to produce sensory feedback for themselves.

Physical and Cognitive Skills

Instructional devices have been developed to improve physical qualities such as muscle strength, range of motion, gross-motor coordination and eye-hand coordination. However, the use of a systematic program that trains a gradual progression of skills is often more important than the technological sophistication of the training instrument. This point is well illustrated in a study by Horner (1971) of a 5-year-old mentally retarded child with spina bifida. A set of parallel bars was used to build increasingly complex movements through systematic reinforcement. This device was used to establish prerequisite behaviors which could lead to ambulation with crutches. Similarly, a machine for gradually improving the power of arm and leg movements while performing a workshop activity has been described by Bonde-Petersen, Wolff, and Henriksen (1972).

Simple devices have also been used to train cognitive skills. Johnson, Firth, and Davey (1978) utilized a commercially available vibrator as a means of providing reinforcement that proved to be more effective than social praise in teaching a series of visual discriminations to profoundly retarded adults. Doughty (1976) states that student desks can be adapted to provide vibration. He recommends this alteration as an efficient and effective means to provide reinforcement during instruction of the profoundly mentally retarded.

Teaching machines have been constructed to improve physical development (see Figure 4). One example is provided by Ball et al. (1977) in their training of two mentally retarded quadriplegic adults. The subjects, when extending their limbs, closed a switch on a goniometer which resulted in auditory reinforcement from an AM radio. The device also recorded the total amount of time that the switch was closed. Results indicated that the auditory reinforcement greatly increased the number of leg movements produced by one of the subjects. Zuromski and his associates were able to develop similar behaviors with severely to profoundly mentally retarded infants and young children (Accrino & Zuromski, 1978; Zuromski, Smith, & Brown, 1977). They trained upper limb movements through the use of mercury switches which activated tapes of music and peoples' voices. Reinforcement alternatively increased right and left arm movements (Zuromski et al., 1977). In addition, two of the subjects demonstrated a simple visual discrimination (Accrino & Zuromski, 1978). However, difficulties were encountered in that it appeared that subjects would habituate to the reinforcing stimuli. Schroeder (1976) found that auditory-visual reinforcement (projected slides and tape recorded music) increased rope pulling responses of two nonambulatory profoundly mentally retarded chil-

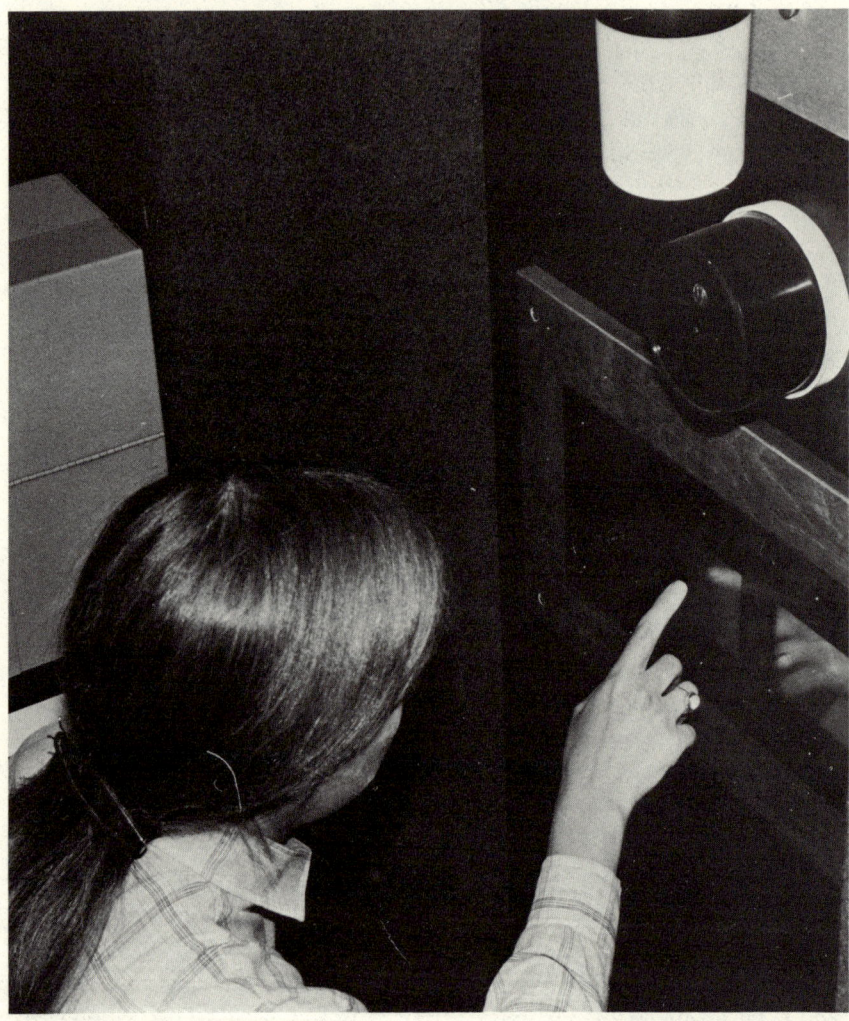

FIGURE 4. On the left, a researcher demonstrates a choice response on a laboratory-based teachinng machine. Above the response panel are fixtures for providing additional discriminative cues. Token reinforcement is delivered automatically (not shown). The right side (p. 541) shows

dren. In this study difficulties were not experienced in habituation to reinforcing stimuli. There were some indications that one child preferred slides which displayed familiar persons rather than those which showed outdoor scenery. The advantage of using automated stimuli lies in eliminating the natural tendency for teachers to ignore the minimal kinds of responses that are emitted

part of the solid-state and electromechanical equipment required to process responses, program stimulus and reinforcing events, and monitor the behavior of the subject. Courtesy of Paul E. Touchette, Eunice Kennedy Shriver Research Center, Waltham, Massachusetts.

during the early stages of response differentiation with profoundly mentally retarded students.

The objectives of teaching machine programs frequently stress the development of visual-discrimination skills. Early examples were reported by Hively (1960, 1962, 1964). Slides were displayed on a visual display panel. The panel contained several touch-sensitive windows that included a sample window and a row of two or more response windows. The subject had to locate and press the response window that displayed the same pattern as the sample window. Correct performance resulted in food reinforcement and presentation of the next problem. Problems were presented so that a gradual progression of task difficulty would be achieved. Sidman and Stoddard (1966) used a different task format. Their display panel consisted of eight windows and the subject had to locate the odd window in the array. Correct responses led to presentation of the next item. Incorrect responses, however, resulted in no change in the display. When a correct response eventually occurred, the previous slide was repeated. This procedure provided the opportunity for subjects to learn from their errors. The investigators reviewed the cumulative records of subjects' responses to identify consistent error patterns and revise the program so errorless learning could be approximated. Bijou (1968) improved on the matching to sample format by requiring subjects to attend to the sample window by pressing it in order to present a display on the matching windows. Edwards and Rosenberg (1966) developed a teaching machine for aphasics that allowed access to visual discrimination programs at different complexity levels. Occasional test trials were included so that correct responses would direct the subjects to more advanced programs, while incorrect responses would result in the presentation of a remedial program.

The question exists as to whether teaching machines are more effective than conventional teaching methods. It can be argued that the failure of teaching machine programmers to achieve low error rates with mentally retarded populations indicates that these devices often fail to provide the degree of precision in differential reinforcement that Skinner had originally proposed. A review by Greene (1966) indicates that teaching machines provide only modest improvements over classroom methods in instruction of academic subjects to mentally retarded populations. However, parameters of both programmed and classroom instruction were not defined in these studies. Issues regarding amount, emphasis, or quality of instruction are not addressed in most comparison studies. A well-controlled study by Russo, Koegel, and Lovass (1978) found that autistic children performed better with teacher supervision, either in classroom instruction or in the use of a teaching machine than was achieved by unsupervised use of the device. The authors attributed the differences to the observation that these children engaged in greater off-task behavior when teacher supervision was absent. Schroeder (1976) filmed eye movements of a profoundly mentally retarded boy when solving a matching to sample task on a teaching machine. He concluded that the boy displayed distinctive fixation patterns which were correlated with a rational solution to the discrimination problem. This study, though, prevented nonattentive behaviors from occurring by utilizing a padded head rest. Thus, it appears that antecedent conditions such as attention factors are also important correlates of performance on teaching machines.

Cognitive skills other than visual discrimination can be taught through the use of instructional devices. Bergmann (1977) describes a device to improve visual tracking skills of handicapped individuals. Ramey and Finkelstein (1978) used contingent audiovisual stimulation to increase vocalizations of babies from low socioeconomic families. This technique was more effective than either noncontingent stimulation or no stimulation. Tashjian (1980) used lights and music as reinforcers for vocal responses of six profoundly mentally retarded, multihandicapped children. Subjects were separated into three groups and were presented tape recordings of their own voices or the sound of others addressing them by name. In addition to the tape recorded stimuli, the groups differed on the type of vocal response which was required to receive the reinforcement. Random vocal production, imitation, or appropriate vocal responding represented the different response categories. Contingencies were mediated by automated contingency control devices with voice analysis capabilities.

Social responses can also be trained through instructional devices. Samaras and Ball (1975) used a "cooperation machine" to teach mentally retarded adults to perform an activity simultaneously. Supervisors also trained the subjects to share food rewards which were delivered by the device. The authors observed that the task fostered more social behavior among the participants.

Although most teaching machines for the mentally retarded have been developed for research purposes, this technology is becoming more commercially available. Roberts (1976) reports that programs have been designed for the severely and profoundly mentally retarded with instructional systems such as DISTAR, Dubnoff, Rebus, and Systems 80. However, to justify the cost of these devices, manufacturers (and researchers) need to demonstrate that the use of automated teaching programs, whether or not the user is supervised on the device, produces results that are not available with teacher-alone instruction.

Computers as Instructional Devices

Teaching machines are usually designed to present a program in which the presentation of stimuli to a subject is strictly controlled with a limited number of response alternatives available, and reinforcement provided only if a "correct response" has been chosen. In developing their program, teaching machines have incorporated several aspects of emerging computer technology. However, some recent applications of computer technology for instructional purposes have utilized an alternative approach.

Rather than presenting a limited number of possible response alternatives with identifiable correct choices, some computer-based devices offer an expanded set of effective responses, none of which are considered preferable. The computer is used as a control system for a display of some kind, while the storage capacity of the computer makes a variety of constructional outcomes possible. Operators are encouraged to explore a range of contingent stimuli in the form of visual displays, audio soundtracks, or both. This permits not only brief sensory events as reinforcement for operating manipulanda, but also brings into play the possibility of exploring temporal and spatial patterning of stimuli. Learning of more complex cognitive skills becomes a possibility as a result.

One of the first applications of computerized instruction in this manner was reported by Colby and his associates (Colby, 1973; Colby & Kraemer, 1975; Colby & Smith, 1971). A program was developed to stimulate the acquisition of language by autistic children. The program consisted of a series of games that provided the children with opportunities to play and interact with symbols. In one game, a child presses a letter on a keyboard (e.g., "H"), a visual display shows the letter, and an audio track pronounces its name. In another game, pressing the key "H" results in a display of a running horse with the accompanying sound of the horse's hoofs. Colby (1973) reports that programs such as these have increased autistic childrens' use of expressive language.

Geoffrion and Bergeron (1977) have developed a computer system to teach reading and language skills. The system, labelled CARIS (Computer-Animated Reading Instruction System), has been tested with children who are afflicted with handicaps including mental retardation, deafness, and cerebral palsy. Rather than using a keyboard, the children use a light pen to choose a word from a list of nouns on a visual display. The chosen word is then drawn by the device on a display screen (cathode ray tube) and a list of action verbs appears. Through the light pen, one of the verbs is chosen, and the screen subsequently displays the previously drawn object performing the action. Incongruous as well as natural relationships can be pictured (e.g., "house jumps," "dog flies," "boy walks"). Through exploring the different combinations of available nouns and verbs, the general meaning of each word occurs. The authors report that the system has been successful in increasing the sight vocabulary of several children. Presently, programs are being designed that will increase demands placed on the system operator by requiring them to spell a whole word before an object or an action will be displayed.

The use of computers to teach adaptive living skills has been reported (Brebner, Hallworth, & Brown, 1977; Hallworth & Brebner, 1979). Programs have already been written to teach educable mentally retarded and cerebral-palsied children coin recognition, shopping, budgeting and banking, calendar use, job application, clothing selection, and reading and arithmetic skills. These skills are taught by means of a computer-controlled random-access slide projector which projects its images on a rearview screen. Images are selected on the basis of selections made on a keyboard. The authors describe a range of modifications to both input and output devices to overcome particular handicaps. One example is the use of a large TV monitor which can display enlarged characters to aid those with poor vision. Computer-controlled audio input devices are being tested with adolescents who have severe physical handicaps that prevent operation of a keyboard.

Goldenberg (1979) has explored the use of computers to teach autistic, cerebral palsied and deaf children geometric and mathematical relationships. Operators instruct the computer to trace a line on a visual display or to move a robot (with a pen attachment to trace its movement) across a piece of paper. Patterns are constructed by instructing the computer to move the pen (nicknamed the "turtle") forward, backward, left or right via a keyboard, to draw arcs, to erase unwanted drawings, and to store and later retrieve particular patterns. By utilizing the computer's storage capabilities, a sequence of steps can be repeated, and increasingly complex patterns may be formed. The author describes an adolescent with cerebral palsy who was able to "draw" a complex geometric figure with little preliminary instruction. Storage of operator input can be instructional in other ways. Rubinstein and Goldenberg (1978) stimulated language development in deaf children by establishing a computerized "post office" where participants could record private messages to classmates which could be retrieved at a later time. Spelling errors could be ignored by the computer, or could be corrected at a later time.

The use of computers as teaching machines remains at an infancy stage. It seems to have advantages over more traditional teaching machines in that a larger set of stimuli are available to the operator. Hallworth and Brebner (1979) report the development of a microprocessor-controlled videodisc player which will have a capacity to present 54,000 color images. This is a dramatic increase over the 80 images which were available through their random-access slide projector. It should be noted, however, that most of the pilot work with the new computerized instruction has been tested with higher functioning handicapped populations (i.e., cerebral palsied, mildly mentally retarded individuals). This contrasts with the previous discussion of teaching machines where the severely and profoundly mentally retarded were often the focus of study. Finally, investigators studying applications of computer technology for instructional purposes need to increasingly document achievements that have been gained by their subjects. The presently available literature discusses software development, and presents excerpted records of handicapped users' interactions with the devices as data. However, in order to gain increased acceptance and to justify the substantial financial cost, improved methodological rigor will have to be incorporated into future studies.

Audiovisual Media

Audiovisual media in the field of mental retardation have primarily served as educational tools. Traditional activities include the production of tapes and films for public awareness and student education, the use of videotape to record informational lectures, and the compilation of resource libraries of media aids (Greelis, 1974). Today, however, innovative approaches attempt to use audiovisual media to enhance skill development of specified target groups of children. Television shows such as *Sesame Street* and *The Electric Company* attempt to teach academic and preacademic skills to a nationwide audience of children and, in particular, the youth of low socioeconomic families who are known to have a greater chance of reading difficulties in the early primary grades. Mauk (1971) describes a variety of projects which include the use of slide presentations, videotape, and motion pictures to promote skill development in the mentally retarded and in those who work with them.

Olson and Rardin (1979) were able to reduce hyperactivity in three learning-disabled boys through photographic mediated self-modeling. Pictures of on-task and off-task behavior were taken of each of the boys in their classroom. When the pictures were later made into slides, the students individually viewed the ones in which they were pictured. By pushing one of two available buttons, they could identify their classroom behavior as either attending or nonattending. Correct identification of attending behavior resulted in food reinforcement. Treatment sessions over time required finer discriminations of on-task and off-task behavior. Although the study is flawed by the absence of adequate control procedures, results suggest that the treatment process was effective in reducing a broad range of nonattending behaviors.

Most reports of using audiovisual media for skill development have utilized videotape with closed-circuit television monitors. Marshall and Goldstein (1970) report that the use of this medium was more effective than other consultation procedures in conveying diagnostic information to mothers of mentally retarded children. Interactions between parents and their children who were diagnosed as hyperactive, were videotaped by Furman and Feighner (1973). Review of these videotapes and instructional feedback was described as an effective method for improving specific interaction skills. Panyan and Patterson (1974) used videotape in two ways to improve the skills of attendants who trained nonambulatory mentally retarded children. Training sessions were recorded with video equipment, and then reviewed by the attendants without additional informational feedback. At a later time, the trainers were exposed to a prerecorded videotape in which appropriate training behaviors were modeled. Data based on behavioral observation attempted to demonstrate that the latter training procedure was more effective. However, Bricker, Morgan, and Grabowski (1972) report that the quantity and quality of interactions between attendants and institutionalized clients were improved only when a reinforcement system that identified and rewarded correct interactions was utilized in conjunction with videotape review.

Other investigators have attempted to directly promote skill development in mentally retarded learners through instructional videotapes. DeRoo and Haralson (1971) increased the productivity of mentally retarded adults by videotaping work sessions. Subjects viewed the film immediately afterward and were required to identify behaviors which competed with productivity. Therapists cued the subjects by stopping the videotape at critical points and by providing verbal feedback without the use of videotape. Other studies (Gibson, Lawrence, & Nelson, 1977; Nelson, Gibson, & Cutting, 1973) demonstrated that the combination of videotaped modeling with verbal instructions and feedback is more effective than either method alone when teaching specific social skills to the mentally retarded. Greelis and Kazaoka (1979) used videotape to provide visual feedback to a mildly mentally retarded girl and to differentially reinforce the distinction between appropriate and tantrum behavior. Training sessions involving the girl and her teacher were filmed during a baseline period. Treatment consisted of exposure to a videotape which presented the following sequence:

1. 30 seconds of the subject engaging in appropriate, on-task behavior
2. 60 seconds of a Popeye cartoon
3. Repetition of the previous two steps
4. 30 seconds of the subject engaging in a tantrum
5. Then 60 seconds where the viewing screen was blank

This 6-minute sequence was repeated four times to comprise a 24-minute treatment session. Training sessions were then presented later in the day under the same conditions that existed during baseline. Results indicated that tantrums were quickly eliminated after presentation of the videotape. However, the amount of on-task behavior did not correspondingly increase. The authors surmise that treatment effectiveness could have been increased if off-task behaviors as well as tantrums were followed by negative consequences on the recorded videotape.

The combination of videotape with closed-circuit television monitors appears to be the most promising application of audiovisual media instruction. It has greater flexibility and less cost than other film media. Although many investigators have used prerecorded sequences to provide modeled instruction, videotape also offers the unique opportunity to present immediate visual feedback to the subject through life-observation and instant replay of completed action (Greelis, 1974). The studies reviewed above also suggest that mere observation of previously videotaped behavior is not an effective instructional procedure. Rather, instruction is maximized when videotape viewing is combined with verbal feedback or with differential reinforcement procedures.

Instructional Devices within Aversive Paradigms

It is recognized by the professional community that positive reinforcement strategies are preferable to the use of aversive stimulation to effect behavior change (Harris & Kapche, 1978; Martin, 1975). However, some behaviors, such as differential reinforcement of other behaviors (DRO) or differential reinforcement of incompatible behaviors (DRI), have not always responded well to indirect reinforcement strategies. Behaviors such as self-injury, ruminative vomiting, and aggression also pose considerable health and safety risks to mentally retarded clients and those with whom they interact. Devices providing aversive stimulation may be considered in cases that meet these criteria. However, the use of aversive devices needs to be monitored carefully. Treatment settings considering the use of this equipment should establish Human Rights Committees which include members of the community so that a shared decision-making process can determine whether a substantial health risk exists and that alternative treatment options have been exhausted.

Current interest in aversive procedures was stimulated by the treatment approach of Lovaas and his associates for self-injurious behavior (SIB) exhibited by autistic and retarded children (Bucher & Lovaas, 1967; Lovaas, 1969; Lovaas, Freitag, Gold, & Kassorla, 1965; Lovaas & Simmons, 1969). Dramatic reductions in SIB occurred when it was followed by electric shocks. These effects were demonstrated under conditions that approximated a laboratory setting. Difficulties have been encountered by several investigators in trying to generalize results to other settings (Corte, Wolfe, & Locke, 1971; Lovaas & Simmons, 1969; Risley, 1968). In response to this problem, Wilbur, Chandler, and Carpenter (1974) developed a portable shock device to reduce SIB. The battery-powered device is attached to a belt which is worn by the client. Electrodes are placed on the back or the stomach. A "Band-Aid" switch is placed over the abused area. When the client strikes himself on the Band-Aid, a switch is closed, and a brief shock is produced. The event is recorded by an automatic counter. This approach can be successful when injury results from a very specific response topography. However, difficulties were encountered by Wilbur et al., (1974) in that the client frequently removed the Band-Aid switch. Another approach to reduce SIB in multiple settings is to deliver electric shocks through a remote-controlled device. Prochaska, Smith, Marzilli, Colby, and Donovan (1974) discuss treatment of a headbanging child with such a device. An experimenter was constantly present when the subject was at school or on the bus. The child's parents were trained to operate the shock device so that treatment could be continued at home. At school, experimenters observed the child from behind a one-way mirror and, at other times, the shock transmitter was hidden from view so that the subject could not determine who was delivering the shock. The treatment was successful in quickly eliminating headbanging and other self-destructive behaviors. Duker (1976) used a remote-controlled shock device to reduce two types of SIB exhibited by an institutionalized female adolescent. Headbanging against a wall was eliminated by delivering a series of shocks that were terminated when the girl sat in a chair away from the wall. The therapist initially guided the girl to the chair to demonstrate how the shocks could be terminated. Avoidance conditioning then occurred by delivering the series of shocks whenever she approached a wall, and terminating them when she sat in a chair. This escape–avoidance approach quickly eliminated all headbanging against the wall. A second response topography, hitting the head with fists, was contingently followed by a single electric shock. This behavior was also substantially reduced when therapists monitored the subject's movements. Attempts to train attendants to use the equipment resulted in treatment with reduced reliability and effectiveness.

Linscheid and Cunningham (1977) used a shock device to eliminate ruminative vomiting in a severely malnourished nine-month-old infant. Shock intensity was set at a low level so that a startle response, and not crying, would be elicited from the infant. Rumination was virtually eliminated after three days of treatment, and follow-up revealed that this success was maintained.

Although electric shock is the most widely known aversive stimulus, the use of a loud, auditory stimulus has also proved successful. Kazdin (1973) was successful in reducing speech deficiencies in mentally retarded adults by contingently pairing the target behavior with a loud noise. However, this treatment procedure was less effective than an alternative response–cost procedure (withdrawal of tokens). Auditory stimuli have long been used to reduce nocturnal enuresis. Mowrer and Mowrer's (1938) bell and pad is an example of this. Although this approach to enuresis has usually been interpreted in a classical conditioning paradigm (a conditioned stimulus, recognition of bladder pressure, is strengthened through paired association with an unconditioned stimulus, the alarm), Tough, Hawkins, McArthur, and Van Ravenswaay (1971) argue that it is essentially a punishment procedure. Lovibund (1964) altered the Mowrer and Mowrer (1938) approach by following the enuresis-produced alarm with a second, more intense signal. This approach clearly involves following a response with an aversive stimulus. Hansen (1979) used a similar device in the context of an escape–avoidance treatment design. Nocturnal-enuresis triggered the initial alarm as before. The child, though, could avoid the second, more aversive sound by quickly getting out of bed and turning off a switch.

The use of aversive stimuli to reduce problem behaviors continues to be controversial. When they meet guidelines for effective punishment as detailed by Azrin and Holz (1966), rapid results can be attained. However, some fear that this powerful effect may result in an overuse of this treatment approach (Gathercole, 1976). Others may question whether electric shock is appropriate to reduce such behavior as stuttering (Martin & Siegel, 1966). In addition, instances where shock-producing apparatus (electrodes, belts containing battery-powered shock transmitter) have been successfully faded from use have not been well documented. A final criticism is that aversive stimuli, particularly shock devices, can present life threatening consequences themselves (see reviews and critique by Butterfield, 1975a,b). The involvement of a Human Rights Committee and, if necessary, a technical consultant in monitoring the use of aversive devices should help to insure that this equipment is utilized infrequently and responsibly.

Communication Devices

Communication devices serve many functions. Some, like the teaching machines described in the previous section, can be used to communicate in a limited sense with teachers for purposes of instruction. Others, which form the basis of the present section, can potentially help facilitate communication *between* individuals.

Speech occupies a preeminent place in interpersonal communication. However, for many mentally retarded individuals, this vehicle of expression is often underdeveloped or is blocked because of cognitive, physical, or other limitations. It is with this population that the development of supplemental or alternative modes of communication can help unlock a communication potential.

Within the past decade, there has been considerable work on developing nonspeech communication systems for the mentally retarded. These efforts have taken various directions. For a long time, attention focused primarily on the development and utilization of various gestural systems of communication, such as mime (Balick, Spiegel, & Greene, 1976; Levett, 1969), and manual sign language (Bricker, 1972; Fristoe & Lloyd, 1977; Kopchick, Rombach, & Smilovitz, 1975; Richardson, 1975). Recently, interest has increasingly shifted to communication systems that employ various kinds of hardware to help overcome the lack of speech.

As yet, no exhaustive classification scheme of device-assisted communication systems has evolved. Despite their seeming complexity, such systems have two basic features: a *symbol system* for representing information, and a *device* to indicate or transmit symbols or symbol components. The large number of ways these two features may be combined afford a variety of communication systems. Three main types are usually distinguished: (1) manipulable symbol systems, where the user communicates by picking up a type of manipulable language symbol (such as a plastic letter of the alphabet) and placing it on some form of display (such as a wooden tray, magnetic board, tabletop, or other surface); (2) communication (conversation) boards, where the user communicates by indicating directly (e.g., with a headstick pointer or patterned movements of the eyes) or indirectly (e.g., by means of electronic control systems) the particular symbol desired from a limited array available on some type of surface; and (3) electronic communication systems, where the user encodes and transmits symbols by means of control mechanisms and one or more electronically activated displays.

Symbol Systems

A major objective of all device-assisted methods of communication is to help the user gain access to, or develop, systems of symbolic formulation and expression. A basic knowledge of the nature of symbols and symbol systems is therefore essential to understanding the range of possible assistive devices.

Briefly, a symbol is something that stands for something else. Two types of symbols can be distinguished. First, there are symbols which resemble the thing they are intended to represent (e.g., a "stick figure" of a human male, standing for the concept "man"). Secondly, there are symbols which are more or less arbitrary, in that they bear no relationship to their referents in terms of appearance (e.g., the printed word "dog," standing for the concept "dog"). At times, both classes of symbols are used in combination (e.g., Rebuses). Individual symbols usually form part of a symbol system, whose members share a common derivational history, various criterial features for inclusion in the set, and associated rules (syntactic, semantic, and pragmatic) governing permissible combinations and sequences of two or more elements.

It is important to point out that most symbols can usually be encoded in more than one physical medium and spatial dimension—including 2-dimensional and 3-dimensional solids, light, or sound. Depending on the medium selected, they can be made available to one or more sensory modalities—including visual, auditory, or tactile. For example, the letters of the English language can be represented in 2-dimensional solid form (e.g., written or printed letters on a piece of paper), 3-dimensional solid form (e.g., plastic letters of the alphabet), light (e.g., subtitles of foreign movies), and sound (e.g., saying, or speaking, each letter in a word). Through these various mediums, letter symbols could be made available to sight, touch, and hearing.

Symbols and symbol systems are not intrinsic to any particular device-assisted system of communication, although some may lend themselves more to one than to another.

At present, there are no clearly established guidelines for selecting one symbol system over another. The subject is complex and will undoubtedly demand a good deal of consideration in the future. Factors that will need to be weighed in relation to each system (a number of which are reviewed in more depth by Silverman, 1980) include:

1. The specific medium in which symbols can be conveyed (this might be important, for example, in relation to an individual's sensory deficits or strengths).
2. The type of symbol involved (e.g., symbols that resemble referents may be easier to acquire than arbitrary symbols).
3. The rules for combining or sequencing symbols (e.g., syntactic and semantic rules may differ in terms of complexity and, concomitantly, in terms of learning).
4. The ability of the system to convey information concerning the past, present, or future, as well as concrete or abstract ideas (such factors would be important, for example, in relation to an individual's current and/or anticipated communication needs).
5. The restrictiveness of the system, in terms of acceptability to others (e.g., the least restrictive system would generally be preferable).
6. Whether, or to what degree, the system would be understandable to relatively untrained or unsophisticated observers (this might be especially important, for example, in terms of the amount of reinforcement the other person receives for helping the individual to communicate).

With these points in mind, the following are among the symbol systems which have already been used, or which could be potentially used, in association with device-assisted communication systems for the mentally retarded.

Artificial Speech

The English language is available in spoken form by means of machine-generated (recorded or synthesized) speech. Words, phrases, or sentences can be generated, or reproduced, which are more or less structurally equivalent to spoken English.

Picture Systems

Two-dimensional photographs or drawings, used singly or in combination, can form the basis of a nearly limitless variety of symbol systems. Such systems appear to be especially useful for communicating basic needs and wants.

English Language (Spelled)

This is a highly flexible system which needs little explanation. It consists of 26 conventional elements (the letters of the alphabet), which are combined to form words, which in turn are concatenated, according to syntactic and semantic rules of combination, to form meaningful phrases or complete sentences.

Rebuses

Rebuses are used in a predominantly pictographic symbol system which uses a single line drawing, several drawings, or a combination of letters of the alphabet and drawings, to represent standard English words. They can be used singly, or combined in the same manner as English words, to form meaningful phrases or sentences. A dictionary-like compilation of rebus symbols has been prepared by Clarke, Davies, and Woodcock (1974), which contains rebuses for more than 2,000 words.

Blissymbolics (or Semantography)

This is a pictographic, idiographic, and arbitrary symbol system developed by Charles K. Bliss (Bliss, 1965). The system consists of about 100 basic elements. These can be used without modification, or combined in various ways to form a vocabulary of almost infinite size. While most Blissymbols are semantically based (i.e., they encode meaning), a few encode strictly grammatical information. the English word equivalent (or other language equivalent) is always printed under each Blissymbol. Vocabulary items can be used alone or, concatenated in a fashion similar to the linguistic structure of English (or some other language).

Premack's Plastic Symbol Language

A symbol system was developed by David Premack (Premack, 1970, 1971; Premack & Premack, 1974) to investigate the ability of the chimpanzee to acquire human language. As originally described, the system consists of pieces of plastic, each representing a specific word, that are backed with metal so that they will adhere to a magnetized slate. Sentences are formed by arranging symbols vertically on a magnetized writing board. Rules for sequencing symbols were derived from an analysis of the English language. Individual symbols are abstract in configuration and do not resemble the word or concept they are intended to represent.

Yerkish Language

Developed by von Glaserfeld (1977) for the LANA Project at Yerkes Regional Research Center (Rumbaugh, 1977), this system was also developed to study language acquisition of the chimpanzee. Yerkish consists of nine abstract design elements, readily discernible from each other, which can be used singly, or in combinations of two, three, or four (by superimposing one on the other), to yield 225 different lexigrams. Each lexigram is reproduced on one of seven background colors, that categorize lexigrams on the basis of meaning (e.g., a blue background signifies lexigrams that can encode activities). Lexigrams generally correspond to a single English word and can be combined in a manner roughly corresponding to English syntactic and semantic structure to form longer messages. Yerkish symbols are arbitrary; their meaning is assigned through training.

Braille

This alternative method of encoding and decoding spelled English was developed by Louis Braille in 1824 for use by the visually impaired or totally blind. There are 63 characters in the system, which are made from raised dot patterns. The characters represent letters of the alphabet, numbers, and frequently used letter combinations. Braille can be used to encode any word or sentence in the English language. Characters can be "written" by a device called a slate, or by a Braille typewriter. The system is usally decoded (read) by passing the fingers lightly over the characters.

Manipulable Symbol Systems

The use of manipulable symbols for purposes of remediating communication deficiencies of the mentally retarded was initially stimulated by the work of Premack (1971, 1972). The major research question underlying his work was: "Can apes be taught language?" Investigators before him had attempted to teach chimpanzees to *speak* (i.e., to produce the sounds and words involved in human speech), but with only limited success (Hayes & Hayes, 1954; Kellogg & Kellogg, 1933). Premack concluded that the major limiting factor of this approach was the complex response typography involved in producing oral speech, and he therefore devised a plastic-word system that could be used for teaching the subject to communicate.

Premack was successful in teaching his chimpanzee subject to "read" as well as to "write" by means of manipulable symbols. The subject eventually acquired a functional vocabulary of over 130 words. The overall training program was an eloquent piece of behavioral research which included a functional analysis of language behavior, step-by-step training procedures, and errorless training methods where only one unknown was introduced at a time. This pioneering work served as the basis and impetus for a good deal of subsequent research. The potential applicability of this work to the needs of many developmentally disabled persons was always clear.

Drawing on his earlier work, Premack (Premack & Premack, 1974) later successfully adapted the plastic symbol system for use with an 8-year-old autistic child who was totally lacking in speech. As part of the program, the authors tested the generalization of the plastic symbol system to the child's natural language, spoken English. They found that some generalization did occur and speculated that the acquisition of the artificial plastic symbol system might prove to be a useful "crutch" which could be discarded later for helping language deficient persons acquire natural language.

Following Premack's work, Carrier and his associates (Parsons & Carrier, 1977; Schmidt, Carrier, & Parsons, 1971) attempted to replicate the same basic procedure with three severely mentally retarded children (aged 8, 12, and 14) and with seven 2- to 3-year-old Down's syndrome children. They had two questions in mind: first, "Can severely impaired, nonverbal children with either a history of failure or a low probability of success in conventional commuciation therapy learn the Premack system?", and second, "Can linguistic rules, learned by using the geometric symbols developed by Premack, be used to facilitate learning of spoken language with children in the target population?" (Carrier, 1976, p. 528). The answer to both questions was affirmative, since every subject learned part or all of the Premack system, and all showed at least some transfer to spoken responses.

By 1974, another successful training program based on Premack's symbol system was reported. McLean and McLean (1974) reported a detailed account of a training procedure for teaching functional communication skills to nonverbal autistic children. The three children selected for the study had no functional speech, and had consistently failed to benefit from traditional speech and language training. By the end of the program, two of the children were able to use symbols expressively. Importantly, the authors were able to demonstrate interexperimenter and intersetting generalization, as well as maintenance of trained responses.

Carrier (1976) furthered his work on investigating the use of Premack-type symbols with mentally retarded persons. Sixty-two severely and profoundly mentally retarded institutionalized children (7-16), who had no speech for communication purposes, served as subjects. Of the 62 initially selected, 60 learned the motor behavior (picking up a symbol and placing in on a tray) prerequisite to the training procedures. Using carefully controlled procedures, Carrier devised a training program for teaching the use of 10 nouns. All 60 subjects completed the training successfully and demonstrated generalization to posttest (magazine) pictures. The mean time required to complete the training was approximately two hours, and error rates for all subjects were low.

The success of this study, coupled with previous positive findings by Carrier and his associates, stimulated the development of a more comprehensive set of training programs (based on similar behavioral methodology) referred to as the *Non-Speech Language Initiation Program (Non-SLIP)*. This program, which is commercially available (Carrier & Peak, 1975), is not intended as a total language training program. Rather, it utilizes Premack-type symbols in an effort to introduce the fundamental cognitive operations involved in learning and using symbol systems or languages (Carrier, 1976). The basic assumption made is that learning to use the symbols will facilitate the acquisition of other ways of communicating.

Despite some promising beginnings, many questions and issues still remain regarding the use of Premack-type symbols with the mentally retarded. The most serious issue is the question of whether or not training in the use of such a system actually does facilitate the acquisition of other, more desirable, communication methods. To date, research is insufficient to draw any firm conclusions. The importance of the question is underscored by the fact that the standard Premack-type symbol system does not readily provide the user with a functional communication system for use in the natural environment (such symbols are totally unintelligible to untrained observers).

Another issue that needs to be clarified is that of selection criteria; for example, who would most benefit from training in the use of Premack-type symbols, and when would the system be the system of choice in preference to some other type of communication mode? While answers are not yet in, the rule of thumb in the past seems to have been to use the system with persons who are severely or profoundly mentally retarded, who are more or less totally lacking in functional speech, who have consistently failed to respond to traditional speech therapy, and who possess sufficient motor function to make the prerequisite motor responses. As our knowledge of Premack-type symbols and their use with mentally retarded persons expands, these criteria will probably need to be reconsidered.

Several advantages of this type of approach should also be noted. The cost of components is minimal. The motor movements involved in the system do not appear to require the same degree of elaborate differentiation as would be involved in oral speech. The symbols can be both seen and felt, which might be of particular advantage for persons with visual acuity problems. Finally, because symbols are on permanent display during the process of encoding messages, they place minimal demands on factors involving short-term memory and sustained attention.

One major disadvantage of the Premack-type communication system is that the user is limited by physical space requirements as to the number of symbols that would be practical to have freely available. It is estimated that probably no more than 75 Premack-type symbols could be arranged conveniently within the reach of the user (Silverman, 1980).

It should also be noted that other systems based on a manipulable symbol format could also be developed. In fact, almost any of the symbol systems listed earlier could be utilized for this purpose. Pictures, English language words, Blissymbolics, Rebuses, or Yerkish language symbols could all be translated into manipulable symbols by reproducing the respective symbol elements on individual pieces of material. Moreover, English word equivalents could be written under Yerkish symbols and reproduced on a small piece of plastic. Some such systems could potentially offer distinct advantages over the Premack-style manipulable symbol system in terms of their intelligibility to the dominant linguistic community.

Communication Boards

Communication board systems can vary along several parameters including size, shape, portability, construction materials, the number of symbols involved, the arrangement of symbols on a display, the type of symbol system utilized, and the methods by which the user indicates the symbol (or symbol sequence) to be communicated. General information regarding the design and clinical application of communication boards is available in several excellent sources (McDonald, 1976; McDonald & Schultz, 1973; Silverman, 1980; Vanderheiden & Grilley, 1976; Vanderheiden & Harris-Vanderheiden, 1976).

The use of communication boards with the mentally retarded is a relatively recent development, that appears to have been stimulated largely by reports of the successful use of such systems with cerebral-palsied children (e.g.,

McDonald & Schultz, 1973; Sayre, 1963), and the emergence of Blissymbolics as an alternative symbol system for the nonverbal mentally retarded (Fristoe & Lloyd, 1978; Harris-Vanderheiden, 1976b; Harris-Vanderheiden, Brown, MacKenzie, Reinen, & Schiebel, 1975; McNaughton, 1976; Olson, 1976). Today, communication board systems are used widely throughout the field of mental retardation, but formal experimental research on such systems is extremely limited.

One of the few experimental investigations of communication boards is that of Reid and Hurlbut (1977). These authors examined the effects of a training program developed for teaching the use of communication boards to nonvocal multiply handicapped mentally retarded adults. The communication board system used required the subjects to point to one or more pictures on a board, each of which had an appropriate descriptor word printed underneath. The training approach was based on a task analysis of skills that the authors considered to be necessary in order to learn to use the system effectively. Thus, training involved the coordinated movements necessary to point to various areas on the board, as well as pointing to various word-pictures in response to a verbal request (e.g, "Where would you like to go?"). Another important aspect of the study was to investigate generalized functional use of the system in the subjects' natural environment. The results of this study indicated that a pointing reponse, in association with a communication board utilizing word-picture symbols, is a viable means of developing functional communication for severely mentally retarded and physically handicapped persons.

Blissymbolics is currently the symbol favored for utilization in conjunction with communication boards for the mentally retarded. However, as indicated by Archer (1977), there are many questions that need to be asked and studied in relation to this symbol system. For example, although it has been suggested that Bliss symbols are easier to learn than traditional English orthography (e.g., Harris-Vanderheiden *et al.*, 1975), this has not been clearly established through formal research. The possibility of using printed words alone instead of Bliss symbols needs to be considered. For instance, Fristoe and Lloyd (1979) have pointed out that even some of the most severely mentally retarded persons can learn sight reading, and in the present society, this system would seem to offer special advantages over all others. Much work is needed on comparing the similarities and differences in the cognitive skills required to learn Bliss symbols, as opposed to those necessary for learning to read words (Archer, 1977). Blissymbolics also should be compared to other symbol systems such as Yerkish, Rebuses, and picture systems (photographs or drawings)—all of which could potentially be used with communication boards.

Another area that needs to be studied involves the methodology for teaching Bliss symbols. Current instructional programs are largely based on intuition and have not been formally evaluated (e.g., Harris-Vanderheiden et al., 1975; McNaughton, 1976; Vanderheiden & Harris-Vanderheiden, 1976). Among the factors that will need to be considered are: (1) the construction and resulting discriminability of stimuli; (2) the sequence of instruction; (3) the rate of instruction; (4) the nature of appropriate reinforcement during training and reinforcement schedules; (5) shaping and fading techniques; and (6) procedures for facilitating use of the system in the individual's natural environment.

Electronic Communication Devices

In the past, severe physical handicaps and motor limitations, especially an inability to use the speech musculature, effectively precluded many people from communicating symbolically. Recent technological developments, especially in the areas of control systems and electronic displays, are increasingly helping more and more people gain access to symbolic expression.

Progress in the development of control systems has been such that it would be difficult to conceive of any child or adult who is so severely impaired that he or she could not theoretically be helped to communicate more adequately. Virtually any type of differentiated response by a person can be used to operate electronic control systems that could be linked to devices for encoding and transmitting messages. Muscle movements that can serve this function include those of the trunk and lower extremities (e.g., any movement of a leg, rotation of the hips, or shoulder movement), those of the upper extremities (e.g., movement of the arm, wrist, or one or more digits), or those of the head, face, or neck (e.g., movement of the head from side to side, looking from left to right, or smiling).

Even if a person cannot make controlled body movements, it may still be possibile to communicate. Research is currently examining the possibilities of using electrical signals from the nervous system, such as muscle action potentials (EMG) or brain waves (EEG), to control electronic switches and displays for purpose of symbolic communication (see Silverman, 1980; Vanderheiden, 1976a). Vanderheiden (1976a) has speculated that a computer program could be devised that would be capable of decoding particular EEG patterns in order to start and stop a scanning indicator that could be moved around a symbol system display. Another EEG pattern would order a printer to type out the indicated message in English. Although highly speculative, this suggestion illustrates the optimistic view held by some regarding the role of the computer in facilitating interpersonal communication by the handicapped (cf. Goldenberg, 1979).

There have also been technological advances in the types of displays that are used in electronic communication systems. Electronic displays can involve representing messages on a screen, printing out messages on paper, signaling messages by means of noise or light patterns generated by the display, or making messages audible in the form of speech. Some representative displays that have been developed (or utilized) to serve such functions include: television screens, LED (light-emitting-diode) displays, rotary scanning displays, strip printers, electric typewriters, and speech synthesizers.

But although inventions and innovations are taking place at a rapid rate in the field of interpersonal communication, there appears to be very little focus or direction within the considerable volume of emerging literature. Scarcely any attempts have been made to formally evaluate the more sophisticated of the currently available electronic communication systems specifically with the mentally retarded. (For a possible exception, see Hagen, Porter, & Brink, 1973.) The vast majority of published reports consist of clinical demonstrations of the efficacy of a system, rather than controlled research, and most studies involving developmentally disabled persons have focused on cerebral-palsied (or other physically handicapped) children of normal or near normal intelligence (e.g., Bullock, Dalrymple, & Danca, 1975; Harris-Vanderheiden, 1976a; Hill, Campagna, Long, Munch, & Naecker, 1968; Law, Lewis, & Parks, 1980; Morasso, Sandini, Suetta, Tagliasco, Vernazza, & Zaccaria, 1978; Park, Roy, Warrick, & Cote, 1979; Workman, 1979).

Clearly, there is a great need for future research aimed at exploring the use of sophisticated electronic communication systems for the mentally retarded. It is likely that such studies have not already been undertaken because of factors such as the relatively high cost of components, lack of public awareness of the availability of such systems, the desire of most researchers to have quick and positive results, and assumptions regarding the basic limitations of mentally retarded persons in the area of communication.

One of the most exciting developments that is currently taking place in connection with electronic communication systems is the recent interest in artificial (machine-generated) speech (Freidman, Cheung, Entine, & Bartell, 1979; Vanderheiden, 1976b; Warrick, Nelson, Cossalter, Cote, McGillis, & Charbonneau, 1977). As Warrick et al., (1977) note, there are many advantages in speech output systems, especially as compared to strictly visual outputs. They represent the possibility of communicating from a distance, such as from one side of the room to another or from outdoors. They would facilitate the users ability to address more than one listener at a time. Perhaps most importantly, synthetic speech would have a high degree of acceptability and intelligibility to persons within the users natural environment. We possess the knowledge to produce pocket-sized synthesizers (Warrick et al., 1977) and the day may come when such devices will be used with mentally retarded persons.

Observation and Recording Equipment

The two mainstays of behavioral assessment and applied research in mental retardation are direct visual observation and paper and pencil recording systems. This reflects in part the dominant orientation of workers in this field to conduct client training and assessment in natural environment settings. It may also be related to the relative lack of technological sophistication of many human service professionals, the insufficient development of suitably portable and rugged instrumentation, and funding constraints. Nevertheless, the role of instrumentation in behavioral assessment is well-established. Instrumentation may be used to effectively (1) detect responses; (2) display and store information accurately and conveniently; (3) determine the passage of intervals of time. Useful devices may facilitate combinations of these functions, or may aid in assessment by providing one function alone.

Response Detection

There are several potential advantages to using instrumentation to detect the occurrence of responses. Responses or their specific characteristics may be too subtle (or too frequent, or may be masked by other events, etc.) to allow reliable detection. Examples of this include psychophysiological measures like GSR, EMG, or EEG. Discussions of these variables were provided in the section on biofeedback applications. Instrumentation may be helpful where observer presence would tend to inhibit the behavior of interest or would drastically alter setting conditions. For example, the presence of the therapist may become discriminative for the availability of programmed consequences, as often occurs when punishment is used to suppress undesirable behavior (Birnbrauer, 1976). Ball, Sibbach, Jones, Steele, and Frazier, (1975) attempted to deal with this problem by using an automated shock delivery system that was triggered by an accelerometer mounted in a special jacket to suppress rapid body movements associated with aggressive responses. Other situations where instrumentation would be helpful are those where observer presence would be inconvenient because of constraints on staff time, where many simultaneous responses must be measured accurately, when response characteristics involve discrete physical parameters like force or wetness, or when reinforcing events must be provided with minimal delay following detection.

The characteristics of various kinds of response detection systems are discussed in Rugh and Schwitzgebel (1977). One class of typical arrangement involves the use of a transducer to change the event into an electrical signal that can be processed for storage in an easily quantifiable form. Some applications have included a mercury switch mounted on an earphone to detect the duration of headtilting (Ball, McCrady, & Hart, 1975), a self-winding wristwatch worn on the subject's arm and ankle to measure gross activity (Schulmann & Reisman, 1959), or a voice-operated-relay to accurately confirm increases in a mentally retarded youngster's voice volume (Jackson & Wallace, 1974).

One major area of application of automatic detectors has been in toilet training. Foxx and Azrin (1973) described a comprehensive toilet training program for retarded individuals in which simple electronic devices are used to alert trainers to the occurrence of eliminations. As previously noted, moisture detector alarms can be mounted in the toilet so that trainers can be sure to reinforce appropriate eliminations, or they can be installed in training pants to alert trainers to the occurrence of inappropriate eliminations (see also Azrin, Bugle, & O'Brien, 1971; Hansen, 1979; Litrownick, 1974; Mahoney, Van Wagenen, & Meyerson, 1971). Blue litmus paper, which turns pink when urine touches it, was suggested by Foxx and Azrin (1973) as a less expensive response detection system. Mowrer and Mowrer (1938) introduced the use of an alarm system to signal the advent of nocturnal bedwetting. Commercial products are now readily available consisting of a battery operated alarm and a wetness detector installed in a pad which is placed in the bed. Azrin, Sneed, and Foxx (1973) employed an operant based multiple-component teaching procedure to eliminate nighttime bedwetting in severely mentally handicapped clients in which a urine-alarm was used to detect bedwetting. Because some clients got out of bed and urinated inappropriately on the floor, another alarm was activated by a switch attached to the bed that closed when the weight of a person was added to the weight of the bed. Those who left the bed could then be quickly prompted to return to bed unless they were on their way to the toilet.

Research on the productivity of mentally retarded workers in sheltered workshops often involves recording the permanent products of their labor (e.g., Martin & Morris, 1980). Reinforcement is often provided on a piecework basis, or for the retarded worker's average productivity as a percentage of the nonretarded worker's expected productivity on the same task. However, Tate (1968) and Schroeder (1972a) described systems whereby the work related responses of mentally retarded clients could be measured directly by wiring elements of the work task to electromechanical programming and recording equipment. Schroeder (1972a,b) used such a system to record the use of tools like soldering guns, nut drivers, and pliers, and was able to automatically program the workspace of each subject on an assembly-line independently. Resulting parametric studies revealed lawful relationships between rate of tool usage and various schedules of independently programmed token reinforcement, required response force, magnitude of reinforcement, and interaction effects of some of these variables (Schroeder, 1972b). The system involved the use of instrumentation not only to detect work behaviors accurately, but also provided for the accurate storage of response data on counters and cumulative recorders and provided automatic delivery of token reinforcement on ratio and interval schedules. Because of ongoing maintenance requirements, an electronically wired sheltered workshop may be more valuable as a research tool than as a vehicle for managing sheltered workshop programs, but improvements in cost efficiency of microprocessor control systems and miniaturization may change the picture in the future.

Other useful response detection devices vary with regard to the characteristics of the handicapped individual and the goals of the training or assessment program. Lindsley's (1964) concept of behavioral prosthesis included the use of various mechanical devices to allow individuals with relatively undifferentiated or minimal response repertoires to register functional responses in controlling environmental events. For very young or severely mentally retarded individuals, contingency awareness *per se* may represent a useful and appropriate educational goal. In support of this notion, Ramey and Finkelstein (1978) provided data suggesting that infants' experience with response-contingent sensory stimulation enhanced their learning of new response-reinforcement relations in a new setting. Lindsley (1963) described a bassinet mounted foot panel that infants could press to see a movie whose projected brightness was programmed on a conjugate (rate analogue) reinforcement schedule. Simple response registration mechanisms have a variety of uses in assessment, in response differentiation, and as prosthetic control devices. Three simple response detection devices shown in Figure 5 are used with handicapped infants enrolled in the Early Intervention Program at Rhode Island Hospital's Child Development Center. These levers, pushbuttons, and cylinder wheels activate microswitches that can operate slide projectors, tape recorders, and a variety of electronic toys. Awareness of controlling relations and differentiated response repertoires can theoretically be built on to increase functional competence in handicapped infants during future years. Zuromski, Smith, and Brown (1977) have described a mercury switch in a plastic-covered metal capsule that can be fastened to a severely handicapped child's body to enable even those youngsters with such minimal motor control that they would be unable to grasp, pull, or press a microswitch-based manipulandum to control contingent events. Other experimenters have used simple wooden levers

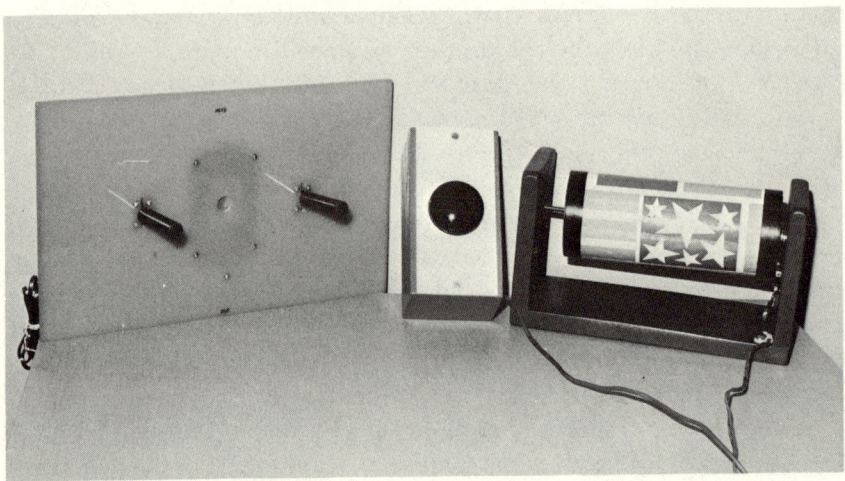

FIGURE 5. Manipulanda designed for use with multiply handicapped infants. From left to right, levers, enlarged push button, and cylinder wheel. Courtesy of E. Rollins, Early Intervention Program, Child Development Center, Providence, Rhode Island.

(Haskett & Hollar, 1978) or loops of rope (Murphy & Doughty, 1977) as manipulanda. Operant responding on simple manipulanda has provided the basis for accurate assessment of nonverbal mentally retarded individuals' auditory (Friedlander, Silva, & Knight, 1973; Lloyd, Spradlin, & Reid, 1968; Myerson & Michael, 1960; Silva, Friedlander, & Knight, 1978) and visual abilities (Friedlander & Knight, 1973; Macht, 1970). Thus, the operant lever still has much to contribute in the analysis and remediation of behavior, and useful devices can be either homemade or commercially purchased from suppliers of specialized adaptive equipment. For example, the Prentke Romich Company (Shreve, Ohio) and J. A. Preston Corporation (New York, New York) both sell a variety of switches designed to be operated by mouth, head, hand, or foot action.

An example of the application of more advanced technology to response detection has recently been reported by Tashjian (1980). Profoundly retarded subjects have been taught to produce imitative vocalizations through the use of a microcomputer system. The computer is programmed to cue and recognize the acoustical properties of several vocalizations and also provide contingent sensory reinforcement for imitative responses. The system is capable of data storage and of performing preliminary data analysis while on-line. Similarly, Goldenberg (1979) reports that a number of severely handicapped youngsters have been able to acquire expressive nonverbal communication skills through the use of a computer graphics program. In one case, a severely spastic athetoid quadriplegic teenager learned to produce graphics on a keyboard through the use of a drawing program that had been modified to partially compensate for typing errors that were made by postresponse accidental key strokes or motor-accuracy related errors. Although still highly experimental and somewhat costly to introduce, these systems suggest that future generation computer-based teaching machines will be capable of utilizing almost any set of reliable responses that a handicapped person can make. Their advantage lies in the ability of programmers to develop software capable of processing response data so that some of the "noise" associated with motor or neurological handicaps can be filtered out.

Storage of Observational Data

Some kinds of behavioral data still require human observers to use their judgments to determine whether or not a response has occurred. These data consist of molar events that are defined in part by the environmental context in which they occur. For example, vigorous gross motor movements involving both arms and legs may occur quite appropriately during sports activities, but they would not be discriminable from aggressive attacks on others by accelerometers attached to the subjects extremities. Human observers are capable of categorizing a large number of acts and may easily shift the focus of data collection from one individual to another in a group setting.

Design and use of observational data systems are thoroughly critiqued in a recent book edited by G. P. Sackett (1978). Useful instrumental includes devices for direct preservation of samples of complex behavioral events through film, videotape, and audiotape (e.g., Brechner, Linder, Meyerson, & Hays, 1974; Christensen, 1979). Recordings can be utilized as the primary data source with behavioral sequences coded from them or they may be analyzed adjunctively to aid in establishing the reliability of field observations (Rojahn, 1978; Rojahn & Wool, 1979; Schinke & Smith, 1979). Audiotape may also be used to preserve narrative descriptions for later analysis from typed transcripts, although the process is extremely time consuming. Other devices range from paper and pencil systems used with beeping recycling timers for use with interval data systems (Greenberg, 1979), mechanical counters which preserve only the frequency of targeted events (Lindsley, 1968), handheld printing calculators for interval or interval-frequency recording (Edelson, 1978), homemade timers and counters built into clipboards to form a kind of hybrid system with limited ability to sample duration on some events combined with written observations (Frankel & Weber, 1978), to digital event recording systems capable of preserving several coded behavior categories as well as sequence and duration information. The multichannel strip chart recorder with each pen wired to a separate push button mounted on a keyboard is an example of the latter (eg., Baker & Whitehead, 1972). More advanced keyboard recording devices that store data on computer-readable material are becoming available and will provide some data processing functions as the observations are recorded. (Sackett, Stephenson, & Ruppenthal, 1973). Some of these systems provide not only a means of coding multiple events, convenient short-term storage, rapid transfer of data to computer disks, editing, and format selection, but also can preserve information regarding sequence, duration, and frequency of data for analysis with recently developed $n = 1$ statistics (see Gottman & Notarius, 1978). Holm (1978) provides a detailed discussion of the relative merits of these recording systems.

Conclusion

This chapter has attempted to broadly review the areas in which instrumentation has been used to aid therapists and researchers working with the developmentally handicapped. Devices have been used to extend the capabilities of either the handicapped client through increasing functional interacation with objects or people, or to extend the capabilities of the researcher and professional in overcoming problems involving measurement or human resources. Two major areas of concern appear to emerge from this discussion.

The first is that many prosthetic aids have not been fully evaluated. Their relative functional value to a client is rarely objectively determined as compared to a different prosthesis or no prosthetic intervention at all, let alone their long-term effects on the acquisition of differentiated adaptive skill repertoires. It seems possible that in some cases adaptive devices can become an end in themselves, unnecessarily limiting the handicapped person's ability to do without them. Devices once marketed or described in the rehabilitation literature do not appear prominently in the behavior analysis literature. The reason for this is not immediately clear. Examples of the relative lack of analysis include devices for mobility, positioning, and control or switching systems. An exception is the use of instrumentation to aid in toilet training, which has a long history of development and controlled comparison. Controlled research is needed to determine whether or not individual prosthetic devices do in fact provide immediate as well as long-term benefits to clients. Clearly, evaluation of prosthetic devices should include their functional effects on social as well as nonsocial variables. Examples of possible approaches to evaluation were noted in studies describing the use of adaptive clothing with self-injurious clients (Rojahn et al., 1978, 1980). Thus, research possibilities include both the development of new devices and the thorough assessment of their use in various environmental contexts.

The second theme involves the exciting prospects of further development of prosthetic strategies for the handicapped and of useful instrumentation for research dissemination. Microprocessor technology and improved engineering knowledge of man-machine interfacing can greatly extend the range of feasible prosthetic strategies. The computer appears to have tremendous potential value as a prosthetic communication aid and as a stimulating and flexible teaching machine. However, cost and accessibility remain significant obstacles for future development. Refinements in software development and prototype design will require collaboration between behavioral and educational specialists and computer scientists and engineers. These developments will have to precede final product design and demonstration, and only then will demonstrably useful systems engender the kind of market demand that will make their production cost effective to the manufacturer. Until that time, consumers will bear the cost of research development as well as that of the parts and labor involved in making the product. Unique and custom-made devices will always be relatively expensive, with prospects for moderation only in terms of dissemination of the design and technical knowledge involved.

Dissemination, however, is another area where technology can be helpful. Electronic medias are becoming more important in the transmission, storage, and use of scientific and technical information. Experiments are under way to determine the value of the telecommunications in the Developmental Disabilities field, including video and audio conferencing, computer mediated message linkages between DD centers, and data transmission (Alternate Media Center, 1979). Networks of specialists interested in solving the instrumentation design and modification problems of handicapped users may be organized through the use of telecommunications. In addition, handicapped persons who may be unable to use conventional communication devices because of oral-motor or speech problems, may be able to communicate over long distances through the use of a computer mediated communication system and a telecommunication network. Finally, service programs in geographically remote areas may be able to have faster access to experts and resources located in urban centers through teleconferencing and information-sharing networks (Johansen, Vallee, & Spangler, 1979). This can potentially reduce transportation costs, and can avoid the costly need for local research and development of instrumentation applications already in use elsewhere.

The National Association of State Directors of Special Education has recently provided a systematic model for the dissemination of assistive devices (NASDSE, 1980). The model uses the state or region capable of serving about 700 students per year as the recommended capacity parameter. It calls for the construction of an assistive device center within each region. The center concept requires coordinated interagency planning and provision of multiple funding sources in order to be successfully established. The program envisions the center as a regional resource with the capability of (1) evaluating and following individual students referred for assistive devices; (2) device procurement and periodic modification at no cost to the student; (3) inservice and preservice technical training of community professionals; (4) public education; (5) providing a continuing communication link among agencies; and (6) providing a communication link between agencies and its own repository of technical information. This report is also useful as a partial directory of federal, state, and corporate technical and funding resources for persons interested in exploring further the concept of an assistive-device center. (At this writing the report is available for a small charge from NASDE, 1201 Sixteenth Street, N.W., Washington, D.C., 20036.)

The Education for All Handicapped Children Act of 1975, P.L. 94-142, and rehabilitation legislation pertaining to adults, appear to provide a basis for public funding of the necessary interventions, both technological and professional, that will lead to wider use of prosthetic strategies. Psychologists function under legal and ethical constraints that affect their use of devices in many ways (Schwitzgebel, 1978). Ethical principles under which psychologists operate (APA, 1977) regarding client welfare, competence, and public statements, encourage the use and scientific investigation of new psychological approaches. If followed closely, the guidelines appear to promote strategies for the evaluation of devices, for safety, and for the continuing education of psychologists, the consequence of which is the application of successful new technologies. Other professions, including engineering, medicine, and education, do not always have an equivalent set of clearly stated ethical guidelines, although pertinent legal regulation may affect these groups more or less equally. For example, legal classification in the United States of some devices like biofeedback instrumentaion, electric shock devices, and even enuresis-wetness detectors as medical devices, appear to require the active collaboration of physicians regarding their use, despite the behavioral functions for which they clearly may be intended (Schwitzgebel, 1977). While the collaboration of computer and engineering specialists may often be more pertinent, it would be premature, indeed, to omit the contribution of any profession having a body of knowledge and skills that could aid the handicapped in enhancing their skills and functional capacities.

ACKNOWLEDGEMENTS

The patient work of Tracy Andrews in preparing the manuscript through various stages is gratefully acknowledged. We thank Lorraine McCann for helpful comments and Nancy Bruce of the Brown University Library for assistance with the computer bibliographic search.

REFERENCES

ABRAMSON, E. E., & CROCKER, R. W. Rapid elimination of out-of-seat behavior by the use of response cost and reinforcement. *Behavioral Engineering.* 1978, 4, 103–105.

ACCRINO, S. P. & ZUROMSKI, E. S. *Simple discrimination learning with sensory reinforcement by profoundly retarded children.* Paper presented at the Eastern Psychological Association Convention, Washington, D.C., April 1978.

ALTERNATE MEDIA CENTER. *Telecommunications and service to the developmentally disabled, Vol. 2: Application possibilities.* New York: New York University, School of Arts, May 1979.

AMERICAN PSYCHOLOGICAL ASSOCIATION, *Ethical standards of psychologists.* Washington, D.C.: Author, 1977.

ARCHER, L. A. Blissymbolics—A nonverbal communication system. *Journal of Speech and Hearing Disorders,* 1977, 42, 568–579.

AZRIN, N. H., & HOLZ, W. C. Punishment. In W. K. Honig (Ed.), *Operant behavior.* New York: Academic Press, 1966.

AZRIN, N. H., BUGLE, C., & O'BRIEN, F. Behavioral engineering: Two apparatuses for toilet training retarded children. *Journal of Applied Behavior Analysis,* 1971, 4, 249–253.

AZRIN, N. H., SNEED, T. J., & FOXX, R. M. Dry bed: A rapid method of eliminating bedwetting (enuresis) of the retarded. *Behavior Research and Therapy,* 1973, 11, 427–434.

BAKER, J. G., & WHITEHEAD, G. A portable recording apparatus for rating behavior in free-operant situations. *Journal of Applied Behavior Analysis,* 1972, 5,, 191–192.

BALICK, S., SPIEGEL, D., & GREENE, G. Mime in language therapy and clinician training. *Archives of Physical Medicine and Rehabilitation,* 1976, 57, 35–38.

BALL, T. S., & IRWIN, A. E. A portable, automated device to training a hyperactive child. *Behavior Therapy and Experimental Psychiatry,* 1976, 7,, 185–187.

BALL, T. S., MCCRADY, R. E., & HART, A. D. Automated reinforcement of head posture in two cerebral palsied retarded children. *Perceptual and Motor Skills,* 1975, 40, 619–622.

BALL, T. S., SIBBACH, L., JONES, R., STEELE, B., & FRAZIER, L. An accelerometer activated device to control assaultive and self-destructive behaviors in retardates. *Journal of Behavior Therapy and Experimental Psychiatry,* 1975, 6, 223–228.

BALL, T. S., COMBS, T., RUGH, J., & NEPTUNE, R. Automated range of motion training with two cerebral palsied retarded young men. *Mental Retardation,* 1977, 15, 47–50.

BALL, T. S., MCCRADY, R. E., & TEXFIRA, J. Automated monitoring and cueing for positive reinforcement and differential reinforcement of other behavior. *Journal of Behavior Therapy and Experimental Psychiatry.* 1978, 9, 33–37,

BARRETT, B. H. Behavior analysis. In J. Wortis (Ed.), *Mental retardation and developmental disabilities* (Vol. 9). New York: Brunner/Mazel, 1977.

BARRETT, B. H. Communitization and the measured message of normal behavior. In R. York & E. Edgar (Eds.). *Teaching the severely handicapped.* Columbus, Ohio: Special Press, 1979.

BEDNAR, M. J. (Ed.). *Barrier-free environments.* Stroudsburg, Pennsylvania: Dowden, Hutchigon & Ross, Inc., 1977.

BERGEN, A. *Selected equipment for pediatric rehabilitation.* Valhalla, New York: Blythedale Children's Hospital, 1974

BERGEN, A. *Selected equipment for pediatric rehabilitation: Supplement I.* Valhalla, New York: Blythedale Children's Hospital, 1975.

BERGMANN, K. A visual tracking machine. *American Journal of Occupational Therapy.* 1977, *31,* 421-424.

BIJOU, S. W. A functional analysis of retarded development. In N. R. Ellis (Ed.), *International review of research in mental retardation* (Vol. 1). New York: Academic Press, 1966.

BIJOU, S.W. Studies in the development of left-right concepts in retarded children using fading techniques. In N.R. Ellis (Ed.), *International review of research in mental retardation* (Vol. 3). New York: Academic Press, 1968.

BIRNBRAUER, J.S. Mental retardation. In H. Leitenberg (Ed.), *Handbook of behavior modification and behavior therapy.* Englewood Cliffs, N.J.: Prentice-Hall, 1976.

BLISS, C. K. *Semotography (blissymbolics)* (2nd ed). Coogee, Sydney, Australia: Author, 1965.

BONDE-PETERSEN, F., WOLFF, C.E., & HENRIKSEN, E. A new training device for rehabilitation during workshop training. *Scandinavian Journal of Rehabilitation Medicine,* 1972, *4,* 188-190.

BORTNER, E. The transfer commode. *American Journal of Occupational Therapy,* 1979, *33,* 655.

BREBNER, A., HALLWORTH, H. J., & BROWN, R. I. Computer instruction programs and terminals for the mentally retarded. In P. Mittler (Ed.), *Research to practice in mental retardation: Education and training* (Vol. 2), Baltimore, Maryland: University Park Press, 1977.

BRECHNER, K. C., LINDER, D. E., MEYERSON, L., & HAYS, V. L. A brief report on a device for unobtrusive visual recording. *Journal of Applied Behavior Analysis,* 1974, *7,* 499-500.

BRICKER, D. D. Imitative sign training as a facilitator of word object association with low-functioning children. *American Journal of Mental Deficiency,* 1972, *76,* 509-516.

BRICKER, W.A., MORGAN, D. G., & GRABOWSKI, J. G. Development and maintenance of a behavior modification repertoire of cottage attendants through TV feedback. *American Journal of Mental Deficiency.* 1972, *77,* 128-136.

BROWN, D. M., DEBACHER, G. A., & BASMAJIAN, J. V. Feedback goniometers for hand rehabilitation. *American Journal of Occupation Therapy,* 1979, *33,* 458-463.

BUCHER, B., & LOVAAS, O. I. The use of aversive stimulation in behavior modification. In M. R. Jones (Ed.), *Miami symposium on the prediction of behavior: Aversive stimulation.* Coral Gables: University of Miami Press, 1967.

BULLOCK, A., DALRYMPLE, G. F. & DANCA, J. M. Communication and the nonverbal, multihandicapped child. *American Journal of Occupational Therapy,* 1975, *29,* 150-152.

BURNETT, L., MCLAUGHLIN, T. F., & HUNSAKER, D. Instruction-following behavior of an entire third-grade classroom: Effects of a timing device, public posting, and teacher praise. *Behavioral Engineering,* 1978, *5,* 37-40.

BUTTERFIELD, W. H. Electronic shock—safety factors when used for the aversive conditioning of humans. *Behavior Therapy,* 1975, *6,* 98-110. (a)

BUTTERFIELD, W. H. Electric shock—hazards in aversive shock conditioning of humans. *Behavioral Engineering,* 1975, *3,* 1-28. (b)

CARRIER, J. K., Application of a nonspeech language system with the severely language handicapped. In L. L. Lloyd (Ed.), *Communication assessment and intervention strategies.*

Baltimore: University Park Press, 1976.

CARRIER, J. K., JR , & PEAK, T. *Program manual for non-SLIP (non-speech language initiation program).* Lawrence, Kansas: H. & H. Enterprises, Inc., 1975.

CARTER, C. Crutch splints for a quadriplegic child. *American Journal of Occupational Therapy,* 1979, *33,* 526-527.

CATALDO, M. F., BIRD, B.L., & CUNNINGHAM, C. E. Experimental analysis of EMG feedback in treating cerebral palsy. *Journal of Behavioral Medicine,* 1978, *1,* 311-322.

CATALDO, M. F., RUSSO, D. C., & FREEMAN, J.M. A behavior analysis approach to high rate myoclonic seizures. *Journal of Autism and Developmental Disorders,* 1979, *9,* 413-427.

CATANIA, A.C. Chomsky's formal analysis of natural languages: a behavioral translation. *Behaviorism,* 1972, *1,* 1-15.

CATANIA, A. C., & BRIGHAM, T. A. *Handbook of applied behavior analysis: Social and instructional processes.* New York, Irvington, 1978.

CHOMSKY, N. *Aspects of the theory of syntax.* Cambridge, MA: M.I.T. Press, 1965.

CHRISTENSEN, A. Naturalistic observation of families: A system for random audio recordings in the home. *Behavior Therapy,* 1979, *10,* 418-422.

CHRISTOPHER, R. P. Recent advances in mechanical aids in the management of children with brain damage. *Southern Medical Journal,* 1974, *67,* 399-405.

CLARKE, C. R., DAVIES, C. O., & WOODCOCK, R. W. *Standard rebus glossary.* Minneapolis: American Guidance Service, 1974.

COLBY, K.M. The rationale for computer-based treatment of language difficulties in nonspeaking autistic children. *Journal of Autism and Childhood Schizopreniea,* 1973, *3,* 254-260.

COLBY, K. M., & KRAEMER, H. C. An objective measurement of nonspeaking children's performance with a computer-controlled program for the stimulation of language behavior. *Journal of Autism and Childhood Schizophrenia,* 1975, *5,* 139-146.

COLBY, K. M., & SMITH, D. C. Computers in the treatment of nonspeaking autistic children. In J.H. Masserman (Ed.), *Current psychiatric therapies.* New York: Grune & Stratton, 1971.

CORTE, H. E., WOLF, M. M., & LOCKE, B. J. A comparison of procedures for eliminating self-injurious behavior of retarded adolescents. *Journal of Applied Behavior Analysis,* 1971, *4,* 201-213.

DALY, D.A., & JOHNSON, H. P. Instrumental modification of hyernasal voice quality in retarded children: Case reports. *Journal of Speech and Hearing Disorders,* 1974, *38,* 500-507.

DE ROO, W. M., & HARALSON, H. L. Increasing workshop production through self-visualization of videotape. *Mental Retardation,* 1971, *9,* 22-25.

DOUGHTY, N. R. An inexpensive vibratory chair. *Journal of Applied Behavioral Analysis,* 1976, *9,* 140. (Abstract)

DUKER, P. C. Remotely applied punishment versus avoidance conditioning in the treatment of self-injurious behaviors. *European Journal of Behavioral Analysis and Modification,* 1976, *3,* 179-185.

EDELSON, R. I., & SPRAGUE, R. L. Conditioning of activity level in a classroom with institutionalized retarded boys. *American Journal of Mental Deficiency,* 1974, *78,* 384-388.

EDELSON, J. L. An expensive instrument of rapid recording of "in vivo" observations. *Journal of Applied Behavior Analysis,* 1978, *11,* 502.

EDWARDS, A. E., & ROSENBERG, B. An automated branching device for the assessment and training for visual discrimination. *Perceptual and Motor Skills,* 1966, *22,* 488-490.

FAVELL J. Reduction of stereotypes by reinforcement of toy play. *Mental Retardation,* 1973, *59,* 254-258.

FAVELL, J. E., & CANNON, P. R. Evaluation of entertainment materials for severely retarded persons. *American Journal of Mental Deficiency,* 1977, *81,* 357-361.

FAVELL, J. E., MCGIMSEY, J. F., & JONES, M. L. The use of physical restraint in the treatment of self injury and as positive reinforcement. *Journal of Applied Behavior Analysis*, 1978, *11*, 225-241.

FERNANDO, C. K., & BASMAJIAN, J. V. Biofeedback in physical medicine and rehabilitation. *Biofeedback and Self-Regulation*, 1978, *3*, 435-455.

FERRARA, C., & HILL, S. D. The responsiveness of autistic children to the predictability of social and nonsocial toys. *Journal of Autism and Developmental Disorders*, 1980, *10*, 51-57.

FINLEY, W. W., NIMAN, C., STANDLEY, J., & ENDER, P. Frontal EMG-biofeedback training of athetoid cerebral palsy patients. *Biofeedback and Self-Regulation*, 1976, *1*, 169-182.

FINLEY, W. W., NIMAN, C. A., STANDLEY, J., & WANSLEY, R. A. Electrophysiologic behavior modification of frontal EMG in cerebral-palsied children. *Biofeedback and Self-Regulation*, 1977, *2*, 59-79.

FINNIE, N. R. *Handling the young cerebral palsied child at home.* New York: Dutton, 1975.

FIRESTONE, P. The effects and side effects of time-out on an aggressive nursery school child. *Journal of Behavior Therapy and Experimental Psychiatry*, 1976, *6*, 79-81.

FLETCHER, S. G. Theory and instrumentation for quantitative measurement of nasality. *Cleft Palate*, 1970, *1*, 601-609.

FOXX, R. M., & AZRIN N. H. *Toilet training the retarded: A rapid program for day and nighttime independent toileting.* Research Press: Champaign, Illinois, 1973.

FRANKEL, F., & WEBER, D. A portable low-cost timing apparatus for collection of observational duration data. *Journal of Applied Behvior Analysis*, 1978, *11*, 522. (Abstract)

FRIEDMAN, R. B., CHEUNG, S., ENTINE, S., & BARTELL, T. Verbal communication aid for nonvocal patients. *Medical and Biological Engineering and Computing*, 1979, *17*, 103-106.

FRIEDLANDER, B. Z., & KNIGHT, M. S. Brightness sensitivity and preference in deaf-blind retarded children. *American Journal of Mental Deficiency*, 1973, *78,*, 322-330.

FRIEDLANDER, B. Z., SILVA, D. A., & KNIGHT, M. S. Selective responses to auditory and auditory-vibratory stimuli by severely retarded deaf-blind children. *Journal of Auditory Research*, 1973, *13*, 105-111.

FRIEDLANDER, B. Z., KAMIN, P., & HESSE, G. W. Operant therapy for prehension disabilities in severely retarded young children. *Training School Bulletin*, 1974, *71*, 101-108.

FRISTOE, M., & LLOYD, L. L. Manual communication for the retarded and others with severe communication impairment: A resource list. *Mental Retardation*, 1977, *15*, 18-19.

FRISTOE, M., & LLOYD, L. L. A survey of the use of nonspeech systems with the severely communication impaired. *Mental Retardation*, 1978, *16*, 99-103.

FRISTOE, M., & LLOYD, L. L. Nonspeech communication. In N.R. Ellis (Ed.), *Handbook of mental deficiency, psychological theory and research*, (2nd ed.). Hillsdale, N. J.: Lawrence Erlbaum, 1979.

FURMAN, S., & FEIGHNER, A. Video feedback in treating hyperkinetic children: A preliminary report. *American Journal of Psychiatry*, 1973, *130*, 792-796.

GARDNER, J. F., LONG, L., NICHOLS, R., & IAGULLI, D. M. *Program issues in developmental disabilities: A resource manual for surveyors and reviewers.* Baltimore: Paul H. Brookes, 1980.

GATHERCOLE, C. E. Remotely applied punishment versus avoidance conditioning in the treatment of self-injurious behaviours. *European Journal of Behavioural Analysis and Modification* 1976, *3*, 186-187.

GEOFFRION, L. D., & BERGERON, D. R. *Initial reading through computer animation.* Paper presented at the annual convention of the American Educational Research Association, New York, April 1977.

GERTENRICH, R. L. A simple adaptive drinking device for mental retardates lacking arm-control (pilot project). *Mental Retardation*, 1970, *8*, 51-52.

GIBSON, F. W., LAWRENCE, P. S., & NELSON, R. O. Comparison of three training procedures for teaching social responses to developmentally disabled adults. *American Journal of Mental Deficiency*, 1977, *81*, 379-387.

GIRDANO, D. A. Buying biofeedback. In T. X. Barbar, L. V. DiCara, J. Kamiya, N. E. Miller, D. Shapiro, & J. Stoyva (Eds.), *Biofeedback and self-control 1975/76*. Chicago: Aldine, 1976.

GOLDENBERG, E. P. *Special technology for special children: Computers to serve communication and autonomy in the education of handicapped children*. Baltimore. University Park Press, 1979.

GOTTMAN, J. M., & NOTARIUS, C. Sequential analysis of observational data using markov chains. In T. R. Kratochwill (Ed.), *Single subject research: Strategies for evaluating change*. New York: Academic Press, 1978.

GREELIS, M. Media stimulation and exceptional children. *Mental Deficiency*, 1974, *12*, 30-31.

GREELIS, M., & KAZAOKA, K. The therapeutic use of edited videotapes with an exceptional child. *Academic Therapy*, 1979, *15*, 37-44.

GREENBERG, M. R. A pocket sized multipurpose timer. *Behavioral Engineering*, 1979, *5*, 147.

GREENE, F. M. Programmed instruction techniques for the mentally retarded. In N. R. Ellis (Ed.), *International review of research in mental retardation* (Vol. 2). New York: Academic Press, 1966.

GRIFFIN, J. C., PATTERSON, E. T., LOCKE, B. J., & LANDERS, W. F. Toward automated physical therapy with the nonambulatory profoundly retarded via operant conditioning. *Behavioral Engineering*, 1975, *3*, 72-73.

GROVE, D. N., DALKE, B. A., FREDERICKS, H. D., & CROWLEY, R. F. Establishing appropriate head positioning with mentally and physically handicapped children. *Behavioral Engineering*, 1975, *3*, 53-59.

HAGEN, C., PORTER, W., & BRINK, J. Nonverbal communication: An alternate mode of communication for the child with severe cerebral palsy. *Journal of Speech and Hearing Disorders*, 1973, *38*, 448-455.

HALLWORTH, H. J., & BREBNER, A. Development of computer-assisted instruction at V.R.R.I. In R. I. Brown & M. B. Bayer (Eds.), *Research, demonstration and practice: 10 years of progress*. Calgary, Canada: Vocational and Rehabilitation Research Institute, 1979.

HAMPSTEAD, W. J. The effects of EMG-assisted relaxation training with hyperkinetic children: A behavioral alternative. *Biofeedback and Self-Regulation*, 1979, *4*, 113-125.

HANSEN, G. D. Enuresis control through fading, escape, and avoidance training. *Journal of Applied Behavior Analysis*, 1979, *12*, 303-307.

HARRIS, A., & KAPCHE, R. Behavior modification in schools: Ethical issues and suggested guidelines. *Journal of School Psychology*, 1978, *16*, 25-33.

HARRIS, F. A. Treatment with a position feedback-controlled head stabilizer. *American Journal of Physical Medicine*, 1979, *58*, 169-184.

HARRIS-VANDERHEIDEN, D. Field evaluation of the auto-com. In G. C. Vanderheiden & K. Grilley (Eds.), *Nonvocal communication technique and aids for the severely physically handicapped*. Baltimore: University Park Press, 1976. (a)

HARRIS-VANDERHEIDEN, D. Blissymbols and the mentally retarded. In G. C. Vanderheiden & K. Grilley (Eds.), *Nonvocal communication techniques and aids for the severely physically handicapped*. Baltimore: University Park Press, 1976. (b)

HARRIS-VANDERHEIDEN, D., BROWN, W. P., MACKENZIE, P., REINEN, S., & SCHIEBEL, C. Symbol communication for the mentally handicapped: An application of blissymbols as an alternate communication mode for nonverbal mentally retarded children with motoric impairment. *Mental Retardation*, 1975, *13*, 34-37.

HASKETT, J., & HOLLAR, W. D. Sensory reinforcement and contingency awareness of profoundly retarded children. *American Journal of Mental Deficiency*, 1978, *83*, 60-68.

Hayes, K. J., & Hayes, C. The cultural capacity of chimpanzees. *Human Biology*, 1954, *26*, 288-303.

Hill S. D., Campagna, J., Long, D., Munch, J., & Naecker, S. An exploratory study of the use of two reponse keyboards as a means of communication for the severely handicapped child. *Perceptual and Motor Skills*, 1968, *26*, 699-704.

Hively, W. An exploratory investigation of an apparatus for studying and teaching visual discrimination, using preshool children. In A.A. Lumsdaine & R. Glaser (Eds.), *Teaching machines and programmed learning: A source book.* Washington, D.C.: National Education Association. 1960.

Hively, W. Programming stimuli in matching to sample. *Journal of Experimental Analysis of Behavior*, 1962, *5*, 279-298.

Hively, W. A multiple-choice visual discrimination apparatus. *Journal of Experimental Analysis of Behavior*, 1964, *7*, 387-389.

Hoffman, A. M. & Morris, W. W. *Clothing for the handicapped, the aged, and other people with special needs.* Springfield, Illinois: Charles C Thomas, 1979.

Holm, R. A. Techniques of recording observational data. In G. P. Sackett (Ed.), *Observing behavior, Vol. II: Data collection and analysis methods.* Baltimore: University Park Press, 1978.

Holt, K. S. Deformity and disability in cerebral palsy. *Developmental Medicine and Child Neurology*, 1963, *5*, 620-631.

Horner, R. D. Establishing use of crutches by a mentally retarded spina bifida child. *Journal of Applied Behavior Analysis*, 1971, *4*, 183-189.

Horner, R. D., & Keilitz, I. Training mentally retarded adolescents to brush their teeth. *Journal of Applied Behavior Analysis*, 1975, *8*, 301-309.

Jackson, D. A., & Wallace, R. F. The modification and generalization of voice loudness in a fifteen-year-old retarded girl. *Journal of Applied Behavior Analysis*, 1974, *7*, 461-471.

Jackson, G. M. The use of visual orientation feedback to facilitate attention and task performance. *Mental Retardation*, 1979, *17*, 281-284.

Johansen, R., Vallee, J., & Spangler, K. *Electronic meetings: Technical alternatives and social choices*, Reading, Mass.: Addison-Wesley, 1979.

Johnson, D., Firth, H., & Davey, G. C. L. Vibration and praise as reinforcers for mentally handicapped people. *Mental Retardation*, 1978, *16*, 339-345.

Kantor, J. R. Man and machines in psychology: Cybernetics and artificial intelligence. *The Psychologcal Record*, 1978, *28*,, 575-583.

Kazdin, A. E. The effect of response cost and aversive stimulation in suppressing punished and nonpunished speech disfluencies. *Behavior Therapy*, 1973, *4*, 73-82.

Kellogg, W. N., & Kellogg, L. A. *The ape and the child.* New York: McGraw-Hill, 1933.

Kopchick, G. A., Jr., Rombach, D. W., & Smilovitz, R. A total communication environment in an institution. *Mental Retardation*, 1975, *13*, 22-23.

Lang, P. J., & Melamed, B. G. Avoidance conditioning therapy of an infant with chronic ruminative vomiting. *Journal of Abnormal Psychology*, 1969, *74*, 1-8.

Law, J., Lewis, J., & Parks, A. L. Using the verbalizer with a nonverbal cerebral palsied child: A case history. *Behavioral Engineering*, 1980, *6*, 19-24.

Lawrence, P. D., & Horne, S. J. Input modes: Their importance in the clinical application of electronic aids for disabled persons. *Archives of Physical Medicine and Rehabilitation* 1979, *60*, 516-521.

Lent, J. R., LeBlanc, J., & Spradlin, J. Designing a rehabilitative culture for moderately retarded adolescent girls. In R. Ulrich, T. Stachnik, & T. Mabry (Eds.), *Control of human behavior* (Vol. 2). Glenview, Illinois: Scott, Forsman, 1970.

Levett, L. M. A method of communication for nonspeaking, severely subnormal children. *British Journal of Disorders of Communication,* 1969, *4,* 64-66.

Lindsley, O. R. Experimental analysis of social reinforcement: Terms and methods. *American Journal of Orthopsychiatry,* 1963, *33,* 624-633.

Lindsley, O. R. Direct measurement and prosthesis of retarded behavior. *Journal of Education,* 1964, *147,* 62-81.

Lindsley, O. R. A reliable wrist counter for recording behavior rates. *Journal of Applied Behavior Analysis,* 1968, *1,* 77-78.

Linscheid, T. R., & Cunningham, C. E. A controlled demonstration of the effectiveness of electric shock in the elimination of chronic infant rumination. *Journal of Applied Behavior Analysis,* 1977, *10,* 500. (Abstract)

Litrownik, A. J. A method for home training an incontinent child. *Journal of Behavior Therapy and Experimental Psychiatry,* 1974, *5,* 77-80.

LLoyd, L. L., Spradlin, J. E., & Reid, M. J. An operant audiometric procedure for difficult-to-test patients. *Journal of Speech and Hearing Disorders,* 1968, *33,* 236-245.

Lovaas, O. I. *Behavior modification: Teaching language to psychotic children.* New York: Appleton-Century-Crofts, 1969.

Lovaas, O. I., & Simmons, J. Q. Manipulation of self-destruction in three retarded children. *Journal of Applied Behavior Analysis,* 1969, *2,* 143-157.

Lovaas, O. I., Freitag, G., Gold, V. J., & Kassorla, I. C. Experimental studies in childhood schizophrenia: Analysis of self-destructive behavior. *Journal of Experimental Child Psychology,* 1965, *2,* 67-84.

Lovibund, S. H. *Conditioning and enuresis,* New York: Macmillan, 1964

Low, N. Cerebral palsy. In H. Barnett & A. Einhorn (Eds.), *Pediatrics.* New York: Appelton-Century-Crofts, 1972.

Lynch, J. J., & Paskewitz, D. A. On the mechanisms of the feedback control of human brain wave activity. *Journal of Nervous and Mental Disease,* 1971, *153,* 205-217.

Macht, J. Examination and re-evaluaton of prosthetic lenses employing an operant procedure for measuring subjective visual acuity in a retarded child. *Journal of Experimental Child Psychology,* 1970, *10,* 139-145.

Macurik, K. M. An operant device to reinforce correct head position. *Journal of Behavior Therapy and Experimental Psychiatry,* 1979, *10,* 237-239.

Mahoney, K. VanWagenen, R. K. & Meyerson, L. Toilet training of normal and retarded children. *Journal of Applied Behavior Analysis,* 1971, *4,* 173-181.

Malpass, L. F. Programmed instruction for retarded children. In A. A. Baumeister (Ed.), *Mental retardation: Appraisal, education and rehabilitation.* London: University of London Press, 1967.

Marshall, N., & Goldstein, S. The effects of three consultation procedures on maternal understanding of diagnostic information. *American Journal of Mental Deficiency,* 1970, *74,* 479-482.

Martin, A. S., & Morris, J. L. Training a work ethic in severely mentally retarded workers: Providing a context for the maintenance of skill performance. *Mental Retardation,* 1980, *18,* 67-71.

Martin G., & Palotta-Cornick, A. Behavior modification in sheltered workshops and community group homes: Status and future. In L. A. Hamerlynck (Ed.). *Behavioral systems for the developmentally disabled: II. Institutional, clinic, and community environments.* New York: Brunner/Mazel, 1979.

Martin, R. *Legal Challenges to behavior modification.* Champaign, Illinois: Research Press, 1975.

Martin, R. R., & Siegel, G. M. The effects of response contingent shock on stuttering. *Journal of Speech and Hearing Research,* 1966, *9,* 340-352.

Mauk, W. C. Applied media: The philosophy and technique. *Rehabilitation Record,* 1971, *12,* 1-5.

Mayhew, G. L., Enyart, P., & Anderson, J. Social reinforcement and the naturally occurring social response of severely and profoundly retarded adolescents. *American Journal of Mental Deficiency,* 1978, *83,* 164-170.

McDonald, E. T. Design and application of communication boards. In G. C. Vanderheiden & K. Grilley (Eds.), *Nonvocal communication techniques and aids for the severely physically handicapped.* Baltimore: University Park Press, 1976.

McDonald, E. T., & Schultz, A. R. Communication boards for cerebral palsied children. *Journal of Speech and Hearing Disorders,* 1973, *38,* 73-88.

McLaughlin, T. F., Brown, D., Malaby, J. E., & Dolliver, P. The comparative effects of a timing device and group and individual contingencies for on-task behavior and academic responding in a special education class. *Behavioral Engineering,* 1977, *4,* 11-15.

McLaughlin, T. F., Dolliver, P., & Malaby, J. E. A timer game: Effects for on-task behavior and generalization for academic behavior for an entire special education class. *Contemporary Educational Psychology,* 1979, *4,*, 172-174.

McLean, L. P., & McLean, J. E. A language training program for nonverbal autistic children. *Journal of Speech and Hearing Disorders.* 1974, *39,* 186-193.

McNaughton, S. Bliss symbols: An alternative symbol system for the nonvocal prereading child. In G. C. Vanderheiden & K. Grilley (Eds.), *Nonvocal communication techniques and aids for the severely physically handicapped.* Baltimore: University Park Press, 1976.

Morasso, P., Sandini, G., Suetta, G., Tagliasco, V., Vernazza, T., & Zaccaria, R. Logos: A microprocessor-based device as a writing aid for the motor handicapped. *Medical and Biological Engineering and Computing,* 1978 *16,* 309-315.

Mowrer, O. H., & Mowrer, W. M. Enuresis: A method for its study and treatment. *American Journal of Orthopsychiatry,* 1938, *8,* 436-459.

Mulick, J. A., & Schroeder, S. R. Research relating to management of antisocial behavior in mentally retarded persons. *The Psychological Record,* 1980, *30,* 397-417.

Mulick, J. A., Hoyt, R., Rojahn, J., & Schroeder, S. R. Reduction of a "nervous habit" in a profoundly retarded youth by increasing toy play. *Journal of Behavior Therapy and Experimental; Psychiatry,* 1978, *9,* 381-385.

Murphy, R. J., & Doughty, N. R. Establishment of controlled arm movements in profoundly retarded students using response contingent vibratory stimulation. *American Journal of Mental Deficiency,* 1977, *82,* 212-216.

Myerson, L., & Michael, J. L. The measurement of sensory thresholds in exceptional children. *Monographs in Somatopshchology,* No. 4. Houston: University of Houston Press, 1960.

National Association of State Directors of Special Education. *Assistive devices for handicapped. A model and guide for a statewide delivery system.* Washington, D. C.: NASDSE, Inc., February 1980.

Nelson, R. O., Gibson, F. W., & Cutting D. S. Videotaped modeling: The development of three appropriate social responses in a mildly retarded child. *Mental Retardation,* 1973, *11,* 24-28.

O'Brien, F., Azrin, N. H., & Bugle, C. Training profoundly retarded children to stop crawling. *Journal of Applied Behavior Analysis,* 1972, *5,* 131-137.

Olson, K. A., & Rardin, M. W. Reducing hyperactive behavior in the classroom by photographed mediated self-modeling. In L. A. Hamerlynck (Ed.), *Behavioral systems for the developmentally disabled: I. School and family environments.* New York: Brunner/Mazel, 1979.

Olson, T. Return of the nonverbal. *Asha,* 1976, *18,* 823.
Orelove, F. P., & Hanify, C. D. Modifying school buildings for the severely handicapped: A school accessibility survey. *AAESPH Review,* 1979, *4,* 219-236.
Ottenbacher, K., Malter, R., & Weckwerth, L. A toilet seat arrangement for children with neuromoter dysfunction, *American Journal of Occupational Therapy,* 1979, *33,* 193.
Panyan, M. C., & Patterson, E. T. Teaching attendants the applied aspects of behavior modification. *Mental Retardation,* 1974, *12,* 30-32.
Park, G. C., Roy, O. Z., Warrick, A., & Cote, C. Mechanical pointer for use with handicapped children. *Medical and Biological Engineering and Computing,* 1979, *17,* 246-248.
Parsons, S., & Carrier, J. K., Jr. *A proposed language program based on David Premack's program for Sarah, a chimpanzee.* Paper presented at the meeting of the Oklahoma Speech and Hearing Association, Oklahoma City, April 1977.
Paskewitz, D. A. Biofeedback instrumentation: Soldering closed the loop. *American Psychologist,* 1975, *30,,* 371-378.
Patterson, F. R., Jones, R., Whittier, J., & Wright, M. A. A behavior modification technique for the hyperactive child. *Behavior Research and Therapy,* 1965, *2,* 217-226.
Popovitch, P. P., & Kilfoil, J. O. Custom handles of dental acrylic to promote self-sufficiency of handicapped patients. *Archives of Physical Medicine and Rehabilitation,* 1978, *59,* 440-442
Premack, D. A functional analysis of language. *Journal of Experimental Analysis of Behavior,* 1970, *14,* 107-125.
Premack, D. Language in chimpanzees. *Science,* 1971, *172,* 808-822.
Premack, A. J., & Premack, D. Teaching language to an ape. *Scientific American,* 1972, *277,* 92-99.
Premack, D., & Premack, A. J. Teaching visual language to apes and language-deficient persons. In R. L. Schiefelbusch & L. L. Lloyd (Eds.), *Language perspectives: Acquisition, retardation, and intervention.* Baltimore: University Park Press, 1974.
Prochaska, J., Smith, N., Marzilli, R., Colby, J., & Donovan, W. Remote-control aversive stimulation in the treatment of headbanging in a retarded child. *Journal of Behavior Therapy and Experimental Psychiatry,* 1974, *5,* 285-289.
Quilitch, H., & Risley, T. The effects of play materials on social play. *Journal of Applied Behavior Analysis,* 1973, *6,* 573-578.
Ramey, C. T., & Finkelstein, N. W. Contingent stimulation and infant competence. *Journal of Pediatric Psychology,* 1978, *3,* 89-96.
Reid, D. H., & Hurlbut, B. Teaching nonvocal communication skills to multi-handicapped retarded adults. *Journal of Applied Behavior Analysis,* 1977, *10,* 591-603.
Richardson, T. Sign language for the SMR and PMR. *Mental Retardation,* 1975, *13,* 17.
Rincover, A., Cook, R., Peoples, A., & Packard, D. Sensory extinction and sensory reinforcement principles for programming multiple adaptive behavior change. *Journal of Applied Behavior Analysis,* 1979, *12,* 221-233.
Risley, T. R. The effects and side effects of punishing the autistic behaviors of a deviant child. *Journal of Applied Behavior Analysis,* 1968, *1,* 21-34.
Roberts, B. Instructional materials for severely/profoundly retarded learners. *Mental Retardation,* 1976, *14,* 39-42.
Rojahn J. Validity and reliability of data from naturalistic observational studies: Problems and alternatives. *Behavioral Analysis and Modification,* 1978, *2,* 296-305.
Rojahn, J., & Wool, R. Inter-and intra-observer agreement as a function of explicit behavior definitions in direct observation. *Behavioral Analysis and Modification,* 1979, *3,* 211-228.
Rojahn, J., Mulick, J. A., McCoy, D., & Schroeder, S. R. Headbanging and self restraint in two

profoundly retarded adults. *Behavioral Analysis and Modification*, 1978, *2*, 185-196.

ROJAHN, J., SCHROEDER, S. R., & MULICK, J. A. Ecological assessment of self-protective devices in three profoundly retarded adults. *Journal of Autism and Developmental Disorders*. 1980, *10*, 59-66.

ROMANCZYK, R. G., COLLETTI, G., & KASHINSKY, W. Enhancing the delivery of educational and treatment services: Utilizing real-time micro computer technology on a programatic basis. *Proceedings of the Thirteenth Annual Gatlinburg Conference on Research in Mental Retardation and Developmental Disabilities*, 1980. (Summary)

RUBINSTEIN, R., & GOLDENBERG, E. P. *Using a computer message system for promoting reading and writing in a school for the deaf*. Paper presented at the Seventh Annual Conference on Systems and Devices for the Disabled. Houston, Texas, June 1978.

RUGH, J. D., & SCHWITZGEBEL, R. L. Instrumentation for behavioral assessment. In A. R. Ciminero, K. S. Calhoun, & H. E. Adams (Eds.), *Handbook of behavioral assessment*. New York: Wiley, 1977.

RUMBAUGH, D. M. *Language learning by a chimpanzee: The LANA project*. New York Academic Press, 1977.

RUMBAUGH, D. M., & SAVAGE-RUMBAUGH, E. S. Chimpanzee language research: Status and potential. *Behavioral Research Methods and Instrumentation*, 1978, *10*,, 119-131.

RUSSO, D. C., KOEGEL, R. L., & LOVAAS, O. I. A comparison of human and automated instruction of autistic children. *Journal of Abnormal Child Psychology*, 1978. *6*, 189-201.

RUSSO, D. C., BIRD, B. L., & MASEK, B. J. Assessment issues in behavioral medicine. *Behavioral Assessment*, 1980, *2*, 1-18.

SACKETT, G. P. (Ed.), *Observing behavior Vol. II: Data collection and analysis methods*. Baltimore: University Park Press, 1978.

SACKETT, G. P., STEPHENSON, E., & RUPPENTHAL, G. C. Digital data acquisition systems for observing behavior in laboratory and field settings. *Behavior Research Methods and Instrumentation*, 1973, *5*, 344-348.

SAMARAS, M. S., & BALL, T. S. Reinforcement of cooperation between profoundly retarded adults. *American Journal of Mental Deficiency*, 1975, *80*, 63-71.

SAYRE, J. M. Communication for the nonverbal cerebral palsied. *CP Review*, 1963, *24*, 3-8.

SCHINKE, S. P., & Smith, T. E. A videotape character generator for training and research. *Behavioral Engineering*, 1979, *5*, 101-104.

SCHMIDT, M. J., CARRIER, J. K., JR., & PARSONS, S. *Use of a non-speech mode for teaching language*. Paper presented at the American Speech and hearing Association Convention, Chicago, 1971.

SCHROEDER, S. Visual-motor performance and receptive language learning in a severely visually impaired profoundly retarded boy. *Research and the Retarded*, 1976, *3*, 1-13.

SCHROEDER, S. R. Automated transduction of sheltered workshop behaviors. *Journal of Applied Behavior Analysis*, 1972, *5*, 523-525. (a)

SCHROEDER, S. R. Parametric effects of reinforcement frequency, amount of reinforcement, and required response force on sheltered workshop behavior. *Journal of Applied Behavior Analysis*, 1972, *5*, 431-441.(b)

SCHROEDER, S. R., PETERSON, C. R., SOLOMON, L. J., & ARTLEY, L. J. EMG feedback and the contingent restraint of self-injuries behavior among the severely retarded: Two case illustrations. *Behavior Therapy*, 1977, *8*, 738-741.

SCHROEDER, S. R., ROJAHN, J., & MULICK, J. A. Ecobehavioral organization of developmental daycare for the chronically self-injurious. *Journal of Pediatric Psychology*, 1978, *3*, 81-88.

SCHROEDER, S. R., MULICK, J. A. & SCHROEDER, C. S. Management of severe behavior problems of the retarded. In N. R. Ellis (Ed.), *Handbook of mental deficiency, psychological theory and research* (2nd ed.). Hillsdale, N. J. Lawrence Erlbaum, 1979.

SCHROEDER, S. R., SCHROEDER, C. S., ROJAHN, J., & MULICK, J. A. Self-injurious behavior: An analysis of behavior management techniques. In J. L. Matson & J. R. McCartney (Eds.), *Handbook of behavior modification with the mentally retarded.* New York: Plenum Press, 1980.

SCHULMAN, J. L., & REISMAN, J. An objective measurement of hyperactivity. *American Journal of Mental Deficiency,* 1959, *64,* 455-456.

SCHULMAN, J. L., STEVENS, T. M., SURAN, B. G. KUPST, M. J., & NAUGHTON, M. J. Modification of activity level through biofeedback and operant conditioning. *Journal of Applied Behavioral Analysis,* 1978, *11,* 145-152.

SCHWITZGEBEL, R. K. Federal regulation of psychological devices: An example of medical political drift. In B. D. Sales (Ed.), *Psychology in the legal process.* New York: Spectrum, 1977.

SCHWITZGEBEL, R. K. Suggestions for the uses of psychological devices in accord with legal and ethical standards. *Professional Psychology,* 1978, *9,* 478-488.

SEIFERT, A. R., & LUBAR, J. R. Reduction of epileptic seizures through EEG biofeedback training. *Biological Psychology,* 1975, *3,* 157-184.

SIDMAN, M., & STODDARD, L. T. Programming perception and learning for retarded children. In N. R. Ellis (Ed.), *International review of research of mental retardation* (Vol. 2). New York: Academic Press, 1966.

SIEGEL, R. K. Stimulus selection and tracking during urination: Autoshaping directed behavior with toilet targets. *Journal of Applied Behavior Analysis,* 1977, *10,* 255-265.

SILVA, D. A., FRIEDLANDER, B. Z., & KNIGHT, M. S. Multihandicapped children's preferences for pure tones and speech stimuli as a method of assessing auditory capabilities. *American Journal of Mental Deficiency,* 1978, *83,* 20-36.

SILVERMAN, F. *Communication for the speechless.* Englewood Cliffs, N. J.: Prentice-Hall, 1980.

SKINNER, B. F., The science of learning and the art of teaching. *Harvard Educational Review,* 1954, *24,* 86-97.

SKINNER, B. F. A case history in scientific method. *American Psychologist,* 1956, *11,* 221-233.

SKINNER, B. F. Teaching machines. *Science,* 1958, *128,* 969-977.

SKINNER, B. F. Why we need teaching machines. *Harvard Educational Review,* 1961, *31,* 377-398.

STOLUROW, L. M. Automation in special education. *Exceptional Child,* 1960, *27,* 78-83. (a)

STOLUROW, L. M. Teaching machines and special education. *Educational and Psychological Measurement,* 1960, *20,* 429-448. (b)

STOLUROW, L. M. *Teaching by machine* (Cooperative Research Monograph No. 6, U. S. *Office of Education).* Washington, D. C.: U. S. Government Printing Office, 1961.

STRANG, H. R., & GEORGE, J. R., III. Clowning around to stop clowning around: A brief report on an automated approach to monitior, record, and control classroom noise. *Journal of Applied Behavior Analysis,* 1975, *8,* 471-474.

TASHJIAN, T. Contingent sensory stimulation and productive vocal responding in profoundly retarded/multiply handicapped children. *Proceedings of the Thirteenth Annual Gatlinburg Conference on Research in Mental Retardation and Developmental Disabilities,* 1980. (Summary)

TATE, B. An automated system for reinforcing and recording retardate work behavior. *Journal of Applied Behavior Analysis,* 1968, *1,* 347-348..

TILLER, J. E., MASEK, B. J., & WALKER, L. C. A system for monitoring and modifying noise levels in the classroom. *Behavioral Engineering,* 1974, *1,* 20-23.

TOUGH, J. H. HAWKINS, R. P., MCARTHUR, M. M., & VAN RAVENSWAAY, S. Modification of behavior by punishment: A new use for an old device. *Behavior Therapy.* 1971, *2,* 567-574.

TREFLER, E., WESTMORELAND, D., & BURLINGER, D. A feeding spatula for cerebral palsied children.

American Journal of the Occupational Therapy, 1977, *31,* 260-261.

TUCKER, D. J., & BERRY, G. W. Teaching severely multihandicapped students to put on their own hearing aids. *Journal of Applied Behavior Analysis,* 1980, *13,* 65-75.

VANDERHEIDEN, G. C. Introduction and framework. In G. C. Vanderheiden & K. Grilley (Eds.), *Nonvocal communication techniques and aids for the severely physically handicapped.* Baltimore: University Park Press, 1976. (a)

VANDERHEIDEN, G. C. *Synthesized speech as a communication mode for nonvocal severely handicapped individuals.* Madison, Wisonsin: Trace Research and Development Center for the Severely Communicatively Handicapped, 1976. (b)

VANDERHEIDEN, G. C., & GRILLEY, K., (Eds.). *Nonvocal communication techniques and aids for the severely physically handicapped.* Baltimore: University Park Press, 1976.

VANDERHEIDEN, G. C., & HARRIS-VANDERHEIDEN, D. Communication techniques and aids for the nonvocal severely handicapped. In L. L. Lloyd (Ed.), *Communication assessment and intervention strategies.* Baltimore: University Park Press, 1976.

VON GLASERSFELD, E. Signs, communication, and language. *Journal of Human Evolution,* 1974, *3,* 465-474.

VON GLASERSFELD, E. The yerkish language and its automatic parser. In D. M. Rumbaugh (Ed.) *Language learning by a chimpanzee: The LANA project.* New York: Academic Press, 1977.

WARRICK, A., NELSON, P. J., COSSALTER, J. G., COTE, C., MCGILLIS, J., & CHARBONNEAU, J. R. Synthesized speech as an aid to communicating language for the non-verbal. *Proceedings of the Workshop on Communication for the Non-verbal Physically Handicapped.* Ottawa, Canada, June 1977.

WEHMAN, P. (Ed.) *Recreation programming for developmentally disabled persons.* Baltimore: University Park Press, 1979.

WESTLING, D. L., & MURDEN, L. Self-help skills training: A review of operant studies. *The Journal of Special Education,* 1978, *12,* 253-283.

WHITMAN, T. L., & SCIBAK, J. W. Behavior modification with the severely and profoundly retarded. In N. R. Ellis (Ed.), *Handbook of mental deficiency, psychological theory and research* (2nd ed.). Hillsdale, N. J.: Lawrence Erlbaum, 1979.

WILBUR, R. L., CHANDLER, P. J., & CARPENTER, B. L. Modification of self-multilative behavior by aversive conditioning. *Behavioral Engineering,* 1974, *1,* 14-25.

WILSON, C. W., & HOPKINS, B. L. The effects of contingent music on the intensity of noise in junior high school economics classes. *Journal of Applied Behavior Analysis,* 1973, *6,* 269-275.

WOLFENSBERGER, W. (Ed.). *The principle of normalization in human services.* Toronto: National Institute on Mental Retardation, 1972.

WOOLDRIDGE, C., LEIPER, C., & OSTON, D. Biofeedback training of knee joint position of the cerebral-palsied child. *Physiotherapy of Canada,* 1976, *28,* 138-143.

WOOLDRIDGE, C. P., & RUSSELL, G. Head position training with the cerebral palsied child: An application of biofeedback techniques. *Archives of Physical Medicine and Rehabilitation,* 1976, *57,* 407-414.

WORKMAN, A. A. Communication system for the nonverbal severely disabled. *American Journal of Occupational Therapy,* 1979, *33,* 194-195.

ZUROMSKI, E. S., SMITH, N. F., & BROWN, R. *A simple electromechanical response device for multi-handicapped infants.* Paper presented at the 85th Annual Meeting of the American Psychological Association, San Francisco, September 1977.

14 Human Sexuality in the Mentally Retarded

WILLIAM D. MURPHY, EMILY M. COLEMAN, AND
GENE G. ABEL

INTRODUCTION

The purpose of this chapter is to review the current information on human sexuality and the mentally retarded. This is an area that has received increased attention in the last 5 to 6 years. At the present time the area is in its infancy in terms of a research base. Currently much of the writing is based on opinions, case reports, and surveys reflecting various aspects of sexual behavior in the mentally retarded.

The current chapter will try to summarize some of this information in six major sections. The first section will deal with the physical development, sexual behavior, and sex role development of the mentally retarded. The second section of the chapter will summarize the results of a survey we have conducted on the sexual attitudes and educational policies of residential institutions for the mentally retarded. This will provide baseline information on programs available throughout the country. The third section examines attitudes toward sex and the mentally retarded. The fourth section will summarize the information on sexual education in the mentally retarded. The fifth section considers the controversial area of sterilization in the mentally retarded, attempting to evaluate the data raised by both the opponents and proponents of sterilization. Finally, we will end the chapter with a discussion and case presentation of the mentally retarded sex offender.

Throughout the chapter, we will attempt to point out needed areas for research. The goal for this chapter will be to (1) provide the reader with basic background information in the area of human sexuality and the mentally

---

WILLIAM D. MURPHY AND EMILY M. COLEMAN • Deparment of Psychiatry, University of Tennessee Center for the Health Sciences, Memphis, Tennessee 38104.   GENE G. ABEL • Department of Psychiatry, Columbia University, New York, New York 10027.

retarded and (2) hopefully stimulate more controlled research on the number of extremely important issues that arise in this area.

Sexual Development and Behavior

The first section of this chapter will review some of the relevant information related to the physical, sex role development, and sexual behavior of the mentally retarded. Although not the focus in the present chapter, one should be aware that sexuality includes much more than an orgasmic response and the capability of such. As sexual behavior is part of interpersonal behavior (Evans, 1977; Pattullo, 1975), any program focusing on the sexuality of the mentally retarded must also focus on relationships and the retarded individual's knowledge of such relationships (Evans, 1977). Procedures for training of heterosocial skills (Curran, 1977) need to be adapted for use with mentally retarded, for without such skills, level of sexual development and sexual knowledge will find little outlet for appropriate expression. Data relevant to social skills training will be reviewed later in the chapter.

Physical Development

The biology of normal sexual development has been clearly presented in a number of sources (Kolodny, Masters, & Johnson, 1979; McCary, 1978). As is well known, at conception the X or Y chromosome from the male sperm is added to the X chromosome of the female to produce either the XX or XY genetic code for females or males, respectively. In the first weeks of fetal development, the male and female fetus are indistinguishable. After the first weeks, differentiation begins to occur at three levels: the external genitalia, the internal sex structures, and the brain (Kolodny *et al.*, 1979). This differentiation occurs as the result of circulating testosterone; without appropriate levels of testosterone at appropriate times, development will be in the female direction regardless of genetics (Kolodny *et al.*, 1979).

In the area of mental retardation, there are physiological abnormalities such as Klinefelter's syndrome and the Prader-Willie syndrome that are associated with mental retardation and disorders of sexual development (Becker, 1972; Hamilton, Scully, & Kliman, 1972; Johnson, Myhre, Ruvalcaba, Thuline, & Kelley, 1970; Kolodny *et al.*, 1979; Raboch, Mellan, & Starka, 1979; Zarate, Soria, Canales, Kastin, Schally, & Toledano, 1973, 1974). Geneticists or endocrinologists can probably list many more such disorders, but in terms of the total mentally retarded population, this group would be a small subpopulation. In designing sexual programs for the mentally retarded, it is important to be aware of this subpopulation and of appropriate treatments such as testosterone replacement in Klinefelter's syndrome (Becker, 1972; Johnson et al., 1970). The majority of the mentally retarded, however, will not have these clear genetic or endocrine dysfunctions (Meyerowitz, 1971), so we will therefore turn to presenting basic data on the mentally retarded where the contribution of genetic or endocrine factors is less clear.

One of the most frequently cited studies of sexual development is the Mosier, Grossman, and Dingman (1962) study of 613 (334 males and 279 females) mentally defective residents at Pacific State Hospital in California. Subjects were between the ages of 10 and 20, represented a variety of diagnostic categories, and had IQs across the range of mental retardation. The results indicated some delay in development of secondary sexual characteristics of mentally retarded males and females, with more delays found in the lower IQ groups. Rundle and Sylvester (1973) found that puberty in the mentally retarded is more diffuse and varied than in normal individuals. That is, with the mentally retarded population, there are a number of subpopulations, some showing normal sexual development and others showing delayed development.

In addition, Salerno, Park, and Giannini (1975) studied ovulation in 97 mentally retarded females. Again, these persons appeared delayed in secondary sex development, with the mongoloid group tending to be the most delayed when compared to the brain damaged or the undifferentiated group.

Basically the data indicate that as a group, the mentally retarded are delayed in sexual development, with delay more prominent in lower IQ and mongoloid groups. However, although the mentally retarded develop more slowly, the majority do develop sexually (Meyerowitz, 1971, Morgenstern, 1973b). In terms of programming, this suggests a number of considerations. First, the mentally retarded do mature sexually, albeit more slowly, and therefore need knowledge of human sexuality as does the rest of the population. Secondly, because of increased variability and the possibility of different subgroups existing within the mentally retarded population, sex education programs must take into account this variability. Not only must one consider the individual's age, IQ, and adaptive-behavior level, but also the level of physical development. Even though sex education is provided for a group of individuals similar in IQ and age for example, the individuals could vary widely in levels of physical/sexual development. Finally, regarding this last point, there is the need for the mentally retarded person to know that sexual development is variable, and that in most cases they will develop normally. As normalization proceeds and more mentally retarded children are brought into the mainstream, the possibility of social self-esteem problems will arise when the mentally retarded compare themselves sexually to their nonretarded peers. Most of us (at least the honest ones) may remember comparing our genitals, pubic hair or breast developments to peers, and some may remember embarrassment at finding less development than that of others around us. As the mentally retarded individuals are exposed to more nonretarded peers, they are likely to have the same experience and will need reassurance as to their own normalcy in this area.

Sex-Role Development

A second aspect of sexual development is sex-role development or the identification and adoption of socially defined modes of behavior based on sex. A number of authors have found that the mentally retarded differ from the nonretarded in terms of sexual identification, as measured by the sex of the first person drawn on the Draw-a-Person test (Fisher, 1960, 1961; Morgenstern, 1973b). For males, Fisher (1960) found no difference for mentally retarded or nonretarded children, but adult male retarded persons drew the male figure less frequently than the nonretarded adults. For females, the opposite was true. The authors suggested that differences in sexual identification may lead to difficulties in other areas of sexual development. However, Morgenstern (1973b) found in a test developed to measure sex-role recognition that although some delay was observed, this became progressively less as the mentally retarded individual became older. These data would suggest that with the type of measure used in this study, these individuals do learn "appropriate" sex-role behavior.

A final study (Biller & Borstelmann, 1965) compared male to female mentally retarded individuals across three aspects of sexual development: (1) sexual identification as measured by the Draw-a-Person test, (2) sex-role preference measured by a variant of the IT Procedure (Clark, 1963), and (3) sex-role adoption judged via a rating scale which measured masculine behavior and was completed by cottage parents. Results indicated reliable sex differences for the Draw-a-Person test and the IT Procedure, with males showing male identification and male-role preference, and females showing female identification and female-role preference. No differences were found between male and female mentally retarded subjects on the rating scale of sex-role adoption. The authors concluded that this measure assessed social adaptation rather than sex-role adoption.

A number of words of caution are needed in interpreting the above data. First, the measures used are somewhat questionable, and the concept being measured (sex-role development) is one that is undergoing continual cultural redefinition Abelson (1977) has suggested that programs are needed to focus awareness of who is male and female. This seems very appropriate, but there should be concern that in designing such programs we do not include and reinforce sexual stereotypes. Biller and Borstelmann's (1965) observation that their measure of sex-role adoption actually measured social adaptation is an example of this. Possibly the mentally retarded person's deficit in sex-role development is an asset that should be reinforced rather than changed. The mentally retarded citizen, because of cognitive and social deficits, needs as many options open as possible and does not need options closed because they do not fit cultural definitions of sex role.

Sexual Behavior

In considering human sexuality in the mentally retarded, it is valuable to have some baseline data to determine what the mentally retarded individual's sexual behavior is, if such behavior differs from the nonretarded, and if so, for what reasons. Some basic data in this area have been presented by Gebhard (1973) concerning 84 white males with IQs between 31 and 70 drawn from the files of the Institute for Sex Research. It should be noted that the majority of these cases were interviewed while in penal institutions or other institutional settings. The comparison group was 477 white males with no history of institutionalization or criminal behavior.

It is difficult to summarize all the data presented by Gebhard (1973), and we refer the reader to the original publication for details. The two findings that are important for the current discussion are (1) the mentally retarded men in this study frequently engaged in sexual behavior, and (2) that institutionalization is the major factor effecting such involvement. For example, Gebhard (1973) found that in the mentally retarded sample, 77% had engaged in heterosexual petting, and 61% had engaged in coitus. This compared to a 90% and 80% frequency respectively for the control group. However, when only those mentally retarded individuals who had spent less than one quarter of their postpubertal life in institutions were investigated, the differences between the controls and the mentally retarded became nonexistent. Homosexual behavior followed the same pattern, with institutionalization being the major factor effecting this behavior.

Additional data on reported sexual behavior in institutions come from Mulhern (1975), and Moore, Thuline, and Capes (1968). Mulhern presents survey data from a questionnaire mailed to 82 institutions for the mentally retarded, with a return rate of 84%. Of interest to this section are the data for occurrence of 11 sexual behaviors ranging from masturbation through heterosexual intercourse to homosexual behavior. Eighty-one percent of the respondents reported that masturbation occurred in their institutions, 70% reported that heterosexual intercourse occurs, 75% reported that homosexual behavior between males occurs, and 69% reported that homosexual behavior between females occurs. The remainder of the behaviors were all reported to be occurring by over 70% of the institutions, with the exception of prolonged kissing in public and petting in public which were rated as occurring by only 48% of the respondents. Of interest is the finding of a discrepancy between what was rated as occurring, and what was permitted by institutional rules. Although masturbation was permitted by 70% of the institutions, a much smaller percentage reported that other sexual behaviors, such as heterosexual intercourse (8%), male homosexuality (9%), or female homosexuality (8%) were allowed. Although this type of survey data does not provide a reliable frequency of occurrence, it does suggest that sexual behavior is occurring in institutions, whether it is permitted or not.

Moore et al., (1968) present one of the few comparisons of various diagnostic categories of the mentally retarded in terms of sexual behavior. Moore et al., compared 536 mongoloid to 536 nonmongoloid retarded persons in terms of a number of "maladaptive behaviors." Sexual behaviors included were homosexual activity, heterosexual activity, exhibitionism, and child molestation. No differences were found between the groups in this institutional study. This is interesting in that the mongoloids are found to be delayed in sexual development physically, but apparently not delayed in terms of their sexual behavior, although age of testing may be a factor.

A final institutional study that sheds some light on the often raised question as to the mentally retarded person's ability to control their sexual behavior comes from Edgerton and Dingman (1964). These authors made a naturalistic study of "dating" behavior of mentally retarded individuals at Pacific State Hospital. Campus passes which gave hundreds of patients unsupervised access to large areas of the hospital were allowed. During a 1-year period, the authors made observations (many nonobtrusive and unknown to the individuals) of the interactions between male and female patients. One of the first observations was the skills the individuals displayed in making complex arrangements for private meetings which were considered beyond their intellectual capacity compared to other areas of their functioning.

The second observation was that the individuals adhered to "proper rules of conduct" on dates, and showed little indication of lack of impulse control. Sexual behavior was limited almost totally to necking and petting although because of lack of supervision any sexual behavior would have been possible. This report seems to suggest that the mentally retarded are capable of complex social interactions and seem to adhere to the rules governing the society in which they live. This finding is in contrast to continuing stereotypes suggesting that the mentally retarded have little impulse control.

When moving from the institutional setting to the community setting, we could find little data to provide any adequate baseline of sexual practices for the mentally retarded. Gebhard's data would suggest that, if anything, sexual behavior is more frequent in the community, given that institutionalization suppressed various sexual behaviors. Carruth (1973) reports anecdotal data on interviews with staff members of halfway houses, but this provides little data on what the actual sexual behavior of the mentally retarded persons was in the community. This area is one requiring additional research.

Literature reviewed in this section suggests that the majority of the mentally retarded develop adult sexual capabilities and feelings as do most nonretarded adults, and that most mentally retarded persons are acting on their sexual capabilities. It is also clear that for many years sexuality among this group was a taboo subject (Money, 1973), and many mentally retarded citizens were not given adequate information regarding their own sexuality. Currently some of these biases are changing. The remainder of the chapter will be devoted to the current status of sexuality in the mentally retarded.

A Survey of Sexual Attitudes and Educational Policies

In order to gain a more accurate idea of the current status of sex education and attitudes toward sexuality in facilities for the mentally retarded, questionnaires were sent to institutions selected from the 1979 Directory of Inpatient Facilities for the Mentally Retarded. Information was obtained on the existence and extent of sex education programs, as well as attitudes and policies toward contraception, masturbation, and homosexual and heterosexual activities of the mentally retarded. The results of this survey are summarized here (Coleman & Murphy, 1980). Further details may be obtained from the authors. The number of returned and completed questionnaires was 131, a response rate of approximately 40%. The age range of the mentally retarded residents was from newborn to 98 years old, with a mean age of 34 years. The IQ range included all five mental retardation categories (profound through borderline) with 44%, reporting patients in all categories, I–V.

Eighty-four percent of the respondents reported providing a sex education program. Most programs (58%) were implemented and maintained by staff from various disciplines, including nurses, social workers, chaplains and educational staff. Physicians and psychologists were usually not involved. The nursing staff was most often the active group. Topics covered in the sex education programs varied widely. All programs included information on anatomy and physiology, and over half (57%) also considered descriptions of various sexual activities, correction of common sexual myths, contraceptive information, family planning, and information regarding reproduction, masturbation, and homosexuality. The remaining programs dealt with only a few of the above subjects or were considerably expanded by discussing examining body awareness and image, self-care and grooming, relationship skills, lifestyles, sex roles, forced sexual encounters, decision-making, sexual responsibility, venereal disease, self-concept, and the effects of drugs on sexual responding.

Twenty-four percent reported encountering no problems at all in instituting the sex education programs. The most frequent difficulty was an adverse reaction from the staff, although several respondents noted that this was a minimal negative reaction and/or was on the part of only a few staff members. In spite of these initial difficulties, 78% of the respondents reported no negative side effects due to the sex education program. None reported an increase in inappropriate sexual activity, although one unwanted pregnancy was reported. Thirteen percent reported dissent among staff which seems to corroborate the report of initial adverse reaction from staff. The remainder noted occasional incidents of inappropriate discussion of sexual activity during academic class, or misunderstanding of material. The need to consider staff reaction, especially if the sex education program is simply tacked on without discussion to an overly long list of tasks, is crucial.

Ninety-five percent of the facilities reported providing social activities (dances, supervised dating, etc.) encouraging heterosexual interactions. However, only 66% provided contraceptive counseling, and only 15% provided private areas for sexual activity. One respondent felt that if the mentally retarded client was smart enough to find a private place for sex, someone should be looking for alternative living arrangements in the community for the person. In general, policies toward contraception for the mentally retarded seem to be very haphazard. The most frequent contraceptive alternative seemed to be giving "the pill" to women known to be sexually active.

Sexual acting out appears to be relatively infrequent among this population. Thirty-six percent never or rarely act out sexually; 56% sometimes act out sexually, and 8% usually or always act out sexually. Unfortunately, no attempt was made in the questionnaire to define "acting out." A variety of behaviors from private masturbation to rape could have been assumed under the term.

Finally, attitudes toward the sexuality of the mentally retarded were explored in the questionnaire. Respondents rated their approval/disapproval of sex education for the mentally retarded on a 5-point Lickert scale, and their attitudes toward four different sexual activities (masturbation, heterosexual petting, intercourse, and homosexual behavior) conducted in private by the mentally retarded individual.

As one would expect, the most favorable attitude was towards sex education for the mentally retarded, with 75% of the respondents strongly approving. Interestingly, masturbation was ranked a close second, with 88% somewhat strongly or strongly approving, compared to 89% somewhat strongly or strongly approving of sex education. Regarding sexual activity involving others (i.e., heterosexual petting and intercourse), however, the approval rate dropped sharply and the disapproval rate increased, until equal amounts of approval and disapproval were expressed regarding homosexual behavior (23% strongly disapproved of homosexual behavior, and 23% strongly approved).

Attitudes toward marriage of the mentally retarded were considered in a questionnaire item borrowed from Mulhern (1975). The majority of respondents (60%) felt that the mentally retarded should be permitted to marry and have children. Often qualifications were added however. For example, one respondent wrote that the mentally retarded should be permitted to marry and have children, if they have good, high level jobs, personal skills, and a sense of responsibility. If this is not the case and birth control methods cannot be monitored, then the respondent felt the mentally retarded should be permitted to marry contingent on sterilization. Only 2% felt that the mentally retarded should not be permitted to marry, and 8% felt that marriage should be contingent on sterilization for the mentally retarded. Thirty percent of the respondents felt marriage should be contingent on use of other birth control methods.

Most respondents felt their responses required qualification due to the age, degree of social ability, or IQ levels of those involved. Factors identified as important included involvement of the resident in social groups (peer and family), determination of informed consent in sexual activity with other residents, consideration of the level of maturity and acceptance of responsibility in relation to IQ and social ability. Many emphasized that each situation requires an individual determination made by an interdisciplinary treatment team. One respondent stated "Physician, social worker, psychologist, and nurse must always be involved, and mutual consensus *must* be reached."

In reviewing the questionnaire results, an inconsistency arises. While the majority of the responding residential facilities for the mentally retarded strongly approved of sex education for the mentally retarded, and in fact provided sex education, acts other than masturbation by the mentally retarded were disapproved of, and in many cases forbidden. Obviously, mixed messages are being sent if on one hand, sexuality is taught to be a natural part of oneself and on the other hand, sexual behavior is denied even when birth control precautions and responsible decision-making have been considered. Administration and staff probably fear reprisal from parents, guardians and the community for acknowledging the sexuality of the mentally retarded. However, ignoring or denying a complex situation has not been an adequate solution. Under such circumstances, sexuality can easily become distorted or exploitive. Helping and allowing a mentally retarded person decide if, how, when, where and with whom to have sex is not easy. Forcing sexual activities underground does not make it easier.

Attitudes toward Sexuality

Attitudes are a major determinant of behavior and a major factor in decision-making. The attitudes toward sexuality of the parents and caretakers of the mentally retarded, as well as the mentally retarded themselves, affect institutional programming, rules and regulations, and essentially, the sexual behavior of the mentally retarded. In this section, we will review the major studies and findings regarding the attitudes of the mentally retarded and of their parents and caretakers.

Parental Attitudes

The initial research on attitudes toward sexuality of the mentally retarded concerned mostly the parents of the mentally retarded. Their role was becoming increasingly apparent in terms of education and influence upon the sexuality of their mentally retarded children. The overall stressful impact of a child's deficiency on both the mother and the father has been documented (Cummings, Bayley, & Rice, 1966; Cummings, 1976; Grebler, 1952). In addition to this frustration of raising a mentally retarded child, parents feel particularly uncomfortable when having to deal with their child's sexuality. Many researchers have noticed the discomfort parents feel regarding sex education of their mentally retarded children (Alcorn, 1974; Dupras & Tremblay, 1976; Fisher & Krajicek, 1974; Goodman, Budner, & Lesh, 1971; Hall, Morris, & Barker, 1973; Hammer, Wright, & Jensen, 1967; Turchin, 1974; Turner, 1970). This discomfort often results in an avoidance of sex education in the home and a preference for sex education to be given outside of the home. These studies also seem to indicate that parents focus first on the unavoidable, that is care and cleanliness of body, public masturbation and that parents' provision of sex education is then confined primarily to facts about birth. Interestingly, the sexist double standard appears omnipresent, and affects the mentally retarded too. For example, in Turchin's study (1974), the mothers felt masturbation was more appropriate for their sons than for their daughters.

Obviously, facing the sexuality of their mentally retarded children is a dilemma for parents. Personal sexual difficulties, a lack of knowledge regarding sexuality, and anxiety in discussing sexuality, as well as the real and imagined dangers facing their children can be involved (L. Goodman, 1973). Goodman describes various parental responses to a mentally retarded child's sexuality. He provides examples of a realistic sophisticated response from secure well adjusted families as well as a desexualizing response in which the child's sexuality is simply ignored. Other possibilities are the "pseudo enlightened response," "the over sexualized response," and "the sex-is-sinful response." The most frequently occurring category of response is some variation of the honest "I don't know." Goodman notes that the most frequently raised specific parental questions concern the limited judgment of the mentally retarded prism in evaluating sexual opportunity, vulnerability to seduction, promiscuity, homosexuality, and excessive masturbation. While these fears may often be unfounded, and preventive measures taken are often over-reactive, the anxiety of parents is real. Goodman suggests utilizing factual material, clarification and interpretation to assist parents in dealing with their child's sexuality.

Attitudes of the Mentally Retarded

More recently, the attitudes of the mentally retarded individuals themselves have been studied. Surveys conducted in this area suggest many parallels and similar dynamics between the normal population and the mentally retarded. For example, there appears to be a wide range of comprehension and of attitudes toward sexuality among the mentally retarded (Edmonson & Wish, 1975; Hall, Morris, & Barker, 1973; Hall & Morris, 1976). As in the normal population, this variability is affected by experience. For instance, in Hall and Morris's study (1976), those who lived in coed quarters tended to have higher sex knowledge scores.

The effects of the double standard as well as the increased options of community living are reflected in Edmonson's study (Edmonson, McCombs, & Wish, 1979). Mentally retarded women in the community had the most conservative attitudes on dating, marriage, intercourse, pregnancy, intimacy, and alcohol and drugs. Mentally retarded men in the community had the most liberal attitudes on dating, intimacy, intercourse, and masturbation. Following traditional patterns, it seems that the males had the most to gain from a liberal sexual attitude while the women felt they had the most to lose. Most of the institutional residents wanted to get married, whereas most of the community residents were neutral about marriage. Marriage may seem more a mark of success and prestige to the institutionalized who are denied status in terms of career, money, children, etc. Those in the community may be more able to achieve a sense of self-respect through means other than marriage.

Unfortunately, the mentally retarded seem to have absorbed many of the negative attitudes toward sexuality of those around them. For instance, in an earlier study by Edmonson and Wish (1975), over half of the 18 moderately mentally retarded men interviewed felt that masturbation (an activity usually frowned on in institutions) was wrong on first questioning. Given the frequency of masturbation, this attitude seems guaranteed to produce guilt. Robinson (1978) provides an example of the mentally retarded person learning inappropriate restrictive attitudes from the nonretarded. In his study, 32 mentally retarded young mothers were found to have significantly more protective controlling and punitive attitudes toward their children than a control group of mothers who had completed two or more years of college. Interestingly, the mentally retarded mothers regarded their own mothers as even more protective, controlling, and punitive than they were. Robinson concludes that programs for mentally retarded youngsters should place more emphasis on child-rearing and family life in order to help counteract inappropriate attitudes that mentally retarded children learn from their own parents.

Attitudes of Caretakers

The attitudes of caretakers of the mentally retarded are also important. In discussing the management of the sexuality of the mentally retarded in institutions, Hirayama (1979) notes that sexuality is one of the most sensitive and troublesome issues faced by institutional personnel. The lack of consensus among institutional staff and administrators, the lack of clear guidelines and policies, the lack of institutional directions, and the lack of knowledge about the sexuality of the mentally retarded "not only perpetuate the existing confusion but also contribute to continuous deprivation of the sexuality of the mentally retarded." A major obstacle is the attitudes of administrators, staff and parents. Myths describing the mentally retarded as oversexed, undersexed, and/or lacking control die hard. Hirayama concluded that sex education for the mentally retarded is essential but not sufficient alone because the problems concerning sexuality of the mentally retarded lie in the attitudes of the people around the mentally retarded rather than in the mentally retarded persons themselves. This lack of consensus and restrictive attitude regarding sexuality is reflected in both studies by Deisher (1973) and Mitchell, Doctor, and Butler (1978). Not only are these restrictive attitudes different than those voiced by academicians, but also the caretakers' attitudes seem to be more restrictive than that of the general population (Mitchell et al., 1978; McEwen, 1977).

In summary, in reviewing the information on the attitudes of the parents of the mentally retarded, of the mentally retarded themselves, and of the caretakers of the mentally retarded, one finds common elements of frustration, ignorance, and repression toward the sexuality of the mentally retarded. Given this attitudinal framework, the often noted research bias in the literature described in subsequent sections of this chapter is more understandable.

Sex Education

In this section of the chapter, the literature demonstrating the need for sex education of the mentally retarded will be described and several specific sex education programs will be considered in more detail. The limited number of actual studies on sex education and on the related area of social skills of the mentally retarded are then outlined. Finally, practical suggestions for teachers and parents and some relevant resource materials on sex education of the mentally retarded are given.

Demonstrated Need

Almost as emotionally charged as the issues of marriage and sterilization for the mentally retarded is the subject of sex education (Sengstock & Vergasor, 1970). Perhaps this is because "opponents" of sex education for the mentally retarded, and even those undecided parents, administration officials, school staff, etc., fear that sex education will lead to sexual activity, marriage, and the need for sterilization. Even sex education for intellectually normal children sparks a fear that open discussion of sex will lead to a society "overwhelmed by a tide of uncontrollable sexual behavior and experimentation" (Gendel, 1966). In spite of the fact, or perhaps because of the fact, that it is such an emotionally related issue, writers have been prolific in this area, although controlled data have been lacking (Balester, 1972).

In contrast, the proponents of sex education emphasize the rights of the mentally retarded to sexual expression and the role of sex education in the normalization process (Bass, 1974a,b; Delp, 1972; Friedman, 1972; Gordon, 1972; Gupta & Singh, 1973; Hall & Sawyer, 1978; Perske, 1973). Friedman (1972) notes that the mentally retarded have little opportunity to satisfy their sexual needs without exploitation or punishment from authorities. To defend ourselves against these issues, we have denied the need of the mentally retarded to act sexually or questioned their ability to function in normal roles. Kempton (1975) feels that the negative effects of a sex education program have been exaggerated and that teachers should be prepared for a few loud protests and then analyze the motivations behind them.

Shindell (1975) agrees, stating that no normalization process can be complete or successful without consideration of its socialization component. Further, Shindell feels the mentally retarded are a particularly vulnerable group because of the nature of their handicap. Without exposure to information and training for sexually appropriate behavior, the mentally retarded often respond inappropriately to attention, give affection without discrimination, and do whatever is requested of them without questioning. They are more likely to believe myths because of difficulty in distinguishing what is real and what is not. Due to the restrictions of an institutional environment, or even differential treatment in the home, the mentally retarded do not have opportunities as normal children do to validate their information and thereby develop control of sexual needs and appropriate social skills through peer group activities.

As Shindell (1975) points out, normalization must include socialization skills and sexual behavior as part of the interpersonal/social behaviors. Shukla and Khoche (1974) and Richardson (1978) have shown in surveys that mentally retarded citizens have as much or more difficulty in emotional and/or interpersonal areas of their lives as they do with housekeeping or job skills. Furthermore, Rosen, Floor, Baxter, Horowitz, and Weber (1971) have shown that ⅓ of a group of 49 previously institutionalized women were having major sociosexual problems outside the institution which led to serious adjustment problems. It was also found that those who had sexual problems outside the institution were having similar problems when institutionalized. It is clear that training programs need to include sociosexual education along with more traditional training in job and home care skills.

A final reason for sex education programs is simply that the mentally retarded citizen is engaging in sexual activity and surveys to date suggest that they do not have the information to make informed decisions regarding their sexuality (Demery, 1978; Fisher & Krajicek, 1974; Hammer, Wright, & Jensen, 1967). Continued denial of the existence of sexuality in the mentally retarded has not and will not in the future change the existence of sexual activity. It seems time to accept this act and provide the information needed by the mentally retarded so that they can direct their own sexual behavior.

Actual Programs

The following is by no means an exhaustive review of the sex education programs of the mentally retarded. It is rather an attempt to describe a few programs exemplifying various approaches and goals of sex education.

Examining actual sex education programs for the mentally retarded, one sees a progression from a tentative limited approach seemingly designed to benefit the institution involved, rather than giving the mentally retarded individual a more global and liberal approach to deal with emotional and physical needs. To illustrate this progression, two programs presented in the literature will be described.

In 1957, Kratter and Thorne described an "experimental" program at Caswell Training School, State School for Exceptional Children, Kingston, North Carolina. Given the sexually repressive climate of the time, Kratter and Thorne are to be congratulated for their courage and persistence in initiating a sex education program for the mentally retarded. This conservative climate is reflected however in their implied goals and limited scope of the program. For example, anatomical differences were not discussed but personal hygiene was. The institutional staff obviously benefitted from the girls' handling of menstruation, but perhaps fear of ensuing sexual activity prevented discussion of such basic information as anatomical differences in the sexes. The educators seemed to be willing to push heterosexuality in order to eliminate "regression" to homosexuality and masturbation. But even this allowance of heterosexuality was very guarded. Topics emphasized the limitations and tremendous responsibilities of parenthood and the restrictions of society regarding sexual attractions. One teacher commented that it was difficult for the mentally retarded persons to understand why kissing and holding hands was all right, but yet they could not do it. This is difficult for the present authors to understand also.

The authors noted that typical reactions among the students to the program were embarrassment, shyness, blushing, obvious discomfort, resentment, and refusal to listen, although a few students were open and frank. The authors also provided a reasonable explanation of this reaction on the basis of the former restrictive attitude of the institution, in which kissing was almost regarded as "an unforgiveable sin." The authors felt that much of the usual heterosexual behavior that would normally have occurred in society was in the institution replaced by an exaggeration of fantasy about sexual matters and by secret discussion on sexual matters with same-sex groups. Anxiety was always present about punishment that would be forthcoming should the nature of these discussions become known to the house parent. Given this history, it is certainly understandable that both the students and the teachers would be somewhat wary and uncomfortable initiating sexual topics in the classroom.

In spite of these fears and anxieties, one can already see this program progressing from its initially limited stage to a more involved one. The authors themselves suggested more intensive instruction of teachers, and progressive development of programs from age 10 and up. As early as several months after this initial report, another appeared (Thorne, 1957) again describing this program. The author reported being "very pleased" with results to date. At this time no adverse reports of student reactions were forthcoming. Indeed many students were reported eager to learn and very appreciative. No pre-post data are offered, however. Another index of change is that by this date, discussion of anatomical differences was included in the program as well as training in personal grooming and hygiene.

An example of a sex education program at the other end of the spectrum is a program offered at Camp Kohai, a summer camp in Ontario for mentally retarded children with learning disabilities and behavioral difficulties (Lebrun & Hutchinson, 1977). The fact that the program is offered in a camp setting seems significant since camps are not usually expected to provide sex education programs while residential settings would seem to be required to do so. In addition to formal sex-education classes, the children at the camp begin sex education informally by exploring their senses. Simone Lebrun, the codirector of Camp Kohai, explains that the educators first focus on the individual's sense of touch. The children begin by touching their own bodies, for example, touching their arm in different ways by pressing softer or harder, and by making circles. After the children feel comfortable about touching themselves, they move on to touching others through gentle games. This acceptance and encouragement of their senses is certainly in contrast to earlier programs such as the one at Caswell in which touching of both self and others was actually punished rather than encouraged. Lebrun considers it "old fashioned" to teach human sexuality by simply giving biological and factual information. She considers this approach unnecessarily clinical. The children had information and facts which were useless because the facts were not related to feelings.

One can see from these two descriptive extremes of sex education programs that there is a need to provide factual information on the individual's level and to encourage the exploration of the subject's body, senses, and self-concept.

Programs have also been designed to teach specific issues of sex education, that is, contraception (Fiedler & Tyler, 1975; David, Smith, & Friedman, 1976), marriage education (Abbott & Ladd, 1970; Hartman & Hynes, 1975), social skills (Humphreys, Forehand, Cheney, & Adams, 1977), menstrual hygiene (Pattullo & Barnard, 1968), and teacher training (Kempton, 1972; Johnson & Magarick, 1972). This seems a beneficial expansion of sex education programs for those individuals needing more detailed information or practice in certain areas. Programs and studies considering contraception for the mentally retarded are presented in the section on sterilization and social skills studies are considered separately later in this same section.

One example of a specific program that makes excellent use of behavioral principles is presented by Pattullo and Barnard (1968). Pattullo and Barnard analyzed the components of menstrual hygiene into individual concrete steps that can be consistently reinforced or shaped step-by-step. The mother is identified as a key person in teaching menstrual hygiene since one of the difficulties in teaching menstrual hygiene is that menstruation does not occur as frequently as elimination for instance. The role of the nurse and teacher are also instrumental as role models for the mother in order to demonstrate consistency with the child. Pattullo and Barnard provide a detailed report of the learning experience of Olga, a 14-year-old severely mentally retarded child who was able to learn to manage menstrual hygiene. They also interviewed 25 mothers whose daughters were mentally retarded and had reached menarche. The interviews revealed some common problems and helpful suggestions. At times, the daughters rejected menstruation because they did not understand its physiology. Some attempted to remove the sanitary pad as soon as it was stained, showed anger and sullenness on observing the flow, and some persistently sat on the toilet in an attempt to evacuate the sanitary pad. Mothers could be helpful in conveying the message that menstruation is a universal female experience by permitting their daughters to observe them at menstrual grooming. Pattullo and Barnard also suggest that the mothers avoid making demands on their daughters at menstruation, since irritability and fatigue were observed frequently.

Pattullo and Barnard's program demonstrates that through careful use of learning principles the mentally retarded are able to manage a bodily function. One criticism of this program however, is a possible squeamishness on the authors' part to allow the mentally retarded to actually explore and become familiar with their bodies. One wonders why the authors insist on sanitary napkins rather than tampons. Many women use tampons today and this may very well be an easier method to teach than sanitary napkins. The possibility that the authors are wary of the mentally retarded girls becoming aware of their bodies is reinforced by the author's description of "modesty training."

They suggested the child be told to keep her knees together when she sits, keep her blouse buttoned and her skirt down, not put her arms around boys, etc. These directions seem understandable, but in teaching individuals what is appropriate and inappropriate regarding their bodies and behaviors, we should be careful not to teach them to be ashamed of their bodies.

Studies of the Results of Sex Education

Given the previously noted furor and debate over the results of sex education, few studies available on the subject provide valuable information.

Initial evidence of the effectiveness and usefulness of sex education for the handicapped population comes from a study by Bloom (1969). Her subjects were not mentally retarded, but psychiatrically disabled ($n = 33$) and physically disabled ($n = 31$). These 16-to-19-year-old high school students were from low or lower-middle socioeconomic class in New York City. Obviously this is a select group, and caution should be used in generalizing results. However, elements in these subjects' backgrounds such as stimulus deprivation, a lack of consensual validation of ideas by peers, and anxiety regarding sexual areas seem to be identical with the problems experienced by mentally retarded children. Both groups showed a highly significant increase in sexual knowledge after the course. The physically disabled group showed no significant difference in anxiety measures at the end of the course. However, the emotionally disturbed group had a significant decrease on the Taylor Manifest Anxiety Scale. The authors speculate that this difference may be the result of the routine discussions of bodily functions and the normal exposure of the body in hospital settings that children with physical disabilities may be accustomed to. The emotionally disturbed children may have had more anxiety about bodily functions as a result of the lack of consensual validation from peers and adults through isolation. The authors conclude that severely physically and emotionally disabled adolescents want and can learn from a course in sex education. Additionally, a course in sex education does not appear to be anxiety producing to any harmful extent, and in fact reduced anxiety among the emotionally disturbed youngsters.

Bennett, Vockell, and Vockell (1972) looked at the effect of a sex education program on nine educable mentally retarded women between the ages of 17 and 23. Interestingly, most of the women had already been involved in sexual activity socially. For example, six had "steady boyfriends." The women attended 12 classes altogether (3 classes per week for 4 weeks). The women were administered the Sex Information Inventory for girls as a pretest and posttest.

Although no actual data are presented, the authors state that knowledge regarding sexual terminology, menstruation, birth control, and sexual intercourse increased considerably on the posttest. Contrary to the teachers' wishes and expectations, the women reported a greater permissiveness toward premarital sex as well as a greater reluctance to touch vaginal areas (even if in private) after completion of the course. The authors believe that this greater permissiveness toward premarital sex may have been the result of one of the women in the group voicing strongly the opinion that sexual intercourse was a good idea for two people who were in love. Regarding the reluctance to touch the vaginal area, the authors speculate that this could possibly have been a result of focusing attention on an issue that had not previously occurred to the mentally retarded women.

As a result of the course, the authors make specific suggestions. First, teaching basic facts to the class as a whole is not effective. For example, in this class those who had previous knowledge regarding venereal disease learned more, while those who did not know anything about venereal disease did not subsequently learn anything about it through the course. The authors suggest giving a pretest and providing specific instructions for those who show shortcomings in specific areas on a pretest. Secondly, the authors suggest that in teaching the student to make accurate discriminations, as many examples as possible of both positive and negative distinguishing characteristics should be given. For example, over emphasis on a single characteristic, such as female breasts to distinguish women should be avoided since there are also additional cues available. Appropriate discrimination training would also seem essential in dealing with touching the vaginal area in private versus in public. Finally, the authors advise a more intensive program to deal with sexual exploitation. The girls showed a greater willingness on the posttest to discuss exploitation by a strange man with the teacher or an adult than on the pretest. However, over half of the women stated that they would still keep it a secret if a strange man put his hand on her breast. Finally, regarding the unexpected increased preference for premarital sex, the authors suggest introducing prestigious models who would verbalize and exhibit the desired behavior (that is, no premarital sex). This would seem effective in influencing the group's opinion in that direction, but it also seems to be "stacking the deck" and denying the women the process of decision-making and the right to sexual expression.

Finally, one study was uncovered which examined the effects of a pilot sexuality-training workshop for staff at an institution for the mentally retarded (Wilson & Baldwin, 1976). The experimental group consisted of 32 volunteers for the workshop. The comparison group was made up of 32 selected staff members who did not volunteer to participate in the workshop. Although the experimental group was significantly younger than the comparison group, no differences were found between groups on general or educational level. Pretest results on a questionnaire developed by the authors to assess the subjects' knowledge and attitudes toward sexuality indicated that participants volunteering for the workshop were not more knowledgeable about human sexuality than the nonparticipants. However, the participants did demonstrate more tolerant attitudes about sexuality than nonparticipants on the pretest. Additionally, the posttest results of the experimental group indicated improved knowledge regarding sexuality and modified attitudes regarding sexuality. In the comparison group, no significant changes from pretest to posttest were found. The authors caution against one potential effect of voluntary training: the staff may become polarized into factions with differing levels of tolerance towards sexuality, subsequently interfering with positive institutional change.

Social Skills Studies

The goals and issues of sex education and social skills are closely interwoven. An essential part of sex education is learning how to cope socially and sexually with others. One of the goals usually envisioned in sex education is sexual acceptance and satisfaction. Often this involves delicate interactions with others.

More studies are available on the effectiveness of social skills training and assertiveness training for the mentally retarded than on the effectiveness of sex education for these persons. Perhaps this is due to a history of the application of learning principles to social competence skills, whereas this history is not evident in sex education. There are more studies available in this area than in the area of sex education and the studies are generally more adequately controlled.

Many operant training programs have successfully dealt with social impairment by training the mentally retarded in socially appropriate communication (Davis, 1978; Humphreys, Forehand, Cheney, & Adams, 1977; Piccari, 1977). Krieger, (1970) used a videotape model and social reinforcement to increase the frequency of appropriate statements of male mentally retarded adolescents during a vocational counseling interview. Nelson, Gibson, and Cutting (1973) taught a moderately retarded male to use grammatically correct questions, to smile, and to discuss socially appropriate topics. Seitz and Hoekenga (1974) used modeling procedures with a mother and her mentally retarded child to change the role of the child from a passive recipient to an active communicator. Assertiveness training has been shown to be effective with both mentally retarded children (Fleming, 1977) and mentally retarded adults (Bangs, 1977). Mentally retarded junior high school students have learned to facilitate their own reintegration into the school system by employing newly learned social effectiveness skills with their teachers (Halpert, 1978).

The above studies indicate the ability of the mentally retarded, whether child, teenager, or adult, to benefit from social-competence training applied to a variety of situations. The training techniques are obviously available and effective, and as noted in previous surveys, the need for social competency is sorely evident among the mentally retarded. Further, it seems that this use of learning principles and adequate pre-post measurement could profitably be extended to other areas, that is, heterosocial skills, marriage education, birth control use, and child rearing skills. Also, further work is needed to define appropriate skills and to program generalization.

Practical Suggestions

Hall (1979) has written that we really need no more studies attesting to the necessity of sex education for the mentally retarded; what is needed is development of teaching methodology as well as information about their attitudes and knowledge about sex and methods to assess sex education programs. Vockell and Mattick (1973) have noted that one reason for the lack of research is the absence of any adequate procedure for evaluation of sex education for the mentally retarded. In any case, "how-to" suggestions are frequently offered in the literature. Some of these questions seem sensible and are commonly and uniformly agreed on; others, however, are the source of much controversy. Unfortunately, none are based on solid research data.

Most authorities in the field of sex education for the mentally retarded agree that simple terms and repetition of facts are essential (Bass, 1974; Gendel, 1968; Kempton, 1977; Morlock & Tovar, 1971). Bass (1963) further suggests that in teaching the mentally retarded it should be assumed that they have less information and more misinformation. Most also agree on the importance of tailoring information to the individual (Reich & Harshman, 1972). Since the mentally retarded vary so widely in abilities and adaptability, the level of understanding each student can reach must be determined (Kempton, 1977). Only then can realistic teaching methods and achievement goals be established. The subject matter and teaching method must always be adapted to the individual's intellectual abilities, stage of development and particular needs. Many educators also insist on visual aids and materials, as well as natural events in the environment to further demonstrate sexual information (Bass, 1974). Although at least one writer feels the use of animals to illustrate reproduction to the mentally retarded may be confusing because of limitations in conceptual generalization (Gendel, 1968), most encourage the use of animals and pregnant women to teach reproduction (Secker, 1973). Because of the mentally retarded person's short attention span and lack of interest in the environment (DeBlassie & Cowan, 1976) the use of simple terms, repetition, individualized presentation, and natural visual aids seem particularly sensible.

Recently there has also been an emphasis on self-concept and body image as well in sex education for the mentally retarded (Shuman-Carpenter, 1977). Secker (1973) suggests beginning sex education with work on body image. DeBlassie and Cowan consider the child's self-concept to be a major concern in counseling.

One point of controversy among sex educators for the mentally retarded is the value of expertise and training versus good will. Many educators have emphasized the need for training of teachers (Adams & Sestak, 1967; Blom, 1972; Reich & Harshman, 1972). In-service training on sexuality of the mentally retarded as well as mandatory courses on sex education in the teachers' education have been called for. Meyer (1970) notes that all teachers do not have the personal qualities required for teaching sex education, that is, some teachers are too domineering in teaching style or lack sufficient warmth to establish a relationship with their pupils. Johnson (1973) notes that many people with sexual problems of their own are creating the atmosphere in which children grow up. To counteract this, he feels teachers not only need to know the basics of the subject matter but must also have come to terms with their own sexuality. Additionally, teachers should be informed about the characteristics of the particular group they are teaching and be comfortable with both the technical and slang sexual words.

In contrast to this extensive training of teachers and comprehensive curriculum is Sol Gordon's approach (1971a, 1972, 1973b, c). According to Gordon, more important than expertise is attitude and good will. He points to the "anti-sex" attitude of many staff and institution administrators, whose so called sex education is devoted to stopping masturbation, homosexual, and heterosexual activity. Gordon has stated repeatedly that the mentally retarded, and perhaps also normal persons, do not need to know many facts about sex. He suggests basic points sex educators need to communicate, including: (1) masturbation is a normal sexual expression; (2) all direct genital sexual behavior takes place in private; and, (3) intercourse risks pregnancy. Both Gordon and Johnson are obviously in agreement on the importance of sex education for the mentally retarded, but there is a difference in emphasis.

Reich and Harshman (1972) suggest that the school sex education program be carefully planned, taught by teams, and provided on an individual as well as group basis. Parents should be included in the program, and ample opportunity for feedback given. Blom (1972) advises that the guidelines be based on what is known about the psychology of children, that is, their interests and cognitive capacities, rather than what adults think children should know. Further, Blom advises that the opportunity to be excluded from sex education class be available.

Whether sex education classes for mentally retarded or for children of average intelligence should be conducted with both sexes present is debated. Morlock and Tovar (1971) suggest separating the sexes in order to minimize anxiety. One possibility is asking the students their preference, and/or allowing a vote to decide whether the boys and girls would like to meet together or separately. Also some classes could be coed, others not. One noted benefit of sex education for normal IQ children has been an increased ability and comfort in discussing dating relationships, reproduction, and so forth, with each other and with the opposite sex included (Mueller, 1971). Given the sometimes puritanical attitude and sexual embarrassment of the mentally retarded, coed groups may be advantageous in developing a realistic and comfortable attitude toward sexuality. Secker (1973) encourages mixed classes for the mentally retarded in their last years in school, at least in order to provide some experience with the opposite sex.

Adams and Sestak (1967) offer what seems a politically pragmatic approach to implementation of sex education in the school system. The suggestions were not given specifically with the mentally retarded in mind, but given the controversy over sex education for the mentally retarded, it would seem wise to follow this cautious plan. The support of school officials should be obtained, and an *ad hoc* committee of key community people formed to give recommendations. Patrons, parents in the school district, and members of the board of education should be kept informed. Once the committee report has been accepted by the board of education, the actual development of the sex education curriculum guide can be undertaken. Adams and Sestak suggest that this be written by a group of male and female teachers as a summer project for which they set aside time and receive payment. A teacher's manual should be developed with instructional activities listed sequentially by grades. Now that more standardized curriculum guides are available, this step may not be needed. In any case, in-service orientation sessions for all of the teachers is recommended. Finally, the actual instruction should get under way with as little fanfare as possible.

In a similar article by Sengstock (1972) dealing specifically with implementation of sex education programs for the mentally retarded, many of the above guidelines are restated. He also suggests an ongoing public relations program and evaluation of the sex education program. Self-analysis questions are offered to teachers to sensitize them to their role, such as: How do you keep yourself conscious of your student's home/institutional situation when your own lifestyle is so much different?

Suggestions for Parents

Sex education for the mentally retarded is often characterized by passing the buck. Schools emphasize the importance of the parents' role in sex education, while parents want their children to be educated outside the home because they feel inadequate to handle sex education themselves (Fisher & Kjajicek, 1974; Goodman, Budner, & Lesh, 1971; Hall, Morris, & Barker, 1973; Hammer, Wright, & Jensen, 1967). As a result, little information is actually given by parents in the home.

The parents' role in sex education was explored by Goodman, Budner, and Lesh (1971). Interviews were conducted with 15 parents of mentally retarded youngsters, eight female and seven male. The age range was 15–19 and the IQ range 55–70. All the parents wished their child would marry and the authors feel that this seemed to be a "regression to an earlier fantasy of the child's normalcy." The parents were worried about the danger involved in telling their children about sex and that this might provoke their children to inappropriate sexual expression. Parents made only minimal effort or none at all to give their mentally retarded children sexual education and felt inadequate in giving their children information in this area. Fourteen of the 15 parents voiced serious concern that their child might be sexually molested. As a result there was greater control over their child's independent activities than would be indicated by intellectual limitation alone.

As a result of these interviews, the authors give suggestions for parent groups on sex education. They feel it is imperative that the group explore feelings, not just receive didactic information. When the parent considers the child's sexuality and how to deal with it, the parent is also forced to face the whole pattern of adjustment to the mentally retarded. Subjects to be covered in parent groups of sex education programs include: introductory background to the physiology and anatomy of sex and reproduction; physical and emotional adjustment problems of mental retardation; social and marital potentials and limitations of the mentally retarded; fears and anxieties of parents over present and future sexual behavior of their child; methods of communicating constructively with the mentally retarded; understanding appropriate and inappropriate limits on the mentally retarded person's sexual behavior; and alternatives available in planning with the mentally retarded for psychosexual adjustment in adulthood. Concerns, experiences and suggestions can be shared. Valente (1975) suggests starting with a homogeneous group of parents, that is, those whose children's IQ is between 70 and 60.

Guidelines for parents on an individual basis have also been offered. In a readable pamphlet for parents available through the Association for Retarded Citizens, Gendel (1968) emphasizes the importance of not only responding to the child's questions about sex but also initiating questions on the subject. He suggests that family habits regarding dress and privacy not be changed for a mentally retarded child. Others disagree, stating that a mentally retarded person should not be exposed to whatever the family pattern is, to the sight of sexual differences, and that the parent should wait for the child to ask questions (Morlock & Tovar, 1971). In our opinion, this prohibition seems another denial of the mentally retarded person's sexual expression or ability to control sexual expression. Gendel repeats the simplify-repeat-reinforce formula advocated for school teachers of the mentally retarded. One caution for parents following Gendel's pamphlet is his bias, not presented as such, against parenthood for the mentally retarded. It is interesting that he stresses the individual variability in development of the mentally retarded but not individual variability in terms of capacity for parenthood.

Kempton, Bass, and Gordon (1971) have also written a guide for parents, *Love, Sex and BirthControl for the Mentally Retarded* (1971). The pamphlet is also available in Spanish. The authors suggest short explanations (5 to 10 minutes at any one session) and using the child's language as well as adult terms. Basic explanations and pictures are presented as well as suggestions regarding puberty, masturbation, dating, sexual intercourse, venereal disease, birth control, marriage, and children. For additional information on preparing the mentally retarded girl for puberty, Pattullo (1969) has written a helpful pamphlet.

Bass (1974) reassures parents that sexual development in their mentally retarded child may be delayed. Reflecting her prosterilization viewpoint, she emphasizes the importance of explaining genetic factors and substitutes for parenting. Schlesinger (1977) encourages parents that sex is a normal part of everyone's life, and therefore their mentally retarded child's interests in sex is perfectly natural. Parents should also realize, however, that just as in the normal population, there is a range of interest in sex among the mentally retarded; their children should not be stereotyped regarding sexuality. Questions should be answered in a straightforward manner. Not all that looks and sounds like sex is sexual in meaning. Teachers sometimes mistake simple fidgeting and wiggling in a classroom seat for attempts at masturbation and parents may make similar mistakes. Finally, Schlesinger recommends that parents should not expect to have all the answers themselves, and should feel comfortable in asking for assistance from teachers, therapists, nurses, etc.

Many parents are unsure how to respond to masturbation and/or vulgar sexual words in their mentally retarded children. Masturbation is one of the most common sexual practices. Ninety-five percent of men and 80% of women masturbate at some time in their lives (Kinsey, Pomeray, & Martin, 1948, 1953). There is no reason why the mentally retarded should be excluded. Goldstein (1972) writes of a mother who upon discovering her child masturbating, first wanted to reprimand him. Stopping herself, she said instead "I bet that felt good!" and was rewarded by a look of gratitude and a better relationship with her son who felt understood. Excessive or continuous masturbation by a mentally retarded child may be the result of boredom and lack of stimulation. In addition to providing an adequately interesting environment, the parent may also need to explain calmly that masturbation is best enjoyed in private. Vulgar or obscene language is best dealt with in the same straightforward and calm manner, explaining its inappropriateness and giving the proper word. "Bad" words may be an effort to gain the parent's attention, so the wise parent should give approval to appropriate language and behavior.

Parents may also worry about sexual exploitation of their retarded child. Although this fear may be exaggerated, the child should be taught when, where and to whom affection is given. As should children of normal IQ, mentally retarded children should know how to protect themselves. Allowing indiscriminate affection and trust of strangers is a disservice to any child. "Cute" can quickly become inappropriate and even dangerous.

Resource Materials on Sex Education for the Retarded

Attention must also be given to resource materials on sex education for the mentally retarded including curriculum guides and other instructional materials for both parents and the mentally retarded themselves. In 1970, Meyen noted the paucity of sex education materials applicable for use by the mentally retarded. The situation improved somewhat in the last decade. Resources including printed materials as well as visual aids and sources for additional assistance are offered in *A Resource Guide in Sex Education for the Mentally Retarded* published jointly by the American Association for Health, Physical Education, and Recreation and the Sex Information Education Council of the United States (1971). Editors Bass and Gelof in the *Sexual Rights and Responsibilities of the Mentally Retarded* (1972) provide lists of appropriate books for the mentally retarded as well as a list of curriculum guides. Further suggestions are offered by Bass (1974) and in *Social and Sexual Development: A Guide for Teachers of the Handicapped* (Meyers, 1971).

The Gendel (1968) and Kempton, Bass, and Gordon (1971) pamphlets for parents of the mentally retarded have already been discussed. We will only make a few observations on several of the other resource materials available.

Essential Adult Sex Education for the mentally retarded (EASE) is a curriculum guide developed by Zelman and Tyser (1979). It is well organized and able to be tailored to the individual easily. Pre-post tests for each section are given, allowing progress of each student to be monitored as well as allowing evaluation of the program. In composing the curriculum, the authors asked mentally retarded persons what they wanted to know. On the basis of their own research using EASE, the authors note differences between the experimental group who used EASE, and the control subjects at the .0001 level. The mentally retarded students improved significantly in each of four areas (biological, sexual behavior, health, and relationships). Further, class, age, and sex were not significantly related to gain scores.

A series of nine slide presentations entitled, *Sexuality in the Mentally Handicapped* was developed by Kempton and Hanson (1978). This resource material too has the advantage of being individualized to the students. Slides can be included or excluded given the capabilities of the individual or group. The authors suggest that the presentations be spaced over a period of weeks to months and that the series of sections of it be repeated, as overteaching is often necessary with the mentally retarded. Topics include parts of the body, male and female puberty, social behavior, human reproduction, birth control, venereal disease and sexual health, marriage and parenting.

Kempton (1978) has reported on a questionnaire evaluation of sex education programs for the mentally retarded using this slide series. The results are based on 31 returned questionnaires out of 110. Although the actual data are not presented, Kempton reports that positive changes toward maturity in attitude were reported unanimously. In addition, the sex education programs resulted in more communication and interaction between sexes. Most of the mentally retarded persons in the programs were very interested in sexuality, and after initial discomfort, enjoyed the discussions. Although these results are obviously preliminary and limited, no dramatic negative behavior was reported and considerable benefits were noted as a result of the program.

Sol Gordon has published several sex education books for the mentally retarded and for teenagers of normal intelligence (Gordon, 1969, 1971b, 1973a, 1979). One of these is particularly significant given its nonsexist approach. In *Girls Are Girls and Boys Are Boys so What's the Difference?* (1979), Gordon shows the potential of both girls and boys without jeopardizing their sense of gender identity. This book is for normal IQ children age 3 to 7 and uses pictures and simplified prose. Besides giving basic facts about reproduction and differences, he clearly points out that girls may climb trees and boys may enjoy playing house. He realistically notes that some women do not want to get married or become mothers and that almost no one enjoys cleaning house. Although some suggested careers are beyond the capacities of the mentally retarded, such as lawyers, doctors, this sense of the freedom of choice and avoiding unnecessary sexual stereotyping is still crucial for the mentally retarded. This approach is especially refreshing given the past resource materials in this area. In *A Resource Guide in Sex Education for the Mentally Retarded* (1971), sexist approaches are disguised as efforts to teach gender identification. In order to demonstrate masculinity and feminity, the reference suggests asking boys to perform such chores as moving desks while girls wash the tops. Children are to emulate adults at various social functions, with girls pouring coffee and serving boys (for example). Boys are to be scheduled in industrial art shops and girls in home economics. Girls are encouraged to be file clerks, receptionists, and waitresses, while boys are offered jobs such as working in tire shops, as bus boys or custodians. The mentally retarded face enough limitations, without having to face limitations imposed by sexual stereotyping. Why purposely teach what many are striving to overcome?

Another book of Gordon's worthy of note is *Ten Heavy Facts about Sex* (1971b). It uses a very humorous comic-book layout to get across basic information about venereal disease and birth control and clarifies some sexual myths. It also offers sensible guidelines for decisions about having or not having sex. A final innovative sex education book is a two-volume set by Block (1979). One volume is entitled, *For Kids Only: The Illustrated Sex Family Album* and the other is *For Parents Only: Do-It-Yourself Guide Book*. The two volumes are meant to be used in conjunction and offer imaginative exercises to explore the sexuality of children. Although not written specifically for the mentally retarded, several exercises in the book present issues from the mentally retarded's point of view. For example, one story involves the worries and false assumptions of a mentally retarded girl who is attracted to a nonretarded boy. "We made love. He'll never leave me now, even when he finds out I'm retarded." Although many parents may have difficulty accepting its liberal style (for example, all of the cartoons are naked drawings of family members) the book offers a unique opportunity to help children deal with sexual issues while also aiding parents to become aware of and to help their children's sexuality.

Sterilization and the Mentally Retarded

Throughout this chapter it can be seen that there is an increased interest in sexuality with the mentally retarded and an increase in human sexuality programs for them. We have also seen that there has been a discrepancy between information given through sex education and what is allowed by caretakers in terms of sexual expression. That is, sex education has become acceptable and is considered appropriate, whereas oppression of the mentally retarded citizen in this area continues.

When we move to the controversial area of reproductive rights, this discrepancy is highlighted even further. As pointed out by Beckman-Brindley and Tavormina (1978) normalization entails not only certain rights but also certain responsibilities to society. In terms of reproductive freedom, this translates into the mentally retarded citizen's ability to raise children and whether society should be forced to take responsibility for these children.

In this section of the chapter, we will attempt to outline the views of both proponents and opponents of sterilization. In addition, we will review some of the information related to their arguments, such as the ability of the mentally retarded to rear children, the genetic consequences of allowing mentally retarded citizens to reproduce, and the ability of these persons to effectively choose and use other forms of contraception. Finally, we will discuss the current legal status of sterilizaton of the mentally retarded.

Since much of the data in this area are opinion based on limited systematic investigations, we will highlight issues and unresolved questions without attempting a study-by-study review. Throughout the review we will also point out the ways behavior therapists could provide valuable skills in remediating current deficits in the literature.

Before moving on to what data are actually available, we would like to raise one further point. If the research questions raised above (i.e., the ability to raise children or ability to use other forms of birth control) were answered positively, then the need for sterilization would be greatly reduced. However, if the questions are answered negatively (which is highly probable for certain groups of mentally retarded individuals) what will be the approach to sterilization? We are still left with the basic question of whether one segment of society has the right to dictate limitations to another. This is a moral, ethical, and at times, religious question that can never be answered completely on the basis of research data alone.

Proponents

One of the leading proponents of voluntary sterilization as a means of birth control for the mentally retarded is Bass (1963, 1964b, 1978). Since her writings represent the views of other proponents, we will briefly summarize them. It should be noted that Bass and other writers who espouse a similar philosophy generally call for voluntary sterilization. The question of whether the mentally retarded can give voluntary consent will be discussed later.

Basically the arguments for sterilization (Bass, 1963, 1964a,b, 1978; Neville, 1978; Thompson, 1978) include an inability to effectively use other forms of birth control, a reduction in the number of mentally retarded offspring (the eugenics argument), the inability of the mentally retarded to serve as effective parents, and the reduction of sexual deviance and/or exploitation of the mentally retarded. The argument is also put forward that if these individuals are freed from fear of reproduction, then a more normal role in society, including marriage, can be assumed.

Opponents

The arguments against sterilization have been based on a number of issues, including a lack of data to support the views of the proponents, the legal difficulties surrounding voluntary consent, and the ethical implications of fostering society's wishes on a minority group.

Petchesky (1979) in a recent review of the literature has summarized the arguments against sterilization and the abuses that in the past have been associated with the procedure. Petchesky points out that many of the issues stated by the proponents are conjecture. That is, there is limited indication that the mentally retarded cannot use other forms of birth control and little evidence that the majority of mental retardation is genetically determined. In terms of parenting, Petchesky correctly points out that there are no studies comparing the abilities of the mentally retarded and the nonretarded parent to raise children. We would also point out that there is no clear data relating IQ level (at least in the mildly retarded group) to parenting ability.

In addition, there is no reason to believe that sterilization would somehow decrease the sexual deviance or exploitation in the mentally retarded (Hall, 1979; Petchesky, 1979) since sterilization does not change sexual functioning. Females would still be open to sexual exploitations and males could still be charged with sexual crimes (Petchesky, 1979).

Burt (1973), in reviewing the legal difficulties in sterilization, makes a comparison between compulsory sterilization in the mentally retarded and compulsory sterilization for women who are found to be carrying defective children. For example, since Down's syndrome can be diagnosed *in utero*, should sterilization be mandated by the state when such a diagnosis is made? Or, Murphy (1973) observes that sickle cell disease could be eliminated in one generation by sterilizing all the carriers. It seems clear that when the eugenics position is taken, one has a difficult time not justifying its use in other areas with genetic transmission is even more clearly mapped than in the mildly mentally retarded.

Two other arguments against sterilization relate to the validity of the IQ test (Murphy, 1973), and to whether the state of being mentally retarded is permanent (Begab, 1974; Chez, 1971; Tarjan, 1973). Both of these arguments of course relate to the difficulties in defining mental retardation. As Begab states "drastic changes in a child's life experience can alter IQ, up or down, and adaptive behavior is even more malleable" and, "a significant number of mentally retarded persons are recognized and function as impaired only during their school-age years." Given our ability to modify what we label intelligence, especially among the mildly retarded to whom sterilization is mainly aimed (Neville, 1978; Petchesky, 1979), we are hard pressed to suggest a relatively permanent procedure since the condition fluctuates in severity.

Anecdotal data related to the above come from Tarjan (1973), who wrote on the experience at Pacific State Hospital once sterilization was ended. He observes that community physicians used to write to the hospital requesting details regarding the sterilization procedure because many patients were seeking reversals. The letters indicated that many patients were now no different from their general patient population and "that in fact, some had proven themselves adequate mothers of children from their husbands' previous marriages." Although this type of data cannot be accepted from a purely scientific ground, it also cannot be ignored and should provide impetus for further studies on individuals' social competence over time.

In the preceding two sections we have attempted to briefly outline the arguments for and against sterilization. The next sections are designed to summarize in more detail data relevant to some of these major arguments.

Eugenics Argument

The eugenics argument has two major thrusts. The first is that the mentally retarded reproduce at a higher rate than the nonretarded, thereby decreasing the overall intelligence of the population. The second argument is that the offspring of the mentally retarded are more likely to have marked cognitive deficits, and it is unfair to submit children to such a handicap if it can be prevented.

Related to point one are the data summarized by Reed and Anderson (1973) on a rather extensive study of families of mentally retarded individuals in Minnesota. The data they presented represent information on 289 probands institutionalized at the Fairbanks School between 1911 and 1918. All subjects had IQs of less than 69. The descendants of the grandparents of these probands were traced to 1969. This resulted in information on up to seven generations and more than 8,000 people.

One of the findings of these data was that the fertility rate was lower for those with IQs below 70 (2.09 offspring per person), while highest for those with IQs of 131 and above (2.98). The lower fertility rate was partly the result of the fact that many of the mentally retarded individuals did not reproduce (31% had no children). Similar findings were observed by Book (1959). Helbig (1973), in separately reanalyzing the data from Book regarding nonmarried and married subjects (both mentally retarded and controls) finds equal fertility rates for the mentally retarded and controls within each marital status group. Regardless of intellectual level, nonmarried have a lower fertility rate than married subjects. In Book's sample, the mentally retarded had much lower marital rates, so that when married and nonmarried subjects were combined, their families rates appear lower.

From the eugenics standpoint, the issue is that the mentally retarded are not over populating whether due to lower fertility rates or lower marital rates. The majority of studies seem to indicate a lower than average number of offspring among this group (Charles, 1957; Floor, Baxter, Rosen, & Zisfein, 1975; Peck & Stephens, 1965), although there are exceptions (Shaw & Wright, 1960). Therefore, the use of sterilization for reducing this overreproduction does not seem to be supported by the data. To be completely fair, however, one has to realize that the majority of data were collected when institutionalization was more common, when segregation of the mentally retarded was the standard operating procedure, and marriage was uncommon. Whether the fertility trends will change as normalization experiences increase is a question for future research.

The second factor suggested in the eugenics argument is the increase in mental retardation among the offspring of mentally retarded parents. Among 25 studies done between 1913 and 1961, mental retardation rates in offspring range from 2.5% to 83%, with much of the variability being ascribed to different criteria for determining mental retardation (Bass, 1963). Another problem is the means by which the samples are chosen. Priest, Thuline, LaVeck, and Jarvis (1961) chose to study families where at least two siblings were institutionalized in a facility for the mentally retarded. With this criterion they found that 48% of the total of 477 siblings (including the institutionalized siblings) were mentally retarded and 7% were of questionable intellectual level. Such a criterion probably selects families who have demonstrated a higher rate of mental retardation and may not clearly reflect the overall number of cognitively impaired persons in the population. The rate of mental retardation in families might be much lower if families with only one institutionalized sibling were included.

Again probably the most complete data, at least in this country, come from the Minnesota studies, although the subjects examined in these studies for genetic tracings were institutionalized. This may have led to the selection of only the more severely mentally retarded cases where family mental retardation rates might be higher. In defense of these data, it should be noted that only 10% of the total sample over the generations studied were institutionalized (Gerald, 1973). Reed and Anderson (1973) present data on 7,778 children in which both parents, one parent, or neither parent were mentally retarded.

The offspring where both parents were mentally retarded had a mean IQ of 74. When only one parent was mentally retarded, the mean IQ of the offspring was 90, and when neither parent was mentally retarded the mean IQ of the offspring was 107. In Ireland, Scally (1973) found very similar data in the offspring of families where for the majority one parent was mentally retarded.

In summary, the information reviewed does suggest an increase in mental retardation which is especially prevalent if both parents evidence the syndrome. Although it seems to be established that the incidence of mental retardation is increased in the offspring of the retarded, does this justify sterilization?

First we must consider what the result would be if all mentally retarded citizens were sterilized. Reed and Anderson (1973) developed a theoretical model based on their data to predict what the decrease in mentally retardation would be if no retarded individual reproduced. The drop would be only .3%. In addition, it must be realized that 83% of the mentally retarded are from nonretarded parents. Therefore, massive sterilization would only slightly reduce the mentally retarded population. If one is interested in reducing the rate of mental retardation, Begab (1974) has outlined numerous possible factors that could be modified, including the deleterious effects of increased drug usage by pregnant women, environmental pollutants, cigarette smoking, improved medical care (which leads to more children surviving than they would in the past), malnutrition, and numerous social environmental factors. It could be argued that those recommending sterilization are looking for the least expensive means of reducing mental retardation, but in fact such procedures are not very effective.

The second question relates to the genetic versus environmental determinants of mental retardation. This review is especially pertinent for the mildly mentally retarded. The studies above do not answer this question. As most researchers are aware, only a few causes of mental retardation have clear genetic links (i.e.,

Down's syndrome, Tay-Sachs disease). Although it is not our purpose to dwell on the nature–nurture controversy, it does suggest other means of assisting the offspring of the mentally retarded. For example, with the advent of day-care centers and early stimulation projects, would figures cited above be reduced? Haber (cited in Begab, 1974) studied 50 newborns whose mothers had IQs below 70. Subjects were randomly assigned to a control and experimental group. The experimental group and their families received intensive intervention, including early stimulation and efforts to modify the family environments. At 66 months the experimental subjects had an IQ score of 125, and the controls' IQ was 92. Although this is only one study and such procedures are expensive, they seem more humane than sterilization. This is one area where behavior therapists should be able to be of assistance.

A final genetic argument raised by Murphy (1973) states that a "gene pool should be far from perfect because its variability makes possible a more subtle adaptation of the species." Such an argument suggests that it may be unwise to tamper with a gene pool unless we are certain what the long-term ramification will be.

Child Rearing Ability

With the exception of Mickleson's reports (1947, 1949), most data on child rearing practices of the mentally retarded come from studies which have mainly focused on their general community or marital adaptation (Andron & Sturm, 1973; Berry & Shapiro, 1975; Bowden, Spitz, & Winters, 1971; Charles, 1957; Floor, Baxter, Rosen, & Zisfien, 1975; Mattinson, 1973; Peck & Stephens, 1965; Scally, 1973; Shaw & Wright, 1960). In general, most of the literature favor the rights of the mentally retarded to marry but add the requirement that contraception or voluntary sterilization be urged (Bass, 1963, 1964a).

Although marriage is acceptable, there is still the concern about the care received by the children of mentally retarded parents. Mickleson (1947) presents interview data and clinical ratings on 90 families that included 105 parents who had been institutionalized in facilities for the mentally retarded. The mean IQ of the 105 was 58.6. Forty-two percent were rated as providing satisfactory care, 32% were rated as giving questionable care, and 26% were rated as having given unsatisfactory care. The authors looked at a number of factors related to care and the following five interrelated factors emerged: (1) number of pregnancies; (2) number of children in the home; (3) mental health of the parents (especially the mother); (4) degree of harmony between the husband and wife; and (5) adequacy of income. The mother's IQ and the mental status of the parents were not related to adequacy of care. Shaw and Wright (1960) have also observed that small families seem to adapt more successfully than large ones.

In interpreting the results, one may be struck by the fact that 26% of these children were being given unsatisfactory care, a number that appears rather large. However, the study suffers from a lack of an adequate control group. Would these results be any different if a sample of nonretarded parents from similar socioeconomic classes were judged as to their parenting skills? It is important to note that the factor that emerged as a predictor was socioeconomic status and not parental IQ. Another factor that might be of importance was the high frequency of these parents who had been institutionalized for a good portion of their lives and, therefore, were probably not exposed to normal social experiences (exposure to younger siblings) that might improve parental care. These two factors, lack of an adequate control group and reliance on the study of adults who had institutional histories, are confounding factors in all the data we could locate regarding the ability of mentally retarded individuals to effectively parent.

The remainder of studies cited earlier were, as stated, focused mainly on either general adaptation of the mentally retarded in the community or adaptation to marriage. Therefore, the data on child rearing are secondary. All of the information in these studies is drawn from interviews and the interviewers' interpretation with no objective measurement of the children's function or the skills of the parent. What must be kept in mind is that the subjects have spent a considerable part of their time in institutions and control groups are lacking.

Despite these limitations, some factors do emerge from these studies. One factor is the variability in the data that might be a result from the author's own bias. For example, Berry and Schapiro (1975) point out in their survey that the care is poor and does not live up to middle-class standards, while Floor, Baxter, Rosen, and Zisfein (1975) make the same observations in terms of middle-class standards, but suggest that the majority of the children were receiving appropriate attention. This highlights the problems that arise when one tries to define appropriate parenting.

Another factor discussed previously is that smaller families seem to do better than larger ones (Mickelson, 1947; Shaw & Wright, 1960). In addition, Scally (1973) suggests that married couples do better than single mothers. In his study, approximately one half the female parents were raising their children alone, which might account for his rather high rate of inappropriate care. What these data seem to indicate is that the mentally retarded citizens face many of the problems of nonretarded parents. That is, a large family, low income, and single parenting create difficulties in child rearing that may appear exaggerated when those doing the judging are from different socioeconomic levels.

In terms of sterilization, the above data leave many questions unanswered. Although it is evident that some of the offspring of the mentally retarded are receiving less than adequate care, it is not clear that this is due to the parents' IQ. In cases where abuse or neglect are observed, children can be protected by child abuse laws (Burt, 1973). It is unclear, given that many parents do not adequately parent, why the mentally retarded are chosen as a group whose reproductive freedom is challenged (Burt, 1973; Fotheringham, 1971; Gupta & Singh, 1973).

A final factor that has received little attention in the literature is the trainability of the mentally retarded individual regarding the provision of adequate parental care and a concurrent lack of data on objective means of assessing adequacy. Mickelson (1949) reviewed the effect of supervision, sterilization, and institutionalization on the 90 families presented above. Much of this supervision was of a social-casework nature, and included supportive counseling, counselor availability, direct services to children, making resources available, etc. The results of this study seem to suggest that the mentally retarded parent can be helped, although factors involved in this improvement are not clear. Since many individuals received multiple services, any interpretation of the effect of social approaches to helping these families is confounded.

Given the current legal restrictions against sterilization (Petchesky, 1979), mentally retarded individuals will continue to become parents. Investigation of the value of behavioral-based training programs and home-based behavioral programs are needed. The mentally retarded are not the only population at high risk of being poor parents, but they are a population that seems to have received little help in learning appropriate parenting skills. Before accepting sterilization as the only means of protecting the children of the mentally retarded, we need to determine that these parents are not amenable to other interventions.

Ability to Use Other Forms of Contraception

Bass (1963, 1964b, 1978) reports that few studies addressing the ability of the mentally retarded population to use birth control methods have appeared, but then concludes that experts agree that the use of contraceptives is beyond the cognitive capacity of these persons. In addition, there are very limited data on training the mentally retarded to use contraception.

In our review of the literature, we found little data that could provide any guidelines in this area. LaVeck and de la Cruz (1973) review various forms of birth control. They suggest that the IUD may be the best method, since it does not require any specific intellectual skills or motivation. They feel that the oral contraceptive regime may not be applicable to most mentally retarded persons, but at present have no data to support their position.

A number of investigations (David, Smith, & Friedman, 1976; Fiedler & Tyler, 1975; Goodman, 1973) describe successful contraceptive education programs for the mentally retarded, although conclusions are not based on systematic data collection. Basically, these studies report that with specialized training material geared to the intellectual level of the mentally retarded, these persons could learn appropriate birth control procedures. There was some suggestion that previous sex education experience was valuable in understanding contraceptive measures (David, Smith, & Friedman, 1976). Finally, an interesting observation can be drawn from Mickelson (1949). The major service offered for family planning was sterilization—in only one family was there evidence of an effort to provide birth control information. Even without such education, 7% to 8% of the couples were practicing birth control. One wonders about the necessity of sterilizing 53 of the families in this study since no effort had been directed toward providing alternative forms of family planning.

One final form of birth control that could replace sterilization is the use of Depo-Provera (medroxyprogesterone acetate), an injectable progesterone which needs to be given only once every 3 to 6 months (Bass, 1978; LaVeck & de la Cruz, 1973). However, at the current time the drug is not approved by the FDA as a means of birth control.

Obviously, studies of various training programs and the development of new training programs are needed before one concludes that voluntary sterilization is the only means of contraception available to the mentally retarded. There are, however, still some nagging issues to be considered. First, in protecting the mentally retarded from civil liberty abuses associated with sterilization by using other forms of contraception, we are at the same time removing certain rights. The major forms of effective birth control used by women (which unfortunately are the major focus of many of the clinical reports) have serious side effects. It seems logical that mentally retarded women should have the same rights to control their bodies as nonretarded women. This again raises the question of voluntary consent which will be discussed later.

A second factor that cannot be ignored is that no matter how successful we are in training appropriate birth control, is this being done for the individual's benefit or for the caretaker's and society's benefit? Are new and better birth control procedures and training programs just a more palliative means of denying the mentally retarded the right of parenthood? Voluntary consent seems to be just as much an issue in these procedures as with sterilization.

Finally, we would like to raise one more point brought to our attention by Susan Daniels, editor of *Sex and Disability*. Dr. Daniels pointed out that much of the argument over rights to bear children distracts from the true problem; motivation to have children. Has society given the mentally retarded the idea that true normality can only be obtained through childbearing? This is an issue that has been raised often by the woman's movement. We need to question whether mixed messages are given to the mentally retarded. It is possible that the desire to reproduce would be much less if all members of society would realize that the worth of a human being can be achieved in many ways other than through reproduction. We need to provide alternatives for the mentally retarded individual (in fact all members of society) for defining self-worth.

Attitudes towards Sterilization

So far we have dealt with the professionals' opinion regarding sterilization and have attempted to review the data relevant to these various arguments. We would now like to turn to attitudes of the non-professional and the mentally retarded themselves. Again, data are lacking in this area and what is available can be criticized on numerous grounds for its lack of methodological rigor.

Two studies were found (Bass, 1967; Whitcroft & Jones, 1974) that investigated the attitudes of parents and others toward sterilization. Bass (1967) collected attitude data on 132 normal parents of mentally retarded children who were located through local parent groups. Of the total sample, 59.85% approved of sterilization. Religion affected approval rate, with Protestants reporting a 71.62%, Catholics a 16%, Jewish a 60%, and those stating no religion a 72.72% approval rate. Subjects' attitudes on a 1–11-point scale followed the same pattern. The total group mean for attitude was 7.48, with those stating no religion and Protestants having the most positive attitude (8.59 and 8.43 respectively). Catholics reported the most negative attitude, and those who were Jewish were close to the population mean. There were small but significant positive correlations between attitude and intensity of feeling (.3939 $p < .01$) and attitude and information (.2670 $p < .01$).

Bass points out that one of the major limitations of the study occurred in soliciting subjects—those groups most opposed to sterilization refused to participate. Additionally, the questions asked were in terms of sterilization in general. It is possible that the results would change if parents were specifically asked about sterilization of their own children.

Whitcroft and Jones (1974) investigated the attitudes of the parents of the mentally retarded ($n = 325$), professionals ($n = 306$), and others ($n = 38$) toward sterilization. The parents were recruited from a group of individuals attending state, district, and local meetings of associations for mentally retarded children—again a possibly biased sample. Eighty-eight percent of the parents and 80% of the total population (including parents) approved of sterilization. Another interesting finding was that of the total sample, only 13% thought that the mentally retarded could maintain a marriage, only 11% thought that they could raise children, and only 19% thought they could understand sterilization.

These attitudes raise some interesting points. For instance, it appears that caretakers feel highly favorable toward sterilization. However, one wonders for whose benefit? It is of concern that both parents and professionals seem to underestimate the ability of the mentally retarded to rear children, and especially to maintain marriage. The judgment of parents and professionals in regard to the ability of the retarded to understand sterilization brings into question whether voluntary consent is possible in this group. It is possible that the groups surveyed were heavily loaded with parents of severely and profoundly retarded persons whereas the data we have reviewed were concerned with the mildly retarded. Future surveys should seek the attitudes of parents and professionals across varying levels of mental retardation.

Turning from the attitudes of caretakers to the attitudes of the mentally retarded themselves we found even less well-controlled data. Bass (1963, 1964b) cites a study by Popenoe and Gosney (1946) published by the Association for Voluntary Sterilization. Since this publication was not readily available, we will summarize Bass's interpretation. This study was a survey of 6,255 mentally ill and mentally retarded persons sterilized in California. They found that the general reaction to the operation was one of indifference. One out of seven reported dissatisfaction, but gave no "rational reason" (rational in whose mind is unclear). Although we are unable to locate the Popenoe and Gosney article, we located a 1929 article by Popenoe which apparently contains similar data. In this population, it was stated that no attempt was made to systematically collect the opinions of the mentally defective "because we felt that their evidence would be of little value." They did state that for those released from psychiatric hospitals (presumably mentally ill rather than mentally retarded) only one of seven was dissatisfied. This raises the question of whether the data cited by Bass are really applicable to mentally retarded.

Similarly, Butler (1945) in reviewing the results of 4,310 sterilized patients from Somona State Home in California reports, and we quote:

> I feel sure that the vast majority are happier and better off in many ways than if kept in institutions. There are several reasons that discharged patients are happier because they have been sterilized. They tend to marry in their own mental level and with no children both may assist financially. The defective girl does not go through the stress of pregnancy and the couples do not have to worry about care of offspring. (p. 513)

We do not doubt that many of the patients were happier outside of the institution but some hard data are needed to support the remainder of this unsubstantiated claim. It is important to remember Tarjan's (1973) discussion of the lack of effect of discontinuing sterilization in California.

A final study indicating lack of negative side effects from sterilization was reported by Perrin, Sands, Tinker, Dominguez, Dingle, and Thomas (1976). They reported data on 20 patients (19 females and 1 male) aged 10.5 to 19.5 years ($x = 16$) who were sterilized between 1970 and 1973. Eight patients had IQs under 30, 9 had IQs between 31 and 50, and 3 had IQs between 51 and 60. Of the high IQ subjects, one had hemiparesis, one spastic diplegia, and a third suffered from incapacitating menstrual bleeding. Nine of the females had tubal ligations, 10 had abdominal hysterectomies, and the one male had a vasectomy. Long-term follow-up (18 months—4 years) indicated no adverse personality changes and no postoperative depression. This study is somewhat different than others we have reviewed in that the subjects were more severely mentally retarded than in the majority of reports from California or they had complicating physical disorders. In addition, sterilizaton was performed under a strict protocol and was not a condition for release from an institution, as appeared to be the case in California. Under these conditions and with these patients, the sterilization did not seem to have an adverse effect.

However, the outcome may be different with the more mildly retarded. Andron and Sturm (1973) in a survey of marital happiness of 12 mentally retarded couples, found that 7 had been sterilized. Four reported the operation had not been clearly explained and most of the females had been told that it was an appendectomy. One male reported that he had been told the operation was reversible. Another woman reported that she had been sterilized during an abortion which had been described to her as a treatment for a stomach ailment. Andron and Sturm (1973) report that 5 couples were unhappy because they could not have children, and another 5 couples changed the subject when children were discussed. Since 3 of the 12 couples were naturally sterile in addition to the 7 who had been surgically sterilized, it is difficult to interpret the data clearly from the 5 couples who expressed negative feelings. We cannot be sure that this number included only those who had been sterilized or also a proportion of those who were naturally sterile.

One of the better interview studies in this area comes form Sabagh and Edgerton (1962). As part of their follow-up of mentally retarded patients released from institutions into the communty, they interviewed and questioned 50 subjects about sterilization. The investigators found that most subjects could understand sterilization, and that 68% of the sample expressed disapproval. Sex differences were apparent in that 35% of the males approved whereas only 9% of the women approved.

In conclusion, we would like to point out how others have interpreted the Sabagh and Edgerton data. Bass (1964b) indicated that the Edgerton low rate of approval occurred because many of the women married Mexicans who place a high value on fertility (apparently this was received from a personal communication from Dr. Edgerton), and that many of these subjects had been sterilized involuntarily. Bass (1978) in interpreting the Edgerton data stated that these individuals "were mostly Latin American with a background of strong approval for fertility." Demographic data presented by Sabagh and Edgerton indicated that 14% of the population were Mexican. It is possible that many married Latin Americans, but we wonder how the change occurred in their ethnic background by 1978. Our concern is that investigators marshal data and interpret it to fit their own view, a problem that seems to color the area of sterilization. In defense of Bass and other proponents, they have never called for involuntary sterilization. However, history seems to indicate that many patients were sterilized against their will, or that subtle (or not so subtle) forms of coercions were used, such as hospital release being dependent on receiving the operation. This had led to the current legal situation which will be reviewed next.

Legal Status

To understand the current legal situation surrounding sterilization in the mentally retarded, one must understand the history of its use and abuse in the United States. Much of the abuse and the legal ramifications of such have been well reviewed (Hepner, 1979; Linn, 1977; Soskin, 1977; Petchesky, 1979; Wolfers & Wolfers, 1973). We will only attempt to summarize their comments here.

Wolfers and Wolfers (1973) present an interesting historical perspective on the use of vasectomies in the United States. The first vasectomy in this country was performed by Dr. Henry Sharp on a reformatory inmate incarcerated for public masturbation. In 1907, Dr. Sharp had data on 176 minors who were sterilized for excessive masturbation. By 1909, he had also collected data on 280 patients who received vasectomies as defective individuals." By 1939,

> Sterilization had been recommended for leprosy, tuberculosis, epilepsy, alcoholism, insanity, sexual deviation, moral turpitude, mental defect, criminal conviction, Huntington's chorea, 'hereditary' deafness and blindness, severe physical deformity, popurism, neurasthenia, syphilis, rape, drug taking, carnal knowledge and ultimately chicken stealing! For almost all of these indications it was, what is more, performed under compulsion in one place or another between 1907 and 1939. (Wolfers & Wolfers, 1973, p. 197)

Although no one would suggest sterilization of adolescents who masturbated (or many of us would be in serious difficulty), or for the other disorders listed above, we must look at this information in a historical perspective. During the time Dr. Sharp was working, masturbation was thought to be the root of many of the ills of society. As knowledgeable professionals we can look at this past abuse with pride in our current advanced information, but one wonders what our colleagues 24–40 years from now will say about current attitudes toward, and practices of, sterilization in the mentally retarded. Are we as sure of our knowledge of retardation as Dr. Sharp must have been regarding the ill effects of masturbation?

Another abuse was the use of sterilization as a prerequisite for release from institutions. Examples of this come from the articles reporting on the California experience with sterilization (Butler, 1945; Popenoe, 1929). It is clear from these reports that sterilization was required for release from institutions—a notable example of how coercion can be applied to the mentally retarded.

In terms of our current situation, Krischef (1972) reported that 24 states had statutes permitting sterilization. It would seem, however, that the actual number of sterilizations being done was greatly decreased from the early part of this century.

This decrease is partly due to the current legal situation which arose from two major sources. First, sterilization in the past has been disproportionately applied to women, minorities, and those from lower socioeconomic statuses (Petchesky, 1979). The second factor which led to federal intervention was the highly publicized case of the Relf sisters (*Relf* v. *Weinberger*) who had been sterilized in a federally funded clinic under threat of losing their welfare benefits if they did not consent. Many other legal challenges to compulsory sterilization have occurred since that time. These have been previously reviewed (Hepner, 1979; Linn, 1977; Petchesky, 1979; Soskin, 1977).

These abuses led to federal guidelines (Federal Register, 1978) which delineated procedures that must be followed when federal financing is involved in sterilization. These guidelines have been summarized by Petchesky (1979). The two most important guidelines for this chapter are: (1) the requirement that sterilization must be voluntary, and (2) a moratorium on sterilization for those under 21, those involuntarily institutionalized, and those defined as legally incompetent.

The interpretation of these guidelines has seemed to rule out sterilization for the mentally retarded and the institutionalized when federal money is involved. For those not institutionalized or when other payment sources are available, the question of sterilization still seems to be open. It is highly likely, however, that given the number of court cases that have appeared (Petchesky, 1979), many physicians will be reluctant to perform sterilization on the mentally retarded.

Although federal guidelines would seem to provide protection to some mentally retarded persons, there still is a question raised regarding what type of protection is needed for those not involved in federal programs. It seems clear that parental consent is not adequate. Soskin (1977) reviewed the legal status of this question and concluded that "substituted" consent is not adequate and the interest of parents is not always the same as the interest of the child. Clear guidelines and procedures are needed for the physician in the community who may be requested to perform sterilizations.

The second problem is that in protecting the mentally retarded, we may also be denying the right to choose a relatively safe form of contraception. As we pointed out previously, most forms of birth control have potentially serious side effects. By not allowing the mentally retarded to choose a relatively safe form of contraception we are sentencing them to the use of more dangerous forms. This leads to the question of whether the mentally retarded can give voluntary consent, and whether guidelines be proposed that allow review by an unbiased group to insure that consent is truly voluntary. Petchesky (1979), Soskin (1970) and Bayles (1978) have outlined what is required for legal consent. They conclude that the consent first must be truly voluntary and no forms of coercion should be applied (i.e., release from an institution). Secondly, the procedure must be explained in a way that is understandable to the person and all risks must be explained (such as, the limits on the reversibility of the procedures). Thirdly, alternative procedures and their risks need to be presented including other forms of birth control, abortion if an unwanted pregnancy occurs, and the availability of services to assist in child care if a child is born (Soskin, 1977). Fourth, the person must be capable of understanding the information (Bayles, 1978).

Can the mentally retarded understand sterilization? According to the data by Sabagh and Edgerton (1962), which were not objective, they can. Other evidence from the Social Knowledge and Attitude Test (Edmonson, McCombs, & Wish, 1979), a sex education test for the mentally retarded, suggest that the mentally retarded do have more knowledge of human sexuality than is usually assumed. Also this test indicates that procedures can be adequately developed to objectively assess sexual knowledge in the mentally retarded. Further work is needed by behavioral scientists in designing other objective means of assessing the mentally retarded's knowledge of sterilization and other forms of birth control. We may also find that with increased sex education for the mentally retarded, beginning at a younger age, their understanding of sterilization may be greater.

A second question concerns procedures for guaranteeing that the consent is voluntary. Soskin (1977) and Hall (1979) have reviewed the guidelines presented by Judge Frank Johnson in the *Wyatt* v. *Aderhold* case. These guidelines have been directed towards the institutionalized, but have applicability in other situations. First, the guidelines remove the guardian from the decision process and place decisions in the hands of a committee composed of professionals, the general public, minorities, and the residents of the facility (Soskin, 1977). If the patient has been declared legally incompetent, then the committee must still decide if the patient has truly given voluntary consent for sterilization and is uncoerced. In this case, the committee's decision must be reviewed by the court that had declared the patient incompetent. As Soskin (1977) points out, this does not clearly answer all the questions but it does serve as a guideline that could be adopted in a number of situations. We would also suggest that attempts be made to evaluate such procedures from their inception to provide a further check on the adequacy of such guidelines and to provide modification as needed.

Conclusion

We have attempted in this section to review the current information related to sterilization realizing that the majority of it does not meet criteria for scientific acceptance. Even with these limitations, our interpretation would be that at the present time there is no justification for involuntary sterilization of the mildly retarded. We feel that guidelines do need to be developed so that voluntary sterilization is an option for the mentally retarded. We also are in need of more information on severely and profoundly retarded and guidelines need to be developed dealing with sexuality in this group.

Other areas of research have been outlined in this section including such questions as parent training, training in alternative forms of contraception, developing objective measures of parenting skills, and developing objective means of assessing the mentally retarded's knowledge of birth control. We hope that that investigators in the area of mental retardation will attempt to provide the much needed data in this area.

THE MENTALLY RETARDED SEX OFFENDER

The general public seems to fear that a mentally retarded individual in the community increases the risk of sex offenses. Berdiansky and Parker (1977) in a survey of difficulties encountered in opening 51 group homes for adult mentally retarded persons in North Carolina found that fear of sexual deviance was raised as an issue in 26% of the cases. The issue was resolved in only 10% of the cases where it was raised. The public's fear of sex offenses among the mentally retarded has the possibility of interfering with normalization and movement of the mentally retarded into the community.

The purpose of this section of the chapter is to review data available on the actual prevalence of sex offenses among the mentally retarded and outline a possible behavioral assessment and treatment strategy that could be adopted. We will also present case histories of mentally retarded offenders seen in our project at the end of this section.

Prevalence

Meyerowitz (1971) states that the mentally retarded are overrepresented among those charged with sex offenses but many of the offenses are rather harmless such as public masturbation or indecent exposure with sexual assault being infrequent. However, no data are presented to substantiate this observation.

When one turns to reports with more substantive data, one finds a great deal of variability in reports. Selling (1939) reported data collected from the Psychopathic Clinic of the Recorders Court in Michigan. Of 551 individuals who were charged with indecent conduct, 43% had IQs below 70. Also in this series were 192 cases charged with rape, attempted rape, or statutory rape. In this group approximately 51% had IQs below 70.

This early study suggests an extremely high rate of sexual offenses for the mentally retarded. However, this data are not supported by later research. Gebhard, Gagnon, Pomeroy, and Christenson (1965) found a good deal of variability in retardation rates among various categories of sexual offenders in their survey of the sexual behavior of incarcerated sex offenders. The highest percentage of mental defectives (their term) was found among heterosexual offenders versus children: approximately 1/7th to 1/5th were classified as mentally retarded (undefined psychometrically). They point out, however, that many of these cases seemed to arise from the individual's seeking of attention or affection rather than sexual gratification. Other categories that seemed to be over represented by the mentally retarded included: homosexual offenders versus children (10%), voyeurs (12.5%), and exhibitionists (12.5%). They also reported that the majority of heterosexual aggressives versus children were persons with mental defects (undefined) or pathology in conjunction with alcoholism or heavy sporadic drinking, however they did not report what percentage of the population was represented. Other offense categories such as heterosexual offenders versus adults or minors, heterosexual aggressors versus adults or minors, homosexual offenders versus minors did not seem to have an over representation of the mentally retarded.

Other studies seem to support the lower rate found by Gebhard et al., (1965). For example, Christie, Marshall, and Lanthier (1977) found the mean IQ of incarcerated pedophiles and rapists at their facility to be within normal limits. The mean IQ of the rapists was 101.86 ($SD = 17.10$) and for the pedophiles 93.30 ($SD = 16.41$). This suggests that although the mean IQ of the pedophiles was somewhat below the population mean, they did fall within normal limits.

Mohr, Turner, and Jerry (1964), in their study of pedophiles and exhibitionists evaluated at the forensic clinic in Toronto, found the mean IQ of 47 pedophiles to be 98.4 with only 4% of the sample falling below an IQ of 79. This is somewhat less than the 9% that would be expected in the population to have IQs below 79. Results for exhibitionists were quite similar, with mean IQ being 103.6 and only 3% of the population falling below 79.

Similarly, MacDonald (1973) reviewed the literature on intellectual level of exhibitionists and found rates of mental retardation ranging from 2% (Taylor, 1947) to 16% (East, 1924). The majority of data available on retardation rates indicate similar patterns to that described above (see Christie et al., 1977; MacDonald, 1973; Mohr et al., 1964 for reviews).

In general, the data reviewed do not suggest an over representation of the mentally retarded in the sexual-offender population, although there might be a slightly higher rate than would be expected from population statistics alone. The rather large percentage reported by Selling (1939) apparently represents some kind of selection factor in terms of arrest rates or referral rates to that clinic. The fact that some of the data reviewed suggest a slight increase in the mental retardation rate among arrested or convicted sex offenders would be expected. The mentally retarded individual, because of poor social skills and cognitive ability deficits, would probably be more likely to be apprehended than the nonretarded. This differential arrest rate, and probably a differential conviction rate, could explain the lower IQ of sex offenders. Even if this was not the case, the data in no way support the notion that the mentally retarded individual in the community increases the rate of sexual offenses.

Treatment

Although it is doubtful that the mentally retarded are at any more risk to commit a sexual offense than the nonretarded, there are sex offenders with marked cognitive deficits. From a clinical standpoint, these individuals create numerous problems in assessment and treatment. Our major problem is the lack of relevant data with which to design adequate, empirically defined assessment and treatment procedures. Our own survey found that the vast majority of institutions for the mentally retarded had no programs for sex offenders. A survey of the literature also failed to show reports describing treatment programs for the mentally retarded sex offender. We were able to locate two single case treatment studies (Lutzker, 1973; Wong, Gaydos, & Fuqua, 1979) of mentally retarded sexual offenders and one single case report of the treatment of public masturbation in a 7-year-old boy (Cook, Altman, Shaw, & Blaylock 1978). We also unscientifically surveyed our colleagues in the area of sexual deviation and found that although they had treated mentally retarded sex offenders, their success was variable and they also knew of little data to provide assistance. For example, Wolfe (1979) in a personal communication reports success with three to four mentally retarded individuals and failure with approximately twice that number. Their clinical observations suggested that the crucial element seemed to be the patient's support system in the community.

Although there may be other reports in the literature of the treatment of mentally retarded sex offenders, we were unable to locate them, suggesting

TABLE I
The Behavioral Assessment and Treatment of Sexual Aggressives

Behavioral excess or deficits	Treatment methods	Assessment methods
Excessive arousal to deviant stimuli	Aversion-suppression methods: 1. Covert sensitization 2. Electrical aversion 3. Odor aversion 4. Chemical aversion 5. Biofeedback assisted suppression 6. Satiation	Penile recordings; self-report; clinical interviews
Deficit arousal to non-deviant sexual stimuli	Generations of arousal to non-deviant cues: 1. Masturbatory conditioning 2. Exposure 3. Fading 4. Systematic desensitization	
	Social skills deficits	
Heterosocial skills	Heterosocial skills training	Behavior role playing procedures
Assertive skills	Assertive training	
Sexual performance	Sexual dysfunction treatments	Self-report inventories
Gender role behavior	Gender role, motor behavior training	Sex education test Clinical interviews

that they are not readily accessible. Therefore, we are left with a problem of considerable clinical significance, while lacking objective data to provide guidance. One solution to this problem is to adapt procedures developed for the treatment of the nonretarded sex offender. Table I presents an update (Murphy, Abel, & Becker, 1980) of a behavioral model of sexual deviation proposed originally by Abel and his colleagues (Abel, Blanchard, & Becker, 1976, 1978; Barlow & Abel, 1976). This table presents areas of excesses and deficits, possible assessment procedures within each area, and possible treatment procedures in each area. Since the procedures for assessment and treatment have been well reviewed in the references cited, we will briefly outline the various areas as they relate to the mentally retarded. It should be noted that the areas can be independent—not all offenders will need treatment in all areas. It should also be realized that there are different degrees of validity and reliabilty associated with the various outlined assessment and treatment procedures that are beyond the scope of this section to review completely.

The first two areas relate to either excesses in deviant sexual arousal (a defining characteristic of sexual deviance), or deficits in nondeviant sexual arousal. The procedures for assessing this area include penile recordings and self-reports such as card sorts or frequency counts. The applicability of penile recordings for the mentally retarded is unexplored. However, there is some indirect data suggesting possible difficulties. One difficulty is raised by the Gebhard *et al.* (1965) observation that for some classifications of sexual offenders, the offense is motivated by attention and affection rather than sexual gratification. However, this observation was based on self-report, a procedure which is highly unreliable with sex offenders in general and probably just as unreliable in the mentally retarded. Those who work with pedophiles, for example, realize that many attribute their behavior to seeking affection not sex, while penile data indicates clear sexual arousal to pedophilic stimuli (Abel, Becker, Murphy, & Flanagan, 1979).

A second observation (Gebhard, 1973) was that the mentally retarded individual is less responsive to visual stimuli than the nonretarded individual. Again, these data were based on self-report and not penile data. More objective data are needed in this area comparing the mentally retarded to the nonretarded on capability of arousal to a variety of sexual stimuli including slides, audio stimuli, and video stimuli.

The other form of assessment in this area is self-report used in conjunction with penile recordings. In general, we employ two types of self-report, a card sort composed of written descriptions of deviant and nondeviant behavior which are rated on a –3 to +3 scale of pleasure. The second form is a frequency count of the deviant and nondeviant behavior in which the patient is engaging, in addition to a count of deviant and nondeviant fantasies. The card sort creates problems in terms of the individual's ability to read, although we have found that we can substitute the written material with pictures (i.e., pictures of adult women and pictures of children) and have the subject rate these rather than rating the verbal statements. At times, depending on the level of mental retardation, subjects were rated on a bipolar scale of either pleasurable or nonpleasurable responses, rather than the +3 to −3 scale.

The frequency count also creates problems in terms of the subject's ability to discriminate deviant and nondeviant fantasies and to remember to record when they are occurring. We have found that it is extremely useful to try to have family members also observe the patient's behavior. Although it is sometimes impossible to get accurate frequency counts of the occurrence of deviant and nondeviant behaviors, there are at times various indirect behavioral manifestations of the deviant behavior that can be noted by family members. For example, some offenders will show typical patterns either before or after their offenses. Family members will note the patient is having problems because of increased irritability or increased restlessness. We recommend that in interviewing the patient and the family members, attempts be made to identify some of these indirect behavioral characteristics. Family members can then keep a count of them and provide at least an indirect count of possible deviant behavior. In working with the mentally retarded sex offender, we cannot stress enough that cooperation must be obtained from the patient's support system if one expects to have any success.

When we move to the treatment procedures for decreasing deviant arousal and increasing appropriate arousal, we again run into a number of problems. A number of the procedures require a certain level of cognitive abilities that may be beyond the capacity of mentally retarded individuals (covert sensitization, systematic desensitization, and possibly satiation therapy). In addition, ethical difficulties arise when using aversive procedures such as electrical aversion. However, it might be possible to use such procedures as odor aversion (the pairing of deviant stimuli with valeric acid) which to the general public probably appears less inhumane than electrical aversion. Again, in terms of increasing arousal, such procedures as systematic desensitization may require cognitive abilities beyond the capabilities of the mentally retarded. Procedures such as classical conditioning and fading do not have sufficient clinical data associated with them to determine their effectiveness and we need further data in this area. A procedure that we might recommend for the mentally retarded is that of exposure. This procedure requires that the subject view video material depicting heterosexual (or homosexual if that is the patient's adult orientaton) stimuli. Our general procedure is to have the patient view 30-minute erotic films. The rationale behind the procedure is that lack of nondeviant arousal results from lack of nondeviant fantasies. Exposure to stimuli material provides fantasy material which the patient can then incorporate into his own sexual fantasies in addition to possibly reducing anxiety to such stimuli. This may lead to increased sexual arousal to appropriate stimuli. The technique is rather simple and does not require excessive cognitive abilities.

Basically, in the area of sexual arousal in the mentally retarded, we need more objective data on the validity of penile responses in these patients and more objective data on the applicability of the various treatment procedures described above. Although we are making the assumption that some procedures like covert sensitization are not appropriate, it is possible that for many mildly retarded individuals such procedures might be effective. Only further research will answer this question.

When we move to the second area listed, that of social skills deficits, there are a number of subgroups included: heterosocial skills, assertiveness skills, empathy skills, and gender-motor behavior. These are areas that have been found to have possible deficits in nonretarded offenders and we feel certain that for mentally retarded offenders they will be as important or even more important. It is highly likely that these various areas of social competence (especially heterosocial skills and assertiveness skills) will present difficulties for the mentally retarded, given that many have spent a good deal of their time in institutions and therefore have not had the opportunity to learn appropriate skills. Again, as with deviant and nondeviant arousal, the assessment procedures for these deficits have not been applied to the retarded sex offender. Those familiar with the behavioral literature will know that there are numerous publications in the area of assertiveness training and heterosocial-skills training. The problem in the applicability of these skills to sex offenders have been recently reviewed (Murphy et al., 1980). The problems of generalizability of laboratory measures of social competence will likely be as large a problem with the mentally retarded individual as it is currently with the nonretarded. It is also not clear what social skills the mentally retarded need to learn to function in their environment. Are the social skills used among mentally retarded individuals different than the social skills of the general population? Are there underlying similarities? These are research questions that need to be answered so that appropriate assessment procedures can be designed for this important area. In terms of treatment in this area, our general procedure has been the use of standard behavioral social-skills training procedures including behavioral rehearsal, modeling, video feedback, and social reinforcement. It is likely that similar procedures, although simplified, will be applicable to the mentally retarded. The major issue, however, will be what behaviors need to be trained and, as in most behavioral treatments, how these will be generalized to the natural environment. (See the chapter by Matson *et al.*, for a more detailed discussion of these and related concerns.)

The final area listed is that of sexual dysfunctions and sexual knowledge. The sex education literature concerning the mentally retarded has been well reviewed already. Sexual knowledge inventories for the mentally retarded are available currently for use in assessment (Edmonson, McCombs, & Wish, 1979). When we turn to sexual dysfunction (impotence, premature ejaculation, retarded ejaculation), we have very little data on this problem in the mentally retarded in general and no data in regard to the problem in mentally retarded sex offenders. Sexual dysfunctions are problems observed clinically in sex offenders and it is likely that the problem will also be observed occasionally in the subgroup with marked cognitive deficits. Treatment procedures used with the nonretarded are generally sex dysfunction treatments (Annon, 1974, 1975) involving information giving, permission giving, communication training and structured sexual exercises. It is likely that similar procedures can be adopted for the mentally retarded, taking into account differences in levels of understanding.

Although the section on treatment has been somewhat brief, the majority of information presented has been adopted from other publications which clearly outline the rationale and the relationship of the various areas listed in Table I to sexual deviation. What is needed at this point is more objective data relating these variables to the mentally retarded sex offender and the development of alternative procedures for both assessing and treating various excesses and deficits in mentally retarded sex offenders. Our clinical experience would suggest that the model is applicable but that the procedures we currently have available are not sufficient to adequately measure these variables, and the treatment procedures we have need much further development for their application to the mentally retarded.

We will conclude this section and the chapter with two case histories of the evaluation and treatment of two mentally retarded sex offenders.

Case 1 (Jerry)

The subject was a teenage male, referred from a local psychiatric adolescent unit for evaluation. Jerry had been accused by his sister of engaging in sexual interactions with her 7-year-old daughter. The patient denied the incidents. Other history taken from the patient indicated that he was accused of raping a 12-year-old female when he was age 13, but he again denied this charge. He did admit to physically assaulting the girl. Jerry admitted to having little sexual experience of any type and reported having had sexual interactions on only two occasions in his life. He denied that he ever masturbated. He also reported that he had difficulties ejaculating although his history was questionable in the whole area of sexual experience. He admitted to deficits in heterosocial-skills (ability to interact with women) and to deficits in sexual knowledge.

His social history indicated that he lived with his mother until she died approximately three years before we saw the patient. At that time he moved in with his sister whom he accused of abusing him. His father, with whom he had little contact since age 5, lived in another state. He reported that he had 10 brothers and sisters (he was the second youngest). One brother was in prison for rape.

The mental status exam suggested that the patient was mildly mentally retarded, and there was some indication of previous psychotic type episodes. At the time he was seen he was on a phenothiazine and was not overtly psychotic. He still seemed to be suffering from a grief reaction following his mother's death which he had not resolved. There was also a history of past suicide attempts.

To try to determine the patient's sexual arousal pattern, his penile response was measured to pedophile cues (Abel, Becker, Murphy, & Flanagan, 1979) and to rape cues (Abel, Blanchard, Becker, & Djenderedjian, 1978). The pedophile cues are a series of seven audiotapes, six dealing with young children, increasing in aggressiveness from a child initiated sexual activity to a pure physical assault. The seventh stimulus in this series is an adult female for comparison purposes. The data from this are presented in Figure 1. As can be seen, the patient showed high sexual arousal to the majority of the child stimuli except for the pure assault and showed adequate heterosexual arousal. This was consistent with the history of sexual assault of young children and suggested that there was a possibility of aggression being used.

The rape cues are a series of video stimuli depicting a mutually consenting sexual interaction, a rape, and an aggressive stimuli devoid of sexual connotation. The results were a 70% erection to the mutual stimuli, a 59% erection to the rape stimuli and no erection to the aggression stimuli. This gave the patient a rape index of .84% (rape stimuli divide by mutual stimuli) which is in the borderline area between a rapist and a normal.

It can be concluded that the patient has sexual arousal to children and a

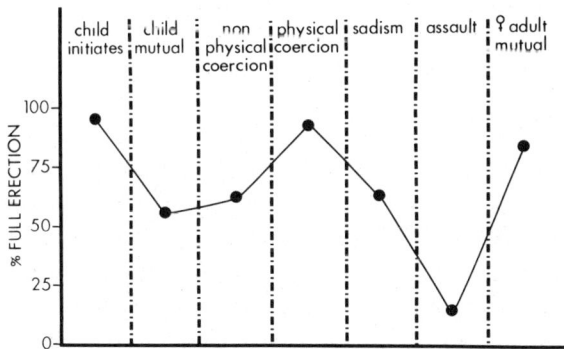

FIGURE 1. Erection responses of a retarded offender to pedophilic stimuli

probable arousal pattern to aggressive sexual interactions. Other assessment indicated that the patient was deficit in heterosocial skills as indicated in the interview and was deficit in his sexual knowledge. Following this assessment, the patient was released from the hospital to a brother who had young males but no young females in the home. Because of the patient's intellectual level, we did not feel that we had any aversive procedures (such as covert sensitization) to use to reduce deviant arousal. We were reluctant to suggest electrical aversion since the patient was hospitalized and was under court order. We did not feel that he was able to give informed consent for such a treatment. Therefore, we began his treatment with sex education and social skills training. His social skills training has been going fairly well as has his sex education but the major problem has been getting him to attend treatment sessions. Apparently the brother with whom he was living did not insist that Jerry make his treatment appointments and therefore his attendance to treatment has been rather sporadic. Also on our last penile assessment prior to this writing, he has continued with high deviant-sexual arousal. Because of this, if we can continue the patient in treatment, we are going to attempt to use covert sensitization possibly associated with valeric acid (odor aversion) in an attempt to reduce his arousal.

This case indicates that some of the measures adopted for nonretarded offenders seem to be applicable and were reflective of this patient's history. However, as we have observed in the past, the mentally retarded sex offenders' (and other offenders, in addition) motivation to continue in treatment is sometimes difficult to obtain. We also see that we are somewhat handicapped in appropriate procedures to reduce deviant arousal when the subject's ability to give informed consent is questionable.

Case 2 (John)

This patient was a 38-year-old male when he was first seen by our project in 1976. He had referred himself and in fact had forced his parents to bring him to our program for treatment. He was estimated to be in the moderately retarded range but seemed to have insight into his difficulties controlling his sexual urges toward young children. This insight and motivation to control his behavior was much beyond his intellectual level at least when judged by educational accomplishments or adaptive behavior.

His sexual history indicated that he first began involving himself with young children at age 12 when he began having sexual interactions with seven- or eight-year-old girls. This continued until age 30 when he was arrested and sent to prison. Other relevant sexual behavior was that from age 17 to age 30 he had been involved sexually with animals and he began "window-peeping" at age 28 which continued until his arrest. At age 26 John was married and reported that his wife was cold and did not like sex. Other than his wife, he seemed to have little sexual experience with adult women.

During his first year in prison he apparently became rather paranoid and at the time we were seeing him was still on Mellaril and Cogentin. Since being started on medication, he was unable to ejaculate but was currently masturbating to fantasies of young children.

While in prison, the patient had been treated with electrical aversion therapy and felt that it had been successful in decreasing his deviant arousal, at least initially. However, since his release from prison, his urges had been increasing over the years until he felt that he could no longer control his behavior. At this point he initiated treatment contact because of his fear that he would return to prison for life. His family was also interviewed at this time. Although they were trying to deny the problems, they were supportive and agreeable to any type of treatment we felt necessary.

In this case, our penile assessments proved less than helpful in that he showed very little erection to any stimuli, either to adult women or to children. It was difficult to determine whether this was secondary to the psychotropic medication or reflected his lack of arousability to visual stimuli alone.

In this case, the patient was under no coercion, and had referred himself. Also, the patient was interviewed by the patient advocate working for our project and who gave consent for his treatment. Because the patient had found electrical aversion effective in the past, and was requesting the same treatment, we treated John with a series of sixteen electrical aversion sessions over a 3-month period. He was also given pictures of adult women to use when masturbating at home. This was designed to replace the fantasies of young children he had been using in his masturbatory sessions.

We have followed him since our initial contact at least once every 6-months up until the present time. From the patient's self report, interviews with his parents, and interviews with a sister who is close to the patient, there are no indications of any return of his pedophilic behavior. In this case, there are indirect behavioral measures of his tendency to act out. The usual signs of the patient having problems are increased irritability, temper outbursts, and social withdrawal. These behaviors have not been reported by his parents, sister, or the patient over this 3-year period.

In this case, adequate erection baseline data was not available, but other sources indicate a successful treatment outcome. The use of electrical aversion raises numerous ethical problems which we attempted to deal with by (1) obtaining permission from the patient; (2) obtaining permission from his family; and (3) having an outside patient advocate evaluate the patient to determine his ability to give informed consent. In addition, the patient was under no legal coercion to participate in treatment. We feel that we were able to ethically provide a treatment that has been helpful to the patient over a 3-year period. We feel the risks involved in the treatment were greatly outweighed by the cost to potential victims of this patient and the cost to the patient himself in terms of reincarceration for pedophilic behavior.

References

Abbott, J. M., & Ladd G. M. Any reason why this mentally retarded couple should not be joined together? *Mental Retardation, 1970, 8,* 45–48.
Abel, G. G., Blanchard, E. B., & Becker, J. V. Psychological treatment for rapists. In M. Walker & S. Brodsky (Eds.), *Sexual Assault.* Lexington, Mass.: Lexington Books, 1976.
Abel, G. G., Blanchard, E. B., & Becker, J. V. An integrated program for rapists. In R. T. Rada (Ed.), *Clinical aspects of the rapist.* New York: Greene & Stratton, 1978.
Abel, G. G., Blanchard, E. B., Becker, J. V., & Djenderedjian, A. Differentiating sexual aggressives with penile measures. *Criminal Justice and Behavior, 1978, 5,* 315–332.
Abel, G. G., Becker, J. V., Murphy, W. D., & Flanagan, B. *Identifying dangerous child molesters.* Paper presented at the 11th Banff International Conference on Behavior Modification, Banff, Canada, March 1979.
Abelson, A. G. Development of core gender identity and gender constancy in retarded and normal children. *Dissertation Abstracts International, 1977, 38,* 1324.
Adams, J. B., & Sesiak, M. E. Sex education—A sensible approach. *The Journal of School Health, 1967, 37,* 222–225.

ALCORN, D. E. Parental views on sexual development and education of the trainable mentally retarded. *Journal of Special Education*, 1974, 8, 119-130.
ANDRON, L. & STURM, M. L. Is "I do" in the repertoire of the retarded? A study of the functioning of married retarded couples. *Mental Retardation*, 1973, 11, 31-34.
ANNON, J. S. *The behavioral treatment of sexual problems (Vol 1). Brief therapy.* Honolulu, Hawaii: Enabling Systems, 1974.
ANNON, J. S. *The behavioral treatment of sexual problems (Vol 1). Brief therapy.* Honolulu, Hawaii: Enabling Systems, 1974.
BALESTER, R. J. Sex education: Fact and fancy. *Journal of Special Education*, 1972, 5, 355-347.
BANGS, T. W. Assertive training for non-assertive developmentally disabled adults. *Dissertation Abstracts International*, 1977, 38, 3411.
BARLOW, D. H., & ABEL, G. G. Recent developments in assessment and treatment of sexual deviation. In W. E. Craighead, A. E. Kazdin, & M. J. Mahoney (Eds.), *Behavior modification: Principles, issues, and application.* Boston: Houghton Mifflin, 1976.
BASS, M. S. Marriage, parenthood and the prevention of pregnancy for the mentally deficient. *American Journal of Mental Deficiency*, 1963, 55, 318-333.
BASS, M. S. Marriage for the mentally deficient. *Mental Retardation*, 1964, 2, 198-202.(a)
BASS, M. S. Marriage, parenthood and prevention of pregnancy for the mentally deficient. *Eugenics Quarterly*, 1964, 11, 96-111.(b)
BASS, M. S. Sex education for the handicapped. *The Family Coordinator*, 1974, 23, 27-33.
BASS, M. S. Surgical contraception: A key to normalization and prevention. *Mental Retardation*, 1978, 16, 399-404.
BASS, M. S., & GELOF, M. (Eds.), *Sexual rights and responsibilities of the mentally retarded.* Proceedings of the Conference of the American Association on Mental Deficiency, Region IX, Newark, Delaware, 1972.
BAYLES, M. The legal precedents in sterilization of the retarded: In whose interest? *Hastings Center Report*, 1978, 8, 37-41.
BECKER, K. L. Clinical and therapeutic experiences with Klinefelter's syndrome. *Fertility and Sterility*, 1972, 23, 568-578.
BECKMAN-BRINDLEY, S. N., & TAVAMINA, J. B. Normalization: A new look. *Education and Training of the Mentally Retarded*, 1978, 13, 66-68.
BEGAB, M. The major dilemma of mental retardation: Shall we prevent it? *American Journal of Mental Deficiency*, 1974, 78, 519-529.
BENNETT, B., VOCKELL, E., & VOCKELL, K. Sex education for EMR adolescent girls: An evaluation and some suggestions. *Journal for Special Educators of Mentally Retarded*, 1972, 9, 3-7.
BERDIANSKY, H. A., & PARKER, R. Establishing a group home for the adult mentally retarded in North Carolina. *Mental Retardation*, 1977, 15, 8-11.
BERRY, J. M. & SHAPIRO, A. Married mentally handicapped patients in the community. *Proceedings of the Royal Society of Medicine*, 1975, 68, 27-30.
BILLER, H. B. & BORSTELMANN, L. J. Intellectual level and sex role development in mentally retarded children. *American Journal of Mental Deficiency*, 1965, 70, 443-447.
BLOCK, W. A. *Do-it-yourself illustrated human sexuality book for kids.* Trenton, New Jersey: Prep Publications, 1979.
BLOM, G. E. Some considerations about the neglect of sex education in special education. *Journal of Special Education*, 1972, 5, 359-361.
BLOOM, J. L. Sex education for handicapped adolescents. *Journal of School Health*, 1969, 39, 363-367.
BOOK, J. A. Fertility trends in some types of mental defects. *Eugenics Quarterly*, 1959, 6, 113-116.
BOWDEN, J., SPITZ, H. H., & WINTERS, J. J. Follow-up of one retarded couple's marriage. *Mental Retardation*, 1979, 9, 42-43.
BURT, R. A. Legal restrictions on sexual and familial relations of mental retardates—Old laws,

new guises. In F. F. de la Cruz & G. D. LaVeck (Eds.), *Human sexuality and the mentally retarded*. New York: Brunner/Mazel, 1973.

BUTLER, F. O. A quarter of a century's experience in sterilization of mental defectives in California. *American Journal of Mental Deficiency*, 1945, 49, 508-513.

CARRUTH, D. G. Human sexuality in a half way house. In F. F. de la Cruz & G. D. LaVeck (Eds.), *Human sexuality and the mentally retarded*, New York: Brunner/Mazel, 1973.

CHARLES, D. C. Adult adjustment of some deficient American children. *American Journal of Mental Deficiency*, 1957, 62, 300-304.

CHEZ, R. A. Mental disability as a basis for contraception and sterilization. *Social Biology*, 1971, 18, S120-S126.

CHRISTIE, M. M., MARSHALL, W. L., & LANTHIER, R. D. *A descriptive study of incarcerated rapists and pedophiles.* Unpublished manuscript, 1977.

CLARK, E. T. Sex role preference in mentally retarded children. *American Journal of Mental Deficiency*, 1963, 67, 606-610.

COLEMAN, E. M. & MURPHY, W. D. A survey of sexual attitudes and sex education programs among facilities for the mentally retarded. *Applied Research in Mental Retardation*, 1980, 1, 269-276.

COOK, J. W., ALTMAN, K., SHAW, J., & BLAYLOCK, M. Use of contingent lemon juice to eliminate public masturbation by a severely retarded boy. *Behaviour Research and Therapy*, 1978, 16, 131-134.

CUMMINGS, S. T. The impact of the child's deficiency on the father: A study of fathers of mentally retarded and of chronically ill children. *American Journal of Orthopsychiatry*, 1976, 46, 246-255.

CUMMINGS, S. BAYLEY, H., & RIE, H. Effects of the child's deficiency on the mother: A study of mothers of mentally retarded, chronically ill and neurotic children. *American Journal of Orthopsychiatry*, 1966, 36, 595-608.

CURRAN, J. P. Skills training as an approach to the treatment of heterosexual-social anxiety: A review. *Psychological Bulletin*, 1977, 84, 140-157.

DAVID, H. P., SMITH, J. D., & FRIEDMAN, E. Family planning services for persons handicapped by mental retardation. *American Journal of Public Health*, 1976, 66, 1053-1057.

DAVIS, P. J. Social skills training of retarded adults: A comparison of modeling procedures. *Dissertation Abstracts International*, 1978, 39, 373-374.

DEBLASSIE, R. R., & COWAN, M. A. Counseling with the mentally handicapped child. *Elementary School Guidance and Counseling*, 1976, 10, 246-253.

DEISHER, R. W. Sexual behavior of retarded in institutions. In F. F. de la Cruz & G. D. LaVeck (Eds.), *Human sexuality and the mentally retarded*. New York: Brunner/Mazel, 1973.

DELP, H. A. Sex education for the handicapped. *Journal of Special Education*, 1972, 5, 363-364.

DEMERY, M. M. A comparison of the cognitive development of retarded women in the domains of human reproduction, physical causality and physical conservation. *Dissertation Abstracts International*, 1978, 38, 6644-6645.

DUPRAS, A., & TREMBLAY, R. Path analysis of parents' conservatism toward sex education of their mentally retarded children. *American Journal of Mental Deficiency*, 1976, 81, 162-166.

EAST, W. N. Observations on exhibitionism. *Lancet*, 1924, 23, 370-375.

EDGERTON, R. B., & DINGMAN, H. Good reasons for bad supervision: Dating in a hospital for mentally retarded. *Psychiatric Quarterly Supplement Part 2*, 1964, 221-223.

EDMONSON, B., & WISH, J. Sex knowledge and attitudes of moderately retarded males. *American Journal of Mental Deficiency*, 1975, 80, 172-179.

EDMONSON, B., MCCOMBS, K., & WISH J. What retarded adults believe about sex. *American Journal of Mental Deficiency*, 1979, 84, 11-18.

EVANS, E. C. Assisting retarded people into the community. *Australian Journal of Mental Retardation*, 1977, 4, 16-19.

Federal Register 43:217 (Nov, 8, 1978) 521465-175.
Fiedler, D. E., & Tyler, J. C. Reaching the forgotten: Contraception for the institutionalized woman. *Advances in Planned Parenthood*, 1975, *10*, 160-163.
Fleming, R. R. Training passive and aggressive educable mentally retarded children and assertive behaviors using three types of structured learning training. *Dissertation Abstracts International*, 1977, *38*, 2363.
Fischer, H. L., & Krajicek, M. J. Sexual development in the moderately retarded child: Level of information and parental attitudes. *Mental Retardation*, 1974, *12*, 28-30.
Fisher, G. M. Sexual identification in mentally retarded male children and adults. *American Journal of Mental Deficiency*, 1960, *65*, 42-45.
Fisher, G. M. Sexual identification in mentally subnormal females. *American Journal of Mental Deficiency*, 1961, *66*, 266-269.
Floor, L., Baxter, D., Rosen, M., & Zisfein, L. A survey of marriages among previously institutionalized retardates. *Mental Retardation*, 1975, *13*, 33-37.
Fotheringham, J. B. The concept of social competence as applied to marriage and child care in those classified as mentally retarded. *Canadian Medical Association Journal*, 1971, *104*, 813-816.
Friedman, E. Missing in the life of the retarded individual—sex: Reflections on Sol Gordon's paper. *Journal of Special Education*, 1972, *5*, 365-368.
Gebhard, P. H. Sexual behavior of the retarded. In F. F. de la Cruz & G. D. LaVeck (Eds.), *Human sexuality and the mentally retarded*. New York: Brunner/ Mazel, 1973.
Gebhard, P. H., Gagnon, J. H., Pomeroy, W. B., & Christenson, C. V. *Sex offenders*. New York: Harper & Row, 1965.
Gendel, E. S. Sex education patterns and professional responsibility. *Southern Medical Journal*, 1966, *59*, 411-416.
Gendel, E. S. *Sex education of the mentally retarded child in the home*. Paper presented at the Council for Exceptional Children Convention, New York, New York, 1968.
Gerald, P. S. Physical and biological aspects (session two): General discussion. In F. F. de la Cruz & G. D. LaVeck (Eds.), *Human sexuality and the mentally retarded*. New York: Brunner/ Mazel, 1973.
Goldstein, J. Sex education and the trainable. In M. S. Bass & M. Gelof (Eds.), *Sexual rights and responsibilities of the mentally retarded*. Proceedings of the Conference of the American Association on Mental Deficiency, Region IX, Newark, Delaware, 1972.
Goodman, L. The sexual rights of the retarded—A dilemma for parents. *The Family Coordinator*, 1973, *22*, 472-474.
Goodman, L., Budner, S., & Lesh, B. The parent's role in sex education for the retarded. *Mental Retardation*, 1971, *9*, 43-45.
Goodman, R. Physical and biological aspects. In F. F. de la Cruz & G. D. LaVeck (Eds.), *Human sexuality and the mentally retarded*. New York: Brunner/Mazel, 1973.
Gordon, S. *Facts about sex for today's youth*. Fayetteville, New York: Ed-U Press, Inc., 1969.
Gordon, S. What adolescents want to know. *American Journal of Nursing*, 1971, *71*, 534-535.(a)
Gordon, S. *Ten heavy facts about sex*. Syracuse, New York: Ed-U Press, 1971.(b)
Gordon, S. Missing in special education: Sex. *Journal of Special Education*, 1972, *5*, 351-354.
Gordon, S. *Facts about VD for today's youth*. Charlotteville, Virginia: Ed-U Press, 1973.(a)
Gordon, S. *The sexual adolescent: Communicating with teenagers about sex*. North Scituate, Massachusetts: Duxburg Press, 1973. (b)
Gordon, S. A response to Warren Johnson. In F. F. de la Cruz & G. D. LaVeck (Eds.), *Human sexuality and the mentally retarded*. New York: Brunner/Mazel, 1973.(c)
Gordon, S. *Girls are girls and boys are boys so what's the difference?* Fayetteville, New York: Ed-U Press, Inc., 1979.
Grebler, A. M. Parental attitudes toward mentally retarded children. *American Journal of Mental Deficiency*, 1952, *56*, 475-483.

Gupta, S. & Singh, M. V. Marriage and sex education of mental retardates. *Child Psychiatry Quarterly*, 1973, *6*, 15-17.

Hall, J. E. Sexuality and the mentally retarded person. In R. Green (Ed.), *Human sexuality: A health practitioner's text* (2nd ed.). Baltimore: Williams & Wilkins, 1979.

Hall, J. E., & Morris, H. L. Sexual knowledge and attitudes of institutionalized and noninstituionalized retarded adolescents. *American Journal of Mental Deficiency*, 1976, *80*, 382-387.

Hall, J. E., & Sawyer, H. Sexual policies for the mentally retarded. *Sexuality and Disability*, 1978, *1*, 34-43.

Hall, J. E., Morris, H. L. & Barker, H. R. Sexual knowledge and attitude of mentally retarded adolescents. *American Journal of Mental Deficiency*, 1973, *77*, 706-709.

Halpert, J. J. Social effectiveness and reintegration of mentally retarded pupils. *Dissertation Abstracts International*, 1978, *39*, 1475.

Hamilton, C. R., Jr., Scully, R. E., & Kliman, B. Hypogonadotropinism in Prader-Willi Syndrome—induction of puberty and spermatogenesis by clomiphene citrate. *The American Journal of Medicine*, 1972, *52*, 322-329.

Hammer, S. L., Wright, L. S., & Jensen, D. L. Sex education for the retarded adolescent: A survey of parental attitudes and methods of management in fifty adolescent retardates. *Clinical Pediatrics*, 1967, *6*, 621-627.

Hartman, S. S., & Hynes, J. Marriage education for mentally retarded adults. *Social Casework*, 1975, *56*, 280-284.

Helbig, D. W. Physical and biological aspects. In F, F. de la Cruz & G. D. LaVeck (Eds.), *Human sexuality and the mentally retarded*. New York: Brunner/Mazel, 1973.

Hepner, P. J. Sexual expression and the mentally retarded: The lawyer's role. *Sexuality and Disability*, 1979, *2*, 38-46.

Hirayama, H. Management of the sexuality of the mentally retarded in institutions: Problems and issue. In D. Kunkel (Ed.), *Sexual issues in social work*. Honolulu, Hawaii: University of Hawaii, School of Social Work, 1979.

Humphreys, L., Forehand, R., Cheney, T., & Adams, S. V. Training retarded individuals in communication skills: An experimental program. *Journal of Clinical Child Psychology*, 1977, *6*, 33-37.

Johnson, H. R. Myhre, S. A., Ruvalcaba, R. H. A., Thuline, H. C., & Kelley, V. C. Effects of testosterone on body image and behavior in Klinefelter Syndrome: A pilot study. *Developmental Medicine and Child Neurology*, 1970, *12*, 454-460.

Johnson, W. R. Sex education of the mentally retarded. In F. F. de la Cruz & G. D. LaVeck (Eds.), *Human sexuality and the mentally retarded*. New York: Brunner/Mazel, 1973.

Johnson, W. R., & Magarick, R. H. Training undergraduates to give physical education and sex education to retardates and their parents. In M. S. Bass & M. Gelof (Eds.), *Sexual rights and responsibilities of the retarded*. Proceedings of the Conference of the American Association on Mental Deficiency, Region IX, Newark, Delaware, 1972.

Kempton, W. Training program in institutions and the community. In M. S. Bass & M. Gelof (Eds.), *Sexual rights and responsibilities of the mentally retarded*. Proceedings of the Conference of the American Association on Mental Deficiency, Region IX, Newark, Delaware, 1972.

Kempton, W. Sex education—A cooperative effort of parent and teacher. *Exceptional Children*, 1975, *41*, 531-535.

Kempton, W. The mentally retarded person. In H. L. Gochras & J. S. Gochros (Eds.), *The sexually oppressed*. New York: Association Press, 1977.

Kempton, W. Sex education for the mentally handicapped. *Sexuality and Disability*, 1978, *1*, 137-146.

Kempton, W., & Hanson, G. *Sexuality and the mentally handicapped: Nine slide presentations for teaching the mentally handicapped individual*. Santa Monica, California: Stanford Film Associates, 1978.

Kempton, W., Bass M., & Gordon S. *Love, sex, and birth control for the mentally retarded: Guide for parents*. Philadelphia: Planned Parenthood Association, 1971.

KINSEY, A. C., POMEROY, W. B., & MARTIN, C. E. *Sexual behavior in the human male*. Philadelphia: W. B. Saunders Co., 1948.

KINSEY, A. C., POMEROY, W. B., MARTIN, C. E., & GEBHARD, P. H. *Sexual behavior in the human female*. Philadelphia: W. B. Saunders Co., 1953.

KOLODNY, R. C., MASTERS, W. H., & JOHNSON, V. E. *Textbook of sexual medicine*. Boston: Little, Brown & Company, 1979.

KRATTER, F. E., & THORNE, G. D. Sex education of retarded children. *American Journal of Mental Deficiency*, 1957, *62*, 44–48.

KRIEGER, G. W. An exploratory study of the effect of model-reinforcement counseling on the vocational behavior of a group of male retarded adolescents. *Dissertation Abstracts International*, 1970, *30*, 4776–4777.

KRISHEF, C. H. State laws on marriage and sterilization of the mentally retarded. *Mental Retardation*, 1972, *10*, 36–38.

LAVECK, G. D., & DE LA CRUZ, F. F. Contraception for the mentally retarded: Current methods and future prospects. In F. F. de la Cruz & G. D. LaVeck (Eds.), *Human sexuality and the mentally retarded*. New York: Brunner/Mazel, 1973.

LEBRUN, S., & HUTCHINSON, P. Human sexuality: Expanding self-awareness in a leisure setting. *Journal of Leisurability*, 1977, *4*, 6–8.

LINN, B. Involuntary sterilization—A constitutional awakening to fundamental human rights. *Amicus*, 1977, *2*, 34–40.

LUTZKER, J. R. Reinforcement control of exhibitionism in a profoundly retarded adult. *Proceedings of 81st Annual Convention of the American Psychological Association*, 1973, *8*, 925–926.

MACDONALD, J. M. *Indecent Exposure*. Springfield, Ill.: Charles C Thomas, 1973.

MATTINSON, J. Marriage and mental handicap. In F. F. de la Cruz & G. D. LaVeck (Eds.), *Human sexuality and the mentally retarded*. New York: Brunner/Mazel, 1973.

MCCRARY, J. L. *McCrary's human sexuality* (3rd ed.). New York: D. Van Nostrand, 1978.

MCEWEN, J. L. Survey of attitudes toward sexual behavior of institutionalized mental retardates. *Psychological Republic*, 1977, *41*, 874.

MEYEN, E. L. Sex education for the mentally retarded: Implications for programming and teacher training. *Focus on Exceptional Children*, 1970, *1*, 1–5.

MEYERS, R. *Social and sexual development: A guide for teachers of the handicapped*. Special Education Curriculum Developmental Center—An In-Service Training Project, 1971.

MEYEROWITZ, J. H. Sex and the mentally retarded. *Medical Aspects of Human Sexuality*, 1971, *5*, 94–118.

MICKELSON, P. The feebleminded parent: A study of 90 family cases. *American Journal of Mental Deficiency*, 1947, *51*, 644–653.

MICKELSON, P. Can mentally deficient parents be helped to give their children better care? *American Journal of Mental Deficiency*, 1949, *53*, 516–534.

MITCHELL, L., DOCTOR, R. M., & BUTLER, D. C. Attitudes of caretakers toward the sexual behavior of mentally retarded persons. *American Journal of Mental Deficiency*, 1978, *83*, 289–296.

MOHR, J. W., TURNER, R. E., & JERRY, M. B. *Pedophilia and exhibitionism*. Toronto: University of Toronto Press, 1964.

MONEY, J. W. Some thoughts on sexual taboos and the rights of the retarded. In F. F. de la Cruz & G. D. LaVeck (Eds.), *Human sexuality and the mentally retarded*. New York: Brunner/Mazel, 1973.

MOORE, B. C., THULINE, H. C., & CAPES, L. Mongoloid and nonmongoloid retardates: A behavioral comparison. *American Journal of Mental Deficiency*, 1968, *73*, 433–436.

MORGENSTERN, M. Community attitudes toward sexuality of the retarded. In F. F. de la Cruz & G. D. LaVeck (Eds.), *Human sexuality and the mentally retarded*. New York: Brunner/Mazel, 1973. (a)

MORGENSTERN, M. The psychosexual development of the retarded. In F. F. de la Cruz & G. D. LaVeck (Eds.), *Human sexuality and the mentally retarded*. New York: Brunner/Mazel, 1973. (b)

MORLOCK, D. A., & TOVAR, C. S. Sex education for the multiple handicapped as it applies to the classroom teachers. *Training School Bulletin*, 1971, 68, 87-96.

MOSIER, H. D., GROSSMAN, H. G., & DINGMAN, H. F. Secondary sex development in mentally deficient individuals. *Child Development*, 1962, 33,, 273-286.

MUELLER, E. E. Introduction of sex education: An American school in Tunisia. *The Journal of School Health*, 1971, 41, 376-382.

MULHERN, T. J. Survey of reported sexual behavior and policies characterizing residential facilities for retarded citizens. *American Journal of Mental Deficiency*, 1975, 79, 670.

MURPHY, E. A. Effects of changing sexuality on the gene pool: A response to Sheldon Reed. In F. F. de la Cruz & G. D. LaVeck (Eds.), *Human sexuality and the mentally retarded*. New York: Brunner/Mazel, 1973.

MURPHY, W. D., ABEL, G. G., & BECKER, J. V. Research issues. In D. Cox & R. Dartzman (Eds.), *Exhibitionism: Description, assessment, and treatment*. New York: Garland Press, 1980.

NELSON, R. O., GIBSON, R., & CUTTING, D. S. Videotaped modeling: The development of three appropriate social responses in a mildly retarded child. *Mental Retardation*, 1973, 12, 24-28.

NEVILLE, R. The philosophical arguments. *Hasting Center Reports*, 1978, 8, 33-37.

PATTULO, A. W. *Puberty in the girl who is retarded*. New York: National Association for Retarded Children, 1969.

PATULLO, A. W. The socio-sexual development at the handicapped child: A preventive care approach. *Nursing Clinics of North America*, 1975, 10, 361-372.

PATULLO, A. W., & BARNARD, K. E. Teaching menstrual hygiene to the mentally retarded. *American Journal of Nursing*, 1968, 68,, 2572-2575.

PECK, J. R., & STEPHENS, W. B. Marriage of young adult male retardates. *American Journal of Mental Deficiency*, 1965, 69, 818-827.

PERRIN, J. C., SANDS, C. R., TINKER, D. E., DOMINGUEZ, B. C., DINGLE, J. T., & THOMAS, M. J. A considered approach to sterilization of mentally retarded youth. *American Journal of Diseases of Children*, 1976, 130, 288-290.

PESKE, R. About sexual development: An attempt to be human with the mentally retarded. *Mental Retardation*, 1973, 6, 6-8.

PETCHESKY, R. P. Reproduction, ethics, and public policy: The federal sterilization regulations. *Hasting Center Reports*, 1969, 9, 29-41.

PICCARI, J. F. Effects of personal adjustment training on mentally retarded adults. *Dissertation Abstracts International*, 1977, 37, 7063-7064.

POPENOE, P. Eugenic Sterilization in California. *New England Journal of Medicine*, 1929, 201, 880-882.

PRIEST, J. H., THULINE, H. C., LAVECK, G. D., & JARVIS, D. B. An approach to genetic factors in mental retardation. *American Journal of Mental Deficiency*, 1961, 66, 42-50.

RABOCH, J., MELLAN, J., & STARKA, L. Klinefelter's Syndrome: Sexual development and activity. *Archives of Sexual Behavior*, 1979, 8, 333-339.

REED, S. C., & ANDERSON, V. E. Effects of changing sexuality on the gene pool. In F. F. de la Cruz & G. D. LaVeck (Eds.), *Human sexuality and the mentally retarded*. New York: Brunner/Mazel, 1973.

REICH, M. L., & HARSHMAN, H. W. Sex education for handicapped children: Reality or repression. *Journal of Special Education*, 1972, 5, 373-377.

Relf v. Weingerger, 372 F. Supplement 1196 (D.D.C. 1974)

A resource guide in sex education for the mentally retarded. Washington: Sex Information and Education Council of the US and American Association for Health, Physical Education and Recreation, 1971.

RICHARDSON, S. A. Careers of mentally retarded young persons: Services, jobs, and interpersonal relations. *American Journal of Mental Deficiency*, 1978, 82, 349-358.

ROBINSON, L. H. Parental attitudes of retarded young mothers. *Child Psychiatry and Human Development*, 1978, 8, 131-144.

ROSEN, M., FLOOR, L. J., BAXTER, D. X., HOROWITZ, J., & WEBER, C. Socio-sexual problems in mentally handicapped females. *Training School Bulletin*, 1971, 68, 106-112.

RUNDLE, A. T., & SYLVESTER, P. E. Evaluation at physical maturity in adolescent mentally retarded boys. *Journal of Mental Deficiency Research*, 1973, 17, 89-96.

SABAGH, G., & EDGERTON, R. B. Sterilized mental defectives look at eugenic sterilization. *Eugenics Quarterly*, 1962, 9, 213-222.

SALERNO, L. J., PARK, J. K., & GIANNINI, M. J. Reproductive capacity of the mentally retarded. *The Journal of Reproductive Medicine*, 1975, 14, 123-129.

SCALLY, B. G. Marriage and mental handicap: Some observations in Northern Ireland. In F. F. de la Cruz & G. D. LaVeck (Eds.), *Human sexuality and the mentally retarded*. New York: Brunner/Mazel, 1973.

SCHLESINGER, B. The mentally retarded and sexuality. *Canadian Medical Association Journal*, 1977, 117, 567-568.

SECKER, L. Sex education and mental handicap. *Special Education*, 1973, 62, 27-28.

SEITZ, S., & HOEKENGA, R. Modeling as a training tool for retarded children and their parents. *Mental Retardation*, 1974, 12, 28-31.

SELLING, L. S. Types of behavior manifested by feeble-minded sex offenders. *Proceedings from the American Association on Mental Deficiency*, 1939, 44, 178-186.

SENGSTOCK, W. L. Family living education for the mentally retarded. In M. S. Bass & M. Gelof (Eds.), *Sexual rights and responsibilities of the mentally retarded*. Proceedings of the Conference of the American Association on Mental Deficiency, Region IX, Newark, Delaware, 1972.

SENGSTOCK, W. L., & VERGASOR, G. A. Issues in sex education for the retarded. *Education and Training of the Mentally Retarded*, 1970, 5, 99-103.

SHAW, C. H., & WRIGHT, C. H. The married mental defective: A follow-up study. *Lancet*, 1960, 1, 273-274.

SHINDELL, P. E. Sex education programs and the mentally retarded. *Journal of School Health*, 1975, 45, 88-90.

SHUKLA, T. R., & KHOCKE, V. A study of the adjustment problems of mentally retarded children. *Indian Journal of Mental Retardation*, 1974, 7, 4-13.

SHUMAN-CARPENTER, B. S. The effects of two methods of therapy on the body image of emotionally disturbed, retarded female adolescents. *Dissertation Abstracts International*, 1977, 37, 6831-6832.

SOSKIN, R. Voluntary sterilization—safeguarding freedom of choice. *Amicus*, 1977, 2, 40-44.

TARJAN, G. Sex: A tri-polar conflict in mental retardation. *Monographs of the American Association of Mental Deficiency*, 1973, 1, 175-183.

TAYLOR, F. H. Observations on some cases of exhibitionism. *Journal of Mental Sciences*, 1947, 93, 631-638.

THOMPSON, T. Sterilization of the retarded: In whose interest? The behavioral perspective. *Hastings Center Report*, 1978, 8, 29-32.

THORNE, G. D. Sex education of mentally retarded girls. *American Journal of Mental Deficiency,* 1957, *62,* 460-463.

TURCHIN, G. Sexual attitudes of mothers and retarded children. *Journal of School Health,* 1974, *44,* 490-492.

TURNER, E. T. Attitudes of parents of deficient children toward their child's sexual behavior. *Journal of School Health,* 1970, *40,* 548-550.

VALENTE, M. Brief guide to office counseling: Sexual advice for the mentally retarded and their families. *Medical Aspects of Human Sexuality,* 1975, *9,* 91-92.

VOKELL, E., & MATTICK, P. Sex education for the mentally retarded: An analysis of problems, programs, and research. *Education and Training of the Mentally Retarded,* 1973, *7,* 129-134.

WHITCROFT, C. J., & JONES, J. P. A survey of attitudes about sterilization of retardates. *Mental Retardation,* 1974, *12,* 30-33.

WILSON, R. R., & BALDWIN, B. A. A pilot sexuality training workshop for staff at an institution for the mentally retarded. *American Journal of Public Health,* 1976, *66,* 77-78.

WOLFE, R. W. Personal communication, December 27, 1979.

WOLFERS, D., & WOLFERS, H. Vasectomania. *Family Planning Perspectives,* 1973, *5,* 196-199.

WONG, S. E., GAYDOS, G. R., & FUQUA, W. *Reducing approaches to children in a mildly retarded pedophile: Operant control in the natural environment.* Paper presented at the 13th annual meeting of the Association for the Advancement of Behavior Therapy, San Francisco, December 1979.

Wyatt v. Aderhold, 368 F. Supplement 1382 (M.D. Ala. 1973).

ZARATE, A., SORIA, J., CANALES, E. S., KASTIN, A. J., SCHALLY, A. V., & TOLEDANO, R. G. Pituitary response to synthetic luteinizing hormone-releasing hormone in Prader-Willi Syndrome, prepubertal and pubertal children. *Neuroendocrinology,* 1973-74, *13,* 321-326.

ZELMAN, D. B., & TYSER, K. M. *Essential adult sex education for the mentally retarded.* Madison, Wisconsin: The Madison Opportunity Center, Inc., 1979.

Index

ABAB Design, 179-180
AB Design, 178-179, 182
Achievement tests, 166-167, 200
Adaptive behaviors, 39
Adaptive equipment, 525, 527-528
Advocates, 320
Aggressive-disruptive behavior, 246-247, 262-264
Alternating treatment design, 181-182
American Association on Mental Deficiency, 78, 87, 88, 91, 170, 171, 173, 183
American Association on Mental Deficiency Adaptive Behavior Scale, 170-171, 173
Anticonvulsants, 472-481
Antidepressant/Antimanic drugs, 490-492
Association for Advancement of Behavior Therapy, 78
Attitudes toward mentally retarded. *See* Philosophy of programming
Autism reversal, 272-276, 294

Behavior modification, 8-15, 28,
  guidelines for, 73-79
  services, 79-88
Behavior therapy, 159
Behavioral assessment, 159-212
Behavioral rehearsal, 327-329
Biofeedback, 533-538
Brown v. *Board of Education*, 22-23, 100, 107
Butyrophenones, 470, 471

Checklists, 170-173, 202-203
Classroom behavior, 189-190
Cleanliness training, 250-259

Client centered practices, 381-382
Community survival skills, 220
Communication boards, 559-561
Community placement, 41, 50, 51, 56, 57, 63
Computers, 545-548
Compulsive behavior, 438-439
Communication devices, 552-559
Consultation, 45
Contact Desensitization, 84
Controlling people. *See* Ethics

De-institutionalization, 19-20, 37-38
Developmental model, 17
Diagnosis and classification, 161-162
Direct observation, 173-177, 203-204
Donaldson v. *O'Connor*, 15
Depression, 437-438
DSM III, 459
Dressing skills, 227-232, 235-236
Due process. *See* Legal issues

Electronic communication devices, 561-563
Ethics, 62-64, 501, 504
Eugenics, 5-6, 613-616
Event sampling, 176
Exhibitionism, 439
Extinction, 84

Functional movement-positive practice, 266
Funding, 41-45, 353-355

Generalist versus specialist training model, 384-385
Generalization, 53, 277-281, 313-314, 345-353

Group homes, 50, 54–55

Habilitation, 100, 374–376, 378–380
Halderman v. *Penhurst State School and Hospital*, 24–25, 70, 72–73, 97, 102, 120
Human sexuality, 583–645
Humanistic legalism, 22–26
Hyperactivity, 439
Human Rights and Ethics Committee, 89–91
Human rights. *See* Ethics

Inappropriate behavior, 311
Individual Education Plan, 109
Intelligence, 162–163, 165–167, 200, 421
Interobserver reliability, 176
Interviews, 167–170
Intrusiveness, 85–86

Language development
 assessment of, 195–198
Lead poisoning, effects on mental retardation, 129–158
 cohort studies of, 139–144
 epidemiological studies of, 14–146
 in etiology of hyperactivity, 136–139
 legal issues, 73, 623–626
 and nutrition, 148–149
 and pica, 146–148
 subclinical levels, 133–134
 toxicity of, 151–153

Mainstreaming, 20–22
Maintenance, 53, 314–315, 338–340, 403–408
Manual guidance, 83
Mealtime skills, 219–221, 244, 261–262, 402–403
Medical model, 10, 103
Milwaukee Project, 318–319
Mobility devices, 528–529
Modeling, 84, 326–327
Multiple baseline design, 180, 334

NARC, 27, 88
Negative influences in community placement, 40–41
Negative practice, 84
New York State Association for Retarded Children v. *Rockefeller*, 71–72

Normalization, 15–21, 38, 409
Nutrition, 223–224

On task behavior, 439–541
Oral hygiene training, 267
Overcorrection, 84, 241–301
 rationale for, 242–243
 components of, 281–284
 practicality of, 290–292

Restitution. *See* Overcorrection

Positive practice. *See* Overcorrection
Parent–child interactions, 308
Parent training manuals, 322–325
Parental stress, 307–308
Parenthood, 304–305
Philosophy of programming, 1–29, 97–98, 241–242
Physical development, 584–586
PL 91-517, 105
PL 93-112, Section 504, 111–117, 518
PL 94-142, 107–111, 114, 117, 121, 320, 518, 570
PL 94-103, 105
Prosthetic strategies, 519
Psychoactive drug, 457, 516
 prevalence of, 460–463
 dosage levels, 496–498
Psychiatric narrative, 173–174
Psychopharmacology, 457
Psychotic speech, 436–437
Phenothiazines, 465–470
Phobias, 432–436
Physical and cognitive skills, 541–545
Physical punishment, 84
Prevention, 305–306, 317–319
Program Review Committee, 88–89
Public masturbation, 439

READ Project, 343–344
Reinforcement of incompatible behaviors, 84, 273–275
Research Review Committee, 91–92
Reserpine, 471–472
Response-cost, 84
Restrictiveness, 85–86
Rights. *See* Ethics
Role-playing, 81, 325–326
Rouse v. *Cameron*, 98

Satiation, 84
Self-feeding, 215–216, 219
    acquisition of,
    deceleration of, 216–219
Self-control, 84, 430–431
Self-help skills, 51, 183–189, 213–240
    history of, 213–214, 529–533
Self-injurious behaviors, 271
Sex education, 595–602, 603–611
Sex-role adoption, 586
Sexual attitudes, 589–595
Shaping, 84
Single subject designs, 204
    See also AB Design; ABAB Design;
    Multiple baseline design;
    Alternating treatment design
Social learning, 422–430

Social skills, 418, 419–432
    assessment of, 190–193, 524, 602–603
Social validation, 232–234
Socioecological programming, 376–378, 381, 385–386
Sterilization, 611–623
Stereotyped behavior, 264–271
    assessment of, 198–199
Stimulants, 482–488
Supervision, 234–235
Symbol systems. *See* Communication devices

Tardive Dyskinesia, 502–503
Time-out, 28, 84, 260
Time sampling, 175–176
Title XX, 42